W9-BTO-823

Teaching Language Arts

Teaching Language Arts

Carole Cox
Louisiana State University

Allyn and Bacon, Inc.
Boston London Sydney Toronto

For my parents, Alice and Gordon D. Shirreffs

A Division of Simon & Schuster
160 Gould Street
Needham Heights, Massachusetts 02194-2310

Managing Editor: Mylan Jaixen
Series Editor: Susanne F. Canavan, Sean Wakely
Production Administrator: Annette Joseph
Production Coordinator: Susan Freese
Editorial-Production Service: Publishers' Graphics
Text Designer: Denise Hoffman, Glenview Studios
Cover Administrator: Linda K. Dickinson
Cover Design: Art Directions

Library of Congress Cataloging-in-Publication Data

Cox, Carole,
Teaching language arts / Carole Cox.
p. cm.
Includes bibliographies and index.
ISBN 0-205-11071-1
1. Language arts (Elementary)—United States. 2. Reading (Elementary)—United States—Language experience approach. I. Title.
LB1576.C755 1988
372.6'044—dc19 87-30732
CIP

All photographs (including cover) by Stuart T. Spates.

Cover photo: Four second-grade students from Audubon Elementary School in Baton Rouge, Louisiana, are actively engaged in the type of individualized, interactive, and integrated language arts learning experience described throughout this book. From left to right, Sandra, Michael, Phillip, and Lindsay are talking about playing characters they have created in a script they have been writing and revising and intend to dramatize. Their idea to do their own story drama emerged after their teacher read Maurice Sendak's Caldecott Award–winning picture book *Where the Wild Things Are* aloud to the class, and they discussed and dramatized the story. (See Chapter 10 for more on drama.)

Printed in the United States of America
10 9 8 7 6 5 4 3 2 1 93 92 91 90 89 88

Overview

Contents

Chapter Eight

Chapter Nine

Chapter Ten

Drama in the Classroom 348

Chapter Eleven

The Media Arts 390

Chapter Twelve

Chapter Thirteen

Preface

Point of View

Teaching Language Arts is designed for use in preservice and inservice language arts methods courses and as a professional reference for the practicing teacher. My interest in writing this text first arose from a professional need as an instructor of such courses and later from a more personal need to further clarify and understand my own point of view towards teaching children a no less significant subject than the effective and meaningful communication in the English language.

The approach to teaching language arts that I describe in this text is one that centers around three main principles of language arts instruction.

1. Instruction in the language arts should be individualized, or child centered—giving children the power to exercise control and ownership over their own language—and respectful of the ideas, language, and culture of a diversity of learners.
2. Instruction in the language arts should be interactive—always meaning seeking—as children use language to express themselves and make sense of their world—and always focused on literacy, in its many dimensions and for everyone, as learners engage in the process of using language for their own purposes.
3. Instruction in the language arts should be integrated—connecting all language modes, all language arts, and all curriculum areas.

Above all, I wanted to create a text that not only clearly explains such principles and practices in teaching language arts in the elementary school but makes them come alive for the reader as well. The book is illustrated throughout with examples of real teachers in real classrooms with real children involved in actual applications of the principles that have guided the development of this book. I wanted the voices of these children and these teachers to join mine, to add a feeling of the sense and style as well as the substance of language arts learning and teaching.

Plan of the Text

While I believe that all the language arts are really one, impossible to separate, I have nonetheless divided the text into chapters to make the content manageable. Chapter 1, "The Language Arts Teacher and the Art of Teaching Language Arts," describes what happened one day in a fourth-grade classroom and how one teacher approaches the art of teaching language arts. Theory and research to support an individualized, interactive, and integrated whole-language approach are explained, and strategies for deciding what to teach, what materials to use, how to organize and schedule the day, and how to teach a lesson for the first time are described. The concept of a "ripple effect" of integrated language and literacy experiences is presented in this chapter and will be carried throughout the rest of the text. Chapter 2, "Children and Language," and Chapter 3, "Talking and Listening," expand on the principles and practices presented in Chapter 1 and explain how children's language and literacy events in their lives become the basis for language arts instruction.

The next four chapters focus on different aspects of the writing-process approach to teaching, which integrates the skills and substance of writing across the curriculum: Chapter 4, "The Development and Uses of Writing"; Chapter 5, "Shaping Writing for Self-Expression"; Chapter 6, "Talking, Writing, and Grammar"; and Chapter 7, "Spelling, Handwriting, and the Writing Conventions."

While examples of literature and reading across the curriculum are infused throughout the entire text, Chapter 8, "Teaching Literature in the Elementary School," and Chapter 9, "Reading As a Language Art," provide specific models and methods for using literature in the classroom and for literature-based reading instruction, both for the beginning teacher and for the practicing teacher who would like to know more about how to extend and go beyond the basal reader.

The next three chapters provide in-depth coverage of those language arts that are always acknowledged but often neglected in teacher education: Chapter 10, "Drama in the Classroom"; Chapter 11, "The Media Arts"; and Chapter 12, "Research and Study Skills." Each of these chapters provides not only a theory and a rationale for the integration of these areas into language arts instruction but also a specific and extensive explanation of how to do it—and how to do it in the context of teaching the other language arts.

The last chapter, Chapter 13, "Language Arts for Every Child," a guide to help the beginning or new teacher to put it all together, is illustrated with examples of how an excellent teacher at each of the grade levels K–5 approaches the art of teaching language arts.

Chapter Organization

Each chapter is divided into the same main sections with the type of organization that has proved useful in my classes as a way to clarify course content.

- *Objectives.* A list of objectives is presented in the form of questions for readers to ponder and begin to form their own answers as they read the chapter.

- *A Child's View.* Here, the words from the children themselves give a first feeling for the chapter content before the reader begins to read for deeper understanding.

• *Centering Ideas.* This section gives examples of real children and real teachers in real classrooms—slices of classroom life. These examples serve as a center around which the reader can begin to focus on the special emphasis of each chapter.

• *Making Connections.* This section provides information that helps to develop understanding, to cast teaching approaches into the appropriate theoretical, historical, social, cultural, or instructional context, or to demonstrate and communicate curricular structure. The material shows connections with models, individuals, theories, and research—past and present; relationships with the other language arts, the content areas, and other areas of the curriculum; and other broad educational goals and topics such as the development of self-concept among children, home and school connections, multicultural education, and special education.

• *Teaching Children.* This section offers specific teaching approaches and classroom applications, including strategies, activities, units, and resources that may be easily and effectively put to use by students in field-based practicums or in their own classrooms. Also included are descriptions of "Featured Teachers" as well as transcripts of real language interactions in the classroom.

• *Summing Up.* The synthesis of the main points of the chapter content is designed to help readers review and reflect on what they have read.

• *Looking Further.* This section suggests opportunities for exploring the chapter content more deeply: discussion questions for lecture classes; topics and activities for small-group discussion; ideas for observation and action research; teaching applications to try out in the classroom; and ways to develop teaching resources.

Special Features of the Text

This text contains a number of special features.

• *Marginal Notes.* Definitions, expanded explanations, examples, references for further reading, related children's books and media, and teaching suggestions and resources are given in the marginal notes. Since an integrated approach to teaching language arts is one of the main ideas underlying the text, the marginal notes also include extensive cross-references to related sections of the text.

• *Featured Teachers.* Descriptions of real teachers provide actual classroom applications and bring the content to life.

• *Visuals.* The text is richly illustrated with samples of children's drawing and writing, with charts, diagrams, and reproductions of teaching materials, and with photographs picturing the actual teachers and children discussed in the text.

• *References.* Source materials and suggested readings are organized by chapter at the end of the book.

Acknowledgments

The collaboration with my husband, Stuart Spates, did not result only in his producing a set of photographs created especially for this book. What also happened is that, in many cases, I began to write about what I had observed as he took photographs and as we talked about what was taking place in the classroom. Our joint efforts added a whole new dimension to the book and helped me to clarify many of the things I wanted to say in this text.

My former advisor at the University of Minnesota, Robert Dykstra, not only always encouraged me to be myself but first suggested I do a language arts text—and *still* be myself. Hiram Howard and Sue Canavan, at Allyn and Bacon, responded in similar fashion to my inquiry about writing this text and allowed me to do so.

My students over the years have always been a source of motivation, helping me to consider what it means to teach language arts. Much of what is included in this text is a result of my interactions with them.

Many reviewers have made excellent and insightful comments and suggestions and have done much to shape the content of the text: Linda Gambrell (University of Maryland); Victoria Chou Hare (University of Illinois at Chicago); Jane McPherson (Solomon Schechter Academy of Dallas); Nancy Mangano (Kansas State University); Mary Lou Maples (University of Tennessee); Lynda Markham (Alma College); Carl Personke (University of Wisconsin at Madison); Eileen Tway (Miami University of Ohio); and Karen Wood (University of North Carolina).

The "Featured Teachers" and my other teacher friends made the content come alive for me. They shared their time, their classrooms, their ideas, and their materials—and I thank them: Pat Abbott, Phyllis Crawford, Avril Font, Phyllis Fuglaar, Marion Harris, Gene Hughes, Mauretta Hurst, Kathy Kay, Steve Ketcham, Jo Anne La Motte, Lynn Lastrapes, Orlena McKenzie, Sunny McMullen, Margaret Mattson, Nora Miller, Pat Peabody, Willa Richardson, Diane Roberts, Diane Rushing, Joyce Ryder, Sarah Sherman-Siegel, Alice Shirreffs, Nancy Shaver Toms, Ann Torregrossa, Karen Watkins, and Glynn Wink.

For special support, counsel, and encouragement, I acknowledge my friends Lois Joseph, Judy Young, and Lucy Jones; my friend and colleague Lea McGee; and Brad Shields of Entré Computers who consistently outwitted the gremlins I know are living in my word-processing program.

And to my five-year-old, Gordon Spates, and my three-year-old, Elizabeth Spates, who have spent most of their lives asking, "Are you *still* working on the book, Mommy?" and to my seventeen-year-old, Wyatt Cox, who asks, "Are you going to finish that thing before I leave home to go to college?" I can now say, "No!" "Yes!" and "Thank you for your support!"

Teaching Language Arts

Chapter One

The Language Arts Teacher and the Art of Teaching Language Arts

Objectives

Look for answers to the following questions as you read this chapter.

- What is the art of teaching language arts?
- What are individualized, interactive, and integrated language and literacy experiences?
- When you begin to teach language arts,
  - What will you teach?
  - What materials will you use?
  - How will you organize your classroom and schedule your day?
  - How will you begin to teach lessons?
  - How will you begin to integrate the curriculum through the language arts?
- How would you describe an effective teacher of the English language arts?

A Child's View

Here is how Monica, grade 4, compared last year's classroom to this year's, where her teacher takes an individualized, interactive, and integrated approach to language and literacy experiences, and children choose many of their own topics of study: "Last year I didn't like it as much 'cause a lot of times you just had to do stuff the teacher told you. And I did it but I didn't like it very much. It was boring. But in this class you go do things because you want to and are willing to work at it. Then the whole thing works out better."

Centering Ideas

What is the art of teaching language arts? Let's eavesdrop on a fourth-grade classroom one morning in April in order to find some answers to this question. Note how the teacher approaches the language arts as **individualized, interactive,** and **integrated** experiences.

A Slice of Classroom Life

Beginning the Day

While the teacher, Avril Font, takes care of such business as record keeping, roll taking, and lunch count, the children are involved in a choice of individual language and literacy events, such as writing in diary journals or reading the newspaper or a library book.

Sharing Experiences

Avril tells the class to meet her in the reading center. Here are excerpts of what follows as the children talk, listen, and interact about things that are important to them.

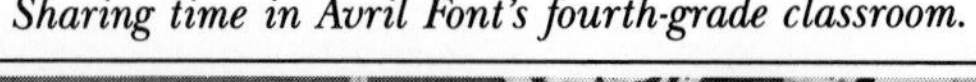

Sharing time in Avril Font's fourth-grade classroom.

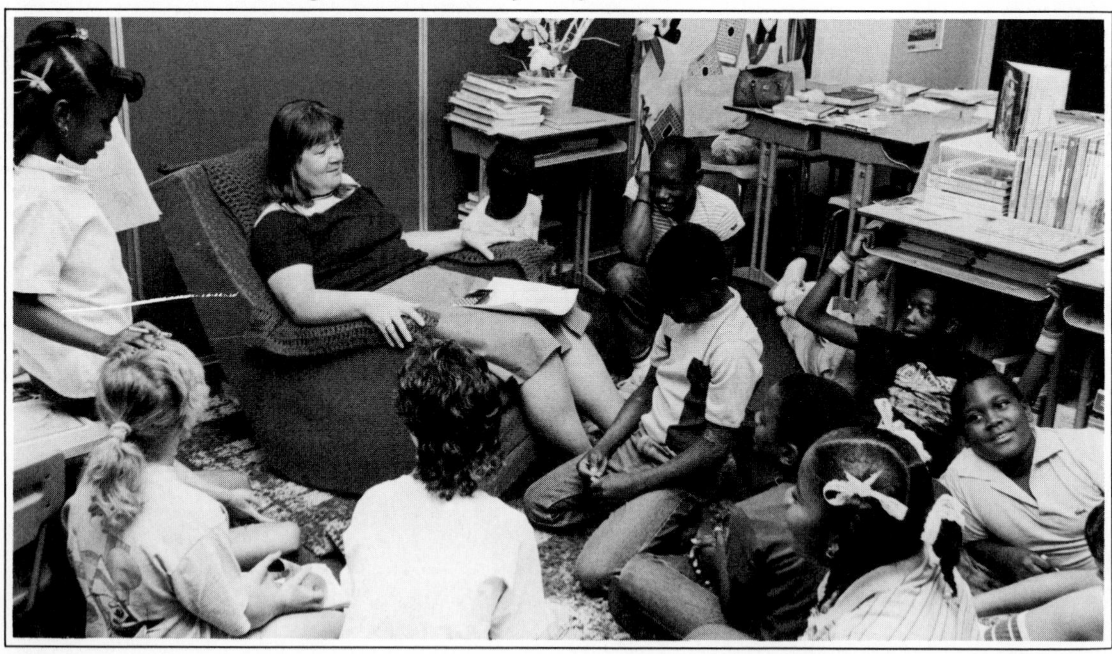

Teacher: OK, let's share.

Child: Mrs. Font, my Paw Paw made things out of acorns for a craft show. I'll bring them in to show.

Teacher: That's a neat idea for a story. Why don't you write down some ideas?

Child: OK.

Child: I got an idea of something to write about. I put a glass on the door to listen to my older sister talk on the phone. But I couldn't hear.

Teacher: Try putting it on the wall. I bet that will work.

One child reads from a book, often used during sharing. It tells what is special about each day.

The Book of Days, by Elizabeth and Gerald Donaldson (A&W Publishers, 1979)

Child: Hey, it says here that it's William Shakespeare's birthday today!

Teacher: Who is he?

Child: A famous writer.

Child: He wrote poetry.

Child: He wrote literature.

Teacher: Right. He wrote plays and poetry. Have you ever heard of *Romeo and Juliet?*

Child: Yeah.

Child: Over Easter, I was watching Channel 27 and they had *Romeo and Juliet,* scene 2.

Planning the Curriculum

Avril notes topics of interest that emerged as the children talked and listened and interacted, and merges these with subjects in the curriculum, topics of study suggested in curriculum guides, as well as special events that come up during the year. Note how she helps children get organized for group work in different subjects that will become integrated through language and literacy activities.

Language Arts and Reading

Teacher: What are we doing in language arts?

Child: I'm going to start a story about pizza.

Teacher: Why?

Child: 'Cause my Mama works in a pizza place.

Teacher: Good. Keep writing. We'll get them ready to make into books. We'll have sustained silent reading after recess. Those of you who have finished your basal reader story can take the test. Continue to read your library books. You can also read the newspaper. And after lunch I'll read the next chapter of *Wind in the Willows* aloud.

See Chapter 9, "Sustained Silent Reading (SSR)"

The Wind in the Willows, by Kenneth Grahame, illus. by Michael Hague (Holt, Rinehart & Winston, 1980)

Social Studies and Science

Teacher: OK, let's plan social studies for today. Who would like to go to the library and research William Shakespeare? [*Show of hands*] When you come back, discuss what you find with each other, and begin to think about how you might share your research with everybody else. What else are we doing in social studies?

Child: St. George and the dragon. We're making transparencies for the overhead projector.

Teacher: You're doing a terrific job with your research. What else?

Child: The maypole group. We have to practice the maypole dance.

Child: We did well yesterday.

Teacher: Yes, you really did. I brought the maypole ribbons. Aren't they great? In science, you're doing research for reports, and posters to share what you find out with the rest of the class.

Child: Me and him want to do guppies. My cousin got 'em in an aquarium.

Teacher: Why don't you two see if you can find out how to make an aquarium?

Child: OK. Can we go to the library?

Teacher: Yes. Take some notes and we'll make some plans to do it.

As you can see, Avril Font uses many means to encourage, support, and guide children's language and literacy experiences in the classroom and across the curriculum. And she has chosen to use these means because they reflect her view of how children learn to use language and become literate:

> The first essential is to try to build on their ideas and language and extend all language arts experiences into all aspects of teaching and learning. I believe that oral language is the basis for the development of literacy. The more they use oral language, the more they can read and write. Their own language must be used, reinforced, and extended into all areas of the curriculum. I see language as multifaceted, even tactile. A lot of people think sharing and planning together is a waste of time. It's not. The more they share and plan together the more verbal they become. They talk to each other more, discuss more in small groups. I try to add a veneer of standard English and I do use means to correct nonstandard language, but if we don't build on the ideas and language that are already there when children come to school, we are building on sand.

Small-Group Work. Students will now begin or continue to work on the activities they have planned together with Avril. Note how Avril provides opportunities for individualized and interactive learning, and integrates the curriculum through the language arts, as you read excerpts from the dialogue that takes place between her and the children as they work on many projects throughout the day.

Students working together in small groups in a classroom where learning experiences are individualized, interactive, and integrated across the curriculum.

Writing Center. Several students are writing and discussing their stories with Avril and other students.

Child [*reading aloud, savoring the sound*]: *My Day at the Movies,* by Lestreca.

Teacher [*reading the story*]: I like it, but it seems a bit long in places. Do you think you could eliminate some information? Read it to me. Are there some things you could leave out?

Mina is writing a book called *My Mom the Seamstress* and discusses, with Avril, what other words she can use besides *seamstress.* In the thesaurus she finds the word *couturière* and remembers that's what her mother was called in Japan when she went to school and learned to sew without a pattern (see Figure 1–1).

Social Studies Groups. Avril moves among the groups working on different topics in social studies as they talk, read, write, and create materials to report on their topic. One group is preparing for the maypole dance.

Teacher: Where is the maypole gang? [*Several children are on the floor arranging the ribbons for the dance.*]

Child: Mrs. Font, what's this word?

1

2

Figure 1–1
Pages from My Mom the Seamstress

Teacher: Czechoslovakia. It's a country in Europe.

Child: Yeah, I was gonna say that. [*Speaking slowly*] C-z-e-c-h-o-s-l-o-v-a-k-i-a. [*Snapping her fingers as she says each syllable*] Czech-[*snap*]-o-[*snap*]-slo-[*snap*]-vak-[*snap*]-i-[*snap*]-a-[*snap*]! Right?

Teacher: Right.

Child: Look. It says here that in Czechoslovakia boys put trees under their sweetheart's window on May Day.

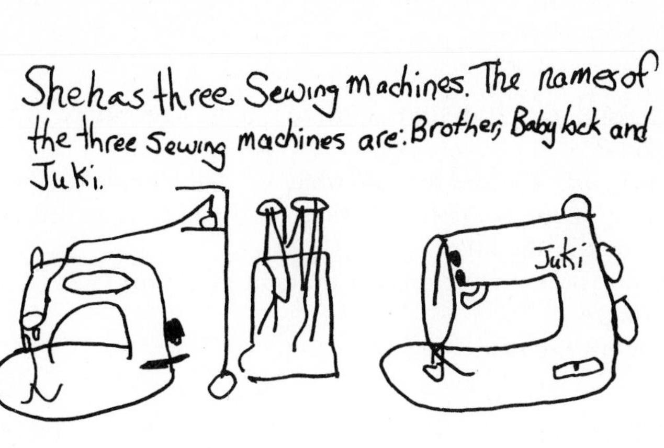

3

The three sewing machines do different things
Brother does 5000 stitches in one minute. Baby lock sews and
weaves. Juki dose everything.

Brother

Baby lock

Juki

4

Child:	Mrs. Font, there was an article in the paper and it said it's danced by girls [*makes a face*] and didn't explain why it's danced.
Child:	They don't know much.
Child:	They could read about it in the encyclopedia.
Teacher:	You read a lot. I'm impressed.

Saint George and the Dragon, by Edmund Spenser, retold by Margaret Hodges, illus. by Trina Schart Hyman (Little, Brown, 1984), winner of the Caldecott Medal, awarded annually by the American Library Association for the most distinguished picture book published in the United States that year

Several other students are reading and talking about plans to show the events in the life of St. George on overhead transparencies and by dramatizing the story in a book.

Child: Mrs. Font, me and him want to know were there really dragons?
Teacher: Look it up. Try looking up what we call dragons today. I think there are some big reptiles on the Galapagos Islands. Let's look in the atlas.
Child: Why do you want the atlas? I thought everything was in the dictionary.
Child: 'Cause it's the name of a place.

The Shakespeare group has also gone to the library and returned with books. They are reading, taking notes, and talking about his life and how they could share what they are finding out with others.

Tales From Shakespeare, by Charles and Mary Lamb (Dutton, 1957)

Child: Mrs. Font, it says he served with a company of actors. [*She makes a V for victory sign.*] I want to be an actress.
Child: Mrs. Font, it says here he wrote "Mary Had a Little Lamb."
Teacher: I don't think so.
Child: It says!
Teacher: Read it again.
Child: Oh. It says his plays were written as stories for children by Charles and Mary Lamb.
Teacher: That's how I read Shakespeare when I was young. Why don't you see if you can find that book in the library?

Science Groups. As Avril comes up, several children want to tell her about their research on different animals and on the posters they are making.

Teacher: How's your work coming?
Child: We got some books on aquariums. We're gonna start working on making one.
Child: [*reading about animals in a book*] Mrs. Font, what does *droppings* mean? It says, "But their presence is revealed by their tracks and droppings."
Teacher: Go look it up.
Child: [*returning with dictionary*] Mrs. Font, I don't get it.
Teacher: I'll tell you what it is. When animals go to the bathroom, the little brown things they leave behind. Excrement.
Child: You mean like dog doo?
Teacher: Yes.

One Teacher's Philosophy of the Art of Teaching Language Arts

Avril Font has been teaching for fifteen years and is considered a **teacher artist** by her principal, peers, parents, and students. She has a definite approach to the way she directs learning experiences in her classroom, which directly affects the way she teaches language arts.

> First, I believe that teaching should be child oriented and stem from the ideas, interests, language, and unique talents of each child. We have to individualize learning experiences. I also know that you are not going to be able to teach everything to every child, but you can teach them the mechanism to look it up and other ways to finding out more about it themselves. You have to be able to say "I don't know" and not be afraid to make mistakes in front of children. I spell incorrectly on the board all the time. The children check me out by looking it up in the dictionary.
>
> Second, I believe learning experiences must be relevant and integrated together. Why Shakespeare? Because someone noticed it was his birthday when reading a book of days they like. It was the same place they found out about St. George and the dragon, and the maypole, and decided they wanted to learn how to do it. It was relevant to their interests, and integrated many subjects together. Why have them do their own science? Why read and write and draw and make books and build things like aquariums? The texts are boring. I love science and do all hands-on science and we get so much more out of it by working together in cohesive groups.
>
> And third, we do almost all of our work in these small cohesive groups. We work as a team in here. They work in groups, but their work is individual. They just spend a lot of time sharing, planning, discussing, helping each other, interacting.

Avril's philosophy—and the philosophy behind this book—centers on three important principles of learning and teaching language arts, namely, that language and literacy experiences should be (1) individualized, (2) interactive, and (3) integrated across the curriculum.

Making Connections

Let us look at each of these three principles more closely. What do we mean when we say that language and literacy experiences are individualized, interactive, and integrated across the curriculum?

Individualized Language and Literacy Experiences

Child Centeredness

The purpose of individualized language and literacy experiences is to develop every child's potential to use language and to give children the power to exercise control and ownership over their own language. Child-centered language and literacy experiences can be defined as those which originate with the ideas, interests, and language of children.

In child-centered classrooms, teachers plan time to observe and listen to children express their ideas and interests, and also plan specific times for sharing these and planning together, as Avril Font does every day. During these times she notes topics of interest and helps children to plan activities around them. Plans follow children rather than the other way around.

Current Theories and Research

Many studies of child language and cognitive development are available to guide the teacher. However, perhaps the most widely accepted theory is that of Jean Piaget (1952), who has provided teachers with a description of the cognitive and language development of children.

Piaget explains that children are able to structure a view of reality through the interaction of their internal maturation and their experiences in the world. And while teaching cannot accelerate the child's advancement through certain required stages of development, neither will this development take place without experiences. Piaget explains his theory of cognitive development through the use of several key ideas and a description of stages in the growth of the child. Reading Piaget often triggers the *aha* response as you begin to think of children you have known or stories your parents told you about your own thoughts and language as a child. As you read these key ideas about the stages in the growth of children, think about what it means when a child says "I used to think . . ."

Key Ideas in Piaget's Theory. Young children learn to organize their experiences and adapt to the environment through the processes of assimilation, accommodation, and, finally, equilibration. For example, have you ever watched a baby put anything and everything into its mouth, including its feet? Piaget would explain that the young child is assimilating the new object to the old process of eating. The baby is classifying, or putting this new and unknown thing into an already existing mental category or operation.

The Red Balloon (Macmillan Films)

My son Gordon started to call any balloon a *red balloon* after he saw the beautiful French film *The Red Balloon.* He also called any animal smaller than a goat a *kitty.* These are both examples of **assimilation,** or classifying an object into an already existing mental category or operation. It is the same process by which a child learns to grasp things and moves from grasping its own hands, to grasping a rattle or a spoon, and eventually a crayon, pencil, or paintbrush.

When Gordon was older, he nearly had a nervous breakdown at the grand opening of a toy store, where balloons of different colors were being given away, because he was asked whether he wanted "a yellow balloon, a pink balloon, or a blue balloon." He kept changing his mind, naming first one and then another, until he decided he wanted "a yellow, a pink, *and* a blue balloon." Gordon had **accommodated** his existing category of balloons from *red balloons* to adjust to the reality of balloons of different colors. He had also ceased calling dogs, rabbits, and squirrels *kitties* and called them dogs, rabbits, and squirrels.

The processes of assimilation and accommodation interact as the young child continues to adapt to the environment, and **equilibration** is the self-regulatory process by which a balance is achieved between the two processes. The concepts developed during these ongoing processes are related to other concepts in the child's mind; Piaget refers to these concepts as **schemata.** Gordon was building his schema for small animals, and further refining it as he interrelated them in his mind. As he encounters other small animals, or any other animals, he will build these into his original schema as he gains in experience. In Piaget's theory, building on children's past experiences is an important part of their future learning experiences.

Stages in Cognitive and Language Development. In Piaget's theory, the cognitive stages are patterns of cognitive structures or mental operations that children go through at different ages. The order of these is always the same, although different children will vary in the time it takes them to go through each stage (Piaget, 1964).

1. ***Sensorimotor stage, from birth to two years***

During the **sensorimotor stage,** children learn about the world and learn to recognize and identify objects, grasping them and putting them into their mouths, learning to make a distinction between their own self and their environment through exploration and discovery. They are learning how to learn. This is a preverbal stage during which children acquire the practical knowledge that forms an underlying structure for later knowledge.

2. ***Preoperational thought, from two to seven years***

During the stage of **preoperational thought,** children begin to learn the symbols for things, or their names. This is the beginning of vocabulary development and of true language which is primarily egocentric, or centered around the self. They are also beginning to develop concepts of good and bad, learning to draw, and developing an intense interest in the symbolization of objects through pretending and play.

3. ***Concrete operations, from seven to eleven years***

During the **concrete operations** stage, children begin to reason logically, or to perform in their heads tasks that they previously had to learn by manipulating objects, although they still need reference to familiar objects and actions. They can follow a set of directions, grasp concepts related to things they already know about, and form simple mental relationships even though they do not always understand how they are able to do these things. They also begin to develop socialized thought and speech because they can focus on more than one thing at a time.

4. *Formal operations, from eleven to fifteen years*

During the **formal operations** stage, children begin to be able mentally to leave the physical world and enter the world of symbols, concepts, relationships, abstract properties, axioms, and theories. They can also understand their own reasoning powers.

The significance of Piaget's theories for teaching language arts is that teachers need to provide opportunities for children to experience, explore, and discover the world around them. Learning implies action on the part of the learner as children interact with their environment in a classroom where there are many opportunities to explore, experiment, and solve problems with adult support.

The Teacher As Researcher

While knowledge of a theory of child development is important as you begin to learn the art of teaching language arts, you should also consider that you yourself are becoming a child development theorist. Your views will expand not only through the findings of others but through what you yourself find as you question, observe, and think about the children you are teaching. Every time you enter the classroom, consider yourself as a researcher and your students as informants.

Goodman (1978) has coined the term *kidwatching* to denote the process of observing children in the classroom. She and others (Merek, Howard, & Goodman, 1984) offer suggestions for teachers to let their teaching behavior be guided by their observations of children's behavior.

- Watch for a child's success in a language or literacy experience, including reading and writing, and extend this to a new and different experience. For example, when a child proudly talked about his grandfather making things out of acorns for a craft show, Avril Font suggested the boy write some ideas for a story about it. And to some other children who had written stories and poems, Avril suggested they bind them into books.

- Watch for children actively exploring new experiences and ask questions like "Why do you think that is true?" or "What's happening here?" For example, Avril asked such questions while the maypole group struggled to arrange the ribbons for the maypole dance.

- Watch for children who are having trouble with an experience; talk to them about it and lead them to discover a solution if they cannot yet do so themselves. For example, when two boys wanted to know whether dragons still exist, Avril asked questions, made suggestions, and guided them to reference materials for some answers.

• Watch and trust children's ability to learn and your own ability to learn from them. For example, Avril carefully observed the two boys planning to make an aquarium as they began to find books on the subject and decide on their own how they would do it.

Respect for the Ideas, Language, and Culture of a Diversity of Learners

Every learner is different from every other learner in some way. In a child-centered approach to teaching, these differences are something to be respected, valued, and built upon in order to meet the needs of every child. Language arts instruction, and all instruction, should be responsive to the uniqueness of a large number of ethnic and cultural groups. Among the many forms these cultures may take are racial identity, ethnic heritage, national origin, political orientation, language, customs, traditions, religion, beliefs, sex, age, socioeconomic level, geographic region, and any combination of these.

Interactive Language and Literacy Experiences

Seeking Meaning

Children use language above all to seek meaning as they express themselves and try to make sense of their world. As teachers and children interact with each other and respond to their experiences, the goal is always to find and create meaning in what they do. In a **whole-language view** of language arts instruction, this principle clearly establishes the purposes for teaching (Goodman & Goodman, 1981):

- The purpose of language use for learners is to focus on the communication of meaning.
- The purpose of listening and reading experiences is to understand, or the comprehension of meaning.
- The purpose of speaking and writing experiences is to create, or the expression of meaning.

Encouraging Active Communication

Active communication should occur among learners and in authentic contexts for learning as students engage in the process of using language for their own purposes. In a recent look at young language users on their way to becoming literate, Harste, Woodward, and Burke (1984) suggest that language is a social event and always involves two language users, one of which can even be a book, or some other form of written language. And it is the interaction or transaction between these that results in meaningful language and literacy experiences.

The significance of this principle with respect to teaching is that for the learner's purpose real language interactions are more useful than isolated language elements that are taught and tested. The language arts are social processes and should be taught in real, meaningful, and natural interactions among students.

Focusing on Literacy

The teaching of reading and writing should have a central role in the classroom. Drawing on the idea that language arts instruction is meaning seeking and is a social event, Harste, Woodward, and Burke (1984) make the following suggestions to teachers for focusing on literacy.

- Since reading and writing are tools to get things done, teachers need to help children use these tools to support all other aspects of learning.
- Reading and writing should be central to all classrooms, and recommended practices include:
  - filling the classroom environment with print;
  - making reading and writing areas central to the classroom organization so that children will have many opportunities to use books, paper, and pencils; and
  - making use of any opportunity to present print naturally.
- Introduce children to as many opportunities as possible for using print in many contexts:
  - have them write journals, letters, and stories to be bound into books;
  - have them read newspapers, message boards, recipes, menus, and other forms of environmental print; and
  - have them read many predictable books with patterns they can hear and enjoy and respond to over and over again.

Integrated Language and Literacy Experiences

Connecting the Language Arts and Connecting the Curriculum through the Language Arts

See "When Teachers Decide to Integrate the Language Arts," by Marilyn Hanf Buckley, in *Language Arts,* 63 (1986), 369–377.

You are a language arts teacher all day long. Whatever the subject or grade you teach, the medium of communication is language in any one of its many forms. It would be an oversimplification, however, to suggest that the importance of language in school learning is simply as a vehicle for absorbing other subject matter. If by language we mean a system of possibilities for representation, expression, and communication, it is much more than a tool: language permeates human thought and life.

The **language arts** have often been defined simply as listening, speaking, reading, and writing. But such a definition merely deals with the tip of the iceberg, as it were. More accurately, you might visualize the language arts as including just about everything that occurs inside a person's head, some of which is expressed through the forms of audible and visible language—speaking and writing, facial expressions, gesturing, play and games, scribbling, drawing, acting out, laughing—and other activities which are not as observable—listening and reading, observing, feeling, imagining, dreaming, visualizing, and above all, thinking.

Some important aspects of the language arts reflect and transmit cultural content—literature and the electronic media, for example—while other aspects are more likely to be classified as artistic—drama, song, and movement. The language arts also include a study of the traditional skills leading to communication in a language: handwriting, spelling, grammar, usage, and the mechanics of writing. And newer skills, such as computer keyboarding and the use of electronic equipment and software such as tapes, video, film, and floppy discs, are all part of the language arts.

Language arts teachers today face the formidable task of clarifying all of these facets of the language arts as they help children make sense of their world through language. Integrating the teaching of language arts offers a theoretical and curricular structure upon which to build a meaningful language arts program.

Language modes function together as children learn to use and control language. Loban (1976) provided support for this notion in a longitudinal study of the language development of 338 children from kindergarten through the twelfth grade. He found that there is a positive correlation among reading, writing, listening, and speaking abilities and that proficiency in listening and speaking are the foundations for proficiency in reading and writing. He also suggests (1979) how to achieve this proficiency:

> The development of power and efficiency with language derives from using language for genuine purposes and not from studying about it. The path to power over language is to use it, to use it in genuinely meaningful situations, whether we are reading, listening, writing, or speaking (p. 485).

The Problem-Solving Approach to Learning

Teachers must create a classroom environment that helps children seek and find the points of connection among what they know, what they want to know, what they do, and what they come to know. This integration of the curriculum also supports points of connection that should occur in an interdisciplinary and humanistic education. In order to put such an approach into practice, the teacher must see to it that children are immersed in a whole-language environment that provides a purposeful climate for learning. Thus the children will be actively engaged in the pursuit of learning and knowledge. The need to learn and to know arises as children ask questions about things they want to know, as they formulate hypotheses to test and answer these questions, and even as they just follow hunches or whims that lead to inquiry.

Humanistic Qualities

Language skills cannot be removed from the context of the cultural content of English and the other humanities. No doubt you must consider accountability, particularly so in view of the great national investment in time, energy, and funds to support the teaching of what are known as basic skills. A strict subskills approach, on the other hand, flies in the face of what we know about how children learn and use language, and it may also leave behind a curriculum stripped of meaningful content, a skeleton without flesh or muscle to move it. However you perceive the learning and teaching process or design and structure your teaching, it should be full of the means to transmit human culture in the humanistic tradition of education: to convey the content that mirrors the ideas and feelings men and women have sought to embody and express throughout time, through literature, philosophy, history, music, art, and drama, as well as through science and mathematics; and to teach the skills necessary for effective communication and transmission of this culture. The art of teaching language arts requires that teachers not only know theories and techniques, but make use of these to convey content as they meet the emotional, social, and intellectual needs of children.

Teaching Children

As you consider what different theories and research convey to the teacher about teaching language arts and begin to make your own decisions about how you will teach them, you will also begin to consider the practical questions of day-to-day teaching:

- What will you teach?
- What materials will you use?
- How will you organize your classroom and schedule your day?
- How will you begin to teach lessons?
- How will you begin to integrate the curriculum through the language arts?

Let us consider Avril Font's answers to these questions, and then look at ways in which you can begin to find your own answers.

What Will You Teach?

Avril Font uses three main sources of ideas to determine what she will teach: (1) state curriculum guides; (2) special events throughout the year (seasons, holidays, current events); and (3) the children in her class.

At the beginning of the year Avril checks state curriculum guides for her grade level for suggested teaching topics; she also gets ideas from special events throughout the year. As the semester progresses, however, her main source of ideas for planning come from the children.

Here are some practical ways in which you can find out about your students at the beginning and throughout the year, so you can use their interests and ideas as a basis for planning what to teach.

- *Writing Autobiographies.* During the first few days of school, ask the children to write a short autobiography, and write one yourself. Read yours to them and invite them to read theirs out loud too.

- *Most Important Person Display.* Announce that the children will each have a small bulletin board or space available for a week to show things that are important to them and tell others about them if they wish. Display items from the whole class during the first week. The following week, set up a display about yourself, baby pictures and all. On subsequent weeks, feature one child at a time, and after he mounts his display, let him tell the class and you about it.

"Most Important Person" things to bring to school: books, toys, trophies, things made, records, baby clothes, photograph album

- *Journal Writing.* Allow some time every day for journal writing, and you write too. Have the children read out their entries only if they volunteer. Even when they choose not to share what they have written, their writing will have triggered thinking and probably talking about their ideas.

See Chapter 4, "Writing about Ourselves and about Others."

- *Parent Conferences.* You may learn things from parents that you will not learn about from the children: family situations, travel, cultural background, and so on.

- *Sharing Experiences.* It is important to let children know that they can share things that are important to them when they come to school. Be flexible and unsurprised by what turns up. You should make opportunities for such interactions available daily, at all grade levels; they will become a primary source of information for you when you think about what you will teach.

- *Interest Inventory.* You can also use a simple interest inventory at the beginning of the year. Children can respond with simple lists or with more extensive writing, or you can interview younger children. Keep the questions simple so that the children will not think you are fishing for certain answers.

Items for an interest inventory: things I like, things I don't like, things I know how to do, things I would like to do, my family, my friends

What Materials Will You Use?

In Avril Font's classroom, children are assumed to have a great deal of control over their own learning. Supplies are readily available to them in special areas around the room and in large storage cupboards. The room is full of books and other printed material and boasts of many pieces of media equipment such as an overhead projector and a computer (on a rolling cart) which she shares with other teachers.

But in Avril Font's room, as in other child-centered classrooms, the real raw material for teaching language arts originates with the children themselves—their thoughts, their experiences, their impulses, and their language. Ashton-Warner (1963), an early and lyrical advocate of a child-centered approach to teaching, comments: "I reach a hand into the mind of a child, bring out a handful of the stuff I find there, and use that as our first working material" (p. 3).

Again, the main source of topics and materials will be the children themselves: the experiences they share in class, their ideas and suggestions and questions, and other materials that support their language and literacy experiences.

Children's Experiences

Children can draw on many of their own experiences for materials, including:

- *Shared experiences.* Descriptions—verbal, written, drawn, danced, acted out—of objects or people, or events created in or out of class.
- *Home experiences.* People, pets, and things from home—books, records, pictures, awards, stories of experiences—sports, trips, movies, music.
- *School experiences.* Other classes—music, art, physical education—library experiences, assemblies, parties, fights in the schoolyard.

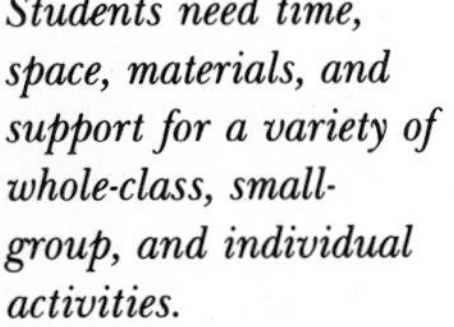

Students need time, space, materials, and support for a variety of whole-class, small-group, and individual activities.

- *Content experiences.* Science experiments, social studies research, guest speakers, field trips, letters to the editor of newspapers on issues of concern.
- *Arts experiences.* Art and music appreciation, creations, song, dance, drama, films.
- *Organic experiences.* Growing things, cooking and eating, animals and other living things, classroom nature collections.
- *Cultural experiences.* Holidays; ethnic and cultural traditions, events, and celebrations; social and community events and movements.
- *Media experiences.* Television, film, music, video, and computers in the life of the child.

Finally, don't forget to draw on your own experiences. You can create great interest and enthusiasm in the classroom by sharing some of yourself with your students.

Children's Literature

The single most valuable set of materials you can use are good children's books. In addition to the school library, a classroom library is an essential component of any elementary program. Most important, however, is your knowledge of children's books and your skill in using them in a language-based integrated curriculum.

Books on children's literature: *Through the Eyes of a Child: An Introduction to Children's Literature,* 2nd ed., by Donna E. Norton (Charles Merrill, 1987); *Children and Books,* 7th ed., by Zena Sutherland, Dianne L. Monson, and May Hill Arbuthnot (Scott, Foresman, 1985); *Literature and the Child,* by Bernice Cullinan et al. (Harcourt Brace Jovanovich, 1981); *Children's Literature in the Elementary School,* by Charlotte S. Huck, Susan Hepler, and Janet Hickman (Holt, Rinehart & Winston, 1987)

Media

In addition to the chalkboards and bulletin boards found in almost every classroom, the great variety of electronic media should be there as well; if they are not permanent fixtures they should be readily available from the library or media center. The following media are useful for teacher and child creations, as instructional materials, or for self-expression.

a record player
an audio-cassette player, blank tapes, and earphones
an overhead projector, blank transparencies, and overhead projector pens
a slide projector
a camera and film for prints and slides
a filmstrip projector and blank filmstrips
16-mm and Super-8 film projectors and film
video equipment and video tapes
a computer, with word-processing program and other software

Supplies and Equipment

In addition to the usual paper and pencil supplies, a classroom should have at least some of the following types of equipment and supplies needed in many experiences where children can be actively involved in problem solving.

art materials for a variety of media
science supplies and equipment
cooking equipment and utensils
rhythm and other musical instruments
materials for costumes and properties for drama
puppet-making materials and puppet stage
a flannel board and materials
found objects for a variety of activities
typewriters

Reference Books and Sources

While the library will have a large selection of reference sources, your classroom should contain as many as possible of the sources listed below, readily accessible for children actively engaged in research and problem solving.

a dictionary
a thesaurus
an encyclopedia
an atlas
a file cabinet for pamphlets, magazine clippings, articles

Language Arts Textbooks

Language arts textbooks provide descriptions of experiences and exercises in each of the language arts. The books may be designed for whole-class, small-group, or individual activities. But while these texts may present a picture of a total language arts program, using such a text for daily activities is not really compatible with a whole-language approach to teaching individualized, interactive, and integrated language arts. Language arts textbooks are not the curriculum.

On the other hand, a language arts text may be used selectively as one of many materials and resources available to the student and the teacher. Here are several suggestions for using such a text.

- Use a language arts textbook to introduce a concept or skill needed by students for a particular purpose. For example, most textbooks will have a well-developed section that explains the basic form of a letter, and gives variations for different letter-writing needs. If a class or a group has reason to write a letter, and it seems important to put it into the correct form, the textbook can be used to introduce the necessary skills.

- Use a language arts textbook to reinforce a skill or a convention children have discovered or invented themselves. For example, punctuation skills will develop naturally and beautifully when children have many opportunities and reasons to write for their own purposes. Many times, however, they will want to know an acceptable form because it is important to them to communicate clearly. The textbook can provide answers to questions they may have about the proper use of such conventions.

- Use a language arts textbook as a reference source. For example, students may have questions about the correct form for writing a script if they want to use this form to create and present some ideas of their own, or to translate a story or book into dramatic form. They can use a textbook for reference as they shape their ideas into a script.

How Will You Organize Your Classroom and Schedule Your Day?

A Room for Teaching Language Arts

Avril Font has organized her room around a reading center, which consists of a large rug with bookshelves full of books on one side, large overstuffed easy chairs at each end, and lots of floor pillows for curling up with a good book or to listen and talk during sharing and planning time. Around this center are six tables formed by pushing four student desks together; each of these tables is a home base for four children. Two large tables are designated work centers with appropriate materials and space for group work in writing, science, and mathematics (see Figure 1–2).

A Schedule for Teaching Language Arts

Avril's schedule follows a certain routine. Of course she must work around school schedules and special subjects taught by other teachers, but she has developed a very flexible schedule over the years to allow for much individualized and small-group work in all subject areas.

9:00–9:15	Business, journal writing, personal reading
9:15–9:45	Sharing and planning in the reading center
9:45–10:15	Group work: language arts and reading, social studies, science, and mathematics
10:15–10:30	Recess
10:30–11:00	Reading: sustained silent reading
11:00–11:30	Physical education
11:30–12:00	Group work: language arts and reading, social studies, science, and mathematics
12:00–12:30	French
12:30–1:00	Lunch
1:00–1:15	Reading aloud
1:15–1:30	Recess
1:30–3:00	Group work: language arts and reading, social studies, science, and mathematics

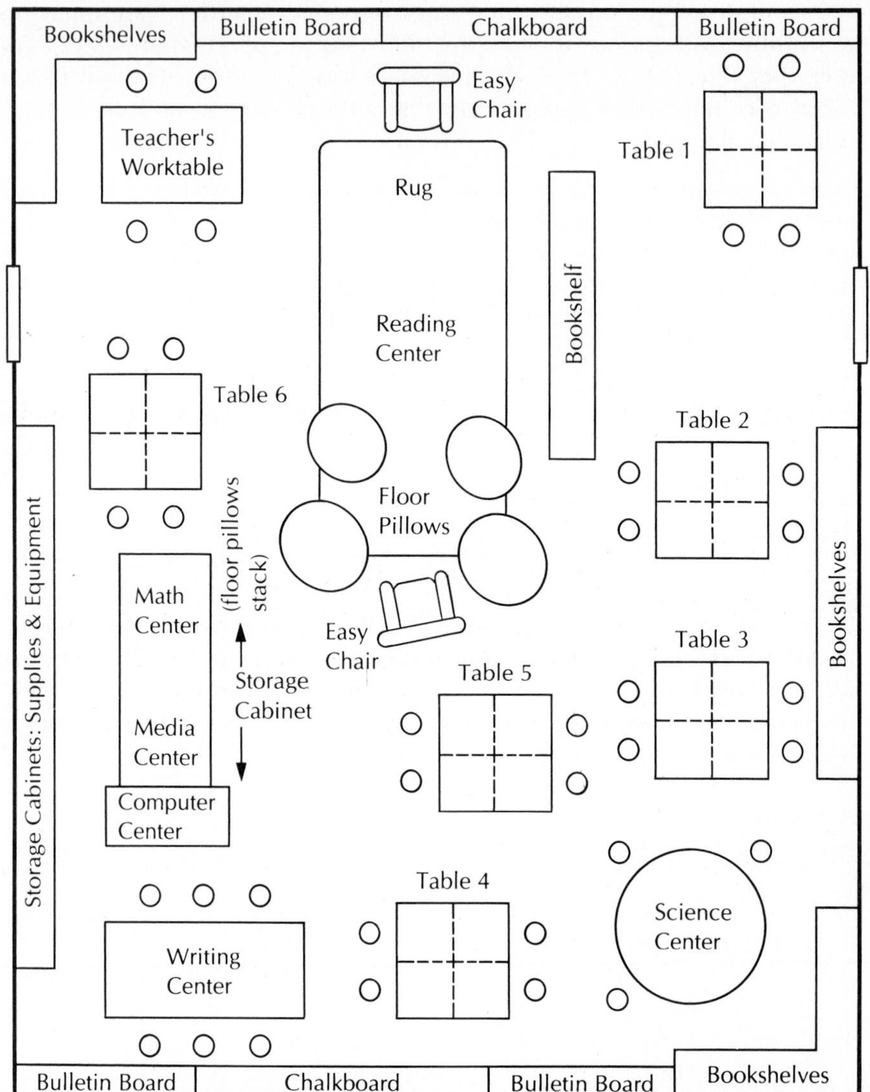

Figure 1–2
A Diagram of Avril Font's Classroom

Organizing the Classroom

In planning your teaching program, you need to consider how you will organize your classroom and materials, your children, and your time. Your room environment should be planned with the following components in mind.

- The room should be filled with print and with well-organized displays and shelves, and the students should have easy access to books and other materials.

• There should be space for children to work, and a variety of work areas which are both flexible and movable: clear table surfaces for large art and construction projects, open floor spaces for movement and drama, tables and chairs that can be rearranged for discussion and other small-group activities.

• Include private places, for small-group planning, reading, rehearsing, sustained silent reading, and writing.

• Create centers such as process centers with materials for writing, creating media, and subject centers with research and other materials on a specific topic of interest.

Organizing Children. The way you organize children and their experiences should allow for the following activities:

• *Whole-class activities.* These can include initiating experiences, both planned and spontaneous, book sharing, presentation of materials, class discussion, exchanging ideas, establishing certain key ideas, goals, or concepts, dealing with words or questions, or identifying directions to pursue.

• *Small-group activities.* As a way of varying experiences for different children, encourage discussion and planning between and among children by grouping students with similar interests, and let them practice problem solving.

• *Individual activities.* Allow plenty of time for children to work alone, reading, writing, making things, and so on. This does not mean that the children should be working separately on the same task but they need an opportunity to use language as they seek meaning through the language arts, and they need to do so in their very own way.

• *One teacher/one child activities.* Plan as much time each week as you can for one-to-one contact, conferencing, or just talking with each child.

Organizing Time. You will also have to organize time and have a schedule, but in an integrated approach to teaching you will not be able to divide the day into neat periods of one subject at a time. During any given period, if the children are actively involved in a subject and activities that interest them, you may find that you have covered all the required subjects for that day, as well as a few that are not required.

Furthermore, the process experiences like writing and drama, which are the glue holding an integrated curriculum together, take a great deal of time in one chunk: time to brainstorm, organize, plan, procrastinate, revise, daydream, argue, resolve, take risks, and produce. What is really important is that children become actively involved in the ownership of their own learning experiences.

How Will You Begin to Teach a Lesson?

How will you put the principles suggested in this chapter into practice the first time you teach a language arts lesson? If you are in a field experience practicum where you may not know the children well before you plan, or if you are teaching your first class or teaching at the very beginning of the year, a good way to begin is with a **pattern for writing.** You can plan a first lesson around a letter or counting pattern, or a poem or rhyme or song, or a book with a predictable language pattern.

Avril Font did this with her class at the beginning of the year when she found that several of her students had never visited the state capitol buildings even though they lived in the capital city of their state. As they began talking about the state, Avril began listing all the things they knew about their state on the blackboard and suggested they create an ABC of the state. For each letter of the alphabet, they brainstormed to find a word that began with that letter; thus the alphabet became a pattern around which they organized their words and ideas.

The class first did this as a whole group with one ABC for all, then each child did her own as they began to read and find out more about the state in individual and small-group work. After a field trip to the state capitol, they researched many topics about their community and reported these in many ways, which included binding and publishing an ABC book.

Sample Lesson Plan: An Alphabet Pattern

Here is what a lesson plan for your first experience might look like.

Level: Primary to Middle Grades

Purpose

1. Children will share ideas on a topic of interest in a large group.
2. Children will brainstorm ideas related to this topic.
3. Children will listen to a pattern (language sequence, poem, book with a predictable pattern) and adapt their ideas to compose a new pattern.
4. Children will read and respond to what they have written.

Teaching Sequence

1. Invite children to exchange ideas on any topic they choose.
2. Identify a topic of interest to many children and expand on the topic by asking questions such as:
   What else do you know about this?
   Have you had any experiences with this?
   What are some other words for these things?
   What else would you like to know about this?
   How could we find out more about this topic?

3. Create a word wall by recording the responses of the children on the chalkboard. Encourage many ideas and accept and praise all.
4. Suggest a way to organize these ideas into a pattern for writing, such as the alphabet.
5. For each letter of the alphabet, take suggestions from children for a word on their topic that begins with that letter, and record these on the chalkboard.
6. Take suggestions also for a sentence for each letter and record the sentences.
7. Encourage children to read and respond to the ABC they have written.

Extending Activities

1. Children can gather in small groups or write their own ABC on this or another topic.
2. Children can illustrate their ABC.
3. The ABCs can be published in several ways:
   mounted on the bulletin board,
   bound in books, or
   drawn on a transparency with permanent colored markers and shown on the overhead projector.
4. Children can pantomime or dramatize their ABCs in a group.

Evaluation

Observe whether or not the purposes of the exercise have been met.

1. Did the children participate in the exchange of ideas?
2. Did they suggest words and ideas related to the topic during the brainstorming period?
3. Were they able to relate their ideas to the pattern and compose them in a new pattern?
4. Were they able to read and did they respond actively to the pattern they wrote?

One Child's Pattern: My Louisiana Book

Here is the ABC pattern written by one child in Avril Font's class. Bridget wrote, illustrated, and bound *My Louisiana Book.* The cover depicts a large red crab, and the book itself consists of a page with a letter, sentence, and picture for each letter of the alphabet.

***My Louisiana Book* by Bridget**

A is for the Acadian people.
B is for Baton Rouge, the capital city.
C is for Creole cooking.

D is for downtown Baton Rouge.
E is for Exxon where my Daddy works.
F is for the Louisiana flag.
G is for the governor.
H is for Henry Shreve who founded the city of Shreveport.
I is for Louisiana Indian mounds.
J is for the pirate Jean Lafitte.
K is for King Cotton.
L is for the city of Lake Charles.
M is for a Mardi Gras parade.
N is for the city of New Orleans.
O is for the Old State Capitol.
P is for pelican, the state bird.
Q is for quay, where we tie up our boats.
R is for the Mississippi River.
S is for the Louisiana State Seal.
T is for old Beauregard Town.
U is for Louisiana State University.
V is for vegetable soybeans.
W is for the War of 1812 when the Battle of New Orleans was fought.
X is for Xavier University in New Orleans.
Y is for yams.
Z is for zydeco Cajun music.

Patterns for Talking and Writing

You can use many other predictable language, poem, rhyme, or book patterns to introduce language arts experiences to a whole class of students and later extend to small-group and individualized activities.

Hosie's Alphabet, by Leonard Baskin (Viking, 1972), is a beautifully illustrated ABC book with a word describing an animal for each letter of the alphabet, such as *bumptious baboon* and *carrion crow.*

See "I Can Read! Predictable Books as Resources for Reading and Writing Instruction," by Lynn K. Rhodes, in *The Reading Teacher,* 34 (1981), 511–518.

Letter and Counting Patterns. Plan lessons around letter and counting patterns, including such common place things as the alphabet, a number sequence or a person's name. The name of a place, event, or holiday or a word on a topic of interest are also good subjects.

Poetry, Rhyme, and Song Patterns. Mother Goose and nursery rhymes provide familiar patterns for children to work with. Poems and songs with regular meter are also useful.

Predictable Pattern Books. Here is a beginning list of picture books with predictable language patterns, including letter and counting patterns; poetry, rhyme, and song patterns; and picture books with a predictable pattern text.

Hosie's Alphabet, by Leonard Baskin (Viking, 1972)
The Very Hungry Caterpillar, by Eric Carle (Putnam, 1981)

The House That Jack Built, by Janet Stevens (Holiday House, 1985)
Millions of Cats, by Wanda Gag (Coward-McCann, 1956)
There Was an Old Woman, Steven Kellogg (Parents Magazine Press, 1974)
I Know an Old Lady Who Swallowed a Fly, by Nadine Bernard Westcott (Little, Brown, 1980)
Old MacDonald Had a Farm, by Tracey Campbell Pearson (Dial, 1984)
Over In the Meadow, by Ezra Jack Keats (Scholastic, 1973)
London Bridge is Falling Down! by Peter Spier (Doubleday, 1967)
Johnny Crow's Garden, by L. Leslie Brooke (Warne, 1986)
Green Eggs and Ham, by Dr. Seuss (Beginner Books, 1960)
One Fine Day, by Nonny Hogrogian (Macmillan, 1971)
The Fat Cat, by Jack Kent (Scholastic, 1971)
Goodnight Moon, by Margaret Wise Brown (Harper & Row, 1947)
Brown Bear, Brown Bear, What Do You See? by Bill Martin, Jr. (Holt, Rinehart & Winston, 1970)
Shoes, by Elizabeth Winthrop (Harper & Row, 1986)
Fortunately, by Remy Charlip (Parents Magazine Press, 1964)
The Important Book, by Margaret Wise Brown (Harper & Row, 1949)
Whose Mouse Are You? by Robert Kraus (Macmillan, 1970)
The Judge, by Harve Zemach (Farrar, Straus, 1969)

How Will You Begin to Integrate the Curriculum through the Language Arts?

The Ripple Effect

One way to think about planning and teaching a curriculum integrated through the language arts is in terms of a **ripple effect.** The focus of a ripple effect is any idea, experience, or subject that does for instructional possibilities what a pebble does when thrown into a body of water. It creates an ever-widening circle of ripples, some becoming waves that create more ripples. Sometimes you will plan a "pebble," and other times it will occur spontaneously. When you think of teaching as a ripple effect of ideas, you don't always know which pebble will make the most waves. Sometimes the pebble you plan and pick out very carefully will plop and sink, and the ripples will be few. Perhaps the children lacked interest or you lacked enthusiasm, or the subject just was not exciting enough to carry the waves.

Sometimes, however, the children will hand you a pebble and the effect of its hitting the water will continue long after it is lost from view. And the longer the ripples last, the wider the circle they will form to reach into all areas of the language arts and the rest of the curriculum as well. Several pebbles were tossed out in Avril Font's room on the morning in April described earlier.

Figure 1–3
Pages from a book about Shakespeare Written by Students in Avril Font's Fourth Grade

Shakespeare became a hot topic for a group of children who read and wrote about him and shared what they had learned by writing and illustrating a story about his life and publishing it in book form (Figure 1–3). The children who were curious about an aquarium read and wrote about it and put together an aquarium and stocked it with fish, which they also studied. Other pebbles had already been tossed and sometimes the ripples merged with new ones created. As some of the children were learning about St. George and the dragon and about the maypole dance, they connected these ideas about English history and traditions with what children in another group were learning about Shakespeare.

A Ripple Effect: The Community

Let us look at a very simple type of pebble that is often found in classrooms, especially at the beginning of the school year, as it was in Avril Font's class. Children are naturally curious about and interested in their community and often know a great deal about different aspects of it. This is a good topic to look into because many learning resources are available. And studying the local community can lead to learning about other communities in the country and the world.

What might a ripple effect about the community look like? Figure 1–4 illustrates how language and literacy experiences on this subject can act as a pebble and create a ripple effect that can extend into all parts of the curriculum.

Figure 1–4 *A Ripple Effect: The Community*

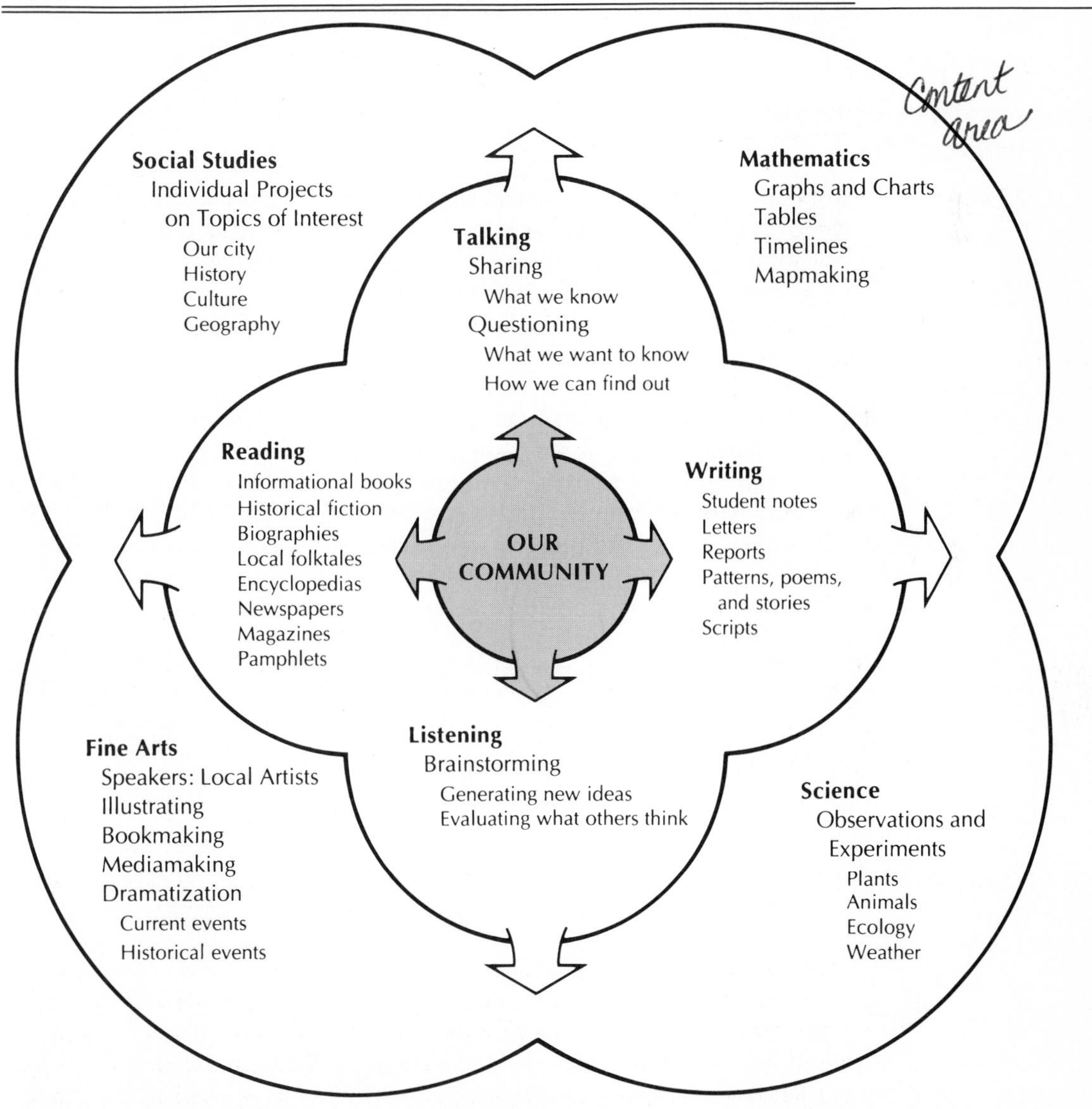

Who Is an Effective Teacher of Language Arts?

Her principal, peers, parents, and especially her students consider Avril Font to be an extremely effective teacher. It is not unusual to hear Avril's students tell a class visitor, or anyone else, that "Mrs. Font is the best teacher I ever had. I really learn a lot in here."

While I was observing in her class, thirteen-year-old Donald, who had already been retained twice, confided in me that even though he had done well enough on all the tests required by the school system and the state to move on to fifth grade—this was the first time in four years he had not had to repeat a grade—he wished he had failed because he wanted to be in Mrs. Font's room again!

Characteristics of Effective Teachers of Language Arts

What do we know about teachers who are effective teachers of the language arts? What are their characteristics? Extensive research on teacher effectiveness in the English language arts (Berman & McLaughlin, 1978; Brookover, 1976; Brophy, Downing, Evertson, & Anderson, 1979; Peters & Blues, 1978; Rosenshine & Berliner, 1978) has revealed the following characteristics of effective teachers:

1. Effective teachers maintain a fairly personal classroom environment with major emphasis on the self-expression of students in interpersonal oral and written communication and in response to literature and how it relates to their own ideas and lives.
2. Effective teachers plan for more class time in discussions and questioning and less for formal lessons or lectures.
3. Effective teachers are instructional and classroom leaders and good managers.
4. Effective teachers have a preference for complexity in learning experiences and a higher tolerance for ambiguity and uncertainty.
5. Effective teachers believe their students can learn, and believe in themselves and their ability to teach effectively.

Summing Up

Individualized language and literacy experiences are child centered. They stem from the ideas, interests, and interaction of individual children. Such practices can be informed by research and theory on the cognitive development of children as outlined by Piaget. He explains that children are able to structure a view of reality through the interaction of their internal maturation and their experiences in the world. Key ideas in this theory are those of adaptation to the environment (which children do through the processes of assimilation), accommodation, and equilibration. Children progressively develop a schema, or a structure, upon which to build new concepts.

Piaget also describes the developmental stages in the cognitive development of the child: sensorimotor, from birth to two years; preoperational thought, from two to seven years; concrete operations, from seven to eleven years; and formal operations, from eleven to fifteen years. While all children pass through all these stages, in Piaget's theory, not all of them will progress at the same rate.

In addition to considering the child's interests and development, teachers should respect the diversity of ideas, culture, and languages children bring to school, reflecting the multicultural character of our nation.

Interactive language and literacy experiences in a whole-language classroom are always focused on seeking meaning. The Goodmans (1981) remind us that the purpose of listening and reading experiences is to understand meaning, and the purpose of speaking and writing experiences is to create meaning. Harste, Woodward, and Burke (1984) also suggest that a whole-language classroom reflects the fact that language is social, that it is a place where teachers encourage active communication, and that the focus of teaching in such a classroom is always on literacy, on the development of reading and writing, and on the life experiences that support the growth of these skills.

Effective teachers of language arts, such as Avril Font, maintain a fairly personal classroom and believe that all of their students are capable of learning.

Integrated language and literacy experiences connect all the language modes, and this connection in turn will support the development of each of these modes, as Loban's research (1976, 1979) has shown. In order to achieve this connection effectively, teachers should take a creative, problem-solving approach to teaching and integrating the curriculum through English language arts experiences that are firmly rooted in a humanistic view of education.

This chapter has also shown ways in which teachers can begin to answer some of the practical questions about getting started in teaching the language arts: what to teach, what materials to use, how to organize and schedule a day, how to begin teaching lessons, and how to begin to integrate the curriculum through a ripple effect of ideas and activities.

Finally, a summary of research on teaching effectiveness in the English language arts enumerated the characteristics of effective teachers and can serve as a guide to you in considering the choices you can make from among the many models, materials, and methods presented in the rest of the text.

Looking Further

1. Brainstorm to compile a list of all the ways in which Avril Font created individualized, interactive, and integrated learning experiences in the language arts. If possible, do this in small groups after reading and discussing with others what happened in her classroom.

2. Observe in a classroom and note to what extent the teacher creates individualized, interactive, and integrated learning experiences.

3. Write a brief autobiography and share it with others in your class, or ask a group of children to write theirs, and then share yours and theirs with each other.

4. Start a journal, focusing on your interests, ideas, and plans for your future as a teacher.

5. Create an interest inventory for a grade level you would like to teach. Administer it to a child of the appropriate age and analyze the responses to see if the questions you asked gave you important or insightful information about the child. Plan an experience for the child based on the inventory.

6. Make a list of some of the important experiences in your life you could tell your class about when teaching, and describe how you would build on these in the classroom.

7. Review several language arts textbooks, noting their strengths, their weaknesses, the parts you would use, and the parts you would not use.

8. Draw a floor plan of the way you would like your classroom to look. Discuss your plan with others in your class and compare your plan with theirs.

9. Outline a lesson plan for a specific grade level and on a specific topic that would use a language or literature pattern. Use the lesson plan format in this chapter. Teach your lesson if possible.

10. Examine three of the pattern books listed in the chapter and describe how you might use each one to structure a language arts lesson.

Chapter Two

Children and Language

Centering Ideas

Five Days with Apples

Further Adventures with Apples

Making Connections

Children Learning and Using Language

Culture, Language, and Language Arts and Reading

Language Is Alive and Changing

Teaching Children

Vocabulary and Concept Development through Language Interaction

Language and Literature Patterns for Language Arts and Reading

Playing with Language

Learning about Language

Observing Children Using Language

Summing Up

Looking Further

Objectives

Look for answers to the following questions as you read this chapter.

- How do you base language arts instruction on the ideas, interests, and language of children?
- How do children learn and use language?
- What is the relationship of culture and language and how does it affect student success in language arts and reading?
- What are some strategies for encouraging the development of language control and use among children and teaching them about language?

A Child's View

Here is how fifth-grade students responded to questions about language:

What is Language?

- "Language is like prepositions, nouns, verbs."
- "A form of communication through the mouth."
- "Language usually means what you speak and write. But it can also mean how you think and perceive things."
- "Language is how to write. If you know words you just can't slap them down on a piece of paper. Words and sentences need meaning to make sense and do their proper functions."

How Do You Get It?

- "Probably some nut thought of it to give kids more work!"
- "It comes natural, like a wolf's instinct to hunt."
- "You get your language from your voice box. And school."
- "It is learned by real-life experiences and influences."
- "Language helps you to think, be imaginative, communicate, and express your feelings. Without it we'd lose a lot."

Centering Ideas

How would you go about teaching individualized, interactive, and integrated language and literacy experiences for the first time, for example in first grade? And how do you base language arts instruction on the ideas, interests, and language of children? Look for answers to these questions as you read the following description of what actually happened in one first-grade classroom during the first five days of the school year.

Five Days with Apples

Day 1: An Apple for the Teacher

Marion Harris teaches first grade in Denham Springs, Louisiana. On the first day of school, three of her students bring her apples. Really. She thanks the children, displays the apples prominently on her desk, and forgets all about them. Marion does not like apples.

Day 2: Apples as Pebbles

When the children ask her why she has not eaten the apples, Marion hedges slightly on the truth and says that she wants to share the apples in a special way. This starts a ripple of excitement in the classroom. Observing this, Marion listens to the children speculate and begins to think in earnest how she might really share the apples. Even more important, she considers how she might build on the children's interest and use the apples as pebbles to start a ripple effect of individualized, interactive, and integrated language and literacy experiences based on the ideas, interests, and language of the children in her new first-grade class.

Day 3: A Story Riddle, Small-Group Discussions, and Writing

Marion Harris remembers a story riddle about apples from her student teaching days. She seats her class in a circle on the floor, and tells a story about a little girl who was bored. It was Saturday and there wasn't any school. And she had nothing to do. When she told her mother how she felt, her mother told her to go outside and look for a little round red house with no windows or doors, a chimney on top, and a star inside. She told the little girl that she would find the little house near a big tree in the backyard. The little girl went outside and looked and looked and finally found the little round red house with no windows or doors, a chimney on top, and a star inside under a big tree in the backyard.

Marion tells the children that this is a riddle and they will have to guess the answer. A lively discussion follows as the children try to guess what it was the little girl found. Someone suggests an apple, but another child says there is no star inside. Marion takes this as her cue to cut an apple in half horizontally and show the children the star-shaped seed pocket inside.

Then she organizes the children into small groups, gives each group an apple, and asks them to observe it: look at it, touch it, smell it, and then compare their observations with those of the other children in their group so that if all the apples were together, they could still pick out their own. She also suggests that they might wish to take notes and gives them small pieces of paper and pencil to do so (Figure 2–1). The children begin to look for clues that will help them distinguish their own apple. They all talk, and some write, as they look. Here are excerpts from their discussions.

Teacher: What do you think is different about your apple?
Child: I see a line. Right here. Uh-huh. Dots. It has little dots. It doesn't have a stem.
Child: Pass it around! I like the little red dots. You like 'em? It has yellow dots too.
Teacher: Yes. I like them.
Child: Yeah. We're doin' tricks with it. We like it.

Teacher: What's different about this one?
Child: It's got green on it and a little light red streak. The bottom is shaped like a star. It doesn't have a chimney.
Teacher: Mm-hm. Oh yes, I see.
Child: It has a green mark. It goes like this [*makes a gesture like an arc in the air*]. It's like a rainbow or something.

Some of the children take notes during these discussions, using drawing and writing—usually a combination of pictures and words—to symbolize and record their experiences. Finally, Marion collects the apples in a bag and asks a child from each group to find that group's apple and discuss his choice with the others.

Child: It'll help to know if yours has a stem. [*Chooses an apple and shows it to the group.*]
Teacher: [*Observing the children's reactions*] Danielle's not sure. Brad and Brady say no.
Child: Yup, 'cause there's the green spot.
Child: We had a big one but that one's too little.
Child: Whose had a streak? Yours did? Is this it?

After more discussion and apple exchanges, each group reclaims the apple they agreed was their own.

Figure 2–1
Children's Notes about Apples

Day 4: Estimating the Number of Seeds in an Apple and More Talking and Writing

During the discussion of what to do with the apples, someone suggests making a pie. Feelings are mixed on this issue.

Child: Are we gonna put 'em in a pot?
Child: No! Sick! Not *our* apple!

The pies win, and it is time to cut the apples.

Teacher: Let's try to guess how many seeds are in each apple before we cut them.
Child: Thirteen hundred. [*Laughter from others.*]
Child: You can't see anything. I'm not guessing.

Marion Harris shows first-grade students the star-shaped seed pocket in an apple after a storytelling session.

Child: Four. There's four in every one.
Child: I think four could be right, or five or six.

More guessing follows and each group eventually comes to a consensus on an estimated number of seeds, which they write down. The children watch as Marion cuts each apple open and they count the seeds and compare the actual number to their estimates.

Child: There's a trap door for the seeds.
Child: Can we eat 'em?
Child: [*Counting*] Three . . . four . . . five. Danielle was right.
Teacher: You hit the jackpot on this one!
Child: Man, we won. [*Laughter.*]

Day 5: Cooking Apple Turnovers and Playing with Words

The apples simmer slowly with some cinnamon on a hot plate as Marion makes plans with the class to cook apple turnovers. The children discuss a recipe which Marion writes on a large piece of chart paper as they watch. They measure and mix the dough, then they each take a piece of waxed paper, some dough, and some flour to keep the dough from sticking to their hands as they smooth and spread the elastic dough flat to wrap the

First-grade students observing, talking, and taking notes about apples.

apples in. They continue to talk, and some of them start to imagine, rhyme, and play with the dough, with the flour, and with words.

Child: Yuck!
Teacher: How does it feel?
Child: Feels like Play-doh. I eat it. Yum, yum. It's squishy.
Child: It's white. I like *flour* 'cause it's *powder.* [*Emphasis on italicized words as in a rhyme scheme.*] Gimme some flour.
Child: [*In a sing-song voice*]

Patterned after the Mother Goose rhyme "Pat-a-Cake, Pat-a-Cake, Baker's Man"

Pat-a-cake, pat-a-cake, baker man.
Pat-a-cake, pat-a-cake, make the glue.
Pat-a-cake, pat-a-cake, come on my hand.
Pat-a-cake, pat-a-cake, put some on.
Pat-a-cake, pat-a-cake, roll it up.
Pat-a-cake, pat-a-cake, put 'em in the pan.
Pat-a-cake, pat-a-cake, throw 'em in the pan.

Child: Hmmmmm. It keeps getting smaller. I pushed my fingerprint in it. Watch it get littler and littler.
Teacher: Mash out the edges.

Child: [*Mashing*] This thing is getting *pain* out of me! It's hard to flatten. My hand is stuck.
Child: Mine must be a pancake. I'll throw it up and catch it. It might fall on my head. Crash!
Child: This is yucky. Won't ever taste good. Pow, pow, pow!

As they continue to struggle with the sticky dough, their behavior and language becomes more playful, and they begin to imagine.

Child: [*In a sing-song voice while swinging a long piece of dough forward and back*] I'm fishin'. Fishin' with my rod. Fishin' with my rod, wishin' with my rod. Wishin' I had a fish. Gotta go fry my fish. Fishy rod, fishy rod. Sticky food, sticky food.
Child: Mine's a little bitty shell turtle. His head's right here.
Child: Mine's sticky. A sticky ball. It's a stickball.

Marion puts a dab of cooked apples on each semiflattened piece of dough. The children fold the pieces over, pinching them together around the edges, and cook them in a pan of hot oil. The spontaneous word play continues: **personifying** (giving human attributes to) apples, rhyming, combining words to make new ones, using **onomatopoeia** (words that imitate a sound) and **assonance** (repeating vowels without repeating consonants—as in *stony/holy*—as an alternative to rhyme), and making **metaphors** (words or phrases used in place of another, denoting the similarity between them).

Child: The apples are frying. They're dying. No, they're swimming in the grease.
Teacher: What does it sound like?
Child: Popping!
Child: Looks like a clam. A shell. A clamshell.
Child: A frying egg.
Child: Looks like a crab. A crawfish. Look at the crab's mouth.
Teacher: Whose little clam is this?
Child: That long one is mine. It looks like a hot dog.

When all the apple turnovers have been cooked, cooled, and eaten, Marion encourages the children to recall words they have used. They watch her create a **word wall** by writing the words on strips of paper for different categories (see Table 2–1). When the word wall is finished, the class discuss and choose and combine some of their words into a pattern for writing called a cinquain, which Marion writes on a large piece of chart paper and later displays on a bulletin board.

A **word wall** is a collection of words brainstormed by children on a subject of interest and recorded by the teacher for all to see.

Cinquain Pattern

Line 1. One word: the title
Line 2. Two words: describe the title
Line 3. Three words: tell an action
Line 4. Four words: tell a feeling or description
Line 5. One word: refer back to title

Apple Pies
Snapping, sizzling
Floating in the grease!
Yummy, great, delicious
100% good!

Table 2–1 *Word Wall for Apple Turnovers*

Colors		*Texture*	*Action*	
brown	*T:* What was brown? *C:* After we fried 'em.	icky	squashed	*C:* the pies
		yucky	frying	*C:* we watched
white	*C:* When we first made 'em. Flour. Sugar.	slimy	patting	
		like Play-doh	spooned	*C:* the apples
yellow	*C:* The pot. The oil.	sticky	cooked	
		stiff	rubbing	*C:* your hands
		greasy	sprinkled	*C:* cinnamon, sugar
		smushy		
		hot		

Shapes		*Feelings*	
circles		happy	
ball		sad	*C:* when they were dying
clam	*T:* Brian said he saw one that was clam-shaped.	glad	
crab	*C:* Crab-shaped!	good	
oyster		smiling	
long-shaped		great	
hot dog	*T:* Lance said he saw one that was shaped like a hot dog. *C:* Miss Harris, I know a word. [*a child who had not spoken earlier*] *T:* Jeremy?	jumpy	*C:* I felt like I was gonna jump up!
round	*C:* We seen some round. *T:* That's great, Jeremy. We have circles and balls but we don't have round.		
turtle shell			

Size		*Taste*	*Sounds*	
small	*T:* What's another word for small?	good	popping	
little	*T:* Good!	yucky	bubbling	
big	*T:* Another word?	yummy	snapping	*C:* like Rice Krispies
large		great	crackling	
huge		delicious	sizzling	*C:* like this—Sssssss
		terrific		
		100% good		

A word wall and pattern writing for apple pies.

Further Adventures with Apples

During the weeks that follow this first week of school, Marion extends the ripple effect started by apples. The children write more apple words and patterns and make their own books of apple words and pictures for others to read. They plant seeds from the apples they ate, as well as other types of seeds, in order to investigate plants and growing things. They try more estimating—like the weights of apples—and experiment with dividing apples into fractions. Marion reads them stories and shows filmstrips and films about Johnny Appleseed and others who grow food and other products people need. They use a variety of art media, including some made from apples: straw-blow and sponge paintings of apple trees, apple block prints, and carved and dried apple heads. And they continue to experience, observe, talk, share, write, read, draw, and dramatize as their thoughts and language become the center of a curriculum integrated through teaching the language arts (see Figure 2–2).

Eat the Fruit, Plant the Seed, by Millicent E. Selsam (Morrow, 1980); *Tall Tale America,* by Walter Blair (Coward-McCann, 1944); and the film *Johnny Appleseed* (Aims Instructional Media, 1968)

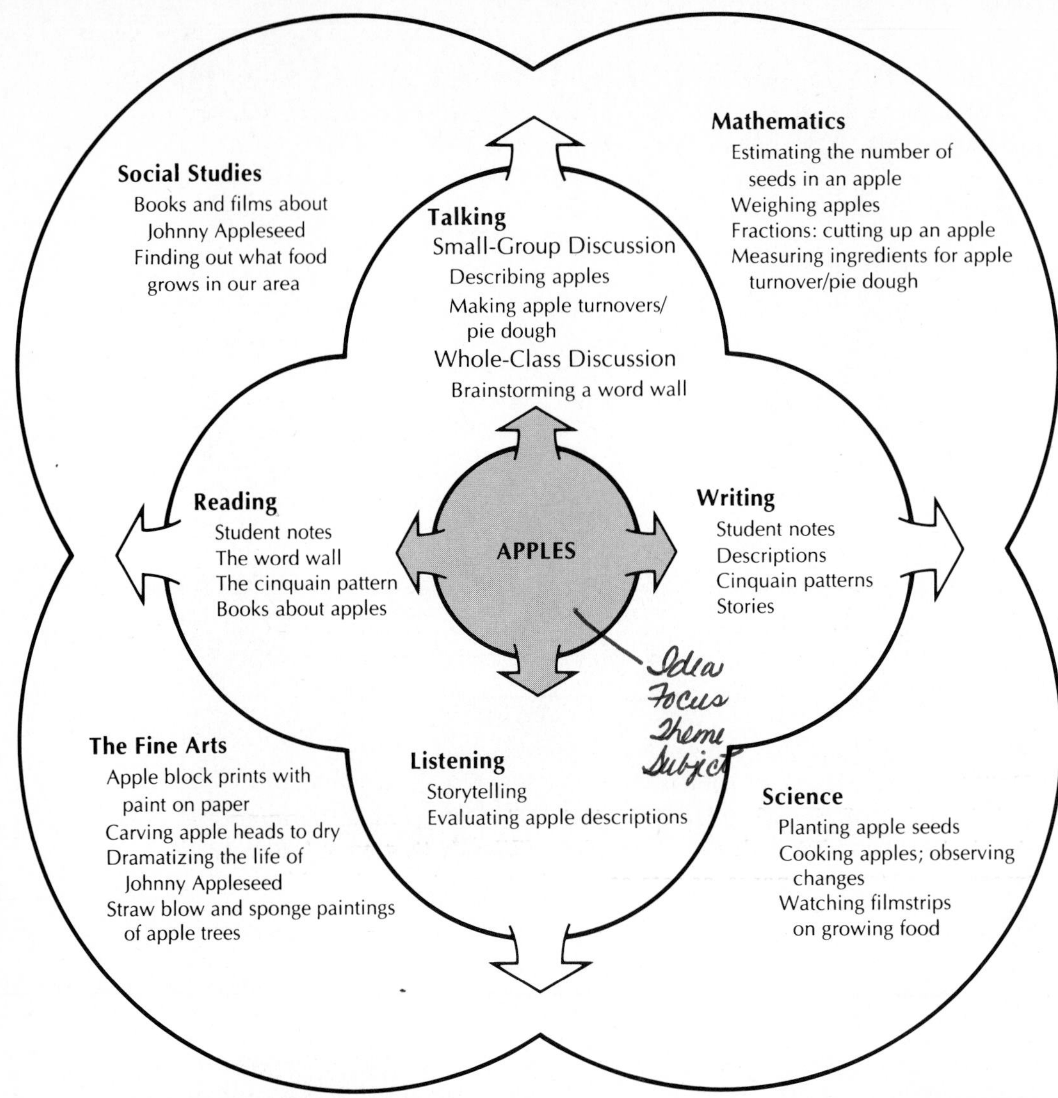

Figure 2–2 *A Ripple Effect: Apples*

Making Connections

What do the experiences of this first-grade class during the first few days of school tell us about how children learn and use language? And what are the implications for teaching language arts?

Studies of the language of school-age children (Chomsky, 1969; Loban, 1963; Monroe & Rogers, 1964; Strickland, 1962) have shown the following characteristics of their language development.

1. Children have acquired most of the basic structures of English before they enter school and have a vocabulary that may range from 3,000 to 48,000 words.
2. As children progress through the grades, they use longer sentences, make more use of movables and subordination, use fewer short utterances, and use more common linguistic patterns.
3. Children between five and ten years old are not simply expanding their use of syntactic structures but are still in the process of acquiring new ones.
4. Children improve the effectiveness and control of their language by degree of flexibility, expansion, and elaboration of elements within already learned language patterns.
5. Children who are more proficient in oral language use a greater degree of subordination, are more sensitive to the conventions of language, score higher on vocabulary and intelligence tests, and perform better in reading and writing.

A Definition of Language

Halliday (1973) offers educators a definition for language from a sociolinguistic point of view that is particularly relevant to understanding children's language in a classroom setting: "We shall define language as 'meaning potential,' that is, as sets of opinions, or alternatives, in meaning, that are available to the speaker-hearer" (p. 64).

Language Use

Halliday also provides a model for interpreting the child's early language development, one which describes a set of functions of language that most children have learned to use by the time they come to school. As the children master these functions, they are learning how to mean; the meaning potential they are building up is a measure of what they can do with language.

Table 2–2 summarizes Halliday's categories of the functions of language, illustrates each category with examples from the children's dialogue during their discussions of apples in Marion Harris's first-grade classroom, and describes the types of language arts experiences, related to each category, which can help children expand their own meaning potential.

The Role of the Teacher in Language Development

How can teachers capture and extend the facility for using language that even young children like these new first-graders bring to school? Some

Table 2–2 *Children's Model of Language*

Children's Model of Language	*Example*	*Experiences*
Instrumental		
Language as a means of getting things done; satisfaction of material needs. The *I want* function.	"Gimme some flour for my hands."	Solving problems; getting things to get the job done.
Regulatory		
Language as an instrument of control; the language of rules and instructions. The *Do as I tell you* function.	"Pass it around."	Giving ordered sequences of instructions; converting these to rules, including conditional rules, as in explaining the principles of a game.
Interactional		
Use of language in interaction between self and others. The *Me and you* function.	"3 . . . 4 . . . 5! Danielle was right! Man, we won!"	Language in groups: listening, talking, dialogue, discussion, interaction.
Personal		
Language as a form of the child's own individuality. The *Here I come* function.	"This thing is getting pain out of me."	Speaking to express and make public their own unique and individual feelings, attitudes, and to discover what these are through interaction with others; the *self as speaker.*
Heuristic		
Knowledge of how language has enabled the child to explore the environment: a means of investigating reality, a way of learning about things. The *Tell me why* function.	"Whose had a streak? Yours did? Is that it? It'll help to know if yours has a stem." "Miss Harris, I know a word."	Question and answer routines; metalanguage, or a language for talking about language—words like *question, answer, knowing, understanding.*
Imaginative		
Using language to create their own environment; exploring their own minds, including language itself. The *Let's pretend* function.	"I'm fishing. Fishing with my rod. Fishing with my rod, wishing with my rod. Wishing I had a fish. Gotta go fry my fish. Fishy rod, fishy rod. Sticky food, sticky food."	Create worlds of their own; stories and dramatic games based on content, but not limited to make-believe copy of real world occupied by people, things, and events; world of pure sound—rhythmic sequences of rhyming and chiming syllables; nonsense; poems, rhymes, riddles and linguistic play; more metalanguage words like *story, make up, pretend.*

Table 2–2 *Continued*

Children's Model of Language	*Example*	*Experiences*
Representational		
Communication of content. The *I've got something to tell you* function.	"It's got green on it. And a little red streak. The bottom is shaped like a star."	Telling about the real world; expressing propositions; conveying messages with specific reference to the processes, persons, objects, abstractions, qualities, states, and relations of the real world.

Adapted from Halliday, 1973.

researchers suggest that this may be more a matter of building on the language children have already learned at home than the initiation of language and learning events by the teacher. In a comparison of adult–child conversations at home and school, Wells and Wells (1984) found that children played a much less active role in conversation in school than they did at home. They initiated fewer interactions, and what they said was syntactically and semantically simpler. Like Tizard, Carmichael, Hughes, and Pinkerton (1980), Wells and Wells found that schools were not providing a linguistically rich environment, and that all of the homes they observed provided more opportunities for learning through talk with an adult.

The classroom interaction described at the beginning of this chapter is one example of how a meaningful context for language use based on language interaction—between teacher and child as well as among the children, and including riddles, storytelling, dialogues, question-and-answer exchanges, large- and small-group discussions, problem-solving situations, and a lot of language play—started a ripple effect created by the apple pebble. Just this one topic allowed the children to explore the options and alternatives in meaning available to them as they used the many functions of language already in their repertoire. And Marion Harris built her teaching approach on the meaning potential that these language experiences, centered around apples, had for these children.

If learning language is, as Halliday suggests, learning how to mean, how do teachers help students do this? Piaget (1962), and Vygotsky (1962), another scholar of the thought and language of children, offer two points of view that may help you think about the meaning potential of children's language.

Piaget argues that thought precedes and is separate from language. He bases this view on his observations of children at play: they demonstrated through the manipulation of objects that they understood certain concepts and could solve certain problems without verbalizing them. Children learn to understand language as they first assimilate and then accommodate language symbols to their symbolic structures. In the search for meaning, children symbolize before they verbalize.

Vygotsky suggests that adult language plays a more active role, that it is a center around which the child forms thought complexes, similar to Piaget's schema or symbolic structures. These develop as a result of the child's interaction with adults. This theory contradicts Piaget's notion that the language of adults helps children verbalize structures that have already developed through the manipulation of objects in their environment.

Obviously, the role of the adult and the language of the world surrounding the child—particularly adult language—is important in both theories. Piaget sees the adult as a person who creates situations in which children discover meaning themselves. Vygotsky sees the verbal interaction between adult and child as a primary means for children to achieve this meaning potential.

In Marion Harris's class, examples of both theories at work could be found. Children were primarily involved in self-discovery as they flattened the sticky, elastic, and stubborn dough and tried to get it to stay flat without poking holes in it. Language usually followed as a description of what they had already done. Adult guidance and verbalization initiated the estimating episode when Marion suggested what they might do and introduced them to the concept of estimating.

Both Piaget's and Vygotsky's theories have much to say to teachers who want to help children make the most of language in order to achieve the meaning potential it has for them as speakers and learners. Interaction is critical, whether it consists of dialogues with the teacher, or situations where the teacher is a listener and observer as children adapt their thoughts and language, or the interaction between children of the same and of different ages.

In a year-long study of language interaction in a first-grade classroom, Dillon and Searle (1981) found that teacher talk tended to dominate in the role of explaining and evaluating and thereby limited child language in both quantity and purpose.

When thinking about this interactive nature of language, you should also consider that sometimes in education—as in art—less is more. A child absorbed in a serious struggle with stubborn dough that will not do what she thought it would and who is talking to herself about it at the same time, sometimes in beautifully descriptive and figurative speech—"this thing is getting *pain* out of me"—should not be interrupted by a teacher's comments, questions, or perhaps even presence.

Teachers must strike a balance between the power and potential of both self-discovery and interaction in the development of thought and language, what Vygotsky calls "the zone of proximal development" (1962, 1978): the range between what children can do alone and what they can do in collaboration with an adult. Knowing when to talk and when not to talk, then, are integral albeit intuitive parts of the art of teaching language arts.

Knowing a Language

As children learn how to use language to gain access to meaning, what exactly is it that they know how to use? What do we really know when we know a language? We know sounds that signify certain meanings and we are able to understand the meanings of sounds produced by other human beings, for language is a uniquely human attribute. We understand the system that links sounds and meanings. This link, by the way, is arbitrary: that which we call an apple is still an apple in any other language.

When you know a language, you are also able to combine words into phrases and phrases into sentences, you know how to produce new sentences never spoken before, and you can understand sentences you have never heard spoken before. You can create an infinite number of sentences from a finite number of words.

English: *apple*
French: *pomme*
Spanish: *manzana*
German: *apfel*

Chomsky (1968) focuses on this creative aspect of language in his development of a generative theory of language. He was also particularly interested in the difference between a speaker's competence (or subconscious control of the linguistic system that generates the language used in a specific situation) and performance (or the actual use of the language). This linguistic competence, or what we know, is a grammar, or knowledge of the elements and rules we use to speak a language. The three systems that interact in language are: a system of sounds, a system of meanings, and a system of sentence formation.

System of Sounds: Phonology. When you know a language, you are able to make sounds that have meanings and to understand the meaning of sounds that other people make. **Phonology** is the study of the patterns and systems of human language. **Phonetics** is a system of classifying these speech sounds, not to be confused with **phonics,** which is a method of teaching unfamiliar words in print based on the sound–letter correspondences in the spoken language.

The phonology of each language includes a set of basic building blocks called **phonemes,** or segments of sound that make a distinction between the meanings of words, and the sequences of these segments that make sense in a language.

For example, the children in Marion Harris's class knew the difference between the meaning of the word *pat* and similar words when they talked about "patting the dough" because as English speakers they knew the difference a phoneme would make at the beginning of other similar words such as *hat, cat, fat, sat, mat, bat,* or *rat* (*-a-tat-tat*). This same knowledge would also tell them the difference between *fry,* in "frying the pies," and *try, pry, cry,* and *wry.* There are about forty phonemes in English but only twenty-six letters in the English alphabet to represent these sounds. Sounds in words are represented by **graphemes** in written language.

System of Meanings: Semantics. When you know a language, you are able to produce sentences with certain meanings and to understand the meanings of sentences that other people make. **Semantics** is the study of linguistic meaning.

Morphemes are the smallest units of meaning in each language; they are sequences of phonemes that cannot be divided without losing meaning. Morphemes combine to form words, which may be made up of more than one morpheme. For example, the word *apple* cannot be reduced without a loss of meaning. It is called a **free morpheme** because it functions as a unit of meaning by itself. To create the plural *apples,* we add another morpheme: *–s.* This is called a **bound morpheme** because it cannot function as a unit of meaning by itself.

Examples of other types of bound morphemes are prefixes like *un-, il-,* and *im-,* and suffixes like *-ness, -y, -ly,* and *-ing.*

When you know a language, you know the morphemes, their meanings, how they may be combined to form words, and how to pronounce them. The vocabulary of morphemes and words in a language is called the **lexicon.**

As a proficient speaker of a language you are familiar, as are the children in Marion Harris's class, with **homonyms,** two words that look and sound the same but have different meanings ("looks *like* a rainbow" / "I *like* 'em"); **synonyms,** two different words that have a similar meaning ("*mash* out the edges" / "it's hard to *flatten*"); and **antonyms,** two words that have opposite meanings (*happy, sad*); you know that morphemes and words may be combined to form compound words (*fingerprint, rainbow, pancake*); and you understand **idioms,** sequences of words with one meaning that goes beyond the meaning of the individual words ("*you hit the jackpot!*").

When you know a language, you also know about **reference,** using words or sentences that may have meaning but do not refer to anything in the real world ("there's a *trap door* for the seeds"); **paraphrases,** restating a phrase or sentence in another form ("the apples are *frying*" / "they're *dying*"); **ambiguity,** using phrases that may have two different meanings (a *frying* egg); and **anomaly,** using words and phrases that are strange in the given context ("the apples are *swimming* in the grease").

You also know and understand how to use the terms that describe these concepts, such as *word, sentence, morpheme,* or *synonym.* These are part of a **metalanguage,** or language used to describe and talk about language ("Miss Harris, I know a *word*").

System of Sentence Formation: Syntax. When you know a language, you know the rules of **syntax,** which enable you to combine words in sentences that express your ideas, and you are able to understand the sentences produced by other people to express their ideas. Meaning in a sentence is partly determined by word order, and word order is one of the things that syntactic rules determine.

You know a language when you know whether a sentence is grammatical and obeys these rules or is ungrammatical and does not obey them. For example, the children in Marion's class would know which of the following sentences are grammatical and which are ungrammatical:

1. Brad and Brady say no.
2. Brady and Brad say no.

3. Brad and Brady no say.
4. Brad and Brady no.

If the rules that you know are the same as theirs (and they are if you speak English), you would know that examples 3 and 4 are ungrammatical. Children know how to form sentences that are grammatical sequences of words. They would also know which of these sentences is ambiguous:

1. The boy caught fish with fight.
2. The boy caught fish with rods.

Syntactic rules in the grammar of a language (1) account for the grammaticality of sentences, (2) determine the ordering of morphemes, (3) reveal ambiguities, (4) determine the grammatical relations between different parts of a sentence, and (5) relate one sentence to another without changing meaning.

If you think example 1 is ambiguous—who had the fight, the boy or the fish?—something in your knowledge of the underlying grammar of English told you so. Such a grammar exists in the head of any speaker of any language. When you know a language, what you know—your **linguistic competence**—is represented by that grammar. And all grammars include the following:

- Phonological rules, which specify the sound patterns of the language and how sentences are pronounced,
- Semantic rules, which characterize meanings of sentences in the language,
- A lexicon, or vocabulary of a language (words and morphemes) specified by phonological, syntactic, and semantic properties, and
- Syntactic rules that mediate between meaning and sound.

Culture, Language, and Language Arts and Reading

Most of the children in Marion Harris's first-grade class have spent their whole lives in Denham Springs, Louisiana, a small town in a rural area near Baton Rouge. Her class is also ethnically very diverse. These factors have influenced their language, just as they influence everyone's language. We are all linguistically different.

A Language Community

Sociolinguists describe the phenomenon of **language community** in terms of the different ways we can look at a person's language. Speakers are members of a language community when they regard themselves as users of the same language. Each speaker in a language community has a personal speech pattern called an **idiolect;** systematic differences of speech pattern among speakers of a language community stemming from differences in social group or geographic region are called **dialects;** and when speakers choose from the range of varieties of use within a dialect, they are using what is called a **register.**

Some factors that determine a person's idiolect, dialect, and register are age, sex, health, size, personality, emotional state, grammatical idiosyncrasies, profession, ethnic heritage, family situation, geographic region, race, and social group. How a person uses language in different contexts and even the passage of time influences that person's speech habits during the course of a lifetime.

For example, Marion Harris and the children in her class are part of a language community that uses English in the classroom. Each person in this classroom, however, has a personal idiolect, different from that of the others, and most speak a southern dialect—specifically, that of south Louisiana—subject to variations related to their cultural heritage.

Language Variation and Literacy

What does this variation in language mean for the teacher when the fundamental role of the school is perceived by many to be the teaching of literacy, particularly reading and writing in standard English? Whereas society may expect you to teach standard English to nonstandard English speaking children, theories of learning tell you that you need to be able to communicate and interact closely, even intimately, with each child. And that means understanding and valuing each child's language. On the one hand, language differences may be perceived as a barrier to a formal education, and on the other hand, they may be seen as the only useful means to achieve it.

What, then, do you as a teacher need to know about the relationship of culture and language to language arts education in order to be able to teach any child in a multicultural country such as ours? A major issue in multicultural education over the years has been whether or not nonnative English speaking students or those who speak a nonstandard dialect have more difficulty in learning to read. Connections between culture and comprehension have been studied by sociolinguists (Labov, 1972; Shuy, 1969) who began systematically to describe certain American dialects, particularly the dialects of black Americans, and to research the significance this might have for teaching reading.

There is a keen interest nowadays in the correspondence between processing of knowledge, on the one hand, and on the other, a child's prior experience, linguistic and cultural heritage, and situational differences, as these factors influence the child's comprehension and interpretation of text. The reading failure of children with limited knowledge of English has often been attributed to the mismatch between children's first or native language—the language they speak—and the language in which they are taught to read. The underlying assumption is that reading acquisition is dependent on the oral language repertoire. Studies of children who had Chinese (Mae, 1980), French (Bradley, 1979), and Spanish (Gunther, 1979) linguistic backgrounds suggest that efforts to teach reading in English should be preceded and accompanied by instruction firmly rooted in an understanding—and if possible, use by the teacher—of their native language as well as oral language experiences in English.

The issue of whether or not children who speak a nonstandard dialect will have more difficulty learning to read print in the standard dialect is a long-standing one. Some studies have found that there is an inverse association between the density level of black dialect usage and reading achievement (Johnson, 1970; Torrey, 1972), and that the better readers among black, lower-socioeconomic-status children are those who produce significantly more standard English features when their oral language proficiency is measured (Fechter, 1978). On the other hand, there is ample evidence to suggest that use of the black dialect does not critically interfere with a child's potential to learn to read (Goodman, 1965; Melmed, 1971; Ruddel, 1965) or with a child's reading comprehension (Goodman, 1978; Liu, 1973; Rigg, 1974; Sims, 1972).

Other evidence, however, suggests that a teacher's limited knowledge of dialect differences can make a difference in the educational progress of these children. Cunningham (1976–1977) found that teachers corrected significantly more black-dialect-specific misuses in reading, and both Politzer and Hoover (1977) and Harber and Beatty (1978) report that teachers have lower expectations, lower estimates of intelligence, and lower ratings of performance for children who speak a black dialect than for children who are speakers of higher-status dialects.

Furthermore, children themselves appear most sensitive to teacher attitude to their speech. In a recent study of language in the classroom, Lucas (1983) found that fourth-grade children who spoke a black English vernacular used this vernacular much less frequently when the teacher was present in small-group discussions than when the teacher was not present.

The results of these many studies suggest that not only should teachers know about language differences and what they mean, but that they should understand Labov's (1978) conclusion that

> the principal problem in reading failure is not dialect or grammatical differences but rather a cultural conflict between the vernacular culture and the schoolroom . . . not so much in the dialect differences themselves as in the ignorance of those differences . . . [and] teachers of reading must begin to make the fundamental distinction between a mistake in reading and a difference in pronunciation (pp. 43–44).

Your attitude towards linguistically different children is as important as your awareness of their language differences. Baldwin's message (1981) for teachers of culturally and linguistically different children is that a child "cannot be taught by anyone whose demand, essentially, is that the child repudiate his experience and all that gives him sustenance" (p. 51).

Language Is Alive and Changing

One of the immutable rules of language is that language is alive and changing. The reasons language changes include the passage of time, geographical separation, and borrowing from other languages. These changes may be phonological, syntactic, semantic, or lexical. Lexical changes, for example, can include changes in word meaning, word loss, or word addition. Sometimes words are coined—created to fit a specific purpose—and become a part of the language. In Marion Harris's class, for example, one child compared the texture of pastry dough to that of Play-doh, a commercial brand of a plasticinelike substance whose name has come to have a generic meaning for children's modeling compound.

Other such brand names that have found their way into the English language include Kleenex, Jell-O, and Xerox.

Teachers should be aware of language change because of the effect it has on children's language, and the effect children's language has on the language in general. Many changes in language occur because of children's restructuring of the grammar of a language as they learn and play with language. And children should be made aware of language change for the power this knowledge may give them over their own language as an access to meaning.

There are many different ways you can help children gain control over their thoughts and language and gain access to meaning in the classroom through the art of teaching language arts. As you learn and practice these techniques, keep in mind that language is alive and changing and that any approach you take to teaching language arts should connect first with children and their language, whole language that is natural, self-generated, contextual, and functional, and whose variability is allowed to grow.

Teaching Children

When Marion Harris began to teach language arts at the beginning of the year, she saw the ripple effect of ideas, interest, and language that a few apples caused in her room. Table 2–3 summarizes the children's behavior and Marion's observations and subsequent actions.

Once you begin to base language arts instruction on the ideas, interests, and language of children, there are several strategies you can use on any subject or in any context to help children develop and use language.

Vocabulary and Concept Development through Language Interaction

One of the best reasons to create a classroom where children are actively engaged in interesting experiences, often generated by their own spontaneous interests, rather than a classroom where children spend their time listening to the teacher, copying prerecorded messages off the board, or filling in blanks on a worksheet, is that it will lead to knowing about things, or the development of concepts. Concept development is an integral part of the way children learn and understand and use the names for things.

Table 2–3 *What the Children Did/What the Teacher Did*

What the Children Did	*What the Teacher Did*
showed interest in apples	observed their interest in apples
talked and questioned about apples	listened to talk and answered questions
discussed and guessed riddle	told a story riddle
	organized children in small groups
observed and discussed apples	encouraged observation and talk about apples
in small groups	listened and observed discussions and interacted with children
played with language	listened to language play
shared words and ideas	recorded vocabulary which emerged from experiences, and read aloud to children
composed words in a pattern	introduced a language pattern for writing
continued to experience, talk, write, dramatize, interact	expanded on these activities and integrated with other areas of the curriculum

Here is a general strategy for concept and vocabulary development in a whole-language environment.

A Strategy for Vocabulary and Concept Development

Experience Things. Attach names to things the children have come to know through experience—either prior experiences at home or in school, or experiences of interest to children throughout the school year, such as cooking and eating, holidays, field trips, or class visitors; math, science, and social studies activities; and literature and media. Here are some ideas for helping children experience things through using words:

- Set aside a special time to build on words and ideas the children bring from home.
- Read aloud every day to the children, including upper-grade children.

Tell the Names of Things. Do not make the children guess; do not patronize them by limiting your vocabulary; and do not hesitate to introduce new words and use them in context as Marion Harris did with the word *estimate.* For example, you might write on the board a *word for the day* that captures their interest, and lead them to discuss and use the word so it enters their vocabulary easily.

Show Words. Write words on the blackboard, on chart paper, show them with the overhead projector, put them on bulletin boards, on children's papers—everywhere. And resist the temptation to tell children to look up a word to find out how to spell it: if they cannot spell it, they will have difficulty finding it in the dictionary. Here are some ways to show words:

- Label things in the classroom, even the children: use stick-on labels with their names, jobs, roles in drama, and so on.
- Create word walls on subjects of interest, as Marion Harris did when the children brainstormed words about apples.
- List words the children will need for specific purposes, and display the words on the blackboard or bulletin board.

Talk about Words. Read the words you and the children write, use them in context, and discuss their meanings as well as different aspects of their meanings, such as synonyms, antonyms, compounds, and idioms. For example:

- Talk about word choice in writing.
- Use a thesaurus and dictionaries to expand meaning and to aid in writing.

Write Words. Provide materials and ideas for ways in which the children can record special words and words they will use when they write; for example:

- Have the children create a personal or class dictionary, with a page for each letter and space to record words. (Marion Harris's students made apple books using words from their word wall.)
- Start a word file, with words on file cards in alphabetical order, or a word ring, with words on strips of heavy paper attached to a metal ring.

Classify and Use Words. During discussions or brainstorming periods, develop classifications of words according to criteria established ahead of time. Marion Harris did this when she helped the children group words in categories, such as color and texture, on the word wall they developed around apples. As children categorize in this way, they are growing in their ability to conceptualize and understand relationships among words. Here are some of the ways you can classify words during any kind of language or literacy experience related to any other subject.

• *Synonyms* are words that have similar meanings. Playing with synonyms is more than just a way for children to add another meaning for a word to their vocabulary. It is a means for them to choose the *one* right word as they seek to make meaning. Poets do this and so do children.

• *Homonyms, homophones, and homographs.* Ambiguity is one result of the presence of homonyms in a language, and children can explore this phenomenon by experimenting with homonyms, homophones, and homographs. Homonyms are words that look and sound the same but have different meanings: *bear* (*an animal* or *to carry*). Homophones are words that sound the same but have different meanings and spellings: *bear/bare; flour/flower; to/too/two; pair/pear/pare.* Homographs are spelled alike but differ in meaning and sound: *read, wind, tear.* Riddles, jokes, and poems are often based on these ambiguities and children enjoy brainstorming lists of homophones. Here is an example of fourth-grade humor: "What do you call a naked grizzly? A bare bear." They can also write and illustrate cartoons using the wrong word from a homophone pair.

The King Who Rained and *A Chocolate Moose for Dinner,* by Fred Gwynne (Messner, 1981)

• *Antonyms* are pairs of words that are opposite or nearly opposite in meaning. Children can search for and collect these in a book of opposites.

Antonyms: Hot and Cold and Other Words That Are as Different as Night and Day, by Joan Hanson (Lerner, 1972); *Push–Pull, Empty–Full: A Book of Opposites,* by Tana Hoban (Macmillan, 1972); *Fast–Slow, High–Low,* by Peter Spier (Doubleday, 1972); *Opposites,* by Richard Wilbur (Harcourt Brace Jovanovich, 1973)

Debbie

Semantic Mapping

Semantic mapping is a specific strategy for teaching and expanding students' vocabulary and concept development. Johnson and Pearson (1984) define *semantic maps* as "diagrams that help children see how words are related to one another" (p. 12), and they suggest the following strategy to use for semantic mapping:

1. Choose a key word related to the children's ideas, interests, or current area of study.
2. Write the word in the middle of the chalkboard or on a large piece of chart paper.
3. Brainstorm words related to the key word and classify them in categories that you or the students suggest.
4. Label the categories that emerge. For example, categories for the words on the semantic map for apple (Figure 2–3) might include:
   - **a.** Colors
   - **b.** Shapes
   - **c.** Textures
   - **d.** Taste
   - **e.** Food
   - **f.** People
5. Discuss the words and their relationship and meaning with children.

Semantic maps help children to see words in new contexts and to understand important relationships among words. Such maps can be created for

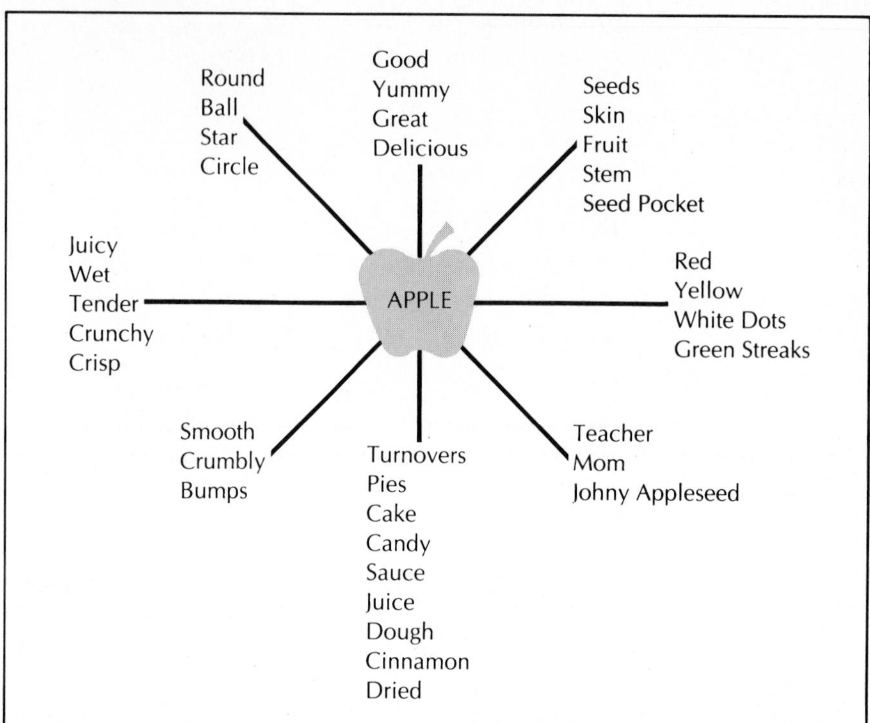

Figure 2-3
Semantic Map for the Word Apple

words across the curriculum, as students need and use words for reading and language arts, and in the content areas as well.

Language and Literature Patterns for Language Arts and Reading

Predictable language patterns can be used to expand concepts and vocabulary, to integrate experiences in the content areas and the arts and humanities through writing and reading, and to stimulate play with words, language, ideas, and images. They can be used with a whole class or with individual children—to initiate classroom writing experiences at the beginning of the year for younger children or to motivate older, reluctant readers and writers.

Predictable language patterns provide an opportunity for individualizing many language arts skills including reading. For example, Avril Font used a simple alphabet pattern to help her fourth-grade class organize their ideas as they talked about their state. Marion Harris had her class use a poetry pattern, the cinquain, to organize the words they had brainstormed and classified about apples.

★ Rhonda

Featured Teacher of the Year Phyllis Crawford: Using Predictable Language Patterns

Principal Phyllis Crawford is a former classroom teacher, reading specialist, and Louisiana Teacher of the Year. She describes (1981) how she uses predictable language and literature patterns, especially to teach language arts and reading.

> Pattern writing is one effective method I use to teach skills, content, expand language, integrate the arts, and encourage reading and writing. Since language has a rhythm and melody that children need to anchor in their ears, reoccurring patterns enable children to successfully unlock the printed page.
>
> From the repeated language pattern, children are able to easily anticipate the sequence of what comes next. The patterns provide a natural and enjoyable stimulus for children to write their own variations. These writings then become a motivational source for reading by the child author and others (from the Preface).

Language Patterns for Writing. The following are some sample patterns for writing that Phyllis Crawford has used in her classes; examples were written by her students. Many patterns can be found in books.

See Chapter 5, "Shaping Children's Writing" and Chapter 6, "Playing with Words, Sentences, and Sense."

- *Brown Bear, Brown Bear, What Do You See?* This is the first book in Bill Martin's Instant Reader series; it is ideal to read to young students, letting them predict the pattern from the repeated sentences and pictures. The pattern is that of question-and-answer, between one animal and another animal of a different color "looking at me." Phyllis Crawford used this pattern when her first-graders were learning about the five senses and the parts of the body. Here is a sample of what the children wrote:

Instant Readers, by Bill Martin, Jr. (Holt, Rinehart & Winston, 1970)

Beautiful Eyes, Beautiful Eyes, What Do You See?

Beautiful eyes, beautiful eyes, what do you see?
I see a smelling nose looking at me.
Smelling nose, smelling nose, what do you see?
I see chattering teeth looking at me.

- *I Love My*... This is another pattern adapted from a predictable-pattern book based on the alphabet. Here is an example written by children:

I Love My Anteater with an A, by Dahlov Ipcar (Knopf, 1964)

Superman

I love my Superman *with an* s *because he is* superior.
I dislike him with an s *because he is* strange.
His name is Samson. *He comes from* space.
He lives on stars *and* suns. *And he is a man of* steel.

Phyllis Crawford makes tacos with a class as part of concept and vocabulary development leading to pattern unity.

• *If I Were*... This pattern is based on the parts of speech (in italics in the example below). Children add a noun, two adjectives describing the noun, and a verb. This example was written by first-graders:

If I Were a Pig

If I were a pig, *a* plump, filthy pig,
If I were a pig, *this is what I would do.*
I would grunt, grunt, grunt, grunt, grunt, grunt.
That's what I would do.

Phyllis Crawford extends pattern writing by copying the pattern onto tag board, and putting copies of the words that the students filled in on

Sandie 294-9855

smaller tag board squares for them to match to the pattern. After the children are able to match the cards with the chart, they try to do it without the chart. Phyllis uses this technique to teach new words and story sequence.

She also uses this pattern to introduce the thesaurus to her young students by having them search for synonyms for words they have already used. For example, for *filthy* they found *dirty, unclean, grimy,* and *grubby.* For *plump,* they found *stout* and *corpulent.* She also encourages them to find antonyms for the words they have used.

• *Just around . . .* Here is a pattern Phyllis Crawford has adapted from the poem "Just around the Corner" by Leland Jacobs. Her students wrote about their school, which is named Audubon.

Just around Audubon

Just around Audubon
You just might find
Some very pretty teachers
That are really nice and kind

Just around Audubon
You just might meet
A gray-haired principal
Walking on his feet.

Her students extended this pattern by finding homophones for some of the words, putting both of them on tag board strips, and illustrating each one of the pair: *some* and *sum; feet* and *feat; mite* and *might; meet* and *meat; principal* and *principle.* They were also delighted to find a trio: *you, yew,* and *ewe.*

• *The Most Important Thing . . .* This is a pattern Phyllis has used which is adapted from Margaret Wise Brown's *The Important Book.* Here is an example written by children who were learning about their state:

The Important Book, by Margaret Wise Brown (Harper and Row, 1949)

Louisiana Gumbo

The most important thing about gumbo is that it's a
scrumptious, thick soup.
It's highly seasoned with Tabasco.
It's full of shrimp, crabs, and oysters.
It's flavored with powdery filé.
But, the most important thing about gumbo is that it's a
scrumptious, thick soup.

• *Over in the Meadow . . .* Preservice teacher Nancy Shaver helped the first-grade students in her field-experience practicum write this pattern based on the old counting song "Over in the Meadow." Each number from one to ten inspires a verse about an animal mother and her baby. Nancy's

Over in the Meadow, by Ezra Jack Keats (Scholastic, 1973)

group of ten students each wrote a verse about a familiar animal in their own environment.

Down along the Bayou

Down along the bayou in the grass and the sun
Lives an old mother alligator and her little alligator one.
"Chomp," said the mother. "I chomp," said the one.
So he chomped and was glad in the grass in the sun.

Playing with Language

In *From Two to Five* (1971) Chukovsky collected examples of language play to support his contention that children are linguistic geniuses: "A bald man has a barefoot head." "A mint candy makes a draft in your mouth." "A grasshopper's husband is a daddy hopper."

The children in Marion Harris's class played spontaneously with language—with expansions of nursery rhymes they knew, and with sequences of rhyming and rhythmic syllables, assonance, personification, and pure nonsense. Teachers should recognize, encourage, support, and extend this genius children display spontaneously for playing with language and making meaning.

A Strategy for Supporting Language Play

You can support children's language play in several ways.

- Value children's playful language inventions as they occur spontaneously, and encourage their efforts at language play.
- Play with language yourself, share the results, and create a playful atmosphere towards language in your classroom.
- Describe forms of language play with examples from literature and life.
- Plan regular sessions for language play.
- Integrate forms of playful language activities with other subjects.
- Present children's products: display in class, collect in a class anthology, dramatize, put to music, create a filmstrip, and the like.

Types of Language Play

Here are some types of language play to recognize or introduce into the classroom.

- *Riddles.* A riddle is a puzzling question solved by guessing. Riddles describe things in terms of other things as in this old nursery rhyme riddle:

Little Nanny Etticoat
In a white petticoat
And a red nose:
The longer she stands
The shorter she grows.
(Answer: a candle)

Riddles can help children explore word meaning, ambiguity, and humor in language. They can also preserve and tap a child's own metaphorical processes as he reads and writes his own. Children hear, read, and repeat riddles like "When is a door not a door?" (when it is ajar) and "What has four or more wheels and flies?" (a garbage truck), and they love to create their own riddles as well. Other types of riddles include:

See "Riddling: A Playful Way to Explore Language," by Linda Geller in *Language Arts,* 58 (1981), 669–674.

- *Puns.* A pun is a play on words using sounds and meaning: "Two coin collectors got together for old dime's sake." Children can make up their own puns given a subject like the title, author, and subject of a book: "*Playing in the Traffic* by Ima Fool (Safety)."

See "A Riddle or Pun Makes Learning Words Fun," by Eleanore S. Tyson and Lee Mountain in *The Reading Teacher,* 36 (1982), 170–173.

- *Conundrums.* Conundrums are riddles based on an imagined likeness between things that are unalike and using a pun in the answer: "What is purple and conquered the world?" (Alexander the Grape) and "What did the goblin say to the ghost?" (Spook for yourself). Children often create a question to go with a pun they have already created for an answer.

- *Hink-Pinks.* Hink-pinks use a question-and-answer form, with the words of the answer in rhyme and in meter. Geller (1981) cites examples of hink-pinks created by ten-year-old Tom, who preferred to write hink-pinks rather than required sentences with spelling words and new vocabulary. Several of his hink-pinks were related to a class study of the Middle Ages: "What do you call a sad gargoyle?" (a pout spout) and "What do you call a servant who works in the center aisle of a church?" (a nave slave) (p. 673).

Learning about Language

Featured Preservice Teacher Karen Watkins: A Unit about Language

Karen Watkins developed and taught a unit on language to a fifth-grade class to which she was assigned for field experience as part of her teacher preparation. She describes (1981) her purposes:

> My purpose was to show students how important and fascinating language can be and help them explore the nature and history of language and word origins to better understand their own language heritage, to develop vocabulary and spelling skills, oral and written language, and the use of the dictionary, thesaurus, and other reference works. I developed folder activities for a center on language study and connected these with our basal reading program, spelling skills, and social studies.
>
> We also studied homonyms, antonyms, compounds, idioms, word blends, and clipped words, especially in the context of our basal reading lessons. In addition to learning more about language, I feel this unit increased the self-concept of my students. They considered themselves to be poor students in many ways and were very enthusiastic when we started to study this challenging subject.

See "Children's Books for Language Exploration," by Ruth Noyce and Flora Reser Wyatt in *Language Arts,* 55 (1978), 297–301, 357.

Here are some of the activities Karen Watkins used with her class:

Words from History, by Isaac Asimov (Houghton Mifflin, 1961)

1. *How Languages are Related.* Students used a map of the world and a language tree to trace the origins of Indo-European languages. American dialects, especially our own, were studied and charted on a map of the United States.
2. *Where Do Words Come From?* Each student researched the origins of several words, located them on a map of the world, and found Old and Middle English spellings.

Codes, Ciphers, and Secret Writing, by Martin Gardner (Simon and Schuster, 1961)

Words on the Map, by Isaac Asimov (Houghton Mifflin, 1972)

3. *Code Language Folder.* Each student created her own code, wrote a message in it, and presented it to others who tried to decode it. The class also discussed better-known theories of language origin, such as the bow-wow, pooh-pooh, and ding-dong theories.
4. *Names of Families, Cities, and Towns.* Students researched their own family names and those of others, used the telephone book to analyze familiar last names in this area, and researched the names of towns here.
5. *Acronym Folder.* Some of the students created acronyms and other students tried to unscramble them.
6. *Slurvians.* These are familiar names or sayings changed by using new words with slightly different sounds. Example: *Little Red Riding Hood* became *Ladle Rat Rotten Hut.*
7. *Palindromes.* These are words, phrases, and even sentences that read the same backwards and forwards. The children collected these from the newspaper and saved them in a class book.
8. *Mexico Day.* The class studied the history, culture, customs, people, and language of Mexico, especially Spanish speakers in the United States and influences of Spanish on English and vice versa. Students wore tags with their names in Spanish, we danced La Raspa—a type of hat dance—and made nachos and tacos and then wrote triantes (a language pattern) about them.

See Chapter 6, "Classifying Words."

Learning about Language Change

Children can also discover how language changes by collecting language samples. For example, fifth-grader Kelly developed a questionnaire on the 1960s as a social studies project (see Figure 2–4). She surveyed people between the ages of 33 and 40 and analyzed the slang and sayings of the times and summarized some of her findings this way: "I learned how many different things people used to say that they don't say anymore because we use different language now. It was neat. I liked doing it. Some of the sayings I got were really lush."

One way in which people can actually try to change language is by creating *sniglets.* The word was coined by Rich Hall (1984), who defined it as follows:

> *Sniglet* (snig′-lit): *n.* any word that doesn't appear in the dictionary but should.

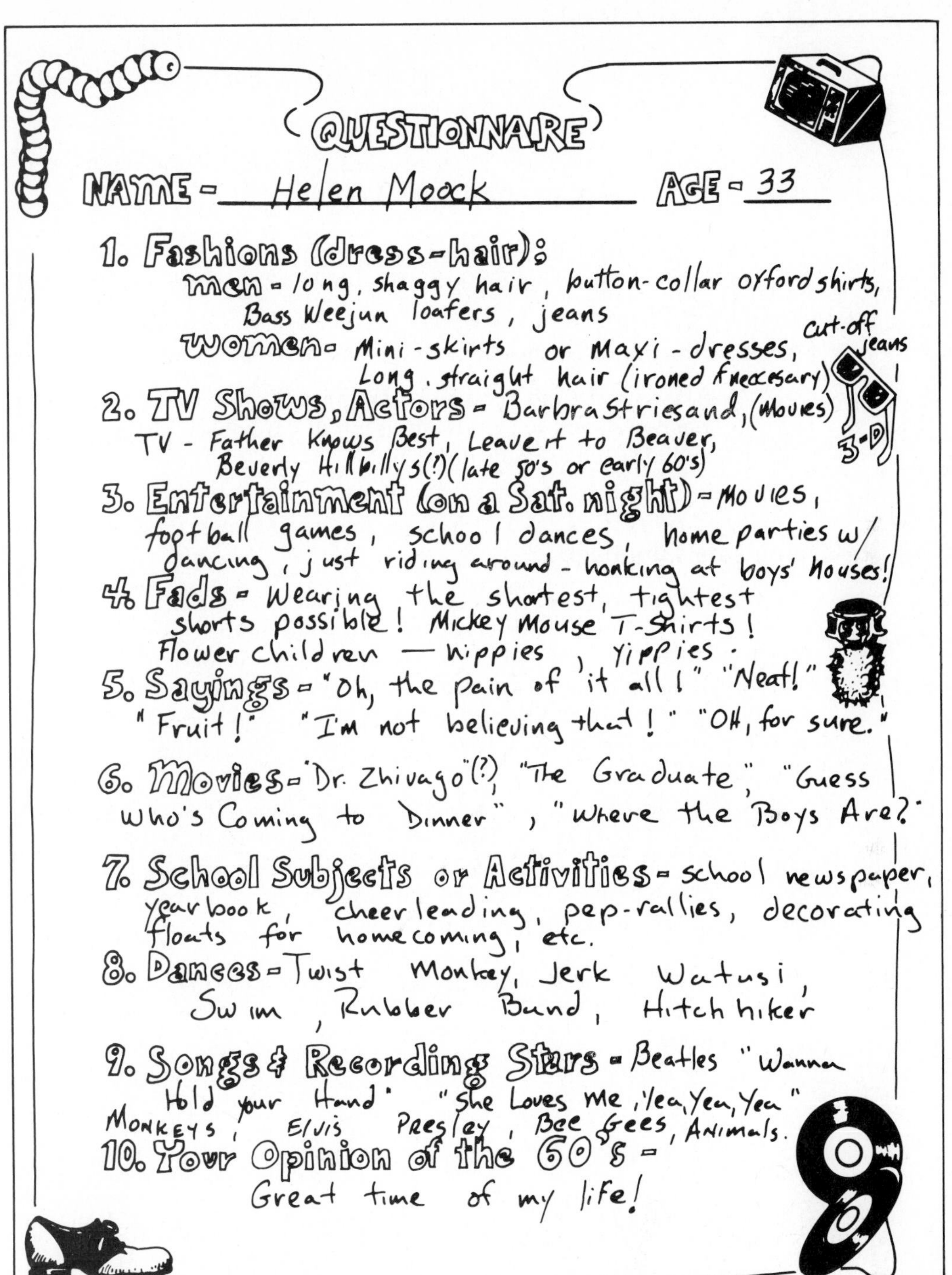

QUESTIONNAIRE

NAME - Helen Moock AGE - 33

1. Fashions (dress-hair):
men - long, shaggy hair, button-collar oxford shirts, Bass Weejun loafers, jeans
women - Mini-skirts or Maxi-dresses, cut-off jeans
Long, straight hair (ironed if necessary)

2. TV Shows, Actors - Barbra Striesand, (Movies)
TV - Father Knows Best, Leave it to Beaver, Beverly Hillbillys(?) (late 50's or early 60's)

3. Entertainment (on a Sat. night) - Movies, football games, school dances, home parties w/ dancing, just riding around - honking at boys' houses!

4. Fads - Wearing the shortest, tightest shorts possible! Mickey Mouse T-Shirts! Flower children — hippies, yippies.

5. Sayings - "Oh, the pain of it all!" "Neat!" "Fruit!" "I'm not believing that!" "Oh, for sure."

6. Movies - "Dr. Zhivago"(?), "The Graduate", "Guess who's Coming to Dinner", "Where the Boys Are?"

7. School Subjects or Activities - school newspaper, yearbook, cheerleading, pep-rallies, decorating floats for homecoming, etc.

8. Dances - Twist, Monkey, Jerk, Watusi, Swim, Rubber Band, Hitchhiker

9. Songs & Recording Stars - Beatles "Wanna Hold your Hand" "She Loves Me, Yea, Yea, Yea"
Monkeys, Elvis Presley, Bee Gees, Animals.

10. Your Opinion of the 60's -
Great time of my life!

Figure 2–4 *Questionnaire for an Interview*

Here is an example from his book.

> *Alponium* (al-po′-neeum): *n.* (chemical symbol: Ap) Initial blast of odor upon opening a can of dog food.

Students can create their own sniglets. The following examples were created by my son Wyatt, a sniglet aficionado:

> *Spork* (spork): *n.* The plastic eating utensil provided in fast-food restaurants which is a combination of the bowl of a spoon and the tines of a fork.
>
> *Foon* (foon): *n.* See above.
>
> *Absenphoneomenon* (ab′-sen-fo-nom′i-non): *n.* Condition during which the phone call you've been waiting for all day comes during the only five minutes you are out of the house.

Observing Children Using Language

As you observe and listen to your students, you are constantly in the process of learning about children and their language in the classroom setting. What you learn becomes the core around which you design instruction. The size of the space between what the children know and can do and what you do about it—Vygotsky's (1962) "zone of proximal development"—can only be determined by an assessment of the stage the children are at in the development of their use of language.

Given the restraints on a teacher's time, such means of evaluation must be simple and easy to implement. You are not likely to have time to tape-record and transcribe language samples while eating lunch with twenty-five first-graders, or on yard duty with the entire upper-grade population. Here are some simple strategies:

1. *Gain awareness of how children learn language,* how they use it in the classroom, and how you will interact with them on the basis of their language.
2. *Observe children,* watch and listen as they talk—to themselves, to each other, to you. Observe them in small groups and during whole-class discussions in the context of what you know about children and their language. Take time to focus on individual children in different settings.
3. *Keep anecdotal records* in a loose-leaf binder or on file cards. Note language behaviors like children's use of language structures, vocabulary, dialect and language differences, use of language, and language play.
4. *Use an observation sheet for language use.* Figure 2–5 shows a simple form adapted from Halliday's description of children's models of language.

Name(s)________________________________ Date/Time____________

Activity____

Situation____

Language Function	Examples	Notes
Instrumental		
Regulatory		
Interactional		
Personal		
Imaginative		
Heuristic		
Informative		

Figure 2–5
Children's Use of Language

You may adapt this for one child or a group, as a checklist, or to record actual language samples, and as a place to note ideas for planning instruction in response to how children use language. Observations and records like these can become a guide for your thinking about and planning language arts experiences.

Summing Up

Basing language arts instruction on the ideas, interests, and language of children requires an awareness of how children learn and use language, what they know when they know a language, and the effect of culture and language differences on language arts and reading development.

Teachers should be aware that children know a great deal about their language when they enter school and that they continue to gain control over their thoughts and language and gain access to meaning by using language in a way that expands their ability to elaborate and use it with flexibility.

Halliday (1973) suggests a useful definition of language for teachers—language as meaning potential—and offers a model which describes the functions of language as children seek to fulfill that meaning potential. The theories of Piaget (1962) and Vygotsky (1962, 1978) shed some light on the relationship of thought to language, and on just what is meant by *meaning;* and they have significant implications for the classroom teacher planning language experiences to integrate learning.

What you know when you know a language can be characterized as a grammar representing a speaker's linguistic competence. This grammar includes the following properties: rules of phonology, semantics, and syntax, and a vocabulary or lexicon. It is also important to remember that we are all linguistically different, and the teacher's positive attitude towards each child's dialect and/or second language is a critical factor in that child's success in school.

The first-grade talk and language interaction in Marion Harris's class gives you a glimpse of what actually goes on in a classroom where the teacher is aware of children's language, the nature of language, and language differences and takes cues from the children in order to plan for instruction in a room where language is seen as natural, creative, self-generated, contextual, and functional, and where its variability is allowed to change and grow.

Looking Further

1. Diagram a possible ripple effect of learning and teaching experiences for a specific grade level around a topic that might interest the students. Include experiences for listening, speaking, reading, writing, literature, fine arts, mathematics, science, and social studies.

2. Observe in a classroom and record the children's language as they interact in a large or a small group. Analyze and classify their language and how they use it according to Halliday's model of children's language.

3. Make a list of all the factors that could influence your personal idiolect. Compare your list to those of others, and discuss how they are alike and how they are different. Use examples of your own speech to explain these differences.

4. Develop a semantic map with others in your class or with a group of children. How could you use this map to plan further learning experiences?

5. Read a patterned language book to children, discuss it, brainstorm a word wall of associated words and phrases, and write a pattern based on the book.

6. Start your own file of books, poems, songs, jump rope rhymes, jingles, and the like that use a pattern and that you might use in the classroom.

7. Describe and give examples to a group of children of some of the types of language play explained in the chapter. Invite them to write their own.

8. Start a file of books about language for children.

9. Invent a sniglet.

Chapter Three

Talking and Listening

Centering Ideas

Listening to Stories and Talking about Them
Watching Films and Talking about Them

Making Connections

How Listening and Talking Take Place in the Classroom
How Listening and Talking Are Taught
Listening, Talking, and Literacy

Teaching Children

Teaching Talking and Listening in Any Context
Strategies for Teaching Talking and Listening
Observing Talking and Listening in the Classroom

Summing Up

Looking Further

Objectives

Look for answers to the following questions as you read this chapter.

- What kind of talking and listening takes place in the elementary classroom?
- How are listening and talking taught?
- What is the relationship between talking and listening on the one hand, and reading and writing on the other?
- What are some approaches and strategies for teaching talking and listening?

A Child's View

Here is how children told Pace (1981) what they knew about listening and talking as they completed a story which "dealt with the adventures of a spider. Jump could ______ very well, but couldn't get anyone to listen to him. Jump knew no one was listening to him because ______."

- How you know when people are not listening: they talk to someone else; they read; they don't look at you.
- To get someone to listen: ask kindly; tap their shoulder and wait; clear your throat; say excuse me and then talk.
- How to be a good listener: don't talk; pay attention; keep your ears open; watch the talker; listen to everybody.
- How to be a good talker: talk to everybody; everybody listens to you.
- Whom they like to talk to: mother; friends; other family members; people who listen carefully.
- The best thing to listen to: stories (the kind you listen to as well as have read to you).
- They like to talk about: friends and playing.
- On teachers: "The most important thing to do is to mind" (p. 153).

Centering Ideas

What kind of talking and listening takes place in the elementary classroom? Kathy Lee teaches second grade. During the week before Halloween, she reads stories and shows films about monsters to her class.

As you read excerpts from these book and film talks, consider what they can tell you about how teachers and children use language in the context of the classroom. How are the talks alike? How are they different? And what do these comparisons tell us about active language interaction, about learning to talk and listen, and about talking and listening to learn?

Listening to Stories and Talking about Them

Kathy first reads two books about monsters in the way many teachers share books with young children: she reads the text, shows the illustrations, and asks questions about the book as she reads aloud.

Where the Wild Things Are, by Maurice Sendak (Harper & Row, 1963); winner of the Caldecott Medal

Book Talk: **Where the Wild Things Are**

Teacher: [*pointing to title*] What does it say, Kipper?
Child: [*reading*] *Where the Wild Things Are.*
Teacher: That's right. And the picture looks like . . . ?
Child: A monster.
Teacher: I think this is a pretty good one for Halloween. [*Noise from the children.*]
Teacher: What kind of feet does it have?
Child: Human feet.
Teacher: Maybe this one can be for one of the days we're celebrating this month. What day is that?
Child: Columbus Day?
Teacher: This [*points to Wild Thing*] will be for Halloween and this [*points to boat*] will be for Columbus Day. [*Noise from the children.*]
Teacher: OK, [*reading*] "The night Max wore his wolf suit and made mischief of one kind . . ." What's he doing?
Child: Looks like a cat or a fox.
Teacher: ". . . and another."

Kathy reads through the rest of the book in this way.

The Dragon of Santa Lalia, by Carol Carrick (Bobbs Merrill, 1971)

Book Talk: **The Dragon of Santa Lalia**

Teacher: [*points to title*] What does it say?
Child: [*reading*] The dragon and . . . the dragon of the san . . . ta . . . la . . .

Teacher: You're pretty close.
Child: Lala?
Teacher: The Dragon of Santa Lalia.
Child: Lalia.
Teacher: OK, [*reads some more*] . . . do you see all that I just read?
Child: Uh-huh.
Teacher: [*continues reading*] can you see all that?
Child: Uh-huh.
Teacher: [*continues reading*] Do you see it yet?
[*Noise from the children.*]

Kathy reads through the rest of the book in this way.

Watching Films and Talking about Them

During the same pre-Halloween period, Kathy Lee also shows films about monsters and talks about them with her class afterwards. The following dialogue illustrates two of these "film talks."

Film Talk: The Dragon's Tears

The Dragon's Tears (Contemporary Films, 1962)

[*After the film is over*]
Teacher: How were the story and the movie about dragons alike?
Child: They both had a dragon in 'em.
Child: They both started alike with the school out in front . . . the school . . .
Child: Um, they were both dragons and they both came from the hills and um, they both had fire.
Child: I know! this one, um, all the water came out of his ears and all the popcorn started coming out of the other dragon's nose.
Child: One put flowers in the tree and the other one made popcorn.
Child: That lady wasn't afraid of that other dragon and the boy wasn't afraid of this dragon today.
Teacher: Very good. Would you be afraid of the dragon today?
Several children: NO!
Teacher: What would you do if you went out for recess now and you saw a dragon on the playground? Frank?
Child: Uh, I'd make friends with it and I'd feed it.
Child: I'd come in here and shut the door and get right under the desk.
Child: I would pet it.
Child: I'd make friends with it and call it with a whistle.

Teacher: Oh, like a dog?
Child: Ride it. Go over it and ride it and walk up his tail.
Teacher: Go up his tail? How big do you think these dragons were?
Child: Well, it's up to the ceiling.
Child: Uh, two times the height of, uh, one of, uh, how big was that? Uh, as high as . . . I mean to the middle of . . . that curtain. Two times as high as that. Two of those.
Child: Mrs. Lee, do you know what I'd do with the dragon?
Teacher: What?
Child: I'd use it for my popcorn popper.

Clay, The Origin of the Species (Phoenix Films, 1964)

Film Talk: Clay, The Origin of the Species

Teacher: Well, what did you think of it? What did you think of all those creatures?
Child: I liked the animals and people and boats and the Statue of Liberty.
Child: And a president. President Lincoln.
Child: A man eating. Something that eats everything that comes by. A lizard.
Child: And a whale and an elephant and a deer.
Child: Yeah, and a cow and a gingerbread boy.
Teacher: What do you think was the most unbelievable thing that happened in there? We saw a lot of funny things, but what really made you go "wow" or something?
Child: I know. When the dinosaurs were playing and they kissed. [*Laughter*]
Child: I liked that, uh, that, um, one dinosaur, um, ate the other one.
Teacher: Do you think you could make things like you saw in the film?
Several children: Yeah!
Teacher: What would you like to make?
Child: You could make anything you want to.
Child: Mrs. Lee, could we make something together?
Teacher: Would you like to make something together?
Child: Yeah. We'd like . . . two people to work in a group, you know, work together.
Child: Could we do it right now?
Teacher: I think maybe later on today we'll make some clay things.
Child: We're gonna make something good. We're gonna make a clown like a football player.
Child: See, I could bring a ball.
Child: Will we have prizes? Let's say they all get a prize.
Child: Yeah! Me included.

Child: We'll run the movie through again.
Child: We'll have prizes and show the movie and then we'll have it all together!

Making Connections

How Listening and Talking Take Place in the Classroom

Each of the dialogues in the preceding section involved a teacher and children listening to and talking about monster stories in books and on film. But did you notice any differences in the way listening and talking occurred? Look over them again in terms of the following ways to classify and analyze more closely how the teacher and children used language.

1. ***Who talked and who listened?***
   Count the number of times the teacher and then the children talked in each discussion and figure the ratio of teacher talk to child talk.
2. ***How did the teacher talk and listen?***
   Classify the questions of the teacher as either **closed questions**—clearly implying only one acceptable answer; or **open questions**—inviting more than one possible answer (Barnes, 1971).
3. ***How did the children talk and listen?***
   Classify the children's answers as either *closed* or *open* as defined above.

Did you find that, during the book talks, the teacher did more talking and asked more closed questions which only required that the children had listened as she read the book to give her the correct answer, and that the children talked less than she did and answered with short one-word answers which could be verified by information from the book? Did you also notice that the children did not interact with each other, and that they made noise unrelated to the talk?

Did you find that, during the film talks, the teacher did less talking (and consequently more listening), asked more open questions which invited more than one possible answer and then built new questions on these answers, and that the children talked more than she did? Did you also notice that the children interacted with each other, listening to each other and responding to each other in a way that often led the discussion in a new direction? In one class, then, with the same teacher and the same children, very different types of listening and talking experiences can take place.

Halliday (1973) suggests ways in which teachers can help children use language most effectively as they talk and listen:

1. Use models of language which do not fall short of those of children.
2. Take into account each child's linguistic experiences and probe their richest potential.
3. Consider how children will use language in school and later in life.
4. Help children use language in meaningful ways in social contexts.

Closed versus Open Questioning Styles

What is the relative significance of the closed and open styles of asking questions in terms of a teacher's approach to the teaching of talking and listening? When Kathy Lee read stories to her class in the typical way many teachers share books with children, she made use of the closed questioning style.

The use of this technique of asking leading questions has its benefits, as Chomsky (1972) and Snow, Dubber, and de Blauw (1980) have found, since it resembles the structure of many other types of school lessons in which a given book provides a topic, contextual support, and a focus for attention. Cazden (1983), however, cautions that

> there are differences too: classroom lessons are notably less responsive to the child's growing language competence. Instead of self-destructing, the structure remains much the same across grades, and only the content of the slots, the teacher's questions and student's answers, increase in complexity. Furthermore, students don't get a chance to take over the adult role. For such opportunities, peer dialogues are essential (p. 10).

Kathy Lee used a more open questioning style in discussing the films, perhaps because the discussion did not take place *during* the film viewing, or because films are not as frequently used in schools and are therefore not subject to traditional teaching routines as books are. In any case, this type of discussion has been shown to benefit students in language growth because it allows them to have more control over their use of language.

In extensive studies of communication in classrooms, Flanders, King, and Cazden (1974) found that when classroom interaction shifted from a narrow, teacher-dominated discussion seeking an expected response, to more child-initiated discussions where the teacher was more flexible and paid more attention to children's ideas and opinion, the children developed a more positive attitude towards the teacher and school work. In addition, the children learned more as measured by subject matter tests adjusted for initial ability.

Unfortunately, the same researchers also found that teachers spent little time on engaging students in the kind of intellectual experiences such as those Kathy Lee's students practiced during film talks: analyzing, synthesizing, speculating, hypothesizing, and theorizing.

Wells and Wells (1984) suggest that the problem may be that we as teachers have a

> less than wholehearted belief in the value that pupil's talk has for their learning. Many of us have years of being *talked at* as students and have probably unconsciously absorbed the belief that, as teachers, we are not doing our job properly unless we are talking, telling, questioning, or evaluating. But all the time we are talking, we are stopping our pupils from trying out *their* understanding in words. We are also depriving ourselves of valuable information about the state of their understanding and thus of an opportunity to plan future work to meet their specific needs (p. 194).

How Listening and Talking Are Taught

Research also informs us about the different ways in which listening and talking are taught in the classroom.

Listening

1. ***Children do a lot of listening in the classroom.***

Of the 68 percent of each day spent in communication, listening leads with 45 percent, followed by 30 percent for speaking, 16 percent for reading, and 9 percent for writing (Rankin, 1928). Students spend two-and-a-half hours out of five during the school day in listening, more than twice the amount of time teachers think they do (Wilt, 1950, 1974).

2. ***Teachers do a lot of talking in the classroom.***

Teacher talk dominates classroom communication, with the result that children spend a great deal of time listening to the teacher rather than in active language interaction with other students (Fox, 1983).

3. ***Teaching listening has not always been considered important in language arts education.***

Little attention has been paid to teaching listening in classrooms: fewer than 1 percent of language arts texts devote space to the teaching of listening (Brown, 1967; Wilt, 1974).

4. ***Listening can be improved through teaching.***

Active approaches to teaching listening can vastly improve listening learning (Childers, 1970; Devine, 1978; Marten, 1978).

5. ***Some approaches to listening are better than others.***

Pearson and Fielding (1982) summarized the findings on teaching listening comprehension and concluded that such teaching can be improved by:

- practicing the same skills usually taught in reading comprehension;
- active verbal responses during and after listening experiences;

- listening to literature read aloud;
- practicing comprehension in other language modes, such as reading and writing; and
- focusing on teaching listening, which makes children more aware of their listening behavior.

Talking

1. ***Children talk more than they read or write.***
   During two thirds of the day in any classroom, someone is talking, and children speak about twice as much as they read and three times as much as they write (Flanders, 1970).

2. ***Teachers talk more than children.***
   From kindergarten through graduate school, teachers talk more than all the students combined; two thirds of the time that someone is speaking it is the teacher (Flanders, 1970).

3. ***Speaking is not taught as systematically as reading or writing.***
   Teachers teach and use reading and writing, rather than oral language competencies, as measures of student achievement, and children really have few opportunities for listening to and using functional types of oral language. The language arts texts emphasize writing and grammar skills much more than speaking, and virtually ignore listening. Curriculum guides provide little help to the teacher who would like to develop listening and speaking skills among students (Brown, 1967; Davidson, 1968; Goodlad, 1984; Silberman, 1970).

4. ***Speaking is important.***
   Theorists and researchers such as Moffett and Wagner (1983) and Britton (1970) have continued to stress the significance of talking and listening and using language effectively in classroom discourse.

5. ***Some approaches to speaking are better than others.***
   Students participate much more freely in discussions led by other students; students who have been trained to lead discussions encourage more divergent and analytic contributions; and teacher questioning formats revised from those usually found in classrooms can extend students' thinking and participation in discussions (Barnes, 1976; Wilcox, 1976).

Research, theories, and implications for teaching such as these suggest that teachers need to build and expand on the growing ability of the young learner to communicate, through modeling, supporting, and above all, encouraging interactive discourse in meaningful social contexts which fulfills the real needs and purposes of children.

The idea that spoken language is basic to learning to read is not new. In 1908 Huey, a pioneer of reading theory whose ideas are still timely today, maintained that children who learn to read for themselves do it in the same way as they learned to speak.

Spoken Language and Learning to Read

A review of the research on the relationship between the development of spoken language and learning to read (Cox, 1984) shows that researchers continue to affirm that a child's experience and knowledge of the linguistic organization of spoken language is basic to her ability to learn to read. To put it another way, students may have difficulty in learning to read if they are hampered in their efforts to recognize and exploit syntactic structures they would normally learn as they learn to speak.

Language-Different Children

The relationship of reading achievement to the spoken language of bilingual or limited-English speaking students has also been investigated. In studies of Native American students, Simpson (1977) found that six-year-old Crow and Cheyenne children lacked linguistic readiness for first-grade reading programs, and Sharpes (1982) found that older Native American students with a low level of overall language ability and oral language proficiency in English also had problems with reading; there was some indication that learning a new language was interfering with their learning to read. Bilingual students may have difficulty in learning to read unless the teacher takes into account their native tongue and their cultural and linguistic heritage and provides experiences in spoken English to support the teaching of reading.

On the other hand, some researchers, such as Levy (1973), have analyzed the vocabulary, syntax, and metalinguistic knowledge of children who speak a black dialect and found them to have a comparable linguistic maturity to middle-class white children and to demonstrate an adequate development of oral language for beginning reading instruction.

"Writing Floats on a Sea of Talk"

As interrelated parts of the whole of language, listening and talking are tied to writing as well as to reading. Researchers who have recently paid a great deal of attention to younger emergent writers (Dyson & Genishi, 1982) call writing "as much an oral activity as a written one" (p. 126), since talking works in concert with the expression of ideas in writing. Britton (1970) expresses it another way: "Writing floats on a sea of talk" (p. 164).

While the assumption has often been made that the development of speaking precedes and leads the way to writing—as Vygotsky (1978) suggests when he describes the development of written language as part of a unified and historical line which begins with speech and proceeds through make-believe, play, and drawing to writing—recent research such as that of Clay (1979) implies instead that writing is part of a unified and simultaneous whole of language development, comprising listening, talking, writing, and reading.

Implications for Teaching

The growing body of research on the importance of oral language to other language functions such as reading and writing suggests several implications for teachers practicing the art of teaching language arts.

1. Teachers should create a healthy climate for learning oral language in the classroom to support the teaching of reading and writing.

2. Teachers should emphasize certain aspects of oral language that appear to be most important in relationship to the teaching of reading:

- expanding the children's vocabulary;
- encouraging the children to use spoken language patterns with flexibility;
- increasing the children's sensitivity to both the conventions and the varieties of language forms; and
- raising the children's levels of metalinguistic awareness (knowing what they know about language).

3. Teachers should systematically provide for the practice of specific reading comprehension skills such as sequencing (putting ideas and information in the correct order), inferencing (finding what is missing by making connections between what the reader already knows and the text), and finding the main idea through listening.

4. Teachers should emphasize methods of teaching language arts and reading which help the children use and understand connections among the language arts: thinking, listening, speaking, reading, and writing.

5. Teachers should recognize and exploit the children's prior experiences and linguistic and cultural heritage in concert with the integrated teaching of language, reading, and writing.

6. Teachers of bilingual or limited-English speaking students should be careful to take into account those students' native language when developing methods of teaching them to read and write and provide experiences in spoken English to support reading and writing instruction.

7. Teachers of students who speak a nonstandard dialect should be aware that dialect differences do not critically interfere with a student's potential to learn to read. They should be particularly aware of the meaning equivalence between standard English and nonstandard dialects, lest such a lack of awareness lower their expectations of intelligence and performance for these students.

Teaching Children

As a result of some of the interactions that took place during the book and film talks in Kathy Lee's class, a ripple effect of language arts experiences spread across the curriculum. For example, after viewing the film *Clay*, the children brainstormed ideas for making things with clay as they saw in the film; this led to their making an animated film using the claymation technique. Talking about using a dragon for a popcorn popper led them to read and learn more about both dragons and popcorn, and to have a popcorn-popping session. These and many other learning experiences rippled out from the initial pebble of book and film talks about monsters (see Figure 3–1).

Teaching Talking and Listening in Any Context

Using the ripple effect of experiences that resulted from the book and film talks about monsters in Kathy Lee's class as examples, let us look at ways teachers can support and direct talking and listening in the classroom.

Experiencing

The students in Kathy Lee's class

- listened to books read aloud by the teacher and
- viewed films about monsters.

More monster books: *My Mommy Says There Aren't Any Zombies, Ghosts, Vampires, Creatures, Demons, Monsters, Fiends, Goblins or Things*, by Judith Viorst (Macmillan, 1973); *There's a Nightmare in My Closet*, by Mercer Mayer (Dial, 1969); *Trolls*, by Ingrid and Edgar Parin D'Aulaire (Doubleday, 1972)

Good experiences for listening and talking are those which stimulate the children's senses, emotions, and ideas. Chapter 1 suggested a broad spectrum of shared experiences relevant to teaching language arts. A teacher may carefully plan such experiences, by providing for pets in the classroom, for instance, or by having the students gather materials for a resource unit in social studies or science, participate in art or drama activities, or do some cooking in the classroom. Other experiences may arise spontaneously, but these can be the most welcome of all, sparking unexpected delight in learning and language experiences: children sharing a personal experience; children connecting with each other's interests, feelings, and ideas; sudden weather changes; holiday or seasonal moods and magic. In the final analysis, an experience is only as good as the impact it has on children's feelings, ideas, language, and means of self-expression.

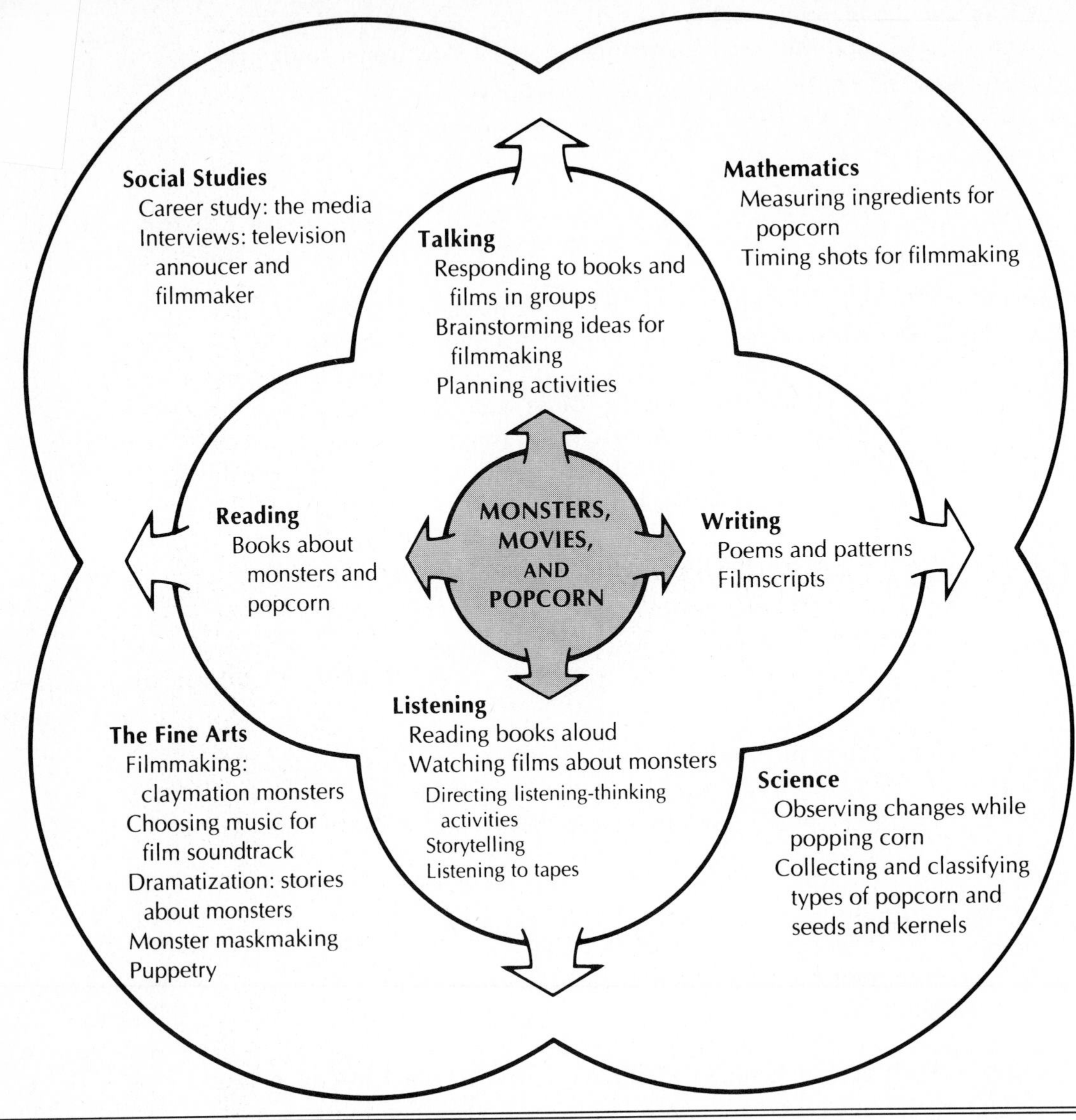

Figure 3–1 *A Ripple Effect: Monsters*

More monster films: *A Little Girl and a Gunny Wolf* (Paramount Communications, 1971); *Where the Wild Things Are* (Weston Woods, 1976); *Custard the Dragon* (Weston Woods, 1964)

Sharing

The students in Kathy Lee's class

- shared ideas in response to books and film and
- shared ideas for new experiences they might create.

Shared experiences can become the basis for shared meaning among children through talking and listening. This does not mean that every child will have the same experience, or will experience the same event in the same way. But considering that you are one teacher with thirty or so children, sharing becomes a basis for interactive communication—talking and listening in a social context. Sharing is also important as the basis for an esprit de corps among the children, a sense of community as they live and learn together in the classroom.

Here are some ideas for a systematic approach to sharing:

1. Establish a regular time every day when children are free to share anything of interest to them.
2. Create other opportunities for sharing:
   - book and media sharing,
   - resource units in social studies,
   - science experiments,
   - music,
   - guest speakers,
   - cooking.
3. Seize spontaneous opportunities for sharing:
   - interest in a current or media event,
   - class problem or conflict to resolve,
   - suggestion from a child for a special activity.

Time for sharing is the factor that the teacher can most easily control. Specific and ample time must be allowed for sharing teacher-planned, child-initiated, or spontaneous events.

Cazden (1985) gives three reasons why specific sharing time is important:

1. It may be the only official time for children to talk.
2. It may be their only opportunity to talk about important personal experiences.
3. It supports children's creation of their own narratives.

Discussing

The students in Kathy Lee's class

- brainstormed ideas for activities and projects that grew out of their sharing after experiencing books and films and
- discussed activities in small groups with each other and with the teacher.

Here are some instruction techniques, organizational patterns, discussion activities, and teacher questioning strategies that can be used to teach listening and talking.

Brainstorming and Problem Solving. Brainstorming is a technique used to produce many ideas from a group for the purposes of problem solving. It encourages imagination, flexibility in generating ideas, and much listening and talking in discussions. This technique can be used on any topic across the curriculum, and is especially useful during a planning session for future activities. The children in Kathy Lee's class were spontaneously brainstorming when they thought of "all the things you can do with a dragon":

Make friends with it.
Feed it.
Pet it.
Call it with a whistle.
Ride it.
Walk up its tail.
Use it for a popcorn popper.

Brainstorming sessions can be conducted with the whole class or in small groups. Ideas can be recorded on the blackboard or chart paper with smaller children; older children may record their own ideas. All the children can take notes or keep their own list of ideas.

Here are some specific guidelines for a planned brainstorming session:

1. Invite ideas—to expand a subject, solve a problem, or plan future activities.
2. Encourage all kinds of ideas—humorous, whimsical, or even nonsensical—and a great number of ideas.
3. Suspend comments or judgments in the initial stages.
4. Record all ideas.
5. Encourage the children to respond to each other's ideas, and to bounce new ones off old ones. Hitchhiking of one student's ideas on another's is valued.

Brainstorming can be used during any of the following stages of problem solving (Parnes, Noller & Biondi, 1977).

1. *Fact finding:* a consideration of the problems, questions, and unorganized information we deal with, and awareness of the information already at hand.
2. *Problem finding:* identifying the essence of the problem and working on it in a way that will help find a solution.
3. *Idea finding:* generating ideas.
4. *Solution finding:* proposing solutions and developing criteria to evaluate them.
5. *Acceptance finding:* developing a plan of action.

These students are brainstorming ideas for making a videotape production about a monster like Godzilla.

Organizational Patterns and Activities. Here are several ways to group and organize students for discussions.

1. ***Whole-class or large-group discussions.***

Teachers can provide a structure and support for times when the entire class needs and wants to talk. Discussions should be invitations to talk as well as listen: this may be in contrast to the planned lesson for which the teacher has a specific type of interaction and a specific content in mind. It is important to create a framework for discussions, and ideally this is done in collaboration between teacher and students. For example, you could together establish some guidelines for class discussions:

Listen to each other.
Contribute ideas.
Respond to what others are saying.
Take turns.

At first some such signal as handraising may be required to establish turns in speaking. But after the children have had plenty of opportunities to practice discussing in a positive situation, this should become unnecessary. In point of fact, handraising can have the negative effect of causing the children to direct their remarks exclusively to the teacher, the one who acknowledges their turn to speak. But children need time to listen and talk to each other without the teacher as intermediary.

2. ***Small-group discussions.***

Children also need time to talk to each other without the physical presence of the teacher. This may happen in situations where they will solve a problem together: plan a group research activity, conduct a science experiment, or prepare a scene for creative drama. At other times, they may simply share their ideas with each other: after a film, before a holiday, during a class, or at a time of community or national problems. Conventions for listening and talking established in whole-class discussions can be adapted for small groups.

3. *Dialogues.*

Having two children—or an adult and a child—listen and talk together provides the greatest amount of listening and talking time for each. There are many formats which lend themselves to dialogue.

- *Problem Solving in Pairs.* Pairs of students can work together to solve problems, for example by doing research on a topic related to a content subject, by planning for a class event such as a film festival, or by devising a puppet play based on a book both children have read or a basal reader story they both liked.

- *Interviews.* Students may plan questions and conduct interviews of community people such as a firefighter or television reporter, school personnel, or parents with special interests. They may also interview each other. In fact, a good technique for bringing students together at the beginning of the school year is to have them interview each other and then report the results of each interview to the rest of the class, perhaps in connection with the most-important-person bulletin board display described in Chapter 1. Some simple questions which could be developed out of a whole-class discussion include:

  "What is your name, where were you born, and where do you live?"
  "How old are you and when is your birthday?"
  "Do you have any brothers or sisters [pets, hobbies, and so on]?"
  "What is your favorite [subject, book, food, color, record]?"
  "What do you like to do [for fun, after school, on weekends]?"

Students may also play the part of characters taken from literature, media, history, current events, science, social studies, mathematics, or the like, being interviewed by other students, for example:

Contemporary sports, political, or entertainment figures.
Favorite characters from books or films.
Historical characters, such as Henry VIII and each of his six wives for a point–counterpoint approach.

Haley-James and Hobson (1980) cite some benefits of classroom interviewing.

Having guests in the classroom increases student interest in listening, speaking, reading, and writing.

Children enjoy the feeling of success and control when they interview.

Interviews encourage a natural integration of the language arts.

Children write more and use a more specific vocabulary for interviews.

Caddie Woodlawn, by Carol Ryrie Brink (Scholastic, 1975), is based on the author's recollections of her grandmother's childhood stories.

The *Foxfire* books by Eliot Wigginton—*Foxfire* and *Foxfire 2* (Doubleday, 1972, 1973) and *Foxfire 3–6* (Anchor/Doubleday 1975, 1977, 1979, 1980)—are excellent sources for experiences in oral history and cultural journalism.

See "Cultural Journalism: A Bridge to the Past," by Mary Olson & Barbara A. Hatcher, in *Language Arts,* 59 (1982), 46–50.

- *Oral History.* A specialized type of interview results in the creation of an oral history. To do this, the students identify, interview, and tape-record the words of members of their family or community who have memories of special events in the past. In addition, they collect and classify artifacts, photographs, and documents relating to the interviewee and present the completed history in spoken form to their own and to other classes, to the whole school, or to community audiences, or in written form by publishing it in the local newspaper, or by creating their own newspaper or their own books. The students can use books like *Caddie Woodlawn* as models for creating an oral history.

  Oral histories can be an exciting approach to integrating the curriculum through language arts. Rosen (1982) describes a teacher in East London who encouraged students and community members to tell stories to school audiences, recorded them on tape, transcribed them, made books of these accounts, and combined these with video recordings of the storytellers to add a visual dimension.

- *Writing Conferences.* Dialogues between teacher and child can become oral preparation for writing, and for rewriting during writing conferences. Children can also engage in dialogue together as they prepare to write, and then discuss each other's writing, in peer-evaluation settings.

See Chapter 4, "Talking to Children about Their Writing."

- *Dialogue Journals.* Dialogue journals are written conversations. Children make journal entries on any topic and teachers write back in response. These journals may be exchanged one or more times a week, or on an individually scheduled basis. They are valuable because they make connections between thinking and language, between speaking and writing, and between teacher and child.

  Staton (1984) makes several suggestions for the practical logistics of using dialogue journals:

See Chapter 4, "Writing about Ourselves and about Others."

See "Writing and Counseling: Using a Dialogue Journal," by Staton, in *Language Arts,* 57 (1980), 514–518.

use small bound notebooks, not spiral, that can be decorated and filled quickly enough so that children feel success when they get a new one to fill;

journal writing should occur at free times throughout the day, whenever students have questions, ideas, or a message, rather than during an assigned time when they really may not feel like writing these;

establish a regular place and time to turn in and pick up journals;

teachers should write back immediately, and may need to take journals home to do so;

more frequent, brief entries seem to work best;

return journals the first thing in the morning the next day and give students ample time to read and respond in writing in return.

Reporting

The students in Kathy Lee's class

- told scary stories about monsters and Halloween,
- dramatized *Where the Wild Things Are,*
- created puppets to perform the story of *The Popcorn Dragon,* and
- made a Super-8 animated film about clay monsters.

What has happened as a result of experiencing, sharing, and discussing can be reported in a variety of ways.

Oral Reporting

See Chapter 10, "Scriptwriting." Chapter 4, "Writing Class and School Newspapers" and "Writing Reports."

Describing what has occurred in a small group or problem-solving pair
Response to literature, media, or storytelling
Results of social studies research or science experiment
Explaining results as a contribution to further activities
Playwriting in small groups
Committee work for a planned event such as a class newspaper

Writing and Drawing

Writing nonfiction accounts
Writing newspaper articles or letters to the editor
Making announcements and labels for projects
Creating visual displays
Drawing, painting, making murals
Illustrating writing and making books

Dramatizing

See Chapter 10 on drama in the classroom.

Storytelling and puppetry
Drama and reader's theatre

Mediamaking

See Chapter 11 on the media arts.

Tape recordings and video recordings
Transparencies, slides, and filmstrips

Strategies to Support Children As They Create Oral Texts

As a result of her extensive research on children's language, and on children and teachers listening and talking together, Tough (1979) has suggested five strategies for teachers to support children as they create oral texts, as described by Davis (1983).

1. *Orienting and inviting* children to talk about ongoing events or explain a phenomenon occurring at the time.
2. *Enabling, stimulating* the child to give a full response to the teacher's request for information by asking for more detailed explanation or justification.
3. *Informing,* adding new information to that provided by the child.
4. *Sustaining,* encouraging added dialogue participation by using verbal and nonverbal means.
5. *Concluding,* anticipating the ending of the dialogue in such a way as to complete it without leaving the child with the impression that the teacher has lost interest in what was being said (p. 169).

Strategies for Asking Questions

Questions are among the most valuable tools teachers have to support listening and talking in the classroom, as well as critical thinking and comprehension. A review of the research on questions in the classroom (Christenbury & Kelly, 1983) verified that

1. questions help students comprehend more as they read;
2. students who ask questions themselves learn more about subject matter;
3. questions help children discover their own ideas and argue and sharpen critical thinking skills;
4. questions help children function as experts and interact among themselves; and
5. questions give the teacher invaluable information about student ability and achievement.

The implications of this type of research can serve as a guide for thinking about questions and practicing those questioning techniques that most effectively create a climate for critical listening and speaking. While many questioning hierarchies have been developed and described, Christenbury and Kelly found that the research does not posit the superiority of any one over another; in fact, the research shows that hierarchies are not conclusive or even always useful when applied in the classroom. Here is what Christenbury and Kelly suggest:

- Use a questioning schema, but do not let it use you.
- Follow your students' lead.
- Be flexible with your questions.
- Do not always play it safe.

As a model for questioning, they suggest a conversation with your friends. You would talk as equals, encouraging the comments of others, allowing them to wander off onto points that interest them, and pausing between ideas. You would neither dominate nor allow your friends to dominate the conversation. There would be a genuine give-and-take atmosphere. As in all human interchange, talk would be allowed to swell, trail off, and even fall silent. In such a climate, given a topic of mutual interest, it is hard to imagine that questioning would fail.

Here are two examples of questioning strategies. The first type is non-text related. It could be used with or without reference to a book or other reading material. The second, Manzo's ReQuest, is specifically designed for use with a textbook or could also be used with a basal reader story.

Closed and Open Questions. A very simple and practical yet effective way to phrase and monitor the questions you ask is to think of them as open or closed (Barnes, 1971).

- **Open questions** are those which invite more than one possible answer.
- **Closed questions** are those which clearly imply only one correct answer.

While both types of questions have important uses, research has shown that teachers tend to focus more on literal, closed questions as Kathy Lee did in the book talks. Make an effort to ask open questions as well, those which require students to think and then explain or justify their answer. Research has shown again and again the importance of using these higher-order, open questions because of their positive effect on understanding, thinking, and achievement in reading (Redfield & Rousseau, 1981).

The ReQuest Procedure. A procedure which includes guidelines for the questioning behavior of both students and teachers while reading a basal reader story, a text in the content areas, or other informational material is called ReQuest (Manzo, 1969). Here are the steps to this procedure, which can be used with an individual student or a small group.

1. The students and the teacher read the first sentence silently, and take turns asking questions about what it means.
2. The students ask questions first, which the teacher tries to answer with the book closed. Suggest to the students that they might ask the

kinds of questions a teacher might ask. Those students who are listening but not asking could ask that a question be clarified. The teacher should be prepared to explain her answer.

3. The students close their books and the teacher asks questions, ideally in a way that models good question-asking behavior.
4. The same procedure is used with the next sentences in the first paragraph, up to the third paragraph. The objective is to get the students to listen, think, and talk, with the teacher himself modeling good question-asking.

Other questioning strategies specifically related to teaching literature, writing, reading, drama, and study skills will be described in other chapters.

See Chapter 9, "Question–Answer Relationship," and Chapter 8, "Talking about Books."

Reading Aloud

Research has demonstrated the benefits of reading aloud to children. Preschoolers whose parents have read to them have gained in language development and literacy through expanded vocabulary, eagerness to read, and success in beginning reading in school (Teale, 1981). Another study (Cullinan, Jaggar, & Strickland, 1974) showed that black, linguistically different school-age children increased their language repertoire to include more standard English without negating their own dialect, and showed gains in vocabulary and reading comprehension as a result of read-aloud experiences in the classroom.

Guidelines for Reading Aloud. Trelease (1985) describes in detail several approaches to reading aloud both at home and school.

- *Read-Aloud Do's*

  Remember that the art of listening is an acquired one which must be taught and cultivated gradually.
  Vary the length and subject matter of your readings
  Follow through with reading. (Don't leave your class hanging for three or four days between chapters and expect their interest to be sustained.)
  Stop at a suspenseful spot each day.
  If you are reading a picture book, make sure the children can see the pictures easily.
  After reading, allow time for discussion and for verbal, written, or artistic expression.
  Do not turn discussions into quizzes or pry interpretations from the child.
  Use plenty of expression in reading and read slowly.
  Preview the books before you read.

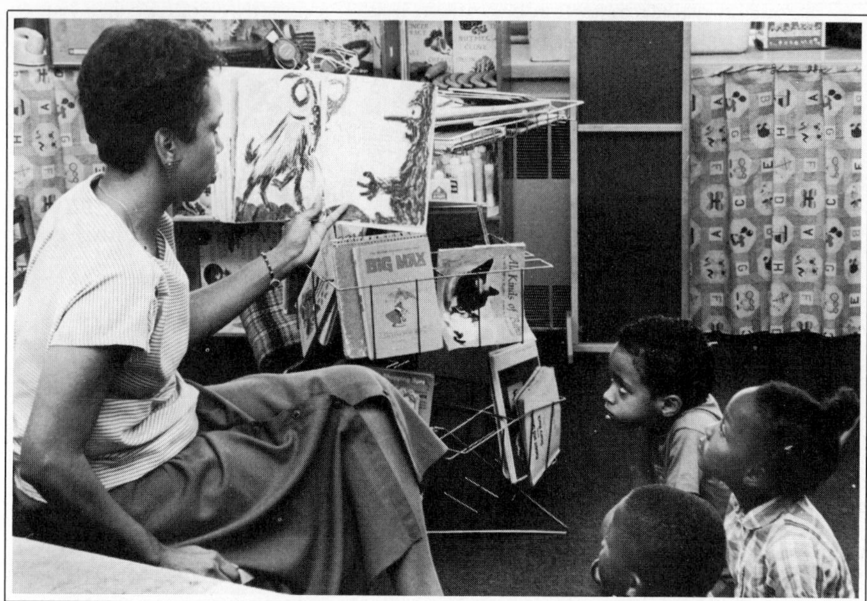

Reading aloud should take place in every classroom, every day—for older students as well as younger ones.

See *Books Are By People* (Citation, 1969) and *More Books by More People* (Citation, 1974), both by Lee Bennett Hopkins.

Bring the author to life, as well as the book, by adding a third dimension when possible: eat blueberries as you read Robert McCloskey's *Blueberries for Sal* (Viking, 1948) or visit the owls at the zoo in conjunction with Farley Mowat's *Owls in the Family* (Bantam, 1981).

- *Read-Aloud Don't's*

  Don't read stories you don't like yourself.
  Don't continue reading a book once it is obvious it was a poor choice.
  Don't feel you have to tie every book to the curriculum.
  Don't be unnerved by questions during the reading. Answer and discuss.
  Don't use the book as a threat or turn it into a weapon.

Consider several criteria for choosing a good read-aloud book. A good read-aloud book should

1. be fast-paced in its plot, allowing the children's interest to be hooked soon,
2. contain clear, rounded characters,
3. include crisp, easy-to-read dialogue, and
4. keep long descriptive passages to a minimum, at least at the start.

Trelease cites *James and the Giant Peach* by Roald Dahl (Bantam, 1978) as the finest read-aloud he has ever known. Other books from his Treasury of Read-Aloud Books include:

WORDLESS BOOKS

The Adventures of Paddy Pork, by John Goodall (Harcourt, 1968)

A Boy, a Dog, and a Frog, by Mercer Mayer (Dial, 1967)

PICTURE BOOKS

Alexander and the Terrible, Horrible, No Good, Very Bad Day, by Judith Viorst (Atheneum, 1976)

Frog and Toad Are Friends, by Arnold Lobel (Harper & Row, 1979)

SHORT NOVELS

The Reluctant Dragon, by Kenneth Grahame (Holiday House, 1953)

A Taste of Blackberries, by Doris B. Smith (Scholastic, 1976)

NOVELS

Bridge to Terabithia, by Katherine Paterson (Avon, 1979)

The Lion, the Witch, and the Wardrobe, by C. S. Lewis (Macmillan, 1970)

POETRY

The Golden Treasury of Poetry, by Louis Untermeyer (Golden, 1959)

Where the Sidewalk Ends, by Shel Silverstein (Harper & Row, 1974)

See Chapter 8, "Reading Poetry."

ANTHOLOGIES

The Fairy Tale Treasury, by Virginia Haviland (Dell, 1980)

Zlateh the Goat and other Stories, by Isaac B. Singer (Harper & Row, 1966)

Directed Listening Thinking Activity (DLTA). The purpose of a DLTA is to focus attention on stories read aloud. Since a similar kind of reasoning takes place in both listening and reading comprehension, it is an important strategy for the teaching of reading as well. The main teaching tool in DLTA is the use of questions to activate prior knowledge and solicit predictions from the children and then focus their attention on the story (text) to verify these predictions as students construct meaning from the text (Stauffeur, 1980). Here is a teaching sequence that can be used with any story read aloud, including children's literature, a basal reader story, or a student-written text. The sequence incorporates sample questions referring to the book *Where the Wild Things Are.*

See Chapter 9, "Directed Reading Thinking Activity."

1. ***Before Reading***

   Introduce the book and tell something about it.

   > *"This is a book about a little boy and an adventure he had."*

   Encourage students to examine the illustrations.
   Discuss any experiences or related concepts, and identify words they may need to know.

   > *"What do you think a Wild Thing is?"*

   Invite students to respond to the story; present the book enthusiastically.

   > *"As I read, you can ask questions or share your ideas."*

2. ***During Reading***
Ask the children to make predictions about what will happen in the story.

"What do you think might happen to Max because he's making mischief?"

Read and then stop to verify their predictions.
Solicit brief summaries.

"What's happened to Max so far?"

Continue to ask the children to make predictions and give their reasons for thinking as they do.

"What do you think will happen next. Why?"

Ask them to respond to events, characters, and ideas in the book.

"What do you think of Max, or the Wild Things, or sailing away from home?"

3. ***After Reading***
Talk about the book.

"What did you think of the book?"

Ask for a summary of the sequence of events.

"What happened to Max first? Next? Last?"

Ask for personal reactions to the story.

"Did you like the book? Why or why not?"

Review new and interesting words.

"How would you describe a Wild Thing? What's a rumpus?"

4. ***Extending the Reading Experience***
Read related books.
In the Night Kitchen, by Maurice Sendak (Harper & Row, 1970)
There's a Nightmare in My Closet, by Mercer Mayer (Dial, 1969)
Encourage children to respond to the story.
Write a story about an adventure or monsters.
Draw a picture.
Make monster masks.
Dramatize the story.

See Chapter 10, "Integrating the Elements of Drama."

Storytelling

Although there are so many books available for children today, and although children are constantly being exposed to television and other visual media, they never seem to lose their fascination with storytelling. Or, as one first-grade child put it as I was about to read a picture book of a favorite folktale she knew I knew by heart: "Tell it with your face!"

The tools of the storyteller are so deceptively simple and so basically human that storytelling is often neglected as a way of teaching talking and listening. It is also a wonderful way to share traditional literature, and stories of the past—the historical past or even your own past.

Stories are everywhere. Young children love to hear stories about when they were a baby. And the important storytellers in your life are often people in your own family. For example, my mother's tales of growing up in a German- speaking family on a farm in southern Illinois in the 1920s and 30s never ceased to fascinate me. I especially enjoyed her stories about stuffing peat moss in her little brother's knickers so he couldn't walk, or putting frogs in the strawberry baskets and crow's eggs in the chicken egg cartons destined for sale in Chicago. And now I find that my own children like to listen to me tell about growing up in California in the San Fernando Valley in the 1950s and 60s, just as I liked to hear my fourth-grade teacher tell stories about what it was like when *she* was a girl there.

Children should be encouraged to tell stories too. In a review of research about children creating and telling their own stories, developmental

Can you guess which story this teacher is telling?

Sources of stories for storytelling:
The Arbuthnot Anthology of Children's Literature, by May Hill Arbuthnot (Scott, Foresman, 1952)
Black Fairy Tales, by Terry Berger (Atheneum, 1970)
Grimm's Fairy Tales by the Brothers Grimm, by E. V. Lucas (Grosset & Dunlap, 1945)
Anthology of Children's Literature, by E. Johnson, A. Sickels, F. Sayers & C. Horowitz (Houghton Mifflin, 1977)

psychologist Wolfe (1984) emphasizes the primacy of the oral language arts as children learn what she calls *long language,* a reflection of their growing knowledge of the construct of scripts, temporal organization, cohesion, and literary genre through experience and practice with storytelling and dramatization as they build up to the more complex *long language* of discussions, reports, and fiction.

Teachers Telling Stories. The teacher is usually the primary storyteller in the classroom.

• *Finding and keeping stories.* In addition to your own experiences, and stories you have heard others tell, folk literature is a traditional source for stories. Younger children enjoy timeless tales like *The Three Billy Goats Gruff, The Three Pigs,* and other tales of three. Tales like *Jack and the Beanstalk* and *The Gingerbread Man* are foolproof too. And any good collection of stories will give you other tales to tell.

You can start a story file on 5 × 7 cards or in a looseleaf notebook. Write down the story and its source. List your audience, and notes on props and related resources such as music and related stories. Include an anecdotal record of responses, and ideas for future tellings. (See Figure 3–2.) Marion Harris started such a file as a student teacher, and referred to it to tell her class the story riddle of the "Little Round Red House with No Doors or Windows and a Chimney On Top" (see Figure 3–2).

Figure 3–2
Saving Stories for Storytelling

FRONT	BACK
Story	Source Audience Props Related Resources Related Stories Responses to Tellings Ideas for Future Tellings

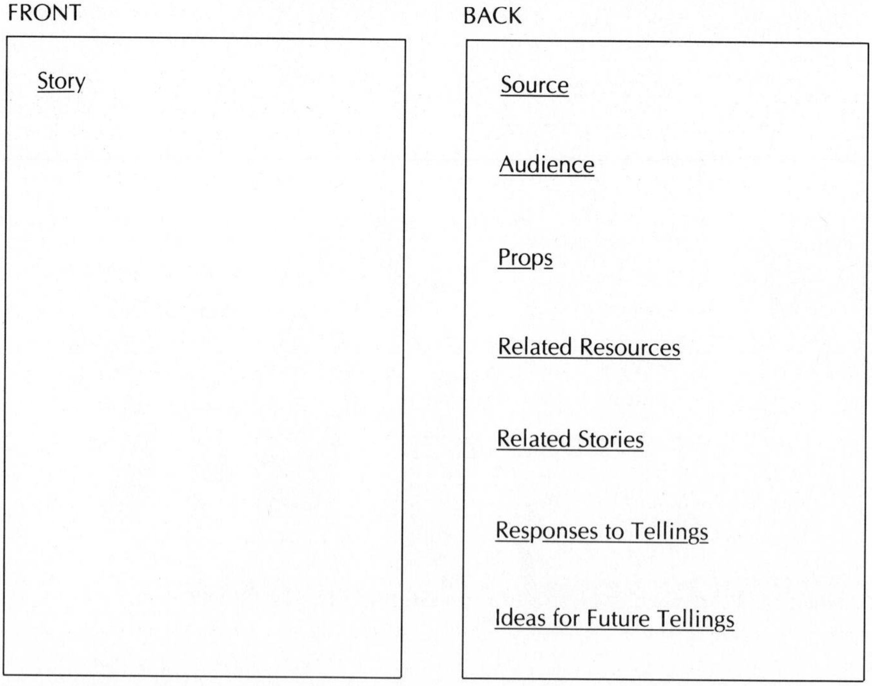

• *Telling stories.* Ross (1980) advises that, above all, you should know the story very well. He also describes a pattern for approaching storytelling that works well for him.

Storyteller, by Ramon Royal Ross, 2nd ed. (Merrill, 1980). See also *Children's Literature through Storytelling & Drama,* 2nd ed., by Nancy E. Briggs & Joseph A. Wagner (Wm. C. Brown, 1981).

1. Read the story aloud several times. Get a feel for the rhythm and style.
2. Outline the major actions in the story, where one ends and another starts.
3. Picture the characters in the story carefully. Describe them in your mind.
4. Picture the setting of the story. Make a map in your mind.
5. Search out phrases in the story that you'd like to work into the telling.
6. Start to tell the story aloud to yourself. Try different ways of saying things.
7. Practice gestures which will add to the story.
8. Prepare an introduction and conclusion before and after the actual telling.
9. Practice telling the entire story, complete with intonation, colorful phrases, gestures, sequence, in a smooth and natural fashion. Also, time the story as you practice.

Tape record a telling and listen for areas where you might improve your delivery. Watch yourself in a mirror during a telling and observe your posture, gestures, and the overall impression of the story.

At Sally K. Ride Elementary School in Houston, Texas, teachers use a story apron with many pockets which hold a toy or other token representing a story. Children choose one and the teacher tells that story. Other such props are story hats or necklaces with story charms.

• *Props for storytelling.* While props are not necessary, some teachers like to use them for storytelling, especially with younger children. I like costumes, and would use a black cape and witch's hat for telling scary stories in autumn.

I also like mood makers: candles, music, or incense. Other props include picture cards and flannel boards and, of course, puppets. Puppetry, a special mixture of storytelling, art, movement, drama, and magic, is one of the best possible mediums for children to listen and talk and share stories as they express themselves.

Children Telling Stories. Children will often want to tell stories about what is going on in their lives. Look for signs that they have something to say and make time to listen yourself or let them tell the class as well. Such stories often come up at unexpected moments, such as during a basal reading lesson, when the story reminds them of something that has happened to them. These times are important. Listen and let them talk.

See "Storytelling in the Classroom: Not an Impossible Dream," by Kathryn Farnsworth, in *Language Arts* 58 (1981): 162–167.

There are many ways to structure children's storytelling experiences, and one of the most effective is to encourage them to tell their stories through puppetry.

Puppetry. Children are natural puppeteers. Watch any young child with a stuffed animal, a toy car, or any object which can become an extension of his own body and voice and ideas, and you will see a born puppeteer.

Rather than planning specific puppetry activities, have materials and books on puppets available in the classroom, and recognize the need for puppets as part of the storytelling experience.

• *Ideas for puppetry* will often occur in the course of experiencing a story. Sources of story ideas for puppetry are many.

BASAL READER STORIES. Some of these are actually written as play scripts and may even include suggestions for puppetry. Others can be developed into oral scripts by children if it is a story they seem to want to dramatize and puppets seem a logical way to do it.

FOLKTALES. Folktales are an excellent source of puppet play ideas. You may read a story aloud, or children may find one they like in a book they are reading themselves.

PICTURE BOOKS. A favorite picture book is often one that children will act out anyway after repeated readings, and puppetry is an excellent way to extend this experience.

• *Materials for puppetry* can be collected by you or donated by parents. Many puppet-making materials are everyday found objects. Make them available to children and let them use their imaginations as they create puppets.

Tools: scissors, tape, glue, paint, marking pens, stapler
Bodies: fingers, hands, and feet
Paper: construction paper, plates, bags, crepe, paper cups, cardboard, envelopes
Cloth: scraps, yarn, socks, gloves, scarves, handkerchiefs, mittens, hats
Sticks: tongue depressors, ice cream sticks, twigs, dowels, old wooden spoons
Fancy things: feathers, buttons, sequins, beads, costume jewelry, ribbons
Odds and ends: boxes, milk cartons, styrofoam, cotton balls, Ping-Pong balls, fruits and vegetables, gourds, leaves, moss, pine cones

• *Making simple puppets.* Many puppets can be made very quickly and simply.

Draw directly on fingers, hands, tongue depressors, or ice cream sticks, with washable markers or paint.

For stick puppets, attach a paper plate, cutout, or styrofoam cup to a stick and decorate.

For paper bag puppets, decorate or draw directly on the bag.

For hand puppets, use gloves, mittens, boxes, fabric, a handkerchief wrapped with rubber bands, or an envelope over the hand.

Puppet Making through the Grades, by G. Hopper (Davis, 1966); *Making Easy Puppets,* by Shari Lewis (E. P. Dutton, 1967); *Hanimals,* by Mario Mariolti (Green Tiger Press, 1982); *Puppets for Play Production,* by Nancy Renfro (Funk & Wagnalls, 1969)

Many other types of puppets are possible. Children may also use informational how-to books on puppetry to research and make their own puppets.

- *Staging puppet plays.* The best staging devices for puppets in the classroom are the simplest:

A table turned on its side and draped with a dramatic-looking cloth

A quilt held by two reliable students or draped over a broom-stick balanced on two chairs

A cardboard box on a table, with the puppeteers seated behind on low chairs

A picture story book which includes a history of puppet drama along with a script is *Punch & Judy: A Play for Puppets,* by Ed Emberly (Little, Brown, 1965)

Puppet stages can be built, but are not necessary to fulfill the real purpose of the drama: to encourage the thinking, listening, talking, and imagination of children as they create oral texts to share with others through puppets.

Puppet stages are a nice addition to a classroom, but there are many simpler ways to share puppets.

Classroom Media Centers for Listening and Talking

You can organize a classroom listening and viewing center, with a tape recorder, record player, earphones, and filmstrip machine. Here, children can listen to and view some of the wonderful stories recorded professionally on tape, records, and filmstrips. An excellent source of children's literature on media is Mary Alice Hunt's *A Multimedia Approach to Children's Literature* (American Library Association, 1983). It lists, for example, Maurice Sendak's *The Nutshell Library* (Harper, 1962), a collection of four small books: *Alligators All Around,* an alphabet book; *One Was Johnny,* a counting song; *Pierre,* a moralistic tale; and *Chicken Soup with Rice,* a story of the months of the year. For each of these, a filmstrip, record, and tape are available from the publisher.

Chicken Soup with Rice is a set of wonderful poems that have been set to music and are sung by Carole King, a friend of Sendak's. Children can listen, read along, and sing the poems with the recordings. Each month, a poem from this book could be featured in a listening center.

Activities to extend this listening and reading experience could include talking about plans to make puppets or dramatize the poem, make costumes to present it, using the poem as a pattern for more writing, or cooking and eating chicken soup with rice on a cool October day, and discussing and reporting on that experience.

A classroom listening center—for enjoyment and learning.

Observing Talking and Listening in the Classroom

As you observe the kind of talking and listening that takes place in the classroom, it is just as important to consider how the teacher talks and listens as it is to consider how the children talk and listen.

In any communication event, you may compare the quantity and quality of your language with that of the children. Consider the way such a comparison was made in the section on Centering Ideas between the way Kathy Lee and the children in her class used language in book talks and in film talks. You may use the observation sheet shown in Figure 3-3 yourself or invite another teacher, aide, or interested person to do it for you. Periodically check yourself as you assess not only the language of children, but your own language, in the process of building the framework that will in turn support the children in building their own language structures.

It may be useful to you to evaluate several types of activities, such as reading, social studies, science, or mathematics, and compare them over a period of time to help you make decisions about the way you may best support and structure the children's efforts to make sense.

Figure 3-3
Talking and Listening in the Classroom

Date/Time______________________________

Activity______________________________

1. *Who talked and who listened?* Count the number of times the teacher and the children talked in discussions.

   Teacher______________________________

   Children______________________________

2. *How did the teacher talk?* Classify the teacher's questions as closed (implying only one answer possible) or open (implying more than one answer possible).

   Closed______________________________

   Open______________________________

3. *How did the children talk?* Classify the children's answers as closed (implying only one answer acceptable) or open (implying more than one answer acceptable).

   Closed______________________________

   Open______________________________

Summing Up

Teachers must understand how talking and listening and language are used in the classroom as children use language to seek meaning. To this end, teachers can become aware of their own use of language and employ means such as open rather than closed questioning styles to support children's growing language competence.

Research has shown that while listening and talking are important, neither of these skills is systematically taught; teacher talk tends to dominate the classroom. This is unfortunate, since listening and talking are basic to learning to read and write. Teachers can support literacy development in many ways by creating a healthy oral language climate in the classroom. Ways to do this include expanding vocabulary, encouraging flexibility and sensitivity to use of language forms, raising metalinguistic awareness, practicing comprehension skills, connecting the language arts, and understanding and building on the student' prior experience and linguistic and cultural heritage.

One approach to teaching talking and listening in any context is to plan many opportunities for students to experience, share, discuss, and report on topics of interest to them. Instructional strategies include brainstorming and problem solving, interviews, oral histories, writing conferences, and dialogue journals. Many useful teacher questioning strategies are available, such as an open questioning style and the ReQuest procedure.

Other ways to develop talking and listening include reading aloud and Directed Listening Thinking Activity (DLTA), storytelling, puppetry, and activities in listening and media centers. Finally teachers can better understand and monitor the quantity and quality of oral language in the classroom through the use of systematic observation techniques.

Looking Further

1. Observe in a classroom and analyze a language sample according to the following criteria:

- Who talked and who listened? Count the number of times the teacher and then the children talked during your observation.
- How did the teacher talk and listen? Classify the questions of the teacher as either closed—clearly implying that only one answer is acceptable—or open—inviting more than one possible answer.
- How did the children talk and listen? Classify their answers as either open or closed, as defined above.

2. Poll several teachers across several grade levels on whether or not they have a regular planned time for sharing in their classrooms. If they do, ask them why. If they do not, ask them why not. List several ways you could plan sharing time in your schedule.

3. Plan and implement a brainstorming session on any topic with a group of children. Record their ideas and list several learning and teaching experiences which could result.

4. Write and carry out an interview with another person in class, and let the other person interview you. Each of you share the results of the other's interview with the whole class.

5. Read aloud to a group of children and plan several ways to extend the reading.

6. Start a file of what you think would be good read-aloud books.

7. Read a picture book to a group of children and follow the teaching sequence of a Directed Listening Thinking Activity (DLTA).

8. Choose and prepare a story for storytelling according to the guidelines suggested in this chapter. Create one prop for your story.

9. Start a file of stories to tell.

Chapter Four

The Development and Uses of Writing

Centering Ideas
- Real Writing at an Early Age
- The Development of a Real Writer

Making Connections
- Writing As a Way of Knowing
- The Development of Children's Writing
- The Interactive Nature of Reading and Writing
- Writing across the Curriculum
- The Teacher As Writer: A Model for Children
- Writing As a Way of Knowing How to Teach

Teaching Children
- A Classroom for Real Writing
- Writing about Ourselves and about Others
- Writing to Get Things Done
- Editing and Revising
- Publication of Writing
- Evaluation of Writing

Summing Up

Looking Further

Objectives

Look for answers to the following questions as you read this chapter.

- What is real writing?
- How do children learn to write?
- What is the relationship between writing and reading?
- Where does writing fit in the curriculum?
- How can teachers learn from writing?
- How do you set up a classroom for real writing?
- What are some strategies for teaching writing about yourself and other people, and writing to get things done?
- How do you teach editing and revising of writing?
- How do you help children publish writing?
- How do you evaluate writing?

A Child's View

Here is how a group of fifth-graders answered the question "What is writing?"

- "The symbols of the alphabet, which put together make words, which make sentences, which make paragraphs, and so on."
- "Writing can be almost anything you want it to be. It can be a way of communicating with each other instead of talking, expressing yourself in a poem or story, recording important data, an article, or writing out math problems. It is an absolute necessity."
- "When you write something you give someone else something to read. It also gives you something to do on rainy days."
- "Writing is making up things that you wish you could do but making someone else be able to do it. But it can be just something to keep for yourself."

Centering Ideas

How do children learn to write? When do they begin? Are there stages in learning to write, as there are in learning to speak? And just what do we really mean by writing? You may be able to find answers to some of these questions by deciding which of the following are—or are not—examples of real writing.

Real Writing at an Early Age

Elizabeth at Age One

Under the old chestnut table her mother uses to write on at home, Elizabeth finds a pad of the smallest Post-its. She makes a mark on one with a pencil she has also found on the floor, pulls the Post-it off the pad, and sticks it to her arm. She repeats this process slowly and carefully and quietly until she is covered like a bird with square yellow feathers, each with its own curious marking. Then, as her mother watches, she raises and flaps her paper-feathered arms and crows her pride and pleasure in the marks she has made.

Gordon at Ages Two and Three

Under the same table, Gordon scribbles on a piece of paper and then holds it up to show his mother (see Figure 4–1).

Gordon had seen the Walt Disney movie version of the book *Mary Poppins,* by Pamela L. Travers (Harcourt Brace Jovanovich, 1934, 1962).

Gordon: [*holding up his drawing*] Look! Kite!
Mother: [*looking up*] A cat?
Gordon: No. Dat a kite. Like up in da 'ky [*points to the picture and points up*]. Like Mary Poppins. Like little boy in Mary Poppins [*pretends to fly a kite*].
Mother: I like that [*writes the date in the corner of the paper as Gordon watches*].
Gordon: I like dat. You write Gordon?
Mother: Yes [*writes* Gordon *in the corner of the paper as he watches*].
Gordon: What dat? What you write?
Mother: [*points to date*] That?
Gordon: Yeah.
Mother: That's the date today. November twentieth.
Gordon: Oh. You put dat on window?
Mother: Yes. I'll put it on the window. [*She tapes the drawing to the window alongside some of her own papers.*]
Gordon: [*admiring his work on the window*] Give me 'nother paper, Mama.

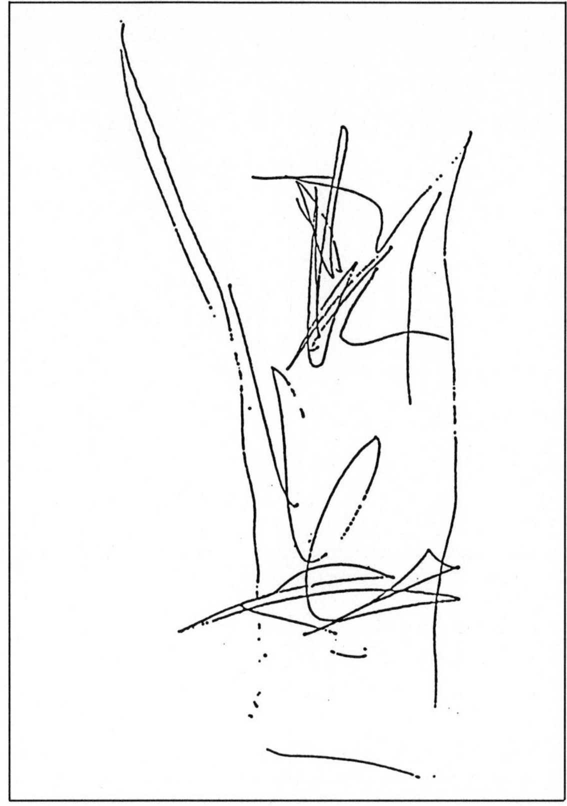

Figure 4–1
Gordon at Age Two: A Kite!

A year later, Gordon is sitting with his mother in a large armchair as she writes in a blank book. He takes the pen out of her hand and scribbles on a page. He says "Look Mama. I write too. I writing a building."

Wyatt at Ages Four through Eight

During a cross-country car trip, four-year-old Wyatt draws pictures of his family, and then narrates what he has drawn to his grandmother as he scribbles large swirls with a red crayon (see Figure 4–2).

A year later, Wyatt draws a picture he says is Alice in Wonderland's sister reading a book to her, draws a line around it, asks for another paper to be glued on to this one to make a book. He then carefully writes letters of the alphabet and numbers he knows, explaining, as he writes, what is happening in the picture (see Figure 4–3).

At age six, Wyatt writes about a trip to the zoo (see Figure 4–4). In the second grade, he writes a story about his dog (see Figure 4–5). At age eight, in the third grade, he writes about a family vacation.

Figure 4–2 *Wyatt at Age Four: Family*

Figure 4–3 *Wyatt at Age Five: Alice in Wonderland's Sister Reading a Book to Her*

by Wyatt

The Zoo.

I am at the zoo. it is fun at the zoo. about 100 animals. at the zoo.

Figure 4–4
Wyatt at Age Six: The Zoo

Arthur

I have a dog named Arthur He is a black tan and white Sheltie. He is fast and jumpy. We have to give him medicine every night because of skin disease. He likes tobe petted and he is 8 moths old.

Figure 4–5
Wyatt at Age Seven: Arthur

The Development of a Real Writer

At nine years old, David has a keen sense of humor and an interest in superheroes and space exploration. During a science unit on the behavior of mealworms, he writes a tongue-in-cheek television script about Superworm, "a famous police agent" (see Figure 4–6).

At ten, he enjoys writing, thinks of himself as a writer, and presents his first book of two typewritten pages to his third- and fourth-grade teacher (see Figure 4–7).

David's interest in superheroes and space exploration waned as he grew older, but his interest in writing continued to grow. He wrote for his high school and college newspapers, and for a local paper after graduation. He began to travel and to write articles about his travels; he is currently working on a novel. He also wrote this same third- and fourth-grade teacher to explain his feelings about writing: "I know exactly how I got to be a writer, can recall the first moment, sixteen years ago, when I first knew I'd be a writer—but I'm not sure why I am a writer. It feels good to know you're there, my first editor, teacher, encourager."

Making Connections

Which of the examples presented in the preceding section represent real writing? David's efforts as an adult are the only ones that have been published. Some of the examples do not even contain recognizable letters or

Figure 4–6
David at Age Nine: Script

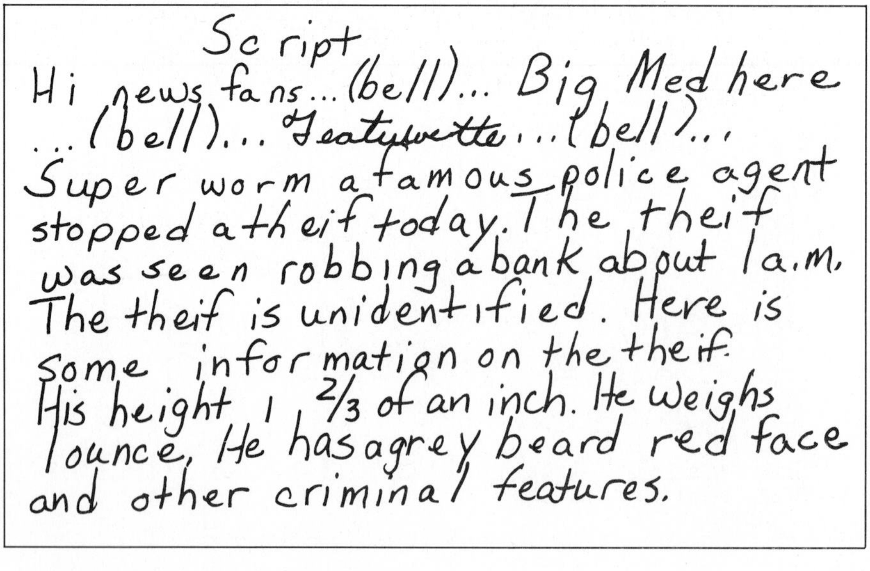

Script

Hi news fans... (bell)... Big Med here ... (bell)... ~~Featurette~~... (bell)... Super worm a famous police agent stopped a theif today. The theif was seen robbing a bank about 1 a.m. The theif is unidentified. Here is some information on the theif. His height 1, 2/3 of an inch. He weighs 1 ounce, He has a grey beard red face and other criminal features.

Run For Space

Looking Back: Six astronauts are in a rocket which,in thirty minutes,will blast off top planet X in the solar system of Zerg which has nine hundred-seventy-three planets,the largest in the galaxy off Zerbelquist,two hundred light years away.Ron,Dave,Beth,Martha, Felicia,and I await the blastoff.It is the year 5469.

Part I: The Blastoff

T/-I8/seconds/

"T–I8 minutes 20 seconds,' Jim Barker flight control captain said, "We've gotten word that Russia plans to beat us to planet X.They're five minutes ahead of us.2

"Don't worry, we'll beat them."Ronald Rowly ,Air Force Col., said.

"T–5 minutes and counting." "Just think," I said "after this we'll be able toar reach as far out into space as we want,explore countless galaxies,and maybe even reach the end of space."

"T–I0 seconds and counting,' said Jim//9876 "9,8,7,6,5,4/3/2/I all systems are go 3,2,I." and then,with an Earth shattering explosionthe Galactus 5 started off.In one day we were a I/8 of the way there. But strange adventures would delay us. . . . .

Part 2: OUR Our Journey

Figure 4–7 *David at Age Ten: Run for Space*

words, and some that do are misspelled, ungrammatical, and messy—including David's earlier writings. In retrospect, however, he thinks of himself as having been a writer when he wrote those earlier pieces as well. What, then, is real writing?

Writing As a Way of Knowing

In the strictest sense, real writing is writing that is bound by the conventions of language and print and can be read and understood by others. Among the examples above, the first real writing would be Wyatt's limited efforts at six. But writing is much more than form and conventions. In the broadest sense, writing is a way of knowing, of discovering what you know as you put down, in the form not only of words and phrases but of scribbles and drawings, your ideas and images and all the other wonderful stuff in your mind that may only become clear to you as you engage in the process of writing it down. Just as you may not know what you are going to say until you say it, so you may not know what you are going to write until you write it. And as you write, writing becomes a way of knowing.

Writing seen thus as a way of discovering what we know is a rather messy process. And as children freely use their innately human symbol-making power, they certainly make a lot of messes. They mark and scribble and gesture and act out and make noise and draw and write and rewrite and crumple paper and make holes in it as they erase, and then they write some more as they revise. In this way, they use written language as a way of discovering what they know and communicating that knowledge to the world.

Even little Elizabeth's crude attempts at making marks place her near the beginning of a timeline of writing development that can now be observed, but that goes back even earlier to the days when she expressed her experience of the world only through play and gestures and speaking. Her gestures and speech, and her marks, are her message to the world: "Here I am!"

In all these examples of writing, from first marks to clear messages, the children are—according to Kelly's theory (1963)—young scientists attempting to interpret the world as they interact with it through a series of active experiments during which they are constantly coming up with and testing new hypotheses. Miller (1977) refers to children at this stage as *spontaneous apprentices.*

The Development of Children's Writing

In the sense of writing as a way of knowing, Elizabeth, Gordon, Wyatt, and David are real writers, or at least they are spontaneous apprentices in the process of developing as writers. They are not, however, following a linear path that leads them from one successfully mastered level of subskills to another. Rather, they are picking their way through a maze of the different aspects of the whole language process, picking up skills in the course of their experiments with language. Sometimes they will move forward quickly in one dimension while losing control over another. They are constantly in the process of experimenting and testing new hypotheses. A piece of writing may end but the process of learning how to write does not. This process has its first beginnings in the actions of the prelinguistic infant as she seeks to make sense of her world and to share what she knows with others.

Symbol Making: Elizabeth at Age One

At age one, Elizabeth is marking and playing and making gestures and sounds associated with these activities. She can only speak four words that are intelligible to most other people, but these words are most often accompanied by facial expressions, gestures, and play, and with certain tones of voice, each with a specific meaning in a specific situation. Just as she learned to say her first words by hearing words spoken to her and interacting with others around her, so she now makes her first marks on paper as a

Mama (cries, frowns, and throws herself forward, reaching: when she needs or wants something),

(continued)

result of having writing materials available and watching others use such materials. And just as gestures were a precursor to talking, so the making of symbols is a precursor to writing.

Scribbling: Gordon at Ages Two and Three

At ages two and three, Gordon also scribbles on paper (not to mention on floors, furniture, and walls). And, like Elizabeth, he takes great pleasure in making symbols which signify his experiences. But there are differences between the efforts of the two children. Gordon intends to use his mother as an audience: he is able to tell her what his scribbles represent, and uses gestures for further elucidation. He is also able to link his drawing to a story he has seen on film or that has been read to him. He is beginning to ask questions about the writing process, and shows that he understands some things about writing. He knows, for example, that certain signs on a page carry a message, such as his name. He also wishes to share his piece and publish it along with his mother's papers that are taped to the window. Later, he uses the word *write* to describe what he is doing. His writinglike behavior, as well as his metalinguistic knowledge of the writing process, is growing.

dada (laughs and bobs up and down: when she wants to play), *bye-bye* (curls fingers in and out: when someone leaves or she wants someone to leave), *oh-oh* (drops or throws down an object, looks at it, at others, and reaches for it: when she drops something or throws it down because she does not want it).

Vygotsky (1978) believes that when even very young children engage in different types of symbol making and using behavior in learning to write and read, they do so by way of transforming various types of shared social behavior—as Gordon did in talking and acting out his "written" message to his mother—and eventually internalizing these through writing and reading.

Piaget (1969) says this symbolmaking function is "the ability to represent something—object, event, conceptual scheme—by means of a *signifier*—language, mental image, symbolic gestures.

Gordon's scribbling is meaningless by itself. Clay (1975) and Holdaway (1978) call such primitive efforts at symbol making *gross approximations* that later evolve into more refined attempts at letterforms, invented words, and pretend sentences as children move towards discovering and using the principles of written language.

Some of the things that children discover about written language from the preschool years through the primary grades are summarized by Dyson (1982, p. 830).

- **Perceptual features:** what it looks like (Clay, 1975);
- **Symbolic nature:** the relationship between print and the formal aspects of speech (Ferreiro, 1978);
- **Structural characteristics:** the conventions that determine how connected discourse is put together, as in the structural features of stories (Applebee, 1978) or the cohesive features that link sentences to form texts (King & Rentel, 1979);
- **Discursive procedures:** the processes by which a dynamic experience is transformed into an explicit, ordered, and linear format (Cook-Gumperz & Gumperz, 1981) and, conversely, by which a linear display is transformed, through both graphic and language cues, into an understood experience (Clay, 1979);

- **Sociocognitive nature:** how meaning conveyed in print relates to the knowledge of both the writer and the reader; that is, that sustained written language, to a greater degree than conversational oral language, must be interpreted independently from the context of a specific or personal situation (Cook-Gumperz & Gumperz, 1981; Donaldson, 1978; Wells, 1981);
- **Functional capacities:** the uses of written language (Goodman, 1980).

Pictures and Print: Wyatt at Ages Four through Eight

At ages four through eight, Wyatt does many of the same things Gordon does, but he takes some new turns in his journey through the writing process maze. His drawings are representational, and he makes it clear that he understands the difference between pictures and print, for he also scribbles abstract but printlike swirls on another piece of paper. These scribbles serve as a story to accompany his pictures, and he pretends to read them aloud to his grandmother, thus demonstrating the tendency of young children to give meaning to their drawing and writing symbols through talking (Dyson, 1983).

At age five, Wyatt practices copying the letters of the alphabet and then freely uses the ones he knows to invent his own words for a story to accompany a picture. He labels his work with his name, which he has also practiced copying. By age six, he is able to write recognizable words, construct a story sequence, illustrate it, and publish it as a book. And by ages seven and eight, he is able to write more extended stories based on his personal experiences. He has mastered certain writing conventions, including spelling, punctuation, and handwriting. And he can communicate his ideas and intentions to a wide audience of readers.

Concepts about Print

Clay (1979) has thoroughly studied how writing develops in children of these ages and describes the concepts about print they are acquiring:

- to understand that print talks,
- to form letters,
- to build up memories of common words they can construct out of letters,
- to use these words to write messages,
- to increase the number and range of sentences used,
- to become flexible in the use of sentences, and
- to discipline the expression of ideas within the spelling and punctuation conventions of English (pp. 11–12).

Clay also found that children spontaneously experimented with their own writing in ways that led them to discover how to write. She describes these ways as concepts and principles. Figure 4–8 demonstrates some examples of these concepts and principles in the drawing and writing sample of a five-year-old.

Figure 4–8 *Five-Year-Old's Drawing and Writing*

The Sign Concept and the Message Concept. Children learn that a sign carries a message and that spoken messages can be written, although they do not always know whether what they write corresponds to what they have said.

The Flexibility Principle. Children learn to experiment with letter forms and discover for themselves the boundaries of print conventions: how far they can go before a letter will lose its identity as a language sign.

The Recurrence Principle. Children repeat forms and patterns and begin to understand that, as in the alphabet, certain of the same elements can recur in variable patterns.

The Generating Principle. Guided by the principles of flexibility and recurrence, young children learn that there are rules for arranging and combining the elements they already know in new and inventive ways. Clay shows that this is a better way to learn to write than simply copying what others have written.

The Contrast Principle. Children experiment with creating contrasts among shapes, meanings, sounds, and word patterns and learn that contrasts can be made between elements at several levels.

The Direction Principle, the Space Concept, and Page and Book Arrangement. Children learn that the pattern of print in the English language moves from left to right and then starts at the left again, and that there are spaces between words. They also learn how to use line and page space to accommodate their writing.

As children learn to put the above concepts and principles into practice, with varying degrees of efficiency, they are moving towards writing that can be read and understood by others without a spoken explanation. As five-year-old Wyatt did in his story about Alice, they will use letters to create wordlike forms. Read (1975) has studied such invented spellings extensively and found that children may come to school with a knowledge of abstract phonological categories and relationships that may result in somewhat bizarre spellings. He suggests that until teachers have a better understanding of this system they should respect it and work with it if only on an intuitive basis. He also found that none of the children he studied had trouble later in learning to use standard spelling.

See Chapter 7, "The Prephonetic Stage."

Writing for Different Purposes: David at Ages Nine and Ten and Older

At ages nine and ten, David can use conventional handwriting, spelling, punctuation, and sentence and paragraph structure. He is able to write extended narratives in different genres with different styles, for different purposes, and for different audiences. On his own, he has composed and typed a very short book. He has a strong writing voice. Perhaps most importantly, David sees himself as a writer, and he will retain that self-image into adulthood, using the remembrance of himself as a writer in the past to sustain the image of himself as a writer in the present. David is gaining control of his writing in many ways. While mastering many of the conventions of writing, he is also learning that revision is part of the writing process: he writes drafts that he knows will not be the last, and he rewrites in order to say things so they will mean what he wants them to mean and will sound the way he wants them to sound. He is also beginning to show a strong sense of story in his writing and developing a sense of style. He writes about action, adventure, and excitement, a characteristic of children at this age noted by both Graves (1983) and Applebee (1978).

Writing: Teachers and Children at Work, by Donald Graves (Heinemann, 1983)

One of the nine-year-olds studied by Graves (1983) and his associate Calkins explain what revision means to her:

> Sometimes when I write a sentence and I realize it doesn't make sense, so I'll cross out part of it and make like a circle and up on a space that is blank I'll write what I wanted to write if I didn't have room on my paper.

> Like here I put, "More and more snow falls. After a long time something amazing happens," but I didn't like the word happens, so I put a little sign and I put the same sign up on top of the page and I put, "starts to form" (p. 4).

Graves (1983) describes another child who learned to spell between the third and fifth grades in the process of learning to revise and rewrite. Since his teacher emphasized that he should concentrate on just setting down information in the early drafts and become more responsible for spelling in the later ones, he moved towards more conventional spelling as he moved towards the final draft:

> The first time, I spell the way I hear them. . . . When I write them I don't think about what they look like, but I don't do this [correcting] while I'm writing, but after I see what they look like" (p. 189).

He usually writes from three to eight drafts. By the time he finishes, correct spelling is important because the piece of writing has become important to him.

The Interactive Nature of Reading and Writing

At age one, Elizabeth crows with delight when she makes a mark on a piece of paper. At age two, Gordon knows that certain letters on a piece of paper say his name. At age four, Wyatt tells what is happening in a picture as he makes scribbles that represent his idea of letters; at age five, he uses real letters to form invented words for a story; and at ages six through eight, he writes stories and books that he reads aloud to others, and that others can read. At ages nine and ten, David writes in different styles he has read in literature and seen in the media. All these children are making a connection among writing, reading, and language.

Both Durkin (1966) and Clark (1976) have found that early readers have usually been, in Durkin's words, "paper and pencil kids," and that they had scribbled, and learned to copy letters and write the names of friends and family members before they could read. Chomsky (1971) also suggests that writing precedes reading.

In a comparison of three classrooms with three different approaches to reading and writing instruction—phonics, skills, and whole-language—De Ford (1981) points to the importance of integrating teaching language processes as a reflection of the "interactive nature of the reading and writing processes in literacy learning" (p. 653). In the whole-language classroom, which used a language experience approach, children's literature, experience centers, and the integration of reading and writing activities, she found that students scored higher on comprehension of predictable stories, on retelling of stories, and on recalling more story information. In writing, these students also produced a greater variety of literary forms:

stories, informational prose, songs, poetry, and newspaper articles; more of these pieces were well crafted; and the students tended to write more about classroom experiences. By contrast, children in the phonics and skills classrooms tended to write on personal or family topics. De Ford concludes that language interaction, such as the supportive relationship between reading and writing, and the freedom of children to discover the many uses of language are foundations of literacy learning.

See "The Author's Chair," by Donald Graves and Jane Hansen, in *Language Arts,* 60 (1983), 176–183.

In a comparison of three children in one first-grade classroom, Graves and Hansen (1983) observed and analyzed what children know about the connection between reading and writing, both seen as acts of composing. In this classroom, children read and wrote every day, saved their writing in folders, and published one of every four pieces as a bound book. These children's books—using both invented and conventional spelling—together with regular trade books became part of the classroom library, which was also a center for teaching reading. Each day, the teacher or one of the children, sitting in what was called the author's chair, would read one of these books while the rest of the children listened, asked questions, and discussed the books. After a year of research, Graves and Hansen (1983) noted three phases in children's understanding of the author concept.

1. ***The Replication Phase: "Authors Write Books"***

   Children playfully invent and imitate their way into reading and writing. They watch and interact with others, then make up their own versions of writing through drawing, spelling, and different uses of the page. They hold up a book and both tell and "read" a story as they have seen others do. They begin to grasp what it is that readers and writers do.

2. ***The Transition Phase: "I Am an Author"***

   In the process of publishing their own books, children begin to understand more about what being an author entails: they learn to choose a topic; they identify with authors they have read or listened to on tape in listening centers; they take an increasing interest in print as a complement to drawing; and they start to analyze what they have written.

3. ***The Option-awareness Phase:***
   "If I Wrote and Published This Book Now, I Wouldn't Write It This Way"

   At this stage, children begin to convey more information by way of implication, expecting the reader to contribute to the message; they increase the use of fictional forms, anticipate the reaction of the audience, and in general become writers who exercise options and anticipate questions from readers. Even as readers, they ask more questions and expect authors to defend their choice of options.

Graves and Hansen (1983) conclude that "readers who are also writers develop a sense of authorship that helps them in either composing process" (p. 183).

Writing does not exist separately from content, context, and use. As with spoken language, children learn how to write in the very process of writing to learn a variety of subjects across the curriculum. Children may be introduced to and learn the various forms of writing in school, but they are just as likely to discover them as they use writing to fulfill specific needs and purposes. During the period of one year in just one subject, nine-year-old David used a great range of types of writing, many of which crossed over into other areas of the curriculum. In an elementary science study unit, David's third- and fourth-grade class was learning about the behavior of mealworms. In the course of their studies of this subject, they used many different types of writing:

- they made labels and signs for an experiment with mealworms,
- they recorded their observations in the form of a log,
- they made notes and summaries of their observations,
- they took notes from reading about mealworms, and
- they reported the findings of the experiment.

From these direct and immediate uses of writing, the children went on to

- gather and tally data,
- create graphs, tables, figures, charts, and diagrams,
- compute and present numerical averages and percentages of findings,
- compile a bibliography,
- write poems about mealworms,
- write fictional stories about mealworms (having spontaneously given names and personalities to the mealworm subjects of their experiments),
- write genre stories, such as *The Adventures of Superworm* and *Another Episode of Dragworm,*
- write pastiches of literature, such as *Wormeo and Juleworm, Abe and I,* and *Swiss Family Worminson,*
- create a script for a Super-8 class-made film called *I Love You, Mealworm,*
- plan props and scenery for filmmaking,
- write directions for filmmaking,
- create publicity for showing the film.

See Chapter 5, Shaping Writing for Self-Expression.

See Chapter 11, The Media Arts.

Many researchers have looked at the types of writing children choose to do and the context they do it in. Britton (1982) and his associates found that as they begin to write children most often choose to write stories, and that they make greater use of what Britton (1970) calls **poetic language**—"language of being and becoming"—than what he calls **transactional**

language—"language to get things done." But other researchers (Bissex, 1980; Harste, Burke & Woodward, 1982; Taylor, 1983) found that children spontaneously write for many different purposes, not just to tell stories.

Teachers who write about writing have found that writing can be a powerful means to teach mathematics (Evans, 1984) and science (Levine, 1985), and that journal writing throughout the curriculum can integrate all types of content through the language arts (Fulwiler & Young, 1982). Applebee, Langer, and Mullis (1986) suggest two major movements that hold the most promise for improving the teaching of writing: (1) students need broad-based experiences in which reading and writing tasks are integrated into their work throughout the curriculum, and (2) instruction in the writing process needs to focus on teaching students how to think more effectively as they write. As you read and experiment with approaches to teaching writing, you will discover many ways in which both teachers and children can use writing as a way of knowing.

The Teacher As Writer: A Model for Children

I once received a teacher love note that made me realize that my students did not connect the type of writing I encouraged them to do with what they saw me do. Wendy drew a picture with the caption, "Mrs. Cox's class writing books and Mrs. Cox writing report cards." I decided then that I did not want children to think that teachers write report cards while children do the real writing. So I began to write in my journal whenever the children did, and did other kinds of writing together with them as often as possible.

There is no doubt that teaching writing can pose a challenge to the teacher who feels less confident about an ability to write than to read. Most teachers consider themselves proficient and even expert readers, but few consider themselves expert writers. This is precisely the problem: Smith (1981) asserts that the greatest myth about who is competent to teach writing is that "people who do not themselves enjoy and practice writing can teach children how to write" (p. 797).

This is not to suggest that you must be a well-known or even a published writer in order to be able to teach. But there are many ways you can model writing behavior, just as you model reading behavior, that will show rather than merely tell your students that writing is important, that it is something we all share and can even enjoy. For example, you can begin to write a piece you can work on as they are writing. At first, you may find it hard to find time, but while the children are absorbed in their own writing, you can concentrate on yours. You may well find that by seemingly doing less (writing alone and leaving the children alone) rather than more (offering to help the children and perhaps breaking their train of thought) you may in fact be doing the most to encourage and support writing in your classroom.

Journal Writing

Start a journal now. It will become a thread that connects you in your future as a student teacher and a teacher with your past, and will help you understand the present.

Curriculum Writing

Participate in curriculum projects, school self-study reports, and other projects that require report writing. You may find you have a great deal to say and learn when you are writing about children, teaching, and learning.

Writing Projects

Through the National Writing Project, teachers across the country participate in summer workshops where they learn to teach writing by writing themselves. Find out if your state has a writing project and become involved. (Write: James Gray, Director, National Writing Project, Department of Education, University of California, Berkeley, CA 94720.)

See "Writing for Publication: Advice from Classroom Teachers," by Barbara Catroppa, in *Language Arts,* 61 (1984), 836–841.

Writing As a Way of Knowing How to Teach

Just as children like Elizabeth, Gordon, Wyatt, and David use writing as a way of knowing about their world, teachers can use writing as a way of knowing how to teach. Participants in the Bay Area Writing Project make the following recommendations of ways to encourage, support, and improve writing in classrooms (Hailey, 1978). These recommendations emerged out of their experiences not only as teachers but also as writers.

- *Talking* should surround the preparation for and process of writing.
- *Rewriting* improves writing as each piece goes through several drafts.
- *Postwriting* involves children sharing, appreciating, and evaluating each other's work.
- *Teaching* should include immediate and meaningful responses to students' writing and regular conferences which focus on meaning, a deemphasis on grading (which in any case does not significantly affect the quality of work), time for writing across the curriculum (not just during a language arts period), and teachers writing as models for students.
- *Reading* and literature experiences improve writing.
- *Interacting* should occur among students and teachers, and there should be an emphasis on experiences and experimentation with language.

Approaches to incorporating these recommendations will be described in the next section and in other chapters throughout this text. Perhaps the most important approach to any method, however, is to think of all children—and yourself—as real writers.

When children have a reason to write and are given opportunities to write, they will write. Given encouragement and guidance from adults, they will write about things that matter to them and their writing will be real. This is such a simple approach to teaching writing that we often tend to overlook it.

On my first day of teaching, I felt I was ready to teach writing with my carefully prepared file of story-starter pictures cut from old magazines and pasted on colored construction paper (a resource I had made for one of my education classes). For a thirty-minute language arts lesson, I had selected a picture for the children to use as a springboard for writing a story.

My class came in from recess, however, already motivated and full of stories about how Fritz and Jonathon had been in a fight in the schoolyard with members of another class over a smear ball game, and what was I going to do about it. Picture forgotten, we had a serious class discussion about fighting. As I watched Fritz's eye get blacker while Jonathon wiped his bloody nose, I laid down what I thought was a reasonable rule: No more fighting or you'll stay in from recess forever. What resulted was a heated discussion over children's rights versus teacher's responsibilities, led by Fritz and Jonathon who claimed I was trying to make them sissies by not allowing them to defend themselves. The debate ended in a sullen stalemate. We never had a language arts lesson or wrote about my selected picture that day, but after lunch I found a pile of passionately written anonymous letters on my desk protesting my autocratic and arbitrary attitude. This was obviously a red-alert situation, and as a new teacher still worried about control and discipline as much as anything else, I knew I had to do something about it.

I tried a more democratic approach. I had the class discuss the problem in small groups, take notes, and generate guidelines for coping with a variety of situations: creating a mechanism for a class agenda to deal with problems like fighting; setting up rules for class discussions of such problems; devising ways of putting their ideas in writing publicly; and drafting a manifesto of children's rights in the context of teacher's responsibility. The children talked and listened and wrote copiously. I will never know how much they would have written about that picture, how much it would have meant to them, or what they would have learned about writing. What I do know is that they became deeply involved in writing guidelines for themselves and others, a kind of manifesto that we posted on charts and published in a class newspaper and later in the school newspaper, and used and revised all that year. By the way, the guidelines were realistic, stringent, and fair. The children were writing for a real purpose, for a real audience, and with real feelings.

This episode convinced me that children do not need teacher-chosen pictures or subjects to write about. Given real reasons, opportunities, and time and support from the teacher, they will write about things that matter to them and subjects that interest them.

A Classroom for Real Writing

With real reasons, real opportunities, and real support from the teacher, real writing is not hard to start or keep going. What is hard to keep going is a teacher-controlled writing lesson which holds no meaning for the children, in which they are simply trying to please the teacher or achieve success according to the teacher's criteria.

There are several elements which are necessary in the classroom to start, support, and sustain real writing.

The Teacher's Attitude

Interest, enthusiasm, and belief in children as real writers are key aspects of a teacher's attitude towards children writing. They quickly perceive the difference between a teacher who is enthusiastic about what they have to say and knows enough about them and their interests to be an enlightened audience for their writing, and one who ignores their meaning in search of errors to correct. And while errors in spelling, poor handwriting, and mechanical mistakes are indeed important, they are not the real basics of writing. Emig (1978), one of the first of many researchers to closely observe students writing development, explains:

> Much of the current talk about the basics of writing is not only confused, but, even more ironic, frivolous. Capitalization, spelling, punctuation—these are touted as the basics in writing when they represent, of course, merely the conventions, the amenities for recording the outcome of the process. The *process* is what is basic in writing, the process and the organic structures that interact to produce it (p. 59).

The Teacher's Role

Much of the recent research on the teaching of writing suggests that the teacher's role is primarily to support rather than to direct children's sense-making efforts as they move towards literacy. In addition to showing interest, enthusiasm, and a believing attitude, then, a major task of the teacher is to give children many opportunities to write about a great range of topics which matter to them and subjects that interest them, and to write in a variety of forms and styles, from class manifestos to first books.

Surrounding Children with a World of Writing. Teachers should make children aware of the power of writing as a way of knowing by surrounding them with a world of writing: children's literature, poetry, nonfiction, magazines, newspapers, and all the other forms of the written word. Literature should be read aloud so that the children will anchor the rhythm of writing in their ears.

Responding Appropriately to Children's Writing. Responding to children's writing is another important aspect of the teacher's role in teaching writing. Sometimes this role has been perceived as that of a copy editor, someone who pays less attention to the substance of the writing but corrects it merely for errors of spelling, punctuation, and grammar, and for illegibility. These conventions are important, but only in the context of what they are trying to do, namely to convey a message. Those teachers who only correct mechanical errors but ignore the message are surely communicating to the child the idea that the message is not important. This in turn creates the problem of inauthentic writing (only write stories which include words you can spell) and gives rise to children's mistaken beliefs about writing (good handwriters are good writers; the fewer the red marks on the paper, the better the writing; neatness counts above all). Probably the worst result is that children do see writing not as a real language function but as a tedious task of copying or of writing what they think the teacher wants to read.

Teachers should focus their responses to writing on the children's motivation for writing and on the resulting message; they should help children learn conventions of writing in the context of real writing.

Talking to Children about Their Writing. Talking about writing is essential. Plan time for several ways to talk about writing.

1. ***Whole-class Discussions***

After the whole class has written on a similar subject, they should discuss, as a class, what they have written. Such discussions, where the emphasis is on sharing and exchanging ideas, will lead to rethinking, rewriting, revising and editing, will support skill development, and will perhaps themselves serve as pebbles to start new ripple effects leading to yet more writing. With the high teacher–child ratio in most classes today, you can do much to support writing through class discussions which involve everyone at the same time. Children can see the process of writing at work as they select topics, mull over words and ideas, make choices, and revise their work as a result of such discussions.

2. ***Small-group Discussions***

Children often write in small groups, solving problems, writing scripts or storyboards for a film, or brainstorming ideas for a newspaper layout. A teacher can work with children in small groups while they write and after they finish writing; they can discuss their writing with the teacher and with each other.

3. *One-on-one Writing Conferences*

Teacher and children may confer spontaneously during a specified writing time when the teacher circulates among the children. Regular conferences may also be scheduled for the teacher to discuss, provide support, and note the progress and needs of each child. It is important for the teacher to keep anecdotal records of such discussions as a running source of information about the child's interests and growth and progress in writing. Samples of the child's writing can be filed so that from time to time comparisons can be made and improvements and needs noted.

During a writing conference, the teacher's role is that of codiscussant rather than judge. Do not have children stand at your desk awaiting your sentence while you read what they have written. Instead, sit side by side with them at a table where you are on the same level and can both see the piece of writing. Let the children talk and ask questions. Withhold judgment. Do not simply wait for the chance to tell them how they can best correct surface errors. Listen first, and then ask the children where they have been in their writing, what problems they are having, and help them find out for themselves where they are going.

4. *Questions for a Writing Conference*

In describing the conference approach of Lucy Calkins (Russell, 1983), an upper-grade teacher lists some of the questions formulated for conferences which she herself has found to apply to any topic:

- What is your favorite part?
- What problems are you having?

The one-on-one teacher/student conference is an important part of the writing process.

- How did you feel?
- Do your paragraphs seem to be in the right order?
- Can you leave out parts that repeat or that fail to give details about your subject?
- Can you combine some sentences?
- Can you use more precise verbs in some places?
- What do you plan to do next with this piece of writing?

5. ***Organizing Conferences***

Graves (1983) has extensively researched and documented the conference approach in the last few years; he offers some "answers to the toughest questions teachers ask about conferences."

- *How do I find the time?* You do not have to correct every paper for every child every time you meet. Writing and conferences are ongoing processes.

  A timetable for a thirty-seven-minute writing period, accommodating about seventeen students, might look like this. First ten minutes: after reviewing writing folders, the teacher circulates the room and helps children who need it. Next fifteen minutes: the teacher holds regularly scheduled conferences with certain children. Next twelve minutes: the teacher holds a conference either with a small group who are applying a common skill, or with children who are at an important point in their writing.
- *How often should I hold conferences?* This will vary, but you should confer with each child at least once a week.
- *What are the other children doing?* Writing, finding more things to write about as they do. It is important to create experience and interest centers in the classrooms, to engage the children's interest, to keep writing materials accessible, and to keep children from interrupting. Class discussions will help children cope by themselves with certain problems such as spelling, what to write about next, and so on.

Graves also recommends teachers to keep conferences short by concentrating on one thing, to teach only one thing per conference, to avoid rushing, and not to talk too much.

The Classroom Environment

See Chapter 1, Figure 1–2.

For real writing to take place, a classroom should provide flexible time and space for writing. Different types of writing require different types of room arrangements. In addition to having their own desk or table, children often need a space where they can be alone to write—in a library corner or a comfortable chair. And when they are in conference with the teacher or other students, children need space and some privacy—a table with a few chairs.

Larger groups, or groups working on large projects such as newspaper layouts or media scripts, need space to spread out, to organize their materials, and to do their writing. Students doing research or reporting need a roomy table close to their reference materials.

Just as the process of writing is not always orderly, neither are the arrangements for writing. Talking, drawing, dramatizing, media making, or simply reading aloud for another person's reaction—all of these are part of the process. A classroom needs to be flexible enough in its arrangements to fit the many needs of young writers.

Materials for Writing

All kinds of writing materials should be available for the children's needs. A center for writing materials should include: a supply of different kinds of paper (all sizes, from small note paper to butcher paper for charts; lined and unlined; different colors and textures; typing paper; art paper); writing and art instruments such as pencils (and a quiet pencil sharpener), crayons, marking pens (water soluble), ballpoint pens, brushes; and related tools such as paints, paper clips, staplers, tape, scissors, paste, and materials for binding books. A filing system in a box, with folders for each child's writing and for group projects, is also valuable.

See "Writing without a Pencil," by Gail E. Tompkins, in *Language Arts,* 58 (1981), 823–833.

A typewriter is a necessity in a writing center. Many children enjoy typing their pieces; some even like to compose at the typewriter. They can type their own books for publication, and type their own newspapers on ditto masters or for photocopying. Even computers and word processors are fast becoming regular fixtures in elementary- and middle-school classrooms.

See Chapter 11, "Information Processing."

Times for Writing. Children should have occasion to write throughout the day: jotting down thoughts in their journals, making notes on long-term projects, recording observations for science or information for social studies, or simply working on their latest story or poem. An idea may come to them at any time and they should feel free to put it down on paper right away. A regular time for writing can be set aside in several ways.

A Sample Daily Schedule for Writing

• *Journal writing (15–30 minutes).* Writing in journals can take place first thing in the morning, even for very young children. A sustained period of private writing like this can help get ideas flowing, identify topics to write about, or simply offer a chance to sort things out, perhaps leaving just one idea or image to pursue.

• *Writing periods (30–45 minutes).* A whole class of younger children might work on language experience stories, while an entire class of older students might write on topics of interest to them. Children in small groups could plan a class project, newspaper articles, or play scripts. Individual children can work on stories, poetry, or books.

• *Free writing (throughout the day).* Children can continue with ongoing pieces and projects when they are not directly involved with another lesson, a special subject class, or testing—whenever they have free time.

Writing about Ourselves and about Others

Most of us have a great deal to say about ourselves and those who touch our lives: family, friends, teachers, pets. Especially at the beginning of the school year when you want to learn as much as you can about your students, you should provide them with many opportunities to write about their lives.

Writing Journals

See "Self-Discovery through Writing Personal Journals," by Sister Therese Craig, in *Language Arts,* 60 (1983), 373–379.

See "Some Helps for Journal Writing," by Ann Toombs Alejandro, in *English Journal,* 70 (1981), 48–49; and "Journal Writing: Stages of Development," by Lenore W. Kintisch, in *The Reading Teacher,* 39 (1986), 168–172.

Students can write in a personal journal every day, both during a regular journal writing period and throughout the day whenever they have ideas they want to record. All that is really needed to get a journal started is a notebook for each child and support from the teacher. Even very young children can begin journals: preschool teachers Elliott, Nowosad, and Samuels (1981) define a journal as "a collection of children's statements, ideas, and thoughts, transcribed by adults and possibly including illustrations. Journals travel back and forth between home and school." The journal becomes a powerful learning and teaching resource, helps parents understand the importance of family activities in their child's learning, and develops reading and writing abilities.

Kindergarten teacher Hipple (1985) has the children write in journals during the first thirty minutes of every day when they are eager to communicate. The journals she uses consist of five pieces of paper stapled together, a page for each day of the week. Children write their name and the date on each page; they receive a new journal every Monday, and the old ones are saved in their folders. They draw, write, give dictation, and talk about and share their journals with the rest of the class.

Primary students can dictate to teachers if they are not already writing independently, and middle- and upper-grade students can make their own blank books to use as journals.

Content Area and Community Journals. Journals are usually personal but they may also be related to classroom experiences and subjects. Over a period of a month, third-grader Eric kept a journal of a mealworm turning into a pupa (Figure 4–9).

Mathews (1984) uses community journals with her first- and second-grade students. She keeps blank books available in various room centers for children to write down their observations or comments. For example, her students kept a record of

- observations of their guinea pig and their rabbit (*Smokey and Rockwell*),
- science discoveries (*Exploring*),

Eric

The Making of A Pupa

Friday, Feb. 20 — His Legs are folding up and he is tightening up. He is getting lighter in color and lighter in weight.

Mon, Feb. 23 — He has turned into a pupa over the weekend. His legs are folded into 4 parts

Wed., March 4 — He is growing wings on the side, There are hair-like things growing on his side. He is growing dark slits where his eyes should be. He is also growing a dark Leathery back.

Thurs. March 5 — His tail tip is growing bigger. His back is even darker and more Leathery.

Mon. March 9 - His vestigal wings are growing.

Wed, March 11 — His vestigal wings are growing even bigger. His legs are getting black and he seems to move more. His tail tip is growing bigger. His back is getting darker.

Tues, March 17 — He dried up!

Figure 4–9
Content Area Journal: The Making of a Pupa

- art projects (*Things We Made*),
- plays and puppet shows (*Pretending*),
- mathematics activities (*What We Did in Math*),
- environmental observations (*Outside Our Window*).

Journals as Sources of Ideas for Writing. Journals can become a source of ideas for children to write about and a place for them to test out these ideas. Journals may also lead to other types of writing. Fourth-grader Andrea was a very private child who wrote more than she talked. She entered into classroom activities only reluctantly, and preferred to write in her journal which soon became a loose-leaf notebook bulging at the seams. She began to write in the persona of a sorcerer's apprentice after listening to the music by Dukas in class and writing about the experience in her journal. Eventually, she wrote a series of dialogues between herself as an apprentice and an imaginary sorcerer. She continued to write about herself as the apprentice and began referring to her journal as her book, which she even took home to write in. Much later, she told me that she had continued working on it even in high school.

Journals as a Literary Form. Journals and diaries are an ancient form of recording the events in people's lives, but they have also become a literary form. Children who have read such diaries may choose to adopt this form themselves. Young Andrea used the form of a fictionalized diary in writing a report on what life was really like in the gold fields of California during the Gold Rush. Her research and report were part of her class study of American history; this is another instance of writing across the curriculum (see Figure 4–10). Here are some examples of children's books written in the form of a diary:

The *Little House* books, by Laura Ingalls Wilder (Harper & Row)

A Gathering of Days: A New England Girl's Journal 1830–1832, by Joan Blos (Scribner's, 1979), winner of the Newberry Medal for most distinguished contribution to children's literature published in the United States that year

Dear Mr. Henshaw, by Beverly Cleary (Morrow, 1983)

Diary of a Rabbit, by Lilo Hess (Scribner's, 1982)

Diary of the Boy King Tut Ankk-Amen, by June Reig (Scribner's, 1978)

Harriet the Spy, by Louise Fitzhugh (Harper & Row, 1964)

Some of the Days of Everett Anderson, by Lucille Clifton (Holt, Rinehart & Winston, 1970)

Anne Frank: Diary of a Young Girl, by Anne Frank (Doubleday, 1952)

Writing Autobiographies

Even young children can write autobiographies. The youngest can draw self-portraits and label them with the things that are important to them. Or

Diary

May 8 1848

Rained this morning. My cousin Bill arrived. Jim nearly shot him down dead. He was on his property. Bill's stayin in are tent. Big Toms and mine. I made a profit of 50¢ today.

May 17 1848

A woman arrived said she was going to mine gold. Insited on her own tent. Wemen. Bill Jim Big Tom and I helped her out. My she's sassy. Things sure will change.

June 2 1848

Gold mining isnt what it seemed to be. I make little profit. What I do make I loose in pokar. I'm in debt to severral people inculeded that woman.

June 11 1848

Food is going up. And my luck is going low. I'm fallen farther into debt.

July 14 1848

I'm movin my family out here. I cant make no money minin. I'll do it with a bar I bout in town.

Figure 4–10
Using the Journal as a Literary Form

the teacher can trace the outline of their bodies on a large piece of butcher paper and let them draw and write on it themselves.

The students can also keep blank books, with a page for each different type of information, to be written in by many students. Give the students a number each and let them write their name on the first page next to their number. Topics for subsequent pages might include birthdays and pets, as well as more subjective categories like favorites: colors, games, movies, music. The children write on each page next to their number.

Older students need little encouragement to write autobiographies and illustrate them with drawings, pictures, or photographs from home. They may also try writing fictionalized autobiographies.

Writing Biographies

See *Ben and Me,* by Robert Lawson (Little, Brown, 1939).

Writing about themselves often leads children to write about others—family members, friends, characters in books, media personalities, sports figures, superheroes, or historical characters encountered in social studies, science, or other content areas. One form of biography is a blend of fact and fiction, such as the story about Abraham Lincoln and his speech writer, a personified mealworm, shown in Figure 4–11.

Figure 4–11
Abe and I: A Fictionalized Biography

ABE AND I

I met Abe when I was accidently mixed up in a cake. Believe it or not, he almost et me! He took one bite and I fell right out. My, was he surprised!

His wife of course wants to throw me out but Abe said I wouldn't do no harm and calls me a cute little feller and sticks me in his pocket.

His wife, Mary, screwed up her face and looked at him. "Abe," she says, "sometimes you puzzle me. Just keep that thing out of my kitchen."

He smiled back at her, put on his coat and stepped outside. He reached into his pocket and took me out. After I introduced myself it took him awhile to get used to the fact I could talk, then finally he said, "Well, I can't stand here talking to you all night. I've got work to do", he says and puts me back in his pocket.

I found out later that night that Ol' Abe was runnin' for President against Mr. Breckinridge. Abe didn't have a very good chance of winning. Breckinridge was a strong man.

At home Abe took me out of his pocket. "Worm," he ways, "if I don't win this election the nation is split 'cause Mr. Breckinridge doesn't want war and ways we ought to let the South secede. I've got to get a speech that will change the people's mind."

"Mr. Lincoln," I says, "maybe I could help you. See, I'm a writer and I have a great idea . . . ."

So for one month I wrote every one of Abe's speeches and he won popularity all over the United States.

And on Nov. 5, 1860, it was assured that Mr. Abraham Lincoln was to be the President of the United States! (And all because of one little mealworm—Me!)

Writing Class and School Newspapers

Publishing is an important part of the writing process. Children can work together to write class and school newspapers on subjects of interest that they want to share with others. For younger children, a bulletin board serves a a fine newspaper, as did notice boards in the days before printing became widespread. Older children can organize and plan a proper newspaper, write individual stories and stories on which they collaborate, create a masthead and design, lay out the paper, and type and reproduce it for distribution to the class or the whole school and to family members. Classes can also work together to produce a school newspaper.

A newspaper's content need not be limited to real or local news. Of course, you may want to start with personal experiences and other topics familiar to the children. But once they have had the experience of brainstorming, organizing, and cooperating on the writing and publishing of a newspaper, there is no limit to how they can use this form for other purposes in writing. For example, they may write a paper from the perspective of a different culture or country they are studying in another class. Or they can go back in time and recreate an earlier period of history in a newspaper. An example of such a newspaper is described on page 141.

Having students write and publish a newspaper is one way of shifting them from totally personal writing, intended perhaps just for themselves or for an audience of one, to writing aimed at an expanded audience of other children in the class, the school, even in the community and the world at large.

Teacher and student collaborate in the writing process as they plan the layout for a class newspaper.

Writing to Get Things Done

Many forms of writing in the classroom occur naturally and spontaneously because they are needed. Britton (1970) refers to such transactional writing as "language to get things done."

Making Labels and Lists

Children can label anything as a form of identification. The first label children often learn to write is their name. Teachers of young children who write names on drawings as the children watch are encouraging children to write their names themselves. Other types of labels used by younger writers are titles, names of other people and objects, dialogue, and the like. Making labels leads easily to making lists. Students can collect words they know and use in blank books with a page for each letter, and add new words as they learn them. Word rings and word files can also be used to compile lists. Other types of lists often used are materials for science experiments, ingredients for cooking, books for research, or people and supplies for parties.

Taking Notes

Taking notes for class discussions and other purposes is a link between writing and other language arts. Young children can dictate their ideas for the teacher to record on the board or on chart paper. Middle-grade children can take notes on experiences, small-group discussions, and books and reference material to contribute to other small-group and whole-class discussions. These notes may consist of a single word or may take more elaborate forms. One purpose for having children take notes is to encourage them to use writing as a means of observing, thinking, and recording, and to move away from the idea of writing as a simple exercise in copying. In a social studies unit, for example, children can make notes on a variety of sources they consult for answers to questions of interest to them. This research may raise new questions, which they can bring up for class discussion. Some will read from texts written for different reading abilities at their grade level. Others who are below or above their grade level can look for information in library books and other materials matched to their own reading level.

Recording Observations

Children can record observations in a variety of contexts. Science study encourages children to record observations as part of the process approach to science. For example, for the Elementary Science Study (ESS) unit, "Where Is the Moon Tonight?" young children are given small pieces of black paper and white chalk to sketch the night sky, and record weather conditions, the time, and the position and shape of the moon over a period of time as they learn to identify the stars and the planets and discover the movements of the planets. These recorded observations become the subject of sharing times each morning.

Elementary Science Study, or *ESS*, (McGraw-Hill).

As part of another ESS unit, "The Behavior of Mealworms," children record various behaviors of mealworms kept in boxes of bran, as a means to test hypotheses. This kind of recording of the real behavior of living things, as shown in Figure 4–12, often leads to fictionalizing these things as well, as in the example of the story about a personified mealworm we saw in Figure 4–11.

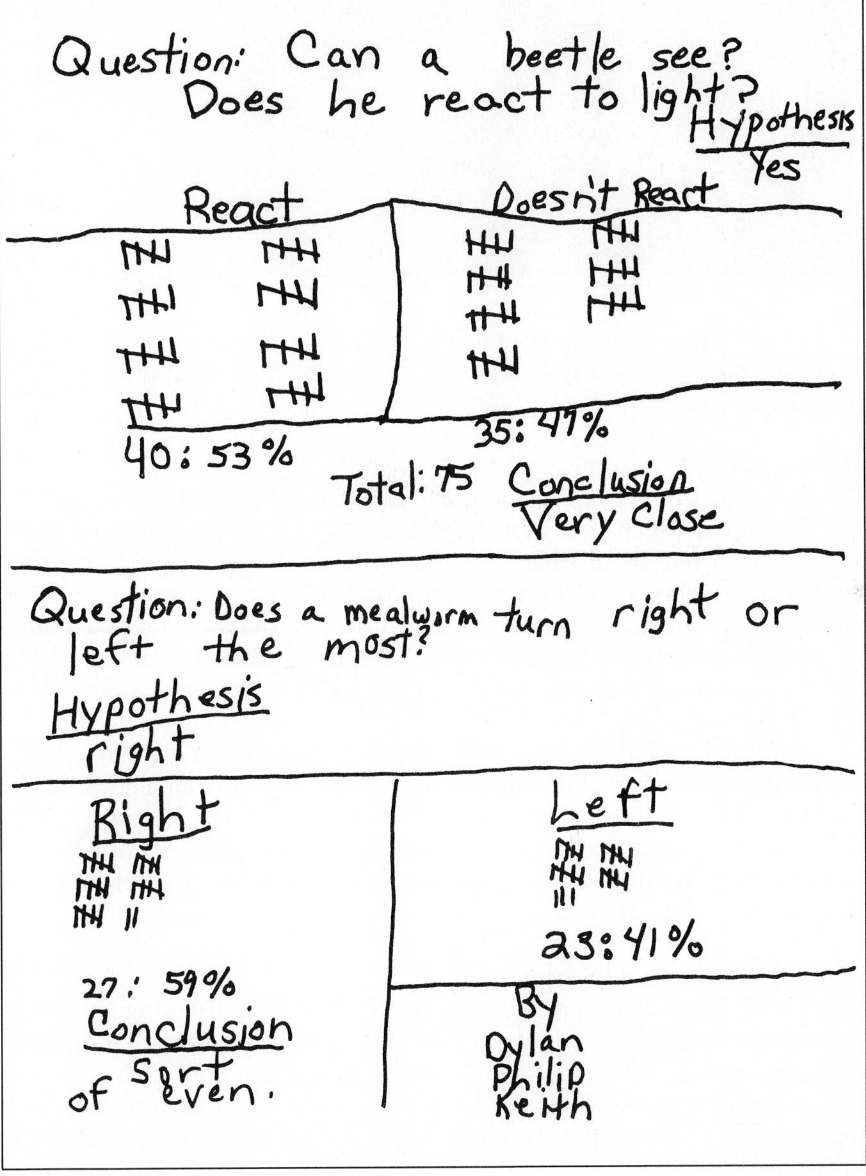

Figure 4–12
Recording Observations of Mealworms

Recording observations in a science center can be an ongoing part of the writing program across the curriculum.

Other aspects of classroom life, such as the rotation of duties, or rosters of class officers and ball monitors, can also provide opportunities to record information.

Writing Letters

See *All About Letters* and *P.S. Write Soon,* published jointly by the National Council of Teachers of English and the United States Postal System (1982).

Letter writing can become as natural as the writing and passing of notes in the classroom, which is a more clandestine but very real form of letter writing. Children should have many reasons and opportunities to write letters in the classroom: to make requests and give replies, to air complaints, to gossip, and just to socialize. Classroom mailboxes and a system of pickup and delivery permits the writing and exchanging of notes with official sanction. If the writer and the reader prefer, of course, mail should remain private.

Children may also send letters outside the classroom for many different purposes: to obtain information on a given subject from a government or other agency if it is not readily available from a nearby source; to get in touch with a favorite author; to question, praise, or criticize a politician; to express their admiration to an entertainment or sports figure; or to air their opinion in a letter to the editor of the local newspaper.

Creating Outlines and Layouts

Organizing ideas in preparation for further thinking, listening, speaking, reading, and writing is an integral part of an integrated approach to teaching language arts. Taking notes and making simple lists lead to the creation of more elaborate outlines and layouts for recording observational findings, writing a newspaper, creating a film script, or blocking a dramatic presentation.

Writing Reports

Children's hypothesizing, experimenting, research, note taking, list making, and outlining should be motivated by a keen desire to learn more about the subject, and to write about it in order to learn. Do not, for example, tell a fifth-grade class that you will study the United States and assign each student a state to write about. Instead, let individual students pursue their own interests within the broad area under study. When you take this approach, the reporting will take many different forms, reflecting the types of students you have, the types of writing they like to do, and the topic each has pursued. The reporting may be straightforward and factual, but it may also emerge as a dramatic presentation, a videotaped talk show, or a newspaper, real or fictional.

For example, after studying American history a fourth- and fifth-grade class began to report what they had learned—and learned as they reported—by writing and publishing a series of newspapers set in each of the eras they had studied. They went about it in the following way.

1. *Identifying Questions to Answer as a Class*

During a class discussion about what was important to know about a country, its people, and its history, they generated these and other questions of interest:

- What happened in the past and why?
- What were the important events?
- What problems did these people have?
- What were the issues of the time?
- Who were the important people and how did they become involved?

In the writing process, research and reporting can take many forms.

- What was their daily life like?
- How did they live?
- What was important to them?
- What were some of their ideas and beliefs?
- How did they express these beliefs?
- What was their art, literature, and religion like?
- Why is a knowledge of how people lived in the past important to us today?

2. ***Gathering Resources***

Both students and teacher contributed to a classroom resource center that included books, magazines, maps, objects and artifacts, photographs, and other printed material and memorabilia found in the library or brought from home. Field trips to historic sites in the area were another source of experiences and information. All these materials were labeled and listed for ease of reference.

3. ***Taking Notes for Group Discussion***

Before making their reports, the students went through an extensive period of experiences—field trips, hearing guest speakers, dramatizations, viewing films and filmstrips—and of reading, note taking, discussing, debating, hypothesizing, and imagining. These activities helped the students to focus on one topic within a particular period to pursue further.

4. ***Researching a Topic***

During this same period, the students began to make notes and write about their topic in depth. They kept records and charted their ideas, and experimented with different forms of writing. New questions emerged during this period, through further discussion, reading, and individual research.

5. ***Reporting***

Since these students had written and published newspapers for their class, their school, and their community earlier in the year, it seemed only natural to go back in time and report what they were researching through a series of newspapers set in different historical periods. They continued to write on individual topics, and to read and research as well, and some of them took editorial responsibility for organizing and planning the newspaper, charting topics of interest as ideas for articles, and creating a layout for the *Colonial Times*. In order to be able to put themselves in the place of the people they were writing about, and to understand the events of the times, they kept searching further and deeper for information which would give them a real feeling for these times and these people. They went beyond simple facts (copying from the encyclopedia was out of the question!) because they wanted to do more than ladle out dull information: they wanted their newspaper to come alive. And so they investigated the language of the time, the historical and regional dialects, and looked at the way things were written, including print graphics of the colonial and revolutionary periods.

In the end, the children produced four newspapers. The *Colonial Times* came first (Figure 4–13). Then they divided into two groups for the revolutionary period, calling themselves patriots and loyalists. Heated debates and public outbursts attended the production of the *Liberty Lion* (Figure 4–14) and *George's Journal,* which voiced the colonial and the British point of view respectively. Finally, the class rejoined forces and chronicled the westward movement in the *Western Times.*

In addition to writing and reporting information in these newspapers, the children dramatized a great deal of what they reported. They wrote speeches and debates for meetings of the House of Burgesses, dialogues of confrontations between Ann Hutchinson and her enemies, and interviews with Benedict Arnold and with a little-known survivor of the Alamo. They wrote scripts that created glimpses into such dark corners of American history as the Salem witch trials, and traveled far away in their imagination with Lewis and Clark and Sacajawea, with the Mandan Indians, and to a barroom in the Gold Country of California.

Editing and Revising

Children (as well as teachers) should have a genuine desire to revise and edit, just as they should have a genuine desire to write in the first place. Since no two writers are alike, the need to revise will not be the same for everyone. The writing process is as individual as a fingerprint. Some people write easily, quickly, and prolifically. Others write more slowly and sparingly, and spend more time revising their work.

For a discussion of two points of view on revising, see "The New Orthodoxy about Writing: Confusing Process and Pedagogy," by Myra Barrs, and "Teacher Intervention in Children's Writing: A Response to Myra Barrs," by Donald Graves, in *Language Arts,* 60 (1983), 829–840, 841–846.

Teachers Editing Children's Work

When encouraging revising and editing children's work, keep in mind the following.

The Self-image of the Young Writer. How does the writer feel about himself? There is a danger with some children—particularly younger or reluctant writers who do not believe they can write—that by suggesting changes in their work you will discourage them from writing at all. It is important, then, to consider the effect of encouraging change on their feelings as well as on their writing.

The Needs of the Young Writer. Why is the child writing and for whom? The more real the writing is to her, the less she needs the teacher to tell her what it should be like. Take your cue from the degree of her involvement in her writing.

The TIMES are
Dreadful
Diſmal
Doleful
Dolorous and
DOLLAR-LESS

Containing the freſeſt Advices, Foreign, and Domeſtick
To all my subſcribers and Benefactors who theſe my weekly
Journall By Mistreſſ Cox'ſ Dame School

BURGESSES DISCUSS COLONIES
Col.William Braxton
Jamestown,Virginia Colony,1661

Last night the legislature and House of Burgesses met to discuss the colonies. Several burgesses made speeches about the people wanting to elect new representatives. Also about the people wanting more protection against the Indians.

Some members complained about the price of tobacco and said that Virginia should pass a law so that th there wouldn't be so much tobacco grown. Some people were afraid that Maryland wouldn't agree with Virginia but Maryland agreed and the Virginia House of Burgesses passed the law.

(assisting reporter-R.Rowley)

DEVELOPMENTS OF PHILADELPHIA

71 people came to Philidelphia in 10 families. The ship only comes twice a year. All of the people are Scots. They are not going to stay in Pennsylvania. They are going to move down to northern Virginia and the Carolinas.

Some people of the city think we should have a police force to watch the merchant's warehouses. Another idea was that we should have clear water. All our water is impure. There is a clear spring on a hill just outside the city. We ought to pipe to somewhere and make a well out of it. The merchants are going to form a company called the Philadelphia Water Company.

The Scientific and Literary → Club was thinking of having a bank but it wasn't a serious matter. One Merchant brought it up and decided to have a bank. It is called the Merchants Bank of Philadelphia.

J.Grinder

NEWS OF THE WITCHES ON TRIAL
Salem Village 1692

Mrs.Phillips will be tried for witchcraft on Saturday. She put apples in her dumplings <u>after</u> they were cooked.

Rev.Samuel Parrises slave,Tituba by name, will be tried for wi tchcraft on Sunday.

Two Indian slaves were hung for Witchcraft one week ago. They were said to have killed a crop.

D.Sternbach

LAWS OF THE BURGESSES PASSED

Last night the House of Burgesses decided on the law that one must pay a tax for protection from savage attack. One burgess said that Indians shall be treated fairly so our colony may live in peace.

It was decided that tobacco be sold at 18 pounds per barrel and if you do not work you shall be punished.

Ben Franklin and
Stan Metzenberg

AN EGG TODAY IS BETTER THAN A HEN TOMORROW. Ben Franklin

EARLY TO BED,EARLY TO RISE, MAKES A MAN HEALTHY,WEALTHY AND WISE.
Ben Franklin

Figure 4-13 The Colonial Times

TO ALL YE PATRIOTS WHO READ MY WEEKLY JOURNAL

SONS AND DAUGHTERS OF THE SONS OF LIBERTY

COX'S 5TH GRADE

REPORT FROM VALLEY FORGE by Gilbert Weston (Guard)

It's been bad here at Valley Forge. Men are in bad shape. I've been here all winter. Every man is starving and sick. No soldier has a piece of clothing in one piece.

Horses are dying. Soon officers will have no transportation. There is hardly enough food to feed the men much less the horses.. Men have to sleep in hay. It can't be fed to horses.

Pants and shirts are in shreds. Boots seem to open and shut their mouths as men walk as though they were starving also. Socks were nothing but webbing and holes. Men were nearly naked. Most were sick or white from cold. The doctor is always busy but he has almost no medicine.

You can believe it or not but all men did not run back home. They have faith in General Washington as I do. The General is not an officer that orders but an officer that works with the men as a soldier. He's fair to us and cares how we are and listens to us.

Winter is letting up. Soon we'll leave here and get back to the war. Back to violence and blood shed and finally to Independence.(Hopefully).

(assisted by Linn Billingsley)

HALE EXECUTED;This is sorry news but Nathan Hale a good friend and a good patriot has been hanged by the British. He was caught as a spy. His words still ring. "I regret that I have but one life to give for my country". He was a good man. Andrea Arnold

LETTER TO THE EDITOR:John Hancock and Samual Adams

Sirs,

It is now that we Americans are in the midst of awar. A war of fighting,killing and many wounded. Many suffer starvation. At Valley Forge men freeze and starve but still they remain loyal. And we must also. Men are fighting so you may not be heavily taxed. They are fighting, fighting not for no taxes only but for America to be one. I think that you must fight also and not sit by the fire complaining of our problems. Please join and fight for your country's rights.

John Hancock
Samuel Adams

(assisted by Andrea Arvold)

JOIN THE MINUTEMEN!

Join the Minutemen! They conquered the British at Concord!
Join and fight the British!
Join and be a Patriot!

We the Minutemen drove the British back many atime at Concord and Lexington and many more.

THE MINUTEMEN WANT YOU!

Contact:David Stenbach,Boston.

Figure 4–14 The Liberty Lion

The Purposes of the Young Writer. What is the child's intent? Your suggestions for changes in a newspaper article, where information needs to be clearly communicated, would be different from those you might make when he is writing a journal, a poem, or some other personal piece.

The Style of the Young Writer. What is the writer's approach? Some children write factual stories based on their experiences and can easily answer questions about what really happened. Others prefer writing fiction. Fantasy emerges strongly in some children's writing, and when they are writing about a country of the mind that they may find difficult to completely visualize themselves, it may be even harder for them to explain it to you. You can help them by providing plenty of opportunities to discuss their writing with you in order to clarify their ideas.

My experience has been that when children care about what they are writing and have a strong sense of their intention as well as their audience—whether they are working on a private journal or on a script for a film they hope will be viewed by millions—they will readily seek revision as they need it. Some writing should not be changed at all because there is no point to changing it. It may be very personal or they may not really care about it at all. But when children have a wider audience in mind as they write, and the writing is real and important to them, they will want to make changes that make it more effective, make it better. They have a concern about conventions and want their work to be correct as to spelling, punctuation, and grammar. As they publish their writing, they become more aware of the needs of the reader and their desire to rewrite to meet those needs grows. Perhaps revision should be seen as answering the need of the child to say clearly what she wants to say, rather than as answering the need of the teacher to have all writing fit his own model of the writing process.

Consider yourself more of a listener than an editor, a practice audience; let children come to you to discover through rehearsal what they are trying to say. You can help them find and follow the path they started on, a Yellow Brick Road which can take them home but where they can also bog down and lose the way.

Children Editing Each Other's Work

See *Writing without Teachers,* by Peter Elbow (Oxford University Press, 1973).

Students can also work in small groups to read and respond to each other's writing. Such small groups may develop naturally, as when children are producing a newspaper or a script for drama or media production. The purpose for responding to each other's writing will then be to improve and resolve the writing as a group.

Students may also work in pairs or small peer editing groups to support each other's writing, to listen, react, respond, and provide a sounding board for ideas. Emphasis in these groups should be placed on a positive attitude and supportive responses.

Guidelines for Peer Editing Groups. Children in a peer editing group should keep in mind the following recommendations.

- Editors should make positive comments, and emphasize strengths as well as places for improvement.
- Writers as well as editors should respect everyone in the group.
- Writers should not apologize or feel what they have written is not good enough. The purpose of the group is to help.
- Rather than arguing, writers should discuss suggestions and then make their own decisions about revision.
- Writers should appreciate the comments and help of the editors.

Techniques for Peer Editing Groups. Elbow (1973) discusses peer editing at length. His ideas are one way to help teachers help children gain control over their own ideas and language through writing. He suggests several techniques for peer editing groups.

1. Summarizing:
   - Give a one-sentence summary of what the writing is about.
   - Give a one-word summary. Pick a word from the writing that best summarizes it, or pick a word of your own you feel best describes it.
2. Pointing:
   - As you listen to the writer read, note words and phrases that make an impression on you.
   - As you respond to the writing, point to these words and phrases.
3. Telling: Tell the writer how you felt as you listened.

Publication of Writing

While some writing is personal, even intimate, and not meant to be shared, it is important that much of what young writers write be shared or presented or published as a means of communicating. There are many ways to publish writing, some of them deceptively simple.

- community journals
- charts and lists used in the classroom
- experience stories dictated to the teacher and written on the board
- stories, reports, drawings, displayed on bulletin boards
- writing folders
- class and school and community newspapers
- bookmaking
- dramatic presentations of scripts
- mediamaking

Whichever method of publication you choose, the emphasis should be on the children's real reasons for writing, and encouraging real writing.

of Writing

The evaluation of writing has been a long-debated and frequently discussed issue in education. The problem is this: if evaluation is a measure of how good a piece of writing is, we must first decide what is meant by good writing, and then decide how to measure it. Agreement has not been reached on either aspect of the issue. As a result, the evaluation of writing has often deteriorated into measurement against a subskills checklist or an artificial division between ideas and mechanics.

Table 4–1 *Holistic Scoring*

Third-Grade Criteria 1976–77				
Rating	***Ideas***	***Style and Vocabulary***	***Handwriting***	***Spelling***
1.	lacks coherency rambling not well developing	limited vocabulary general lack of adjectives	generally not neat inconsistencies in size, formation and alignment	misspells common words omits vowels lacks symbol/sound correspondence
2.	literal translation of topic lack spark noting seems to happen	generally lack attempt to go beyond common words	generally neat	misspells common words phonetic approach to spelling most words
3.	comparative ideas begin to emerge main idea is carried through	attempt to use expanded vocabulary some use of adjectives stronger verb selections	generally neat	occasionally misspells common words attempt to spell difficult words is phonetic
4.	well-developed cohesive ideas creative spark consistent point of view	use of descriptive words use of transitional words and phrases helps flow of writing	generally very neat	correct spelling of common words generally successful attempts at spelling difficult words

From Miles Myers, *A Procedure for Writing Assessment and Holistic Scoring* (Urbana, IL: NCTE, 1980), p. 50.

Some approaches have been made to evaluating the children themselves rather than just their writing, in order to take into account some of the elusive factors of writing. Clay (1979) has developed a rating technique for observing the early progress of young writers. It is meant for use during the first six months of instruction in school and is only intended as a rough scale to measure the students' progress, including the level of their language, the quality of their intended message, and directional principles (in our culture, writing from left to right) and decide their instructional needs.

Here are some other ways to evaluate children and their writing.

Table 4–1 *(Continued)*

Third-Grade Criteria 1976–77			
Mechanical Conventions	***Grammar and Usage***	***Sentence Structure***	***Organization Paragraph Dev.***
misuse of capitals lack of capitalization for proper nouns capitals in middle of words lack of punctuation	incorrect tense shift tense within composition	sentence fragments run-on sentence	lack of paragraphing lacks sequence lacks development of ideas—has beginnings but no middle or end
capitals at beginning of sentence inconsistent capitalization and end punctuation	subject–verb agreement is evident	some awareness of sentence structure sentence fragments sentence patterns are not varied	lack of paragraphing generally indent first paragraph lacks progression of ideas
first word of sentence capitalized capitals sometimes appear in middle of sentence end marks used correctly	satisfactory subject/verb agreement	some variety in sentence patterns most sentences declarative some evidence of sentence fragments or run-ons	lack of paragraphing generally indent first paragraph conclusions are apparent good beginning sentence generally good sequence
uses a variety of mechanics well	possessives are used correctly tense is inconsistent subject/verb agreement is good	varied sentence patterns few sentence fragments and run-ons	lacking paragraphing first paragraph is indented well-developed beginning, middle and end

Writing Folders

All the written work of each child may be saved in a folder, with the date and a note about context, purpose, and setting for writing. These folders may be used to note the students' progress, discuss their writing with them, and plan for further instruction.

Anecdotal Records

During writing conferences, keep an ongoing record of the following information in a loose-leaf notebook with a page for each child:

- the child's name
- the date
- the topic
- the occasion
- the type of writing
- conference notes

Holistic Evaluation

See "Evaluating Students' Writing Holistically—An Alternative Approach," by Carol Greenlalgh and Donna Townsend, in *Language Arts,* 58 (1981), 811–822.

The above techniques are useful for plotting each child's writing development in terms of individual change and growth. But teachers often need to compare children in order to report class progress and grading. Teachers in some school systems have developed ways of evaluating which looks at the piece of writing as a whole and can be used to draw comparisons among children, classes, and other school systems. Table 4–1 shows a set of holistic scoring criteria which grew out of some teachers' concern over the problems of writing evaluation and their experiences as writers and teachers with the Bay Area Writing Project.

Summing Up

Observing children from infancy through adulthood tells us many things about young writers: children want to write, they can write, and they will write and share what they have written with others. But they need the support of parents, teachers, and other adults in their lives who understand their development as writers and who listen to what they are saying as they talk and write.

Children use language—of which writing is one dimension—as a way of acting and expanding on their experiences. They do this in the manner of young scientists who are constantly testing new ideas and creating new experiments for such testing.

Researchers such as Clay (1975) have observed and described the linguistic progress of children as they learn about print in the years from ages four to seven, and Graves (1983) and others have studied primary and middle elementary students' growth in writing. All of these theorists and researchers have emphasized the importance of the interrelationship of the language arts in the development of writing, and have paid particular attention to the connections between reading and writing as young children use language in becoming literate.

Instruction in writing should take into account the importance of writing to learn in learning to write, and the obviously important role of writing across the curriculum. Teachers should also be aware that they themselves need to write in order to teach writing, and that they should provide many and varied opportunities for children to write, support children's writing through their attitude, role, and the classroom environment they create, talk about writing with children, and above all, listen to what the children are trying to say and help them to say it.

Looking Further

1. Observe several kindergarten children writing and collect their writing samples. Analyze these according to Clay's "Concepts about Print."

2. Observe the writing activities in an elementary classroom and compare these with the characteristics of a process approach to teaching writing.

3. Hold a writing conference with a child using suggestions described by Calkins in this chapter.

4. Write a short piece in class and conduct a peer editing group with others according to guidelines described in this chapter.

5. Collect several papers written by children and evaluate them according to the holistic scoring chart shown in Table 4–1.

6. Create a holistic evaluation chart you might use in the classroom.

Chapter Five

Shaping Writing for Self-Expression

Objectives

Look for answers to the following questions as you read this chapter.

- How do young writers find their own voices in writing?
- What are the different modes of writing and how do children use them?
- How do you encourage the creative urge in children?
- How can self-expressive writing become a means to integrate the curriculum?
- How can teachers provide time and opportunities for self-expressive writing?
- What kind of talk supports writing?
- What are some ways teachers can help children shape and publish their writing?

A Child's View

Here is how fifth-grader Stephen defines writing: "Writing is putting your feelings and fantasies down in words and sharing them with other people. You put all of your heart and belief into writing. Writing is you, and it is you in ways you never dreamed of." Stephen expresses some of his feelings in a poem and in a story (excerpted here).

Hate

Harsh, terrible.
Controlling your life.
Can destroy a friendship.
Contempt.

A True Love

From his perch at the window of his tower, Nil, son of the god Non, creator of the region of land, looked out at the world of his father. He could sense a tenseness in the air. "Something is amiss," he thought as he gazed out to the valley of Ithendril where the prince of Ara-Non slept. "I can feel a disturbance in the prophecy lines."

On one of those sparkling September days in the middle west when the light is so clear that everything seems suddenly to have come into sharper focus, I got fall fever and convinced myself that nothing could be gained by staying inside when such a beautiful moment existed outside. My combination third- and fourth-grade class had been noticing and talking about the changes in the color of the leaves and the light and the seasons. I divided the class into several groups and gave each group a different-colored piece of nylon net from the drama trunk.

Outdoors, surrounded by all the colors and the smell and texture of autumn, the children discussed ideas for acting out different colors. In pantomime, the groups communicated their ideas wordlessly through movement and dance and the single prop of some slightly used nylon net. Blue was a waterfall; red was a sunset that suddenly appeared against the skyline between two old elm trees on the only hill on the playground; green was a raucous, snapping, snarling dragon that undulated around the trees and among the children.

Once back indoors, we talked about colors, light, leaves, seasons, sunsets, dragons, and other related matters and started a list of words and phrases describing these experiences and feelings and images of color the children had seen or imagined.

Red

a sunset drifting and floating silently away
a warm and sparkling feeling
like a dancing cardinal with a glowing crown
the feeling when you make a mistake and want to hide

Orange

a leaf in September on its falling journey
the excited feeling of riding a horse
a bonfire on Halloween night
a jack-o-lantern all lighted up by a waxy candle

Green

a grasshopper
a parrot's feather
a dragon that sputters and wiggles from side to side
a room when nobody's in it

Blue

cool
comfortable

like a feather bed
a hot fire
the night when the clock strikes twelve
the future

For the rest of the afternoon, the children wrote and talked about many of these and other feelings and ideas and images they had experienced that afternoon.

On the days following, they continued to experiment with pantomiming colors and looked for music to add another dimension to their movement and dance expressions. Some of the groups took taped music outdoors to work on pantomimes.

One day, the art teacher noticed the children outdoors and took colored slides which she showed to our class. She also brought us some books of paintings and prints representing the history of art, and we looked at and discussed the use of color in art. We also began to read about colors and to look for color imagery in writing in books.

Thus the initial experience of looking at colored leaves became a pebble creating a ripple effect of topics of interest and experiences that continued throughout the year. It expanded into every area of the curriculum and was integrated throughout the language arts, especially through writing for self-expression.

Making Connections

On any one afternoon, young writers may use many types of writing for many purposes and one of the things they learn as they do so is to use their own voice in writing. Their voice is likely to be strongest when they are telling about real experiences, describing their family or pets, or explaining what they know about American history.

Children should also have many opportunities to listen to the voices of established writers and to practice the sound of their own voice speaking in what Britton (1975) calls "poetic language" (including that of stories) and the "language of being and becoming" (as when they describe *green* as a "dragon that sputters and wiggles from side to side").

Such writing is often called *creative writing.* But *all* writing is creative in that it requires that writers make choices, think of new ways to say old things, and flex and stretch the muscles of their voices in writing. Certain types of fiction and fantasy and poetry, however, move beyond the more autobiographical and functional forms of writing to other forms for shaping writing for self-expression, the purpose of which is to let the mind go free and visit places it has never seen, explain things no one has ever experienced, diagram dreams, put the usual in an unusual way, or look at things from the inside out.

Children Write to Find Their Own Voices

See "Wof Stew: A Recipe for Writing Growth and Enjoyment," R. Kay Moss & John C. Stansell, in *Language Arts,* 60 (1983), 346–350.

Children can find their own voice in writing through any experience in any subject and for any reason. The choice of what they will say and how they will say it should be left open in order to let the sound of their own voice come through clear and strong. For some, their writing will be most authentic when it is about experiences inside their head, experiences which may be just as real to them as those that occur in the physical world.

Listen to a young child tell you about the ghost downstairs and how she scared him away while ghost hunting. Or the second-grader who comes in late to class and tells you about a monster he met on the way to school. Or the sixth-grader who acts and talks and writes like the latest hero encountered in books or media. If you listen carefully you will know that these experiences are every bit as real as those that actually happened at home or in school.

Children often roam the world in their minds, or travel through time and space to play out their dreams and conflicts in countries of the mind.

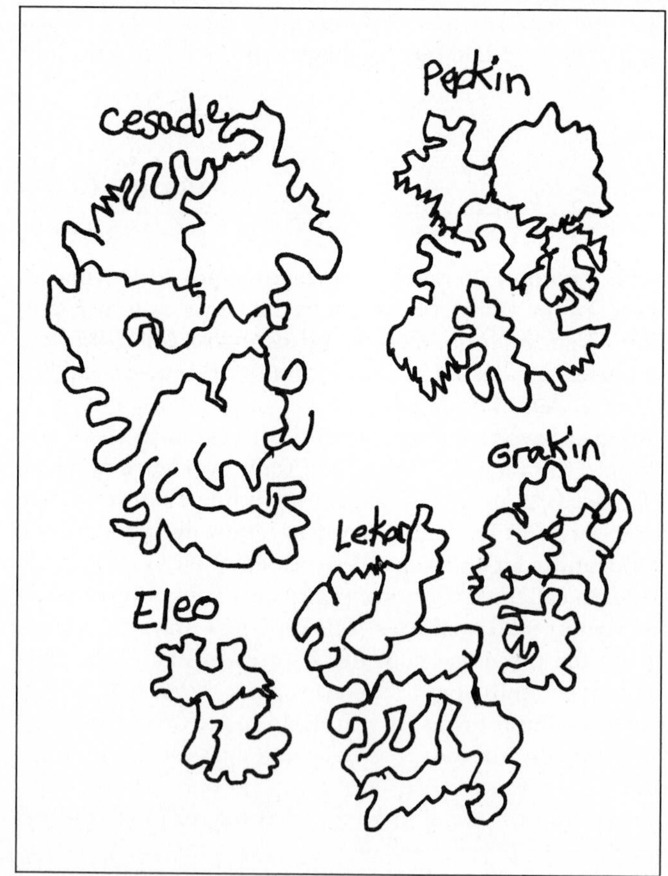

Figure 5–1
My Own Map, by Wyatt

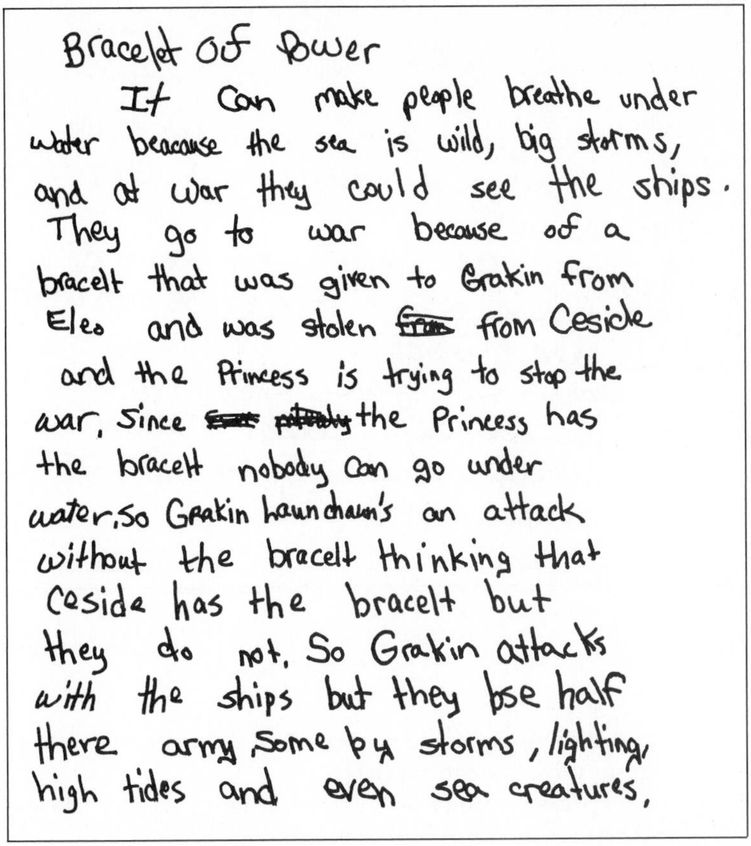

Bracelet Of Power

It Can make people breathe under water beacause the sea is wild, big storms, and at war they could see the ships. They go to war because of a bracelt that was given to Grakin from Eleo and was stolen ~~from~~ from Ceside and the Princess is trying to stop the war. Since the Princess has the bracelt nobody Can go under water. So Grakin launchaun's an attack without the bracelt thinking that Ceside has the bracelt but they do not. So Grakin attacks with the ships but they lose half there army, Some by storms, lighting, high tides and even sea creatures,

Figure 5–2
Writing for Self-Expression:
Bracelet of Power,
by Wyatt

Wyatt, whose writing at ages seven and eight centered around his friends, pets, play, and family, began at age eleven to write about a bracelet of power in a mythical land of Cesadie. He created an entire world with a landscape that he mapped (see Figure 5–1) in order the more carefully to understand and describe its history and the events that took place there. His writing voice at the time came out of the mouth of a "valiant young Prince Cesame" that he had created (see Figure 5–2). And while his narrating voice—as in fulfilling a teacher-assigned topic of his idea of life in the future (see Figure 5–3)—was soft and somewhat weak, his voice as the prince was strong and sure.

See examples in Chapter 4, on "the development and uses of writing."

Modes of Writing

Britton (1975) has studied the different modes students choose and use in writing in school. He has developed categories to describe three function modes students use in writing: the transactional, the expressive, and the poetic modes.

Years

10 years- 10 years from now I will
be 21 and in college and almost
be married.
25 years- 25 years from now I,
will have a job and be married
and have kids.
50 years- 50 years from now
I will be old still, married
and my kids will be gone
and almost married.

Figure 5–3
Writing on a Teacher-assigned Topic: Years, *by Wyatt*

1. The **transactional mode** is used when the writer wants to give information, to record, or to report.
2. The **expressive mode** uses a kind of language that is close to the self and reveals thoughts and feelings.
3. The **poetic mode** is used when the writer shapes ideas to achieve an aesthetic effect.

Britton found that students from ages eleven to eighteen mainly used the transactional mode in school, while the writing of younger students is more expressive and resembles "written-down speech" which tells about their experiences and feelings. Langer (1967) describes this aspect of speech as a way for children to tell "the way things seem to us, the way we feel about things, the way things might be or we should like them to be" and that this type of language will "undergo organization in the direction—ultimately—or verbal art, of poem, story, or play" (p. 65). Other investigators (Bissex, 1980; Newkirk, 1984; Taylor, 1983) have found that young children freely use the transactional mode and attempt to persuade, argue, make requests, and otherwise use writing to exercise power and control. In another study of modes of students' writing in the third, fifth, and eighth grades, using Britton's function categories, Whale and Robinson (1978) found that these students wrote most frequently in the transactional mode in school (63.7%), in the poetic mode next often (18.6%), and in the expressive mode the least (13.9%).

It is interesting to note that while Britton suggests that children's writing develops on a continuum from expressive to transactional to poetic as they grow older and achieve more distance from the self, the third- and fifth-grade students in this study used the expressive mode (11.65%) less often than the eighth-graders (18.22%), and the poetic mode (22.85% and 24.6% respectively) more often than the eighth-graders (8.6%).

The important thing in terms of teaching real writing is that children apparently use a range of writing modes. Teachers should be familiar with each of these modes in order to help children find a fit between what they want to say and how they want to say it in each writing instance.

Encouraging the Creative Urge in Children

Children have the urge to create. We all do. Even very young infants are literally inventing rather than discovering language when they speak their first words or make their first marks on paper (Bruner, 1975; Halliday, 1975). Creativity in connection with education, however, is sometimes seen as limited to certain subjects—such as art, music, drama, or writing fiction—and certain topics—such as fantasy, imaginary creatures, monsters, and space. Many teachers connect creativity only with certain children, and see a dichotomy between children who enjoy and use fantasy themes in self-expression, and those who express themselves, say, by doing well in science. Some students—like David, whom we met in an earlier chapter, who enjoys writing about adventures in space and the possible limits of what humans can find and do there—are labeled creative, while others—like David's friend Stan, who is interested in astronomy, uses his own telescope, and enjoys reading and writing nonfiction—are not. Both these boys know science and both are creative. David exercises his creativity by writing and reading fiction with space themes. Stan exercises his by writing and reading nonfiction with space themes. One prefers fiction, the other prefers facts. Relegating the two to separate categories—as though it were impossible to be interested in science facts and fantasy and fiction at the same time—is one of the more harmful and artificial distinctions we make among children. Albert Einstein must have sensed this false dichotomy when he said, "The gift of fantasy has meant more to me than my talent for absorbing positive knowledge."

See Chapter 4, Figure 4–7.

Creative Thinking

Creative thinking and expression is a need and a prerogative of all children. Many educators have identified and described creative thinking in its own right and shown how it becomes relevant to teaching any subject. Many researchers interested in creative thinking have described models for creative problem solving in all subjects. Techniques such as brainstorming are important jumping-off places for children to think, speak, dramatize, draw, move, or write about any subject.

See Chapter 3, "Brainstorming and Problem Solving."

Supporting the Growth of Creativity

Torrance (1962) has researched the meaning, teaching, and testing of creative behavior for many years, and describes an environment which can help encourage the creative urge in children. The elements of this environment can be used in any teaching situation, but the suggestions and applications listed here are aimed at shaping writing for creative self-expression. As you read the list, some additional ideas may occur to you.

1. ***The absence of serious threat to the self; the willingness to risk.***
   - Personal journal writing that is not evaluated but encouraged as a more private place for recording a free flow of ideas and feelings as a source for topics to write about.
   - Extensive rehearsing and drafting in writing, without editing or correcting, in order to try out new ideas.
   - Withholding of the teacher's immediate judgment of writing.
2. ***Self-awareness: being in touch with one's feelings.***
   - Free choice of topics and modes, the better to find and speak with their own voices.
   - Extensive writing on one topic or in one form, to fully explore these as a means of creative self-expression.
   - Awareness of many forms, such as poetry, writing patterns, and scripts.

Encouraging brainstorming and creative problem solving is an important part of writing for self-expression.

- Plenty of time and many opportunities and materials to experiment with writing.

3. ***Self-differentiation: seeing the self as being different from others.***
   - Sharing writing in a classroom where all forms of writing on all topics are valued and appreciated.
   - Author-of-the-week displays highlighting the selected works of one young author.
   - A variety of publishing and presenting modes: graphics, illustrated poems and stories, media, drama, dance.
4. ***Openness to the ideas of others, and confidence in one's own perceptions of reality or one's own ideas.***
   - Discussing writing with the teacher and other children.
   - Writing conferences.
   - Peer editing groups in which ideas can be freely exchanged.
5. ***Mutuality in interpersonal relations: a balance between an excessive quest for social relations and a pathological rejection of them.***
   - Writing in whole-class or small groups: newspapers, playwriting, media scriptwriting.
   - Compiling anthologies: publishing collections of children's own writing.

Teaching Children

How do you help children find their own voice through different modes of writing, and encourage their creative urges? Especially, how do you do this considering the great emphasis today on basic skills in reading and mathematics, and information in the content areas? One solution is to consider that the most important basics you can teach children are how to think, how to solve problems, and how to create new ideas—and how to apply these skills across the curriculum.

Self-Expressive Writing across the Curriculum

Self-expressive writing is a major tool with which children can shape content and new ideas. It is a means for children to look at information in new ways, perhaps in ways it has never been looked at before, and to act on information and make it their own in writing about it. Poets do this and so do children. The children who began to think about and express ideas about colors one fall afternoon began to look through the eyes of a poet by asking two of the basic questions a poet might ask:

> What are colors really like?
> What would a color be if it were something else?

This initial interest and experience of thinking about colors and asking questions such as these led them to ask more questions in their attempts to find out more about colors throughout the rest of the year:

> Why do leaves (and light and seasons) change throughout the year?
> Why are people different colors?
> What if plants were people?

As children notice and question the relationships they observe between phenomena and concepts and ideas, and spontaneously begin to ask "What if . . . ?" teachers can support this great power of children to hypothesize by integrating process and content and creative thinking. Writing can be the glue that holds together in meaningful ways a variety of seemingly dissimilar concepts, facts, and skills as children use these pieces to solve problems they have hypothesized. In so doing they have a real need to know, and a reason to use their new information and skills. Thus, writing for self-expression—a strong drive on any writer's part—becomes the drive to gain control over information and skills.

Teachers can use many strategies to support children's self-expressive writing, but the emphasis should always be on individualized, child-centered means of helping children find their own writing voice through many modes, on encouraging the creative urge in children, and on making connections among children's experiences and an integrated curriculum.

A Ripple Effect: Color

Here is a more detailed description of what took place in that third- and fourth-grade classroom as the students began to think about colors one September afternoon. Their experience became a pebble that created a ripple effect on the topic of color, cutting across the curriculum and continuing until the end of the school year. Writing for self-expression became one of the primary tools they used to shape their language and understanding of their experiences (see Figure 5–4).

The children chose and used many forms of writing after an occasion, a topic, and a reason to write emerged through classroom experiences, sharing, and talking. What follows is not a comprehensive collection of types of writing, but a case in point of what really happened and how it happened.

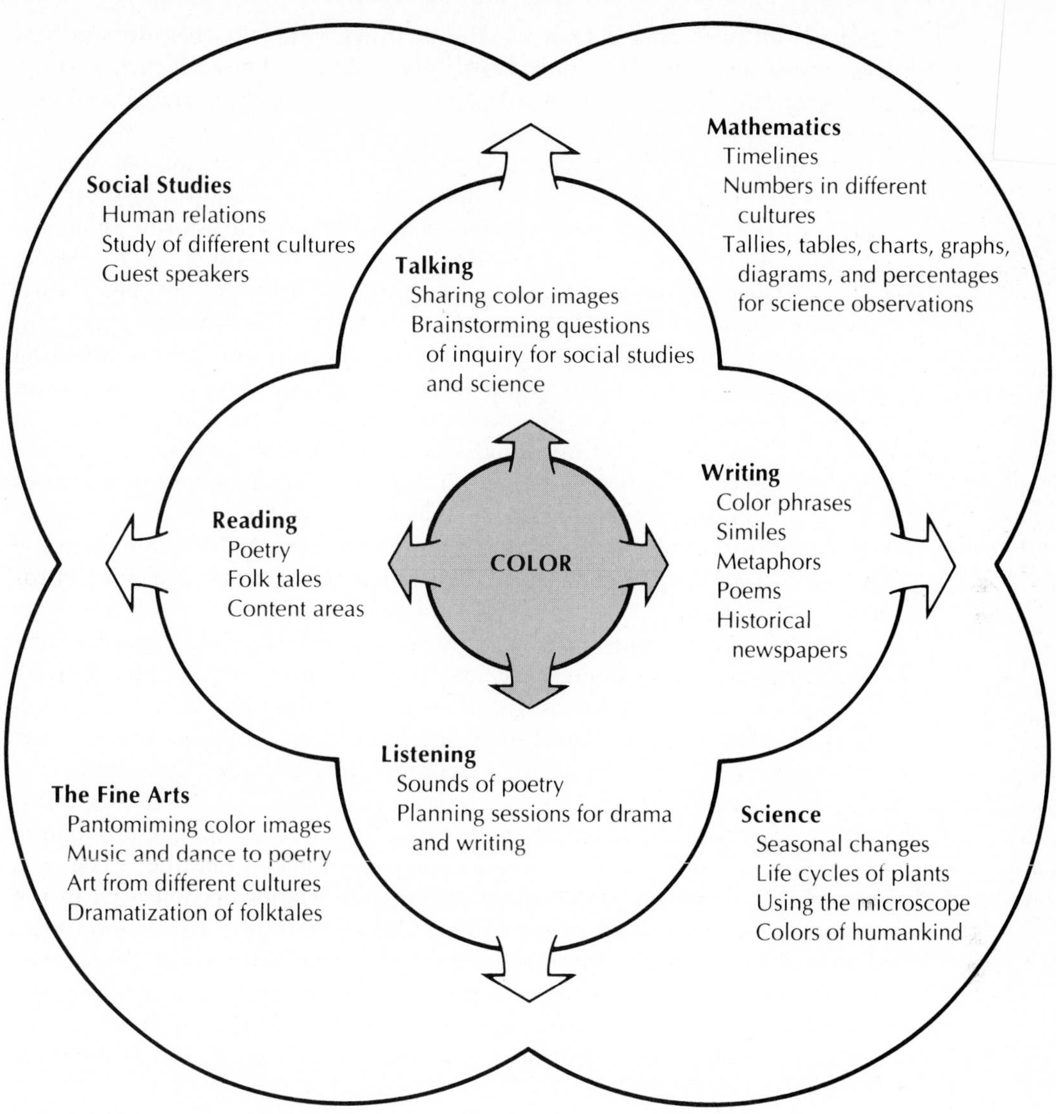

Figure 5–4 *A Ripple Effect: Color*

Expanding Experiences and Concepts; Building Vocabulary; Writing and Reading; Integrating Skills. After talking about the experience of observing colors, brainstorming ideas of what a color might be, and pantomiming an image for each color, the children expand their concepts and vocabulary through lists of words and phrases of color imagery, first written on the blackboard and then transferred on to a large piece of chart paper to save.

See this chapter, "Centering Ideas."

See Chapter 12, "Dictionaries" and "Thesauri."

The children add to this list from time to time, and collect and record their own special words in word banks (personal dictionaries, word files,

Larousse illustrated French–English Dictionary for Young Readers, edited by Martha Fonteneau (Larousse, 1969); *Mi Diccionario Ilustrado,* Marion Monroe (Scott, Foresman, 1971)

"What is Pink?" by Christina Rosetti in *A Random House Book of Poetry,* ed. Jack Prelutsky (Random House, 1983); "I Am Rose," by Gertrude Stein in *Amelia Mixed the Mustard,* poems selected and illustrated by Evaline Ness (Charles Scribner's Sons, 1975); "Vegetables," by Shel Silverstein, and "Josephine," by Alexander Resnikoff in *Oh, That's Ridiculous!* poems selected by William Cole, illustrated by Tomi Ungerer (Viking, 1972)

The Pantheon Story of Art for Young People, by Ariane Ruskin Batterberry (Pantheon, 1975); *The Impressionist Revolution,* by Howard Greenfield (Doubleday, 1972)

boxes, and word rings). They use the dictionary and the thesaurus to find synonyms and new descriptive words about colors. These in turn become spelling words, content for word games, acrostics, and anagrams, and new sight words for reading.

And the children begin to write immediately. That same afternoon, they write notes recording their impressions and feelings and scraps of images. Some write in their journals while others write stories about becoming colors. Several of these stories are revised and edited and displayed.

I also read the children a poem: "*Voyelles*" (*Vowels*), by Arthur Rimbaud, a nineteenth-century French poet. In the poem, Rimbaud links vowels to colors and colorful imagery. Moreover, he was only sixteen when he wrote it—not so much older than these students that they could not imagine themselves speaking with a poet's voice as well. I read the poem first in French, then translate it into English on the board; many of the children save the color words in French. We add some foreign-language dictionaries to the writing center and begin to collect color words in other languages. One student in the class is Japanese, and we seek out other students in the school who speak a language other than English to learn more color words in other languages.

We begin to collect and read poems about colors and related topics. Some are traditional poems, such as "What is Pink?" by Christina Rosetti. Others are more personal and spoken with a strong voice, such as "I Am Rose," by Gertrude Stein. And some are humorous nonsense, such as "Vegetables," by Shel Silverstein, and "Josephine," by Alexander Resnikoff.

Music, Art, and Poetry. After combining music with their color pantomimes, some of the students begin to listen to music while they write, and to write in response to the music. Records and tapes become part of the writing center. So do art prints and art history books, initially loaned to us by the art teacher, but then supplemented by others from the library and from home. Certain artists, especially Picasso, Miró, Chagall, and the Impressionists, capture the children's interest because of their use of light and color. The students also write—and draw and paint—in response to art.

The free and easy style of Mary O'Neill's poems about color makes them accessible as a model for some of the children; and poems about color soon appear in their writing. These poems and other writing are displayed on a bulletin board and the many books of poetry, art, and music are collected below, along with writing materials, including colored paper.

What is White?

White is a dove
And lily of the valley
And a puddle of milk
Spilled in an alley—

A ship's sail
A kite's tail
A wedding veil
Hailstones and halibut bones
And some people's telephones.
The hottest and most blinding light
Is white.
And breath is white
When you blow it out on a frosty night.
White is the shining absence of all color
Then absence is white
Out of touch
Out of sight.
White is marshmallow
And vanilla ice cream
And the part you can't remember in a dream.
White is the sound
Of a light foot walking.
White is a pair of
Whispers talking.
White is the beautiful
Broken lace
Of snowflakes falling
On your face.
You can smell white
In a country room
Toward the end of May
*In the cherry bloom.**

Human Relations and Social Studies. That same autumn, the school system provided interested classes with a consultant in human relations. Marlene Cummings, a black registered nurse, addressed the schools on the physiology of color differences among people. She was motivated by her concern about her own sons who attended predominantly white schools where she felt these differences might not be clearly understood. As part of her presentation, she played a game simulating prejudice and discrimination, and then encouraged children to ask questions. After her discussion with our class, she noticed Mary O'Neill's book in the writing center and commented on her reservations about Mary O'Neill's poem "What is Black?" because of the many negative images used: "things you'd like to forget," "run-down street," "broken cup," "soot spots," "suffering." Along with letters thanking her for coming to class, some of the children who had heard her comments included poems about the color black expressing their responses to the ideas generated by her visit. These poems had undergone extensive rewriting and revisions over several weeks. These young poets had a strong experience to draw on, and a specific audience in mind, as they tested their voices through poetry. Here is one example of such writing.

Black is Beautiful, by Ann McGovern (Four Winds Press, 1969); *Here I Am!* edited by Virginia Baron (Dutton, 1969); *All Us Come Cross the Water,* by Lucille Clifton (Holt, Rinehart & Winston, 1973)

See some of the many books by Verna Aardema: *Tales from the Story Hat: African Folktales* (Coward-McCann, 1960); *Why Mosquitoes Buzz in People's Ears* (Dial, 1975), a patterned story and winner of the Caldecott Medal for the illustrations by Leo and Diane Dillon; and *Who's in Rabbit's House?* (Dial, 1977), a Masai folktale shown as a play performed by villagers in masks, and also illustrated by the Dillons.

Egyptian Hieroglyphics for Everyone, by Joseph and Lenore Scott (Funk & Wagnalls, 1968); *Moja Means One: A Swahili Counting Book,* by Tom Feelings (Dial, 1971)

"Dear Mrs. Cummings,

"You convinced me that black is beautiful. I am very glad you came to talk with us. Now I know what makes the skin black or white. Thank you for your time. Here is a poem I wrote about black.

"Black is Beautiful

Black is a racing horse, galloping full speed
Black is a tree trunk covered with leaves
Black is the ocean deep, deep down
Black is a blackbird's feathery crown
Black is a blackboard
Black is a cat
Black is a ringmaster's tall round hat."

The interests and strong responses triggered by Marlene Cummings's visit suggested a new focus for further social studies investigation: human relations and cultural and racial diversity in America. The class began to gather resources, supplemented by books and ideas and experiences from the children, that created a new ripple in many different directions. One focus was the study of African history, culture, geography, and contemporary social and political structure.

A related investigation took us back in time to ancient Egypt and then to India and to the source of many ideas and inventions we know in our culture today. The children also pursued topics in a study of black Americans from the time of the slave trade to the present. The students found children's books about black Americans that focused on self-image; an anthology of poems written by children from many heritages across the United States; and other books that explore the heritage of black Americans. This literature became a source of material for listening, reading, and writing on students' self-chosen topics in this area.

The children researched many subjects dealing with the black heritage, in philosophy, literature, history, geography, and politics, and reported on them, either in a straight journalistic style in the *Pan-African Press* and *Delhi's Daily,* or by fictionalized reporting in *The Sphinx Speaks.* They also read and acted on what they read in other ways and through other forms of writing. Small groups of children adapted ancient Egyptian myths and Hindu and African folk tales into scripts for story dramatization, and created costumes, props, and publicity for these productions. The study of these cultures and countries spilled over into other areas of the curriculum.

Mathematics and Science. Some of the students read and wrote about the origins of writing and the numerical system and related this to language study as they learned about hieroglyphics and counting in other cultures. In addition, since the original reason for going outside during that first week of school had been to observe and discuss the color of leaves changing in the fall, we began an Elementary Science Study unit called "Budding Twigs." Elementary Science Study units take an inquiry (rather than a textbook) approach to science, using processes such as observation, classification, measurement, prediction, hypothesis, interpretation, and inference.

The types of writing used during this study were labeling, note taking, reporting on these observations in science journals, and reports of findings. Experiences to write about ranged from field trips to nearby forests and arboretums, with a parent acting as a naturalist guide, during which students drew and wrote about changes they observed in trees and plants during the seasons, to a series of experiments conducted in the classroom using branches cut at intervals during the year.

Fiction and writing for self-expression crept into this study too, with the children personifying the plants they were observing, and writing stories about them. This in turn led them to write and produce a play about personified plant people on another planet in *The Tale of an Unfair Election.*

See Chapter 10, "Scriptwriting."

Presenting and Publishing Writing for Self-expression. The color-images and poems started at the beginning of the year became a part of the life of the class, and many of the children continued to revise them and to work on new ones, as well as on other forms of poetry and patterns on other topics. The school board published a number of these pieces in a book called *Dear Mrs. Cummings,* a collection of the letters and other writings from the children after her visits.

Other poems became another aspect of the ripple effect, started by the topic of color, on the arts and language arts. After dramatizing some traditional myths and folktales from other cultures, and writing and producing an original play about personified plants, the children had the idea of presenting these poems in dramatic form for others, and eventually publishing them in an anthology.

This concept took the form of a pantomime/dance presentation. Some of the children worked in groups and some alone, each preparing a poem for presentation. They blocked out movements in pantomime and dance to music that matched the mood of their images. The movements and the music were coordinated with choral readings of the poems, which they had taped. They dressed in leotards or swimsuits of their color, and the only props they used were their original pieces of nylon net. They titled this work *Magic Colors* and presented it in the round in the gym. The audience sat in a large circle of chairs with several spaces for the children to enter and exit. After the audience was seated and the room darkened, the children entered (almost) noiselessly and crouched behind the chairs. As the tape recorder played each poem and its corresponding music, the various groups played out the pantomime/dance they had created.

Language Arts for Every Child. This final experience in what had become an ever-widening set of ripples started by the concept of color the first week of school was greatly satisfying for most of the children, and had a special significance for some. Several of the younger boys had often had difficulty writing for self-expression alone, but were successful when they wrote together or edited their writing in a peer group. And they were especially proud when they pantomimed and published their poems together. Two of the children had speech problems that often inhibited their speaking in class, but they were much more relaxed because they had time to practice reading their poems, and because not they but the tape recorder "read" their poems on the day of the presentation. This was also true of many shy children who usually had trouble sharing what they had written. One student, eight-year-old Mariko, was Japanese and spoke limited English. She was also a beautiful dancer. She extended the slow and halting recording of her poem through the lingua franca of dance.

> ***Silver***
>
> *Silver feels like a fairy that's gliding through the night.*
> *Silver means peace and quiet.*
> *Silver is a sleeping feeling.*
> *Silver is a merry color like bells ringing.*

Writing for Self-expression in an Integrated Curriculum

In teaching the language arts, it is crucial to recognize the central role of the language and experiences of the child in all learning, as well as the importance of writing for self-expression as a means to unify and integrate many areas of the curriculum.

During this schoolyear, poetry became a catalyst for learning about human relations, social studies, science, and mathematics through literature, art, music, dance, and the media. Because poetry is such an important tool for molding experiences and learning through feeling, thinking, listening, reading, and writing, children need access to many forms of poetry for shaping writing for self-expression.

A Day in the Life of Young Writers

What would a day in the life of young writers look like in a classroom where writing for self-expression across the curriculum was supported and encouraged?

Time and Opportunities for Writing

15 minutes: *Journal Writing*

Topics for writing may emerge.

Journal writing gets the juices for writing flowing.

15 minutes: *Sharing*

Sharing encourages thinking out loud, discovering new ideas.

Teachers can support and encourage these ideas as topics for writing.

20–30 minutes: *Class Writing*

Teacher records shared experiences: class stories.

Introduction of new shapes for writing: poems and patterns.

Brainstorming ideas on a topic and planning future projects that can involve writing.

20–30 minutes: *Writing on Topics of Choice*

Planning and drafting new ideas.

Continuing and revising ideas already started.

Conferences with teacher and other students.

Revising and editing writing.

30–60 minutes: *Writing in the Content Areas*

Overlap with writing on topics of choice.

Using a variety of forms for exploring and reporting ideas in the content areas: stories, reports, poems, scripts.

Collaborative efforts with other students: newspaper on a period in history, publicity for a play presentation on a subject in a content area.

15 minutes: *Reading Aloud*

Teacher reads poetry and literature that may become a model for writing, or give young writers new ideas.

These are some of the times and opportunities that exist all day for young writers to write and integrate what they are learning across the curriculum through their writing. Other important times, which will overlap with writing times, are those during which talk is promoted on all subjects of interest to support all forms of writing. Jones (1986) suggests several strategies, based on current research on writing, for promoting such talk based on the functions of "writing talk" in the classroom.

Talk Worth Promoting during a Young Writer's Day

1. Talking to rehearse and expand writing (Graves, 1983; Murray, 1985) talking to generate thought (Smith, 1982).
   a. Hold peer, teacher, and group conferences using questions like:
      "Tell me about [topic]."
      "What have you thought about writing?"
      "How will you begin?"

b. Allow talk and arrange the classroom for mobility and flexible seating, with adequate natural lighting.
c. Read often, read children's writing as literature (Graves, 1983), and learn to "read like a writer" (Smith, 1983); encourage children to share what they read and their impressions of it, by asking questions like:
   "What do you think of it?"
   "How do you suppose [the author] got that idea?"
   "What makes it work for you?"
   "Does this remind you of anything else we've read?"

2. Talking to verbalize writing strategies and decisions (Calkins, 1983; Giacobbe, 1982).
   a. Hold peer, teacher, and group conferences using questions like:
      "How is it going?"
      "How can I help you in this conference?"
      "Why did you . . . ?"
      "I noticed that you [changed/added . . .]. Why?"
      "When you started writing this piece, what were you thinking?"
      "Did anything surprise you about this piece?"
   b. Encourage children to share techniques that work for them—techniques for getting started, choosing topics, getting unstuck.
3. Talking to evaluate efforts (Graves, 1983).
   a. Hold peer, teacher, and group conferences using questions like:
      "What do you think of it so far?"
      "Which do you like best? Why? What would make it better?"
      "If you were going to work on this again, what would you do?"
      "Is there anything you would change?"
   b. Withhold judgment, including praise. Let the author be the ultimate critic.
4. Talking to affirm membership in the writing community.
   a. Treat children like authors. Assume they are capable of making their own decisions and let them do so.
   b. Demythologize literature. Reinforce the idea that books are written by people, and that some people have simply had more experience than others.

Shaping Children's Writing

Introducing poetry and patterns as **models for writing** is one way to offer children a form within which to shape their writing. These forms can be to older students through daily reading-aloud periods. For younger children, they can be presented through poems and patterns dictated by the class and written down by the teacher. Through such experiences, children learn to choose and use these forms for their own images and ideas in writing.

Using forms of poetry for self-expression is a logical outgrowth of children's natural speech which is full of chants, rhymes, songs, and nonsense. Children often spontaneously think and speak and write in the way Frye (1964) describes as the way "the poet thinks, not in logical sequences, but in the most primitive and archaic of categories, similarity and identity: A is like B; A is B. These are categories that appear in poetry as simile and metaphor. 'Eternity is like unto a Ring,' says John Bunyan. 'Grandfather of the day is he,' says Emily Dickinson of a mountain" (p. 7). Frye urges that education "preserve a child's own metaphorical processes, not distort them in the interests of a false notion of reality" (p. 9).

This is not to suggest that, merely because children often use metaphorical language, they are all poets. Poetry is much more complex than that. On the other hand, if children hear poetry read aloud, read poems themselves, and respond to poetry through listening, talking, dance, drama, and art and express their feelings, ideas, and images through forms of poetic writing, then poetry may help them to preserve that way of seeing things special to children—and to poets.

See "But Is It Poetry?" by Myra Cohn Livingston, in *The Horn Book* (December 1975; February 1976).

Poems

A variety of elements can be incorporated into poetry; among these are simile, metaphor, rhyme, syllabic patterns, or concrete poetry.

Similes. A **simile** draws a comparison between dissimilar things using the words *like* or *as.* The first-graders in Phyllis Crawford's class wrote similes about colors. They expanded their concepts about color through many art experiences and a search for color-words in the dictionary and the thesaurus and on their crayon box. They wrote synonyms on colored paper cut into leaf shapes and then invented similes for each color as well.

As yellow as . . . a sweltering sun
refreshing lemonade
a corpulent cat

Writing color-words on cards, they practiced alphabetizing and matching new color-words with the original words (*yellow/saffron*). To explore the effects of color, they made some cooking experiments, such as turning rice yellow with the spice saffron.

The experiences of listening to poetry with vivid images, exploring color words, and writing similes led the children to a study of the five senses, which in turn led to further vocabulary development and the writing of yet more similes.

Smell As reeky as wrinkled, perspiring feet.
Hear As deafening as a hovering helicopter.
See As colorful as an enchanted sunset.
Feel As bumpy as a warted toad.
Taste As yummy as seasoned etoufé.

A well-known example of a well-known metaphor from a well-known poet and playwright: "It is the east, and Juliet is the sun!" *Romeo and Juliet,* Act II. Scene II, by William Shakespeare

See "Exploring Metaphor in Language and Development and Learning," by Linda Gibson Geller, in *Language Arts,* 61 (1984), 151–161.

Wishes, Lies, and Dreams, by Kenneth Koch (Random House, 1970)

Metaphor. A **metaphor** draws a comparison between two dissimilar things by naming the one for the other. Aristotle calls this process of renaming an "indication of genius, since the ability to forge a good metaphor shows that the poet has an intuitive perception of the similarity in dissimilars." Creating metaphors is a way of using language to gain control over ideas and even life, a way of symbolically representing reality. As Britton (1970) puts it: "We symbolize reality in order to handle it" (p. 20). This means of handling reality is not exclusively the domain of the genius or the poet. Children also create metaphors, often fluently and beautifully.

The poet Kenneth Koch (1970) gives some examples of metaphors written by third- through sixth-grade children in New York as a consequence of his suggestion that they "think about a thing being like something else (the cloud is like a pillow) and to pretend that it really was the other thing . . . to say *is* instead of *is like* (the cloud is a pillow)" (p. 147). One example:

> *"Mr. Koch is a very well-dressed poetry book walking around in shining shoes" (p. 144).*

Koch suggests that teachers encourage children to think and write this way through comparison poems. Such poems may be simple metaphors or similes, or they can take other forms:

> *I used to . . . , But now I . . . .*
> *I am a . . . , but I wish I were . . . .*
> *If I were a . . . , I would . . . .*

Rhyme. Poetry need not **rhyme**, but frequently does. Here are several types of rhyming patterns from poetry.

1. *Couplets.* A couplet is a two-line rhymed verse. A first-grader combined his impressions of doing folk dances at school and a trip to the zoo in a couplet which he first chanted and then wrote down and illustrated:

> *A panther*
> *Once was a folk dancer.*

2. *Triplets.* A triplet is a verse in three lines that rhyme.

3. *Quatrains.* A quatrain is a four-line poem with a varied rhyme pattern. A fourth-grader wrote this quatrain after observing mealworms for science study:

> *A mealworm in bran*
> *Is apt to expand*
> *So give the mealworm*
> *A helping hand.*

4. *Limericks.* A limerick is a nonsense poem in which lines 1, 2, and 5 rhyme, and lines 3 and 4 rhyme. Edward Lear popularized this traditional form of verse around 1850.

There was an old man with a beard,
Who said, "It is just as I feared!—
Two Owls and a Hen,
Four Larks and a Wren,
*Have all built their nests in my beard.**

Here is a fourth-grader's limerick:

There once was a man from Mars,
Who liked to eat the stars.
One day he ate twenty.
Oh, man, was he funny.
That silly old man from Mars.

Syllabic Patterns. Some traditional forms of poetry follow a **syllabic pattern** rather than a rhyme pattern.

1. *Haiku.* A traditional Japanese form of poetry, haiku consists of seventeen syllables in three lines in the following pattern: five, seven, five. Haiku are generally written about nature. Here is a fourth-grader's haiku:

Shiny blue water
ripples as the boy throws stones
into the still sea.

2. *Senryu.* Senryu follow the same pattern as haiku but are on a topic other than nature.

3. *Tanka.* Tanka use thirty-one syllables in five lines (seven, five, seven, five, seven) on a nature topic.

Children who have experience writing poems based on a syllabic pattern often make up their own. Fifth-grader Tom did this when he created "Rumble," a simple pattern of one word per line.

Under
boulders
isn't
where
I
want
to
look
today.

*From *The Complete Nonsense of Edward Lear,* collected by Holbrook Johnson (Mineola, NY: Dover Publications, Inc., 1951), p. 3.

Figure 5–5
Concrete Poetry in the Shape of an Israeli Line Dance

Concrete Poetry. In **concrete poetry,** the writing itself takes a representational form. The words can be written in the shape of whatever is being described, or written in and around some other shape. Third-grader Tracey created this poem in the shape of a dance pattern she had learned from Moshiko, a teacher of Israeli folk dances (see Figure 5–5).

Featured Preservice Teacher Pat Peabody: Children Reading and Writing Poetry

Here are some examples of some of the many ways Pat Peabody involved students with reading and writing poetry as part of a field experience for learning to teach reading and language arts.

1. *Poetry Journal.* The students kept a journal in which they recorded favorite poems, phrases, and ideas about things, new ways of thinking about things, and words and phrases that were new and appealing to them.

2. *Poetry Place.* A special area in the classroom included books of poetry that children could add to, poems found in any media, and a bulletin board for displaying copies of poems they liked or wrote themselves.

3. *Word Bank.* The students looked through their poetry journals for favorite words or phrases they had collected, wrote them on 3 × 5 cards secured with a binder clamp, and withdrew from their account when they needed words for writing poetry.

4. *Word Painting and Using a Thesaurus.* The students used their word bank and a thesaurus to paint word pictures:

Word	***Synonym***	***Simile or Metaphor***
daisy	*posy*	*like a little sun*

5. *Who is a Poet?* Students displayed the following sentences about poets on a bulletin board, and discussed these ideas:

"A poet sees things differently."
"A poet looks beyond the obvious."
"A poet looks inside for feelings about the world."
"A poet thinks about feelings."
"A poet chooses from a word bank and paints a poem."
"A poet touches feelings inside others."
"Get inside your world—share it with a poem."

6. *Poetry Walks.* The students went on silent walks and were encouraged to look for some commonly seen object and then write about it something they might not have noticed before or compare it to something else in the form of a simile or metaphor. After these walks, they painted word pictures and illustrated them (see Figure 5–6).

Stories

Children's written narratives may take many shapes depending on their age and developmental level, their interests and experiences, and the topics they choose to write about.

Variations among Children. A very young child's story may consist of just a single sentence, most likely accompanied by a drawing. A first- or second-grader's story may be well constructed in three sentences representing the beginning, the middle, and the end. As students move through the middle grades, their stories become longer and may even turn into short books or longer, ongoing narratives. However, when children are learning to write, length and structure and mechanics are not as important as the children's desire to express themselves, to find their own voice, and to make meaning.

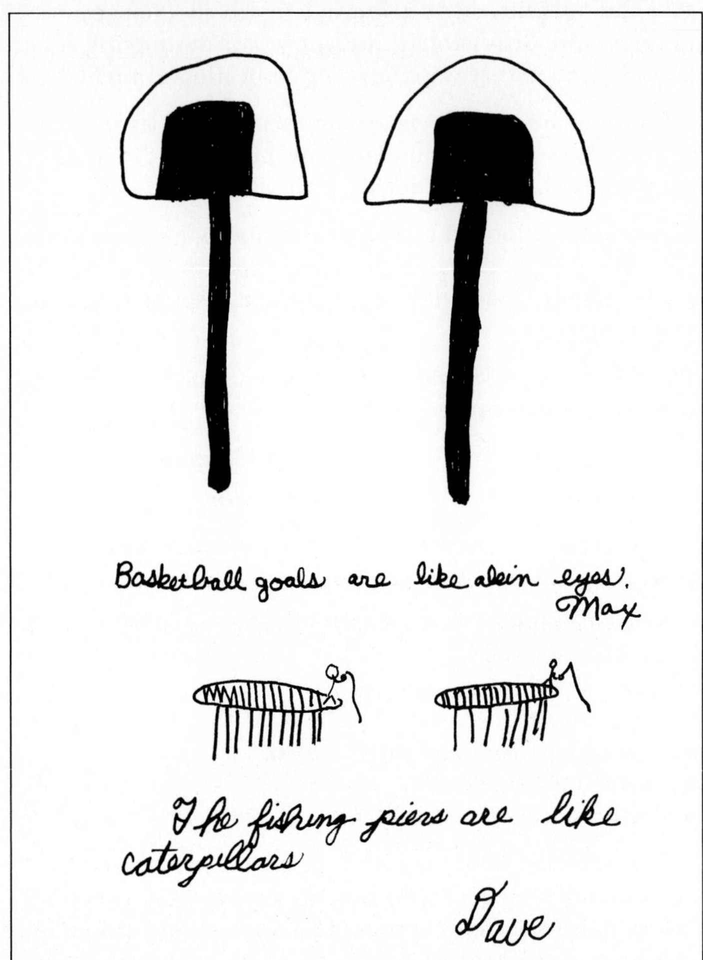

Figure 5–6
Similes Composed by Third-Graders after a Poetry Walk

Motivation. A teacher does not always need to motivate children to write stories, or provide a special stimulus or story starter. Children have many stories to tell and will tell them if you support and encourage their writing efforts. Many of these stories will emerge at first through talking and telling and sharing and interacting with others, in a kind of sorting process preliminary to writing. Other story ideas may appear in journals, during brainstorming sessions, or through specific experiences.

Topics. Everyone has experiences but not everyone is aware that there is a story hidden in there somewhere. Some students have plenty of stories to tell and little trouble finding an idea to write about. Others need support in searching out topics.

Children are stimulated to write if they are allowed to write about something they know. You should be sensitive to the sources young writers can use to find ideas for stories and help them in their search. Recent and rich experiences at home and school, and responses to literature and media, are broad categories to think about. Remember that children need support and guidance, rather than assignments, as they try out their own voice in writing for self-expression. Remember also that stories are where you find them. Below are listed three places children can find topics to write about, or which may trigger a ripple effect with one child that will lead from one topic to another. The list is illustrated with examples of children's writing that emerged from these kinds of experiences, some of which have already been described.

1. Experiences.

a. Writing in response to sensory experiences such as food, experiments, and weather.

Letters to a Ghoul, written by a third-grader after talking about fall weather, Halloween, and an imaginary ghoul trapped in a tree in the school yard.

Invasion of the Killer Popcorn, written by an eighth-grade remedial reading student after the teacher made popcorn and the class wrote patterns about popcorn.

b. Writing in response to aesthetic experiences such as music, art, and drama.

Escape from Bald Mountain, a fourth-grader's response upon listening to Moussorgsky's "A Night on Bald Mountain," program music based on a Russian folktale about the devil's revels one night of the year on a mountaintop.

The House with Eyes, a fifth-grader's response after seeing a reproduction of an Edward Hopper painting of a deserted house.

c. Writing based on school experiences such as topics in the content areas, holidays, field trips, guest speakers, demonstrations, pets, personal relationships, social interaction, games and sports.

The Soccer Champs, a second-grader's imaginary adventures of the players in a world-class soccer tournament.

King Tut and I, a fourth-grader's writing in the form of the diary of a young Egyptian boy who was best friends with the boy King Tut.

d. Writing based on home experiences such as family, hobbies, interests, pets, trips, friends.

Arthur, a second-grader's description of his pet dog.

e. Writing based on journal topics.

My Best Friend, a second-grader's description of his best friend and adventures they will share.

The Secret, a sixth-grader's description and musings about a secret love.

2. Literature.
   a. Writing in response to literature.
      The Station, a fifth-grader's response to several books on the Underground Railroad (her own family's house had been a station on the Underground Railroad, by means of which runaway slaves escaped to freedom before the Civil War).

The Marsh King, by C. Walter Hodges (Coward, McCann, 1967)

      The Young King, a sixth-grader's description of the adventures of a young king in an imaginary land, written after reading Hodges's *The Marsh King,* based on the life of England's King Alfred.
   b. Literature as a model.
      Rabbitrella, a first-grader's tale of a Cinderella rabbit.

Chitty Chitty Bang Bang, by Ian Fleming (Random House, 1964)

      Further Adventures of Chitty Chitty Bang Bang, a play written by third-graders after reading the book by Ian Fleming.

3. The Media.
   a. Writing in response to media such as popular music, television, short films in class, and feature films outside of a school.
      Run for Space, a fifth-grader's short book describing a space adventure, written in response to several popular television shows on space.
   b. Extending characters and plots from the media; adapting the style of real-life sports and media personalities.
      Diaper Boy, a fifth-grader's creation of his own superhero patterned after those in the media.

Genre Writing. The sample of children's writing in Figure 5–7 shows that many children like to read and write in popular genre forms, such as science fiction, historical fiction, realistic fiction, fantasy, and biography, and are influenced by such genres in the media. Various literary and popular genres are well represented in children's books and a familiarity with examples of these may help you to recognize students' interest in one genre or another and encourage their writing in that genre. Thinking in a genre may help them focus their ideas as they write for self-expression.

See these books of myths by Ingrid and Edgar Parin D'Aulaire: *D'Aulaire's Book of Greek Myths* (Doubleday, 1962), and *Norse Gods and Giants* (Doubleday, 1967).

Here are some examples of children's books, arranged in broad categories used to discuss children's literature, which the children may read or have read aloud to them as a way of stimulating their own writing.

1. *Folklore.* Folktales with many variants such as "Cinderella" and "The Gingerbread Man"; fables of Aesop and La Fontaine; Greek, Roman, and Norse myths, and myths from other cultures and times; tales of heroes; legends; tall tales.

See Chapter 8, "Featured Teacher Margaret Mattson: Close Reading of a Classic."

2. *Realistic Fiction.* Mysteries, from Donald Sobol's *Encyclopedia Brown* books to Ellen Raskin's *The Westing Game;* adventure, from R. L. Stevenson's *Treasure Island* to Jean George's *Julie of the Wolves;* sports stories such as those by Matt Christopher.

Figure 5–7
Diaper Boy, by a Fifth-Grader

3. *Historical Fiction and Biography.* Books for younger students by Jean Fritz; Laura Ingalls Wilder's *Little House* books; Scott O'Dell's *Island of the Blue Dolphins.*

See "When Children Write Science Fiction," by Dorothy Marla, in *Language Arts,* 62 (1985), 355–361.

4. *Science Fiction and Fantasy.* Tales of other worlds such as C. S. Lewis's *The Lion, the Witch, and the Wardrobe* series, Lloyd Alexander's chronicles of Prydain, and Ursula Le Guin's tales of Earthsea; stories about personified animals like *Winnie-the-Pooh* by A. A. Milne and *Charlotte's Web* by E. B. White; time and space fantasies such as Madeleine L'Engle's *A Wrinkle in Time,* Lucy Boston's *Green Knowe* books, and Susan Cooper's *The Dark is Rising* series; and science fiction by writers like Robert Heinlein, John Christopher, Sylvia Engdahl, and Anne McCaffrey.

The original *Choose Your Own Adventure* series is published by Bantam books, but there are numerous other versions of this genre by other publishers.

Choose-Your-Own-Adventure Books. A popular type of children's paperback book today is the series *Choose Your Own Adventure* which cuts across a wide range of genres. At first these books were written by Edward Packard as a consequence of telling stories to his own children and giving them a choice of which way the story would go at different points in the plot. Other authors took up the idea and these kinds of books are now available for second-grade through adult reading levels, on appropriate subject matter. Reading and writing choose-your-own-adventure stories—individually, in small groups, or as a class—is an exciting way for some children to become involved in reading and writing a particular genre, and in writing in general.

Here is one possible sequence you can use to help children read and write their own adventures.

1. Read a choose-your-own-adventure book aloud to the class and let them make decisions as a group about which way to go in the story.
2. Start a class collection of such books. Ask children to bring them from home and search garage sales for them.
3. Have the children read such books to each other in small groups, making decisions together along the way. They may also read them by themselves (in fact, they probably do so already).
4. Discuss and identify the structure of a choose-your-own-adventure-book together as a way of getting them started writing. For their own story, they will need to think about and develop the following:
   Genre: adventure, mystery, fantasy, history, mythology, sports.
   Setting: time, place, landscape, some events and scenes.
   Characters: start character sketches of three characters (themselves and two others), their background, physical characteristics, and behavior.
   Plot: describe a basic story and then the first event; at the end of the event, give readers two choices, and write both; continue in this way throughout the story.
   Theme: note the general theme of the book.
5. Now the children can begin to write in small groups, or brainstorm together and then write their own. Children interested in the same genre may want to work together.

Phyllis Fuglaar engages in a writing conference as her students work on their own choose-your-own-adventure stories.

Featured Teacher Phyllis Fuglaar: Writing and Publishing Choose-Your-Own-Adventure Books

Phyllis Fuglaar is herself a published teacher/writer and her combination fourth- and fifth-grade classroom looks like a writing workshop. Throughout the year, Phyllis involves her students in writing in many ways and across the curriculum. Her class regularly publishes newspapers, reports, anthologies, and books by individual authors.

Her students have written a number of choose-your-own-adventure books, and she notes that in the course of this activity they generated many more ideas than usual in prewriting discussions; they worked well in pairs and small groups; they became very involved; their parents often became involved in the book production; the stories were longer than usual; the children learned to edit each other; and all were eager to publish and read to others what they had written. These books also generated a great deal of pride in her classroom: for one child, it was the only project he had finished all year.

One of the children commented on writing this kind of story: "I liked writing this story because whenever I write a story, I always have lots of ideas for an ending, and doing this I can use all those ideas." Other students said that they liked having a partner and that it was fun to make up all the possibilities for different ways for the story to develop.

The books were bound and illustrated, partly in the classroom and partly at home. Figure 5–8 gives an excerpt from one of these books.

Figure 5–8 *Writing Choose-Your-Own-Adventure Stories:* Cave of the White Dwarves

Bookmaking

Teachers like Phyllis Fuglaar, and others who believe that children are real writers, also believe in the value of publishing this writing. Children need to see that their writing is intended for a wider audience than the teacher or family members who might notice it on the refrigerator door at home. Classroom bookmaking, often with the cooperation of the parents, is one way to achieve a wider audience.

How To Make Your Own Books, by Harvey Weiss (Crowell, 1974)

Handmade books can range in complexity from a piece of paper folded in half to hand sewn and bound books. My favorite example of spontaneous bookmaking by a young child is that of Tommy, who took a department store gift box, drew illustrations on the inside, cut the top in pieces on which he wrote a story called *The Football Boy,* and attached the pieces to one side of the box with string laced through holes he had poked with a pencil. What is significant is that he did this entirely on his own, without an example, suggestion, or help from a teacher. Tommy wanted to publish his story and devised his own method to do so.

Different Book Forms

Books can be very simple:

- Stapled sheets with a construction paper cover.
- Heavier paper or cardboard sheets on a metal ring.
- Loose-leaf notebooks with the title on the cover.

Books can also be made in unusual forms:

- Scrolls that can be rolled up.
- Shape books, bound together with a metal ring.
- Books in containers: pages in boxes, tubes, bags.
- Accordion books that unfold and do not need a cover.

Bound Books

Books bound in a more traditional manner can also be made in the classroom. There are several variations on this type of book. Covers can be made with glued paper, fabric attached to cardboard with drymount tissue, wallpaper samples, and many other materials. Pages can be hand sewn or stapled. One easy bookbinding method using stapled pages and Con-Tact paper is shown in Figure 5–9.

Bookmaking should be an ongoing process in a classroom, and parents are ideal partners in this enterprise. They can help by sending materials, and by attending a workshop you give on making books, which will enable them to help their children bind their own books at home or in school.

Audiences for Children's Books

It is not enough to publish children's books; they should also be read. They can be coded and catalogued and become part of a classroom library. Some schools include such books in the school library to make them available to children from other classes. Teachers and librarians can feature the work of young book writers, arranging for volunteer "authors of the day (week, month)" to read their books to others, and producing class and school anthologies that can be distributed more widely. A display of children's books that have been made throughout the year can coincide with class or school book fairs.

See "Sharing Your Students: Where and How to Publish Children's Work," in *Language Arts,* 57 (1980), 635–648.

Other Ways to Publish Children's Writing

Other ways of publishing children's writing are available. For instance, many journals publish art and writing by children. Or, the children may write letters to the editors of journals and newspapers. Drama presentations and media productions are other ways of bringing children's writing to a wider audience and letting them know that there is a reason to use their own voice in writing for self-expression.

See Chapter 11, "Magazines."

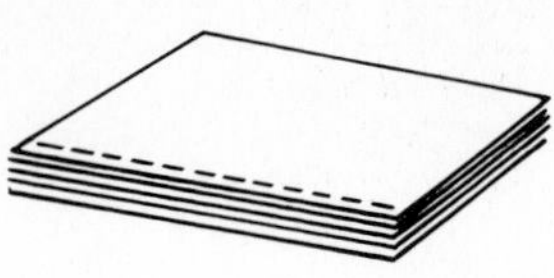

1. Stack the completed book pages and add an extra page each to front and back. Sew or staple the pages together on the binding edge (sewing creates a more durable binding).

2. Cut two pieces of cover cardboard one-fourth-inch larger in each dimension than the page size.

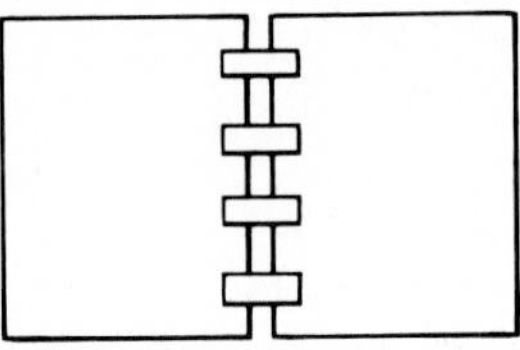

3. Tape the two pieces of cardboard together with a one-fourth-inch separation in the hinge.

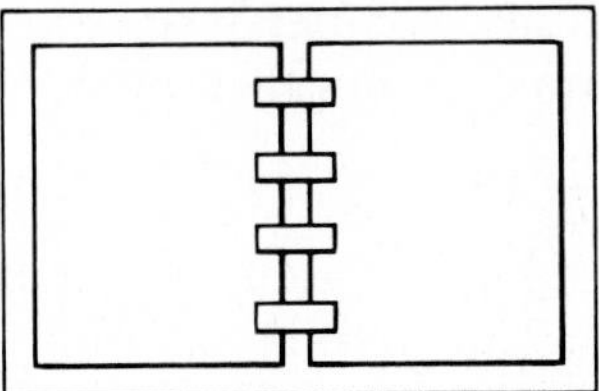

4. Place the cardboard on the cover Con-Tact paper spaced far enough apart for the cover to fold shut. Cut the Con-Tact paper to extend one inch beyond each edge of the cardboard. Peel the backing off the paper; center the cardboard on the cover. Press into place.

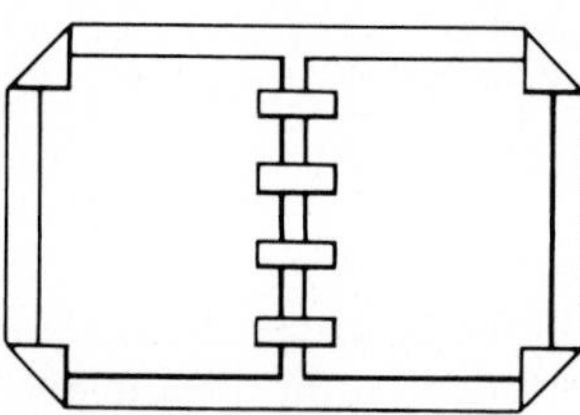

5. Fold the edges of the cover material around the cardboard by folding down first the corners and then the sides.

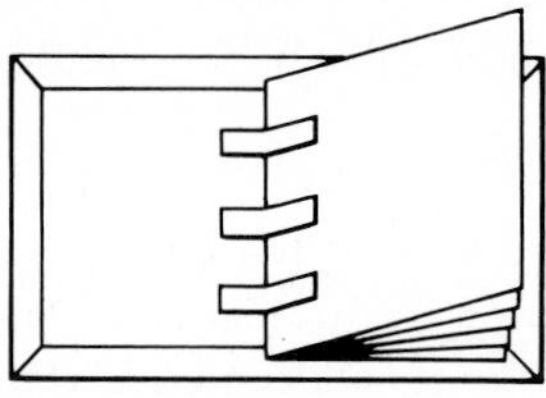

6. Tape the bound edges of the book into the cover. Masking tape will do.

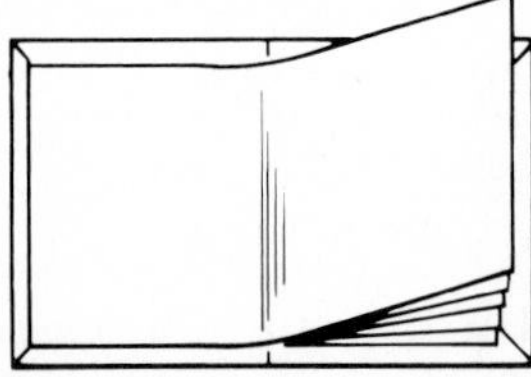

7. Cut two pieces of Con-Tact paper the height of the pages and more than twice the width of the pages.

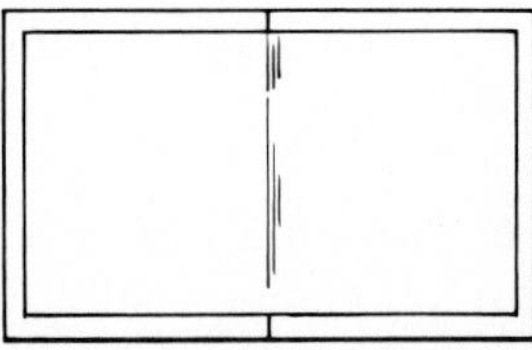

8. Place the peeled Con-Tact paper (inside cover piece) on the inside of the cover to overlap the tape in the hinge, and adhere to the extra page in front and the hardcover front. Repeat this step with the back inside cover.

Figure 5–9 *Steps to Bookmaking*

A young author shares the book she has written and published with an audience of younger students.

Summing Up

Writing for self-expression is one of the ways young writers can use to find their own voice, and gain control over their ideas and language. In schools, such writing is always done in the context of students writing about themselves and others, and more functional types of writing, but the form and content of writing for self-expression is limited only by the distance children can travel in their minds.

Britton (1975) calls this self-expressive, poetic language (including that of stories) "the language of being and becoming." In addition, he suggests that the type of writing students do moves on a continuum towards the poetic as they grow older. However, other researchers have found that students at all levels use poetic as well as expressive and transactional writing in school.

Teachers can create conditions to support the natural creative urge among children in the classroom and there are many specific approaches to daily writing by which they can do this effectively. Many opportunities also exist during each school day to encourage children's self-expressive writing and the talk that supports this or any other kind of writing.

Stories and poetry are forms of writing by which children can express themselves more imaginatively. Their urge to create can be freely exercised and encouraged through these forms, but this type of writing is also a grand means to integrate the curriculum through writing in the content areas. After all, children must write about something, and that something is often a set of related topics that can spread in many different directions into every part of the curriculum.

Teachers should be aware of the many forms of shaping writing for self-expression, from narrative stories to the many poetic forms, and ways to use literature as a model. One important aspect of writing is publishing. Bookmaking, publication in journals, and drama presentations are among the effective ways of letting children know that they are real writers with a real audience. These are the things that can lead young writers to a desire to write and find their own voice in writing for self-expression.

Looking Further

1. In a small group, brainstorm other ways you can support the development of creativity in writing and other language arts experiences. Refer to Torrance's criteria for conditions to support the growth of creativity (pp. 158–159).

2. Develop an approach or a lesson that encourages children to create similes and metaphors. Teach your lesson to a group of children, if possible.

3. Start a file of types of poems and rhymes to use as models to shape writing.

4. Ask to see writing files for several children in one classroom. List and analyze the different types of stories each child wrote. Discuss your findings with the class teacher to discover the source of the children's ideas for writing.

5. Select a poem or book which you think would be a good model to help children with their own writing. Read it to a class and suggest how they might use the work to model their writing. Evaluate the results in the children's writing.

6. Start a file of literature to model writing classified by genre: folklore; realistic fiction; historical fiction and biography; science fiction and fantasy.

7. Follow the procedure to write a choose-your-own-adventure story in small groups in your class on a topic of interest to you and in an adult genre such as murder mystery, detective story, or gothic romance. See if you can also do this with a group of children.

8. Practice making a book yourself, and then try it with children. Refer to Figure 5–9 for instructions on bookmaking.

9. Start a journal of your own. Collect images and ideas to use as a source for self-expression. Share your journal with a group of children, and encourage them to start their own.

10. Choose a poem you like and that you think children will like, too. (See Chapter 8 for ideas.) Brainstorm a possible ripple effect that this poem might create; consider activities across the curriculum. Share the poem with a group of children, and try some of the activities.

Chapter Six

Talking, Writing, and Grammar

Objectives

Look for answers to the following questions as you read this chapter.

- What do children really know about the grammar of the language they speak?
- What is grammar?
- What does research tell us about the importance of teaching grammar?
- What are some of the strategies for teaching grammar in a classroom with an individualized, interactive, and integrated approach to teaching language arts?

A Child's View

Here is how two fifth-graders, Faith and Barbara, responded to the questions, "What is grammar?" and "What do you know about it?"

Faith says:

"Grammar is dots and things that make sense. So that it sounds right. Also so that people can understand what you wrote.

"I know spelling, periods, commas, colons, semicolons, pronunciation, exclamation points, question marks, quotations, parentheses, capital letters, paragraphs, complete sentences, adverbs, adjectives, subjects, noun predicate, verb, preposition, prepositional phrase, infinitive, gerund, present tense, past tense, participles, spaces, letters, punctuation, usage."

Barbara says:

"Grammar is the way that you use words. Slang is bad grammar.

"I know the parts of speech, how to use words properly, when to use words."

Centering Ideas

In a rebus story, a letter, number, or picture replaces a word. Replacements can be linked to both sound (picture of an eye = *I*) and meaning (picture of an eye = *eye*).

Faith and Barbara are best friends and they often fight. They like to work together but this often leads to serious and sincere debates over whatever problem they are trying to solve. At the beginning of the school year, they and their friend Lillian are writing a rebus story that they plan to bind as a book and read aloud to all the kindergarten classes. Barbara has misplaced several days' worth of notes and drafts for the story. Faith is very annoyed, Barbara is very defensive, and Lillian is very quiet as the other two criticize each other's attempts to reconstruct the story and write a new draft.

Grammar in Action

As the friends wrangle over what they had written, what they do and say touches on several major issues of language learning and teaching in schools today:

1. The primary role of meaning in talking and writing.
2. The relationship of children's intuitive knowledge of the rules that govern language production—or grammar—and what grammar may mean to students and teachers in the school context.
3. The teaching of talking, writing, and grammar.

Keep these issues in mind as you read this excerpt from a dialogue among the three fifth-graders.

Barbara [*reading*]: "In Lancaster, Wisconsin, a small eight-year-old boy found a lost cat." *Found* is past tense. Is he finding him right now?

Faith: Are we telling the story over again or is it really happening right now?

Barbara: Half the story is in past tense and half the story is present tense.

Faith: I think it's present tense because, see, he says "How long will I have to stay?"

Barbara: How about "While they're gone, Tommy started walking around"?

Faith [*sarcastically*]: Yeah. That's what we put on the draft you lost. [*She makes a face at Lillian in front of Barbara.*]

Barbara [*upset*]: No we didn't. It doesn't matter, Faith. You don't have to look at Lillian that way.

Faith [*to Lillian*]: What do you like, past or present?

Barbara [*aloud to herself*]: She's gonna say present.

Faith: Present tense. Just keep it present tense.
Barbara [*reading*]: "After several weeks of testing, they found out all the names they needed."
Faith: Yeah. They found out all the names.
Barbara: See! You agreed with me! Needed—past. Found—past.
Faith: But . . . we . . . here I think we could say it was present.
Barbara: Well, make up your mind. I like past.
Faith: I like present.
Barbara [*to Lillian*]: Which do you like?
Lillian: I like 'em both.
Barbara: Oh, I hate it! Now she's gonna use majority rules cause she doesn't care. Faith, uh . . . how come you always use majority rules when you want to get your own way?

And so on. A little later:

Barbara: OK, if we use present tense, how am I gonna say "You tripped over him"?
Faith: How's this for a way? "After several weeks . . ."
Barbara: It's kinda . . . indented.
Faith: I know. But don't you remember you were supposed to have proofread that?
Barbara: Just for grammar.
Faith [*giggles sarcastically*]: A paragraph is part of grammar. And I went through it too but now we don't know because you can't find it.
Barbara: There's no time to argue.
Faith [*sarcastically*]: I'm sorry. OK. You can just redo it all again.

And so on. A little later they are adding rebus pictures to the story.

Faith: You're supposed to have pictures where there would be nouns. But some nouns you don't draw a picture. Like an eye for *I*.
Barbara: *I* is a pronoun. And I don't think they would think about an eye.
Faith: No. Not that way. Not that kind of eye.
Barbara: But I would think they would think about *I*.
Lillian: Anybody have any marking pens?
Faith: I don't like the *eye*.
Barbara: Then *you* change it!
Faith: OK! I'll change it!

The girls continue discussing the types of rebus pictures they will use, trying to decide what kindergartners are likely to recognize, what will be most meaningful for them. They decide they need to be careful because "kindergartners are picky about what they see and hear."

Barbara [*reading what she has just written*]: "The cats came back . . . came back . . . came back . . . came back"? Returned. Do you think they know what *return* means?

Faith: Return? Come on, Barbara. They don't know what that means.

Barbara: "Came back." Accidentally.

Faith: Accidentally? Are they going to know what that means? What's another word for accidentally?

Barbara [*laughing*]: Not-on-purposely! "The cats came back not-on-purposely."

Faith [*sighing resignedly*]: Barbara. Please. Tomorrow, will you just bring your work?

Grammar in Proper Perspective

In order to put grammar in a proper perspective in the context of language learning and teaching, we might move from looking at Barbara's and Faith's definitions and descriptions of what they know about grammar, through their reference to grammatical terminology while writing, to the whole range of meanings associated with the word *grammar.*

Both Barbara and Faith can define grammar and list several things they know about it. Both have had many years of instruction in formal rules

Barbara, Lillian, and Faith talk—and argue—about the book they are writing.

of grammar using textbooks and isolated drills, and they have become quite successful at completing such exercises on grammar tests. What is important to note, however, is that Barbara and Faith would be able to talk and write and communicate effectively without knowing how to define grammar, tell what they know about it, or pass tests on it. Like all children, they came to school with an underlying intuitive understanding of the rules that govern language production and provide the means for conveying meaning. What is really important is the role of grammar in the context of language and meaning in school and in the other areas of life.

To illustrate, let us examine what Faith and Barbara are really doing during their discussion and writing session. In arguing over whether to use the present or the past tense, they are really talking about the sense and meaning of the story and the relative effects on the reader of talking about events in the present or the past. Present and past are not the issue. The issue is what they want their story to mean, and the effect of the sense of each sentence on that meaning. In talking about proofreading and paragraphs, they are really talking about organizing their ideas, about the sequence of each chunk of meaning in the story and how it relates to what came before and what came after. In arguing about an *eye* for an *I*, and about nouns and pronouns, they are really talking about the problem of symbolization in writing and the ambiguity of English because of words that sound alike but have different graphic representation and meanings.

The children's main concern is to communicate effectively with their intended audience of kindergarten readers. So that in discussing whether to say *came back* or *return*, or *accidentally* or *not-on-purposely*, they are concerned about using words to say precisely what they mean and composing so that others can comprehend. Even though Faith and Barbara refer frequently to grammar as an issue in their writing, and frequently use grammatical terminology, the real issue is the primary role of meaning in talking and writing.

In teaching talking, writing, and grammar, teachers need to be especially careful not to assume that some of the means we use to talk about language, such as grammatical rules and terms, are ends in themselves. Our ultimate goal is to help children use language to think and learn and make sense as they talk and write and read. The study of grammar is often defined in terms of basic skills such as spelling, punctuation, pronunciation, and organizing writing. In this sense, grammar is often mistakenly seen as anything that seems to need correcting by teachers: less prestigious forms of speech, dialect and language differences, slang, and writing mechanics. We often talk about grammar as something we need to learn and use because something is wrong with our speech or writing. And knowing more about it will offer a remedy.

What, then, *is* grammar really? We need to know the answer to this question before we know what it means to talk about talking, writing, and grammar and what place grammar really has in learning and teaching in a curriculum integrated through the language arts.

What Is Grammar?

Stop for a moment, think, and write down what you think grammar is and what you know about it. While you may have a very firm idea of what grammar is, based on the role of grammar instruction in your own education, it is really quite an elusive and loaded concept with a long history linking it to everything from philosophy, logic, and rhetoric during the time of the Greeks to literature, composition, and usage, in the present day. Few people would agree on any one description. Weaver (1979) gives a partial list of all the things the chameleon word *grammar* has meant to different people, for different purposes, and in different periods of time.

- ***Grammar is sentence structure.***
  Grammar often simply refers to word order, the function of words, and the grammatical endings of words in a language.
- ***Grammar is usage.***
  Socially acceptable and prestigious language usage is often referred to as *good grammar; bad grammar* is defined as the use of language forms and constructions that are not acceptable to many people.
- ***Grammar is description.***
  Many linguists have attempted to describe the syntactic structure of a language; they call this classification a *grammar.*
- ***Grammar is a process.***
  Psycholinguists have attempted to describe how people are able to create and understand sentences in a language; they refer to this process as *grammar.*
- ***Grammar is a set of rules.***
  In education, grammar has often been thought of as a set of rules for teaching students about some combination of the above: sentence structure, correct usage, descriptions of language, and language processes, as well as mechanics, pronunciation, and whatever else teachers have thought would enable students to speak and write "correctly."

Which of these descriptions of the word *grammar* best fits the one you wrote down may depend on your age, the kind of school you went to, the English book you used, and the beliefs of your parents, English teachers, and school administrators regarding the purpose and importance of teaching grammar. Chances are, however, that whatever your definition of grammar is and whatever you know about it, you were definitely taught something called *grammar,* even though what was called grammar may have little to do with why we now believe we should teach it.

Weaver (1979) also describes some of the many reasons people have given, over the centuries of educational thinking and theory, for the great importance that has been placed on teaching something called grammar.

Historical Reasons for Teaching Grammar

The study of grammar is a way to:

- Learn about and understand how to use a language.
- Learn how to learn about other things that require a scientific investigative approach.
- Learn how to think, since language is a reflection of thought.
- Learn how to learn a foreign language more easily.
- Learn to speak and write in a socially acceptable and prestigious way.
- Learn how to become a better listener, speaker, reader, and writer.

The Ineffectiveness of Teaching Grammar

Over many years, researchers (Ebel, 1969; Harris, 1960; Meckel, 1963; Monroe, 1950; Petrosky, 1977) have explored all the above assumptions. The results of the research have consistently failed to support the assumptions. The findings show that the study of grammar does not significantly improve thinking, logic, achievement in a foreign language, recognizing or using more socially prestigious English, or understanding of sentences, or promote improved listening, speaking, reading, understanding of literature, or writing. These studies also do not support the assumption that the study of grammar will help students systematically to learn about and understand other subjects. They also show that students do not even remember aspects of the formal study of grammar very long after it is taught. In fact, in a review of years of research on grammar and writing, Braddock (1963) asserts that "the teaching of formal grammar has a negligible, or, because it usually displaces some instruction and practice in actual composition, even a harmful effect on the improvement of writing" (p. 38).

Why We Persist in Teaching Grammar

If extensive research over a long period of time has failed to support and even suggests a negative effect of the teaching of grammar as a subject, why do we persist in teaching it? Why are students like Barbara and Faith learning formal rules and terminology today? Why is the subject even included in this book? There are many historical, philosophical, and even political reasons that teachers must be aware of and be able to deal with in facing the issue of whether or not they should teach grammar.

- ***Teaching grammar has a long tradition.***

  From the time of the Greeks and Romans who taught rhetoric as a means to analyze and understand poetry and speak effectively in public, to the current generation of parents and teachers who were themselves taught grammar in schools and may have a deeply embedded belief that it was a necessary part of their education, grammar has a long tradition as an essential subject in school.

- ***Teaching grammar is viewed as a basic skill.***

There is a current nationwide concern over teaching and learning what are called **basic skills.** In many people's minds, grammar is traditionally one of those skills and a foundation for proficiency in learning correct language usage, reading, and writing. Again, this view is not supported by research.

- ***Teaching grammar is an integral part of language arts curricula and textbooks.***

In a survey of representative elementary school English textbooks over a sixty-year period, von Bracht Donsky (1984) found three major trends: (1) less emphasis on writing, (2) more emphasis on oral language, and (3) no change for grammar and sentence construction exercises, what she calls "those nineteenth century die-hards... plodding unerringly along, oblivious to changing times... and educational currents" (p. 797).

- ***Teaching grammar lends itself to testing and has therefore been used as a measure for advancement through the educational system.***

It is much easier to test students' knowledge of a formal rule of grammar or the classification of a part of speech than it is to test the level of social prestige of their speech or the quality of their writing. Standardized tests of the former are still used as a measure of student success. The basic conflict here is between what many people believe and what we know from research on teaching grammar and the nature of child and language development. But despite the centuries-long heritage, practice, and even mythology of the importance of the study of grammar, there is a lack of support for this belief in the research and theory of the more recent past.

How Children Really Learn to Use Language

A more realistic view of how children really learn to use language, including socially prestigious forms of speaking, reading, and writing development, suggests an attitude and approach to the study of grammar that takes into account the intuitive knowledge of the underlying grammar of their language which they bring to school. And there is a vast difference between having this underlying knowledge of language and the ability to use that knowledge, on the one hand, and knowing how to formally describe that same language and its structure and its rules for language production and comprehension on the other hand. When children come to school they have a great deal of knowledge of the former, a working knowledge of their knowledge, as it were. They do not, however, have a knowledge of the latter, of how to describe and explain how language works for them in terms that linguists have devised and teachers have described and drilled. The implication of this fact for teaching is that children need to continue to build on their underlying knowledge of language production. This is best done by having them use language to fulfill real needs and purposes as they seek to make meaning through language—as Barbara and Faith and Lillian did, for example, in writing their rebus story book for kindergartners.

Neither theory nor research supports the traditional deductive approach to the formal study of grammar in which students are taught prescriptive rules, terms, and definitions, and then apply these in isolated exercises by diagramming sentences, or by correcting sentences full of errors and citing the rules involved. A great deal of theory and research, however, suggests that children should have many opportunities to use language in meaningful ways to help them gain control over their intuitive understanding and underlying knowledge of the grammar of their language by putting this knowledge to use. Chomsky (1980) explains how children are continually in the process of constructing their own **internal language system:**

> Children of elementary school age are still actively engaged in acquiring their native language. Language development is much slower than during the preschool years and not as noticeable as in the earlier years, but studies show that it continues in much the same manner as with younger children.
>
> School-age children continue to learn new constructions systematically on their own, using the language they hear around them. They are prepared to construct their own internal language system from inputs that come their way and they benefit from exposure to a rich and varied linguistic environment (p. 56).

See Chapter 2, "Featured Preservice Teacher Karen Watkins: A Unit about Language."

This is not to suggest that students should not learn about language as content or as a subject for study. Students may relish experiencing how language is studied, how it works, and how language is related to thinking; they may be interested in the history of a language, the relationships among language families, language differences, dialects, and language change; they may wish to know how the knowledge of a language is really related to listening, speaking, reading and writing that language, and how grammatical terms serve as a way of talking about these things. But these aspects of grammar should not be taught with the assumption that they are a necessary part of reading and writing development or a remedy for problems in speaking, reading, or writing.

We know that classroom teachers rely heavily on texts and that these texts more often reflect cultural trends and public opinion than sound educational theory (Duffy, 1982). And until educational policy falls more in line with educational theory and research, it may be that materials such as these will be seen as a necessary means of preparing students for end-of-the-year tests, which will move them forward to the beginning of the next year, which in turn will prepare them for another end-of-the-year test. Interestingly enough, we know that students who have not studied formal grammar do as well on tests of formal grammar as those who have.

In the face of public concerns and demands, and administrative policies in response to these, teachers should know something about grammar as long as it remains an educational issue. Your decision as to what to do about the issue of teaching grammar should be based on what you know about grammar.

Grammar in Historical and Linguistic Perspective

In light of the nature of the study of grammar as an educational issue, teachers should be aware not only of what grammar is or is not, and what it can or cannot do, but of how different grammarians have described different models for explaining or using language.

The main types of grammar described below have different histories and theoretical frameworks and provide different models for describing language. Teachers should be familiar with these in order to put the teaching of grammar and their knowledge about grammar in the proper perspective. Table 6–1 compares the features of these various types of grammar, including a historical perspective, main characteristics, educational implications, and some terms, rules, and definitions.

Traditional Grammar

Originally, the **traditional grammar** was a prescriptive grammar for teaching English in medieval times. It had its roots in the study of classical languages and has provided a commonly used terminology for talking about language and a tradition of analyzing and describing the grammar of a language. Eventually, however, the traditional grammar became a set of rules for writing English correctly, based on rules which had been developed for writing Latin correctly. The problem is that English is not a Latin language and that Latin categories and terms do not fit English nor accurately describe it.

During the eighteenth century, traditional language scholars classified the parts of English speech in the same way classical languages were classified; these parts of speech are still found in school books today. Both Faith and Barbara include *parts of speech* in their lists of what they know about grammar, and talk about nouns and pronouns as they argue about using a picture of an eye for the word *I* in writing their rebus story.

In the nineteenth century, linguists began to focus on describing how language forms, such as those which had been studied for centuries before, were related to language use.

Structural Grammar

In devising a **structural grammar,** certain linguists attempted to distinguish between spoken and written language and to analyze the patterns unique to English, taking into account language differences among geographical

Table 6–1 *Comparing Grammars*

Traditional Grammar	*Structural Grammar*	*Transformational Grammar*
Grammar as rules for socially correct usage. Originally provided a basic terminology which teachers and students could use to discuss language.	Grammar as a description of how language is used. Looked at different languages and differences among language uses: idiolect, dialect, and other varieties of language forms.	Grammar as a theory of how language is produced. Meaning was tied to a theory of language which gave it explanatory and predictive power and a way to understand language competence and performance.
BUT:	**BUT:**	**BUT:**
The terms and rules are inadequate and inaccurate and cannot explain how language works. Prescribes rather than describes and doesn't take into account language-different learners.	Does not attempt to explain how meaning is related to use in language.	It is difficult to understand and apply rules, which sometimes sound like algebraic equations.
Eight Parts of Speech noun pronoun verb adjective adverb preposition conjunction interjection	***Form Class Words*** Nouns, verbs, adjectives, and adverbs—words that carry most meaning and are inflected or change form. ***Function Words*** Noun determiners, auxiliary verb forms, subordinators, prepositions—words that are important for structural relationships but have little meaning and do not change form.	***Phrase Structure Rules*** *Noun* N → T + N where N = noun and T = determiner. *Noun Phrase* NP Det N Prop N Pronoun where Noun phrase = determiner plus a noun, proper noun, or pronoun. ***Transformational Rules*** Movement, deletion, insertion, and substitution.
Sentence A group of words expressing a complete thought and possessing a subject and a predicate.	***Sentence*** Each sentence is an independent linguistic form, not included by virtue of any grammatical construction in any larger linguistic form.	***Sentence*** S → NP + VP, or where S (sentence) equals NP (noun phrase) plus VP (verb phrase).

regions and social classes, dialects of different groups, and the idiolect of the individual. These linguists provided much information about how language is really used, in nonstandard as well as standard usage, and about the many varieties of language use such as literary, formal, colloquial, and slang. Anthropological interest came into the picture when the structuralists described Native American languages, for example, and through the 1950s, as they sought to give an accurate description of how English was actually spoken. Unlike earlier linguists, however, they did not relate *meaning* to their descriptions because of the imprecise meaning of the term, and they used categories, or form classes, to classify relationships among words rather than the traditional parts of speech.

Barbara's definition, "Grammar is the way that you use words," reflects the structural linguists' orientation. Knowledge about the language differences that the structuralists sought would help her to explore what she meant when she said, "Slang is bad grammar."

Transformational Grammar

Transformational grammar is a recent attempt to describe not only how language is used, but also the psycholinguistic processes at work as we use it. It also makes the most complete attempt to establish the relationship between sound and meaning in a language. Chomsky (1957) and other linguists challenged the structuralist view that left meaning out of descriptions of language, citing as examples such sentences as:

John is eager to please.

and

John is easy to please.

These two sentences cannot be explained without reference to their meaning.

The transformationalists were most interested in the intuitive knowledge that allows speakers, even very young ones, to create, use, and understand sentences that they have never heard before but that are nonetheless grammatical. They maintain that grammar is more than just a description of speech: it should be a description of the process of how language is produced.

In order to explain this relationship between what we know—or *competence*—and what we say—or *performance*—Chomsky described two levels of language:

1. Surface structure, or form: a string of sounds and letters, words, phrases, and clauses.
2. Deep structure, or meaning: the underlying propositions and relationships among them.

The transformationalists were not as interested in defining terms like *sentence* as they were in explaining the relationship between surface structure and deep structure, and the innate *sentence sense* that tells us when a sentence is grammatical and when it is not in our native language.

Transformational grammar is not a set of prescriptive rules of how to speak and write correctly, or simple descriptions of the language, but an attempt to describe how any speaker of any native language is able to produce language. Chomsky says that a grammar should explain how a language user is able to make infinite use of finite means and that the rules should explain why speakers may create and use a sentence they have never heard before, and others, who may never have heard it either, will understand it. Even very young children are able to do this because they have internalized these rules. Furthermore, even though they learn much about language through imitation, the process they draw on to use language is innate.

Transformationalists explain that a native speaker understands certain basic or kernel sentences: simple declarative sentences in the active voice. These sentences can be transformed by certain phrase structure rules so that the speaker can generate an infinite variety of different and more complicated sentences. Instead of conventional sentence diagrams, transformational grammar uses a tree or branching diagram which can show the pattern common to all sentences with similar syntactic structures (see Figure 6–1).

The Role of Grammar in the Classroom

What does this theory, research, and history about grammar tell us about teaching grammar in the classroom today, especially in light of what we know about how children learn to use language and use language to learn?

We have seen that the formal teaching of grammar is not an effective way to help children improve talking, usage, or writing quality and that, in fact, the time spent teaching grammar may have a negative effect on language learning since it deprives students of some of the time they might use on tasks that would improve language development. But if not grammar, what then? What experiences will help children grow in language fluency, flexibility, elaboration, and control over more and more complex

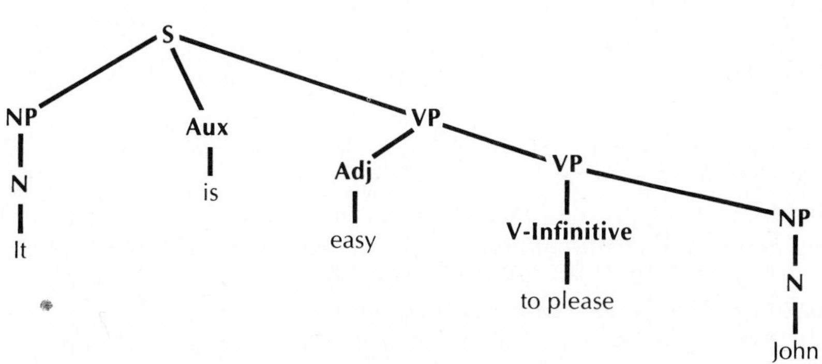

Figure 6–1
Tree Diagram

grammatical structures? What are Barbara and Faith doing in their discussion that really might affect the development of their talking, writing, and knowledge of grammar?

The things they were doing that might really make a difference occur naturally in real language experiences: finding an interest, focusing on meaning, solving a problem, interacting, arguing, playing with language, reading, writing, rewriting, and talking about language. Their experiences were focused on meaning. Their concern was not really whether or not they wrote the story in the past or present tense—a thinly disguised excuse for expressing their anger at each other, anyway—but for saying what they wanted to say the way they wanted to say it to the audience they wanted to say it to. And their teacher supported them in this effort.

The following section on "Teaching Children" describes several strategies that teachers can use to support, encourage, and help children to use language to say what they mean and develop control over their understanding and use of talking, writing, and grammar:

- talking and interacting with others
- playing with words, sentences, and sense
- listening to literature
- revising writing
- heightening awareness of language

Teaching Children

If the grammar of a language is really the underlying knowledge children draw on as they grow in their use of language, then this grammatical knowledge will grow as children actively use language. Barbara and Faith are both able to give definitions of grammar and list quite a few things they know about it. They also use grammatical terms and references to grammar as they revise their writing. What drives their talking and writing, however, are their own interest, ideas, ability, and desire to use language as they practice it in the context of real speaking and real writing for a real purpose and with a real audience in mind.

Barbara and Faith have had instruction in two approaches to learning to use language. Their school is partly departmentalized and two teachers teach language arts in the fifth grade. One of the teachers, Phyllis Fuglaar, individualizes instruction, encourages interaction, and integrates the language arts with the content areas. It was in her class that Barbara and Faith were wrangling over their story revision before writing a final copy and publishing and presenting it as a book to the kindergarten classes.

The second teacher uses a whole-class textbook method to teach formal rules of grammar and grammar terminology, and has the children practice drills and exercises in isolation. This is not unusual, and both approaches may even be used in the same class by the same teacher. What is unusual is that this kind of curricular division and the second teacher's approach to language learning still exists in light of the years of research and practical advice which tell us that this formal approach to grammar does not help children to use language more effectively, or in fact even to understand or cite the formal rules of grammar more efficiently.

If the teaching of formal grammar does not improve writing nor even ensure a knowledge of formal grammar, then what should teachers do instead? In addition to the kind of extensive time spent on talking and writing in Phyllis Fuglaar's class, and language interaction, individualization, and integration with the content areas, here are some strategies and approaches which will provide children with many opportunities to focus on language in use rather than mere language usage, and become involved in active, child-centered language experiences.

Talking and Interacting with Others

Rich experiences with oral language are essential if children are to continue to expand their growing ability to use language fluently and flexibly and to understand how language works. Such experiences can be planned or they may occur spontaneously, but they should all emerge from real experiences that children share as they interact with each other.

For example, Faith and Barbara are putting language to work for their own purposes as they argue over writing. Each is doing her best to convey her ideas, to develop the meaning that is most important to her, and—what is perhaps most significant—to assert herself as the two friends carefully and forcefully express their ideas to each other. And not only do they use words and sentences and organized arguments, but they emphasize these with inflection and facial expressions and gestures registering everything from disdain to dislike to disgust, as they hone their meaning in writing.

Not every small-group discussion or writing session will produce such an authentic exchange between students. They may not care about what they are writing or whether anybody lost a paper. They may not even care whether they write or not. That is why it is important first to engage their feelings to help them generate ideas and words and phrases and sentences in their search for meaning as they continue to learn how to use language for their own purposes. Here are some means for achieving and encouraging this involvement, which can be used as real needs and real occasions arise.

Talking with Each Other

Children need plenty of opportunities to have authentic exchanges with each other on issues and subjects that interest them. Small-group discussions in the context of solving a problem—for example, a class election, a science experiment, or a drama production—are an ideal means to do this.

Arguing with Each Other

Issues often arise that can lead to arguments: whose pencil? whose turn? who's right? or who's in charge? Let the children present their ideas, work them through together, and settle their own arguments through discussion.

Debating with Each Other

Some discussions can be planned to take place either between two children or in a panel group. Various formats are possible: point/counterpoint; panel discussions; debates. The discussions may be tied to content areas, for example, in the form of a debate between Colonist and a Loyalist.

Dramatizing with Each Other

See Chapter 10, Drama in the Classroom.

Arguments, debates, and other kinds of exchanges which require that children use language carefully, forcefully, and creatively can be dramatized through role-playing, improvisational characterizations, and curriculum drama.

Playing Games with Words, Sentences, and Sense

Children learn to use language fluently and flexibly and expand their repertoire of syntactic structures by using language in spontaneous and creative ways. For example, Barbara is playing—and annoying Faith—when she makes up the word *not-on-purposely* as a synonym for *accidentally*. These are the kinds of games children play with language anyway as they flex the muscle of their growing power over language.

See *Word Play and Language Learning for Children,* by Linda Gibson Geller (National Council of Teachers of English, 1985).

In addition to recognizing and encouraging children's spontaneous word play and understanding its relationship to language learning, there are approaches you can suggest they try as they use words and expand them in playing with sentences and sense. These approaches can be part of a repertoire of games and strategies you can draw on as the occasion arises. They may also become part of center activities after being introduced to a group or class. Children will undoubtedly also create variations of their own. The following games may be played by a whole class, a small group, or one child alone, and adapted for different grade levels.

Getting Games Started

Collecting Words. First you need some words. You can generate a word wall on the chalkboard or chart paper for the whole class or a group, or older children can brainstorm their own words on paper. In either case, though, the words should come from the children's own experiences and images, and may relate to recent and specific experiences at home, in school, or in the world.

Debating issues is an excellent teaching strategy to support students' growing control over their language.

The words may be related to more general ideas:

words for Monday . . . or Friday
words for wind . . . or rain

They may be words that express personal feelings:

happy, sad, mad, excited, bored

Or they may be words that elicit feelings:

pretty, frightening, strong, weak, weird,
ugly, beautiful, soothing, musical, harsh, funny

They may also be part of someone's own personal list of words. Children often have a list of special words they save and savor—or detest. Over the years, my son Wyatt has kept a growing list of the latter, including *nougat, pork, snorkel,* and *yawn,* which he says "may be the most mindless word in the world." He does not know why he dislikes them, but children understand that words are connected to feelings, negative as well as positive. Ask students to think about, collect, and share their own special words:

My Special Best Words, by John Steptoe (Viking, 1974), is a picture book about a family's personal language, including bathroom words.

favorite . . . or disliked words
comfortable . . . or strange words
words I used to think meant something else . . . but now I know better

Classifying Words. Several of the examples of ways to generate words are based on suggesting simple two-category classifications, often a contrast (*favorite/disliked*). You can expand this idea and use classification as a reflection of content. For example:

Frederick, by Leo Leonni (Pantheon, 1967), is a picture book about a mouse who collects images and words while the other mice are storing food for winter. When the food is gone, he cheers them with a poem about the seasons.

1. ***The Four Seasons***

   The seasons—spring, summer, fall, and winter—are a classification students are familiar with.

2. ***The Senses***

   The senses suggest another simple classification system. Here is an example of a triante pattern, using the senses as a basis for classifying words, on the topic of the seasons.

Triante Pattern	***Third-Grade Triante***
Line 1: 1 word (title)	*Spring*
Line 2: 2 words (smells)	*Fresh Sweet*
Line 3: 3 words (touch)	*Warm Soft Wet*
Line 4: 4 words (sight)	*Green Colorful Sunny Lively*
Line 5: 5 words (sounds)	*Singing Laughing Whispering Gurgling Buzz*
(Lines 2–5 refer to title.)	

3. ***Word Function***

   The classification of words can also reflect word function. As described in "Making Connections," there have been many ways in which linguists have created categories to classify words. Some were tied to Latin, others to function, and still others to meaning. The names and terms for these categories can be taught to children and the overlap and relationship between them discussed. For example, younger children can find words for naming, describing, and action. For older children, you would call these same categories nouns, adjectives, and verbs. What is important is that children understand that a name by any other name is still a way to think about word meaning and use.

See Chapter 2, "Language Patterns for Writing."

4. ***Word Patterns***

   There are also simple writing patterns which use and expand on the classifications of words with names from traditional grammar.

"Alphabet Pyramid" Pattern	***Example by Second-Graders***
noun	*Superman*
adj. noun	*Strong Superman*
adj. noun verb	*Strong Superman showing off*
adj. noun verb adverb	*Strong Superman showing off superbly*

"My Hands, My Feet" Pattern

Choose the name of something that can do an action, such as hands or feet, and write some of the many action words that are possible. Here are two examples by first-graders:

My hands like to:
squeeze a mop
mess with slop
do the dishes
scoop up fishes

My feet like to:
walk on floors
go through doors
step on bugs
play on rugs

"You Are Too . . ." Pattern

Children can describe things that they are too large, too small, or just the right size to do. Here are three examples by second-graders:

George Shrinks, by William Joyce (Harper & Row, 1986), is a picture book about a child who shrinks to a few inches.

You are too large to do some things like:
fit into a mouse house
swim in a fish bowl
live in a bird cage

You are too small to do some things like:
fly to the moon
lift a whale
eat a watermelon whole

You are just right to do some things like:
climb upstairs
swing up high in a swing
sit in chairs

"Do What, When, and Where" Pattern

Name some living things and list what kinds of things they do (verbs) and where or when they do it (adverbial phrases). Here are four examples by third-graders:

Snakes crawl,
Down the hall.

Kittens sleep.
While I eat.

Witches zoom.
On their brooms.

Bats soar.
Outside my door.

"What Next?" Pattern

Choose a noun and find three adjectives that start with the same letter.

cold, clammy, creepy cave
dark, damp, dreary dungeon
sticky, slimy, slippery swamp

"Concentric Circle" Pattern

One noun, three adjectives, and five verbs are written in a spiral. Or the shape can coincide with the subject's shape. An example by fourth-graders is shown in Figure 6–2.

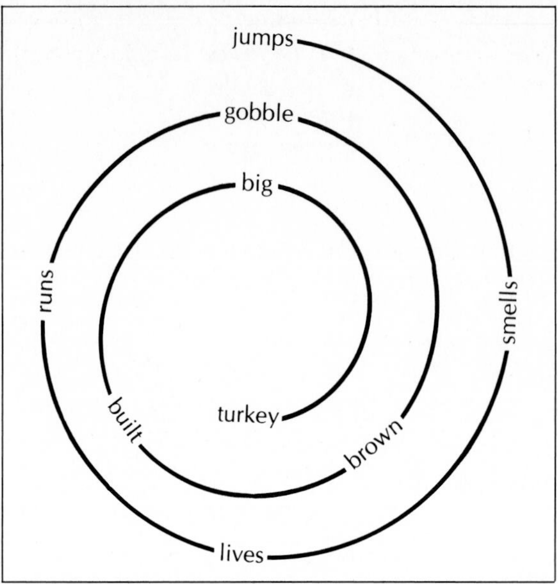

Figure 6–2
"Concentric Circle" Pattern

"Diamante" Pattern

Traditionally, diamante patterns shift from one subject to an opposite in meaning in the fourth line but this is not strictly necessary, as shown here in this example by a seventh-grade remedial reading student:

Pattern	***My Bike***
Line 1: noun	*Tube*
Line 2: adj., adj.	*Black, rubber*
Line 3: verb, verb, verb	*Turning, squeaking, fixing*
*Line 4: noun, noun / noun, noun**	*Wheel, handlebars, chain, pedals*
Line 5: verb, verb, verb	*Crashing, bounding, smashing*
Line 6: adj., adj.	*Broken, bent*
Line 7: noun	*Bike*

*Shift to opposite subject, if used

Combining Words. Children can combine two-word phrases and expand them to form three- and four-word phrases. Here are some examples by third-graders describing animals, using the same letter of the alphabet.

angry alligator
boisterous bear
angry alligator acting ambidextrously
boisterous bear bothering badly

You can proceed geometrically from these short phrases, combining phrases to create sentences. These same students used their short phrases to create an animal alphabet:

A is for the angry alligator acting ambidextrously.
B is for the boisterous bear bothering badly.
C is for the carnivorous cougar catching constantly.
D is for the dangerous dinosaur digging dilligently.

And so on, right up to:

Z is for the zealous zebra zigzagging zestfully.

It usually takes little effort to encourage children to play with words. Here are some specific activities which may themselves be combined, modified, and expanded in many ways that you and your students can think up.

"Name Sentences"

Choose a name or a special word and use its letters in sequence to start each word of a sentence. For variation, use a theme: an advertisement, a slogan, a newspaper headline, or a song, book, or movie title.

"ABC Sentences"

Each line of words must begin with the next letter in a series of the alphabet. Here are two examples written by second-graders:

Doughnuts eaten frantically give heartburn.
Jumping kangaroos land merrily near open pouches.

"Alphabetall Sentences"

Challenge the children to write a sentence using all the letters of the alphabet. Try different criteria: shortest, longest, or sentence with fewest repeated letters. Suggest that they make up their own rules about using letters in the course of the game.

"Newspaper Cut-Up Sentences"

Look for interesting words in the newspaper. Cut them out and arrange in sentences. Variations on this theme include ransom notes, nonsense recipes, hidden messages, and two-word phrases.

"Mad Libs"

This is an adaptation of a commercial word game consisting of a series of partially completed stories, one to a page. One child asks another for words, identified only by the part of speech, to fill in the blanks in the story. The first child writes down the words that the second child suggests, and then both read the result: a grammatically correct but often ridiculous or even hilarious nonsense story.

You could create these stories with words missing, or have children create their own by writing a story and deleting certain words.

"New Worlds in Old Tales"

Children can rewrite familiar nursery rhymes or folk and fairy tales with different words and with a different theme.

"Story Frames"

Even very young children have learned to understand and use the conventional structure of stories including formal openings, formal closings, and the past tense. The children can brainstorm examples of these and write them on separate file cards that can be classified and kept in separate envelopes. Then the children can choose from the envelopes and construct nonsense stories with correct story structure. Here are some examples of parts of a story structure.

Openings:
- Once upon a time . . .
- Long, long ago . . .
- In a galaxy far, far away . . .

Characters:
- a poor woodcutter
- a wicked witch
- a young starfighter pilot

Problems:
- . . . didn't have enough food for his children . . .
- . . . hated a beautiful young princess . . .
- . . . set out to explore space . . .

Closings:
- . . . and they lived happily ever after.
- . . . and was never seen again in those parts.
- . . . and saved the Federation.

"Story Sequence Puzzle"

This is a technique used by reading specialist Phyllis Crawford. After a read-aloud story or a storytelling session, the children discuss the sequence of events in the story and dictate them to the teacher. (This can also be done during an individualized reading conference.) The teacher copies the story onto a piece of poster board and a child illustrates the other side with a scene from the story. The teacher then cuts up the board into rectangles to form a puzzle. When the puzzle is assembled with the story in the correct sequence, and flipped over, the picture on the other side will be correct. Figure 6–3 shows an example, using the story *The Three Bears.*

The Three Bears, by Paul Galdone (Seabury, 1972)

Mother Bear made porridge for breakfast.	Goldilocks broke Baby Bear's chair.
The bears went for a walk.	Goldilocks tried the beds and fell fast asleep.
Goldilocks entered the cottage of the Three Bears.	The bears frightened Goldilocks.
Goldilocks ate the porridge all up.	Goldilocks ran away.

Figure 6–3
Story Sequence Puzzle

Sentence Sense

Sentence Combining. Sentence combining is a technique used to increase syntactic maturity by combining kernel sentences, the simplest statement of ideas, to form more complex sentences.

Antecedents to Sentence Combining. There are three important antecedents to the technique of combining sentences.

1. ***The model of transformational grammar (Chomsky, 1957).***
   "To understand a sentence, it is necessary to reconstruct its representation on each level, including the transformational level where the kernel sentences underlying a given sentence can be thought of, in a sense, as the 'elementary content elements' out of which this sentence is constructed" (pp. 107–108).

2. ***A definition of syntactic maturity (Hunt, 1965).***
   Hunt created a definition of syntactic maturity which he measured by T-units. A *T-unit* is a "minimal terminable unit," or a main clause plus all modifiers. Hunt's research shows that as students mature their written language moves in the direction of more complex patterns.

3. ***A study of sentence combining exercises (Mellon, 1969).***
   Mellon did a study using sentence combining exercises, based on a model of transformational grammar, which showed student gains in writing maturity and quality. Results of the research on sentence combining and its

effects on writing maturity, quality, and reading comprehension have not been consistent, however. Dudley (1983) and the National Council of Teachers of English have identified it as an area in which more research is needed.

See *Creative Approaches to Sentence Combining,* by William Strong (National Council of Teachers of English, 1986). "Playful attention to language" is the key to language learning according to this author who provides twenty creative sentence-combining activities which can be photocopied for classroom use.

Approaches to Sentence Combining Practice. Materials for sentence combining practice are available commercially, and can also be found in many language arts texts (see Figure 6–4). But children themselves can also practice strategies of sentence combining, changing, and expanding using their own words, phrases, sentences, and ideas. This is what Faith and Barbara were doing when they worked together with Lillian to revise their writing, combining, adding to, expanding, moving parts, and changing their sentences. The word and sentence games described above are also ways of combining sentences that are more meaningful than practicing with someone else's ideas and language.

The Five Basic Sentence Patterns. Some of the more common basic **sentence pattern** practices can be used in the same way as described for playing word and sentence games: collecting, classifying, and combining words and sentences into longer discourse. Listed below are the five basic patterns and three types of transformations (Malmstrom, 1968) that can change them into an infinite number of sentences. Children already use the basic patterns when they come to school (Hunt, 1965; Loban, 1976) but they need practice in transforming them. They get this practice by playing with language and talking and writing. Teachers should make the children aware of the basic patterns and transformations during writing conferences and encourage the children to develop facility with language structures through interaction in real contexts. The five basic patterns are shown here, illustrated with examples from the drafts of Barbara, Faith, and Lillian's story, *The Mysterious Cat.*

1. ***Noun Phrase/Subject* + *Intransitive Verb* + *Adverb***
(does not take obj.) (optional)

Monster toys come alive on Mardi Gras.
A glowing cat appears.

2. ***Noun Phrase/Subject* + *Transitive Verb* + *Noun Phrase/Direct Object***
(takes direct obj.)
+ ***Adverb***
(optional)

Tommy finds a stray cat that came from a fight in the street. It drills a hole in the ground.

Exercises Combining Sentences

A. Join the following pairs of sentences by following the directions in parentheses.

1. Penny brought records. Ted brought a record player. (Join with **, and**.)
2. The team must arrive on time. They will forfeit the game. (Join with **, or**.)
3. The bus was ready to leave. Half the team wasn't on board. (Join with **, but**.)
4. The jar of strawberry jelly was open. A spoon lay nearby. (Join with **, and**.)
5. Liz heard a cat. She couldn't see it. (Join with **, but**.)

B. Join the related parts of the sentences in each pair. Follow the directions. Leave out the words in italics.

1. Carl bought tickets. Dot *bought tickets*. (Join with **and**.)
2. You may use tempera paints. *You may use* finger paints. (Join with **or**.)
3. The players were tired. *However, they were* happy. (Join with **but**.)
4. Gordon clapped. *He* cheered. (Join with **and**.)
5. The puppy chewed my shoes. *It chewed* Linda's wallet. (Join with **and**.)

Figure 6–4 *Sentence Combining Practice*

From *Building English Skills,* Silver Level. Copyright 1984. McDougal, Littell & Company, Evanston, Ill. Used with permission.

3. ***Noun Phrase/Subject*** + ***Transitive Verb*** + ***Noun Phrase/Indirect Object*** (can insert *to* or *for*) + ***Noun Phrase/Direct Object*** + ***Adverb*** (optional)

Tommy takes care of the cat.

4. ***Noun Phrase/Subject*** + ***Linking Verb*** + ***Noun Phrase/Predicate Noun*** (forms of *to be,* etc.) (follows a linking verb = NP/Subject) + ***Adverb*** (optional)

So they turn into hedgehogs!

5. ***Noun Phrase/Subject*** + ***Linking Verb*** + ***Adjective/Predicate Adjective*** (substitute for subject) + ***Adverb*** (optional)

It is lonely where we live.

While children already know and use these basic patterns when they come to school, they are still learning to transform these sentences into more elaborate, expanded, complex sentence structures. Much of what has already been described in this chapter, and in other chapters, about children interacting, talking, writing, listening and responding to literature, and playing with language will develop this facility in a natural way when children use language for their own needs and purposes. Teachers should be aware of and encourage the ways in which these sentence structures can be transformed.

Basic Types of Sentence Transformations. Here are three types of **sentence transformations** (Malstrom, 1968):

1. *Changes,* or turning one type of sentence into another type such as a question, a negation, a sentence in the passive voice, or an elliptical sentence (which leaves out everything that is not understood by the context).
2. *Combining,* or putting together several sentences into a compound sentence.
3. *Reducing,* or changing some sentences into smaller parts and inserting them into or combining them with other sentences.

Literature As a Model for Language

The language of literature ringing and singing in children's ears will affect not only the kind of language they appreciate and understand and enjoy but also the kind they use. Chomsky (1972) found that the knowledge of complex language structures varies greatly among children from six to ten and that this knowledge is not necessarily related to age. The children in her study who developed greater facility with language structures sooner were those who had had more exposure to the language of books, both those they had read aloud to them and those they read themselves.

Teachers can support their students' growing acquisition of syntactic structures and use of words by reading aloud, and they should do this frequently and from a range of many different types of books. Literature provides a model of language as children listen and then actively respond as they think, talk, dramatize, draw, read, and write.

Some language will be heard or read and remembered from relatively unacclaimed sources. When writing about a cemetery at Halloween, Faith comes up with the word *blood-curdling* in a brainstorming session with Barbara, and then sheepishly confides to her that she found it in a less-than-literary but ever-popular Nancy Drew book.

It is important to remember, too, that writers for children do not necessarily limit their ideas or art or vocabulary, including those who write and illustrate for younger children, and even those who write what are called *I Can Read* books. Crosby Bonsall, author and illustrator of *The Case of the Hungry Stranger* and other adventures of four members of a Private Eyes Club, explains in a recent interview (Cox, 1985):

> I do not use a word list. . . . It has to sing and it has to be alive, because you're trying to get a child hooked on reading. My task is to polish and make every line as rhymthical and as good as I can because I'm writing economically. Therefore, I care that my words have some lilt. You may use repetition in an *I Can Read* book without repeating a phrase at all. Sometimes it's fine if you have a really good working phrase like " 'Beans,' said Homer," in *I'm Not a Pest.*

Picture books by Crosby Bonsall: *The Case of the Double Cross* (Harper & Row, 1980); *And I Mean It, Stanley* (Harper & Row, 1974); *Mine's the Best* (Harper & Row, 1973); *It's Mine* (Harper & Row, 1964).

Language Style in Children's Books

Wonderful words and language abound in children's books. For example, there are the sleek but deeply embedded sentence structures in Beatrix Potter's classic, *Peter Rabbit.*

Peter Rabbit, by Beatrix Potter (Warne, n.d.)

Listening to literature read aloud is another strategy to support children's growing acquisition of syntactic structures and use of words.

Once upon a time there were four little Rabbits, and their names were—Flopsy, Mopsy, Cotton-tail, and Peter. They lived with their Mother in a sand-bank, underneath the root of a very big fir-tree.

"Now, my dears," said old Mrs. Rabbit one morning, "you may go into the fields or down the lane, but don't go into Mr. McGregor's garden: your Father had an accident there; he was put in a pie by Mrs. McGregor."

Amos and Boris, by William Steig (Puffin, 1983).

And there is William Steig's way with descriptive words in *Amos and Boris,* a picture book about a friendship between a mouse and a whale:

Boris admired the delicacy, the quivering daintiness, the light touch, the small voice, the gemlike radiance of the mouse. Amos admired the bulk, the grandeur, the power, the purpose, the rich voice, and the abounding friendliness of the whale.

Charlotte's Web, by E. B. White (Harper & Row, 1952); *A Wrinkle in Time,* by Madeleine L'Engle (Farrar, Straus, 1962); *The Eyes of the Amaryllis,* by Natalie Babbitt (Farrar, Straus, 1972); *The Girl Who Loved Wild Horses,* by Paul Goble (Bradbury, 1978)

See Chapter 8, "Children's Choices."

Children should hear the style of E. B. White's language in *Charlotte's Web* and Madeleine L'Engle's use of figurative language in *A Wrinkle in Time.* Or the imagery of Natalie Babbitt in *The Eyes of the Amaryllis:*

The beaming sea lay far out, at low tide, much as it had the afternoon before, and it sparkled in the early sunshine, flicking tiny, blinding flashes of light into the air. The horizon, impossibly far away, invited her. This was a mermaid morning—a morning for sitting on the rocks and combing your long red hair.

Children's Awareness of Language

Children are aware of an author's use of language and cited it often as a reason why they liked Paul Goble's *The Girl Who Loved Wild Horses,* a Children's Choice selection. What they admire is Goble's use of descriptive language, imagery, and similes in passages like this:

The horses galloped faster and faster, pursued by thunder and lightning. They swept like a brown flood across hills and through valleys. Fear drove them on, leaving their familiar grazing grounds far behind.

Repeated Patterns in Children's Literature

See Chapter 1, "Predictable Pattern Books."

Many traditional rhymes, songs, stories, and books use sentence patterns which repeat throughout the text. Exposure to such patterns through listening and reading, and then responding through chanting along as the teacher reads, through drama, or through writing similar patterns afterwards, is a powerful means of promoting facility with different grammatical forms and appropriate language usage.

Here are two types of patterns, with examples of books that use a structure of repetition.

1. ***Sentences and sentence patterns repeated in a repeated plot.***

   A familiar example is the Scandinavian folktale, *The Three Billy Goats Gruff.* The character of the Billy Goat is repeated in three sizes, and each repeats the dialogue of the others in three encounters with a troll. Here is the dialogue as written by Marcia Brown in her version of the tale:

> "Who's that tripping over my bridge?" roared the troll.
> "Oh, it is only I, the tiniest Billy Goat Gruff, and I'm going up to the hillside to make myself fat," said the billy goat with such a small voice.
> "Now I'm coming to gobble you up!" said the troll.

This is an excellent story for listening, chanting along, and especially for dramatizing and repeating the dialogue of the billy goats and the troll.

Other stories with a pattern include *The Three Little Pigs, The Three Bears,* and *The Little Red Hen.* Some picture book variations of *The Little Red Hen* are by Paul Galdone (Houghton Mifflin, 1973), Janina Domanska (Macmillan, 1973), and Margot Zemach (Farrar, Straus & Giroux, 1983).

2. ***Sentence patterns repeated in a cumulative plot.***

Other books use cumulative plots in which characters, objects, and actions are introduced and then added on to previous ones as the story unfolds. A classic example is *The House that Jack Built.* Here are the first three lines of such a story written by first-grade children:

> *This is the school that we learn in.*
> *These are the children that go to the school that we learn in.*
> *This is the book that is read by the children that go to the school that we learn in.*

Revising Writing

Children really put their underlying knowledge of the grammar of a language to work when they write. As they begin, they are in the process of organizing ideas, choosing words, constructing sentences, and making sense. **Revision** occurs at all stages of writing and reflects the use of fluency and flexibility and elaboration that children are learning to control.

Stages in the Revision of a Story

Faith, Barbara, and Lillian work through several drafts of their story, as described in the section on Centering Ideas. Over a period of several weeks, they refer back to previous drafts (except for the one Barbara lost) and number their drafts to keep track of them. A closer look at some of these drafts will suggest many ideas for helping children to gain power over their use of written language and will make it clear that children need many opportunities to write and talk about their writing. They also need encouragement, and especially time, to use what they already know how to do with language in order to expand their facility with language structures. Time for talking and revising writing is not *practice* for learning how to master language usage, it actually *is* language in use.

- ***Session 1. Generating topics.***

During the first of several sessions of writing a rebus story for the kindergarten classes in their school, Faith, Barbara, and Lillian talk, interact, doodle, draw, write, rewrite, and reject several topics, words, and names for characters. As you examine their notes in Figure 6–5, think about the process they are going through. They cross out many rejected ideas: monster toy comes alive on (Mardi Gras) Easter; Mary gets stuffed by monster for Easter. Combining some of the remaining ideas, they create new choices, and finally settle on: Tommy finds stray cat; Tommy takes care of cat.

- ***Session 2. Expanding and elaborating ideas.***
  During this session, the three girls revise as they write, making decisions as they go along and leaving their options open (see Figure 6–6).

- ***Session 3. Moving sentences and leaving blanks for future ideas.***
  Now the girls begin to write dialogue for their characters rather than

Figure 6–5
Session 1: Generating Topics

Tommy tan or beige
Joh
"When g i-r-l-/boy cat named Alexander
puts on tee shirt
a glowing cat appears on-shirt-and-finds-out and comes Cat back off shirt and starts
They
to take to girl/boy john ¶ Alexander sa sent me here for help. We need a "human to
Tommy
tests
do experiements on, so that we can become more like humans Because It is lonely,
where on
we live because there are very few of us."

Figure 6–6 *Session 2: Expanding and Elaborating Ideas*

just a narrative of what is happening to them as they did in Session 2. They are also moving whole sentences around within the text:

> *"I don't know how long the tests will take."*
> *"How long will I have to stay?"*
> *"Let me think about it."*

At a juncture where they are not sure where the story is going next, they leave a space and a note to themselves with possible options for next time (see Figure 6–7).

- ***Sessions 4 and 5. More generating, expanding, combining, changing, moving, and leaving blanks.***

These two sessions are periods of intense writing with pauses and breaks where ideas seem to stop, followed by another whole idea-

"After several weeks of testing they make-an-important found
all
out what they needed to know "

fill blank space

Faith

stray-cats
humans become successful LAST
something else

suggestions

Figure 6–7 *Session 3: Moving Sentences and Leaving Blanks for Future Ideas*

generating period during which time they come up with a recipe for a magical mixture:

bat's blood
flies
fingernails
toes
eyeballs
numb
water

- ***Session 6. Reconstruction.***

This is the period described in Centering Ideas, when the three girls try to reconstruct their last draft.

- ***Sessions 7 to 9. Reworking a completed draft.***

Each of the girls writes a complete working draft at home, and then they work together in school to refine their ideas. They change some things, fill in blanks, change some more, and finally produce a final draft.

- ***Session 10. Final proofreading.***

These students are not following a simple linear process of producing an idea, writing a draft, and then correcting it for spelling, neatness of handwriting, punctuation, and paragraph form at the very end. Instead, these functions are recursive: they are occurring at the same time—except, perhaps, for neatness of handwriting!—throughout the writing process.

What is important here is the children's drive to create meaning, and it is this drive that determines the relative importance of conventions at each stage of writing and revising. Furthermore, it is these students' intuitive and underlying knowledge of grammar that enables them to understand not only how to express ideas in English, but also to know that handwriting, spelling, and punctuation are not as important, that they are only surface features of that underlying knowledge.

This is not to suggest that these students and their teacher do not care about these conventions. But they care about them only at the point when they become important to the meaning of the story, when it comes time to share a draft with another writer, and most of all when they prepare to publish their writing as a book for kindergarten students.

- ***Sessions 11 and 12. Publishing the story.***

During these two sessions, the girls plan their book, breaking it up into logical chunks for the book layout, copying it over in large neat print, and adding illustrations for the rebus story where pictures replace certain words. The final step is binding the story into a book.

See Chapter 5, "Bookmaking."

- ***Session 13. Sharing published writing.***

The three young authors read their book to all the kindergarten classes and present it to the kindergarten teachers to place in their class library.

The Importance of Revising

The above example shows the importance of allowing children to have many opportunities and plenty of time and support to generate, expand, elaborate, change, leave blanks, choose, and play with ideas, words, and sentences. It also shows that teachers should let children know that having a lot of ideas is better than having just a few, that they have options and can expand and elaborate on these, that they can leave blanks and make changes; in short, that they have choices. All these are things that language users do when they use language to make meaning, and you should make it clear to your students that they have the power to do so themselves. They know their language and they know how to use it—and they *should* use it.

Heightening Awareness of Language

The experiences described below focus specifically on language as something to learn about for its own sake, something real and alive, something with exciting differences, something with a history as old as the history of humankind.

Listening to the Sounds of Language

Children can listen to tapes and recordings of **language varieties:** literary, historical, regional, or languages other than English. Examples include poets reading their own works, folktales from American regions or other countries, or some of the many recordings of Shakespeare. An excellent source of these is *The Sounds of English: A Bibliography of Language Recordings.* Categories of recordings include:

history of the English language
historical periods of English (Old, Middle, and Early Modern English)
American English
modern non-American dialects
voices of notable Americans
authors reading their own works
regional music

An example of one of the recordings listed is "As If: Poems Selected and Read by John Ciardi."

"As If: Poems Selected and Read by John Ciardi" (Folkways Records)

Appreciating Language Differences

Children can compare their own idiolect and dialect with those of others in their classroom, and their own language with that of their parents, grandparents, and others in the community. They can listen to some of these differences on recordings and note them in the media. Many children's books written in another dialect or language are also available, for example:

Spanish: *Tortillitas para Mama: And Other Spanish Nursery Rhymes,* by Margot C. Griego et al. (Holt, 1981)
French: *Mother Goose in French,* by Barbara Cooney (Crowell, 1964)
West African: *Why Mosquitoes Buzz in People's Ears: A West African Tale,* by Verna Aardema (Dial, 1975)
Quaker: *Thy Friend Obadiah,* by Brian Turkle (Penguin, 1972)
Appalachian: *Did You Carry the Flag Today, Charlie?* by Rebecca Caudill (Holt, Rinehart & Winston, 1971) and *Jim and the Wonder Beans,* by James Still (Putnam, 1977)
Black: *Stevie,* by John Steptoe (Harper & Row, 1986)

See Chapter 2, "Learning about Language."

See "The Origin of Words: A Unit of Study," by Judi Lesiak, in *Language Arts,* 55 (1978), 317–319 for ways in which students can investigate language.

Compiling Language

A very simple way to make children more aware of the nature and varieties of language uses and users is to have them keep a word journal in which they can collect and compare special words, phrases, and expressions. Sources for this kind of collection are everywhere: books, movies, parents, grandparents, friends, songs, rhymes, and so forth.

Assessing Children's Talking, Writing, and Use of Grammar

While there are many standardized tests of the knowledge of formal grammar that claim to be able to measure a child's understanding and use of language structures, what can be more useful to classroom teachers are their own observations in measuring and assessing how well children are developing their speaking, reading, and writing abilities and in learning more about their knowledge of the underlying grammar of their language (Gunderson, 1980). Here is an adaptation of an informal evaluation system based on questions teachers ask themselves to guide their observations of children (Lilja, 1980).*

- *Awareness.* Does the child demonstrate awareness of language as a method of communication for specific purposes tied to meaning?

- *Spontaneous use.* Does the child demonstrate security with language use by freely participating in language activities and showing spontaneity of usage? (Eager handraising and loud sounds of "Ooh-ooh-ooh, Teacher!" demonstrate this.)

- *Using nonverbal signals or body language.* Does the child rely on signals—pointing, head movement, hand symbols—rather than words to communicate meaning?

- *Using baby talk.* Does the child use obvious baby or family talk in speech patterns, word choice, pronunciation, or sentence structure?

*Adapted from Linnea D. Lilja, "Measuring the Effectiveness of Language Education," in Gay Su Pinnell (Ed.), *Discovering Language with Children* (Urbana, IL: NCTE, 1980), pp. 105–108.

• *Using a dialect or regional language.* Does the child use dialect or regional usage to the point where communication with others is inhibited? (Be careful not to assume that because you do not understand such usage, others do not either.)

• *Use of time-, place-, and thought-holders.* Does the child use substitutes for words, such as "uh-huh," "uh-uh," "hmm," to the point where communication is greatly limited?

• *Word choice.* Does the child obviously possess an ample vocabulary to enable her to have meaningful communication with others and express her ideas clearly? Does she know the names of everyday items? Does she use a variety of words and know some synonyms for those words? Is she curious and eager to acquire new words to use? Does she experiment and play with words?

• *Using sentence patterns.* Is the child able to communicate ideas in appropriate sentence patterns? Does he use a variety of such patterns: questions, negations, exclamations, and sentences with varied word order?

• *Clarity of thought structure.* Is the child able to express and communicate ideas effectively in talking and writing?

Summing Up

Three major issues of language learning and teaching in schools today, especially in terms of thinking about teaching, talking, writing, and grammar are:

1. The primary role of meaning in talking and writing.
2. The relationship of children's intuitive knowledge of the rules that govern language production—or grammar—and what grammar may mean to students and teachers in the school context.
3. The teaching of talking, writing, and grammar.

In pondering these issues, it is important to ask what grammar really is, and what is really important for teachers and children to know about grammar. There are many definitions of what grammar is, including sentence structure, usage, a description of a language, and a language process. In education, grammar has been most often perceived as a set of rules for understanding and using some combination of the above, and to enable students to think, talk, or write correctly and well.

The research, however, shows that the study of formal grammar does not improve thinking, logic, achievement in a foreign language, socially more acceptable language usage, or improved understanding of literature, reading, listening, speaking, or writing. Some of the reasons why we persist in teaching grammar despite these findings are that grammar teaching has a long tradition in education, that it is often viewed as a basic skill by the public, that it is an integral part of many curricula and textbooks, and that it is very easily testable.

In order for teachers to know why or why not they should teach formal grammar, they need to know something about the historical and linguistic tradition of grammar study and the three main models of the grammar of a language: traditional grammar (with roots in the study of Latin as applied to learning English since medieval times), structural grammar (with a more recent focus on understanding how language is used and differences among languages and language users), and transformational generative grammar (with Chomsky's revolutionary look at language as a process).

Since neither current educational theory nor research suggests that children need to learn the formal rules of any of these grammars, what should a teacher do instead to support children's growing facility with the structures of their language? Children should have many opportunities to use language in meaningful ways as they gain control over their intuitive understanding and underlying knowledge of grammar. Recent theory and research suggest several strategies for creating a classroom where this can take place.

Children should be encouraged to interact with others, to play games with words, sentences, and sense, to listen to literature, to revise their writing, and to heighten their awareness of language.

Looking Further

1. Write down your definition of grammar and what you know about it and compare it to the definition of others in your class. Analyze the source of your ideas about grammar. Why do you think your definition is what it is? Which definition listed in the chapter comes closest to your own?

2. What are your beliefs about the effectiveness of teaching grammar? In small groups, compare these with the beliefs of others in your class.

3. Ask several teachers whether they teach grammar and why. Compare their answers with the results of your discussions in Question 2.

4. Examine a State Curriculum Guide for a rationale and content of grammar teaching. Evaluate it according to what research tells us about the effectiveness of teaching grammar.

5. Examine several language arts textbooks for their approach to grammar teaching. What type of grammar does it reflect? How does it approach the teaching of grammar? What do you think of its approach?

6. Observe a group of elementary-school children at play during recess or free time. Note any examples of language play. How could you build on these examples for teaching?

7. Create a pattern based on the functions of words and try it out with children. Or, find a pattern in literature which does the same thing.

8. Start a file of books which are outstanding examples of the way words can be used in literature. Create your own classification for these types. Some possibilities include: interesting sentence structures, descriptive words, style of language, use of figurative language, and imagery.

9. Start a file of stories with repeated patterns that you like. Create your own classifications, or use

- sentences and sentence patterns in a repeated plot, or
- sentence patterns repeated in a cumulative plot.

10. Observe children revising their writing in small groups. Note how they are using their underlying knowledge of language as they do so.

11. Start a file of children's books which use another language or a variation of American English.

12. Observe a child and assess her language use according to the questions listed in the chapter.

Chapter Seven

Spelling, Handwriting, and the Writing Conventions

Objectives

Look for answers to the following questions as you read this chapter.

- What is the nature of the English writing system?
- How do children learn to spell?
- What is the relationship between spelling and reading and dialect?
- How do children learn handwriting?
- How do children learn writing conventions?
- How effective are commercial texts for teaching spelling, handwriting, and writing conventions?
- What are some strategies for teaching spelling, handwriting, and writing conventions in a classroom where language arts are individualized, interactive, and integrated across the curriculum?

A Child's View

During the middle of the fall semester, three first-graders are writing while other members of their self-contained classroom are involved in other activities. Michael, Alisha, and Anita are not in a special group for writing, but it just happens to be their free writing period at the same time. During this thirty-minute period, they may write about anything they want and illustrate their stories. Their stories are shown in Figures 7–1, 7–2, and 7–3.

Figure 7–1
Michael's Story

Figure 7–2
Alisha's Story

Figure 7–3
Anita's Story

Centering Ideas

What do Michael, Alisha, and Anita's stories tell us about the development of the **mechanics of writing**—handwriting, spelling, and writing conventions such as capitalization and punctuation—in children's writing? And what kind of implications for instruction can be drawn from what we know about children's development and abilities in each of these areas, and the relationship of these to the development of writing in general?

Keep these three samples of writing in mind as you think about these questions and as you read what current theory and research tells us about the learning and teaching of spelling, handwriting, and writing conventions, and about how we can learn from the children how to teach them.

Making Connections

Writing—including spelling, handwriting, and writing conventions—represents the rather monumental effort of literate human beings to put the living sounds of language into static symbols of print. Writing first emerged from early people's efforts to record their experiences or leave a message for others. They drew on the walls of caves or carved marks in stone. Later these pictures and marks became symbols such as the pictograms of prehistoric cultures and the hieroglyphics of the ancient Egyptians, and different cultures developed different forms of recording sounds through writing.

The ABCs in hieroglyphics.

The English Writing System

Many of these writing systems, or orthographies, have evolved over time. An **orthography** is a code which consists of a set of graphemes (written symbols which stand for a word, syllable, or speech sound in a language). When you know how to spell and have mastered handwriting and writing conventions, you know how to produce these graphics correctly and you know what they mean. There are several types of orthographies: **logographic,** or word writing; **syllabic,** or syllable writing; and **alphabetic,** or sound-to-letter writing.

Many graphemes can represent a single phoneme, for example, the long /a/ sound in *way, weigh, wait, fate, hey, ballet, fiancée, lady.*

Many phonemes can represent a single grapheme, for example, the *o* in *one, do, dot, open, oven, women.*

The most widespread type of writing is alphabetic; English is an alphabetic system. The alphabet used for English derives from ancient Hebrew, Greek, and Roman. Some alphabetic codes, such as the Finnish, Turkish, and Spanish, have a one-to-one correspondence between sounds and letters, while English has what Chao (1968) calls a "many-to-many" correspondence. English has over forty speech sounds but only twenty-six letters of the alphabet to represent them. One, two, or more of these letters may function as graphemes, for example, the *gh* in laugh, which represents the phoneme /f/.

What is the origin of these irregularities in the English language? The answer to this question brings us back to a basic characteristic of language: language changes. Some of the following types of changes have made a great difference in how English is spoken and written.

The transition from Old to Middle English rendered the /*k*/ sound silent when it preceded a consonant at the beginning of a word, but the grapheme *k* remained in the orthography, resulting in irregular spellings like *knife* and *knight*.

French words that brought to England after the Norman Conquest: *ballet, bouquet, restaurant, lieutenant.* Spanish words added to English: *mesa, junta, macho.*

1. *Sound changes.* The pronunciation of sounds and words has changed over the centuries, but spellings have not always changed accordingly.
2. *Borrowed word changes.* Many invasions and occupations of the British Isles, as well as British exploration and colonization, resulted in the addition of words from other languages without changes in their spelling.
3. *Etymological changes.* For example, Renaissance writers wanted to give classical languages and cultures a rebirth and resurrected some Latin spellings. Many of these spellings reinstated voiced letters which had been deleted in the French pronunciation from which the English words were derived.

But just how irregular is English, really? In a study at Stanford University, Hanna, Hanna, Hodges, and Rudorf (1966) investigated the alphabetic nature of American-English spelling, analyzed 173,000 common words, and programmed a computer with the rules of spelling in English. The computer scored as follows on a test of all 173,000 words:

No errors	49% (8,000 words)
One error in phoneme/grapheme correspondence	37%
Two errors	11%
Three or more errors	2%

The researchers conclude that vowel and consonant sounds and their symbols have regular spellings approximately 80 percent of the time and suggest that errors can be corrected through mastery of morphological rules and an approach to spelling that uses recent findings in linguistic research.

Perhaps the most important finding of recent research in linguistics is in the area of the language development of children, and how they really learn spelling, handwriting, and writing conventions.

How Do Children Learn to Spell?

Learning to spell, like learning to speak, is a developmental process. Children begin to internalize what they are coming to know about language systematically, create some flexible rules based on this knowledge, and gradually apply these rules as they begin to spell. This is a developmental, systematic, sequential, and very slow process that is far too complex to rely solely on simplistic teaching strategies like memorizing words from lists or learning rules found in spelling books. Children need to be actively engaged in the writing process and use this knowledge to solve problems, test hypotheses, make mistakes, and make discoveries and inventions, just as they do when they learn to speak.

The Stages in Children's Spelling Development

All children seem to move through the same sequence of stages in learning to spell, regardless of when they begin to write. It seems that children intuitively know a great deal about English orthography, and on the basis of this knowledge they create a hierarchy of concepts which guide their initial spelling efforts. The sequence of the stages they go through indicates that they are establishing internalized rules moving from simple letter–sound correspondences to more complex phonological, syntactic, and semantic knowledge, and that they do this as they use spoken and written language in real and meaningful situations. Several researchers (Beers & Beers, 1981, summarizing Beers & Henderson, 1977; Gentry; 1981, Henderson, 1980; Templeton, 1979; Zutell, 1979) have identified these stages (see Table 7–1).

1. *The Deviant Stage*

Children's earliest writing efforts are scribbles which they begin to create as soon as they can grasp a pencil or a crayon. This scribbling becomes more representational and precise, often accompanied by spoken explanations. Preschoolers soon begin to replace scribbles and drawings with letterlike shapes or actual letters and numbers, often scattered randomly over a page; some can write their name. During this stage, which Gentry (1981) calls the **deviant stage** of spelling development, children are becoming aware that speech can be recorded by means of graphic symbols, even though they do not have a clear, objective understanding of the relationship between sounds and letters in words, or of what words really are.

2. *The Prephonetic Stage*

The next stage, which Gentry (1981) refers to as **prephonetic,** occurs around kindergarten age for many children. It is characterized by one-, two-, and three-letter representations of discrete words, because children have learned that letter names stand for elements of words—usually consonants—and they have more control over both ends of simple words, but more often the beginning. They are still not able to spell many words correctly, and their concept of what a word is is still not clear, but they do know that letters make words and do not invent symbols as substitutes for letters as in the earlier stage.

Before examining the next stage, we should look at the work of Read (1975) and his concept of invented spelling. Read's research demonstrates convincingly that kindergartners predict the spelling of words auditorily in sophisticated ways, and that there are frequently occurring patterns in their

Table 7-1 *The Stages of Spelling Development*

Gentry (1981)	***Deviant*** btBpA	***Pre-phonetic*** MSR	***Phonetic*** MONSTR
Henderson (1980)	***Preliterate Prephonetic*** dog candy bit Cinderella	***Preliterate Phonetic*** D or DJ K or KDE B or BT S	***Letter-Name Strategy*** DIJ KADE BET SEDRLI
Beers & Beers (1981)	***Prereading Stage*** 1. Prephonetic level ABDG—Wally 11 + 02—cat 2. Phonetic level WTBO—Wally KT—cat HM—home GT—get	***Phonetic Stage*** GAT—get TREP—trip FRMR—farmer SCARD—scared JUPT—jumped	
Grades	***Preschool***	***Kindergarten and Beginning First***	***Mid-First***

Adapted from Gentry, 1981.

spelling. He finds that children often use single letters to represent the sound of the full letter name *(PPL = people; BCAZ = because; LFNT = elephant),* omit nasal sounds before consonants *(MOSTR = monster; NUBRS = numbers; PLAT = plant),* and use one letter—particularly *L, R, M, and N*—to stand for a whole syllable *(GRIF = giraffe; NHR = nature).* One of the most revealing aspects of children's spelling that came out of Read's work is the sophisticated set of linguistic criteria children use for decoding which vowel sound to use. Whereas adults are accustomed to the short–long vowel relationships found in spelling, *(extreme/extremity; nation/national),* children, on the other hand, are sensitive to phonetic relationships between **vowel sounds.** Since the sounds in *feel* and *fill* are formed similarly in the mouth, a child might spell both *FEL. Like* and *lock* might both be spelled *LIK.* Moreover, finding that many children think *chair* begins like *truck* and *jar* like *dragon,* Read realized there is very little difference in the sound used in pronouncing *truck* and *chruck* and *dragon* and *jragon.* One of Read's most significant findings is that the children in his study arrived at roughly the same system for spelling, a system that was clearly built on their articulation as well as on their ability to hear and segment speech sounds in words.

Transition	*Correct*
MONSTUR	MONSTER
Vowel Transition	
DOG	DOG
CANDE or CANDY	CANDY
BIT	BIT
CINDARILA	CINDERELLA

Orthographic Stage
GAETF—gate
MAIK—make
SPATER—spatter
RIDDER—rider
SITTIN—sitting
CANT—can't

Morphemic & Syntactic Stage

1. Control of doubling consonants.
   HAPPY
   SMATTERING
2. Awareness of alternative forms.
   MANAGERIAL manage
   REPETITION repeat
3. Awareness of syntactic control or key elements in words.
   SLOWLY SAVED
   PASSED RESTED
   FASTER SLEEPING

End First Beginning Second ***Second–Fourth*** ***Fifth–Tenth***

3. *The Phonetic Stage*

The characteristics described by Read are evident in the stage Gentry (1981) describes as **phonetic,** where spellings include all of the sound features of words as a child hears and articulates them. In other words, the written forms contain every speech sound, recorded in the same sequence in which the sounds are articulated when the word is spoken *(CHROBLE = trouble).* Children pass through this stage at some time between first and third grade.

4. *The Transitional Stage*

The **transitional stage** described by Gentry (1981) begins to occur at the end of the first grade and the beginning of the second grade and precedes stages of more standard spelling. At this stage, vowels are included in every recorded syllable, and familiar spelling patterns are used. Standard spelling is interspersed with invented phonetic spelling *(HIGHCKED = hiked; TODE = toad).* At this stage, children seem to realize that it is necessary to spell words so they may be read by themselves and others and that every word has a conventional spelling as used in print. They also learn that there are various ways to spell many of the same speech sounds and that many words are not spelled entirely phonetically.

5. *The Correct Stage*

After the transitional stage, children continue to gain control over more conventional spelling, but the characteristics and points of change during this **correct stage** are less clear than in earlier grades. While still struggling with consonant doubling and word affixes, many second- and third-graders are already mastering word roots, the past tense, and short vowels, although they still have problems with the position of letters, as in the silent *e* that controls vowels. Along with their growing vocabulary and comprehension of the meaning of words, fourth-graders are acquiring greater familiarity with vowel patterns in relation to stress and meaning in words. From fifth grade onwards, students increasingly understand how meaning and grammatical structure control spelling in English and are becoming better at doubling consonants and at spelling alternate forms of the same word and word endings. In addition to understanding the underlying phonological rules they gained as young children, these older students have now grasped and are able to use knowledge about the importance of meaning and syntax in spelling in English.

Some Examples

In order to connect these research generalizations with some specific children, let us look again at the spelling of the three first graders, Michael, Alisha, and Anita, in terms of Gentry's (1981) classification of the developmental stages of spelling. What stage is each of the children in, and how deep is their understanding of English orthography as evidenced in their writing?

Michael reads his one-sentence story as "There is a plane." *Is* and *a* are spelled correctly, he has written something for every word; and both *ThEHR/there* and *Pne/plane* include letters which represent some of the speech sounds heard in the word. Alisha reads her two-sentence story as "My cat is black and brown. He is cute." *Cat, black, and, he* and *is* are spelled correctly, and the other spellings include all the sound features of the words: *mi/my, brwn/brown, cut/cute.* Anita reads her four-sentence story as "My cat's name is Snow Paws. His last name is Fred. His middle name is Billy. And that is all." Most words are spelled correctly, invented phonetic spellings use familiar patterns, and a vowel is included in every recorded syllable: *Sno/Snow, Pous/Paws, mitul/middle, Bilee/Billy.*

While all three children show behavior typical of first grade, they are at different stages in their spelling development: Michael at the prephonetic stage, Alisha at the phonetic stage, and Anita at the transitional stage.

Spelling and Reading

In a study of the relationship of cognitive development to both spelling and reading, Beers (1980) found that the more that young children know about words in general, the better they are able to spell and read. She questions the practice of teaching spelling in isolation from language arts and reading instruction, and suggests that all these subjects should be taught in an integrated curriculum. The time-honored practices of spelling instruction, such as weekly lists of spelling words unrelated to children's experiences or reading or needs in writing, are of little value in learning spelling. Her research suggests that the spelling strategies of children are most directly related to their growing word knowledge, which in turn suggests once again the need for a curriculum integrated through the language arts in the primary grades.

Looking at good spellers among older students in middle and secondary school, Templeton (1979) also emphasizes the importance of general word knowledge and vocabulary development. He found that mature readers understand words in print that they would be afraid to pronounce and that instruction should take advantage of this understanding of the visual as well as the spoken representation of words for older students. Teachers should develop means to direct their students' attention to the structure of printed words. For example, the logical underlying relationship between the words *equation* and *equanimity* is much more obvious in print than speech. Templeton notes that the more students understand about the logic of word structure, the more they will gain from the printed page as they read, and the better they will spell.

Spelling and Dialect

If children's early spellings are based on phonetically derived strategies, do children who speak a nonstandard dialect or English as a second language use the same strategies as those who do not? Strever (1980) found that students who speak different American dialects follow the same sequential development of spelling strategy patterns as those who do not. She also found that the differences in socioeconomic status do not make a difference in the development of spelling skills. She suggests that these findings discourage the use of methods of spelling instruction that are based solely on studying sound–symbol relationships, or language arts programs that emphasize learning standard pronunciation first since, as students mature, there is little correlation between pronunciation and their spelling and reading skills.

Strever suggests further that the better method is to help children make connections between writing English and the spoken English they have already mastered. Their own language should be the source of instruction: dictations with younger children, stories written by older students, and the use of their own words and language as a source for further word study activities, games, and understanding and use of language patterns in writing. Such an approach also fosters a positive attitude among children and tells them that speaking and writing and spelling are for sharing their ideas and images and feelings with others, and that their ideas are of value no matter what their home culture, language, or dialect.

How Do Children Learn Handwriting?

Graves (1983) has described five general phases in children's handwriting development during the composing process, all of which can occur and overlap during the first grade.

1. ***Get-it-down phase***
   At this stage, driven by the urge to express themselves by making marks—which can start as soon as they are able to hold a marking tool—and letterlike forms, letters, and words, children will put the marks down in random order on a page, and begin to have a general idea of composing from left to right.

2. ***First aesthetics***
   At this stage, children show awareness of the placement of words on the page and the amount of space needed for their story, a desire for a clean, fresh page to write on—and a strong desire to get rid of any mistakes, which can lead to problems with erasers: smudging, tearing the page, and frustration.

3. ***Growing age of convention***
   As they near the end of the first grade, children may show less desire to get their message down and more concern with how it looks to others, so they take more care with word spacing, margins, and writing exactly on the line. This desire also affects spelling and mechanics as they become more aware of their audience.

4. ***Breaking conventions***
   As children gain more mastery over handwriting, spelling, and other writing mechanics, they are also faced with the problem of content in writing; with the help of the teacher, they need to learn that it is all right to change, move, and mess up parts of their writing.

5. ***Later aesthetics***
   When children discover that they can scratch out rather than erase an error, and move and add parts to their writing, they are on their way to understanding that their work is a draft and only a first step towards other drafts and finally a finished product. It is for the final product that they will use special looks and materials: neat handwriting, typewriting, or word processing; clean or special paper; special writing tools such as pens or colored markers; and illustrations and binding for publishing.

During all five stages and throughout their further development in handwriting skills, children are working to control two main elements of **praxis** (the motion of making letters, words, and messages on the space of a page): pressure and control of the page space.

Let us take yet another look at our three first-graders and see what their writing products tell us about their control of handwriting in the context of the writing process as described by Graves (1983). Michael's story shows that, like many children in the get-it-down phase, he understands composing from left to right but has less control over spacing. His beginning awareness of first aesthetics shows up, however, in his attempt to get rid of errors through erasing in his invented spelling of the word *Pne/plane.* His control over pressure varies considerably—compare the *r* and the *a.* Alisha's control of spacing is more developed than Michael's, her pressure more even, and her awareness of first aesthetics strong. She erased and tried to correct five of the nine words, and became particularly frustrated at her attempt to write *cut/cute* as she erased and then smudged and then wrote it over. Anita's control of pressure is good and her awareness of letter and word spacing is growing. Note that she erased four times to achieve correct spacing: *Sno/Snow; name; is* (twice). Anita has entered the growing age of convention. She has obviously carefully pondered—and corrected when necessary—the spacing between words, margins, correct placement of words on the line, and use of the entire paper space. She has not reached the stage of breaking conventions but may soon do so as she quickly and eagerly fills whole pages with her stories; she shows a strong desire to get her message right, to have it say exactly what she wants it to say. The next step for her is to make changes in content and organization, with the help of her teacher, and to move on her way to becoming a writer who rethinks, reenvisions, and revises.

How Do Children Learn Writing Conventions?

Research suggests that children learn writing conventions in the same way they learn to speak, write, and spell: as they solve problems, test hypotheses about language use, and discover how language is used in the context of purposeful expression and communication.

For example, for an entire year, as reported by Graves (1980), Lucy McCormick Calkins observed the way two third-grade teachers taught punctuation. One taught these skills in isolation using daily drills and worksheet exercises, and the other taught them in the context of the writing process as children wrote for an hour a day, three days a week. Table 7–2 shows what the children learned about mechanics during the course of a year. The children who engaged in writing learned more about punctuation because they needed it in order to make sense to their audience and to bring the sound of their own voice through the silence of print. They learned punctuation as they needed it to write.

In an activity-centered first-grade classroom where children wrote from the first day of school, Cordeiro, Giacobbe, and Cazden (1983) analyzed all the writing of the children and the nature of writing conferences between teacher and children for a year. They found that the punctuation marks taught most often were periods (thirteen children) and possessive

Table 7–2 *Teaching the Mechanics of Writing*

Method		
Ms. West		*Ms. Hoban*
daily drills workbook exercises sentences on chalkboard which children correct ditto sheets pretests/posttests little writing		writing an hour a day, three days a week begin with their own information invent and use punctuation for own purposes
	Results	
3.85	Average number of kinds of punctuation children could define/explain of thirteen types: period; exclamation mark; apostrophe; paragraph sign; dash; caret; quotation marks; comma; colon; parentheses; asterisk; semicolon.	8.66

Based on Graves, 1980.

apostrophes and quotation marks (six children each). They also found that direct instruction helped the children learn the correct use of possessive apostrophes and quotation marks, but that the children still got them correct even after having been taught only about half the time. Periods were retaught more than all other conventions combined, but were still used only half of the time required. All the children progressed at about the same rate, but the untaught children did relatively better in the correct use of periods, from other knowledge sources, either written texts or their own developing intuition about the underlying rules of language. In addition, while they were not always able to use periods according to adult standards of conventions in writing, their writing shows strong evidence that they were developing an intuitive and untaught understanding of phrases and clauses, or the structural units that occur between discrete words and complete sentences—in the same way they are struggling at this age with phonological distinctions as evidenced in their evolving invented spelling.

In this sense, they are creating as many errors of commission as of omission, but these errors show they are making hypotheses and gaining control over their own sentence sense on their way to a more complete understanding of the difference between a single word, a phrase or a clause, and a complete sentence. Thus, if they use a period to segment a phrase or a clause rather than a complete sentence, it shows they are making a positive move towards an understanding of sentences and the use of punctuation—in the same way as they move from using a scribble, then a letterform, then a letter for every syllable, then a vowel in every syllable, to a final stage of correct spelling.

Evidence of this growing control can be seen in the three brief writing samples of Michael, Alisha, and Anita. Michael, the least-developed speller of the three, uses capitalization both correctly and incorrectly, and no punctuation. Alisha uses no capitalization, and a period once at the end of the story, but none to indicate the required break between sentences in the middle of her story. Anita uses capitalization correctly in two ways—at the beginning of sentences and to indicate a proper name—and uses periods correctly for four sentences. Her only mechanical error is the omission of a possessive apostrophe in the word *cats*.

The writing of these three first-graders also clearly shows the process children undergo—whatever their age—as they learn spelling, handwriting, and writing conventions. They are generating and testing new hypotheses, and constantly trying out new ideas and methods as they write. Interestingly enough, most children try out the same kinds of things as they move through the predictable stages of development. It is unfortunate that many past teaching attitudes, practices, and materials have not always reflected what we now know about these predictable stages in child development.

What we do know is that we should make the teaching of these skills real, and center them around real ideas and interests, real experiences and language, and the real writing of children. In addition to important aspects of the classroom context for teaching spelling, handwriting, and writing conventions—the teacher's attitude and choice of materials and methods—the following section describes three general strategies which reflect what we know about how children learn to master form and convention in writing: the mechanics of writing as part of writing process, the mechanics of writing applied to the content areas, and games for learning the mechanics of writing.

Teaching Children

First, a Word about Commercial Programs

Spelling texts have traditionally been a primary means of teaching spelling. Such texts are divided into units with word lists and practice exercises related to a particular aspect of spelling instruction. Some educators feel that controlled lists of graded words and direct teaching of rules are an effective way to teaching spelling. No doubt these traditional texts are easy to use since many students can work through a unit by themselves and keep busy while the teacher is with other students. They also make pre- and posttesting and grading easy, since the words and tests are prepared.

But just how effective are these formal materials for spelling instruction? Graves (1977) made an analysis of these texts and compared the results to earlier studies of the content, approach, and effectiveness of basal spelling programs. The earlier studies showed that

1. texts used a variety of approaches with no clear patterns of organization or systematic use of high-frequency words;
2. children spelled better in response-meaning and word-study exercises—which do not require attention to the structural elements of the word but require them to use the word in sentences and writing—than in the course of preparatory exercises on homophones, affixes and inflectional endings, silent letters, initial consonants and blends, vowels, and phonics;
3. a test-corrected-test method—with no formal study with a book—accounted for 95 percent of achievement among children in spelling compared to a spelling book exercise practice and test-study method.

The more recent studies showed that

1. spelling books today include fewer of the least effective exercises—especially phonics, the least effective of all—and more language arts skills exercises—handwriting, synonyms, word origins—although there is no evidence that these contribute significantly to spelling power;
2. more emphasis has been placed on word usage activities, of the kind that do contribute to spelling power.

These studies raise serious doubts about the real usefulness of a formal spelling program using a commercial spelling text. Both the earlier and later studies show that students learn words best when they apply them in writing. Teaching spelling with a text, then, while an easy method for the teacher, is a questionable one in terms of how well children learn to spell.

Language arts textbooks have traditionally been a primary means of teaching writing and writing conventions. Graves (1977) also reviewed these texts in light of what recent research tells us about the writing process. He found that

1. isolated drills on skills—predominantly grammar and punctuation—dominate and increase as students get older;
2. what passes for teaching writing is a situation where the teacher suggests a writing genre—prose, poetry—the amount of writing to be done—sentence, paragraph—and the topic or a story starter.

This method flies in the face of what research and even common sense tells us about the composing process: that children can and will choose their own topics for writing; that they need time to generate ideas and rehearse and plan through talking, drawing, dramatizing, and so on; that they can and will write and rewrite many drafts with the help of the teacher's response and guidance during conferences or small-group experiences as they seek to find their own voice in writing; and that conventions are best taught at the final draft stage of writing, since children have a real need to create a correct copy of their work to publish for others to read.

If you do not use a commercial text as a comprehensive formal program to teach skills, then what should you do? Here are some general strategies and materials for the diagnosis and teaching of these skills, including ways to make effective use of commercial materials.

Strategies for Teaching Spelling, Handwriting, and the Writing Conventions

We know that children at a very early age make marks and later symbols to represent messages they have to tell. And these young writers make natural attempts to create standard orthography in their own language. They use invented spelling when they are not able to use standard spelling, and even make attempts at capitalization, punctuation, and other conventions such as paragraphing. Children naturally want to use the handwriting, spelling, and other writing conventions they observe in the world of print around them.

One of the teacher's main responsibilities, then, is to provide support and materials and methods to help children continue to try out new hypotheses and practice the new generalizations they discover as they test these hypotheses in moving towards mastery over the written conventions of their language. Here are some ways you can do this.

The Teacher's Attitude

Just as you encourage children to talk and exchange ideas freely in the style they choose, so should you encourage them to draw on their own ideas and styles as they write. Accept their drawing and scribbling attempts at handwriting, their invented words, their tries at punctuation. Many children fear writing because they are afraid of criticism for mistakes in handwriting, spelling, and the writing conventions. Some will only write words they think they know how to spell, or words they can copy from wall charts, the glossary of a book, or another child's paper. Consider how this could severely limit their attempts to write sincerely and authentically or to write anything of meaning.

Other children spend much of their time in related diversionary tactics. They stop every time they cannot spell a word. They raise their hands and fidget while waiting for the teacher to spell the word for them. Then they erase the word and ask how to spell another. Or they crumple and throw away the telltale evidence of what they think is bad handwriting. They may think that the first draft must look like a final copy because very often that is what the teacher implies by telling them to check spelling, watch punctuation, write neatly, and copy it over.

Some teachers adopt a search-and-destroy-all-errors-at-all-costs mentality, leading their students to believe that revision means looking for errors to correct quickly rather than making changes that affect the meaning of the message.

This is not to suggest that correct copy and legibility are not important. Of course they are. But few writers show the world their first drafts or their notes. The reader does not know whether they had to look up a word to check its spelling or whether someone else edited their punctuation. And authors spend much time revising before anyone sees their work. For children in school, an audience of teacher and other children is present from the beginning. Both teacher and child must realize that the beginnings of writing are not at all the same as the final product, and that notes and drafts and revisions are meant to be messy and subject to change.

Given enough time and encouragement from the teacher and their peers, as well as a real reason to make their message clear through correct conventions, children will move towards a standardized form of their message. Few children would want a piece of writing posted on the bulletin board or published in a class newspaper or bound in a book if it were full of mistakes. Their awareness of audience and their urge to publish or produce their writing for others is the greatest incentive to make their message clear.

The teacher's role is to support children's early efforts, encouraging them just to *try*—to put down a letter or a picture for a word or just leave a blank for a word they cannot spell—and assuring them that they can edit and revise along the way, with the help of the teacher or their classmates. When children have a real reason to write and a real audience for their writing, the teacher becomes their copublisher and collaborator rather than merely a person with a punitive red pen.

Materials and Methods for Teaching Spelling

Described here is an informal, individualized approach to teaching spelling that takes into account the research on the development of spelling in children and the effectiveness of basal spelling materials and various approaches to teaching spelling. Most school systems begin a systematic approach to spelling in second grade. In kindergarten and first grade, of course, children should be given many opportunities to write for meaning, and invented spelling should be encouraged.

Materials. You might display wall charts of common words used in children's writing, such as the list shown in Table 7-3. Basal spellers may also

Table 7–3 *The Top 200 High-Frequency, High-Utility Words for Reading and Writing*

the	not	more	bear	something
and	out	could	made	eat
a	him	make	good	watch
to	from	house	boy	another
of	got	thing	long	oh
in	so	big	it's	tell
he	or	day	water	much
I	them	play	than	find
it	by	too	after	word
you	what	because	three	night
was	little	how	around	walk
that	if	well	many	father
on	were	man	here	start
is	can	who	call	took
they	know	came	each	friend
his	do	say	our	may
for	me	put	any	still
then	went	been	I'm	show
with	down	that's	try	great
one	no	now	tree	let
she	their	way	dog	baby
said	don't	want	away	most
all	an	its	didn't	never
this	some	these	before	give
my	time	told	work	must
have	other	first	old	head
but	see	take	again	thought
as	look	mother	through	always
at	about	did	year	last
we	will	right	ask	he's
had	just	only	place	every
go	would	where	girl	sometime
there	your	there's	turn	help
be	into	home	hand	read
are	come	think	live	eye
like	back	use	can't	school
up	which	new	run	once
her	has	people	even	Mr.
when	two	very	name	kind
get	over	off	saw	us

From *The Ginn Word Book for Teachers: A Basic Lexicon,* Dale D. Johnson and Alden J. Moe, with James F. Baumann. © Copyright, 1983, by Ginn and Company. Used with permission of Silver Burdett & Ginn Inc.

be a source of such lists. Or you might make lists of words on special topics in your classroom: holiday words; words from the content areas; words the children like. These charts can change according to the children's needs, and can become an aid for word choice in writing. You might also create word study centers, with materials for word play and games, such as those described later in the chapter. Standard dictionaries and thesauruses are further sources of words. Dictionaries for school use are graded, and each class could have a variety of levels of dictionaries, as well as basal spellers.

Fifth-grade teacher Steve Ketcham asked his class to brainstorm a list of synonyms for said. Here are their alternatives: *asked, spoke, told, begged, stated, declared, pleaded, complained, whined, complimented, informed, screamed, yelled, shouted, hollered, advised, warned, cautioned.*

See Chapter 12, "Dictionaries."

A spelling journal for each child—loose-leaf notebook with alphabet dividers—can become a personal list of words the child misspells, needs to use in writing, or just wants to know how to spell. Children often want to know how to spell a word because it intrigues them or excites them or just because it's there. Such words of interest may be personal words, mysterious words, media words, or special dirty words.

Diagnosis and Individualized Instruction. Lists of high-frequency words from the writing of children, showing the percentage of children at each grade level that spell them correctly, have been developed as a source of information for teachers on what should be considered the average difficulty of these words through the grades. For example, the New Iowa Spelling Scale (Greene, 1977) lists 5,507 high-frequency words for grades two through eight. By randomly selecting words spelled correctly 50 to 75 percent of the time at the appropriate grade level to create a test, you can use the Iowa Scale as a diagnostic tool in the classroom. Students scoring from 1 to 50 percent correct are at the frustration level, and below average; those scoring from 50 to 75 percent are at the instructional level, and average; those scoring from 75 to 100 percent are above average; those scoring 90 percent are working at the independent level. You can also use this method by drawing words from a spelling basal that you are sure is based on research of word frequency use: despite the implications that they are, many in fact are not and simply choose words that fit the units or rules they wish to teach (Ames, 1965; DiStefano & Hagerty, 1983; Hinrichs, 1975).

In one week, my four-year-old son asked how to spell *Gordon, Mama, Elizabeth* (his sister), and *dinosaur butt*—the current popular insult at his preschool.

When you have an idea as to the grade-level placement and relative developmental level of each child in your class, as compared to others at this level, you need to observe and assess not just the number but the kind of mistakes they make in spelling. Not all children will be having the same kind of difficulty, or many difficulties at all, and the kind of experiences you provide for them should be individualized according to the needs of each.

Here is a description of common error patterns at different developmental stages and appropriate instructional strategies in response to them.

1. ***Error patterns of beginning spellers (preschool to second grade)***

Common errors at this stage include using a letter name for a sound, omitting nasals before consonants, and confusing vowel sounds with similarly articulated letter names. These normal developmental stages, as described by Read (1971) and others, correspond to Piaget's stages of cognitive development (Zutell, 1979); few of these occur after the second grade.

Learning to spell at this stage should be an integral part of free writing for meaning, and invented spelling should be not only supported but encouraged. Even though many school systems establish formal spelling programs by the second and even the first grade, one study of first- through fourth-graders indicated formal instruction in spelling should not begin until children have developed an understanding of word structure through numerous experiences with words in their own writing and reading (Beers, Beers & Grant, 1977). Other studies showed that no formal instruction is just as effective as a formal program after grade four (Hammill, Larsen & McNutt, 1977; Manolakes, 1975).

2. *Error patterns of developing spellers (second through fourth grades)*

Common errors at this stage include misspelling common words and failure to apply generalizations about some orthographically regular words.

Children at this stage should be actively engaged in simple activities with high-frequency irregular words and difficult words from their own writing. Spelling basals are a source of the former. Practice with the latter can be done by having the students work in small ability groups and pairs, taking words from their own spelling journals. Some simple activities that do not require special materials or direct instruction or supervision by the teacher include (see Figure 7–4)

- **a.** writing the words in sentences,
- **b.** making a crossword puzzle or word-search puzzle for others to solve (duplicate and make available blank grids),
- **c.** scrambling the letters in each other's words and then unscrambling them,
- **d.** creating cloze puzzles for each other by deleting certain letters for another child to fill in (these can be written in story form).

Children working in pairs and groups can play and practice with their own words and then test each other. Research has shown that such a test-corrected-test method accounts for almost all the words learned by students. The children should immediately correct their own spelling tests and rewrite the words they missed. Less able spellers should confer with the teacher as they correct. For older, more able spellers, the teacher can check the spelling journals periodically to note progress.

Students at this stage can be introduced to generalizations about some orthographically regular words that follow regular patterns. For example:

- **a.** *Y-rule.* Words that end in a consonant plus *y* change *y* to *i* before adding *es* or *ed* (*try/tries/tried*).
- **b.** *Final, silent* e. Words that end in silent *e* drop the *e* before adding a suffix beginning with a vowel and keep the *e* when the suffix begins with a consonant (*skate/skating/skates*).
- **c.** *Doubling.* Words in which the final syllable ends in a consonant preceded by a single vowel double the consonant before adding a suffix beginning with a vowel (*hit/hitting*).

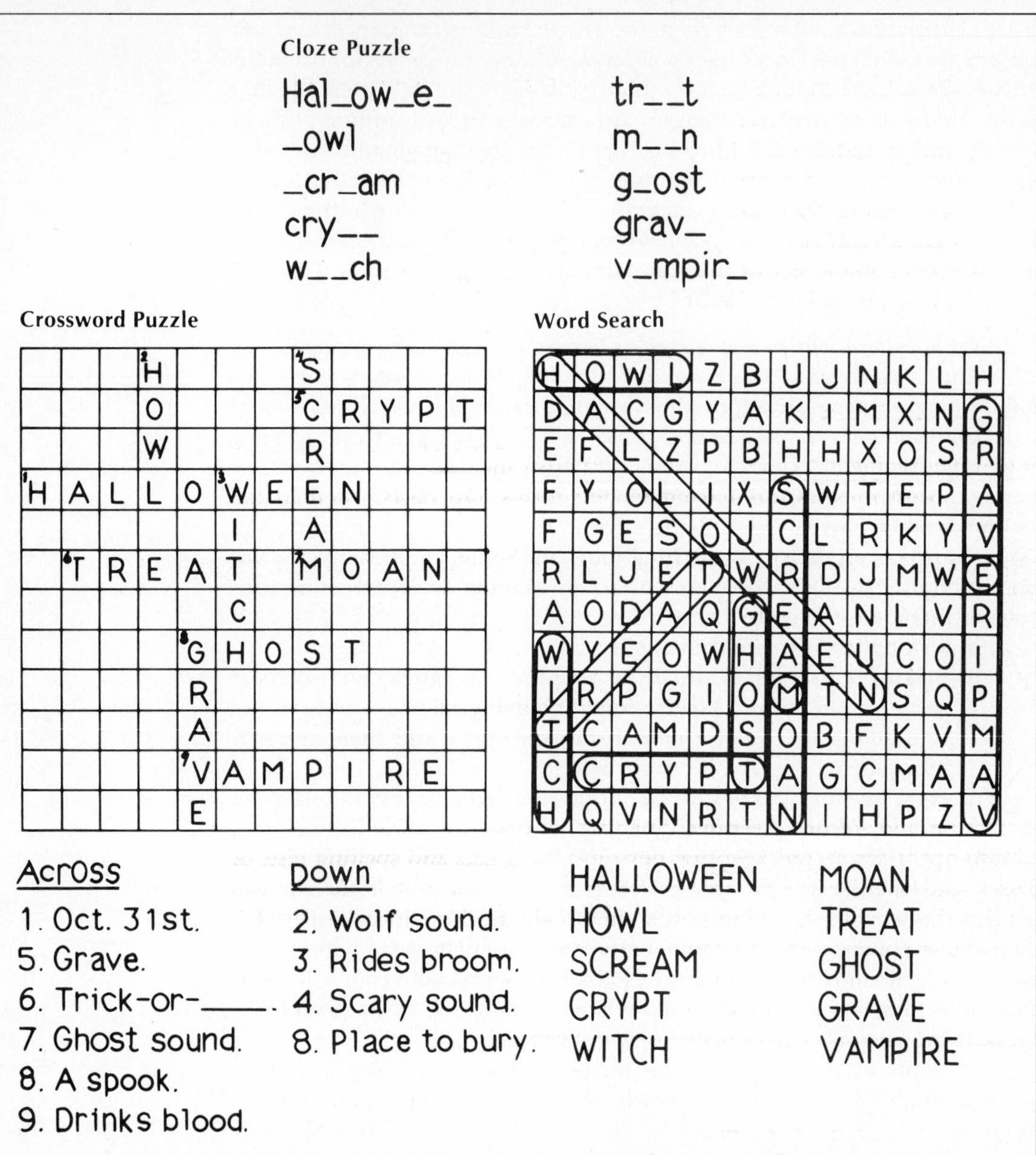

Figure 7–4 *Activities for Developing Spellers*

> **d.** *Plurals.* Most single nouns become plural by adding an *s* or *es* (*cat/cats, dress/dresses*).

Students can become aware of the special characteristics and constraints of the writing system, or orthography, of English by playing in pairs, in small groups, or as a class, games that focus on such recurring patterns. Other patterns may be found and selectively used from basal spellers.

a. By using lists of common root words kept in a folder or file in a work center, even younger children can create categories of as many related words they can think of by changing a word's root to the plural, changing a verb's tense, or making a noun possessive, and can discover how certain words can function as both a noun and a verb, for example, *smile, run, play, heat, laugh.*

b. Older students can play such familiar card games as Rummy, Old Maid, or Authors with a deck consisting of at least ten sets of four cards, each related to one root word, where the object is to make a book of four cards with the same root word.

3. ***Error patterns of older spellers (fifth through eighth grades)***

Students at this level should focus on gaining a deeper understanding of how meaning and form are related in English spelling. They can practice and play with these words having related forms and roots, often in the context of study in the content areas. For example:

a. From the dictionary, compile a list of words whose meaning students are not likely to know. In pairs of small groups, they may select a word, guess its meaning and write it down, then look it up in the dictionary. Whoever comes closest to the meaning scores a point. Examples: *xenophobia, quaff, pyre, mein, entail, cayuse.*

b. Another activity is to create semantic maps for words used in the content areas. This can be done by the whole class together with the teacher or in small groups without the teacher.

See Chapter 2, "Semantic Mapping."

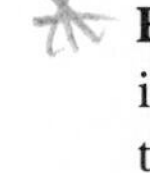

Evaluation and Record Keeping. Spelling journals for each child should include space for record keeping: personal word lists and spelling tests of these words can be dated and kept as an appendix in the back. You can monitor these during writing conferences held weekly with younger children and every few weeks with older children. This system turns a spelling journal into an individualized record of the student's development: words needed for writing, error patterns, and progress in spelling. Words can be checked off when they have been spelled correctly on a test.

Materials and Methods for Teaching Handwriting

Materials. Wall charts of manuscript (printing) for primary grades and cursive (connected letters) through grade eight should be on display. These charts often come in long strips and are traditionally placed on the wall over the chalkboard. Students should also have individual copies of models of writing to use at their desks; this is an important use for a basal handwriting series.

Two commonly used programs (see Figure 7-5 and 7-6) are Parker Zaner-Bloser—the traditional ball-and-stick style—and D'Nealian—an italic

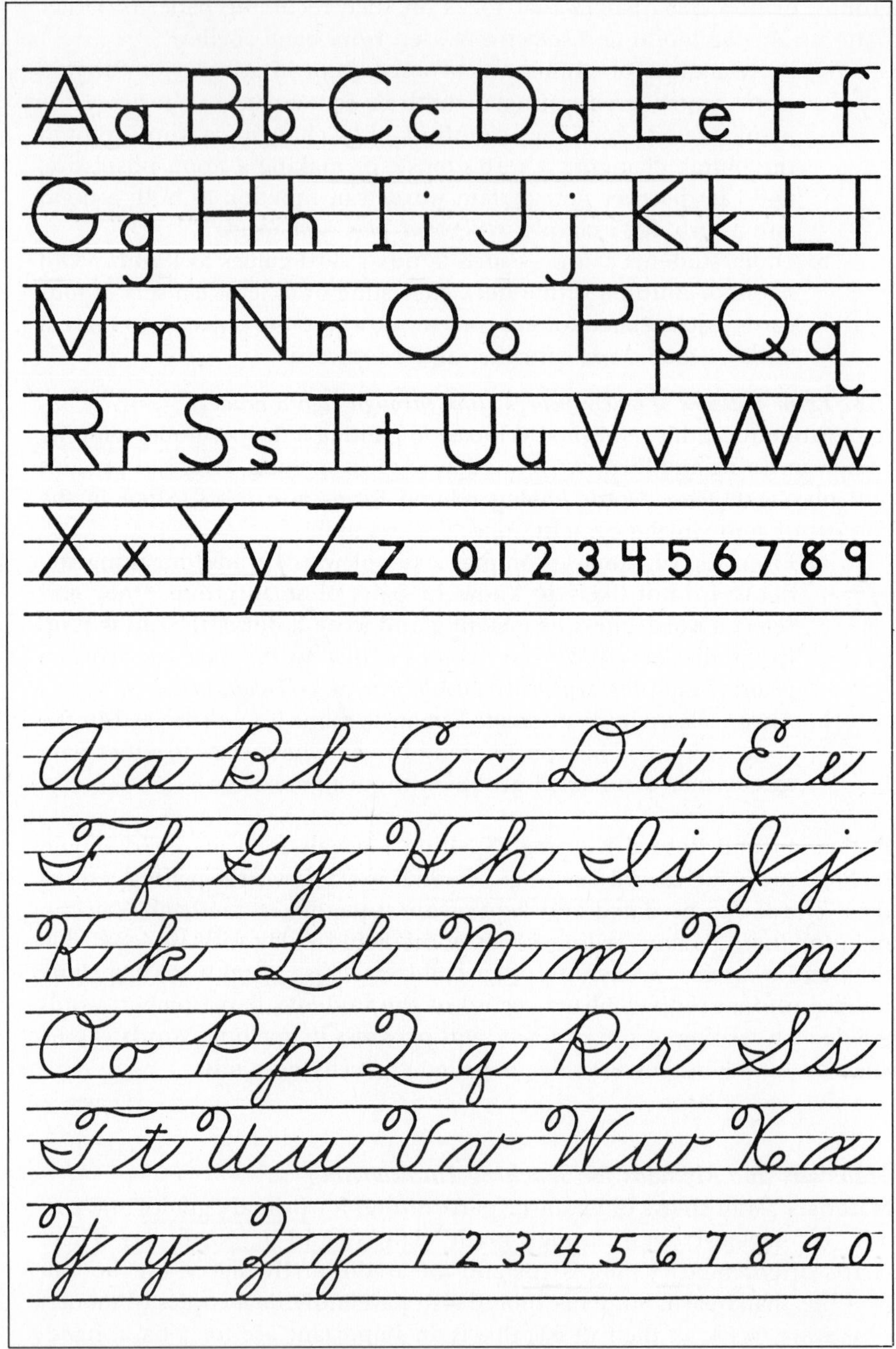

Figure 7–5 *The Parker Zaner-Bloser Alphabet*

From *Handwriting: Basic Skills and Application* (Columbus, OH: Zaner-Bloser, Inc., 1984), pp. 443–444.

Figure 7–6 *The D'Nealian Alphabet*
From *D'Nealian® Handwriting, Grades K–8,* by Donald Thurber. Copyright © 1981 by Scott, Foresman, and Company. Reprinted by permission.

style that attempts to make the transition from manuscript to cursive easier by slightly slanting manuscript letters. Other models of writing in the room are the teacher's board and chart writing, print on display on bulletin boards, in books and on labels, signs, and posters, and children's own writing.

Children should have many different types of materials for drawing, painting, and writing in the room: pens, pencils, paints, crayons, felt-tip markers, and a great variety of papers and other surfaces to draw and write on, such as chalkboards, wipe-off slates, paper plates, and boxes.

Diagnosis, Evaluation, and Record Keeping. You may be tempted to compare a child's handwriting to the models in commercial handwriting series. It seems logical to do so. But unlike spelling, handwriting does not have one agreed-upon form; even these series present different exemplars of good handwriting. Legibility, rather than an exemplary form, should be the standard by which you assess a child's progress in handwriting. Students' handwriting can become less conforming as they get older, a natural function of the preadolescent drive for personal expression through outward appearances, also exhibited by changing mannerisms, clothes, and hairstyles. This is the age when many students adopt a backhand style or a large scrawl with flourishes, or begin to dot their *i*s with little circles or—in extreme cases—hearts or flowers. Again, the issue is not whether an eleven-year-old's *i* is dotted with a smiley face but whether or not the writing is legible and the writer is able to communicate effectively with others. Graves (1978) suggests that teachers observe certain actions denoting change and development in diagnosing and evaluating handwriting (see Table 7–4).

As in spelling, children should be guided towards self-diagnosis of their handwriting. They can keep a folder of their own handwriting samples with a log to note their progress at appropriate intervals as a basis for discussing progress and problems with the teacher. Companies such as Zaner-Bloser provide scales of a variety of handwriting samples with evaluative comments and suggestions for improvement that students may use to evaluate their own writing.

Approaches to Teaching. To encourage the development of motor skills and a sense of space, two important factors in learning to write, younger children should be provided with plastic or wooden letters to handle and sort into categories such as letters that look alike, letters that have stems, or round letters. They can also match upper- and lowercase letters and see that some letters have different representations. They should also have many opportunities to practice free writing and playing with letter and word formation, using pencil and paper, chalk and chalkboard, sand trays, or modeling clay (which they can make themselves) and special activities like making and eating letters from edible clay. Art experiences play an important part in developing a child's motor control and exploration of space on paper.

Table 7-4 *Observing Handwriting*

Observe	*Note*
Use of thumb & forefinger together.	Children lose control with a poor (too tight or loose) grip.
Continuousness of writing.	Stops & starts may be due to problems with idea formulation, or spelling, as well as inexperience with handwriting.
Position of elbows & stability of body axis.	The less elbow motion, the better the speed & ease of writing.
Position of writing surface.	Children learn to accommodate paper to left or right of midline of their body, rather than straight on.
Distribution of strength.	Light & heavy lines show how well they are controlling pressure & suppression of large muscles in favor of small muscles.
Use of writing space.	From letter run together at various angles children learn to delineate spaces between words & sentences as they understand what these units mean.

Based on Graves, 1978.

Writers of all ages should have a comfortable space with the table and chair at correct level and enough room so they are free to move their arms, and without elbows bumping. As you demonstrate a good position for paper and writer, and how to hold a pencil (see Figure 7–7), observe the children as they write. Some have a death grip on the pencil and others choke it like a batter getting ready to bunt. Guide them to a comfortable and relaxed relationship with pencil and paper.

In most American schools, children learn letterforms and manuscript from first through second grades and cursive from somewhere between second and fourth grade. Most practice of these forms, however, should take place as children write, and demonstrations by the teacher should only be used to introduce new concepts—such as the shift from manuscript to cursive—or to focus on whatever problems many of the children are encountering.

See "Let's Go On a Bear Hunt: A Fresh Approach to Penmanship Drill," by Gail E. Tompkins, in *Language Arts,* 57 (1980), 782–786.

The teacher should give as little direct instruction as is needed to provide children with enough control so that they are able to write freely, fluently, and legibly. Handwriting is really learned as children write inde-

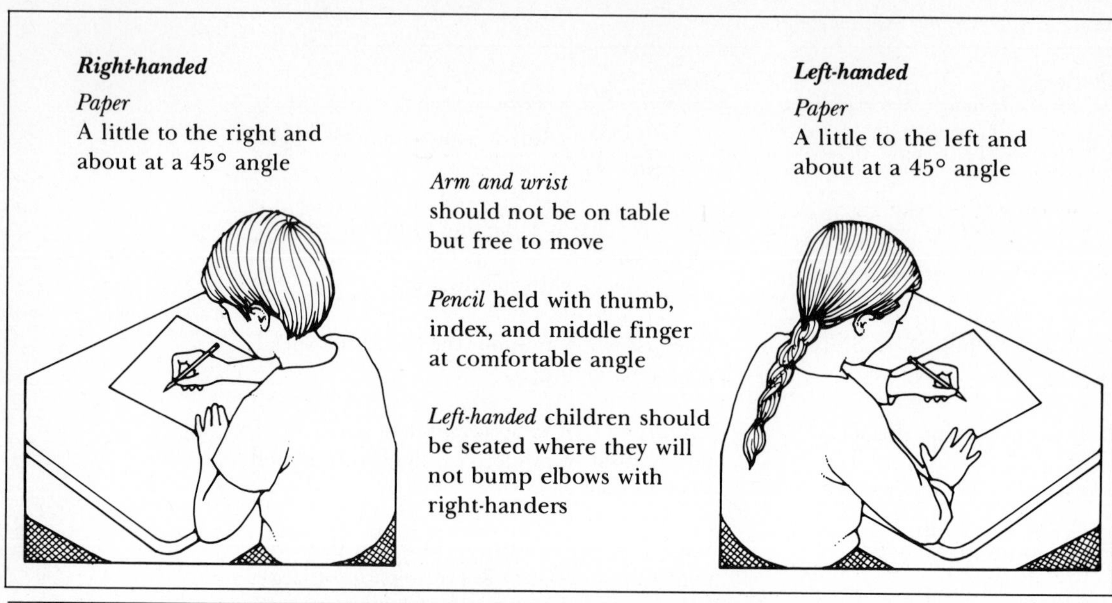

Figure 7–7 *Children, Paper, and Pencil in Proper Position.*

pendently. Appropriate topics for direct instruction include introducing children to the basic letterforms and their variations and to explain the transition from manuscript to cursive. Figure 7–8 shows a teaching sequence for these elements, moving from manuscript to cursive.

Spelling, Handwriting, and the Writing Conventions as Part of the Writing Process

Spelling, handwriting, and such conventions as capitalization, punctuation, and other mechanics are best learned and taught in the context of real writing where children have a real need and a real reason to use these skills. In order to keep these skills in their proper perspective, there are several things you need to remind your students and yourself as you teach skills and writing.

Reminders for Students and Teachers

A reminder for students:

- Get your ideas down on paper even if they are incomplete, messy, or misspelled, or lack conventional form. (You can have writing without conventions but you cannot have conventions without writing.)
- Writing does not always proceed in a logical or linear order. If you cannot finish a thought, leave a blank and go on.

Manuscript

Simple Letters

1. Straight lines | and lines with another stroke t i j k u
2. Circles o and circles with another stroke a d b p g q

Letters with Similar Pattern

1. Open circles c and open circles with another stroke e f
2. Lines and humps n m h r
3. Angles x y v w z
4. A unique letter s

Upper Case

1. Like lower case C O S T K P U V X Z
2. In between F J M N W
3. Unlike lower case A B D E G H I L R Q Y

Transition from Manuscript to Cursive

Show same words in both styles, how they are connected, and the change in slant.

Cursive writing

1. The numbers and arrows on commercial materials show the order and direction of the formation of each letter.
2. Letters with undercurve / - b e f g h i k l r s t u w
3. Overcurve or hump letters m n v x y z
4. Downward curve (- a c d g o
5. Lower loop j p g
6. Upper case letters which share similarities
7. Note that only six letters are really formed differently in cursive: b, e, f, r, s, z.

Figure 7–8
Teaching Sequence for Manuscript to Cursive

- Keep the flow of ideas going.
- Be confident. Write for yourself as well as for others.
- Use your own voice.
- Do not expect to write a perfect paper the first (one, two, three . . .) times.
- Do not apologize for what you have written.
- Be proud of what you like about your writing.

A reminder for teachers:

- Encourage all kinds of writing, all the time.
- Deemphasize the importance of standard spelling and respond appropriately to nonstandard spelling. Remember the natural stages of spelling development.
- Remember that handwriting is for writing and that legibility is the point.
- Withhold the urge to correct every mistake you see until the child expresses a need or concern about his writing.
- Do not edit or push skills on every piece of writing. (Some types of writing do not require the conventions: journals, notes, personal writing. Others do: stories for publication, reports, formal letters, newspaper articles, oral scripts.)
- Show the students how to edit and correct mistakes by doing it yourself—on the chalkboard, on an overhead projector, or on your own writing.
- When you are focusing on one skill, do not talk about all the others at the same time.
- Focus on skills appropriate for each age group and its needs.

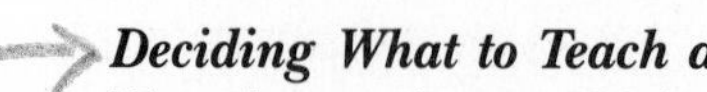

Deciding What to Teach and Organizing Instruction

How do you know which skills to teach? It will depend on the grade you teach, and the level of development of skills in your class. Do not, for example, decide to teach your first grade class a lesson on using periods in punctuation and then evaluate their results as they write. Ask yourself first whether or not they need that skill. Some may have already mastered it. Some may not be ready for it, as the research by Cordeiro, Giacobbe, and Cazden (1983) has shown. And most will have no idea what you are talking about if it does not apply directly to their needs in writing.

As a case in point, look again at the writing samples of Michael, Alisha, and Anita shown at the beginning of this chapter. Anita is obviously not having any trouble with capitalization. She uses a capital letter at the beginning of each sentence and for proper names. Michael and Alisha need help, but each has a slightly different problem. Michael uses capitals inappropriately—in the middle of a word and at the beginning of a common noun. Alisha does not use them anywhere. So you see that examining students' present skills can help you determine what skills you need to encourage, and how you can go about organizing instruction to develop them.

Collecting Writing Samples. At the beginning of the school year, encourage a great deal of free writing: journals, notes, stories. Get writing going at this point, and advise children not to worry about mechanics. (And they *do* worry, especially the older ones.) Collect these samples for a week, put them in a folder for each child, note the needs of each, and then determine the overall needs of the class and the ability levels of all the children. Then begin to think about how you can meet those needs. Here are some possible organizational patterns.

Teaching One Skill to the Whole Class. Upon evaluating the writing samples, you may identify some problem in mechanics—for example, capitalization—that many of the children or even the whole class needs help with. You might start by discussing the problem with the whole class, using the papers they have written. Ask for volunteers to share their problems, and correct them on the chalkboard or on the overhead projector. Be sure to do this only as the need occurs. It is not realistic to determine ahead of time what skills you will focus on or how often because some children, such as Anita, will not need help while others may not be ready for it. This approach is generally suitable for very broad categories of recurring problems. It could also be used to lead the children to an awareness of what these categories are, and how they can begin to check themselves as they write. Cramer (1978) suggests that children ask themselves the following questions as they self-edit:

Did I punctuate the end of each sentence?
Did I use punctuation in other appropriate places?
Did I spell each word correctly or check my spelling for words I was unsure of?
Did I write in my best handwriting?

Use the whole-class or large-group approach with caution and only when it is needed, and keep it in the context of each child's own needs and purposes for writing.

Teaching One Skill to Small Groups. As the semester progresses and you continue to observe children writing and keep writing folders for data with which to plan the teaching of skills, you may discover that certain children all need help or refinement of a skill. You may apply the one-skill/whole-class approach with this group while the other children in the class are writing.

Teaching All Skills to One Child. The bulk of your instruction will focus on assessing individual children's needs as they write throughout the year and will take place in response to their questions about conventions. Mastery of the various writing skills will best occur when they have a real need to get it right—when preparing a newspaper article to be printed, for instance, or writing an important letter. Conventions gain importance as the child develops audience awareness.

Remember that your role is to encourage and support children's sense-making efforts for many types of writing—which will inevitably lead to editing—to focus on meaning and style, and to improve usage so that the student moves towards controlling the conventions of writing in order to communicate with others.

Remember also that when you help children edit you are not correcting a test. In fact, you are not the editor, the child is. And your primary responsibility is to help her to gain control over her own writing. Self-concept is more important than capitalization, and children need to know that you value the former more than the latter. When they feel good about themselves and want to write and do write, they will also want to get it right. Support their efforts to edit themselves, but not at the expense of their self-image as writers. Above all, avoid red pens.

Learning Skills through Individual Conferences. A good example of ways to confer with children about their writing can be seen in this description of how first-grade teacher Mary Ellen Giacobbe uses four types of conferences, with content the first focus and skills the last (Cordeiro, Giacobbe & Cazden, 1983).*

> *Content conference*—I assume the role of learner and by careful listening encourage the writer to teach me about the topic. Once it is established what the writer knows, I ask general questions to help the writer to discover he or she knows even more: "Gee, I didn't know about.... Could you tell me more about ...?" After expanding the topic, I ask questions to help the writer to focus.
>
> *Process conference*—It is helpful for writers to reflect on what they have done in their writing and to consider what they might do next. Questions to help children understand their process include, "How did you go about writing this piece?" "I noticed you crossed this section out. Could you tell me how you decided to do that?" "How did you choose your topic?"
>
> *Evaluation conference*—The child is asked to evaluate each piece of writing and then to pick the best of the last three or four to be "published" (typed on a primary typewriter, sewn and bound into a hardcover book and then reillustrated by the child). The book then becomes part of the class library.
>
> *Editing conference*—When the content is as the writer intends it to be, the child is taught one skill in the context of his writing. For instance, if there

*From Patricia Cordeiro, Mary Ellen Giacobbe, & Courtney Cazden, "Apostrophes, Quotation Marks, and Periods: Learning Punctuation in the First Grade," *Language Arts, 60*(1983): 323–332.

> is a lot of dialogue in a particular story, I might teach the child how to use quotation marks. If the child uses that skill in the next piece of writing, I ask about the usage, and the child decides if it should be added to the list of skills he or she is responsible for during the editing stage of future writing (p. 324).

Giacobbe also describes her record-keeping system for this conferencing approach to writing and learning skills.

> Located in the writing center were two writing folders for each child. The first folder, for work in progress, served as a record-keeping device for both the writer and the teacher. All the titles of books written are listed on the cover. Inside the cover on the left is a list of possible topics to write about (compiled by each child). On the right is the list of skills the writer is responsible for during the editing stage of any piece of writing. On the back of the folder is space for the teacher to keep a record of skills known and skills taught. The other folder is for accumulated work (p. 324).

Learning Skills in Peer Conferences. Students can also edit other students. Here is an example of a fourth-grade peer-editing group, using the method described in the chapters on writing, helping each other edit and revise. One child experienced in this method explains to another how it works.

Child Editor: Editing means to look through it and see if there's any mistakes and revising is like changing the words to make it easier to understand.

Child Author: It's not going to be the final copy?

Child Editor: No.

Child Author: After we revise it do we rewrite it again?

Child Editor: Yeah.

Child Author: This is like a newspaper story about what might happen at Halloween. [*Reads*] "Mystery of Witch and Warlock Continues. In Baton Rouge, on the 31st of October which is Halloween, Robert Trolls said he saw a black evil witch and warlock on a magic broomstick. 'It was a scary sight,' he said. Robert says that at 8:00 at night while he was taking his son and daughter trick-or-treating he saw the witch and warlock. 'My children thought it was very scary,' says Robert Troll. It was a full moon when the witch and warlock came. They made a scary laughing sound and flew away. His wife said that she had seen something fly up in the sky and she . . . (wait) . . . outside to look at it . . . better . . . (wait) . . . outside to see it better but she couldn't see anything. When she came inside it looked like her house had been robbed. 'My diamond ring and necklace has been stolen,' she screamed. Every Halloween people look outside to see what this flying object is and something gets stolen. Only the most valuable stuff gets stolen. So if you see a flying object do not look outside 'cause if you do something will get stolen."

After reading, the peer-editing group discusses the story.

Child Editor: *Evil.* I don't think it should be there. Maybe you could find a better word to describe them.
Child Author: Or maybe leave evil out?
Child Editor: That might sound better.
Child Editor: Why don't you put jewelry instead of stuff. It sounds kinda . . . a little babyish or something.
Child Author: OK. Let's see. Jewelry. Only the most valuable jewelry or her most valuable jewelry. How do you spell jewelry?
Child Editor: J–E–W–E–L–R–Y.
Child Editor: I think you need to indent here to make another paragraph.
Child Editor: He could give a name to the son and daughter. It could be anybody. You know, it's sorta . . .
Child Editor: How about using adjectives to describe them? Or grades in school? Or specific age?
Child Editor: Like *evil.* It describes witch.
Child Author: OK. His fourth-grade son and baby daughter.
Child Editor: You need a comma in the middle here. This looks sorta like a period or something.

Students listen attentively as a classmate reads what he has written in a fourth-grade peer-editing group.

Child Author: Well it shouldn't.
Child Editor: I couldn't really understand the part about his wife. But it's good. It's a good story.

The students continue to discuss all aspects of this story: its content, meaning, style (it was supposed to be a newspaper article), spelling, punctuation, organization, form, and so on. Their discussion shows that they are very aware of the importance of these elements when they are applying them directly to a piece of writing they are sharing and may want to publish.

The peer-editing group followed the same procedure with the three other members, and with the editing and revising advice they received from each other rewrote their pieces the next day. Several of them eventually published their pieces in a fictional class newspaper about Halloween.

This example demonstrates that children can and will take charge of their own needs in writing—the need to make meaning clear, the need to achieve conventional forms in spelling, handwriting, and mechanics, and the need to communicate what they have written—as they occur in the context of real writing.

Spelling, Handwriting, and the Writing Conventions Applied in the Content Areas

Children learn skills in the process of writing freely and often on topics of their own choice. One focus for many types of writing in the classroom, which also gives children a real reason and need to gain control over writing skills, is in the context of learning in the content areas. Subjects across the curriculum become sources of spelling words that the children really need in some of the many types of writing they do for other subjects such as social studies, science, mathematics, and the arts. Handwriting and writing conventions become increasingly important to the children as they publish some of these forms of writing in the content areas. A unit in one of the content areas often becomes the focus for a ripple effect of many other experiences and activities, including the teaching and learning of writing skills.

Finding a Pebble

I stumbled on such a unit one year that cut across the curriculum and was integrated through the language arts. The pebble that started the ripple effect was an educational television show with the intriguing title "Meet the Arts." I wanted to take advantage of televised learning and the topic sounded more intrinsically interesting than "You and Your Teeth" or "Learning about Maps."

Judging from the classroom interest, my choice was justified. This excellent program had my third- and fourth-grade students spellbound from the beginning. A teacher/narrator guided them through stages of the history of art each week, beginning with the cave paintings in Lascaux,

Students learn spelling, handwriting, and the writing conventions as they work together on a report for social studies.

France, and moving through time to the present period. Since art is a reflection of humankind's feelings, ideas, desires, visions, ideals, fears, and drives, art history is really a history of the world from the time human beings first made marks on surfaces to indicate that they were there, that they were aware they had a past, and that there would be a future to note it all. Everything we studied that year was centered around ideas from art as a way to study world history, and was integrated through the language arts.

A Ripple Effect: Culture Graphics

As we continued our study of world history through the arts, one idea that emerged was that all cultures have used some form of graphic symbols to represent their ideas. As the students noticed these symbols, and the similarities and differences among them in their various forms over time, they tried to invent some themselves and raised their awareness and appreciation for all communication systems. They also practiced spelling, handwriting, and the use of writing conventions in the broader context of learning about art, graphics, writing, and human communication.

See *The Bestiary,* by T. H. White (Putnam, 1960). Bestiaries were compilations of what medieval people knew of natural history with sources that went back to the early oral tradition, mythology, Egypt, Greece, Rome, and the early Christian Church.

Medieval Bestiaries. One experience in particular led the children from an initial inquiry to an in-depth study of the many permutations of graphics and writing in our culture. The television show on medieval times showed monks in a monastery painstakingly copying and illuminating book manuscripts, a rare treasure in those days. In an age of fast copying machines that can crank out hundreds of copies in minutes, the idea that one monk might spend a lifetime copying one book was intriguing and romantic to the students and they had to find out more.

As part of our research, we found out about bestiaries and there was nothing to do, of course, but write and illustrate our own manuscripts. After an extended period of creating original manuscripts, patterned after books of the period covering topics from mythology to religion to medical advice and household tips, we went through a period of the study of hand bookmaking, calligraphy, and illumination. By this time, many of the students had a manuscript ready to copy and illuminate, and for several weeks our room was transformed into a medieval monastery. Everyone took a vow of silence and copied and painted their manuscripts with India ink, watercolors, enamel paint, and gold and silver while candles burned and twelfth-century Gregorian chants played in the background.

The importance and value of ideas recorded through pictures and symbols must have become clear to these students and these books became prized possessions, almost obsessions for some. No one was really surprised when the most popular fifth-grade boy in the class—the tallest, most athletic, and most admired both by the girls and by the other boys—burst into tears when he spilled India ink on a nearly completed manuscript page, covering a beautifully illuminated letter he had worked on for days. The boy recovered, because he was also most well adjusted, but his outburst triggered a new attitude of interest, respect, and understanding for the relationship between ideas and words, and symbols and signs, and the links among these, from the time of early human beings right up to a fourth- and fifth-grade class studying spelling, handwriting, and writing conventions in the context of world history.

Handmade Books. The experience with illuminating manuscripts led to an extended interest in calligraphy and other writing systems, further increased by a visit from a graphic artist who taught at the local university. His particular interest was bookmaking, and he created and printed books by hand. He shared many ideas about the process with the students, and left samples of many types of print used by artists such as himself. Intrigued by the idea of a limited edition of handmade books, especially after the painstaking work of copying one by hand, we decided to create a limited-edition book as a class project. Someone had found out that cookbooks are perennial best-sellers. In collaboration with the art teacher, the class put together a collection of favorite family recipes, cut linoleum prints to illustrate each one, printed the text on a handpress, and bound and sold copies.

See Chapter 5, "Featured Teacher Phyllis Fuglaar: Writing and Publishing Choose-Your-Own-Adventure Books."

Modern Graphics and a Time Capsule. The children wrote scripts for commercials to air over the public address system at school, and we moved into the age of new media as we continued to think about culture graphics. This eventually led to an animated filmmaking project, of the sort described

See Chapter 11 on the media arts.

more fully in the chapter on the media arts, and to our initiation into the computer age, as we viewed and responded to computer-generated graphics. In May, after these and many other experiences, we placed samples of our work as well as other signs and symbols from the current culture into a metal time capsule and buried it in the schoolyard as a message to future generations about what we had learned about the past and the use of symbolization in the present.

Games for Learning Spelling, Handwriting, and the Writing Conventions

Playing word games can raise a student's linguistic awareness of the underlying relationship among words and the important relationship between word study, writing, and learning to spell and use other writing conventions.

Word Sorts

Words for games can be drawn from classroom experiences and events, children's books, words from the content areas, and the children's own writing. For example, words related to Halloween are simultaneously exciting and troublesome. First-graders may be reading and writing about and planning to be a witch for *Halloween*—a tricky word itself, and an exciting etymological study. Fifth-graders may be moving on to being *ghouls* and *vampires,* and exploring words like *haunted, bloodthirsty,* and *mummy.* While younger children may be learning about Halloween customs and using words like *trick-or-treat, safety,* and *costume,* older students may be studying about *skeletons* and *bones—femurs* and *fibulas* and the especially popular *coccyx.* These wonderful words can be noted and recorded and collected on labels and word rings and in personal dictionaries, spelling journals, word files, and word banks. Classroom lists of frequently used words for these experiences and events can be written on the board or on chart paper, or on a transparency for the overhead projector. These lists then become a source of material for word and spelling games, related to the students' real interests, experiences, and events. The words can be written on sentence strips to be cut up or put on word cards for classification games.

Beers and Beers (1981) make some suggestions for word classifications and for discussion questions to help children explore meaning elements, syntactic function, and pronunciation of words.*

1. Gather a collection of words that a child knows (word bank, word recognition test, actual reading material).
2. Ask the child to categorize the words under various headings. You may provide the heading based on his or her spelling or encourage the child to seek out the heading.

*From Carol Strickland Beers & James Wheelock Beers, "Three Assumptions About Learning to Spell," *Language Arts, 58,* 5(1981): 573–580.

3. Some examples of these headings are:
   a. Short-vowel words
   b. Long-vowel words
   c. One-syllable words
   d. Describing words (adjectives or adverbs)
   e. Verbs ending in *-ing*
   f. Past-tense verbs
   g. Words with prefixes, suffixes
   h. Words conveying the same meaning
4. Once a category has been filled by the child ask the following questions and discuss the responses with the child.
   a. Why did you put these words together?
   b. What do you find similar to these words (meaning, function, letters, etc.)?
   c. What do you find different about these words? Why do you think they are different?
   d. Why is this a useful category for grouping words? (p. 579)

This type of gamelike approach is called **word sorts,** and there are many variations. Word sort activities draw on children's growing ability to classify similar words, form generalizations about the relationships among these word categories, and then generate hypotheses about patterns among words which they can test with new words they meet as they increasingly discover for themselves how language and words work (Gillet & Kita, 1979, 1980; Sulzby, 1980).

The only materials required are index cards, or small cards you cut yourself, with appropriate words printed on them. Young children seated on the floor or in a word study center, in small groups or individually, can begin to practice sorting objects according to similar properties (buttons, sea shells, dry pasta), or picture cards (animals, objects, fruit) and then move to sorting word cards. They may simply put them in piles, or you may use a sorting card such as a piece of poster paper with the categories drawn on it or a manila folder with columns and a token object or picture to represent a category in each column. Provide a miscellaneous category for words they may not be sure about right away. Observe the children as they sort and provide assistance and immediate feedback. Note the differences among them and the difficulties and successes they seem to be having, to help you plan for future word sort activities. For young children, keep closed categories simple at first. Use only words they are familiar with from their sight vocabulary, words from language experience charts and writing, basal readers, library books, labels in the classroom, or words used in the content areas for older children.

Here are several different types of sorts, starting with those appropriate for younger children and moving on to those appropriate for older children according to what we know about how children learn to spell (Gillet & Kita, 1979).

Teacher's Choice: Closed Sorts. In this version of the game, the teacher states the criterion in advance.

1. *Letters and sounds:*
   initial letters; consonants; vowels; blends; vowel sounds and patterns—short, long, digraphs, r-controlled; homophones
2. *Structure:*
   prefixes; suffixes; affixes; inflection;
   number of syllables; juncture of syllables;
   consonant doubling; dropping *e*
3. *Grammatical function:*
   parts of speech; stress; inflectional endings—*-ed; -ing*
4. *Meaning:*
   root families; etymology; types of words

Children's Choice: Open Sort. In this version of the game, the children establish their own criteria. After a period of sorting objects and pictures and then word cards according to the teacher's criterion, children should be encouraged to play with cards and begin to establish their own criteria for sorting categories. These open sorts may be practiced in a gamelike situation, with two or more children playing traditional games with word cards (Gillet & Kita, 1979, 1980). For example, to play Guess My Group, the children sort their own cards into several categories and the other players try to guess what the categories are. For the game of Concentration, sixteen cards are placed face down on the table. A child turns two cards over, tries to create and justify a category for them, and, if the others accept it, picks up these cards and chooses two more. If the others do not accept the category, another child plays. The child with the most cards at the end of the game wins. Go Fish, Rummy, Old Maid, and other traditional card games can also be played with word sort cards.

Word Sort Searches. Another variation on word sorts is to search for words which fit a category in a written text and circle or underline or write them down. For younger students, this can be done with pages copied from their basal readers, library books, teacher-created texts, or their own writing. These texts can be laminated and written on with a nonpermanent marking pen; thus the marks can be wiped off and the pages used again and again. If the pages are kept in a folder, an answer key could be written on the back for the child to self-check. This procedure could also be used for a children's-choice open sort.

Older students may go on word searches in dictionaries, thesauruses, textbooks, or anywhere they might find words to fit the category they want to use for a word sort. These may be teacher-chosen closed sorts: you suggest a word teaser such as the **phonogram** (word part) *mne,* to see if they can find other words with this element (for example, *amnesia, mnemonic, Mnemosyne.*) Or they might look up word origins to explore common roots of words, for example, *psych,* contained in *psychology, psychiatrist,* and *psychiatric.* Such word searches can be most effectively linked to content area study in an upper-grade classroom, and can lead to other pursuits such as the study of Greek and Roman mythology to learn about the sources of many of the Greek and Latin words in English.

Word Games

Many other kinds of word games require few or no special materials. Some that are useful for spelling are described in the chapter on grammar. Hodges (1981) describes many other games that trigger and then reinforce students' awareness of relationships among words. Some examples are given below.

Letters and Sound Relationships. A number of games can be used to teach the relationship between letters and sounds.

1. *Rhyming Ping Pong.* Two students or teams of students call rhyming words (*cat, bat, fat*) back and forth as quickly as they can. The winner is the last one to have said a word when a signal is given or a timer goes off.

2. *Endless Chain.* Play starts with a word spelled aloud (or written on the board) by one student or team. The next player must spell a word that begins with the last letter or grapheme of that word.

3. *Consonant Cluster Cards.* You or the students make two decks of cards. One deck contains a series of consonant clusters: *bl, br, ch, cr, dr, dw, fl, fr, gr, gl, pl, pr, sc, sch, scr, shr, sl, sm, sn, sp, spr, squ, st, str, sw, thr, tr, tw.* The other deck contains a series of phonograms that can be combined with the consonant clusters to make words: *ad, ale, am, ame, ance, and, ank, at, ate, ave, awl, ay, aze, id, ide, ile, im, imp, ine, ing, ink, ip, ipe, ire, ive, od, ool, oop, op, ope, own, um, ump.*

These card decks can be used for a simple matching game like Solitaire: consonant cluster cards are placed faced up and the child draws phonogram cards and matches them with a consonant cluster to make a word. They may also be used to play a variation of Rummy, with pairs made by combining a cluster and a phonogram.

4. *Phonogram Play.* Challenge the students to make as many words as they can from a given phonogram by adding a consonant or consonant cluster. Use the cards described above. Some good phonograms for this include *ace, ade, ate, ill, ine, ight,* and *ost.*

From Letters to Words. Make a deck of letter cards (you will need at least 200), as follows: for the vowels, 15 cards for the letter *e* and 10 each for *a, i, o,* and *u;* for the consonants, 10 cards each for the letters *c, h, s,* and *t,* 8 each for *b, d, f, g, l, m, n, p, r,* and *w,* 5 each for *j, k, v,* and *y,* and 2 each for *q, x,* and *z.* You will also need to make cards for common two-letter graphemes such as *oo, ea, ee.* These cards may be used to play any number of games using letters to build words. Here are some examples.

A first-grade student sorts words in a game that supports his growing control over the language conventions.

Some commercial word games for spelling: Boggle, Perquackey, Scrabble, Spill & Spell, Word Yahtzee.

1. *Scrambled Words.* In pairs, children try to stump each other by posing scrambled words which the other tries to unscramble.

2. *Building Words.* Each child in a small group receives the same number of cards and tries to make as many words as possible.

3. *Building and Attaching Words.* Older children may attach the words they build in horizontal and vertical strings, as in Scrabble.

4. *Alphabets.* In this variation of Anagrams, students make as many words as possible by rearranging the letters of a given word.*

Some books about codes: *Code Games,* by Norvin Pallas (Sterling, 1971), *Codes and Secret Writing,* by Herbert Zim (William Morrow, 1948), *The Code and Cipher Book,* by Jane Sarnoff and Reynold Fuffing (Scribner, 1975)

Graphic Games

Children can play games with graphic representations of the language. For example, they can

- experiment with their own name (children do this spontaneously as they try out new looks for their signature),
- create graphic representations of words or phrases (such as the ones shown in Figure 7–9; can you guess what they are?),

*Adapted from Richard E. Hodges, *Learning to Spell* (Urbana, IL: ERIC/National Council of Teachers of English, 1981), pp. 18–26.

O hole NE — HOLE IN ONE

ROADS / ROADS — CROSSROADS

T O U C H — TOUCHDOWN

Figure 7–9
Graphic Representations of Words

- write stories in which a letter, number, or a picture replaces a word,
- create their own secret codes and write messages in them (some simple formulas: numbers for letter of the alphabet in order; reverse alphabet; next letter of the alphabet; new symbols for letters),
- use the symbols of a writing system from the past or another culture or another alphabet to create a code or type of hieroglyphics,
- learn a famous coding system such as Morse code and write a message using it.

Summing Up

While often perceived by parents and the public as the outward signs of an educated person who has mastered the basics, in point of fact, correct spelling, legible handwriting, and the writing conventions are merely the tools of the writer. This is not to suggest that handwriting, for example, is not a significant aspect of learning to write. It is important to remember that skills should not be the tail that wags the dog, and take on an importance beyond their usefulness to the writer. They should be taught and learned by children in the context of real language experiences leading to real writing. The research on teaching these skills suggests many practices we should and should not follow in the interests of the development of spelling, handwriting, the writing conventions, and composing among children.

Should-nots for Teaching Spelling

1. Make the following erroneous assumptions about spelling: that it is based primarily on a knowledge of phonics; that rote memorization and copying words over helps; that children should not write if they cannot spell correctly.
2. Rely on commercial spelling programs, with their lists and units, at the expense of time which could be spent on spelling in the context of writing.

Shoulds for Teaching Spelling

1. Be aware of the predictable developmental stages all children go through as they develop spelling strategies, and evaluate each child's spelling progress in terms of these stages.
2. Provide many opportunities and plenty of time for the children to experiment and discover these strategies in the context of real writing for a real audience and for real purposes, and to edit their own writing to find and correct their own errors.
3. Create classroom experiences and activities which expand children's word knowledge by helping them explore similarities and differences among words, meaning elements, and pronunciation.
4. Use a variety of teaching materials and approaches and many individualized experiences to meet the needs of different children.
5. Integrate the teaching of the language arts with experiencing, thinking, reading, speaking, writing, handwriting, and spelling.

Should-nots for Teaching Handwriting

1. Follow a set of commercially prepared materials that follow a lockstep sequence of isolated drills—such as copying rows of circles and slants or words, or simply copying teacher-written sentences off the board—or that teach handwriting through independent drills as though it were an end in itself.
2. Restrict young children to the use of special materials for handwriting, such as wide-ruled paper or large primary pencils without erasers.
3. Ignore the strong connections between the development of spelling, handwriting, and mechanics in the context of composing.

Shoulds for Teaching Handwriting

1. Collect observational data on the individual children and relate this to the data on their development in spelling and writing.
2. Keep handwriting in its proper context of composing and writing for real purposes.
3. Offer the children many opportunities for the exploration of space in art, work, constructions, drama, movement, and dance, as well as in writing.
4. Create a writing center with a variety of writing instruments and paper.
5. Provide enough time for the children to write topics of their own choice as the major way of improving their handwriting. Graves (1983) suggests a minimum of twenty minutes per day for children ages six to nine. Increase time accordingly for older students.

Should-nots for Teaching the Writing Conventions

1. Rely on language arts texts, programmed materials, or dittoed worksheets to teach writing conventions.

2. Become discouraged with yourself or the children if, even after direct teaching and the appearance of correct forms in their writing, some children make the same errors again. While they are gaining mastery over one aspect of composing, they may temporarily lose it in another. Progress is real, but not always steady.

Shoulds for Teaching the Writing Conventions

1. Encourage the children to discover and use the writing conventions as they need them in the context of real writing.
2. In direct instruction, give the children an explanation of a convention based on function and meaning rather than a rote-memory rule ("a sentence is a complete thought") that younger children may not understand.
3. Remember that the use of periods, often a reflection of a more highly developed syntactic sense, may be one of the last forms of punctuation to be mastered, and that first grade may be too early to expect correct use.

Looking Further

1. Collect at least three samples of children's writing from the same class and analyze their stage of spelling development according to Gentry's stages of spelling development described in this chapter. If possible, do this for two different grade levels more than one year apart.

2. Do the same as in Question 1, this time analyzing the children's handwriting according to Graves's stages of handwriting development described in this chapter.

3. Ask several teachers how they teach the writing conventions. Comment on their answers in the light of the study of how punctuation was learned in the two third-grade classrooms described in the chapter.

4. Analyze several spelling textbooks according to what Graves found in his analysis of spelling texts.

5. Collect writing samples from one class and analyze them according to the description of error patterns in this chapter. Suggest activities for children on the basis of your analysis.

6. Play a word game with a group of children to teach spelling according to one of the suggestions in this chapter. See if you can create a word game of your own.

Chapter Eight

Teaching Literature in the Elementary School

Objectives

Look for answers to the following questions as you read this chapter.

- How can you use literature to integrate the language arts and learning across the curriculum?
- How do you choose and use children's books in the classroom?
- How do you create a context for literature in the classroom?
- What are some strategies for talking about and responding to books?
- How can you center the language arts and reading instruction around literature?

A Child's View

Here is a letter written by fourth-grader David to the author of a book his teacher read aloud in class:

Dear Mr. Shirreffs,

I like your books very much. Our teacher read us *Mystery of the Haunted Mine* and I got a copy of *The Secret of the Spanish Desert* from the library. My Mom has ordered it from the bookstore so I will have my own copy.

We are making a play using the characters in your book and I get to be Tuck because I'm tall and funny like him. Could you come and see our play?

Is there really treasure in the desert? How do you find it? Have you written any other books? I would like to read them. . . .

This is the letter David wrote as an adult to his former fourth-grade teacher:

Dear Carole,

I still have your father's books, the two he autographed: *Mystery of the Haunted Mine* and *The Secret of the Spanish Desert.* I had them on my bookshelves in my last flat, and stopped and read them again as I was packing up in preparation for moving. They're in Mom's attic now, with the rest of my books. I'll always treasure them. . . .

"How to Find a Lost Mine" and Other Treasures in Children's Books

See "Gordon D. Shirreffs: An Interview With a Western Writer," by Carole Shirreffs Cox, in *English Journal,* 75 (1986), 40–48.

I discovered the power and importance of literature in the elementary curriculum almost by chance during my first year of teaching. As my fourth-grade class and I quietly pored over some paperback book club order forms, three students approached me excitedly saying, "Miss Shirreffs, there's a book in here with your name on it!" "Impossible," I countered, "No one has a name like that except my family." "It's true," they returned; and they were right. My father, Gordon D. Shirreffs, writes Western novels and has also written many books of historical and regional fiction for children and young adults.

Mystery of the Haunted Mine (Scholastic, 1962; formerly *The Haunted Treasure of the Espectras* (Chilton, 1962). Other children's books by Gordon D. Shirreffs are: *Son of the Thunder People* (Westminster, 1957), *Swiftwagon* (Westminster, 1958), and *The Gray Sea Raiders* (Chilton, 1961).

By now the entire class was interested and many ordered their own paperback copies of *Mystery of the Haunted Mine,* a contemporary tale of mystery and adventure set in the rugged Arizona mountain country that tells about three young people searching for a lost Spanish gold mine which is thought to have been guarded by the spirit of the outlaw Asesino for over fifty years.

The day the books arrived was exciting for the children and significant for me in terms of how I began to perceive the role of literature in language arts education. I had not really been fully aware until then how it is at once easy and essential to integrate language learning and literature. Now, of course, I cannot imagine how it could be any other way. And it was the children who showed me how it should be done.

Here is a road map of what happened in this fourth-grade class in California—and in other classes of mine elsewhere—when one book acted as a pebble that set off a ripple effect of language learning experiences.

Reading the Book Aloud

See Chapter 3, "Reading Aloud," and Chapter 9, "Reading Aloud and Along with Children."

A chapter of the book a day read aloud becomes the high point of the day. Some students read along in their own copies. Others put their heads down on their desks and lose themselves in listening to the story of how Gary, Tuck, and Sue unraveled the mystery of the lost map and the lost gold mine, encountering natural hazards such as the climate and terrain of the Southwest desert mountains and more unnatural ones such as the alleged ghost who guarded the mine and who seemed more real than not.

Providing Time to Talk

In addition to time to read, it is obvious that the children should always have time for talking after reading to give them the opportunity to focus their thinking, develop concepts, clarify their feelings, and share their ideas. Questions to start off a whole-class discussion are simple and open, inviting more than one correct response. For example:

See Chapter 3, "Closed Versus Open Questioning Styles."

> What do you think about what happened?
> What did you like? Not like? Why?
> What do you think will happen next? Why?

Identifying Questions of Interest

Children's questions emerging during whole-class discussions and at other times yield many ideas for ways to expand this literature experience into other areas of the curriculum. For example, what is the desert like in Arizona? Was the treasure real? Whose treasure was it? How did the early Spanish settlers mine for gold? What were the Indians like there? Are there other mines and treasures? Was this one really haunted?

I list these questions on a piece of chart paper and, through further discussions and planning times, these become study questions for new social studies and science inquiries related to topics of interest centered around the American Southwest: its history, geography, culture, people, and myths and legends.

Notable Children's Trade Books in the Field of Social Studies and *Outstanding Science Trade Books,* both available annually from Children's Book Council, 67 Irving Place, New York, NY 10003

Gathering Resources

When one child brings in a map of Arizona saved from a family trip, I invite others to do the same and more maps, postcards, rock collections, Indian artifacts, and a snakeskin or two begin to crowd the table and bookshelf which have become a center for the study of the many topics and activities stimulated by the reading of this book. I learn to find special bibliographies listing related children's fiction and informational books and media to expand the classroom study and literature center.

Helping to Find More Books

In addition to books related to topics of interest for further study, I learn to help the students identify and find books related to their own interests to widen their independent reading and response to literature. Sometimes the choice of books is influenced by the type of book we are reading as a class. For example, after reading *Mystery of the Haunted Mine,* some of the children acknowledge a strong interest in any type of mystery. Others indicate that they like stories of the supernatural. Some lean more towards any kind of adventure story.

I also encourage the children to respond to these books in many individual ways: through talking, writing, art, drama, and media production. These responses become an integral part of several literature-based strategies for the teaching of reading.

A school librarian can be an invaluable aid in helping you match children and books for wide independent reading on all subjects. See also bibliographies such as *Adventuring with Books* (National Council of Teachers of English, 1985).

Integrating Topics of Interest

The tale of the haunted mine starts a ripple effect of experiences that include social studies (history, geography, and Native American, Hispanic, and Anglo cultures), science (geology and ecology of the desert), mathematics, art and music, and folklore—all suggested directly or indirectly by listening to a contemporary mystery with a strong regional and historical setting and mood. Table 8–1 shows the range of some possible topics of interest to pursue and their relationship to the content areas, some possible kinds of learning experiences, and related books for research and for wide independent reading as students work in small groups or read alone.

Keep records of these unit-related books with brief annotations. These may be kept on file cards, in a loose-leaf notebook, or on a computer file.

Ever since that time, I have begun any unit of study by gathering a nucleus of good children's books, both nonfiction and fiction, around which to center opportunities for experiences related to the students' interest. It is also a good idea to keep a record of these books with brief annotations, types of learning experiences, and student responses and results.

Finding Out More about the Author

Insight into an author's method of writing will inevitably tell children a great deal about writing, research, and literature in general. They are usually fascinated to learn about how authors get their ideas and do their research and their writing, and what other books they have written.

A Visit from an Author: Gordon D. Shirreffs

See *Something about the Author* (Gale Research, 1971).

A highlight of our study of the *Mystery of the Haunted Mine* is when the author, my father, agrees to come and talk to my class, having warned me in advance that he is not going to try to answer impossible questions like "Where do you get ideas for your stories from?" But in fact he does just that as he tells my students more stories drawn from his knowledge about the culture and history of the Southwest. First, he gives them the following seriously stated but tongue-in-cheek rules for finding a lost mine:

How to Find a Lost Mine

1. Travel to a remote part of the Southwest desert country that is unmapped and unexplored.
2. Be chased by bandits, desperadoes, and outlaws.
3. Lose your food and water.
4. Become completely lost.
5. Discover a gold mine but not a way of taking the gold with you.
6. Fill an empty tin can (shoe, canteen) with a few gold nuggets.
7. Head for civilization.

Table 8–1 *A Study of the American Southwest*

Topics of Interest	*Response/Learning Experiences*	Books		
		Informational	*Fiction*	*Poetry*
Social Studies				
People of the Southwest:				
Many Cultures	*For each culture:*			
Native Americans	Interview a famous person of past on tape (or pretend to be this person). Cook and eat food of that culture.	*Geronimo, The Fighting Apache,* Ronald Syme	*Sing Down the Moon,* Scott O'Dell	*Out of the Earth I Sing,* Richard Lewis
Hispanic Americans	Read a biography and compare with other students for accuracy, authenticity, and bias. Write a newspaper from point of view of each culture. Cook and eat food of that culture.	*The Hispanic Americans,* Milton Meltzer *Children of the Wild West,* Russel Freedman	*And Now Miguel,* Joseph Krumgold *Child of Fire,* Scott O'Dell	*The Voice of the Children,* Miriam Lasanta
Anglo Americans	Debate a current issue.			
A Long History				
Early Settlement Early Explorers Recent Times	Make a timeline of the Southwest. Dramatize events in *Tree in the Trail*—history of SW along SF trail, Native American to Spanish and Anglo explorers and settlers.	*Tree in the Trail,* Holling C. Holling *With Domingo Veal in San Ontario, 1743,* Marian Montinello	*Walk the World's Rim,* Betty Baker	
Land of the Southwest: A Diverse Geography				
Desert Mountains	Build erosion table, a model of the desert and mountains; observe and record effects of weather on terrain in journals.	*Eight Words for Thirsty,* Ann Sigford *The Gentle Desert: Exploring an Ecosystem,* A. Pringle		*Desert Voices,* Byrd Baylor
Science				
Mineral Wealth				
Geology Mining	Collect, identify, classify and report on properties of rocks, minerals, precious metals. Construct as display with experiments other students could try. Set up a sluice box to experiment with gold mining.	*The Rock-Hounds Book,* Seymour Simon *Secrets in Stones,* Rose Wyler *Gold and Other Precious Metals,* Charles Coombs	*Trapped in Death Cave,* Bill Wallace *Ghosts Beneath Our Feet,* Betty Wright	

(continued)

Table 8-1 *Continued*

Topics of Interest	*Response/Learning Experiences*	*Books*		
		Informational	*Fiction*	*Poetry*
Ecology				
Animals Plants Humans	Write a script and videotape a series of television documentaries on ecology of the Southwest; information and interviews with Native Americans and Hispanics of the past and present, and various personified plants and animals who identify problems, suggest solutions.	*The 100-Year-Old Cactus,* Anita Holmes *The Desert is Theirs,* Byrd Baylor	*Hawk, I'm Your Brother,* Byrd Baylor	*The Earth is Sore: Native Americans on Nature,* Aline Amon
Mathematics				
Culture Mathematics: Treasure Hunting				
Other Cultures	Research and report on Native American number systems. Learn to count in Spanish.	*From Ungskah I To Oyaylee I0,* Lucille Corcas		
Charts Maps	Make maps of Southwest. Make imaginary treasure maps and write stories to go with them.	*Secret Codes and Ciphers,* Bernice Kohm *Understanding Maps,* B. Tannebaum	*The Secret Three,* Mildred Myrick	
Fine Arts				
A Unique Culture				
Art	Make masks. Make mural of Southwest showing people, history, and cultures.	*They Put on Masks,* Byrd Baylor		*The Tree Stands Shining: Poetry of the North American Indians,* Hettie Jones
Music Dance	Listen to Native American and Hispanic music and folk songs. Learn dances from both cultures.	*A Cry from the Earth: Music of the North American Indians,* John Bierhorst		
Humanities				
Literature: Traditional Poetry/Verse Philosophy/ Religion	Storytelling: learn a story and tell for others. Read aloud: write poems and verse themselves. Guest speaker: write interview questions. Stage a ceremonial of Native Americans with pantomime and masks. Dramatize Hispanic ceremony: Los Posados, etc.	*And It Is Still That Way: Legends Told by Arizona Indian Children,* Byrd Baylor *Mask-Making with Pantomime and Stories from American History,* Laura Ross	*The Girl Who Loved Wild Horses,* Paul Goble *Paco's Miracle,* Ann Nolan Clark	*The Whispering Wind: Poetry by Young American Indians,* Terry Allen *The Sacred Path: Spells, Prayers and Power Songs of the American Indians,* John Bierhorst

8. Be caught in a fierce desert sandstorm and stagger or crawl along.
9. Be found unconscious with the can (shoe, canteen) of gold nuggets clutched in your hand, but unable to find your way to the gold mine.
10. You have found a lost mine.

Then he tells them more stories: of mysterious mountains rising up unexpectedly out of the Southwest desert country, their shadows casting an eerie spell over the mind and imagination of anyone who ventures near them; of strange glyphs and signs carved in rough canyon rock which lead a gold seeker to a hidden mine; and of spirits of long-dead *patrones,* men killed at a mine site to become ghostly guardians of these treasures. As he speaks, he spirits the mesmerized fourth-grade girls and boys out of their classroom and leads them over many of the twisting trails that wind through the strange terrain of Southwestern lore, a curious blend of truth and legend of the Indian, Spanish, and Anglo cultures. With my father as beckoning guide, the children trudge through an imaginary desert searching for gold.

Other books about treasure seeking in the Southwest by Gordon D. Shirreffs are: *The Secret of the Spanish Desert* (Chilton, 1964), sequel to *Mystery of the Haunted Mine, Mystery of Lost Canyon* (Chilton, 1963), and *Mystery of the Lost Cliff Dwelling* (Prentice-Hall, 1968).

He also gives them an insight into the process of writing historical or regional fictional by telling the children that everything in his books and stories is based on fact. He did not create his formula for finding a lost mine out of his fertile imagination but from countless tales of prospectors who told of finding and losing a mine under those very circumstances. The Espectros Mountains, which appear in his books, are modeled very closely on the very real Superstition Mountains in Arizona, the site of many mysterious disappearances and unsolved murders documented in local county records.

Espectros means *ghosts* in Spanish.

Perhaps the most tempting nugget of Western lore with which my father tantalizes the children is a description of the old Spanish miners' code, symbols that the early miners carved in the rock to mark their way back to a mine through twisting canyons and dry river beds that could change course after landslides or desert flash floods (see Figure 8–1).

The children are fascinated when the three young treasure hunters decoded these symbols on an old *derrotero,* or map, as they searched for the legendary lost Espectro mine. But when my father explains that these symbols were really used by the Spanish gold miners and might even still be out there somewhere in the wild canyons and rugged foothills of Arizona and New Mexico, idly waiting to lead someone to a lost mine, I could swear I see many young eyes in the class light up with a gleam that could only be described as gold fever.

The students ask many questions that day, questions that stem from their listening, reading, thinking, and responding to literature. For example, there has been a sly rumor going around that perhaps I am the prototype for the character of Sue in the book.

Author: Do you have any more questions you'd like to ask me?
Child: How do you get characters?

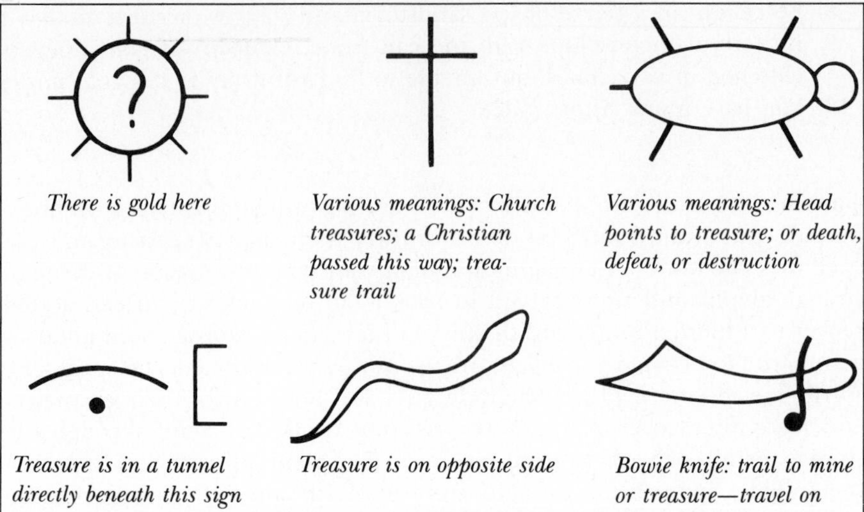

Figure 8–1
Old Spanish Miners' Code

Author: A writer gets characters from the people he knows in life. And they're all around you. Fascinating characters. You really don't have to make characters up.

Child [*a bit slyly*]: Well, I mean, like, we thought maybe Sue sounded a little like Miss Shirreffs. Is that true?

Author: Well, I don't want to embarrass Miss Shirreffs—she'll probably get mad at me if I do—but I might have gotten some ideas about Sue from her. Why do you think she's like Sue?

Child: Well, she likes school, and books and movies.

Author: And she liked languages. Don't forget she was good at languages, like Miss Shirreffs. Anything else? About the way she acts?

Child: Well . . . [*very slyly and somewhat sheepishly*] you said she "inspected her nails" when she thinks she's right or gets nervous. And she talked a lot.

Author [*laughing*]: Yeah, that's true. I'd forgotten about that. But I'm not going to say Sue is Miss Shirreffs. I guess you'll have to decide how real Sue really is. And that's really up to each of you as you read the book or any book for that matter.

You do not have to have a father who writes books in order to integrate literature into your teaching through a shared read-aloud experience. The fact that my students first noticed the book because it was written by somebody with the same name as their teacher just happens to be the reason our attention was drawn to it. Nor is it necessary to have the author talk to the class in person. When I was living in Wisconsin and read this book to my class, they wrote letters to the author—something anyone can do.

What *is* necessary is the willingness to reserve a special time of the day for reading aloud, for talking about books and letting children openly respond to literature, to encourage them to do wide independent reading, and then to use their interests and responses as a focus around which you plan further experiences in language and learning that can be woven throughout the curriculum.

The power of literature in the elementary curriculum is to capture the imagination for a moment, to take us where it has never been before—to other times and places, even to other worlds; to let us empathize with others and discover their needs and pleasures and joys and fears; to let us discover all the moods that can possibly be created by writers of books; and, above all, to discover the power of literature to make us feel and see and understand things we would not otherwise feel and see and understand about what it means to be human.

The importance of literature in the elementary curriculum is that it is a way of knowing about the world. Teachers can foster this way of knowing by extending students' interests; by encouraging listening, thinking, talking, responding, and sharing; by helping students extend their reading independently on a wide variety of subjects; by focusing close reading and research on topics of particular interest; and by integrating language learning and learning across the curriculum.

In order to do all this, and make the most of the treasures to be found in children's books, you should become knowledgeable about several aspects of choosing and using books in language arts education—students' interests and attitudes, understanding literary elements, and issues in children's literature—and about literature in the classroom in general.

Attention can be drawn to books to share in many other ways: one student's recommendation; a favorite book of yours that you recommend; a media tie-in book.

Authors can be contacted through publishers and often send biographical information about themselves and even advice on writing for young readers.

Making Connections

The experience of this fourth-grade class is just one example of how a book can cause a ripple effect of interest, ideas, and experiences with language, demonstrating the power and importance of literature in the classroom. Children's books are available on many topics of interest to start similar ripple effects in other classrooms.

Choosing and Using Books

Children's Interests and Attitudes

Many studies on children's interests in and attitudes towards literature (Purves & Beach, 1972) indicate that children prefer literary to nonliterary presentation of material in books that tell good stories with suspenseful plots and much action; that content seems to be the major determinant of reading interest; and that students' interests show definite development trends.

Examples: picture books and anything by Dr. Seuss.

Children at all ages maintain an interest in stories about children their own age. At an earlier age, they like folktales and fairy tales and stories with fantasy figures, often animals, who represent childlike experiences. These younger children perceive their reading as entertainment and prefer books that do not confine them and that allow a free extension of vicarious experience. As they grow older, students' interest often moves from fantasy to real-life stories when they begin to perceive reading as a way of finding out about the world. Middle-grade students tend to prefer stories of daily life as familiar experience, stories about animals and nature, and tales of adventure. Middle-school students are more interested in reading books about people their own age, perhaps because it allows them to participate vicariously in the activities of peer groups other than their own during this period of moving away from parental control and trying out new identities within the safety of the peer group before choosing and assuming their adult identity as individuals.

Examples: E. B. White's *Charlotte's Web,* Laura Ingalls Wilder's *Little House* books, Bantam's *Choose Your Own Adventure* series, and anything by Beverly Cleary or Judy Blume.

Examples: S. E. Hinton's *The Outsiders, Tex,* and *Rumble Fish,* and Paula Danziger's *The Cat Ate My Gymsuit* and *Can You Sue Your Parents for Malpractice?*

Students' Criteria for Choosing Books. Other studies show that it is extremely important to students to have many opportunities to select their own books rather than merely having books assigned. They like to be able to read at their own speed, they appreciate helpful librarians, and they enjoy having a great number of titles to choose from, especially books that fulfill personal interests. Among the criteria for selecting books are an opportunity to sample the book, its content, the book title, teacher recommendation, illustrations, the author's name, previous introduction by the mass media, and a friend's recommendation.

Research also shows that peers, parents, and teachers can make a difference through recommendations and models to emulate. These factors may be more important than direct instruction, and the teacher's enthusiasm for literature is most important of all. Studies have also shown that parents know more than teachers, who often misjudge students' reading interests. These studies also suggest that teachers consult children more and experts less in assessing their reading interests. Above all, students' interests are influenced by their need to satisfy certain psychological needs: the need to fantasize, explore, or identify with animals, heroes, and children and young adults who provide optimistic models for vicarious experiences.

For a free reprint of each year's list of Children's Choices, write: International Reading Association, 800 Barksdale Road, Newark, DE 19714.

Children's Choices. Since 1973, the International Reading Association/Children's Book Council Joint Committee has conducted an annual poll and published a list of Children's Choices selected by children themselves from among several hundred of the more than 2,500 children's trade books published every year. The books cover subjects and interests from kindergarten through eighth grade. Teams of teachers in five areas of the country, rotating biannually, test the books in the classroom. The results are published each year in the October issue of *The Reading Teacher.*

Analysis of these books reveals the following common characteristics: they usually teach a lesson; they describe the setting in detail; they are generally not sad; they tend to consist of episodic plots involving confrontations among characters with opposing viewpoints; and they are faster-paced than less popular books. Their most notable characteristic, however, is warmth. Evidently children like these books because the characters express their feelings (Abrahamson, 1980; Sebesta, 1979). As for their content, an analysis of the first six years of Children's Choice books reveals the following categories of books in order of preference, beginning with the most liked (and shown here with representative examples) (Greenlaw, 1983).

See *Children's Choices: Teaching with Books Children Like*, edited by Nancy Roser and Margaret Frith (International Reading Association, 1983).

Primary Level

1. Humor
   George and Martha Tons of Fun, by James Marshall (Houghton, 1981)
   Morris and Boris, by Bernard Wiseman (Dodd, 1974)
   The Stupids Have a Ball, by Harry Allard and James Marshall (Houghton, 1979)
2. Make-believe, people, and animals
   The Snowman, by Raymond Briggs (Random, 1979)
   Alexander, Who Used to be Rich Last Sunday, by Judith Viorst (Atheneum, 1979)
   Some Swell Pup, or Are You Sure You Want a Dog? by Maurice Sendak (Farrar, Straus, 1977)
3. Real things, rhyme, and mystery
   Freight Train, by Donald Crews (Greenwillow, 1979)
   Gregory Griggs and Other Nursery Rhyme People, by Arnold Lobel (Greenwillow, 1979)
   Nate the Great and the Phony Clue, by Marjorie Sharmat (Coward, 1978)
4. Fairy tales, sports, and how-to books
   Hansel and Gretel, by The Brothers Grimm, illustrated by Susan Jeffers (Dial, 1981)
   The Littlest Leaguer, by Syd Hoff (Windmill, 1977)
   The Great Thumbprint Drawing Book, by Ed Emberly (Little, Brown, 1978)

Upper Level

1. Adventure, jokes/humor, and informational books
   Frozen Fire, by James Houston (McElderry/Atheneum, 1978)
   Miss Nelson is Missing, by Harry Allard (Houghton, 1978)
   Pyramid, by David Macaulay (Houghton, 1975)
2. Fantasy, mystery, sports, and the supernatural
   Greenwitch, by Susan Cooper (McElderry/Atheneum, 1974)
   The Case of the Baker Street Irregular, by Robert Newman (Atheneum, 1979)

Front Court Hex, by Matt Christopher (Little, Brown, 1974)
The Headless Roommate and Other Tales of Terror, by Daniel Cohen (Evans, 1981)

3. How-to books, biography, historical fiction, poetry
   Model Buildings and How to Make Them, by Harvey Weiss (Crowell, 1980)
   Langston Hughes: American Poet, by Alice Walker (Crowell, 1974)
   Dragon Wings, by Laurence Yep (Harper, 1975)
   Nightmares: Poems to Trouble Your Sleep, by Jack Prelutsky (Greenwillow, 1977)
4. Science fiction, romance
   A Swiftly Tilting Planet, by Madeleine L'Engle (Farrar, Straus, 1979)
   Bargain Bride, by Evelyn Lampman (McElderry/Atheneum, 1978)

The Literary Elements

Even though the content of stories, poems, and books for children varies greatly and is represented in many different types of children's books—picture books, picture story books, fantasy, contemporary realism, historical and regional fiction, traditional verses and tales, poetry and rhyme, informational books and biography, books of jokes, riddles, and word play, and how-to books—good books all share certain literary elements: character, plot, setting, mood, language, and style (Lukens, 1982). Not only should teachers be aware of these elements when evaluating and choosing books for children, but they should also make every effort to foster an understanding of these elements among students as they experience, discuss, and respond to literature.

Sloan (1984) describes eight skills or understandings of literary elements for elementary- and middle-school students. They are shown here with examples of books for primary and upper elementary grades and for middle schools that particularly lend themselves to the development of each understanding through discussion.

1. ***An awareness of plot as a series of incidents or sequence of events through which the initial incident or story problem is resolved.***

   Cumulative folktales like *The Fat Cat,* by Jack Kent, can develop an understanding of sequence for young children as can the episodic plots in Beverly Cleary's books (*Ramona and Her Father,* for example). For older students, literary devices, such as the flashbacks in *Mrs. Frisby and the Rats of NIMH,* by Robert O'Brien, can expand awareness and understanding of plot.

2. ***Skill in following story sequence and predicting possible outcomes.***

   Predictable traditional tales like *The Three Little Pigs* or newer ones like Bill Martin's *Brown Bear, Brown Bear, What Do You See?* for young children, Rebecca Caudill's *Did You Carry the Flag Today, Charley?* and Katherine Paterson's *Jacob Have I Loved* are books that lend themselves to discussions leading to an understanding of story sequence.

3. ***An awareness of the tension between character and incident.***
Stories like Beatrix Potter's *The Tale of Peter Rabbit,* E. B. White's *Charlotte's Web,* Jean Craighead George's *Julie of the Wolves,* and Scott O'Dell's *Island of the Blue Dolphins* all show characters struggling to survive a chance or circumstantial incident in their lives.

4. ***The ability to understand characters through their appearance, relationship to the environment, actions, thoughts, speech, reactions to others, reactions of others.***
Some books for character study for younger children include Ludwig Bemelmans's *Madeline* series and Arnold Lobel's *Frog and Toad* series. Older students can analyze the fascinating characters of Toad, Rat, Mole, and Badger in Kenneth Grahame's *The Wind in the Willows.* (In building a three-dimensional study of a character, students should prove each descriptive statement about a character by direct reference to the text.)

5. ***An ability to note the mood or tone of a book.***
Many picture books focus more on creating a mood than on telling a story: Uri Shulevitz's *Dawn,* Janice Udry's *A Tree is Nice,* or Robert McCloskey's *Time of Wonder.* Certain fantasies for older students are excellent examples of how a writer can create a mood: Natalie Babbitt's *The Eyes of the Amaryllis,* or books by Madeleine L'Engle such as *A Wrinkle in Time* or *A Swiftly Tilting Planet.*

6. ***An awareness of language as a means of establishing tone and mood.***
Some picture books use language in memorable and unique ways to create a mood: the spare, mysterious text of Margaret Wise Brown's *Goodnight Moon* and the irresistible refrain in Wanda Gag's *Millions of Cats:*

> *Cats here, cats there.*
> *Cats and kittens everywhere.*
> *Hundreds of cats, thousands of cats,*
> *Millions and billions and trillions of cats.*

Writers for older children, like Natalie Babbitt, provide examples of how effectively writers can use language to create a mood, as in these first lines from *Tuck Everlasting:*

Natalie Babbitt, *Tuck Everlasting* (Farrar, Straus, 1975)

> The first week of August hangs at the very top of summer, the top of the live-long year, like the highest seat of a Ferris wheel when it pauses in its turning. The weeks that come before are only a climb from balmy spring, and those that follow a drop to the chill of autumn, but the first week of August is motionless, and hot.

See Chapter 9, "Featured Teacher Sarah Sherman-Siegel: Close Reading of a Book with Sixth- through Eighth-Grade Students."

7. ***An appreciation of humor, exaggeration, description, and figures of speech; the ability to form and react to the sensory images produced through language.***
The youngest students easily recognize the element of humor in the nonsense of Dr. Seuss books, somewhat older ones can find it in Peggy

Parish's *Amelia Bedelia* books, and even older ones can enjoy the fantasy of words in Norton Juster's *The Phantom Tollbooth* or the humorous poetry of Shel Silverstein in *Where the Sidewalk Ends.*

8. *An awareness of how setting, mood, and plot relate.*
Some books simply put it all together: *Charlotte's Web, The Wind in the Willows,* or *Island of the Blue Dolphins.* You will find many others as you read yourself and read to children.

An understanding of these elements can best be developed in relaxed discussions where the students interact with the teacher and with each other, sharing ideas, impressions, and images.

Issues in Children's Literature

Today's student is faced with many issues in life, and today's literature for children and young adults describes and analyzes many of these issues. It is important, therefore, for today's teacher not only to know that books on topical interests and issues exist, but that these topics have not always been dealt with realistically, fairly, or humanely, and that each book should be judged not only on interest and literary value, but in terms of human values as well.

See *Children's Literature: An Issues Approach,* by Masha K. Rudman, 2nd ed. (Longman, 1984).

Some general criteria to look for in evaluating books that treat sensitive issues include

1. realistic solutions to special problems such as divorce, adoption, racial and ethnic prejudice, and children with special problems and needs,
2. realistic characters who behave plausibly, humanely, and responsively and are individuals rather than rigid stereotypes,
3. bias-free language,
4. accurate and up-to-date information on subjects of a sensitive nature,
5. good writing and an avoidance of obvious sensational conflict or a too-obvious message, and
6. appropriateness for a student's developmental level.

Here is a sampler of the many good books on many issues of interest to children today:

Family

When the New Baby Comes, I'm Moving Out, by Martha Alexander (ages 5–7; new baby)
I'll Fix Anthony, by Judith Viorst (ages 5–8; sibling rivalry)
A Father Like That, by Charlotte Zolotow (ages 5–8; single parents)
It's Not the End of the World, by Judy Blume (ages 10–12; divorce)

Aaron's Door, by Miska Miles (ages 9–11; adoption)
The Great Gilly Hopkins, by Katherine Paterson (ages 9+; foster child)

Gender Roles

Mommies at Work, by Eve Merriam (ages 5–8)
Philip Hall Likes Me, I Reckon Maybe, by Bette Greene (ages 9–12)

Old Age and Death

Annie and the Old One, by Miska Miles (ages 6–8)

Heritage

Moonsong Lullaby, by Jamke Highwater (all ages; Native Americans)
Roll of Thunder, Hear My Cry, by Mildred Taylor (ages 8–12; black Americans)
Santiago, by Pura Belpre (ages 6–9; Hispanic Americans)
A Boy of Old Prague, by Sulamith Ish-Kishor (ages 9–12; Jewish Americans)

Special Children, Special Needs

The Summer of the Swans, by Betsy Byars (ages 10+; intellectual disability)
Darlene, by Eloise Greenfield (ages 9–12; mobility)
The Bear's House, by Marilyn Sachs (ages 9–12; emotional dysfunction)
Me and Einstein, Rose Blue (ages 8–12; learning disability)
A Hero Ain't Nothing But a Sandwich, by Alice Childress (ages 12+; substance abuse)
Blubber, by Judy Blume (ages 8+; appearance)
Helen Keller, by Micki Davidson (ages 7–10; giftedness, vision, hearing)
The Pinballs, by Betsy Byars (ages 9–12; child abuse)

Literature in the Classroom

What happened between one favorite book and many children and then between many children and many other books, as described in "Centering Ideas," is just one example of the impact of literature on children. Hickman (1980), who has done ethnographic research, observing how children and teachers interact with literature in a real classroom context, describes another.

> Ben's teacher is showing her kindergarten–first-grade group the new selection of books she has brought from the public library to add temporarily to their reading center. When she holds up *Pezzetino,* by Leo Lionni, six-year-old Ben scoots closer from his place within the circle of children on the carpet.

> "Oh, that's my favorite book!" says Ben. He reaches out for it, hugs it to his chest, and kisses the cover. Around the group, nods and smiles show that others recognize this title and seem to understand Ben's feelings about it.
>
> Later in the day, when part of the first-graders' work is to spend ten minutes sharing a book with a kindergartner, it is *Pezzetino* that Ben chooses. Following this sharing, the teacher invites some of the children to talk with her in a small group about their books.
>
> Ben says, "I like *Pezzetino* because of all the colors 'n' stuff, and the way it repeats. He keeps saying it. And there's marbleizing—see here? And this very last page. . ." Here Ben turns to the end of the book and holds up a picture for the group to see. "He cut paper. How many think he's a good cutter?" Ben conducts a vote, counting the raised hands that show a majority of the group believe Leo Lionni to be "a good cutter" (pp. 524–525).

Hickman's (1980) research suggests that Ben's active, engaged, and involved response to this favorite book could occur because of the context for learning about and with literature in his classroom. His teacher had provided a supportive environment and provided many opportunities for him to think and talk about the story. Although she used no formal guide for the study of literature, what she did was critical to Ben's growth in understanding, appreciation, and use of language and literature.

Here are the characteristics of the environment that this teacher created to support a response to literature in her class.

1. Books provided in the classroom are chosen for quality; many are chosen around a focus to stimulate comparisons.
2. Books are accessible, and children are given time to choose and read them.
3. Books are read aloud every day.
4. Books are discussed—by the whole group, by small groups, and by individuals—some in free talk, others centered around a focus including literary conventions.
5. Children can work with literature in many ways—art, writing, drama—and are encouraged to share.
6. Long-term experiences are planned so that children can return to books they know well.

What really makes a difference in how children and favorite books are brought together is the teacher. This is especially true in the absence of formal programs, texts, or systems for teaching literature in most schools. What are some specific implications of the examples in "Centering Ideas" and that cited by Hickman (1980) for teaching and unleashing the power and importance of literature in a curriculum integrated through the language arts?

"Unleashing the power and importance of literature in a curriculum integrated through the language arts" is one of those statements that sound like a good idea, but just how do you really go about doing it? Would it not be easier just to let the stories in a basal reader—or the school librarian—take care of literature in the curriculum?

Descriptions of the power and importance of literature often focus either on one child's reaction to one book, as in Hickman's (1980) ethnographic study, or on an entire class and its reaction to one book, as shown at the beginning of this chapter. What is important to note is that, as for most integrated language arts experiences, the explanations will tend to deal with the kind of interaction that is possible between learners, language, and the classroom environment rather than giving step-by-step instructions for achieving this interaction.

A Context for Literature in the Classroom

It is possible, however, to describe a general context for literature in the classroom—kind of teacher, room environment, overall evolution of method—which teachers often learn through discovery, actually led by the young learners themselves, as I was by my first class. Thereafter, I could anticipate and look forward to the same kinds of experiences that evolved the first time, as described in the road map in "Centering Ideas." Here are some guidelines for creating a classroom where children can lead the way for teachers to discover the power and importance of child-centered and literature-saturated learning in language arts.

Finding and Selecting Books

A main source of books, of course, is the school library. You should also plan to build a classroom collection. Most paperback books clubs for schools offer teachers a free book for a specified number purchased by their students. Garage sales, too, are an excellent source of these same paperback books that other children have read and outgrown.

See Chapter 1, "Children's Literature."

For recommended books or books on specific subjects, the school librarian is an excellent resource. Other good ways of finding out about books are journals, book lists, and the special bibliographies selectively listed here.

Journals

Language Arts
The Reading Teacher
The Horn Book

Children should be able to choose books from a well-stocked classroom collection.

Booklist
School Library Journal
Children's Literature in Education

Book Lists

Adventuring with Books (National Council of Teachers of English, 1985)
Best Books for Children (Bowker, 1981)
The Best in Children's Books (University of Chicago Press, 1980)
The Bookfinder (American Guidance Services, 1981)
Children's Books Too Good To Miss (University Press Books, 1980)
The Elementary School Library Collection (Bro-Dart, 1982)

Specialized Bibliographies

The Black Experience in Children's Books (New York Public Library, 1979)
Books for the Gifted Child (Bowker, 1980)
A Hispanic Heritage (Scarecrow Press, 1980)
Literature by and about the American Indian (National Council of Teachers of English, 1979)
The Single Parent Family in Children's Books (Scarecrow, 1978)

Creating an Environment for Reading

Set up a classroom library and book center. Designate space, shelves, and furniture such as tables for displaying books or children's work, comfortable chairs for reading (a rocker for the teacher?), and other special reading places: floor pillows, beanbag chairs, or a homemade cave with a light in it. Set aside one bulletin board to promote literature and response to literature: start with book jackets or a poster of a book cover; information about an author or a book genre (fairy tales, informational books, realistic fiction); and continue with children's writing, art, or other responses to literature.

Becoming a Model for Reading

The teacher as a model for reading and the teacher's enthusiasm for literature can be most important aspects of integrating literature into the curriculum. Ways to do this are simple:

- Read aloud to children every day, several times a day.
- Read yourself and share your enthusiasm for books with children.
- Try sustained silent reading: set aside a period of time each day when everyone reads silently—nothing else. Be sure to allow time afterwards for book sharing, discussion, and planning response experiences.

See Chapter 9, "Sustained Silent Reading."

Matching Children and Books

Find out what each child's reading interests are to help them find books they will like. Observe the children as they interact with books in the classroom and in the library. Watch, for example, as a first-grader picks up Wanda Gag's *Millions of Cats* over and over, chanting "Hundreds of cats, thousands of cats . . ." again and again; or a fourth-grader reads *Little House in the Woods* and asks the librarian if there are any more books like it; or a sixth-grader systematically seeks out every science fantasy book in the library.

Confer with the children about their reading. Some questions to ask, representative of those used by the Children's Choice teams (Monson & McClenathan, 1979), are:

Is this one of the best books you have read?
How does the book compare with your favorite books?
Should it be in our school library?
Would your friends enjoy reading it?
What did you like best about the book?

Talking about Books

Whole-class and small-group discussions are essential for children to reflect upon and discover their feelings, ideas, and attitudes about their experiences with literature.

Understanding Literary Elements. Discussing the books they have read is also important for developing students' understanding and abilities with

Providing time and places to read is an important part of the classroom literature environment.

regard to literature as described by Sloan (1984). Here are some of the questions she suggests teachers use to guide children to a deeper understanding of the nature of literature as they discuss specific books and begin to see certain qualities of form and structure that all stories share.*

Type of Story

- Every storyteller constructs a make-believe world that may be very like our own or entirely different from it. What signs and signals indicate whether a story will be more fanciful than realistic? (Talking animals; exaggeration; strange, improbable situations, characters, or settings; stories that begin "Once upon a Time.")
- If the world created by the author is far different from the world we know, how does the author make the story seem possible and believable?

Setting and Plot

- Where and when does the story take place? How do you know? If the story took place somewhere else or in a different time, how would it be changed?
- What incident, problem, conflict, or situation does the author use to get the story started?
- How is the story arranged? (Chronological order; individual incidents; flashbacks; told through letters or diary entries.)
- Trace the main events of the story. Is it possible to change their order? Leave any of them out? Why or why not?
- Suppose you thought of a different ending for the story. How would the rest of the story have to be changed to fit the new ending?

*Reprinted by permission of the publisher from Sloan, *The Child as Critic* (2nd ed.). (New York: Teachers College Press, © 1984 by Teachers College, Columbia University. All rights reserved.), pp. 104–106.

- Did the story end as you expected it to? What clues did the author offer to prepare you to expect this ending? Did you recognize that these clues were important to the story when you were first reading or listening to it?

Characters

An example of a discussion about character was described in "Centering Ideas," when a student asked my father about characters in his books.

- Who is the main character in the story? What kind of person is this character? How do you know?
- Are any characters changed in the course of the story? If so, how are they different? What changed them? Does the change seem believable?
- Some characters play a small but important role in a story. Pick out a bit player from the story. Why is this character necessary to the story?

Point of View

- Who is the teller of the story? If the teller is a character in the story, how is the story different from one told by an outside narrator?

Mood and Theme

- Does the story as a whole create a definite mood or feeling? What is the mood? How is it created?
- Did you have strong feelings as you read the story? What did the author do to make you feel strongly?
- What are the main ideas behind the story? How does the author get you to think of them?

Teachers can model reading behavior and share enthusiasm for literature in many ways.

General Questions

- Is this story, though different in content, like any other story you have read or watched? Does it follow a pattern? If so, what is it?
- Think about the characters in the story. Are any of them the same character types you have met in other stories?

...mar ...ading Instruction," by Jill Fitzgerald Whaley in *The Reading Teacher*, 34 (1981), 762–771.

Understanding Story Structure. Another approach to talking about books stems from research (Mandler & Johnson, 1977) on story schema, which is defined as "an idealized internal representation of the parts of a typical story and the relationship among those parts" (p. 111), and resulting story grammars, or the rules that explain the structure of a text and a person's mental image of it, based mainly on traditional folk literature.

From a knowledge of story grammar, teachers can derive questions to support the development of a story schema among children. Furthermore, we know that the questions we ask children about stories they listen to or read are a primary reading comprehension strategy (Pearson & Johnson, 1978) and that the knowledge of story structures developed through these types of questions can support the listener's and the reader's comprehension (Whaley, 1981).

Sadow (1982) suggests that teachers can design questions for talking about books based on Rumelhart's (1975) story grammar. Teachers can first ask themselves generic questions, or *question frames,* as they read and analyze a story, answer these, and derive appropriate questions for classroom use based on this information. Here are some examples of questions about story grammar, based on Scott O'Dell's *Island of the Blue Dolphins.*

For Teacher's Use Only

Question Frames

1. Setting:
   Where and when does the story take place?
   Who are the characters involved?
2. Initiating event:
   What starts the flow of events?
3. Reaction:
   How does the main character react to the initiating event?
4. Action:
   What does the main character do about it?
5. Consequence:
   What is the result of the main character's action?

Answers

1. Setting:
   The story takes place on an island rich with otter off the coast of California in the early 1800s, where a twelve-year-old Indian girl, Karana, lives with her people in the village of Ghalas-at.

2. Initiating event:
   After many of the men in her village are killed by ruthless Aleut otter hunters, Karana's people seek a new home. They send a messenger who sends a ship to take them to another island, but Karana's six-year old brother misses the sailing.
3. Reaction:
   Karana refuses to sail away and leave her brother.
4. Action:
   She dives into the stormy sea and swims back to the island to find her brother.
5. Consequence:
   Since the ship does not return for her, Karana spends the next eighteen years alone on the island after her brother is killed by a pack of wild dogs. She learns to protect herself against the dogs and ruthless otter hunters, and she survives until a ship comes to her island.

For Use with Students

Classroom Questions

1. Setting:
   Who is Karana?
   Where and when does she live?
   What is her life like in the village of Ghalas-at?
2. Initiating event:
   What happens to her village after the Aleut otter hunters come?
   Why do Karana's people seek a new home?
   What happens to her little brother when it is time to sail?
3. Reaction:
   How does Karana feel when she realizes her brother is not on the ship?
4. Action:
   What does Karana do about it?
5. Consequences:
   What happens to her after she jumps into the sea to return to the island to find her brother?

Making Time for Poetry

Poetry should be a natural and integral part of a child's experience with language in the classroom—not just poetry for St. Patrick's Day, School Lunch Week, or Dental Hygiene Month, but poetry for the beauty and truth and joy of it, every day, every week, every month, and throughout the year.

Poetry is often neglected in the classroom (Terry, 1974). This is unfortunate, since experiences with rhyme and rhythm pervade our lives—from pat-a-cake games with baby to Mother Goose to finger plays and songs to TV jingles, popular songs, and college fight yells.

Because poetry is easy to read aloud to the whole class, and because a poem is often the shortest piece of literature and therefore the easiest to share with a whole group, poetry experiences can and should permeate the school day. Finding poetry to pack your curriculum is easy.

Types of Poetry. Poetry can be classified as nonsense, humor, traditional, narrative, lyric, and so on. Or it may be classified around a specific subject, such as the Southwest. Sloan (1984) offers a broader way of thinking about types of poems, which avoids the danger of relegating poetry to the status of afterthought to other subjects. Here is Sloan's classification to help you begin your thinking about how broadly poems can be considered to meet the language and literature needs of children.*

- Poems that express wishes, dreams, and desires, usually of an existence or circumstance better than one presently being experienced.
- Poems that deal with the life and death of humans, animals, birds, and nature.
- Poems that pinpoint a moment in time, a place, a wish, or desire.
- Poems that are simply expressions of feeling or emotion.
- Poems that are rhythmic and verbal representations of work or play.

An example of this last type is "The Pickety Fence," by David McCord**:

The pickety fence
The pickety fence
Give it a lick it's
The pickety fence
Give it a lick it's
A clickety fence
Give it a lick it's
A lickety fence
Give it a lick
Give it a lick
Give it a lick
With a rickety stick
Pickety
Pickety
Pickety
Pick

*Reprinted by permission of the publisher from Sloan, *The Child as Critic* (2nd ed.). (New York: Teachers College Press, © 1984 by Teachers College, Columbia University. All rights reserved.), pp. 82–83.
**From *One Day at a Time* by David McCord. Copyright 1952 by David McCord.

Poetry for Different Ages. Here are some suggestions for types and collections of poems most appropriate for children of different ages.

Mother Goose and Other Traditional Rhymes

The Real Mother Goose, by Blanche Fisher
The Tall Book of Mother Goose, by Feodor Rojakovsky
Brian Wildsmith's Mother Goose, by Brian Wildsmith

Picture Books with Poetic Text

Goodnight Moon, by Margaret Wise Brown
Drummer Hoff, by Ed Emberly
Millions of Cats, by Wanda Gag
Chicken Soup with Rice, by Maurice Sendak

Poems for Younger Children

Every Time I Climb a Tree, by David McCord
The Birthday Cow, by Eve Merriam
The Queen of Eene, by Jack Prelutsky
Cricket in a Thicket, by Aileen Fisher

In the middle grades, children still enjoy poems read aloud and can also read poetry themselves. Many enjoy collections of poems on favorite topics or of favorite types as described in Terry's (1974) study of upper elementary children's poetry preferences. Students in this study liked poems dealing with enjoyable and familiar experiences, that tell stories, and/or that have a strong element of humor, and poems with rhythm and rhyme. The most-liked of one hundred poems read to over a thousand fourth-, fifth-, and sixth-graders, was this one by John Ciardi*:

Mummy Slept Late
and Daddy Fixed Breakfast

Daddy fixed breakfast.
He made us each a waffle.
It looked like gravel pudding.
It tasted something awful.
"Ha, ha," he said, "I'll try again.
This time I'll get it right."
But what I got was in between
Bituminous and anthracite.
"A little too well done? Oh well,
I'll have to start all over."
That *time what landed on my plate*

Looked like a manhole cover.
I tried to cut it with a fork:
The fork gave off a spark.
I tried a knife and twisted it
Into a question mark.
I tried it with a hack-saw.
I tried it with a torch.
It didn't even make a dent.
It didn't even scorch.
The next time Dad gets breakfast
When Mummy's sleeping late,
I think I'll skip the waffles.
I'd sooner eat the plate!

They also liked limericks, like this one by an unknown poet:

From *Laughable Limericks,* edited by Sara and John Brewton (Crowell, 1965)

There was an old man of Blackheath,
Who sat on his set of false teeth.
Said he, with a start,
"Oh, Lord, bless my heart!
I've bitten myself underneath!"

Poetry collections by Lee Bennett Hopkins: *Surprises* (Harper & Row, 1984), *Moments* (Harcourt Brace Jovanovich, 1980), and *My Mane Catches the Wind: Poems about Horses* (Harcourt Brace Jovanovich, 1979)

Reading Poetry. Once you begin to find poems, the best and easiest thing to do is to read them to the children. Poet and poetry compiler Hopkins (1981) has several suggestions for doing this effectively:

1. Select appropriate poems for your students, but also select those you have a genuine love for so that you can share your enthusiasm for poetry.
2. Read the poem aloud several times to yourself to get the feel of the words and the rhythm.
3. Follow the rhythm of the poem by reading it naturally.
4. Make pauses that please you or simply follow what seem to be the natural pauses of the lines.
5. Use a natural voice when reading aloud.
6. Be quiet for a few moments after a poem has been read (p. 321).

See Chapter 5, "Featured Preservice Teacher Pat Peabody: Children Reading and Writing Poetry."

Involving Children with Poetry. Poetry should become an integral part of the school day and the language and literature life of all children. The best way for this to happen is for teachers to become familiar with the wide and wonderful range of poetry for children; to read poems aloud every day; to provide picture books with rhyming texts and appropriate collections of poems in primary grades, and anthologies and single-poet collections in all other grades in classroom libraries; and to encourage the appreciation of poetry after reading through discussion, writing, related media in listening and literature centers, and the integration of poetry into a curriculum integrated through the language arts.

Children's Response to Literature

Much of children's interaction with books will take place informally and incidentally, and without plans on your part. This is bound to happen when children are surrounded by books, are read to, and read for themselves. They will also respond in ways you help plan when you share certain books with them. Above all, let the children and the books themselves guide you in encouraging and supporting their interaction.

Many strategies for this kind of support are described throughout this text in other contexts for learning and teaching language arts, including the following activities:

sharing poetry
language patterns and literature
media centers
reading aloud
storytelling
reader's theatre
puppetry
creative dramatics
story dramatization
adaptation of literature for drama
literature as a model for writing

Here are a few more strategies for encouraging interaction between children and books.

Using Wordless Picture Books. Great numbers of picture books without any text have appeared in recent years, and illustrators like Mercer Mayer (*A Boy, a Dog, and a Frog*) and John Goodall (*Paddy's Evening Out*) have become very popular. There are many ways to use these wordless books in teaching language arts and reading, not only with younger students but with older ones as well (McGee & Tompkins, 1983). These books naturally lead children to tell the story out loud, since it has no text written down. Children can also create their own wordless picture books by composing stories with pictures only—and no text. Role-playing and creative dramatics are natural spin-offs, since children will have to bring to the experience the characterization and dialogue they have discovered for themselves in the story.

Mapping a Story. Young children can draw maps of the settings and actions of favorite picture books, such as *Petunia,* by Roger Duvoisin. Older students can create maps of imaginary worlds after reading books of fantasy, like *The Lion, the Witch, and the Wardrobe,* by C. S. Lewis, or realistic books where children create an imaginary world, such as in Katherine Paterson's *Bridge to Terabithia.*

Singing and Dancing. There are many excellent books whose text is a traditional song: John Langstaff's *Over in the Meadow* and *Frog Went A-Courting;* Peter Spier's *London Bridge Is Falling Down* and *The Fox Out on a Chilly Night,* for example. It would be almost impossible to stop children from wanting to sing, too, and dance as well.

Cooking and Eating. Children (and teachers) can cook and eat foods suggested in picture books, such as the chamomile tea mentioned in Beatrix Potter's *The Tale of Peter Rabbit.* Just a few of the many other picture books dealing with food are folktales such as *The Ginger Bread Man, Stone Soup,* by Marcia Brown, *The Popcorn Book,* by Tomie de Paola, and *Blueberries for Sal,* by Robert McCloskey.

Older children might make fudge according to the secret recipe in Ian Fleming's *Chitty Chitty Bang Bang,* the cookies described in *Little House* books by Laura Ingalls Wilder, and foods from other countries and many cultures in America, as they read informational books or books with regional settings or characters of diverse ethnic heritage.

Literature-Centered Instruction

Once you have created a context for literature in the classroom and discovered the power and importance of literature in the teaching of the language arts, it is an easy leap to creating a literature-centered curriculum. This can be done when a book becomes a pebble that creates a ripple effect of ideas and experiences as described earlier in the chapter. Another way literature can become central to the curriculum is for a teacher to choose a book to read closely with the whole class and carefully plan language arts and other experiences around this book. Here is an example of how one teacher, bored with the basal reader and distressed that her students, even though good readers, did not care about reading and had not read much literature, especially the classics, decided to use one book as a center for her reading and language arts instruction.

Featured Teacher Margaret Mattson: Close Reading of a Classic

See Chapter 9, "Close Reading of a Book."

As a teacher of average to high-achieving fourth-grade students, Margaret Mattson has discovered that using basal readers as the core of the reading program is inadequate.

> The stories are boring, filled with flat characters and predictable plots. The books are filled with short story after short story with no continuity. Students never really got into the stories as one does with good literature. The only rationale for using a certain story is to teach a certain skill. Although students were able to score well on skills tests after completing the prescribed activities, I never felt that they had learned anything that

they actually integrated into their own personal reading processes. Rather, they learned the format, to give the expected answers. It is a superficial type of learning.

At the same time that Margaret was struggling with the value of basals, she was becoming aware of the students' shocking ignorance of classic books. Many associated classics only with Walt Disney movies and seemed unaware that a book preceded the movie. The obvious outcome of these two concerns was her decision to build her language arts and reading program around a children's classic. Here's how she went about it.

Planning Close Reading

Selecting the Book

Margaret chose *Treasure Island* because none of the students had read it and she felt a fantastic classroom environment could be created for it: pirates, mysterious maps, hidden treasure, and the like. Ninety-five-cent paperback copies were available from one of the children's book clubs.

Planning the Unit

Margaret tried to be discriminating. "I didn't want to dissect the book until its magic was gone but I wanted it to be a productive learning experience." She made a list of the concepts she wished to convey and questions for students to consider. She also used basic questions about fiction as a focus for discussions (Felsenthal, 1978):

Character

1. Who is the main character? Is it someone who
   a. really lived?
   b. was made up for the story?
   c. can likely exist?
2. Who are the other characters?
   a. real or made up?
   b. likely or unlikely to exist?
3. What do the characters' speech, action, ideas, or appearance tell you about them?
4. What reasons do the characters have for the things they do?
5. How do the characters feel about each other?
6. Do any characters learn something important in the story?
7. Do they change their attitudes or behavior?

Action or Plot

1. Is the main action of the story
   a. physical?
   b. something that takes place in the imagination?
2. Is the main action
   a. something that really happened?
   b. something made up for the story?
   c. something that would be likely to happen in the world?

Dramatizing a scene from Treasure Island: *while hiding in an apple barrel, Jim Hawkins overhears Long John Silver plot to take over the Hispañola.*

3. What effect does the action have on the characters?
4. What is the primary problem that the characters have?
5. How is the problem solved?

Setting

1. Where does the action happen?
   a. What details tell you that?
   b. Is it a real place? A place made up for the story? A likely place?
2. Does the setting indicate a particular period in history?
3. Could the same story happen in a different setting? Why or why not?

Organizing and Scheduling Experiences

Lessons and activities were to be conducted during at least one-hour blocks of time three days a week. Students were also given thirty minutes a day to read a specific amount and unfinished reading was to be done at home. Impromptu sessions were also held as their interest grew, activities took longer than we expected, or if anyone was having difficulty understanding a portion of the story.

Margaret later organized students into groups, which could change, to work together on different activities.

Creating a Classroom Environment

Margaret made and displayed a huge map of Treasure Island drawn on brown wrapping paper so it looked ancient and suspended a colorful paper parrot from the ceiling. A labeled cross-section of a ship, complete with a Jolly Roger, covered the bulletin board. "Enthusiasm was building. When the books arrived and each student had their own copy, they were really ready to read."

The story was first published in installments entitled "The Sea Cook" in *Young Folks* magazine and appeared in book form in 1883.

Other books by Robert Louis Stevenson are *A Child's Garden of Verses, Dr. Jekyll and Mr. Hyde, Kidnapped, The Black Arrow,* and *The Master of Ballantrae.*

Initiating the Unit

The class learned about Robert Louis Stevenson, that he was a very sickly person who felt the function of literature was to supply adventure to people who lead unexciting lives. Margaret asked the students to respond to that idea. She also told them that *Treasure Island* was the outcome of his supplementation of a map of an imaginary island drawn by his twelve-year-old stepson. He entertained the boy and himself with stories of pirates and buried gold.

Teaching through Close Reading

Session 1. Reading aloud and discussion

Although the students were to read the book independently, Margaret read the first nineteen pages aloud to get them involved in the story. The story begins with a flashback and sets the mood:

> I remember him as if it were yesterday, as he came plodding to the inn door, his sea chest following behind him in a handbarrow; a tall, strong, heavy, nutbrown man; his tarry pigtail falling over the shoulders of his soiled blue coat; his hands ragged and scarred, with black, broken nails, and the saber-cut across one cheek a dirty, livid white.

The class talked about this description of Billy Bones, and the children drew portraits of him. One student remarked that she knew exactly what he looked like because she had seen the movie. This led to an interesting discussion about the adaptation of a book into a movie and the selection of actors to play the roles. The class also discussed their feelings about Billy Bones and how the author created those feelings.

Even though *Treasure Island* contains some unfamiliar vocabulary, Margaret did not introduce words except for the labeled cross-section of the ship, and a chart of nautical and geographical terms displayed and later added to by students. Vocabulary was discussed after students read and was usually deciphered by contextual analysis.

For the next session, students were to read the next four chapters, or the rest of Part One: "The Old Buccaneer."

Session 2. Talking in groups, writing group summaries, and making treasure maps

Each group made a token of cardboard, hid it on the school grounds, and then created a map to aid treasure seekers. Compasses and yellowed paper enhanced authenticity. The students were getting into the mood of the book and referred to Margaret as "One-Eyed Mattson" and her neighbor as "Peg-Leg McGraw" on a map.

Groups then traded maps and were challenged to find the tokens in the shortest amount of time. These were traded for "treasure"—candy coins covered with foil. While this was a good map-reading activity, the main purpose was to put them in the story.

In small groups, the students discussed what they had read and wrote a summary of it and then all the groups interacted. "This was a clarifying experience for them and me. They really interacted and challenged each other. I find these small-group activities to be very productive as it forces students to form an opinion and defend it."

For the next session: read Chapters 7 to 9 of Part Two: "The Sea Cook."

Session 3. Recognizing and discussing the technique of foreshadowing in literature

The class discussed foreshadowing and how authors use it to give clues of what is to come, and how Stevenson used it.

For the next session: read Chapters 10 to 12 of Part Two.

Session 4. Discussing and dramatizing

Groups discussed the story and then took twenty minutes to plan a skit to dramatize one of the most exciting scenes. "The room buzzed with the creative noise of students who were involved and excited about what they were doing, and a much deeper analysis of the story was occurring than any workbook could inspire."

A trembling Jim hid in the apple barrel while a freckle-faced Long John Silver boasted of his infamous past. Dialogue overheard during the planning stage further reinforced Margaret's feeling that students were guiding their own higher-level thinking: "Long John oughta be kind of like two different people, you know? All friendly and polite around the Captain but real mean and bragging when he's not."

The skits were terrific and the students really took off with them. They wanted to do the full story on the stage for other classes. (Children are never overwhelmed by enormous undertakings as teachers usually are!)

For the next session: read Chapters 13 to 15: Part Three: "My Shore Adventure."

Session 5. Painting and writing description

Margaret reread the description of the island and asked students to close their eyes and imagine that they could really see it. They then used watercolors and magic markers to paint what they saw, and then used words to create that picture as well.

Session 6. Discussing cliffhangers

Chapter 14 ends with a cliffhanger and Margaret asked them how many of them kept reading even though the chapter ended. Many hands went up and she challenged "Why? Isn't the end of a chapter a good place to take a break?" The class discussed this and other examples of this technique in this book and others and one student volunteered that soap operas use it as well, and others named other TV shows that do too.

For the next session: read Chapters 16 to 18: Part Four: "The Stockade."

Session 7. Discussing and using point of view in writing

The next three chapters are told from the doctor's point of view rather than Jim Hawkins's. Discussion groups were challenged to uncover the author's motives for changing viewpoints. Advantages and disadvantages of first-person, omniscient, limited omniscient, and objective point of view were explored.

Students rewrote an episode using a different point of view. For example, one wrote a journal for Long John Silver, complete with a tattered paper cover and blots of red ink (blood?) on the pages. Part of an entry reads: "Today me and my friends plotted to take over the Hispanolia. But I said we were going to let them find the treasure and get it on board and wait till we're halfway back to England. Then we would take over. I was so happy just thinking how rich I was going to be. . . ."

For the next session: read Chapters 19 to 21 of Part Four.

Session 8. Student-selected projects

After a discussion of these chapters, each group chose and started a project:

Group 1: A papier-mâché model of the island.
Group 2: A board game based on *Treasure Island.*
Group 3: An etiquette book for beginning gentlemen of fortune.
Group 4: A taped interview of Long John Silver.

For the next session: read Part Five: "My Sea Adventure."

Sessions 9 and 10. Discussing Jim's character and preparing projects

Discussion groups focused on the character of Jim Hawkins: What kind of person was he? If he were transplanted to a different setting, like our classroom, what kinds of problems might he have?

Groups continued to work on projects, repeatedly going back and analyzing the story. Group 1 skimmed for descriptions of the island and listed them before making the model. Group 2 sequenced events in the story to make the game. Group 3 studied the pirates' actions and used informational trade books to create a spoof of an etiquette book with headings like "What to do if you receive the Black Spot." Group 4 had to establish a thorough understanding of the complex character of Long John Silver in order to do the interview.

For the next sessions: Read the remainder of the book, Part Six: "Captain Silver."

When everyone had finished reading the book, the class held more group discussions and were very eager to talk, share their projects, and start new projects. They couldn't be stopped. Here are some of the things they did:

See Chapter 4, "Writing Class and School Newspapers."

- Made *Wanted* posters for pirates.
- Wrote a Bristol news account of the journey.
- Designed book jackets.
- Drew illustrations for unillustrated scenes.
- Wrote secret codes.
- Wrote journals for various characters.
- Adopted many of Stevenson's conventions in their writing.
- Wrote sequels about another trip to the island to recover the remaining treasure.
- Planned a Treasure Island party and came dressed as pirates, made duff—a dessert mentioned in the book—and nibbled on apples and cheese as we watched the Disney movie version of the book. (By tradition, duff was not properly cooked until it could be dropped from the cross-gallant-crosstrees—the highest accessible point on the ship—and not break.)

A Recipe for Duff. In a medium bowl, beat 2 eggs well, add 1 cup brown sugar, 1-1/2 cup chopped raisins, and 1/3 cup shortening and blend. Sift together and stir in 1 cup flour, 1/2 teaspoon salt, 1 teaspoon baking soda. Pour into well-greased 1-quart mold (1-lb. coffee tin is ideal). Cover pudding with waxed paper, then cover tin with a double layer of aluminum foil tied on tightly with string to prevent water from seeping in. Place in large pot of boiling water which should come 3/4 of the way up the side of the tin. Cover pot loosely and boil for 3-1/2 to 4 hours, adding more water as needed. Serve warm with whipped cream.

Teaching and Learning from Close Reading

Margaret sums up: "I plan to continue to use a literature-centered approach to teaching reading and language arts. A literature approach can generate a startling amount of excitement about reading, and I was still able to teach required skills but in a natural and meaningful way." For example, Margaret's students really applied the following skills during this unit:

- **I.** Using context to interpret
  - **A.** unfamiliar words
  - **B.** idioms
  - **C.** figures of speech
- **II.** Identifying story elements:
  - **A.** characters
    1. round
    2. flat
  - **B.** setting
    1. integral
    2. peripheral
  - **C.** plot
    1. flashback
    2. conflict
    3. patterns of action
       - (a) suspense
       - (b) cliffhanger
       - (c) foreshadowing
- **III.** Recognizing and appreciating techniques and elements of style:
  - **A.** point of view
    1. first person
    2. omniscient
    3. limited omniscient
    4. objective
  - **B.** imagery
- **IV.** Style
  - **A.** diction
  - **B.** figurative language
  - **C.** imagery
  - **D.** mood

In the future, Margaret plans to have students select a book they wish to read from several options. They will then work in small groups on various activities such as discussions, oral reading, and book sharing through activities such as dramatizations. "I believe literature should be approached holistically and used as a center to integrate language arts and reading in the classroom because I also believe reading must be approached with enthusiasm and in a global manner." As Polanyi (1958) states: "We can know a successful system only by understanding it as a whole, while being subsidiarily aware of its particulars; and we cannot meaningfully study these particulars except with a bearing on the whole" (p. 19).

See Chapter 9, "Whole-Language and Literature-based Reading Instruction: Alternatives to the Basal Reader."

Summing Up

Discovering the power and importance of literature in a curriculum integrated through the language arts is not difficult if you let your students lead the way, as mine did in the first class I taught. They asked me to read them a book that interested them, and I did. After each reading, they wanted to talk about the book and I learned to guide discussions and ask them questions about the book's plot, characters, setting, mood, style, and theme. They had many questions during these discussions and I learned to listen to them and plan for activities around their interests. They asked for other good books to read and I learned about the wealth of information in informational books for children and how to use them to create learning experiences in the content areas. They responded to these books in discussions and as they listened, talked, wrote, researched, drew, dramatized, and built things, I learned to gather resources and plan opportunities for them to respond in these and other ways to literature. They wanted to share their responses and I learned to provide opportunities for them to do so. And we all learned a lot about literature, language, and learning from each other.

Teachers who recognize the power and importance of literature in the curriculum need to know how to choose and use books based on students' interests and attitudes, the literary elements of the books, issues in children's literature, and the role literature can play in the classroom. Strategies for creating a context for literature include finding and selecting books and resources for each class, creating a classroom environment, becoming a model for reading, matching children and books, talking about books and teacher questioning, making time for poetry, and responding to literature. A major way to encourage response is through literature-centered language arts and reading instruction.

Looking Further

1. Choose a book you like and brainstorm experiences and activities which might result after reading the book aloud to a class.

2. Ask a child or group of children which books and what kinds of books they like and why.

3. Start a file of books that would lend themselves to developing an understanding of the following literary elements among children: plot, characterization, setting, mood or tone, theme, and language style.

4. What do you think is an important or sensitive issue facing children today? Identify and read several books related to that theme.

5. Read and review an issue of at least three of the journals on children's literature listed in this chapter. Which did you prefer? Why?

6. Ask a child the questions used by the Children's Choices teams with reference to a recently read book.

7. Lead a discussion focused around understanding literary elements with questions listed in this chapter.

8. Choose a book you like and develop a set of story grammar questions, or frames, for it. If possible, read the book and use the questions with children.

9. Identify two or three poems for each of the types of poetry listed in this chapter. Compare your choices with others in the class. Keep a list of all the choices to start a file for use in the classroom.

10. Read several poems aloud to children according to Hopkins's suggestions described in this chapter.

11. In small groups, brainstorm as many ideas as you can for ways to involve children with literature.

12. Suggest a book you would use for a close reading in the classroom and explain why you chose it. Suggest several things you might do with children.

Chapter Nine

Reading As a Language Art

Objectives

Look for answers to the following questions as you read this chapter.

- What is reading?
- How do children learn to read?
- How do you assess reading using naturalistic methods?
- What supports success in learning to read?
- How is reading taught today?
- How do you teach reading using language- and literature-based methods?

A Child's View

Here is how young readers responded to the question "What is reading?"

Four-year-old Gordon learned to read without formal reading instruction before he went to school. At age two-and-a-half, he had made the link between signs and print in the environment and meaning. At age three-and-a-half, he practiced memory reading of favorite story books and knew several words by sight. By age four-and-a-half, he is reading fluently. When asked how he does it and what he thinks reading is, he shrugs and replies, "I just follow the words."

At the beginning of fourth grade, Chedrick did not read at all and said he had never read a book. At the end of the year in Avril Font's classroom, he is reading a biography of Patrick Henry in order to write a report on the American Revolution. When asked what he thinks reading is, he grins and replies, "Boy, I got a good brain. I read fourteen pages. I be lookin' at these big words and I be *knowin'* 'em and knowin' what they mean. That's reading!"

Johns and Ellis (1976) asked 1600 elementary-age students "What is reading?" and found that their "views of reading were restricted and often described reading as an activity occurring in classrooms using textbooks, workbooks, and reading groups" (p. 115):

36 percent said reading is an activity using commercial materials
33 percent said they did not know what reading is
16 percent said reading is a decoding process
less than 10 percent said reading is a meaning-getting process

Centering Ideas

The teaching of reading receives more attention than any other aspect of elementary education today, and most people have an image of traditional reading instruction based on their own school experiences. Think about your own background. Is it similar to the following scenario? During a period of sixty to ninety minutes a day, children read stories from a set of graded commercial readers called basals. The teacher works with one of three ability groups at a time, using a teacher's manual as a guide. Those children not working with the teacher are doing independent seat work using workbooks with exercises that usually require answering specific questions related to the story they have read, and practicing skills by filling in blanks or circling multiple-choice questions.

This traditional image suggests that the use of a basal reader program guarantees the successful teaching of reading. As most experienced teachers know, there is more to it than that.

Reading As a Language Art

One of the recent reports on the quality of education in America focused on reading. *Becoming a Nation of Readers: The Report of the Commission on Reading* (Anderson et al., 1985) goes beyond the view of reading instruction as the simple application of a basal reader program to a much broader view of reading as a language art.

> It cannot be emphasized too strongly that reading is one of the language arts. All of the uses of language—listening, speaking, reading, and writing—are interrelated and mutually supportive. It follows, therefore, that school activities that foster one of the language arts inevitably will benefit the others as well. Writing activities, in particular, should be integrated into the reading period (p. 79).

When reading is viewed as a language art, the teaching of reading takes on a different complexion, one which embraces all the complexities of language, thinking, and art itself. As such, reading is very personal, being an individual's act of constructing meaning from print. But reading is also a social act and must always be considered in terms of each specific situation and interaction between reader, text, and context.

While thinking about reading can be as complex, on the one hand, as thinking about thought, language, and human behavior, there are many ways, on the other hand, to approach the teaching of reading as a language art that are simple, albeit deceptively so. Many of these ways are supported as instructional methods by recent research on how, when given the proper support through social interaction, children learn, and learn to take ownership of their own efforts to learn to read and write naturally (DeFord & Harste, 1982; Teale, 1982). This does not, however, minimize the teacher's role in the teaching of reading; in fact, that role explodes when you consider the myriad opportunities that exist every minute of every day first to recognize and then to support, encourage, and direct children's language and literacy development.

A Language- and Literature-Based Reading Lesson

Here is a language- and literature-based reading lesson that first-grade teacher Nora Miller taught her class, which included thirteen transitional students (considered too young for first grade), two children repeating first grade, and eleven others. You will note that she approaches the teaching of reading as a paradoxically complex but also natural process of gaining meaning from print, a process that is highly personal and social at the same time.

As Nora gets comfortable in a rocking chair, the children gather around her enthusiastically and find a seat on the floor. They see she is going to read *May I Bring a Friend?* a picture book about a child who brings a different animal every day of the week to visit the king and the queen.

May I Bring a Friend? by Beatrice Schenk de Regniers, illustrated by Beni Montresor (Atheneum, 1965), and winner of the Caldecott Medal

Child: Yeah! This will be the third time this week you're gonna read that book.
Teacher: Do you know why?
Child: 'Cause we like it.
Teacher: I like it, too. Do you remember the names of the animals in this book?

As the children call out the names, Nora puts sentence strips with the names of the animals on them on the flannel board next to her: giraffe, hippopotamus, monkey, elephant, lion, and seal. Using the same procedure, she puts sentence strips with the names of the days of the week in random order on the flannel board and she and the children talk about the words. When she begins to read the book and show the illustrations, many of the children join in and chant the parts of the story they remember from the two prior readings. They do this naturally and with pleasure. This is a rhyming book with a predictable pattern.*

See Chapter 1, "Predictable Pattern Books."

The King and Queen
Invited me
To come to their house
On Sunday for tea.

*Beatrice Schenk de Regniers, excerpted from *May I Bring a Friend?* Copyright © 1964 Beatrice Schenk de Regniers. Reprinted by permission of Atheneum Publishers, an imprint of Macmillan Publishing Company.

First-grade teacher Nora Miller directs a reading lesson based on the book May I Bring A Friend?

I told the Queen
And the Queen told the King
I had a friend
I wanted to bring.

The King told the Queen
"My dear, my dear,
Any friend of our friend
Is welcome here."

So I brought my friend . . .

The page ends here, and before turning it Nora asks:

Teacher: What do you think will happen next?
Child: He'll bring a friend!
Teacher: Do you know what friend he will bring?
Child: I know! A giraffe.

Teacher: And what day of the week is it?
Child: Sunday!

Nora turns the page slowly, mysteriously, as the children begin to bounce up and down in anticipation.

Child: Look! It *is* a giraffe! I was right!
Teacher: Super. Look at the picture of the king and queen. How do you think they're feeling?
Child: Sad.
Child: Amazed.
Teacher: What do you think they'll do now?
Child: I think she's gonna go [*gestures with fist*] *wow! pow!*
Teacher: Why?
Child: She wouldn't take that. No way.
Teacher: Let's see what happens next.

Nora continues to read the book, asking the children to predict the story sequence, the day of the week, and the animal friend. She also invites responses to the story and illustrations and discusses these with the children. After each section of the story, she asks a child to find the name of the day of the week and the name of the animal friend that day from among the words on one side of the flannel board. After the children choose and say them aloud, they place them in order together on the other side of the flannel board.

When the reading is over, Nora and the class talk about the book—some of them still chanting aloud parts of the text they remember. One child volunteers to spell *Sunday,* and other volunteers spell other days and then the names of the animals. Nora uses this opportunity to ask whether anyone notices some similarities in the words for the days of the week. When *day* is identified, they talk about the structure of the words and the parts of the words added to *day.* Finally, they put the animal names in alphabetical order.

There are several reasons why Nora planned this reading lesson. First of all, she believes in the importance of motivating children to read and enjoy reading through the use of literature and shared language experiences. But she also had several other items on her planning agenda. On the statewide minimum competency reading test, her students had done very poorly in recognizing the names of the days of the week and in sequencing. While Nora does not believe that succeeding on this test is the only way—or even the best way—to measure the progress of children in reading, in her school system they must pass this test in order to move on to the next grade. And so she wove many of the skills and competencies she knows they will need to succeed in real reading situations and on the test, throughout the lesson as the opportunities occurred and as she drew on her knowledge of the reading process and of how children learn to read.

Making Connections

During the language- and literature-based reading lesson described in the preceding section, what was actually happening as Nora Miller taught reading? In order to answer this question, which has broad implications for the way you will teach reading in your own classroom, we must first look at some topics which underlie any approach to reading.

The Reading Process

While most people would agree that reading is the process of getting meaning from written language, not everyone would agree on exactly how this occurs. The reading process has been described in various ways by different reading researchers and theoreticians presenting different models of the reading process, each of which is connected to a different approach to the teaching of reading.

A Linear Model of the Reading Process

The **linear model** of reading, familiarly called the bottom-up model, views reading as a process in which the child learns to recognize first letters, then individual words, and then words in context and finally begins to understand what she is reading (Gough, 1976; LaBerge & Samuels, 1976). This theoretical model—which holds that the reader's job is to figure out the meaning of the text as it was intended by the author—is most often reflected in a sequential approach to teaching reading that breaks reading down into a series of smaller to larger subskills which should be taught in a certain order. An example of this would be a commercial reading program like the basal reader, and other programmed materials, that have a hierarchy of objectives and activities and provide the same text material for all students as well as a teacher's manual that guides the teacher step by step through these materials and the sequence of skills.

A Psycholinguistic Model of the Reading Process

The **psycholinguistic** model of reading proposed by Goodman (1976) is nicknamed the top-down model, although Goodman challenges the classification of this model as simply the opposite of bottom-up (hence, top-down). This model views reading as a process of hypothesis testing where the reader's job is to make predictions as to the meaning of what is being read, based on even minimal actual information. Readers simultaneously test and accept or reject hypotheses as they create meaning by interacting with the text. This theoretical model is reflected in a whole-language approach to teaching reading that includes strategies like language experience and writing, direct experiences and natural literacy events, literature and shared book experiences, and assisted personal reading and writing.

An Interactive Model of the Reading Process

The **interactive model** (Rumelhart, 1977), based on **schema theory** (Rumelhart, 1981), views the reading process as an interaction between the reader and the text. Schema theory explains such a model by explaining how learners acquire, store, and use knowledge in the form of a schema, or packet of knowledge in the mind. The reader's job is to make meaningful connections between prior knowledge, or schemata, and use personal reading strategies, developed and adjusted for each individual purpose in reading, while seeking to construct meaning from print. This theoretical model allows for both bottom-up and top-down processes and is reflected in teaching approaches that emphasize direct reading of word identification skills, vocabulary, and word meaning and comprehension through a variety of direct teaching strategies. These strategies include activating prior knowledge and concept development, teacher questioning methods, teaching story structure, and using patterned books that encourage predictions on the part of the reader.

Nora Miller, a real teacher facing real needs and pressures associated with the teaching of reading today, and with real convictions of her own based primarily on a lot of real experience in the classroom observing and teaching children, uses methods associated with more than one of these models. She is expected to use a basal reader by her school system; the evaluation system in her district is directly tied to and uses basal testing materials. She also uses language experience and patterned language approaches and literature-based reading methods, especially predictable story books and shared-book experiences, including shared experiences in small groups, reading centers, and wide personal reading and writing, and lots of reading aloud to, and sustained silent reading with, her children. And she also does much direct teaching of vocabulary in whole-class and small-group lessons and with the use of games, and makes careful use of questioning to help her students develop their own comprehension strategies.

Nora based her decisions about how to teach reading on her knowledge of the reading process, how children learn to read, naturalistic methods of assessment, factors that support success in reading, and many methods of teaching reading. She must merge these with other factors, such as the reading materials and tests required by her school district.

Children's Reading Development

A recent review of the growing body of research on the development of reading (Mavrogenes, 1986) shows that kindergartners entering school probably already

- know how to make use of and make sense of print in their environment and can associate letters and words with ideas, things, and people,
- know that print is meaningful and has a purpose and communicates concepts and feelings,

- are aware that reading and writing involve certain principles: linearity, direction, spacing, sequencing, patterns, forms, repetitions, and uniformity of size and shape,
- can name some letters, and
- have certain proficiencies in visual and auditory discrimination and are aware of the word-to-word correspondence between writing and talking.

Mason and Au (1986) describe three broad phases of reading development: early reading, formal beginning reading, and emerging mature reading. They caution that each phase can only be described in very general terms because of the great individual differences possible among children of each age.

1. **Early reading** is the period up to the middle or end of kindergarten. At this age, children have many home literacy experiences: storybook reading by parents, seeing their parents use print, using print themselves, and perhaps reciting the alphabet, reading a few familiar words, watching "Sesame Street" on TV, and recognizing signs and labels in their environment. There are several teaching implications here: (a) Teachers should build on the early literacy experiences that children bring to school; (b) keep alive the pleasure in the reading process and tie activities to children's interests through reading stories together; (c) demonstrate the many uses of reading and writing as communication; and (d) develop children's understanding of letter and word patterns.

2. **Formal beginning reading** covers the period from first through third grades, when school experiences shift to the use of basal readers and independent writing. Instruction may focus on identifying words rather than on getting meaning from the text. Children learn to read stories and understand story events, can answer the teacher's questions about their reading, know hundreds of words by sight, can identify new words in context, and can read and work on their own. The teaching implications here are (a) that children should learn to understand what they read as well as recognizing words, (b) that they should be able to do this in a supportive atmosphere that recognizes their interests, and (c) that they should learn to make use of their growing abilities in reading and writing.

3. **Emerging mature reading** is the period from fourth through sixth grades. At this age, children can read fluently and use reading to learn in the content areas, but they may not yet fully realize the importance of comprehending, or getting meaning from print. The teaching implications here are (a) that students need instruction in text comprehension and how to relate what they already know to new information they find in print, and (b) that they should learn how to use many different kinds of print for many different purposes, as well as reading for pleasure.

Naturalistic Methods of Reading Assessment

Another essential part of teaching reading as a language art is to meet the needs of each child through a process of ongoing evaluation. Reading assessment has taken many forms in American education. Moore (1983) suggests several strategies that readers must use in order to develop personal comprehension.

1. self-questioning
2. forming and defending value judgments of a passage
3. comparing and contrasting the content and style of a passage with one read earlier
4. setting and satisfying one's own personal reasons for reading
5. anticipating what is coming in a passage
6. activating prior knowledge of a topic and connecting it with newly encountered information
7. visualizing situations depicted in print
8. adjusting strategies according to one's own personal reasons for reading

Since these skills vary greatly from reader to reader and from situation to situation, they have rarely been assessed, and would not fit any of the traditional test formats if they were. Moore suggests two methods for the naturalistic assessment of these important objectives, as alternatives to the standardized, informal, and criterion-referenced tests more commonly in use.

See the entire April 1987 issue of *The Reading Teacher* on the theme of assessment.

1. Observing students' responses to a range of reading situations during the school day, with different kinds of materials, noting the following, and recording the observations on checklists, anecdotal records, tape recordings, and with samples of work.
   a. In reading groups: predictions about stories, answers to questions, discussion of characters' actions.
   b. During oral reading: types of mistakes and their relationship to understanding the text.
   c. For oral and written assignments: ability to comprehend the materials used.
2. Observing students' comprehension during reading conferences focused on individual reading choices and responses to literature, noting:
   a. retelling of a passage of a book, and
   b. answers to the teacher's questions designed to clarify understandings.

This type of naturalistic assessment has been described by others as ongoing evaluation (Austin, 1958), diagnostic teaching (Strang, 1964), kidwatching (Goodman, 1978), and diagnosis by observation (Cunningham, 1982).

Factors That Support Success in Learning to Read

Reviews of this research (Blair, 1984; Cox, 1984; Kinerk, 1984; Pearson & Raphael, 1984) show that the following attributes and characteristics of students, teacher, classroom environments and instructional techniques, and schools contribute to learner success in reading.

Characteristics of the Child

In addition to general intellectual ability or specific reading ability, certain characteristics of children are related to success in learning to read.

1. Proficiency in oral language, especially the ability to use oral language patterns with flexibility and increased sensitivity to conventions and varieties of language forms.
2. Amount of background knowledge and the ability to draw on this knowledge while reading, including
   - **a.** general knowledge base and varied prior experiences,
   - **b.** metacognitive knowledge, or understanding and appropriate use of cognitive processes and strategies, such as knowledge of the reading process in general, and question-answering strategies, and
   - **c.** cultural and social knowledge.
3. Vocabulary size (the bigger the better).

Characteristics of the Teacher

One of the most consistent findings of research on reading is the great importance of the teacher; certain characteristics of teachers are most often associated with student achievement in reading.

1. Teachers who believe their students can learn to read, communicate that belief to their students, and believe that they themselves can indeed teach them to read.
2. Teachers who put a lot of effort into teaching reading, by
   - **a.** using a variety of materials,
   - **b.** providing differentiated instruction,
   - **c.** keeping records of student progress (including ongoing diagnosis, planned instruction on the basis of individual evaluation, and stated pupil purposes for learning), and
   - **d.** arranging conferences that focus on individual student progress.
3. Teachers who are good planners and managers of classroom behavior, and
   - **a.** spend time and energy at the beginning of the school year getting to know their students,
   - **b.** set instructional goals,
   - **c.** make sure students know what is expected of them,

d. avoid criticism,
e. are enthusiastic,
f. keep students actively engaged in learning tasks at which they are highly successful, and
g. use a positive reward system and emphasize student responsibility and planning.

Characteristics of the Classroom and Instruction

The following characteristics of the classroom and the instructional approach are important in the teaching of reading.

1. Time and opportunities to learn, to become actively engaged in learning experiences, and to experience success.
2. Warm and pleasant but well-managed and task-oriented classrooms.
3. Direct instruction by and interaction with the teacher.
4. More whole-class and small-group experiences rather than individual seat work.
5. An atmosphere that encourages a positive attitude towards school and reading for learning and enjoyment.

Reading Methods Today

Despite the fact that a variety of methods of reading instruction have been historically practiced in the United States, and research has shown that no one single method is superior to any other (Bond & Dykstra, 1967; Chall, 1967)—that there is, so to speak, no teacher-proof method or set of materials—the commercial basal reader program remains the primary method of reading instruction in elementary schools (Shannon, 1982).

A basal reader program consists of a set of graded books used by a class or by groups within the class. All the books include a selection of stories each of which forms the core of a reading lesson. Materials for a basal reader program include

- a set of graded books for group or class, each book containing a selection of stories,
- a teacher's manual, and
- student workbooks.

The method of a basal reader program involves three reading groups; the teacher works with one group at a time while the remaining two groups do seat work or independent reading. The sequence for each group is as follows:

1. *Prereading.* The teacher's manual provides
   - a summary of the story,
   - new vocabulary, with suggestions for teaching,
   - background information for interest and comprehension, and
   - a prereading question.

2. *Silent reading*
    - In the primary grades, the children read one page at a time; the teacher asks comprehension assessment questions taken from the manual.
    - In the later grades, the children read several pages at a time, or the entire story; the teacher asks comprehension assessment questions taken from the manual.
3. *Oral reading*
    - The teacher asks questions for comprehension and final discussion taken from the manual.
    - The primary grades read aloud more, the later grades read aloud less.
4. *Skill development.* The focus is on instruction, with an emphasis on practice in workbooks or worksheets on
    - decoding,
    - word meaning,
    - comprehension, and
    - special activities for less able readers

Several reasons are most often cited for the widespread acceptance and use of basal readers (Shannon, 1983):

1. Reading instruction has been reduced to a kind of management system to certify students' minimum reading competence.
2. Schools want to show that they have a standardized way of judging and granting this competence.
3. Commercial materials make this possible because they use a sequence of testable objectives, a teacher's manual to guide the teacher to meet these objectives, and a test that demonstrates whether or not the teacher has succeeded.

Reading instruction thus becomes the application of a set of commercial materials used throughout a school or system. But since the decision to do this, and the choice of materials to be used, are made at the administrative level, teachers are alienated from the decision-making process with regard to the goals, method, and pace of the teaching of reading.

The overreliance on commercial materials has many critics among theorists, researchers, and practioners in the field of reading, for the following reasons:

1. Not enough attention is paid to the individual needs of students.
2. The system precludes or stymies instructional innovation.
3. The system predetermines the teacher's instructional decisions.

Durkin's research (1978–79, 1981) reveals a fundamental problem with the basals, namely, that less than 1 percent of instructional time during basal reading lessons is devoted to comprehension. This is indeed a problem if you accept the premise that reading is getting meaning from written language, or the comprehension of print.

But if not the basals, what then? The Reading Commission, a joint committee of the International Reading Association and the National Council of Teachers of English, suggests three essential ingredients of programs to teach reading (Goodman, 1986):

1. Since we learn to read by reading, there should be much reading of entire, meaningful, relevant texts.
2. Since readers need to try to make sense out of texts even when they are not sure about them, there should be an atmosphere of risk-taking in any reading program.
3. Since reading is the process of making sense of written language, the focus for both the reader and the teacher should always be on meaning.

I would like to proceed here on the basis of three assumptions. One is that you have had or will take a separate reading methods course using one of the many fine textbooks available that describe and explain in detail the teaching of reading in the elementary school. The second is that that course and text will also describe and explain the content and use of the basal reader in detail. And the third is that you will probably practice using a basal reader in your early field experiences, student teaching, or beginning teaching.

To attempt to deal with any of these in depth here seems redundant, especially considering that what you may not deal with in depth except in a language arts course or a text such as this one are ways to extend and expand and go beyond the basal through language- and literature-based reading instruction, and ways to teach reading as a language art. The focus of the following section will be on such methods.

Teaching Children

One Teacher's Reading Program

Nora Miller uses many strategies to teach reading as a language art all day long. Her daily schedule looks like this:

9:00–9:15	Business/sharing and planning
9:15–9:30	Sustained silent reading
9:30–10:00	Language experience and literature
10:00–11:00	Centers: writing, reading, art, science, social studies

11:00–11:15	Sharing: writing and art done in centers
11:15–12:00	Lunch/bathroom/playground
12:00–12:30	Basal reading lessons: group 1 with teacher
12:30–1:00	Basal reading lessons: group 2 with teacher
1:00–1:30	Recess
1:30–2:00	Basal reading lessons: group 3 with teacher
2:00–2:30	Mathematics: whole-group, hands-on experiences

Nora begins the day with class business and makes many uses of meaningful print with the children: noting the day of the week and writing it on the board; writing down on the calendar special events that will take place that day; helping children put their names, written on cards, into pockets on a job chart for class responsibilities. Children also share at this time, and plan the day; these plans are written on the board, as well.

Sustained silent reading is next, with the children and the teacher each choosing and reading a book and talking about them with the rest of the class. A language experience and literature lesson, such as the one described in "Centering Ideas," becomes the basis for a ripple effect of experiences that take place in small-group learning centers. Here, children respond to the book or experience they have shared, through related reading activities, art, or writing, and do other activities in the content areas integrated through the language arts. Nora feels that a most important part of work in the centers is sharing the art and writing that emerges.

See Chapter 13, "Nora Miller (First Grade)."

In the afternoons, Nora uses a basal reader with three reading groups, divided according to ability. Her school system expects her to use a basal, and the tests that come with a basal series are used as one determinant of whether or not a child passes to the next grade. In addition to working in basal reading groups with the teacher, and doing some independent follow-up work, the children also work in the writing and art centers and spend time in the class library looking at and reading books of their own choice. Nora Miller, like many other experienced teachers, has devised many ways to extend and expand on basal reading lessons in order to teach reading as a language art. Above all, she finds many means to create an environment to support literacy growth in her classroom.

See Chapter 13, "Learning Centers."

Creating an Environment to Support Literacy Growth

Here are some of the many ways in which any teacher can create such an environment.

1. Using environmental print, with permanent and changing displays in the room.
   - letters of the alphabet (manuscript or cursive)
   - calendar: days of the week, month, weather, events
   - class roster: list of children's names

- job chart with pockets labeled for each job to hold the card with the name of the child who has the job for the day
- routing chart for centers and other routines
- labels for parts of the room, furniture, supplies, centers, activities, events, holidays
- words to favorite songs, poems, or sayings
- bulletin boards and space to display children's art and writing and projects related to class theme or unit
- directions: care of class pets, bookmaking, class procedures, saving work, class business

2. Establishing a class library and reading corner.
   - shelves and places to keep and display library books, paperbacks, magazines, newspapers, pamphlets and booklets, books written and published by the children, and reference works
   - places for reading: tables and chairs, floor pillows, and a rocking chair for the teacher
3. Creating centers for direct experiences and ongoing projects and activities: art, writing, bookmaking, content areas, media, games, and special projects.
4. Providing time for reading and writing.
   - reading aloud to the children
   - sustained silent reading periods
   - time for wide personal assisted reading
   - responses to reading through whole-class discussions and small-group interactions, individualized reading conferences between teacher and student, and art, writing, drama, and research projects in the content areas
5. Supporting and encouraging natural literacy events.
   - sharing, planning, and show-and-tell
   - talking about reading experiences and other literacy experiences such as art and writing
   - asking and answering questions about subjects of interest
   - reading directions: games, learning centers, TV guide to select programs, newspaper to note current events of interest, daily lunch menu, how to sign up for a team sport
   - role-playing: spontaneous or planned dramatizations
   - functional writing: names, titles, captions, lists, directions
   - notes and letters: younger students can use a class postal system; older students can be encouraged to write for information, to comment, to communicate
   - class directories or compilations: phone numbers, addresses, birthdays, favorite recipes
6. Broadening the scope of the reading program across the curriculum by providing time for reading in the content areas, not only for reading to learn, but for acquiring background knowledge to support comprehension.

A center for making a bird feeder is one way to create an environment to support literacy growth.

A recent study has shown how important it is not to overstress basic skills in reading instruction to the exclusion of time for instruction in other areas of the curriculum. Singer and his associates (1984) found that schools in the same school system that had a broad curriculum emphasizing the development of vocabularies and general knowledge by providing broad instruction in social studies, science, and the fine arts had significantly higher scores on a system-wide test of essential skills, especially in inferential and interpretive reading, than schools that stressed basic skills only. This finding is supported by the interactive theory of reading, which describes reading as a process of interaction between what is in the text and what the reader already knows. Keep this in mind as you plan a total reading program. Reading is not really an isolable skill that can be taught separately from the rest of the curriculum or the world of the child outside the school.

Beyond the Basal Reader

There are many ways teachers can extend and expand the basal reader and go beyond it through a variety of means, or in fact not use it at all, and still teach reading.

Extending One Basal Lesson

Let us begin by looking at how you might extend one basal lesson. My university students over the years have shown great insight and originality in integrating language and literature experiences into basal reading lessons they found lacking in their specific teaching situations in field experiences where they are often assigned to work with one reading group using the basal reader.

For example, Diane Roberts had taught a basal reading lesson based on an excerpt from Miska Miles's story, *Annie and the Old One.* The purpose of the lesson, as Diane stated in her lesson plan adapted from the basal teacher's guide, was to enable students to recognize, pronounce, and know the meaning of some new words. The technique suggested in the basal guide for doing this was to show a vocabulary word card and define the word in a sentence. The suggested sentences were:

Annie and the Old One, by Miska Miles (Little, Brown, 1971), is the story of a young Navajo girl and her aging grandmother.

1. High, steep banks or cliffs, that is *bluffs,* could be seen in the distance.
2. The flat-topped mountain with steep sides is called a *mesa.*
3. A *hogan* is a house made of stones or logs with a roof of branches covered with earth.
4. In weaving, the *warp* is the thread running lengthwise.

Diane found that her fourth-grade students were not interested in the story and did not really understand the vocabulary words. She decided to extend this basal lesson. Here is Diane's own lesson plan for the next day:

- *Level:* fourth grade

- *Focus:* developing vocabulary words from a story about the Navajo, *Annie and the Old One,* through literature, photographs, objects, and direct experiences

- *Purpose:*
  1. Students will acquire knowledge of vocabulary words encountered in the basal reader story, *Annie and the Old One,* through experiences with objects, photographs, and literature.
  2. Students will be better able to visualize, understand, and appreciate the story.
  3. Students will be able to discuss some aspects of Navajo life.

- *Materials:*
  1. Objects: turquoise stones and ring, sheep's wool, yarn of various colors, handheld loom
  2. Books: *Annie and the Old One, The Native Americans: Navajos*

The Native Americans: Navajos, by Richard Erdoes (Sterling, 1979)

- *Teaching Sequence:*
  1. Tell the children: "Today I want to share with you some things which will help us to learn some things about the Navajo people."
  2. Let children examine and discuss the objects and name them.

3. Read aloud the informational book, *The Native Americans: Navajos.* Discuss Navajo life and explain vocabulary words as they are encountered in the text and photographs.
4. Review the vocabulary words.

- *Extending activities:*
  1. Children can draw a design for a Navajo blanket.
  2. Play Native American String Play game.
  3. Make colored sand and create Navajo sand drawings.
  4. Interview a grandmother or other elderly person.
  5. Encourage writing about the Navajo or the elderly.
  6. Read *Annie and the Old One* aloud.
  7. Provide other books about Native Americans in the classroom.

- *Evaluation:* Observation of oral responses during discussions in lesson and further lessons related to *Annie and the Old One.* A written examination on vocabulary words will be administered at the end of the unit.

Diane found that the time spent in developing concepts through direct experiences and discussion of objects, sharing the informational book about the Navajo, and extending activities made a great difference in the children's interest and understanding not only of the vocabulary words but the world of the Navajo and the beautiful story of the little girl who tries to prevent her grandmother's inevitable death. She notes that

> there was simply not enough time and not the right experiences in the original lesson in the teacher's guide to develop concepts, words, or understanding. What does the word *mesa* mean to children who have grown up in the flat Mississippi River valley? How could they understand a *hogan* from a simple sentence? What does *warp* mean if you've never seen a loom or woven anything? And why should they care if they were not motivated to read the story? An initial test showed they didn't understand the words. If I had been able to expand and extend the story immediately, it would have been successful.

After Diane began to read *Annie and the Old One* aloud to the class on subsequent days and the class began to read, talk, and write about the Navajo, Diane provided more opportunities to extend the story:

A Recipe for Fry Bread. Mix together: 1 c. shortening, 4 c. flour, 1 T. baking powder, 2 T. powdered milk, 1-1/2 c. warm water. Pat into flat circles, fry in hot oil, drain, sprinkle with powdered sugar.

1. The students designed and created a weaving on the hand loom.
2. They made Native American fry bread, ate it, and talked and wrote about it.
3. They dramatized scenes from *Annie and the Old One.*

Extending Any Basal Lesson

Going beyond the basal means modifying the use of the basal and the basal guide from that of a total reading program where every story is read, every teacher direction in the guide followed, and every workbook exercise completed in the exact sequence presented. Basal publishers, in fact, have never advocated such a linear, comprehensive use of their programs.

A first step in a more selective use of the basal is to analyze the scope and sequence in the guide and make decisions about what is most important for a particular class and for individual students. One way to decide is by choosing those objectives and activities that focus on comprehension, or getting meaning from print—the real purpose of reading. In this way you are using the basal guide as a resource but are still in control of your own reading program.

You can also consider the basal reader as just one of many reading materials in the classroom. It is one kind of text, but not the only kind to use for reading instruction. Many of the newer basals use selections from children's literature and have overcome some of the criticisms leveled against them in the past, such as that the content of the stories was banal and centered around white, middle-class, traditional families. Newer basals include characters from many cultural and ethnic groups and depict men and women in nontraditional roles.

Basal series with a meaning emphasis: *Sounds of Language* (Holt, Rinehart & Winston), *Language Experiences in Reading* (Encyclopaedia Brittanica), *Breakthrough to Literacy* (Bowmar), and *Reading Unlimited* (Scott, Foresman)

Many basal publishers also offer supplementary reading materials such as records and tapes, student newspapers, and sets of paperback books tied to the themes in the basal stories.

When you use a basal story, there are many ways to extend and go beyond the basal to teach reading. Here is a selected list:

1. For students of any age:
- teacher questioning techniques
- direct and shared experiences
- discussion
- writing
- small-group and reading center activities

2. For younger students:
- language experience approach
- pattern writing
- directed listening thinking activity (DLTA)
- listening center
- creative dramatics
- story dramatization
- puppetry
- reading aloud
- flannel board
- storytelling
- mediamaking

3. For older students:
- self-selected inquiry or research on topics of interest that emerge as a result of reading a basal story
- study in the content areas
- semantic mapping

directed reading thinking activities (DRTA)
reader's theatre
newspaper publication
fictional journal writing
scriptwriting
play performance
mediamaking

Strategies for Teaching Comprehension Using Any Printed Text

See "The New Face of Reading Comprehension Instruction: A Closer Look at Questions," by Denise Nessel, in *The Reading Teacher,* 40 (1987), 604–606.

The interactive model of reading described earlier views reading as a process of constructing meaning from text. Its practical application is to provide students with strategies that will help them become independent readers who monitor their own thinking while reading. One important teaching strategy to help students achieve this goal is the use of effective questions. Research has consistently underscored the importance of teacher questioning techniques to help students develop ways of monitoring their personal comprehension in order to make the link between their own prior knowledge and the text they are reading (Au, 1979) and to improve their ability to answer questions during reading, especially inferential questions (Gordon & Pearson, 1983; Hansen, 1981; Hansen & Pearson, 1983).

Here are two teaching strategies that use specific teacher questioning techniques to help students monitor their own comprehension as they read. Each of these strategies can be used either with a basal reader story or with any other printed text: children's tradebooks, magazines, newspapers, or stories written by the children themselves.

Question–Answer Relationship

Raphael (1982) has developed an instructional approach to improving both literal and inferential comprehension that can be used with any type of text. This approach is based on Pearson and Johnson's (1978) system for categorizing a question depending on where the reader will find the information to answer it. The premise is that students will do better if they understand the question–answer relationship, or QAR. Here is an example:

Text: The beaver gnawed the tree. The tree fell to the ground.

Three Types of Questions	***Question–Answer Relationship Where is the answer found?***
1. Text-explicit question: answer is explicitly stated in text.	1. *Right There.* The same words that make the question and the answer are found in the same sentence.

Q: "What did the beaver gnaw?" — *A:* "The beaver gnawed the tree."

2. Text-implicit question: answer can be inferred from the text. — 2. *Think and Search.* The answer is there, but not in the exact words used in the sentence.

   Q: "Why did the tree fall?" — *A:* "Because the beaver gnawed it."

3. Script-implicit question: answer comes from the background knowledge of the reader. — 3. *On My Own.* The answer won't be found in words in the story, but in your own head.

   Q: "Why did the beaver gnaw the tree?" — *A:* "(. . .)"

The teacher can explain these three types of questions to the students in practice lessons and encourage them to use the questions independently as they read any type of text.

Directed Reading Thinking Activity

A directed reading thinking activity (DRTA) is a variation of the format of a directed reading activity, such as those used in basal reading instruction. A main difference is that the DRA is carefully scripted with specific questions in the teacher's manual. The DRTA (Stauffeur, 1975, 1980) focuses on active involvement with the text as the students again make predictions and verify them as they read. The teacher uses questions to activate prior knowledge, to introduce and expand vocabulary and word meaning, and to teach word identification skills and, above all, comprehension.

Like the DLTA, the DRTA can be used with any text. Spiegel (1981) suggests that this approach is especially useful when students have a command of vocabulary and background knowledge, and as a major alternative to the Directed Reading Lesson used in basals.

1. Prereading
   - Introduce the selection: show the cover or an illustration and read the title.
   - Ask for predictions about the story: "What do you think the story is about?" and "Why?"
   - Ask the children what they already know about the subject (this is especially useful for informational texts).
   - Write their ideas and predictions on the board or on chart paper.
2. Reading
   - Direct the children to read to verify the predictions they made.
   - Ask: "What will happen next?" and "Why do you think so?"
3. Postreading
   - Discuss the verification of the children's ideas and predictions.

- Encourage the children to find and read sections that prove or disprove their predictions.
- Encourage discussion of those predictions that can neither be proved nor disproved directly by the text, but can be inferred.

The students may read the entire selection first, or you may have them read a section, stop, discuss, and go on.

The focus of reading instruction should always be on comprehension, and there are many ways this can be done, with or without a basal reader. Many language and literature experiences allow the teacher to extend and go beyond the basal lesson, and teacher questioning strategies such as QARs and DLTAs can be used throughout the day with any reading material.

The point is that although basals are currently the primary material to teach reading in classrooms, they are not the only way. Many teachers use the basal but go beyond the suggestions in the teacher's manual in order to meet the needs of their own students, as Diane Roberts did when she extended the story of *Annie and the Old One.* Others go beyond the basal by using many other approaches to teaching reading as a language art, as Nora Miller does in her reading program with language- and literature-based reading instruction.

Whole-Language- and Literature-Based Reading Instruction: Alternatives to the Basal Reader

Let us look now at some specific techniques for teaching reading that are centered around children's language and children's literature and do not use a basal reader at all.

The Language Experience Approach

See Chapter 2 for more examples of the language experience approach in action.

The language experience approach (LEA) uses children's own experiences, their talk, and their writing as the primary material for reading instruction (Ashton-Warner, 1963; Goodman, 1970; Hall, 1981; Stauffeur, 1980; Van Allen, 1976). Experiences and sharing precede talking; the discussion is then written down and read by the children. For younger children, teachers record group talk on the blackboard or on chart paper, or work with one or a few children in small groups. These experiences and the talking, writing, and reading become a springboard for older students to pursue topics or questions of interest through more reading, research, and writing and publishing of what they have written.

Many examples of language experience lessons are given in this text, such as in Chapter 2, which describes how Marion Harris's first-grade class made apple turnovers during the first week of school. While classroom experiences like this are still alive and fresh, you can build on them in the following ways.

Teaching Sequence

1. *Expand direct experiences and develop concepts.*
    - Extend direct experiences through talking, gathering resources, adding books to the class library, and creating displays and centers of interest.
    - Develop concepts through talk and more concrete experiences, and acting on these through art, drama, and writing.
2. *Build vocabulary.*
    - Focus on words the children already know and use during discussions, and add new words along the way.
    - Record and display these words of interest.
    - Write the words on the board or on chart paper while the children watch, read them aloud, let the children write them and save them in personal dictionaries, on word rings, in word boxes or class lists.

See Chapter 2 for techniques to help build vocabulary.

3. *Write and read.*
    - Record words and ideas as children share them and watch you write. This can be done in prose form or in a pattern or poem form. Older students can do this themselves after you have modeled it.
    - Students can write independently or in small groups.
    - Students read as they watch you write the words, read the stories or poems written by groups, read their own writing as they share and rewrite, and read the writing of other children as they discuss it.
4. *Integrate skills.*
    - Skills can be taught in context as the children write and read their own words.
    - Skills become meaningful to the children this way because they are a means for the children to fulfill their own purposes in reading and writing.
5. *Publish.*
    - Writing through the language experience approach is published instantly when it is recorded by the teacher.
    - When children write independently, their writings can be displayed on bulletin boards, read aloud, bound in books, performed as plays, recorded through the media, printed in newspapers or magazines, collected in anthologies, or dramatized, danced, and sung.

Here is an example of a real language experience lesson that follows this teaching sequence.

Featured Teacher Gene Hughes: Using the Language Experience Approach with Remedial Readers

Gene Hughes teaches a special reading class for students who need motivation and help with reading. He has found that one of the most successful approaches with these students is LEA, because most of them have not succeeded with traditional reading methods and because they have a low concept of themselves as readers.

Gene provides many shared experiences for his students, encourages them to talk about these, and uses language experience lessons combined with sustained silent reading and wide assisted personal reading and writing and individualized reading conferences. Gene teaches all the related skills through language experience lessons and through individualized and small-group lessons.

For example, Gene was given a baby crow which he brought to school each day to share with the students. The following language experience story was recorded by Gene as his students dictated it, and it became the basis for further reading instruction: building vocabulary, teaching skills, and strengthening comprehension.

Bart the Crow

Bart is a baby crow. He has black feathers. He is soft. Bart lives in a nest. The nest is a plastic pail filled with hay. Sometimes we take him outside so he can exercise and get fresh air. He has a good appetite. We feed him grapes, baby food, dog food, and puppy chow. He drinks water. He is a good bird and we care about him.

See *The Cry of the Crow,* by Jean Craighead George (Harper & Row, 1980).

See Chapter 13, "Mauretta Hurst (Kindergarten)."

During the semester, Gene's students talked and wrote and read what they wrote about Bart. They also read other books about birds and how to care for them. They were interviewed by the newspaper about Bart and later read about themselves in the story that was printed. When Bart had an accident, they learned to care for his injury and wrote the following language experience story about it, shown here in the same teaching sequence described earlier.

1. *Expand direct experiences and develop concepts.*
Gene gathers the students around him on the floor and gets a large piece of chart paper ready and gets ready to get Bart.

Teacher: When Bart comes out of his cage, he'll be excited.
Child [*excitedly*]: Here he comes!
Teacher: He needs to fly around for a while. His leg's doing better. He's not limping as badly as he was. What's he doing now?
Child: Taking a bath kinda like.
Teacher [*Picks Bart up and pets him.*] Just like a baby. Remember when he couldn't fly?
Child: Now his wings go out.
Teacher: Remember his accident?
Child: Broken leg.
Teacher: Not exactly.
Child: Fractured.

Students share an experience with Bart the Crow as preparation for a language experience reading lesson.

Child: Marco did it.
Teacher: It was an accident and could have happened to anyone. When babies are small their bones are . . .
Child: Tender.
Child: Soft.
Child: Weak.
Teacher: So what did we do when he had the accident?
Child: Took him to the doctor.

2. *Build vocabulary.*

Teacher: What do you call a doctor for animals?
Child: A vet.
Child: A veterinarian.
Teacher: What happened then?
Child: They took a picture of him.
Teacher: What's that called?
Child: I know. An x-ray.
Child: And he was in the hospital.

[*Bart is on the floor moving among the children.*]

Child: He's trying to untie my shoelaces!
Child: He loves to find pencils.

Teacher: Let's talk about his accident. What did we say happened?
Child: He had a fraction.
Child: No. He had a fracture.
Teacher: It didn't happen too long ago so we could start our story with the word *recently*. That means something that happened a little while ago.

3. *Write and read.*
Gene uses a large marking pen to write the story on the chart paper as students dictate it. He is working on the floor with the students around him.

Teacher: "Recently Bart . . ."
Child: Had an accident.
Teacher: How do you spell that?
Child: A-c-c . . .
Child: . . . i . . .
Child: A-c-c-i-d-e-n-t.
Child: Someone picked him up the wrong way.
Child: Bart fractured his leg.
Teacher: How did he act?
Child: He limped.
Child: He curled his toes up.
Teacher: What did we do to make him feel better?
Child: We took him to the vet at LSU.
Teacher: Let's read what we have so far.

[*Student reads.*]

Teacher: What happened next?
Child: The doctor gave him a shot.
Child: And x-rayed him.
Teacher: What did the doctor prescribe for him?
Child: The doctor said he needed rest.
Teacher: How is he doing now?
Child: Fine.
Teacher: Let's put a sentence to tell that.
Child: He's doing fine now.
Teacher: Will someone read the story?

Bart's Accident

Recently Bart had a little accident. Someone picked him up the wrong way. Bart fractured his leg. He limped and curled his toes up. We took him to the vet at LSU. The doctor gave him a shot and x-rayed his leg. The doctor said he need rest. He's doing fine now.

4. *Integrate skills.*

Teacher: I see a little mistake. I wrote *need* here.
Child: Needed. Add *-ed.*

Teacher: What should we use for a title?
Child: *Bart's Accident.*
Teacher: This is an apostrophe. It means the accident happened to Bart.
Teacher: What does LSU stand for?
Child: Tigers.
Teacher: Yes, but the letters LSU are an abbreviation, or a short way to say something.
Child: Louisiana State University.
Child: SU is Southern University.
Teacher: What do we call letters like SU?
Child: Abbreviation.
Teacher: You did a good job on this story. How many sentences long is it?
Child: Eight. It's a long one.
Teacher: Look at the first one. What's the new word that tells when?
Child: Recently.
Teacher: There's also a word that tells the name of a doctor for animals.
Child: Veterinarian.
Teacher: Which word tells you about a special picture?
Child: X-ray.

Students dictate a language experience story about Bart the Crow.

5. *Publish.*

Teacher: Now let's sign our names. You're the authors.
Child: Let's put it in the hall so everybody can read it.
Child: Yeah. Put it by our other ones and the story they wrote about us in the newspaper.

Examples of language experience lessons have been used extensively throughout the text.

Responding to Literature and Learning to Read

Despite the fact that most teachers today use some sort of basal reading series or other system, many educators (Koeller, 1981) advocate a literature-based reading program as an alternative to such a system or in combination with other programs for the following reasons.

Literature for Language Development. For decades, researchers have shown that young children who learned to read naturally, even before they entered school and without any formal training in reading, were read to often at home by parents and other caretakers, and that this contributed to their linguistic development, their growing sense of story, and their eventual success in reading (Chomsky, 1972; Clark, 1976; Durkin, 1961; Thorndike, 1973).

Literature for Developing a Sense of Story. As children are read to or read themselves they are developing what Applebee (1978) describes as a sense of story. For example, three first-graders dictated this story to their teacher.

> *One day King Mike and Queen Elizabeth called for a meeting with their court. Sixteen days later they had a baby and named her Princess Diane. A wicked witch came into the castle and told King Mike that she wanted his magic unicorn. The King said, "No!" "Then I shall kill your daughter," said the wicked witch. Then she left with the princess. The next day, the queen went and got the princess back. They lived happily ever after.*

From exposure to nursery and traditional tales, these young children have learned about story structure, the language of stories, and characters in literature (if not biology) and what to expect from them: kings and queens have power (and princesses), witches are wicked (and steal princesses), and unicorns are magic. This gives them a familiarity with all future stories they encounter that will support their ability to predict what will happen and reduce uncertainty as they learn to read.

Literature for Meaning and Pleasure. Many young children's first real experiences with decoding and understanding print occur when they are interested, absorbed, and even fascinated enough to want to read a story and find its meaning all by themselves. Bettelheim and Zelan (1982) argue for literature-based reading programs and challenge the notion that reading needs to be taught with programmed reading materials such as basal readers, or with an emphasis on skills rather than meaning.

> It is high time that children and teachers were freed of the yoke and the blinders that are the direct result of teaching reading as if its ultimate purpose is the acquisition of decoding skills, and as if the only way to become able to recognize a word is to be exposed to it innumerable times. The truth is that words are learned easily and fast if we are interested in what they mean to us. If we want our children to grow up to be literate, reading must be exciting from the very beginning, and never become a chore the way raking grass is for a first-grader—the symbolic activity with which reading is introduced on the first page of *Janet and Mark,* revealing exactly what the constructors of these primers think learning to read may be best compared to (pp. 305–306).

Literature for Learning to Read by Reading. Pearson and Johnson (1978) describe two strong beliefs about all aspects of reading acquisition.

1. *The importance of reading,* or "learning to read by reading." Pearson and Johnson urge teachers to encourage, promote, provide time for, and reward wide and frequent reading by students, for "as they read more and learn of reading's many pleasures, reading will become the reward itself" (p. 178).
2. *The importance of the teacher,* especially for children who do not come from a home where reading is practiced or valued. Johnson and Pearson urge teachers to be a model for students, to read to them daily, to let them see the teacher read (something besides teachers' manuals and lesson plans), to provide time for free reading daily, to encourage and guide the students, to respond to their reading experiences, and to praise them.

Literature-Based Reading Methods

Reading Aloud and Along with Children. The lap method is more of a natural instinct than a method; it is what parents do when they hold young children on their lap and read favorite stories over and over again, interacting with the child as they do so. As simple as it sounds, there may not be a better way to teach reading, and many children learn to read because they are interested and begin to read along themselves in this secure and pleasurable setting.

Research by Flood (1977) has also shown that there is a preferred way to read to young children, and have them read along with you, which has implications for teachers teaching reading to young children in the classroom, as well as when they read to one child or to a small group, or help teacher aides or parents gain the most benefit possible as they read to children. Flood found that the more actively involved the child is—talking about the story, asking and answering questions—and the more the adult encourages this involvement—by asking warm-up questions, questions during the story, and evaluative questions at the end, and giving positive reinforcement for answers—the higher the child's score is on certain prereading-related tasks. He suggests four steps to follow when reading with children, which can also be applied to teachers and aides in the classroom reading with children.

Sylvester and the Magic Pebble, by William Steig (Simon & Schuster, 1969)

1. Prepare the children for the story by asking warm-up questions. For example, with *Sylvester and the Magic Pebble,* you might ask:
   - Have you ever collected anything?
   - What was it?
   - Does anyone collect rocks?
   - Can you describe one of your special rocks?

   Then tell the children, "We are going to read a story about a donkey named Sylvester who liked to collect rocks."
2. Verbally interact with the children during the reading. Ask and answer many different kinds of questions, for example:
   - Why did Sylvester think the pebble he had found was magic?
   - Why did he wish he would turn into a rock?
3. Reinforce student responses in the course of the reading. For example, if one of the children remarks, "Sylvester's parents were very sad when they couldn't find him," you might reply, "That's right. You're noticing things in the story."
4. At the end of the reading, ask children to evaluate the story. You may want to ask some of the following questions:
   - Did you like the story? Why or why not?
   - How do you think Sylvester and his parents feel now?
   - Did you like Sylvester?

Children who have not been read to a great deal at home need to be read to in school. Cohen (1968) found that second-grade children who are read a story every day are significantly ahead in reading vocabulary and comprehension than those who are not read to. One primary teacher described by Hepler (1982) explains how important she feels it is to read aloud to and read along with other students:

> I read to my children a lot—a whole lot! I'll read anywhere from one to three stories at a time. Sometimes I'll reread a favorite story twice. And I read four to five times a day. I read to the whole group, to small groups of four or five children, and to individual children. While I'm reading to the group I'll encourage them to join in on the refrains. With individuals I may point to words, talk about what a word is. Sometimes I'll frame a word with my hand or put it on the board. I put songs, poems, and refrains on chart

paper so children will try to read them by themselves. And I'll read stories over and over again, just the way children hear bedtime stories. It's not unusual for me to read a book twenty times a month! (pp. 2–3)

Sustained Silent Reading. Reading specialist Crawford (1984) describes her approach to sustained silent reading (SSR):*

See "Getting Started with Sustained Silent Reading and Keeping it Going," by Linda B. Gambrell, in *The Reading Teacher,* 31 (1978), 328–331, and "SSR/Booktime: Kindergarten and First Grade Sustained Silent Reading," by Jim Kaisen, in *The Reading Teacher,* 40 (1987), 532–536.

> Sustained Silent Reading is one of the greatest things that has happened to my teaching career. It has enabled me to take my children far beyond the basal reader, for skills and vocabulary development as well as comprehension and appreciation of literature. And the excitement it generates stimulates learning for both the teacher and children.
>
> The only materials are good reading material at many levels, for many interests: library books, paperbacks, basals, poetry, magazines, newspapers, informational books, etc. To initiate SSR each year, I follow these steps.
>
> 1. *Introduce books to whole class.* I put a pile of 40 to 50 books on the rug in the reading center with the children seated around the edge. I choose a book, read a few pages aloud, make a comment, and then put the book back in the pile. I do this three to five more times and then read at least one entire book aloud. This takes 20 to 30 minutes.
> 2. *Introduce approach.* I say "Today, we are going to read silently, and we're going to sustain ourselves in silent reading. This means that you're going to spend some time with one book, paying attention only to it, reading and re-reading it or looking at the pictures carefully. You know you can read books without reading words. Pictures tell us many things."
> 3. *All select books.* They will scramble into the middle of the pile and immediately grab the book I read all the way through, and next choose the ones which had a few pages read. They must keep the book they choose and can go anywhere in the room to read. I find something to read too.
> 4. *All read silently.* They cannot interrupt anyone else including the teacher—and must stay in the place they have chosen. If they finish reading or looking at the book, they should re-read or look at illustrations.
> 5. *Share books.* Signal the end of reading. (Note children's behavior to determine when to stop. If they are all absorbed in reading, let them continue.) After SSR I share something in order to give the children an idea of the ways that books are shared: tell the main idea or theme of the book, read a passage and relate it to current events or something special in school, share interesting words, phrases, ideas, or illustrations in your book, or tell how you felt about your reading. Children then have a model for sharing their own books.
>
>   Usually four or five children share daily. You may ask questions and invite other children to ask questions which encourage children to think, interpret, infer, and personalize their reading experience. Encourage discussion of ideas and words in the book as well as their personal response to it.

*From Crawford, 1984. Used with permission.

See "How To Use Predictable Books for K–2 Language Arts Instruction," by Gail Heald-Taylor, in *The Reading Teacher,* 40 (1987), 661–665.

Shared Big-Book Experience. This is a natural outgrowth of the read-aloud, read-along lap method. The method recreates the developmental aspects of the natural way children learn to speak, and the conditions under which many preschoolers who come from a literacy-oriented environment learn to read naturally. They are surrounded with good books of high literary quality, which they experience with interested adults who answer their questions and are willing to read favorite books over and over again. And even before young children understand the connections between print and words, they want to share the pleasurable social aspects of the lap method. At eighteen months, my daughter Elizabeth's favorite sentence was "Read to me!" accompanied by the gesture of bashing her targeted reader with a book. No one was exempt, including her four-year-old brother Gordon, who was just beginning to read favorite books himself.

Applied to the classroom, this meaning-centered and process-centered approach builds on the readinglike behavior of young book-bashers like Elizabeth. Holdaway (1979, 1982) describes the approach used by teachers in New Zealand on a national scale. They attempted to adapt the environment of the home bedtime story situation to the classroom. The approach includes three elements.

1. The books had to be those loved by children ages five through seven.
2. The books needed to have the same visual impact from twenty feet away (when used by a teacher with a group or class) that a regular book would have on the knee of a child. (Teachers who used this method made enlarged texts about 30 × 24 inches so that every child could see the print. They used heavy brown paper, charts, overhead transparencies, and slides, when reading to the whole class.)
3. Books need to be represented by the teacher with joy, more as a performance than a lesson, and involve the children in the joy of reading.

After use of this method as a beginning reading method for the first two years of school, children in New Zealand proved equal or superior in reading to those taught by traditional methods. Most significant was the highly positive attitudes among more slowly developing children.

A teaching–learning sequence example of shared big-book experience might look like this (Holdaway, 1982):

1. Opening warm-up.
   Favorite poems, jingles, songs with enlarged text. Teaching of a new poem or song.
2. Old favorite.
   Enjoyment of a favorite story in enlarged format. Teaching of skills in context. Deepening understanding. Unison participation. Role playing, dramatization.
3. Language games, especially alphabet.
   Alphabet games, rhymes, and songs, using letter names. Fun with words and sounds in meaningful situations (not isolated phonic drills).

4. New story.
Highlight of session. Long story may be broken naturally into two or more parts. Inducing word-solving strategies in context, participation in prediction and confirmation of new vocabulary.
5. Output activities.
Independent reading from wide selection of favorites. Related arts activities stemming from new story. Creative writing, often using structures from new story. Playing teacher—several children enjoy favorite together—one acting as teacher. (p. 299)

A teacher interested in trying a big-book shared reading experience might begin with one of the Children's Choices books for 1984: Arnold Lobel's *Book of Pigericks.* Children enjoy other books by Arnold Lobel, and this one lends itself to enlargement and could be shared with a whole class by xeroxing a page on paper, then on a transparency for use with an overhead projector. Here is a suggested teaching–learning sequence for a big-book experience with *The Book of Pigericks* and other stories.

The Book of Pigericks, by Arnold Lobel (Harper & Row, 1983). Other books by Arnold Lobel: *Frog and Toad Are Friends* (Harper & Row, 1970); *Fables* (Harper & Row, 1981)

1. *Opening warm up.* Familiar nursery rhymes, such as "This Little Pig Went to Market," "Tom, Tom, the Piper's Son," "Barber, Barber, Shave a Pig," followed by a new poem from *The Book of Pigericks.*

2. *Old favorite.* Read *The Three Little Pigs.* Teaching skills in context could include identifying words that begin with the letter *p* and words that rhyme with *pig.* Deepen understanding of story structure by identifying the story parts (opening, introduction of characters, identification of problem, repetition of three encounters with the villain, and ending) and remembering other stories that follow a similar pattern, such as *The Three Billy Goats Gruff.*

The Three Little Pigs, by Paul Galdone (Seabury, 1970)

Directing a shared big-book experience: students role-play a favorite nursery rhyme, "There Was An Old Woman Who Lived in a Shoe."

Role-playing and story dramatization could come next, after another reading, as the children volunteer to play out the parts of the pigs and the wolf. Unison participation could occur the first time the story is read, with half the class reading and chanting to the other:

Wolf: Little pig, little pig, let me come in!
Pig: Not by the hair on my chinny, chin, chin!
Wolf: Then I'll huff, and I'll puff, and I'll blow your house in!

See Chapter 6, "Classifying Words," for an alphabet pyramid pattern.
Oh, A-Hunting We Will Go, by John Langstaff (Atheneum, 1974)

3. *Language games, especially the alphabet.* An alphabet pyramid pattern could be created using the *p* words collected during the reading of *The Three Little Pigs.* An alphabet rhyme "This is a . . ." could be created with the words that rhyme with *pig,* also collected during the reading of *The Three Little Pigs* (i.e., "This is a *pig.* This is a *fig.* This is a *pig eating a fig.*). An alphabet song could be created, with other words that rhyme with *pig,* to the tune of "Oh, A-Hunting We Will Go."

Pig Pig Rides, by David McPhail (Dutton, 1982)

4. *New Story.* The highlight of the session could be the introduction of a new story, *Pig Pig Rides,* about a young pig who tells his mother everything he is going to do that day including racing cars and horses, jumping 500 elephants on a motorcycle, and driving a train to China and a rocket to the moon. Children could solve words like *elephants* and *motorcycle* in context with picture clues, begin to predict what Pig Pig might do next, and confirm new vocabulary words such as *please, careful, record,* and *deliver* after reading.

For more pig books and suggestions for using pig literature in primary grades, see *Focus Units in Literature: A Handbook for Elementary School Teachers* (National Council of Teachers of English, 1984)

5. *Output activities.* Independent reading from a wide selection of other books. For example:

Portly McSwine, by James Marshall (Houghton, 1979)
Roland the Minstrel Pig, by William Steig (Harper, 1968)
Pa's Balloon and Other Pig Tales, by Arthur Geisert (Houghton, Mifflin, 1984)
Perfect the Pig, by Susan Jeschke (Holt, Rinehart & Winston, 1980)
The Pig's Wedding, by Helme Heine (Atheneum, 1979)
Paddy Pork's Evening Out, by John S. Goodall (Atheneum, 1973)—a wordless picture book
The Pig's Book of World Records, by Bob Stihe (Random House, 1980)
A Treeful of Pigs, by Arnold Lobel (Morrow, 1979)

Art activities could take place over the next several days, with materials for the following provided in the art center:

See *Perfect the Pig,* by Susan Jeschke (Holt, Rinehart & Winston, 1981), a story about an artist who paints pictures of Perfect, a flying pig.

- *Thumbprint pigs:* An inkpad and paper are all that is needed for children to create characters such as pigs, or anything else, using their own thumbprints.
- *Pig pictures.* Children can draw in response to pig stories, or illustrate their own pig stories.

Creative writing could take place first with the whole group, and then in small groups or individually as children follow the pattern of the story structure of *Pig Pig Rides:* as his mother asks him what he will do that day, he gives a fanciful reply; she asks again, and so on. Other patterns from this teaching sequence could be adaptations of nursery rhymes, the story of *The Three Little Pigs,* or limericks. Or children could write freely about pigs, or anything else they choose.

Playing teacher—several children enjoying a favorite story together—could take place as reader's theatre, where one child guides and reads the mother's part in *Pig Pig Rides* and others take turns reading Pig Pig's lines.

See Chapter 10, "Reader's Theatre."

Individualized Reading. Individualized reading is a method whereby the students themselves select and read a wide range of material, participate in individual reading conferences with the teacher, and work on projects related to their needs, abilities, and reading interests, either in small groups or individually (Stauffeur, 1980; Veatch et al., 1979). This approach can be used with the basal or as a total reading program.

The advantages of such an approach are that it provides for individual differences of interest and ability in reading, emphasizes comprehension and real reading of longer texts and good literature, provides opportunities for the development of skills in the context of real needs in reading, and capitalizes on the interrelationship of all the language arts, including reading.

The individualized reading method does assume that teachers will plan a well-organized system, understood by the students, in the absence of a basal program providing a step-by-step teacher's manual for instruction and evaluation. As for its effectiveness, summaries of the research of the fifties and sixties (Bond & Dykstra, 1967; West, 1964), which tended to focus on a comparison of methods, showed that students make similar progress as with other, more traditional methods.

Here are the major features of an individualized reading program, which can be implemented in any classroom already focused on literature and where reading is viewed as a language art.

- *Self-selection of books of interest.* Classroom libraries should provide a wide selection of books for children, supplemented by school and public and home libraries. Many students also choose to read books ordered from paperback book clubs. Teachers need to be aware of their students' literature interests.
- *Opportunities for extended reading periods.* Students spend the majority of their instructional reading time actually reading a book of their choice.
- *Conferences with the teacher.* Teachers schedule individual conferences on a weekly basis, during which time they discuss the book with the child, note levels of comprehension, reinforce skills, and plan for both group and individual activities.
- *Group and individual activities.* Time for responding to books through a variety of activities is planned with the teacher. Groups may be formed on the basis of interest in a similar subject.

- *Sharing response activities.* Students need to share their responses with others, through art, writing, drama, constructions, and the like.

Featured Teacher Glynn Wink: Using Individualized Reading with Second-Grade Students

See Chapter 13, "Glynn Wink (Second Grade)."

From Monday through Wednesday, Glynn Wink uses the basal reader and teaches other subjects in separate blocks of time. But on Thursdays and Fridays, her schedule changes. Her students go to the computer room and the science laboratory room. In her classroom, the rest of the time is spent moving through five centers related to reading, math, and the content areas they are studying. The children also read independently and come to Glynn for an individualized reading conference. Important features of her program include these conferences and her system of record keeping.

1. *Conferences.* While the other students are reading or working in centers, Glynn calls a student to her desk and asks him to bring the book he is reading. She gets comfortable with the child, and asks general prompting questions, such as:

- What is the book about?
- Tell me about the main characters: Where do they live? What do they do? What are they like?
- What did you like about the book? Not like? Why?
- What is happening now?
- What do you think will happen next? Why?
- Would you please read some of your book to me?

During the reading time, Glynn may just listen, but she may also provide words the child cannot read or does not understand, discuss concepts and vocabulary, or ask or answer questions about the story, its meaning, and the child's response to it. At the end of the conference, she always tells the child, "I enjoyed your reading," and adds other words of praise as appropriate.

2. *Record Keeping.* Each student keeps a spiral notebook with the following information on each page: the book title, a sentence about the book, and the date. Glynn checks off the date and writes a word of praise next to her checkmark and initial. Glynn also keeps a notebook, with a page for each student, and the following information on each page: the child's name, the book title, comments, skills needed, activities, and the date.

To make sure that the children are acquiring the skills they will need to pass the tests used in her school system, which are based on the basal reader in use, Glynn uses the scope and sequence of the basal as a guide. The activities she develops will be suggested by these skills, but also related to interests that the children develop in the course of reading a certain

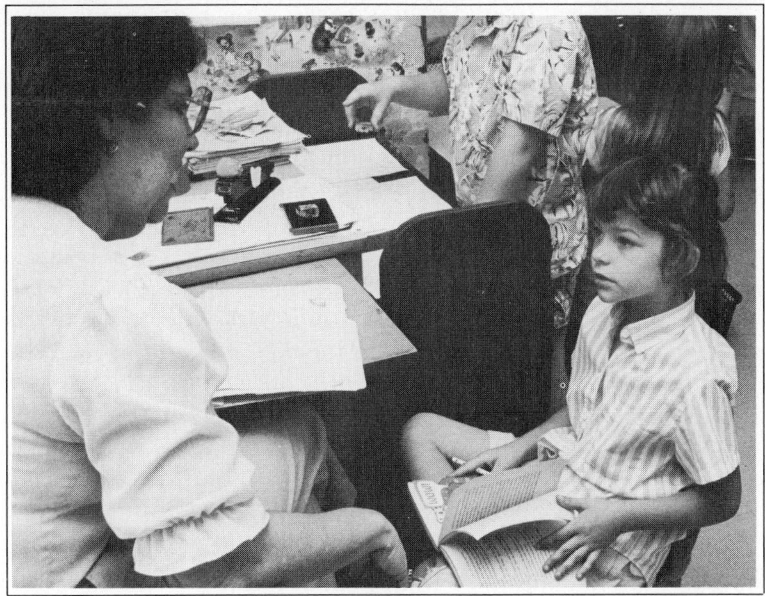

Glynn Wink holds an individualized reading conference with a second-grade student.

book. A teacher using a total individualized reading program can correlate it with the basal in the same way, and even use the basal tests for diagnostic purposes and to make sure that the needed skills to be tested are taught.

Close Reading of a Book. Another way to base reading instruction on literature is by a close reading of one book by a whole class or group of students all reading the same book. In France, where I learned and used this method as a university student, this method is called an *explication de texte.* I began to use it with my own students when I discovered the power and importance of literature in the classroom for teaching all subjects across the curriculum. In fact, I first used it when I read one of my father's books, *Mystery of the Haunted Mine,* to the whole class, and focused everything we did around the interest generated by the book.

See Chapter 8, "Centering Ideas."

I also used it that same year with a small group of boys who were reading well below their proper level. The book we read was Holling C. Holling's beautifully illustrated story about the Santa Fe Trail, *Tree in the Trail.* The book is ideal for a close reading because each two-page spread is a chapter in itself, with a full-page illustration facing a page of text and with marginal illustrations including maps, artifacts, and diagrams, and marginal notes giving additional fascinating information about life among the Indians and other settlers of the Southwest.

Tree in the Trail, by Holling C. Holling (Houghton, Mifflin, 1970). Other books by Holling: *Paddle-to-the-Sea* (Houghton, Mifflin, 1969); *Minn of the Mississippi* (Houghton, Mifflin, 1951); *Pagoo* (Houghton, Mifflin, 1957)

The boys loved this book, and each reading period was an adventure as we let Holling lead us through time and over the trail to the West. It was the first time I had succeeded in so much as getting them to read anything, much less enjoy it. And the rest of the year they devoured other books of Holling's about regional American history.

Featured Teacher Sarah Sherman-Siegel: Close Reading of a Book with Sixth- through Eighth-Grade Students

Here is an example of how a new elementary teacher began to use the close reading method when she found herself teaching reading to sixth- to eighth-graders in a middle school. Not satisfied with the basals available in her school, but told that she had to use a text, she turned to literature.

Sarah chose Natalie Babbitt's *Tuck Everlasting,* a beautiful fantasy about a family who accidentally drink magical waters that give them eternal life. The Tuck family encounters a young girl who learns their secret and must decide whether or not to join them.

Tuck Everlasting, by Natalie Babbitt (Farrar, Straus, 1975)

Sarah began the school year by getting a copy of *Tuck* for each student with the help of librarians and parents. She approached teaching reading to middle-school students through a close reading of this book, or an *explication de texte.*

1. The whole class read an assigned number of pages every night. They were not to read ahead (or if they could not resist, they agreed not to talk about it).

2. Before each reading, the class skimmed the chapter for any unfamiliar words, talked about their meaning, and recorded them in their journals. I had originally prepared vocabulary lists and comprehension questions for each chapter, but found this to be better: why not work on the words I knew they needed? I also found the questions they asked, and those that came up during discussions, were much better than the ones I wrote out ahead of time.

3. They read every night, and made an entry in a special journal: their feelings, reactions, ideas, questions, and so on. To get them started, I gave them a list of twenty-five sentence starters for journal entries such as: "This part reminded me of . . . ," "I liked [didn't like] the way the author used . . . ," "This character reminds me of [another in a book; life] . . . , and "I could see myself in this because. . . ." After a while, they no longer needed these. Journal writing became well established and a source of their comments during discussions.

4. Monday through Thursday I directed discussions and taught skills. Literary elements such as setting, theme, plot, and characterization were identified and discussed in detail. Babbitt's writing is especially good for looking at figurative language, metaphor, simile, and symbolization. Here are some specific activities we did:

- Found a metaphor and did two illustrations: one literal and the other figurative. Displayed them in the classroom.
- Discussed the use of prologue and epilogue in *Tuck Everlasting*—why the author used them and other books might not.

- Natalie Babbitt does not use chapter titles. We discussed why she divided the books as she did and why some chapters are short and others long. The children summarized the chapters and created chapter titles. (I thought they would find this boring but they loved it.)
- Debated the pros and cons of everlasting life with a student mediator and two opposing sides.
- Wrote character sketches.
- Held a mock trial of May Tuck: "Let's suppose May went to jail. You would have to get her off before anyone found out she couldn't die."
- Rewrote the ending.

5. On Friday we held self-directed discussions of 45 minutes each. A new leader each week prepared evaluative questions, guided the group discussion, and evaluated the results on a form.

6. In the end, the students created individual projects.

Obviously there are other ways to teach reading besides exclusively using a commercial basal reader program, and many pressures are at work on teachers as they decide which approach to use. But it is rarely a simple *either/or* choice, and many teachers combine many different strategies.

See Chapter 8, "Featured Teacher Margaret Mattson: Close Reading of a Classic."

Making Choices for Reading Instruction

It may help to think of the options for reading instruction as a menu in a Chinese restaurant. While you will probably choose one main approach, you have other choices you can make as well.

With All Choices

Teacher questioning strategies	Environmental print	Sustained silent reading
Small-group/center activities	Reading for writing	Reading in content areas
Assisted personal reading	Direct/shared experiences	Writing for reading
	Reading aloud	

Choose One

Regular basal	*Selected basal*	*No basal*
Main method; ability grouping; daily basal lessons	Combined with other methods; basal lesson less than daily.	Whole-language and literature-based: language experience; shared big books; individualized reading; close reading

Choose Several

Creative dramatics	Semantic mapping	Independent research
DLTAs	Journal writing	Reader's theatre
Pattern writing	Scriptwriting	Newspaper publication
Flannel board	Story dramatization	Play production
Listening center	DRTAs	
Content area study	Puppetry	
Storytelling	Mediamaking	

Examples of how several real teachers make these choices and plan and teach reading as a language art are described in detail in the last chapter of this text.

Summing Up

The teaching of reading receives a great deal of time and attention in the classroom. The traditional approach to reading instruction is to use a commercial basal reader series. A recent report on the quality of education in America, *Becoming a Nation of Readers: The Report on the Commission on Reading* (1985), suggests instead that reading be viewed and taught as a language art.

Several different models of reading have been proposed by different researchers and theorists: the linear, or bottom-up model; the psycholinguistic, or top-down model; and an interactive model based on schema theory. Each of these implies different types of teaching methods and materials, with some overlap among them as well.

Whichever model or models you draw from, it is important to know how children learn to read. Research tells us a great deal about what kindergartners already know about the reading process when they enter school. Several studies have also described the attitudes, behavior, and understanding of children in the stages of early reading, formal beginning reading, and emerging mature reading.

Many different methods of assessing the reading development of children have been used, and many of these have responded to demands for accountability from outside the schools. More naturalistic methods are possible to assess and meet the needs of each child. Research also tells us a great deal about what factors support success in learning to read, no matter what the method.

While the most common method used to teach reading today is the basal program, a joint commission of experts from the International Reading Association and the National Council of Teachers of English suggests that more time for teaching reading be spent using whole, meaningful texts.

Each teacher's reading program can incorporate many strategies for reading instruction, and this chapter has emphasized those which are alternatives or can be used to extend and go beyond the basal reader. These include creating an environment to support literacy growth, strategies for extending a basal lesson, and teaching reading comprehension using any printed text including a basal reader.

Language- and literature-based reading methods are also described. These include the language experience approach, reading aloud to and along with children, sustained silent reading, shared big-book experiences, individualized reading, and a close reading of a book (or *explication de texte).*

Finally, it may help to think of making decisions about reading in the same way you make choices from a menu in a Chinese restaurant. While you will choose one main entree, or method, there are some items you can have with all entrees, and many others to choose from to accompany your meal as well.

Looking Further

1. Ask a class of children: "What is reading?" Analyze their responses in the context of the way reading is taught in their class.

2. Describe, and discuss and compare with others in your class, your memories of reading instruction in the classroom. Which of the three models of reading described in this chapter did it most reflect?

3. Observe a kindergarten class and note how many of the types of understanding described by Mavrogenes in the chapter are present.

4. Observe a reading lesson and compare what the teacher does with the description of effective teachers of reading in this chapter.

5. Evaluate one classroom according to the suggestions in this chapter for creating an environment to support literacy growth. Which of the suggestions are in evidence? Which are not?

6. Examine the teacher's guide for a basal reader series. Choose one lesson and develop another lesson to go beyond the basal and extend the suggested activities.

7. Read a story to a group of children and follow the teaching sequence for a Directed Reading Thinking Activity.

8. Observe a language experience lesson in action. Identify the parts of the lesson and how the skills are taught.

9. Develop a shared big-book lesson for the primary grades around a concept or theme. If possible, teach the lesson.

Chapter Ten

Drama in the Classroom

Objectives

Look for answers to the following questions as you read this chapter.

- Does drama really belong in the language arts curriculum?
- What are the objectives in teaching drama?
- What relationship exists between drama and reading?
- How can drama be used to integrate the curriculum?
- What is the role of the teacher in drama?
- What are some specific types of drama for the classroom and some strategies for teaching them?
- How do you evaluate progress in drama in the classroom?

A Child's View

Here are some comments made by children who have experienced drama in the classroom.

- "Only 24 hours to Shakespeare!"—Ryan, a third-grader, overheard by his mother the day before he was to participate for the second year in a Shakespeare program at his school.
- "I think it is the funnest thing I've ever done, where I acted out things and learned something at the same time."—Cullen, a fifth-grader, overheard by his teacher after he played in a dramatization of Greek myths.
- "Very, very, very, happy. . . ."—Joni, a second-grader, overheard by another child after she played a witch in a dramatization of a Halloween story written by the class.

Centering Ideas

"Do drama—and Shakespeare—really belong in the language arts curriculum?"

A surprised principal once hastily posed this question to a group of education student observers he was leading unannounced into my room to observe language arts activities in action. They arrived just as my very active third-grade Roman mob playing *Julius Caesar* were streaming out of the classroom screaming "Burn, burn" and "Kill, Kill!" freshly fired up by Carolyn's impassioned delivery of Mark Anthony's "Friends, Romans, countrymen, lend me your ears" oration over Caesar's dead body. But Jeff, leader of the Roman rabble, heard the principal's question to the university students and stopped dead in his tracks, a flashlight with red cellophane covering the lens to simulate a glowing torch poised over his head. He turned to me dramatically and inquired incredulously: "Mrs. Cox, *doesn't he know who Shakespeare is*?"

Julius Caesar, Act III, Scene 2, by William Shakespeare

All Jeff really knew about Shakespeare is that he wrote great plays and poetry, and was considered a master of the English language arts and perhaps the world's greatest storyteller. Since this class had extensive experiences with drama, it seemed only natural that they play Shakespeare's stories as well, especially since he had already conveniently put them in the form of a play.

All I really knew about doing Shakespeare with children was that it generated tremendous enthusiasm, excitement, and extended possibilities for ripple effects of language arts across the curriculum. I also found that Shakespeare's language and ideas are not too difficult for children to read and comprehend at their level of understanding. No one will ever grasp all of Shakespeare at one time—which is one of the reasons we revere him in the first place. His plays are too rich a storehouse of human thought and emotion for easy understanding. But we can return to him again and again, at different times in our lives, and find some new meaning.

My experience (Cox, 1980) has also been that children understand a great deal of Shakespeare, as evidenced by their ability to perform his plays with great feeling, style, and energy. I can think of no way to make elementary age children read, memorize, characterize, rehearse, and present a Shakespearean play without understanding what they are doing or wanting to do it.

As for other forms of classroom drama such as creative dramatics, story dramatization, scriptwriting, reader's theatre, or curriculum drama, these activities are as natural to children as breathing.

The rest of this chapter will explain why and how you can use the ancient art of drama—especially the plays of Shakespeare—as you teach the art of language arts.

Comments by children such as Ryan, Cullen, Joni, and Jeff, who have experienced drama in the classroom, suggest some important reasons why drama should play a leading role in the education of elementary students in the language arts. Drama as a living and learning experience for children has the power to

- spark great enthusiasm and a desire to participate in school activities,
- build a framework within which to develop a positive self-image as well as a positive environment for growing and learning,
- stimulate problem-solving ability, creativity, and thinking, and
- create enjoyment and pleasure in learning in school.

There are many other historical, cultural, psychological, educational, and humanistic reasons why drama should be central rather than merely peripheral to the early education of children.

Drama and Human Development

Drama is central to the human experience. Since primitive men and women first danced around an open fire and used gestures to tell others of their kind about a great hunt or battle by impersonating animals or hunters or warriors, human beings have used songs and movement and action to express feelings and ideas, recount past events, tell a story, or predict the future. Through the centuries, drama has been a natural means for people to communicate about many things: events of daily life or death, dreams and visions, and the power of magic and supernatural beings or of heroes and heroines, gods and goddesses.

The word *drama* comes from the Greek root meaning "to do or live through."

In similar fashion, young children still use gestures and sounds to imitate things they observe in their environment long before they actually speak. Piaget (1962) notes evidence of this innate tendency even during the first few days of a baby's life in the case of his own son, Laurent, who began to cry the night after he was born when he heard other babies in the hospital cry. Furthermore, Laurent would cry in response to Piaget's imitation of a baby's cry, but not to a whistle or other kinds of cries. Just as drama preceded literate man's attempts to express and record ideas and feelings in print or other symbol systems, then, young children come to play and drama naturally as they respond to and communicate with others by imitating life through sounds, gestures, and movement even before they can speak.

Piaget explains that language development goes through three stages: (1) an actual sensorimotor experience with an action or object, (2) the dramatic reliving of this experience, and (3) a word that represents this whole schema verbally.

Drama is a natural part of the evolution of thought and language for each individual in particular, and for humankind in general. And the potential of drama as a learning experience in the elementary language arts curriculum is unlimited. Ward (1957), an early advocate of drama for children, underscores the important role that drama can play in education: "When one notes the eagerness with which children greet both creative and formal drama, he wonders how it can be that education has not long since made use of so deep-rooted an impulse. To ignore it seems a tremendous waste of power" (p. 15).

Drama in the Classroom

A Rationale for Drama

See National Council of Teachers of English/Children's Theatre Association, "Informal Classroom Drama," *Language Arts,* 60 (1983), 370–372.

Other educators over the years have not ignored this potential power of drama education. The Anglo-American Seminar on the Teaching of English in 1966 brought British and American educators together at Dartmouth College. During the course of the seminar, these educators set forth the following rationale for the use of oral communication and drama to foster children's learning of language, and as an integral part of the English language arts curriculum (Duke, 1974).

1. Drama and oral communication should become the centrality of pupils' exploring, extending, and shaping of experience in the classroom.
2. There is a definite urgency for developing classroom approaches stressing the vital, creative, dramatic involvement of young people in language experiences.
3. The importance of directing more attention to speaking and listening for pupils at all levels, particularly in those experiences which involve vigorous interaction among children, should be apparent.
4. The wisdom of providing young people at all levels with significant opportunities for the creative use of language—creative dramatics, imaginative writing, improvisation, role playing, and similar activities—has become increasingly evident (p. 30).

Objectives for Drama

Ward (1957) lists some important objectives of creative drama:

1. To provide for a controlled emotional outlet.
2. To provide each child with an avenue of self-expression in one of the arts.
3. To encourage and guide the child's creative imagination.
4. To give young people opportunities to grow in social understanding and cooperation.
5. To give the children experience in thinking on their feet and expressing ideas fearlessly (pp. 3–4).

Along with these objectives are others which are usually realized if playmaking is well guided: *initiative,* resulting from encouragement to think independently and to express oneself; *resourcefulness,* from the experience with classmates in creating a play which is their own; the freedom in *bodily expression* that comes from much exercise in expressing ideas through pantomime; growth in the *enjoyment of good literature;* and the beginning of appreciation for the drama (pp. 3–9).

A Conceptual Approach to Drama

Siks (1983) quotes Ward—"Drama comes in the door of a school with every child"—and further expands on the "importance of the art of drama to satisfy human needs and to foster the development and learning of children" (p. 3).

> Drama *does* come to school with children, but they don't know or even care that it is called "drama." What children care about are opportunities to join with others in actively expressing their thoughts, feelings, and imaginings. They want to act out some of their impressions about what they did, how they did it, and to reflect on the content—the heart of the enactments (p. 3).

Siks (1983) also outlines the basic assumptions of a conceptual approach to drama in education.

1. The art of drama is a way of learning and knowing about the self and the external world.
2. Drama in education, based on the expressive processes of children's dramatic play, is extended to their creative processes, enabling children to learn to give dramatic form to their feelings, perceptions, and imaginings.
3. Drama is taught as an art by employing and relating its basic processes and concept; it is used as teaching tool to integrate learning.
4. Drama is included, centrally, as an art in the language arts curriculum.
5. The teacher of drama should understand the nature of child development and learning and the nature of drama by experiencing its processes and concepts (p. 5).

British educator Dorothy Heathcote (1981) explains why drama should be at the core of the elementary language arts curriculum.

See also "Learning, Knowing, and Languaging in Drama," by Dorothy Heathcote, in *Language Arts,* 60 (1983), 695–701.

> All drama, regardless of the material, brings to the teacher an opportunity to draw on past relevant experience and put it into use; language, both verbal and non-verbal, is then needed for communication. . . . I am primarily in the teaching business, not the play-making business, even when I am involved in making plays. I am engaged first of all in helping children to think, talk, relate to one another, to communicate (pp. 80–81).

Drama and Reading

One practical application of these rationales and objectives for drama in language learning is to make the connections between drama and the teaching of reading. Both drama and reading involve language, perceptions, concept development, aesthetic appreciation, and ultimately the whole range of experience itself. In the elementary curriculum, both drama and reading are language arts and communication skills that can be integrated in many exciting ways: for motivation, language development, listening, reading, writing, vocabulary growth, reading for purpose and meaning, comprehension and critical reading skills, extending reading, reading as a thinking process, and creative reading. Furthermore, drama provides a framework within which to teach reading as active process. The emphasis here is on *action:* young children acting and reacting to stories through drama as they get ready to read; actively involved with oral language as they think out loud in dramatic activities; actively reading and reacting to children's literature, dramatic literature, and the related reading necessary to mount a play; and the resulting interaction among children, ideas, feelings, experience, and print.

See "Dramatic Improvisation: Risk-Free Role Playing for Improving Reading Performance," by G. Michael Miller and George E. Mason, in *The Reading Teacher,* 37 (1983), 128–131.

Research reinforces the notion of a positive relationship between action-centered experiences with drama and learning to read. For example, Yawkey (1980) found that reading readiness scores on the Gates–MacGinite Readiness Test were higher for a group of five-year-old children who participated in role-playing activities that involved story dramatization and problem solving through dramatization for fifteen minutes a day, five days a week, for seven months than they were for a group that did cut-and-paste activities with a minimum of social interaction. Children's understanding of story content and concepts were improved by the role playing that encouraged these children to think, feel, and act like the characters they were playing in the story.

Pellegrini and Galda (1982) found that among 108 children in kindergarten and in first and second grades, those that engaged in dramatics–thematic–fantasy play developed better story comprehension as measured by a ten-item criterion-referenced test after listening to the story of "Little Red Cap" (a variation of "Little Red Riding Hood") than did those engaged in discussion or drawing activity. The conclusion was that the acting out of the roles of major characters such as Little Red Cap, Grandma, the Hunter, and the Wolf improved the children's understanding of the story because it more actively involved them with the events of the story they heard. Other studies have demonstrated that drama can improve vocabulary, oral reading, reading comprehension, and self-concept (Blank, 1953; Carlton, 1963; Carlton & Moore, 1966).

An important link with reading is formed as children experience drama in response to literature. The following list presents a set of points of connection among reading, literature, and drama using, by way of example, a dramatization of *Where the Wild Things Are* for primary children, and a performance of Shakespeare for middle- and upper-grade children.

Where the Wild Things Are, by Maurice Sendak (Harper, 1963)

1. *Dramatization of literature to encourage interest in and motivation for reading*

Reader interest and motivation are essential for effective reading instruction. Consider for a moment a young child playing the part of Max in *Where the Wild Things Are.* How really interested this child would be in understanding how the wolf-suited Max confronts an island full of monsters and "tamed them with the magic trick of staring into their yellow eyes." Or consider an older student playing the part of Juliet. How really interested she would be in reading her script, or in reading for information about Renaissance costumes, the role of women (or lack of it) in Shakespeare's theatre, or how people behaved or danced at a Renaissance masked ball. In picture books and dramatic literature, there is something to capture the interest of everyone, especially the desire to play exciting characters and share a story with others.

2. *Dramatization of literature to expand vocabulary*

Teachers may become concerned with the level of difficulty of vocabulary in books and plays. The readability level of *Where the Wild Things Are* is grade 3.2. The vocabulary of Shakespeare's plays is not usually considered within the reach of children at all. Let me suggest that the vocabulary of a Sendak or a Shakespeare provides ideal ways to teach difficult words because children will have a real reason to understand and use these words in order to play their parts.

A system of reciprocity is at work here. An interest in and a need to understand words will be helped by the development of an understanding of the character who is speaking the words and the play in which they are spoken. Comprehension supports word identification in the same way that word identification supports comprehension. Understanding a scene and its dialogue will obviously help students understand any words they have not encountered before or do not fully understand. Drama provides a great opportunity to familiarize students with less common abstract words when understanding these words is critical to playing a part.

For example, how can students resist adding a word like *gnashed* to their vocabulary, if it signals the start of a wild monster rumpus, or the word *tyrant* in the context of Macduff's challenge to Macbeth, "Tyrant, show thy face! Turn hell-hound, turn!"—especially if it signals the start of a two-handed broadsword fight to the death.

3. *Dramatization of literature to encourage the development of critical reading skills and comprehension*

Students do more than repeat what they read in dramatizing literature. They must interpret and transform their reading experience to make it part of their dramatic experience and part of their lives. A dialogue is initiated between the writer and the reader, moving the student towards the creation of a role.

Here are some ways in which teachers can encourage the development of critical reading skills and comprehension through drama.

- **a.** Provide a model for comprehension processes, by reading and interacting with the story or play.
- **b.** Stimulate guided discussions of stories and plays, and practice questioning techniques to help students further understand what they have read so they can quite literally act on their reading.

c. Offer feedback pertinent to the playing of a story to reinforce students' active reading, understanding, and reacting to stories and scripts, or offer information helpful for creating a play.

d. Manage the practice and development of certain skills that are ideally taught in the context of dramatizing literature, for example:
   (1) paraphrasing what has been read through discussions of the motivation of characters, how scenes should be played, and what is actually happening during the scene;
   (2) identifying and distinguishing between the main idea of a play or scene and the details peripheral to the plot;
   (3) understanding story structure, plot, and narrative sequence, relying heavily on skills of ordering and understanding the sequence of action;
   (4) identifying cause and effect through analysis of character action and events in the story and their consequences;
   (5) identifying with characters, evaluating character traits, perceiving character relationships, and recognizing the emotional and motivational reactions of characters;
   (6) recognizing, understanding, and appreciating figurative language and multiple meanings of words and passages;
   (7) developing the imagination, forming sensory impressions, and reacting to mood or tone; and
   (8) interpreting and appreciating the symbolic use of language in literature.

4. ***Drama to encourage guided, extended reading***

Shakespeare and His Theatre, by John Russell Brown (Lothrop, Lee, Shephard, 1982); *Shakespeare's England* (American Heritage, 1964); *One Day in Elizabethan England,* by G. B. Kirtland (Harcourt, Brace, Jovanovich, 1962)

Students become highly motivated to read and find out about anything that will help them play a part. Children dramatizing *Where the Wild Things Are* can extend their reading to other picture books about monsters, boats, and islands; many Shakespeare-related topics are of great interest to older students: stage craft, Renaissance costumes and weapons, the life of Shakespeare himself.

5. ***Drama to encourage lifetime readers***

One goal of reading instruction that can be easily lost in the daily shuffle of skills and drills is the creation of lifetime readers. Early experiences with the dramatization of fine literature can create readers who continue to read, enjoy, and really experience literature and drama as they become adults.

A Mixed Art for Integrating All the Arts

Drama is an art form as well as a form of literature. The purpose of drama is to tell a story and the means to tell it is through the actions or speech of the characters. The power of drama is its ability to give form to feelings and to make us feel. The subject of drama is the whole range of human experience—those feelings, conflicts, and needs that may seem confused in real life but that can be organized and clarified and understood through the use of drama.

Drama also embraces the visual and plastic arts—in fact, virtually all the other arts and humanities—and forms a link with our past and our culture that children can understand and enjoy through their own experiences with drama. An early proponent of the arts in education, Mearns (1958) describes the great range of experiences that are possible through drama:

> All the arts combine in the theatre—decor, dance, impersonation, effective speech, the song, pantomime, the projection of personality, art of suppressing self and even ill-will for the sake of unity of effort . . . living together and the art of creative imagination (p. 92).

As a mixed art, drama is a means to develop all the language arts and integrate the curriculum as well. Consider for a moment the mixture of ingredients that can be introduced in a curriculum integrated through drama:

Language

- expressing and responding to human experiences
- organizing and clarifying experiences
- listening
- speaking
- reading
- writing
- visual and nonverbal language, including decor, gesture, movement and mime

Literature

- oral storytelling
- responding to literature in dramatic form
- appreciating and understanding dramatic literature

Art

- theatre arts: set design, costumes, properties, sound, lighting, graphics, media
- other arts: music, dance, song

The Content Areas

- curriculum content as the subject of drama: human relations, social studies, science, mathematics
- drama as an integrating force across all subject matter areas

No matter how you choose to use any of the many forms of drama possible in the classroom and across the curriculum, your focus should always be on the child. Way (1967) maintains that as an educator he is primarily "concerned with the development of people, not the development of drama.... Education is concerned with individuals; drama is concerned with the individuality of individuals, with the uniqueness of each human essence" (pp. 2–3). He emphasizes above all the importance of the role of the teacher in drama in the classroom.

The Teacher's Role in Drama

Way (1967) asserts that

> The most important single factor in the use of drama as a genuine part of education is the teacher.... A really full, generous and compassionate interest in children, irrespective of academic ability or gift, is the first requisite; a knowledge of why to use drama is another; the freedom to approach the matter from where he or she feels happiest and most confident is another... (p. 8).

He also makes the following suggestions for beginning to use drama in the classroom:

> Start from where you yourself are happiest and most confident; this may be the telling of a story or it may be a simple discussion about appropriate behavior in certain situations; it may be the problems of the school play or a discussion of Hamlet's attitude toward Claudius,... it may be a simple concern with sharing physical space and material objects or the complex understanding of racial problems. Start from that point—where you yourself feel interested and confident. Keep reminding yourself that what you are concerned with is the development of everyone, of the manifold facets of human beings; a circle can start at any point on the circumference of the circle. Ultimately there may be only one goal, but the means of that goal are manifold and individual depending on where you, as teacher, are, and growing out of the particular bond you have made with the children or young people you are helping to develop (p. 9).

Choose from those activities on the circle of drama (see Figure 10–1) that you feel will best enable you to help children to learn, live, grow, create, and communicate.

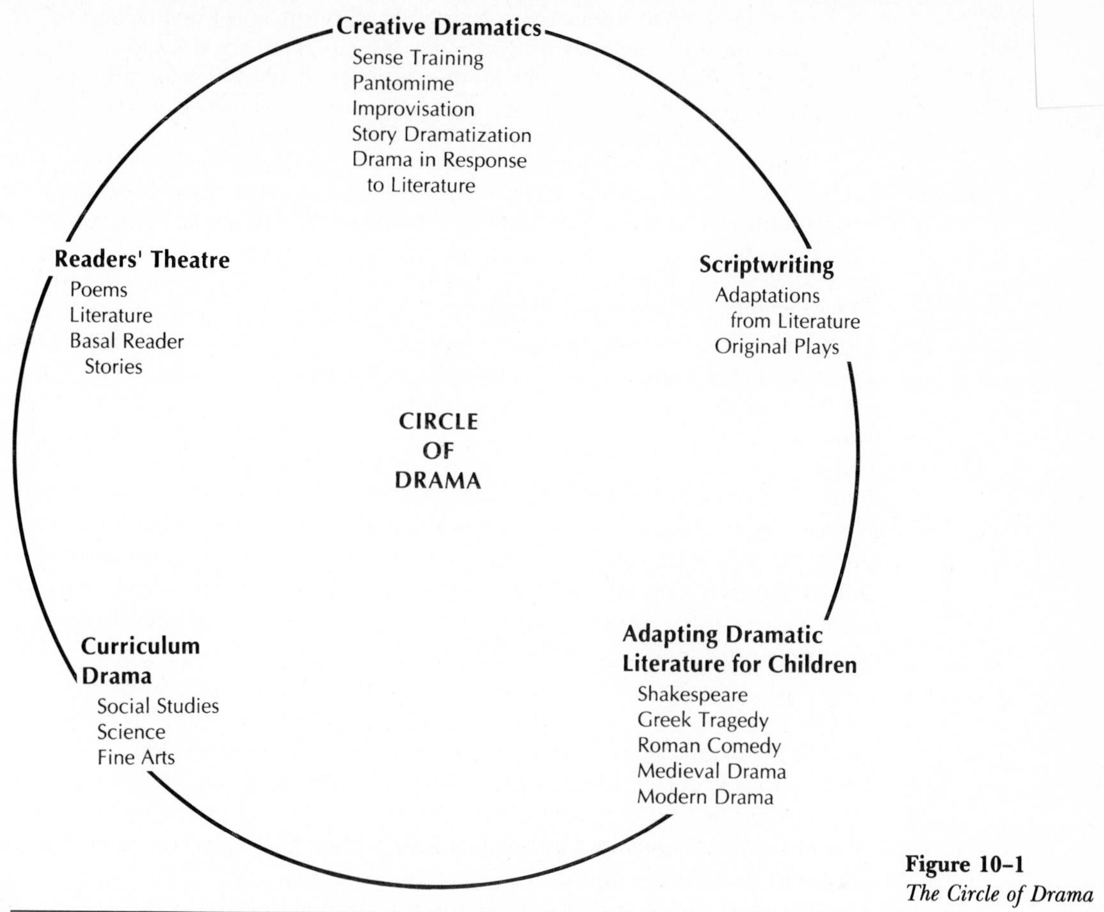

Figure 10–1
The Circle of Drama

Creative Dramatics

The Children's Theatre Association of America (Davis & Behm, 1978) defines creative dramatics this way:

> "Creative Dramatics" is an improvisational, non-exhibitional, process-centered form of drama in which participants are guided by a leader to imagine, enact, and reflect upon human experiences. . . .
>
> The creative drama process is dynamic. The leader guides the group to explore, develop, express, and communicate ideas, concepts, and feelings through dramatic enactment. In creative drama the group improvises action and dialogue appropriate to the content it is exploring, using elements of drama to give form and meaning to experience.
>
> The primary purpose of creative drama is to foster personality growth and to facilitate learning of the participants rather than to train actors for

the stage. Creative drama may be used to teach the art of drama and/or motivate and extend learning in other content areas. Participation in creative drama has the potential to develop language and communication abilities: problem solving awareness, empathy, a clarification of values and attitudes, and an understanding of the art of the theatre.

Built on the human impulse and ability to act out perceptions of the world in order to understand it, creative drama requires both logical and intuitive thinking, personalizes knowledge, and yields aesthetic pleasure (pp. 10–11).

The Elements of Creative Dramatics

Approaches to creative dramatics can come from many directions, and be adapted to many age levels and instructional settings. Creative dramatics is a synthesis of sense training, pantomime and improvisation, and story dramatization.

Sense Training. Activities such as those described below can be developed as warm-up exercises to move children from simple sense training to more elaborate forms of drama. A key to sense training is the concentration ability children develop as they communicate through nonverbal means: facial expressions, gestures, and movement. The emphasis should be on creating confidence and enthusiasm for dramatic expression.

With younger children, these activities can be expansions of their spontaneous play. Observe what they are acting out during unstructured periods of dramatic play and build on these moments as you lead into drama. With older children, begin slowly to give them confidence in their ability to express feelings and ideas with their bodies, to use many language forms through drama, and to create an awareness of themselves as well as a sensitivity to other children.

Here are some ideas for focusing warm-up activities on the senses.

- *Touch.* Try these directions with the children sitting on the floor, each one doing his own activity. You may want to dim the lights to create a secure atmosphere.

  1. "There is a balloon on the floor in front of you. Pick it up. Blow it up. Tie a knot in the end of it and attach a string. Let it float in the air as you watch."
  2. "There is a baby animal crouched behind you. It is frightened. Pick it up. Pet it and comfort it."
  3. "There is a blob of sticky, gooey clay in front of you. Pick it up. Make something from it."

- *Taste.* Try these directions with children in pairs, facing each other. Ask one partner to guess exactly what the other is pretending to eat.

  1. "Make your favorite sandwich and eat it."
  2. "Eat your favorite food."
  3. "Eat something you don't like."

• *Sight.* Try these directions with children in small groups facing each other. Children are to pantomime around the circle. When everyone is finished, let them guess what the others did.

1. "There is a trunk full of clothes in the middle of the circle. Take something out of it and try it on. There is only one of each thing in the trunk."
2. "There is a pile of presents wrapped in boxes in the middle of the circle. Choose one, open it, and take out and use what's inside."
3. "Your favorite toy or game is in the middle of the circle. Pick it up and show how you play with it."

• *Sound.* Try these directions with children standing in small groups. When everyone is finished, see if they can tell what the others did.

1. "I will make a sound [*hit a table with a rhythmic beat*]. Act out what it makes you think of."
2. Give the same direction, but rub your hands together to make a slithery sound.
3. Give the same direction, but make a scraping sound with an object against the blackboard.

Pantomime and Improvisation. Pantomime and improvisation are a natural outgrowth of sense training. Pantomime uses facial expressions, body movement, and gestures to communicate instead of sounds and words. Improvisation adds speech to spontaneous movement and action. The two techniques may lead to more elaborate playing of scenes, story dramatization, or scriptwriting. Ideas for pantomime activities may come from your observations of the spontaneous play of children, or you may want to develop a file of ideas to develop this drama element and relate it to other learning activities in the classroom.

• *A Pantomime File.* Keep a file of ideas to motivate pantomime related to children's experiences, literature, or the content areas. Some topics around which to center these ideas include:

1. animal movement, interaction between children and pets, interaction among animals;
2. play, sports, games, toys, fun places to visit;
3. costumes and other props for inspiration: hats, capes, canes, buckets, baskets;
4. music to stimulate pantomime;
5. nursery rhymes, poems, picture books, folk tales, stories;
6. social studies, science, mathematics, or fine arts subject matter.

• *A Pantomime Play.* Simple pantomime activities can lead into the playing of scenes. For example, children working in pairs could improvise a short scene and lead into improvisation with one child speaking and the other child communicating only through movement.

• *Improvised Scenes.* When children have had experience with pantomime, and have added speech to their play, they will move easily into improvised scenes. Some situations to improvise include:

1. telephone conversations;
2. imaginary journeys: riding in a car, bus, plane;
3. response to stories: original stories written by children or drawn from literature;
4. interaction with media: music, slide projections, film.

See also *Stories to Dramatize,* by Winifred Ward (Anchorage, 1952).

Story Dramatization. When children respond to a story through drama by acting out the actions as they play the characters, they are creating a story dramatization. This kind of drama is still spontaneous and based on improvisation, but follows a plot development. The criteria for choosing stories to dramatize include (Ward, 1957):

1. a worthy central idea or motive;
2. economy of the number of incidents;
3. a climax that is strong yet does not appeal too greatly to any one emotion;
4. a quick and satisfying ending;
5. realistic characters, whether they are supernatural or not;
6. dialogue that gives the impression of natural conversation.

A dramatization of a story about a magic unicorn incorporates all of the language arts.

Integrating the Elements of Drama

Here is an example of how to integrate all the elements of drama in experiences in response to *Where the Wild Things Are.*

Monster Masks. The children can make simple monster masks to set the mood and help them establish distance between the real self and a monster self and develop a characterization either of Max or of a Wild Thing. Use a manila folder for each child; cut it in half and draw and cut an oval in one of the halves for child's face to show through. Cut a strip on the diagonal from the other half and attach this to the mask a little above the ears and across the back to hold the mask in place. Use the remainder of folder to add shapes: ears, horns, hair, teeth. These masks may be decorated with a variety of materials.

Monster Mime. With their masks in place, the children can engage in sense training, pantomime, and improvisation. After reading and discussing the book, lead them through a day in the life of a monster by asking them such questions as:

> "Show me how you sleep, monster, and how you wake up."
>
> "What do you do when you wake up, monster? Do you stretch, growl, do exercises, look mean?"
>
> "How do you get ready for a new day, monster? Do you brush your teeth (tooth)? Do you comb your hair (scales, fur, tentacles)? Do you wear clothes?"
>
> "How do you move around when you are ready for a new day, monster? Do you creep, crawl, slither, lumber, galumph, stagger, stumble, or fall down frequently?"

Monster Dance. With monster movements developed through mime, the monsters can dance. Experiment with a variety of music, and let the children choose their own preferred monster music. You may suggest a series of types of movements for different monsters: walking, marching, jumping, crouching and pouncing, and so on.

Story Dramatization. Maurice Sendak says that the aesthetic problem he was attempting to solve when creating *Where the Wild Things Are* was that of capturing movement and dance on the page of a picture book. He does this beautifully in the wordless sequence which starts when the young protagonist, Max, who has just been made "King of All Wild Things" by the Wild Things themselves, imperiously orders: "Let the wild rumpus start!"

There is a natural point of connection between the developmental sequence of drama activities focused on the theme of monsters and the dramatization of the story by children. Once they have heard and discussed the story and reacted to it and crept inside the character of a monster with masks, mime, and movement and dance, it is a small step to trying on the character of Max or a Wild Thing and then taking the larger step of jumping inside this magical book and living it through story dramatization. Here is a sequence of steps you could follow, as an example of steps for story dramatization of any book.

1. *Reread and discuss the book.* Ask the children to note the number of characters, how they behaved, the sequence of events in the story. Note also the most exciting parts, the climax, and the way the story ends, or is resolved. After several readings, discuss these points and chart the story with the class for dramatization purposes on the board or chart paper.

- *Characters:* Narrator, Mother, Max, Dog, Wild Things, Other (Inanimates such as Trees, Boats, Ocean)
- *Sequence of events:* (1) Max makes mischief. Mother sends him to bed. (2) A forest grows. A boat comes by. (3) Max sails away to where the Wild Things are. (4) Max tames the Wild Things. Max becomes King. (5) The wild rumpus (dance). (6) Max is lonely. He leaves the Wild Things. (7) He sails home. His supper is still hot.

2. *Take volunteers for the cast.* Delegate leadership for the direction of the play to one child at a time. For example, begin with the Narrator and rotate to the other children in turn.

3. *The cast plans and discusses.* The children decide how they will play the scene, who will do what action and where. There are enough parts for Trees, and Ocean, Boats, and Wild Things to involve the entire class. Or, half can play and the other half watch, and then reverse.

4. *Children play the scene.* Allow the Narrator to provide direction for the story initially. Later, as children play the scene several more times, this role will become less important.

5. *Discuss and evaluate after each playing.* Everyone should become involved in this stage. Emphasize the positive. Ask:

- What did you see that you liked?
- Who did something really interesting (exciting, realistic, fantastic)?
- What can we do next time to make it even better?

Scriptwriting

As an extension of improvised, spontaneous drama in the classroom, children may create scripted drama. I believe, however, that if children do use scripts, they should either write them themselves from an original concept or adapt them from a fine children's book or a basal reader story, or use dramatic literature specifically adapted for children.

Children who write original scripts in response to a topic they are pursuing in school, a recent event or experience of high interest to them, literature they have read, shared, and enjoyed, or a combination of these, have a unique opportunity to put their feelings, thinking, and language to work. Writing scripts for plays on subjects they choose puts them to work building ideas, using language as the tool for constructing their own drama. Their real reward comes when they are able to communicate their original ideas, which have undergone revision and refinement in the composing process, to an audience of significant others by literally acting on what they know and bringing their words and ideas to life in the script, production, and performance of their own play. One approach to scriptwriting evolves when all the children in a class become interested in the same topic or event and want to explore it further, to learn what they know about it through selecting, organizing, elaborating, and dramatizing a script they have written.

See *Young Playwrights,* by Gerald Chapman (Heinemann, 1984); "Scriptwriting in Small Groups," by Carole Cox, in *Student-to-Student: Practice in Cooperative Learning,* Classroom Practices Series, ed. by Jeff Golub (NCTE, in press).

Stages in Scriptwriting

1. *Select a topic.* The suggestion to write a play for the first time may come from you, *after* a topic of interest has emerged in the classroom. Some experiences that could stimulate the class to write a play might include:

a children's book read aloud to the whole class,
social studies or science units,
current events of interest to the children,
popular films or other media events,
field trips, or
a combination of these and other interests.

2. *Extend the response to the topic through writing.* Younger children may dictate a group story to the teacher who can record it as part of a language experience story, or the children may write their own stories. Older students may note ideas and extend these through personal writing. Many ideas for scripts will emerge from such writing.

3. *Share stories.* At some point, the children may choose to share what they are writing, and their stories may become a focal point for discussing and extending their ideas into a dramatic script form.

4. *Brainstorm ideas.* Begin with small-group discussions of the focal idea, then move to a whole-class sharing of these ideas.

5. *Block a script.* Begin with more small-group discussions followed by a whole-class discussion of the group's ideas. One way to organize these ideas is to list them under the following headings on the board or a large wall chart. (These new terms may be defined and explained and added to the children's growing vocabulary of drama and script terms.)

synopsis (story idea)
plot
setting
characters
sequence of actions and events

6. *Record the results.* Individual children can record the ideas under each heading and a small group can write them on a chart for the whole class to use as a framework for future discussions and writing.

7. *Divide the sequence of events and actions into numbered acts.* Then divide the class into groups according to their interests and ability to work together.

8. *Write acts in small groups and add dialogue.* This will be an extended period of time of discussing and revising until each group has a working draft they can share with other groups. Many specialized writing skills can be introduced, taught, and reinforced as the children need them to produce a working draft. For example:

- ordering and sequencing events and actions,
- writing in a script form: scene notes, stage directions, narration, dialogue (and quotation marks),
- unity of time and place, and
- consistency of character behavior and language.

9. *Come together as a large group to share act drafts.* Read the first drafts together, and discuss the interaction of the acts and ways to smoothe out the transitions between acts.

10. *Revise the acts in multiple small groups.* The various groups should now work with each other to smooth transitions and continuity between and among acts. Act I group could first work with Act II group, then Act II group with Act III group, and so on.

11. *Review and revise the script as a group.* Leave a copy of the emerging working script available in a writing center so that the children can read and respond to it between writing periods.

12. *Synthesize final script.* Changes will undoubtedly occur as the play goes into production, but a working script that has gone through an extended period of talking and writing is the beginning point for producing a scripted play.

An Example of Scriptwriting

A play was composed by a combination third- and fourth-grade class working in small groups as a natural outgrowth of several interests that were organized, clarified, and communicated to others through dramatization—a demonstration of how natural it is to integrate the curriculum through writing and drama. I had read aloud to the children Gordon D. Shirreffs's *Mystery of the Haunted Mine,* and it generated the ripple effect of ideas, interests, and activities described in Chapter 8. One of these effects was the composing of a play.

See Chapter 8, "Centering Ideas."

The students were excited about the three main characters in this book: Gary, Tuck, and Sue. I noticed they were spontaneously acting these characters. I also, somewhat uncomfortably, realized that Sue was beginning to manifest mannerisms I recognized as my own. (Children often imitate their teachers anyway. You will often hear your own voice and speech patterns in unexpected places when they do not think you are listening.)

Gary, Tuck, and Sue also began to appear in their writing and it seemed only natural at this point to suggest scriptwriting and to organize these improvisational character sketches into dramatic form. We began, of course, with the three main characters, but we still needed a setting, a plot, and a lot of action. At this time, we were studying both the moon and plants in science. This inspired the play's setting, another planet peopled by two races, Plant People and Humanoids. The conflict in the play derived from another interest: a social studies unit on elections during a presidential election year. The play began to take form when they titled it *The Tale of an Unfair Election.* Here is the plot, as summarized by the publicity for the play performance:

> An election takes place on the planet Zot. The election has been rigged by the Humanoid presidential candidate, Taylor. The Humanoids are invaders from a dying planet and have enslaved the native Plant People. Trailing Arbutus, the other presidential candidate, sends his vice-presidential candidate, Leaf, to earth for help to restore free elections for Plants and Humanoids alike.
>
> Leaf meets the Metzenberg children, Gary, Tuck, and Sue, who take him to their father, a famous space scientist who is going on a scientific expedition to Zot. He takes Leaf along and promises to help. The children stow away on the spaceship U.S.S. *Moonbeam* and join their father for many adventures on Zot.

Playing the Script. The play was performed in the round in the middle of the gym, with the audience in a circle of chairs around the action. Spaces were left at intervals in the circle for entrances and exits and the children waited behind screens outside the circle. To create an effect of deep space, the room was dark except for spotlights on the action. Audience members were invited to participate in scenes of political rallies and revolt, so that they became a part of the crowd and of the drama itself.

The Individual Child and Drama. While the play was a special part of the year for everyone, one student in particular appeared to benefit. Jan was the shyest child in the class and often struggled to look people in the eye when she spoke. She was also large for her age, a problem which compounded her shyness and desire to remain unnoticed.

She had become extremely involved with her scriptwriting group, however, and when we took volunteers for the cast, she asked to play the important role of the presidential candidate of the Plant People, Trailing

Arbutus. I think we were all surprised and not at all prepared for the transformation that took place when Jan donned the imperial robes of the leader of the Plant People, a long and flowing hooded affair covered with plastic leaves attached with safety pins. She suddenly stood straighter, to the full advantage of her larger size. And as she gripped her robe and swished it about for emphasis, a voice emerged from inside the hood that none of us had ever heard before. It was similar to the voice of the quiet and very dignified young Jan, but it had a new edge of authority and volume. As they say in the movies, "Jan Andrews *Is* Trailing Arbutus!"

Jan outdid herself in this role and came to relish all drama. The other children recognized her special talent and the transformation that took place when she worked on a script or put on a costume. For Jan, composing a play in the relative safety of a small group and then acting on it in the relative safety of another character was the special way she found her own voice, one that was barely audible during ordinary whole-class activities but that rang forth strong and clear when she created or played a role in drama.

Reader's Theatre

Reader's theatre is to drama in the classroom what oral interpretation is to the theatre arts: participants read and interpret literature aloud from scripts that have been especially adapted. Scripts for reader's theatre can be adapted from many types of literature: texts of picture books for younger children and novels for older children; folk and fairy tales, and other types of traditional literature such as fables, myths, and legends; poetry and songs; and stories and poems from anthologies and basal readers.

In a reader's theatre presentation, the children hold their scripts and refer to them as necessary. Reader's theatre does not require any special costumes, sets, props, lighting, or music. Once the script has been developed, a reader's theatre production can be practiced and performed almost instantly in the classroom.

The Purposes of Reader's Theatre

Reader's theatre has many functions:

- to understand and appreciate literature by actively reacting to reading and sharing stories,
- to encourage the retelling and sharing of a story,
- to experience reading enjoyment through the dramatization of a text,
- to expand oral language and sharpen listening skills,
- to become actively involved in the reading process through rereading, rethinking, and acting on reading,
- to interpret text that has been read, as a means to comprehension,
- to involve all types of children with all types of abilities,

- to improve children's self-concept, and
- to integrate all areas of the curriculum through the choice of stories or texts related to other subjects.

Criteria for Selecting Stories

Stories to be adapted for reader's theatre should have the following characteristics:

- plenty of dialogue and clear prose,
- lively, high in interest, and humorous, with children or personified animals as main characters,
- a good balance of parts of nearly the same size, and
- short story format (especially for the first time).

Some examples of material that works well for reader's theatre are:

Folk Literature for Younger Children

"The Little Red Hen"
"Chicken Little"
"The Three Billy Goats Gruff"
"The Gingerbread Man"
"The Fisherman and his Wife"
"The Three Wishes"

Folk Literature for Older Children

"Rumpelstiltskin"
"The Frog King"
"Cinderella"
"Snow White"
"The Tinder Box"
"East of the Sun, West of the Moon"

Other Books for Younger Children

Amelia Bedelia, by Peggy Parish
The Case of the Scaredy Cats, and other books by Crosby Bonsall
How the Grinch Stole Christmas and *Horton Hatches the Egg,* by Dr. Seuss
Leo the Late Bloomer and *Owliver,* by Robert Kraus
Frederick and *Fish Is Fish,* by Leo Leonni

Other Books for Older Children

Tales of a Fourth Grade Nothing, and other books by Judy Blume
The Reluctant Dragon, by Kenneth Grahame

The Lion, The Witch, and the Wardrobe, and other books in the Narnia series by C. S. Lewis.

Poetry

Where the Sidewalk Ends, by Shel Silverstein
A Light in the Attic, by Shel Silverstein

Other sources of material for reader's theatre are basal reader stories, student magazines, textbooks, and newspapers.

Adapting a Story or Text

This is the procedure for adapting a story or text for a reader's theatre script.

1. Add narrator parts to identify time, place, scene, or characters as needed. One narrator can be added for the whole story, or more than one as in a narrator for each character.
2. Delete lines that are not critical to the further development of the plot, are peripheral to the main actions of the story, represent complex imagery or figurative language difficult to express through gestures, state that a character is speaking, or whose meaning can be conveyed through a character's facial expression, gestures, simple sound effects, or mime.
3. Change any lines that are descriptive but could be spoken by a character or would move the story along more easily if they were changed.

Putting Reader's Theatre into Practice

The following procedure may be used with a whole class, a small group, or an instructional group such as a basal reading group.

1. ***Introduce the story.***

Read or tell the story aloud to young children, or let older children read the story aloud by taking turns. Encourage an extended response period to the story through discussion involving all children. Here are some questions to ask:

What did you think of this story? Why?
How do you think some of the characters felt?
Why did they act the way they did?
How do you know?
How did they express what they were feeling?

2. ***Explain reader's theatre.***

If this is the first time these children have done reader's theatre, explain to them how it works: the physical arrangement and movements (turning in and out of the scene when not involved), the roles of narrators and characters, mime, expression, and the use of scripts.

3. *Cast the story.*

Distribute prepared scripts, made either by yourself or together with the children. An overhead projector is useful in the latter case. Use transparencies of the story and work through the adaptation with students, revising it according to their suggestions as they watch on the overhead. Scripts could also easily be adapted, by a few children or by an individual, on the computer with a word processing program.

Take volunteers for all parts. In the initial sessions, let many different children play each part. They should all become familiar with all the parts, as in improvised drama.

4. *Develop script awareness.*

Read through the script with the students. Stop and discuss actions, characters, mood, expressions, as they go along. Allow them to respond to the story with questions, comments, and reactions to other characters. Continue until they seem comfortable and secure with the script. Encourage them to continue to read and react to their scripts for each successive time. Emphasize reacting to the story, reading with expression, and communicating with an audience through voice, facial expression, and gestures.

5. *Block, stage, and practice playing the script.*

You may plan the physical staging ahead of time with the group, but be ready to revise according to how the script actually plays with an individual group. Accept suggestions for modifications from the students.

A few simple guidelines: narrators often stand, perhaps with a prop such as a music stand to hold the script; characters are usually seated on a chair or stool or even on a table; floor plans should be decided ahead of time and changed as you proceed (there is a minimum of movement around the floor in reader's theatre).

6. *Sharing reader's theatre.*

By the time children have prepared and participated in reader's theatre, their enthusiasm encourages them to want to share with others. There are many ways to make this comfortable for them: stage the production in the round in a classroom, multipurpose room, or library rather than on a conventional stage; share with other children in the classroom first, then with classes of younger children, then with classes of the same age, working gradually towards sharing with adults and parents.

Sample Reader's Theatre Script

The humorous tale of the two infamous friends Morris the Moose and Boris the Bear in *Morris has a Cold,* by Bernard Wiseman, has been adapted in the basal reader *Glad to Meet You.* The script shown here is, in turn, adapted from the basal reader version.

Morris Has a Cold, by Bernard Wiseman (Dodd, Mead, 1978), adapted in *Glad to Meet You,* Second Grade, Level 7 (Ginn, 1982)

Morris Has a Cold

Cast and Setting

Morris Narrator,
(standing)

Boris Narrator,
(standing)

Morris and Boris
(both seated with backs to audience)

Morris Narrator: Morris the Moose said:

Morris: [*turns in*] I have a cold. My nose is walking.

Boris Narrator: Boris the Bear said:

Boris: [*turns in*] You mean your nose is running.

Morris: No. My nose is walking. I only have a little cold.

Boris: Let me feel your forehead.

Morris: Four heads! I don't have four heads!

Boris: I know you don't have four heads. But this is called your forehead.

Morris: That is my ONE head.

Boris: [*growls*] All right. Let me feel your one head.

Boris Narrator: Boris puts his hand on Morris's forehead.

Boris: Your one head feels hot. That means you are sick. You should lie down.

Morris Narrator: Morris lay down.

Boris: [*shouts*] Not HERE! You are sick. You should lie down on a bed. Here is a bed. Come lie down. Put these covers on. No, no. Do not cover ALL of you. Why did you cover your head?

Morris: Because my head has the cold.

Boris: Your head should not be covered.

Boris Narrator: Boris took the covers from Morris's head.

Morris: Ah-choo!

Morris Narrator: Morris let out a big sneeze.

Boris Narrator: Boris covered Morris's head.

Boris: How does your throat feel?

Morris: Hairy.

Boris: No, no. I don't mean outside. How does your throat feel INSIDE?

Morris Narrator: Morris opened his mouth to feel the inside of his throat.

Boris: [*shouts*] NO! NO! NO! Oh . . . just open your mouth. Let me look inside. Your throat is red. I know what is good for it. I will make you some hot tea.

Morris: Hot what?

Boris: TEA. Don't you know what tea is?

Morris: Yes. I know what it is. T is like A, B, C, D . . .

Boris: [*yells*] NO! NO! Tea is . . . Oh, wait, I will show you. This is tea.

Boris Narrator: Boris gave Morris some tea.

Boris: Drink it. It will make your throat feel better. But first, stick out your tongue.

Morris: I will not stick out my tongue. That is not nice.

Boris: [*shouts*] Stick out your tongue!

Morris Narrator: Morris stuck out his tongue.

Boris: [*shouts*] That is not nice!

Morris: I told you it was not nice.

Boris: [*growls*] That is because you didn't do it the right way.

Boris: It is getting dark. Go to sleep. If your cold is better in the morning I will make you a big breakfast.

Morris: A big what?

Boris: Breakfast. Breakfast is . . . OH! Go to sleep.

Morris Narrator: In the morning Morris said:

Morris: My nose is not walking. My one head is not hot. My cold is better. Make me a big breakfast.

Boris: All right. But you have to do something for me.

Morris: What?

Boris: DON'T EVER GET SICK AGAIN!

Adapting Dramatic Literature for Children

Another way to involve children with scripted drama is through the adaptation of dramatic literature—Shakespeare, for example. Just how do you do Shakespeare with children? Here is my own approach (Cox, 1980, 1985).

Shakespeare for Children

Adapting the Script. To prepare a script, I work in a paperback copy of the play, underlining what I think is most important and manageable for the age of children who will use the script and deleting what will take the play beyond their reach: scenes and characters peripheral to the main plot, and long soliloquies. Do not underestimate children, however: I am constantly amazed at their capacity to comprehend and act on Shakespeare's words. And I have never changed his words, never thought I should, and have never found this to be a problem for children who actually play the plays. Children love to roll Shakespeare's words and phrases around on their tongues, savoring the verbal feast. Shakespeare is one way to develop a child's taste for a gourmet vocabulary.

Material in this section on Shakespeare for children has been adapted from Carole Cox, "Stirring Up Shakespeare in the Elementary School," in *Literature—News that Stays News: Fresh Approaches to the Classics,* ed. by Candy Carter (Urbana, IL: NCTE, 1985).

Shakespearian plays that I have adapted for children include *Macbeth, Julius Caesar, Romeo and Juliet, Hamlet, A Midsummer Night's Dream, The Taming of the Shrew, A Comedy of Errors, Twelfth Night, Richard III,* and *The Tempest.*

Shakespeare-related reading for younger children includes *Bottom's Dream,* by John Updike (Knopf, 1969); *London Bridge is Falling Down,* two versions by Ed Emberly (Little, Brown, 1967) and Peter Spier (Doubleday, 1967); *Castle,* by David Macaulay (Houghton, Mifflin, 1977); *Anno's Britain,* by Mitsumasa Anno (Philomel, 1982); and *The Story of an English Village,* by John Goodall (Atheneum, 1979).

A script condensed for children should play about thirty minutes. The original would run two or more hours. As you rehearse, you can add or subtract lines. Many children will be able to add to their parts as the play—and their confidence—develops.

Examples of Scripts. Here are examples of scripts for the two witches' scenes from *Macbeth* adapted for three levels: two versions of Act IV, Scene 1 (for Grades K–1 and 2–3) and one version of Act I, Scene I (for Grades 4 and over).

Grades K–1

SCENE: A cavern. In the middle, a boiling cauldron.
Thunder. Enter the three Witches.

First Witch: Round about the cauldron go.
All: Double, double, toil and trouble;
Fire burn and cauldron bubble.
Second Witch: Fillet of a fenny snake,
In the cauldron boil and bake.
All: Double, double, toil and trouble;
Fire burn and cauldron bubble.
Third Witch: Scale of dragon, tooth of wolf,
Witches' mummy, maw of shark.
All: Double, double, toil and trouble;
Fire burn and cauldron bubble.

Grades 2–3

SCENE: A cavern. In the middle, a boiling cauldron.
Thunder. Enter the three Witches.

First Witch: Round about the cauldron go:
In the poison'd entrails throw.
All: Double, double, toil and trouble;
Fire burn and cauldron bubble.
Second Witch: Fillet of a fenny snake,
In the cauldron boil and bake.
Eye of newt and toe of frog.
Wool of bat and tongue of dog.
All: Double, double, toil and trouble;
Fire burn and cauldron bubble.
Third Witch: Scale of dragon, tooth of wolf,
Witches' mummy, maw of the salt-sea shark,
Root of hemlock digged i' the dark.
All: Double, double, toil and trouble;
Fire burn and cauldron bubble.

Playing Macbeth *in a classroom setting.*

First Witch:	Cool it with a baboon's blood.
Second Witch:	Then the charm is firm and good.
Third Witch:	By the pricking of my thumbs, Something wicked this way comes, Open, locks, Whoever knocks!

Grades 4 and Over

SCENE: Scotland. A deserted place.
Thunder and lightning. Enter three Witches.

First Witch:	When shall we three meet again In thunder, lightning, or in rain?
Second Witch:	When the hurlyburly's done, When the Battle's lost and won.
Third Witch:	That will be ere the set of sun.
First Witch:	Where the place?
Second Witch:	Upon the heath.
Third Witch:	There to meet with Macbeth.
All:	Fair is foul, and foul is fair. Hover through the fog and filthy air.

Drum within

Third Witch: A drum, a drum!
Macbeth doth come
All: The weird sisters, hand in hand
Posters of the sea and land,
Thus do go about, about:
Thrice to thine, and thrice to mine,
And thrice again, to make up nine.
Peace! the charm's wound up.

Enter Macbeth and Banquo

Macbeth: So foul and fair a day I have not seen
Banquo: What are these
So wither'd and so wild in their attire?
Macbeth: Speak, if you can: what are you?
First Witch: All hail, Macbeth! hail to thee, thane of Glamis!
Second Witch: All hail, Macbeth! hail to thee, thane of Cawdor!
Third Witch: All hail, Macbeth! thou shalt be King hereafter!
First Witch: Hail!
Second Witch: Hail!
Third Witch: Hail!
First Witch: Lesser than Macbeth and greater.
Second Witch: Not so happy, yet much happier.
Third Witch: Thou shalt get kings, though thou be none:
So all hail, Macbeth and Banquo!
First Witch: Banquo and Macbeth, all hail!
Macbeth: Stay, you imperfect speakers, tell me more:
I know I am thane of Glamis;
But how of Cawdor? The thane of Cawdor lives,
A prosperous gentle man; and to be king
Stands not within the prospect of belief,
No more than to be Cawdor.
Say from whence
You owe this strange intelligence?
Speak, I charge you.

The Witches vanish

Playing Scenes from Shakespeare. To play these scenes from *Macbeth,* read, and discuss them with your class. Then begin to turn a corner of the room into a witches' cavern on a deserted heath in Scotland: use murals and art created by the children, a large black pot (a wastebasket will do as well), and

Material in this section has been adapted from Carole Cox, "Shakespeare and Company: The Best in Classroom Reading and Drama," *The Reading Teacher,* January 1980. Reprinted with permission of the International Reading Association.

assorted rags, capes, hoods, brooms, and ingredients for the witches' brew ("eye of newt and toe of frog") made by the children from clay or other materials.

Begin to move the children through the scenes as the atmosphere thickens and their interest mounts. With younger children, the three witches can take turns saying their lines while the rest of the class sit in a circle and chant the refrain: "Double, double, toil and trouble; Fire burn and cauldron bubble." Here is one way to go about playing the adapted witches' scene with an entire class in Grades K–3.

1. Divide the whole class into three groups and seat them in a semicircle around a cauldron (a large pot, or what-have-you).
2. Speak the lines; have all the children repeat them softly.
3. Practice chanting the lines softly and with expression until the children are fairly comfortable with them. Enthusiasm and energy are more important here than exactness or enunciation. The lines can be divided as follows:

   First Witch: Group 1.
   All: Entire class.
   Second Witch: Group 2.
   All: Entire class.
   Third Witch: Group 3.

4. Ask for a volunteer from each group to step forward and be a witch at the cauldron. Repeat the lines in Step 3 again with all the children: the standing witches and the seated class.
5. When the children appear confident, let the standing witches say their lines alone while the seated children chant the refrain along with the standing witches.
6. When this succeeds, dim the light and add motions, gestures, and sound effects, and place some Dry Ice into the pot to make it "bubble."
7. Repeat the above steps over several class periods, adding gestures, costume pieces, props, sound effects, and so on, until every child who wants to be a witch has had the opportunity to do so.

Exercise care in handling Dry Ice to avoid accidents. Store in metal container; do not touch with bare hands. To create bubble effect, slowly pour room-temp. water over ice.

Fourth- through sixth-grade children can play the scene with the witches as well as the characters of Macbeth and Banquo. Those children who are not playing a speaking part can support the players with sound effects and the sound of the drum. Every child should have the chance to step into the role of a witch, Macbeth, or Banquo, and serve as a member of the chorus, crew, and audience.

Casting an Entire Play Adapted from Shakespeare. Describe the play and each part while the children have a script in hand. Ask them to think about which part they would most like to play if they could choose. They usually have some questions at this time. How big is the part? How many lines and

As one fourth-grader put it: "The things I like best is when swords bust or someone goes mad."

how many scenes does the character play? What kind of costume does the character wear? What are some things the character does? After such discussion, have them put their heads down and raise a hand as you call the name of the part they would most like to play. If no one else raises a hand, the part is theirs. This procedure usually casts most of the parts. If more than one child wants the part, give them a chance to pick one of the remaining parts. If more than one still wants the same part, they can look over a few lines and read them on the spot for the rest of the class. The children then take a secret vote for the person they feel should have the part.

Children invariably want to play the part that they feel they are most suited for and that is within their capabilities. They all want to do their best, to make the play succeed, and to enjoy it. Letting them select their own parts virtually guarantees all three. Furthermore, children participating in Shakespeare and other drama develop a greater tolerance for sharing and cooperating.

The principal parts are not always the most desired. The role of Hamlet may go begging, for example, while several children want to play his father's ghost. Macbeth may require some coaxing, but the three witches never lack for volunteers. No distinction according to sex need be made when casting Shakespeare. Some of my best Hamlets have been wonderfully intense girls, and Lady Macbeth was once a perfectly ruthless fourth-grade boy. Supernatural creatures such as witches, fairies, ghosts, and monsters are always open to both sexes.

In the case of a large class, major parts can be split. Macbeth's role divides neatly in two, before and after the murder of King Duncan. The part of Lady Macbeth—usually a highly desired role—can be divided into before and after she goes mad. This solves the problem of more children than parts, and gives more than one child a chance to play a meaty role. Three witches times two scenes equals six youngsters who get to chant "Double, double, toil and trouble. . . ."

Rehearsals. The blocking of the play relies heavily on working together as a group and making decisions. Children may also rehearse scenes in small groups, and at different times, depending on your schedule. It is not necessary to come together as a whole group at each rehearsal.

Costumes, Sets, and Properties. The creation of costumes, sets, and props requires that children read and research to obtain ideas from many sources. Children are highly motivated to read extensively and for meaning when the information they are seeking will help them create a Renaissance ball gown for Juliet or a rapier for Tybalt. During this research, students glean ideas from a great range of sources and thereby extend their reading beyond the play's script.

Students often spend more time dreaming and reading about theatre props and costumes than creating them. Items found at home are more than enough to outfit a play. A child's imagination is the best source of sets and costumes, for it can handily transform some cardboard room dividers into Macbeth's impenetrable castle and a few broken branches with children crouched behind them into the entire English and Scottish army. A pair of black tights topped with a belted blouse changes anyone into a Renaissance rake. A child in leotard and tights decorated with colored nylon net is obviously a midsummer fairy.

The Performance. When performance day arrives, teachers may do several things to put the emphasis on children and their language and to minimize technical difficulties. Stages can be avoided. The classroom, multipurpose room, or playground are ideal places to produce Shakespeare in the round, with room for chairs or floor seating. Curtains are not necessary. A door or a tree can serve for exits and entrances. Shakespeare's theatre was actually performed this way, curtainless, in the open, on a thrust stage with an entrance/exit or two in the rear. On a conventional stage, children's voices do not carry well and the children themselves are visually lost and too far removed from their audience. Prompting should be avoided, too, and the emphasis placed on thinking on one's feet. If a line is forgotten, another can be improvised to take its place.

A Renaissance festival may precede a play production, with strolling performers in costume playing recorders or guitars and handing out flowers or pieces of gingerbread and Elizabethan treats. Children will most enthusiastically enter into the spirit of the times of William Shakespeare, throwing aside inhibitions, self-consciousness, and fear of work. As one youngster exclaimed when asked what he thought about doing Shakespeare: "I like everything about it except for when we took breaks."

Other Types of Dramatic Literature to Adapt for Children

In addition to Shakespeare, there are many other types of dramatic literature which may be adapted for children.

Greek Tragedy

Antigone, by Sophocles
Electra, by Sophocles
Prometheus Bound, by Aeschylus

Roman Comedy

The Menaechmi, by Plautus
The Haunted House, by Plautus
The Crock of Gold, by Plautus

Students truly act on the words and ideas of Shakespeare as they play scenes like this one from Hamlet, *in which Laertes wounds Hamlet with a poisoned sword.*

Medieval Drama

Saint George, A Christmas Play (anonymous)
English Passion Plays:
Adam, or Man's Disobedience and the Fall of Man (anonymous)
The Deluge: Noah and His Sons (anonymous)
The Second Shepherd's Play (anonymous)
English Morality Play:
Everyman (anonymous)

Renaissance Drama

Ralph Roister Doister, by Nicholas Udall

Seventeenth and Eighteenth Centuries

Tartuffe, by Molière
The Imaginary Invalid, by Molière
The Physician in Spite of Himself, by Molière

Nineteenth and Twentieth Century

Mary Stuart, by Friedrich von Schiller
Cyrano de Bergerac, by Edmond Rostand
St. Joan, by George Bernard Shaw
Androcles and the Lion, by George Bernard Shaw

Drama is a powerful means to enrich, enliven, and expand learning across the curriculum. **Curriculum drama** is a term used (Kelly, 1981) to "describe a method by which potentially dramatic moments within required studies are identified and developed in order to heighten emotionally the students' response to the curriculum, thus deepening the learning experience" (p. 102). Potentially dramatic moments in the curriculum could include:

- problems of social living in the classroom,
- contemporary social problems and current events,
- reliving events in history,
- stepping into the lives of people of other cultures,
- becoming characters in favorite books,
- dramatizing biographies of famous people,
- bringing myths, legends, and folk tales to life, and
- writing and adapting scripts of fantasy or spin-offs from subjects in the content areas.

Examples of Curriculum Drama

Throughout this book, we have seen several examples of curriculum drama, and drama as an integrating force in the curriculum, including

- Mauretta Hurst's kindergarten class dramatizing the story of *The Three Billy Goats Gruff* after reading the book by Marcia Brown, in conjunction with a visit to the zoo and a study of animals;

See Chapter 13, "Mauretta Hurst (Kindergarten)."

- Marion Harris's first-grade class acting out the life of Johnny Appleseed after she read to them a biography of his life, in conjunction with a study of how things grow and the food we eat;

See Chapter 2, "Centering Ideas."

- a reader's theatre script of the book *Pig Pig Rides* used by second-graders, with one child playing teacher and the others taking turns orally interpreting the script.
- third- and fourth-graders creating group pantomimes of their images of different colors, writing about colors, studying about color changes in nature and the colors of humankind, and adapting ancient Egyptian, Hindu, and African folktales for dramatization as part of their study;

See Chapter 5, "A Ripple Effect: Color."

- Avril Font's fourth-grade class dramatizing the life of St. George, creating a television documentary on Shakespeare's life, and dancing around the Maypole as part of their social studies small-group study.

See Chapter 1, "A Slice of Classroom Life."

- Sarah Sherman-Siegel's sixth-grade students creating and dramatizing a mock trial of May Tuck after a close reading, or *explication de texte,* of Natalie Babbitt's book, *Tuck Everlasting.*

See Chapter 9, "Close Reading of a Book."

In this chapter, examples of curriculum drama and integration of the curriculum through drama have included young children's story dramatization and related art experiences after reading *Where the Wild Things Are;* middle elementary students' writing inspired by literature and content area study in science and social studies, in the fantasy *The Tale of an Unfair Election;* reader's theatre scripts adapted from basal reader stories; and adaptations of dramatic literature, such as Shakespeare, for children. The latter has also been a powerful means to integrate entire language arts units of study, learning in all subjects in a class, and the curriculum in an entire school.

Featured Teacher Lynn Lastrapes: Shakespeare with Second Grade

I recently directed "Stirring Up Shakespeare" at Walnut Hills in Baton Rouge (at the invitation of the principal, Orlena MacKenzie, a believer in the arts in education). Lynn Lastrapes, a second-grade teacher, describes what took place in her classroom as a result:

> I truthfully wondered how second-graders could understand some of the complicated plots and characterizations. Except for your talk to us, I never would have thought to try this myself. I didn't take to Shakespeare until after college and I was an English major! I felt excited, stimulated, and good the whole week. I still do. I loved it for myself, but even more for the way my class took to it. Even poor students loved it. They all seemed to relish the "meatiness" of the stories. There was so much going on. Their interest was thrilling.

Lynn discussed some of the many things that happened in her classroom after introducing Shakespeare.

- The class reads 15–20 minutes of Shakespeare after lunch every day and has completed four plays. The students have been able to remember and compare things from all of the plays.
- Vocabulary has been greatly enhanced, with little effort from Lynn.
- The students' predicting what was going to happen in plays has been fun and meaningful.
- As the class resumed reading each day, it recapped those events that were necessary to understanding that day's part of the play. The students were very accurate in summing up.
- The students could tell the play in their own words.

Material in this featured teacher section (pp. 382–385) has been adapted from Carole Cox, "Stirring Up Shakespeare in the Elementary School," in *Literature—News that Stays News: Fresh Approaches to the Classics,* ed. by Candy Carter (Urbana, IL: NCTE, 1985).

- Everyone drew pictures of scenes from the plays.

- The class found places from Shakespeare's plays on the map.

- The class imagined how various characters felt and students shared how they would feel if they were so-and-so.

- The class listened to music like Mendelssohn's "A Midsummer Night's Dream" and Pavarotti singing the aria "O figli miei! Ah! la paterna mano," in which Macduff is thinking of how Macbeth murdered his children. (According to Lynn, "They were moved, I tell you! Even though it was in Italian, they felt the emotion.")

- The class also listened to Tchaikovsky's "Fantasy Overture to Romeo and Juliet." ("The love theme made one of the boys do a nose dive, but he really loved it inside I think!")

- During Brotherhood Week, the class used *Romeo and Juliet* as one of its stories and talked about the consequences of not being brotherly.

- Several students called Lynn and thanked her for letting them know about an LSU production of *Hamlet.* They went and loved it. ("Second-graders going to *Hamlet* is beautiful!")

Lynn concludes that the "children are clamoring for more Shakespeare. I want to do *The Tempest* next year. I want more, too."

Teachers in other classrooms at Walnut Hills described other classroom activities which ensued:

- The students researched and wrote about Shakespeare's life and related Renaissance topics: food, arms and weapons, music, costumes and clothing; and so on.
- Classes played other scenes from other plays: Mark Anthony's funeral oration in *Julius Caesar;* scenes from *Romeo and Juliet;* and several others.
- Students listened to recordings of Shakespeare's plays and read related books about Shakespeare, his plays, and the Renaissance.

A Schoolwide Renaissance Fair

After two weeks of concentrated school and classroom activities designed for "Stirring Up Shakespeare," Walnut Hills School held a Renaissance Fair in conjunction with a Book Fair. The gym was decorated with the children's art and writings, and teachers, children, and their parents came in Renaissance dress. Renaissance theater treats of mead and gingersnaps were served, and a Renaissance recorder group from LSU played traditional music. Then several classes presented a program of scenes from the plays they had worked on, along with other research projects:

A teacher in Elizabethan dress participates in a combined Renaissance Fair and school Book Fair.

- the witches' scenes, done by kindergarten, first, and second grades;
- the funeral oration scene from *Julius Caesar,* played by third-graders;
- scenes from *Romeo and Juliet,* played by fifth-graders; and
- a report, display, and demonstration of Renaissance arms and weaponry, by fourth-graders.

The event later was the lead article in the award-winning school newspaper *Paw Prints:*

> ***Learning about the Renaissance***
>
> I love the exciting times of the Renaissance! I hope you like to get in touch with the Renaissance world like I do. Dr. Carole Cox Spates, a teacher from LSU, came to Walnut Hills. She showed us books, costumes, and great scenes by William Shakespeare, like *Hamlet,* which was acted out by students.
>
> Then her husband, Mr. Spates, taught us how to use a sword, and how the people used the sword in the Renaissance times. It was a lot of entertainment for me! But, the guy who was fencing against me won the fight.
>
> Thursday, February 16, I came with my parents to a Renaissance party at school. It was very exciting for me too, because I was wearing a Renaissance costume.
>
> —A 5th-Grader

Articles by many children filled the pages. Two of the children's comments underscore the impact of this new approach to the classic: a schoolwide exploration of the life, times, and works of William Shakespeare.

> Shakespeare was a magnificent man. He was a play writer. He wrote plays such as *Macbeth, Hamlet, Julius Caesar,* and *Romeo and Juliet.* Feb. 16 we relived his plays. It was as if Shakespeare were inside us. Shakespeare will always live because of his plays.
>
> —A 5th-Grader

> All around the school of Walnut Hills, kids and teachers have been talking about Shakespeare. Everyone knows he's a wonderful person, and he's been writing stories like *Macbeth, Hamlet,* and more. Even now he's gone, we still are looking back to his stories and enjoying them.
>
> —A 3rd-Grader

Evaluating Drama

Drama evaluation is an ongoing process for both teachers and children. This is also one of the important instances where children can and should be involved just as much as the teacher in evaluating their own progress and the progress of the group. In this way, evaluation becomes a basis upon which to build further instruction. Drama is child-centered rather than criterion-referenced. Both teacher and students need to assess and understand what happened during Monday's session before the one can plan and the other can prepare for and participate on Tuesday.

Another significant aspect of drama evaluation is that the teacher as evaluator is modeling important positive behavior for students' self- and group evaluation. What you say and how you say it will affect how your

An interest in reading Shakespeare is created by dramatizing his plays with children.

students evaluate and plan with each other, which is an integral part of drama activities. Keep in mind that drama is almost invariably a cooperative group effort and that children need to develop skills in this domain as much as in any other. In fact, one of the great benefits of drama is that it develops self-awareness and self-concept within an encouraging and supportive environment among other individuals with whom the children must live and work in order to play and dramatize.

Three types of procedures are relevant for drama evaluation: *observations* by the teacher, *discussions* between teacher and children, and *assessment* of pupil progress and teaching.

1. ***Observations by the teacher serve to develop discussion guidelines and to encourage and reinforce children's responses.***

The teacher can take play notes during any type of drama session to provide guidelines for discussion later. For creative drama activities as well as plays, these may focus on pupil and group progress, words of encouragement and praise, questions you will use to lead later discussions, and suggestions for a direction you would like to the children to move towards as a result of guided discussion.

2. ***Discussions between teacher and children help the children to evaluate themselves and others and to plan cooperatively for future sessions.***

Discussion is a critical component in every type of drama session. Remember that you are a model for the type of constructive evaluation you wish your children to emulate. Types of questions for leading into these discussions include:

- What did you see that you liked?
- What did you enjoy doing or watching?
- Whom did you notice doing something really well (interesting, imaginative, different, humorous)?
- Why did you like what they did?
- What do we need to work on next time? How can we do this?
- What shall we concentrate on next time? (Ideas: concentration, cooperation, teamwork, movement, pace, energy, characterization, dialogue, voice, gestures, space, traffic.

3. ***Assessment of pupil progress and teaching determines the children's progress and the teacher's effectiveness.***

You may wish to keep anecdotal records and logs following an individual child's progress, the group's progress and interaction among children in the group, and the development of specific drama activity. This type of evaluation will be useful for planning and for parent conferences and will serve as a record of successful (or unsuccessful) ideas for future reference.

You may also wish to develop your own questionnaire, tailored to the grade level you are teaching, to the instructional setting, and to the preferred type of drama activity. For example, the oral responses of younger

NAME Ryan GRADE COMPLETED 2

Tell about the play by William Shakespeare.

It is about a man that was contro-
lled by witches. He takes over the kingdom. And is killed bya brave nobleman called Macduff

Which character(s) do you play? Dunkin kennox docter sword

Tell about your character.

Dunkin is the kingof scot land.
Lennox is anodleman
The docter is a docter
Sword is theson of generalSword

What is the most important thing about the play?

Its supernatural

What is the most important thing about your character?

Hes king
nothing
Hes a docter
He fites macbeth

How did you feel about doing Shakespeare

happy

Figure 10–2
Ryan's Responses to Playing Shakespeare

children and the written responses of older children may be collected on a form (see Figure 10–2) that gives insight into children's understanding of the narrative form and content of drama, their part in a particular drama activity (especially plays and adaptations of dramatic literature), and their feelings about participating in drama.

Second-grader Ryan completed the response form shown in Figure 10–2 after playing several parts in a school production of *Macbeth.* I believe that his responses demonstrate that doing drama with children offers great benefits for learning, living, and language both to children and to teachers practicing the art of teaching language arts.

Summing Up

Does drama really belong in the language arts curriculum? The theories, research, and experience of many educators suggest that drama should be central and not peripheral to all learning in the classroom. The work of Piaget (1962) shows that children use imitation to learn, and that they come to play and drama naturally as they learn to communicate with others. American as well as British educators, such as Ward (1957), Heathcote (1981), and Siks (1983) offer teachers rationales and objectives for the use of drama in elementary education. Research on reading instruction also shows the importance of drama as a means to teach reading comprehension, and many opportunities exist for teachers to make connections between teaching reading, literature, and response to literature through drama. As a mixed art, drama is an ideal means to integrate the curriculum through the language arts.

The role of the teacher in drama in the classroom is of critical importance. Drama expert Way (1967) suggests that teachers remember above all to focus on children in drama and begin where the teachers themselves are most natural and comfortable. Many specific types of drama are appropriate for elementary- and middle-school classrooms. Creative dramatics is a process-centered form of drama which consists of experiences with sense training, pantomime and improvisation, and story dramatization. Scriptwriting can be done as a whole-class activity or in small groups with children creating original scripts from their own experiences or in response to literature and other media.

Reader's theatre is a form of script performance where students prepare and then read poems and stories for an audience. Dramatic literature, such as Shakespeare, may also be adapted, shared, and performed in the classroom. All forms of drama activities are ideal means for integrating all aspects of the curriculum.

Looking Further

1. Describe where you might begin experiences in drama, making choices for activities from the circle of drama in Figure 10–1.

2. Try out several of the sense-training activities in small groups in your class. Brainstorm a list of other ideas for sense training to use with children.

3. Start a file of pantomime and improvisation ideas for use with children.

4. List several stories suitable for dramatization with children. Choose one and develop a lesson plan for a story dramatization from it. If possible, try it out with children.

5. Write a script for a one-act play in your class. Try playing the script with children if possible.

6. Identify several stories suitable for adaptation to a reader's theatre script for a given grade level. Adapt one of them into a script and play the script with others in your class. If possible, play the script with children.

7. Adapt one scene from a Shakespeare play according to the suggestions in this chapter.

8. Play the witches' scene from *Macbeth* with a group of children.

9. Adapt a scene from another play for use with children.

Chapter Eleven

The Media Arts

Objectives

Look for answers to the following questions as you read this chapter.

- How are the media arts used in classrooms today?
- Why should the media arts be integrated into the English language arts?
- What are the effects of the media arts on developing literacy?
- How can the media arts be integrated into the teaching of the language arts?

A Child's View

Here are some comments from children using the media arts in the classroom.

A fourth-grader commenting on the filmmaking experience:

> Film is like your grandma's preserved pears. Film preserves memories. Film will show things you are proud of.

Three third-graders who had been brainstorming a video drama:

> We can do anything we want with this video machine. Like Godzilla's fire. Like on that Dr. Pepper commercial and he was burning everything up and they gave him a Dr. Pepper. Fire all over the place. Maybe another planet. We need to make muscles and buildings and a little cable car that flies. And like this could be a time capsule. We need popsicle sticks. And a trap for Godzilla's feet. No trap! Godzilla's trying to save us from creatures from space. We need to make a background, you know how backgrounds move and they change things electronically? And I could get my hamster to talk and Godzilla could save him! Yeah!!!

A fourth-grader telling his teacher about the class newspaper:

> This newspaper is gonna be so neat 'cause everybody in the world will read it and we can tell 'em and show 'em what we're doing and they'll all *love* it.

A fifth-grader to a class visitor:

> Don't worry if you don't know how to use the computer. I'll show you. Do you want to play our Choose-Your-Own-Adventure? It's easy!

Centering Ideas

Photo Essay: Images of the Media Arts in Classrooms Today

Questions:

A. What is happening in each of these photographs?
B. What does this have to do with the art of teaching language arts?

Answers to A:

- Photo #1: Third-graders collaborate at the computer.
- Photo #2: Seventh-graders shoot a Super-8 animated film from an original script they have written, and which they plan to enter in an international student media festival.
- Photo #3: Fifth-graders use a video tape recorder and a television monitor to shoot a dramatized interview with Christopher Columbus on *Meet the Explorer.*

Answer to B:

Continue reading this chapter.

Making Connections

How many of the activities shown in the preceding photo essay were you able to identify, describe, and explain? And how many of these experiences have you had yourself? If all of them, you are well on your way to preparing to meet the needs of children growing up in a world forever changed by new technologies. If few or none, keep an open mind about your potential to teach the media arts because children between the ages of five and thirteen will require skills and understandings in all of these—not to mention in newer forms of technology that are emerging every day—in order to be prepared to live and work in the world they will find as adults. More than 75 percent of children in kindergarten today will eventually be employed in occupations involving the use of computers (West, 1983).

To ignore the media arts because they have not traditionally been a part of school curricula is to ignore the reality of the world we live in. To assume they cannot be an integral part of the learning and teaching of language arts is to ignore what current theory and research and practice about merging the media arts with traditional education tell us.

Photo #1

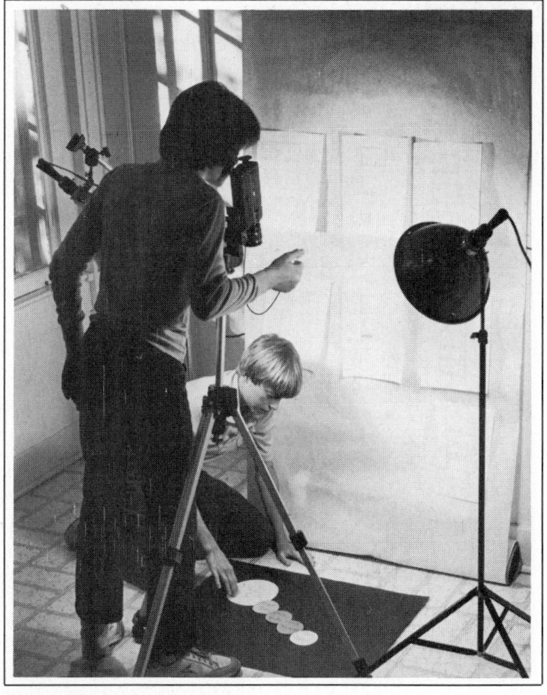

Photo #2

Photo #3

The Media Arts in the English Language Arts

The Commission on Media of the National Council of Teachers of English (NCTE, 1984) has recently proposed a rationale for integrating the media arts into the teaching of the English language arts.

> Each new medium—from the printing press to photography, radio, recordings, film, television, videotape, and the computer—has been hailed as a potentially revolutionary force for changing the forms and functions of human communications. As teachers of English and the language arts, our attention traditionally has focused on communication of knowledge through print, the first medium of literacy. Meanwhile, our students have grown up in an environment that includes the newer auditory and visual electronic media. For them, "acquiring literacy" involves taking into account a wider range of media of communication.
>
> Certainly English and language arts teachers have moved beyond the early view of these media as mere audiovisual aids used only as support for print materials. Increasingly, we are recognizing a need to integrate all communication media into the teaching of English and the language arts. But how can we justify devoting attention to the development of a broadly based literacy when we are expected to focus exclusively on teaching "the basics" of literacy—reading and writing?
>
> We believe that communication today and in the future will mean the ability to understand, use, and control more complex symbol systems in order to function competently. Thus, teaching students to discover meaning and to communicate effectively now requires knowing how electronic media function in the development of language, thought, and knowledge in our culture.
>
> Integrating electronic media into classroom teaching involves not only teaching *through* these media but also teaching *about* them. Whether we are concerned with film, television, or computers, we must provide opportunities for students to use these media. Students can develop the analytic thinking processes of a broader-based literacy through filmmaking experiences (as well as writing experiences), through discussions of television dramas (as well as short stories), and through consideration of values and stereotypes that appear in commercials (as well as in novels and essays). We should also teach about media—their interrelatedness, their unique capabilities, their potential and actual influence (both positive and negative) on human consciousness, their future development.
>
> Integrating media into English and the language arts does not deny the primacy of oral and written language. Although new technologies are changing the means of communication, verbal language is still basic to all media and central to our mission as English and language arts teachers. Natural language forms—printed and spoken—are required, either as part of the actual language of communication (as in movie dialogue, television documentary narration, printed instruction on the screen) or as adjuncts to other communication forms (as in film production notes, stage directions for a television play, artificial computer languages).
>
> Equally important, the thinking skills that underlie communication—inductive-deductive reasoning, making references, supporting value

statements—are best taught in the contexts of all media, verbal as well as visual. Students must learn to understand the power of all media in order to avoid being controlled by them.

In addition, practical considerations—the growing number of jobs in information processing which require competency in the new communication technologies and the increasing use of new media languages in our daily life—make teaching toward a more broadly based literacy absolutely essential. Thus, an expanded concept of literacy is necessary for the development of efficient, effective communication in today's media environment (pp. 1–2).

The Effects of the Media on Literacy Development

There has always been concern both among parents and among educators that as children spend many hours viewing television and films, their potential literacy development is threatened. Results from the 1979–80 National Assessment of Reading and Literature indicate that given a choice of reading a book, watching television, reading a magazine, or going to a movie, half of the nine-year-olds sampled would rather go to a movie. The same response was given by nearly two-thirds of the thirteen- and seventeen-year-olds (National Assessment of Education Progress, 1981). This is certainly an issue of concern to reading and English educators and anyone else interested in the future of literacy in an age increasingly characterized by the proliferation and availability of the offspring of the electronic revolution, such as microcomputers, video games, and the visual media. The underlying assumption implied here, however, is that children's interest in viewing and their interest in reading are inherently mutually exclusive phenomena, and that the more they want to watch, the less they will want to read.

How else does research inform the teacher about the relationship of the media arts to literacy development? In a review of the research, Irwin (1976) found that with the media, as with any learning experience, "It is not so much the media that contribute to success in reading, rather it is the teacher's effective use of technology that determines success in reading" (p. 390). Her recommendation was that, above all, teachers need to be familiar with media research and its effects on reading and language learning. Here is a summary of such research on the various media discussed in this chapter.

Forms of Film

Studies show that the films children like best are those that are most like their favorite stories and books (Cox, 1978, 1982, 1984), that story-related films can improve reading comprehension (Dech, 1975), and that photography in a language experience approach can improve the performance of remedial readers (Goddard, 1977).

Television and Sound and Video Recording

Research has failed to show a negative correlation between the amount of television viewing and academic achievement (Bennett, 1974; Childers & Ross, 1973). In fact, research findings (Dalzell, 1976; Hamilton, 1975; Lamb, 1976) indicate that "Children can learn much from television which will make it possible for them to benefit by responding to print more effectively and with greater understanding" (Lamb, p. 370); that an important variable in learning from television is the amount of discussion and interaction with parents and teacher and opportunities for participation, feedback, and transfer of learning from television after viewing (Cook & Conner, 1976; Diaz-Guerrero, 1976; Flood, 1976; Ienatsch, 1974); and also that reading achievement improves for students who use both sound and video tape recordings in a language experience approach (Schneeberg, 1973; Smith & Morgan, 1973).

Print and Photojournalism

Several studies have shown improved reading achievement and attitudes when communication concepts are taught by encouraging students' personal responses to newspaper reading through discussions and writing. (Berryman, 1971; Board of Education, City of Chicago, 1970; Reid, 1972; Stetson, 1977).

Computer Technology

Results of computer-assisted programs in elementary and intermediate reading skills programs indicate a significant growth in vocabulary and word identification skills (Atkinson, 1973, 1974; Fletcher & Atkinson, 1972; Fletcher & Suppes, 1972) and in achievement of basic skills and improved attitude towards instruction (Saracho, 1982), although this last study reported that students (who happened to be migrant Spanish-speaking children) did not prefer the computer learning environment. The effects of word processing on children's writing include: longer stories, increased revising, and improved confidence and transcribing skills (Phenix & Hannan, 1984), and improved peer interaction and understanding of the audience in the writing process (Bruce, Michaels, & Watson-Gegeo, 1985). Computer programming instruction of young children tends to increase the amount of social interaction (Hawkins et al., 1982) and demonstrates the importance of the teacher's role in supporting a computer learning environment (Genishi, McCollumn, & Stravel, 1985).

Teaching Children

The photographs in "Centering Ideas" show children from the primary- through middle-school grades using and interacting with many media arts. It is important to keep in mind that all these technologies are accessible to all children at all grades. Any six-year-old, for example, can learn to make and to appreciate films, television, and videotaped productions, to understand and use and even produce a newspaper or magazine, to mount a photography show, and to become computer literate—not to mention being able to practice skills at the computer, use a word processor, and learn to program a computer.

All these media arts, then, are for all children, and are limited only by your imagination in their adaptability to specific students, classes, or learning environments. And in an information-processing age, when new technology is changing the way we learn, work, and perhaps think, teachers must learn to use, above all, their imaginations.

Forms of Film

Film Study

Certain films are ideal for helping children to become literate in the usual sense as well as cinema literate (Cox, 1978, 1982), for example, favorite films that are adapted from books or that tell stories. By way of illustration, here are the top ten films chosen from among twenty-five stories rated by 350 fourth- and fifth-graders (Cox 1983b), which are either adapted from a book, a fable, or a traditional folktale, or tell an original story in film form.

1. *The Case of the Elevator Duck* (Learning Corporation of America, 1974)
2. *The Fur Coat Club* (Learning Corporation of America, 1973)
3. *The Blue Dashiki: Jeffrey and His Neighbors* (Encyclopaedia Britannica, 1969)
4. *Clown* (Learning Corporation of America, 1969)
5. *Catch the Joy* (Pyramid, 1970)
6. *The Cow* (Churchill, 1970)
7. *The Daisy* (Macmillan, 1967)
8. *Rock in the Road* (Macmillan, 1968)
9. *Hansel and Gretel* (Encyclopaedia Britannica, 1973)
10. *Hopscotch* (Churchill, 1972)

The *Case of the Elevator Duck,* adapted from the book of the same name by Polly Berrien Berends (Random House, 1973)

Exposure both to good books and to good films such as these provides the students with opportunities to experience, interpret, and evaluate the same or similar stories expressed through two different mediums. Moreover, film introduces into the classroom a dynamic quality that can lead to action-centered responses by children to both literature and film. Films can be shown to the whole class in a short period of time. Immediate response and involvement in the viewing experience and story are possible. Teachers can then quickly and actively exploit the energy and interest generated by film among the children, an energy and interest that can extend into other areas of teaching the English language arts. Some of the more obvious ways the study of film can support literature, reading, and language arts experience in the elementary classroom include concept development, vocabulary development, and development of students' personal responses to film, books, and other forms of narrative through discussion, writing, art, drama, music, dance, filmmaking, and other expressive modes.

The practical question here is how teachers can best orchestrate the teaching of children's films in concert with the teaching of children's literature to enhance each other's potential and at the same time use both print and nonprint media to encourage the growth of literacy among students.

Response Guide for Children's Films. Here is a model for guiding and extending responses to film, especially as these responses pertain to literature, reading, and language arts experiences in the classroom (Cox, 1983c).

1. ***Previewing***

   Films should always be previewed by teachers for suitability and interest; to note concepts, themes, and vocabulary; and to plan for extending the viewing experience.

2. ***Viewing***

   A simple introduction to a film is best, perhaps including a few initiating questions. Avoid curriculum overkill: long explanations, vocabulary lists, and questions that sound as if you plan to give a test on the film after it is shown. Remember that children are already extremely enthusiastic about watching films. A good request to make of children before they view any film is that they remember one thing they see or one thing they hear to share with the group after viewing.

Or, as film critic Pauline Kael puts it, "If you don't think you can kill the movies, you underestimate the power of education."

Figure 11–1 *Film Preference Instrument*

	Boy	*Girl*	*Grade*	*School*
Name ________________	________	________	________	________

How much did you like this film?

Film (title) ____________________

I didn't like it at all.	(I would rather have done something else.)
I didn't like it very much.	(I wouldn't want to see it again.)
It was o.k.	(I wouldn't mind seeing it again.)
It was good.	(I would like to see it again.)
It was great!	(I could see it many times without getting tired of it.)

Weight ratings as follows:

1 = I didn't like it at all.
2 = I didn't like it very much.
3 = It was o.k.
4 = It was good.
5 = It was great!

From Carole Cox, "Film Preference Instrument," in *Measures for Research and Evaluation in the English Language Arts* (Vol. 2), ed. by William T. Fagan, Charles R. Cooper, and Julie M. Jensen (Urbana, IL: NCTE, 1985).

The Film Preference Instrument (see Figure 11–1) can be used to measure and evaluate children's interest in a film and to collect initial information on their responses to the film through their written reactions. This instrument is easily administered in the classroom and can be used from year to year. Ratings of each film can be noted for future reference on the response guide planning form (Figure 11–2).

Figure 11–2 *Response Guide for Children's Films*

Previewing

Title ______________________________ **Rating** __________

Distributor ______________________________ **Date** ________ **Min.** ________

Circle: **color/b&cw** **live/animation** **narration/dialogue** **music**

Audience/Level ______________________________

Vocabulary ______________________________

Annotation

Viewing

Introduction

Postviewing

Watch-and-Talk Groups

Activating and Extending Film Responses

A. Literature

B. Writing

C. Drama, Art, Music, and Dance

Related Resources

3. ***Postviewing***

a. *Watch-and-talk groups.* After the film, immediately put children in small discussion groups and let them talk about the film among themselves. Observe what it was that impressed them, their reactions, their apparent level of understanding. The planning of experiences should not be based on the film's content, but on the interaction between the film and the child and among children as they discuss the film with each other. Take into account what they brought to the viewing experience—a variable with every child and group of children.

b. *Activating and extending film responses.* The film viewing experience is a powerful one, and the showing of a fifteen-minute film—especially if it is a film the children like—could pique their interest and stimulate their responses for weeks and even over a semester or a year.

This kind of interest and stimulation can provide an imaginative teacher with enough raw material to extend and integrate this experience with film art to literature and other experiences. It can also be a unifying experience, one which the entire class is able to share at the same time, or for each individual child's self-expression through writing, drama, art, music, dance, or filmmaking.

See *Films and Filmstrips for Language Arts, An Annotated Bibliography,* by J. P. May (National Council of Teachers of English, 1981).

c. *Related resources.* Related resources to extend the viewing experience can include other films, books, media, or content area teaching materials.

A Sample Response Guide. Figure 11–3 shows a sample response guide developed for a favorite children's film, *The Case of the Elevator Duck.* Suggestions for teaching were based on children's responses to this film and on the experiences that developed out of these responses.

Filmmaking

Super-8 Filmmaking. Super-8 filmmaking with children is a natural outgrowth of film study just as creative writing or bookmaking can develop from literature appreciation (Cox, 1975a). Filmmaking may pose a greater challenge than bookmaking would to a teacher more accustomed to handling print than nonprint media, but teachers who meet the challenge one day at a time will be well rewarded by the great excitement, enthusiasm, and educational potential filmmaking can generate in an elementary classroom (Cox, 1975b, 1983a).*

*Material in this section on filmmaking is from Carole Cox, "Young Filmmakers Speak the Language of Film," *Language Arts,* 60 (March 1983): 296–304, 372.

Previewing

Title THE CASE OF THE ELEVATOR DUCK **Rating** 4.67

Distributor Learning Corporation of America **Date** 1974 **Min.** 17

Circle: **Color** **b&w** **Live** **animation** **narration** **dialogue** **music**

Audience/Level Middle to upper elementary

Vocabulary housing project (introduce: genre, synopsis, pilot)

Annotation

The story unfolds around a semi-classic plot: boy finds duck (but can't keep it because of restrictions against pets in the housing project where he lives); boy finds duck's rightful owner (who can't keep it either), and boy finally finds a home for duck at the day-care center. Characters include: Gilbert, a Black 11 year-old part-time detective; his mother, supportive of his quest to find the duck a home but concerned about the housing authority; a housing policeman; a friend who can't understand why our hero would rather play detective than basketball; the small Spanish-speaking boy who can't tell Gilbert the duck belongs to him because he speaks no English; his adult sister who refuses to take the duck back; and the director of the day-care center who finally takes the duck in.

Viewing

Introduction

Have you ever found an animal that you could not keep? What happened? How did you feel? Have you ever pretended you were a detective or helped solve a mystery? What happened?

Postviewing

Watch-and-Talk Groups

Children's responses included: "I liked it because it was interesting, exciting, funny, etc." They liked the duck because they said they liked ducks, they liked the way the duck kept following the boy and appearing in the elevator, and because he was funny. They liked the way the boy kept trying to find the duck a home, his voice, and because he was funny and nice to the duck. They said the story, action, acting, setting, music were good. Many said they liked it because they like animals, stories about children and animals together, and because they liked detective stories and mysteries. One child said he liked it because "there was a Black boy in it and I'm a Black boy too." Overall response was very positive and children rated this film extremely high.

Activating and Extending Film Responses

A. Literature

1. Story Synopsis/Genre. Write a synopsis based on the book *The Case of the Elevator Duck,* or another detective or mystery book you choose that will become the basis for a new TV series you will star in called *(Your Name), Young Detective.* Use the following outline to help you: (1) Setting, (2) Time, (3) Characters, (4) Plot. Write in the style of the other detective and mystery stories you have read and viewed.
2. Script and Dialogue. Write a script in a dialogue based on your synopsis, which will become the pilot show for the series.

B. Writing

1. Point of View. Write the story of *The Case of the Elevator Duck* from the point of view of one of the other characters: Gilbert's mother, the housing policeman, Gilbert's friend, Julio, Julio's sister, the day-care center director.

Figure 11–3 *A Sample Response Guide for a Children's Film:* The Case of the Elevator Duck

2. Personification. Pretend the duck is a person and write the story from its point of view. Pretend the elevator is a person and write the story from its point of view.
3. Further Adventures. Write about the further adventures of Gilbert or another character from another detective or mystery book. You could start a series of these stories.
4. *E.T. II.* Tell about the time you found an animal that you could not keep. If this has never happened to you, imagine you have found an animal, or any creature (an extraterrestrial?) that you can imagine. What happened?
5. Pattern Writing. Write a poem about a duck using a pattern such as a *cinquain* or another pattern.
   Line 1: one word (title)
   Line 2: two words (describe title)
   Line 3: three words (tell action)
   Line 4: four words (tell feeling)
   Line 5: one word (refer to title)
6. Concrete Writing. Write your poem on a picture or cutout of a duck, or write a poem about a duck in the shape of a duck.

C. Drama, Art, Music, and Dance

1. Dramatization. Dramatize one of the scripts written above as part of a live play, puppet show, videotaped television show, or tape-recorded radio show.
2. Storyboards. Create a storyboard, or shooting script, for a Super-8 filmmaking project, from one of the scripts already written. Storyboards are sheets of paper with 3–4 large squares in the center where scenes are drawn. Space on the left and right can be used to note dialogue, narration, setting, shooting directions, and sound and special effects.
3. Super-8 Filmmaking. Make a film from the storyboard.
4. "The Duck" Dance. Think about three or four ways the duck in the movie moved. Describe them and do your own version of these movements. Find some music with a good beat and put these movements to it in a pattern you can repeat and show and teach to others. Put on the music and do "The Duck."

Related Resources

A. Books. Many mystery and detective books for children are available. Here are a few of the more recent ones on a variety of reading levels.

Anderson, Mary, *Matilda's Masterpiece.* Atheneum, 1977.
Bonsall, Crosby, *The Case of the Double Cross.* Harper & Row, 1980.
Godden, Rumer, *The Rocking Horse Secret.* Viking, 1978.
Sharmat, Marjorie, *Nate the Great and the Phony Clue.* Coward, McCann, 1977.
Sobol, Donald J., *Encyclopedia Brown Carries On.* Four Winds Press, 1980.

B. Films. The following live-action films, some of which are book adaptations, follow a theme and storyline similar to *The Case of the Elevator Duck:* a boy or girl and his or her dog, duck, goat, horse, kangaroo, extraterrestrial?

Clown (Learning Corporation of America, 1969)
Being Right, Can You Still Lose? (Walt Disney Educational Media, 1976)
Me and Your Kangaroo (Learning Corporation of America, 1973)
Phillip and the White Colt (Learning Corporation of America, 1973), adapted from the feature, *Run Wild, Run Free,* from the book by David Rook
Zlateh the Goat (Weston Wood Studios, 1973), adapted from the story by Isaac B. Singer

Figure 11–3 *Continued*

1. ***Materials for Filmmaking***
   a. *Film Folders:* Each child can use a folder with pockets to hold written materials, storyboard forms for script writing (see Figure 11–4), and an idea note pad.
   b. *Equipment:* Many libraries or media centers own most of the following pieces of equipment. Parents—and interested camera stores—are other good sources for borrowed pieces:
      Super-8 camera with cable release for pixelation
      tripod
      photoflood bulb, 250 watts (optional)
      adjustable clamps to hold bulbs (optional)
      Super-8 projector
      Craig Master Splicer, or splicing tapes
      splicing cement (for wet splices)
   c. *Film:* Kodachrome 40 Super-8 movie film

Dialogue	Film Shots	Description
	[ ]	
	(Technical Notes, Sound Effects, Shooting Directions)	
	[ ]	
	[ ]	

Figure 11–4
Storyboard Form

Making films in response to literature in a fifth-grade classroom.

2. ***Basic Steps in Filmmaking***
   a. *Idea Sharing, Brainstorming:* The first real step towards filmmaking, after a period of film study, is idea sharing and some brainstorming—children in small groups exchanging ideas as fast as they can think of them without regard for their practicality, a method I have found very effective to use to stimulate children's ideas for filmmaking. When one strong idea or central theme has emerged, children may continue to develop it as a class, in small groups, or individually.

      Here is an example of brainstorming by a group of fourth-graders who decided to make a space film and then worked as individuals to produce the following lists of ideas, which varied greatly in character, thus providing clues as to how each child might best contribute to and benefit from filmmaking. Some were simple but all-inclusive statements such as "I would like to see space fights and have a hero and evildoers," or "Spaceships fighting at each other. There's some top secret stuff. One ship has it and others are trying to get it. Creatures from other galaxies" (p. 297).

      Some of the children made lists and showed a flair for naming, like the dragons of ancient times (p. 297).

Kondavolin	clone king	Hortu
Electrohead	Read Eye	Princess Prine
Bombrain	Dr. Galaxy	Gornen
zap circle	Planet Man	Ram Finger
safety bubble	The Melkot	Pliton
faz gun	Sisen	

b. *The Plot:* The next step was to let the children share lists, exchange ideas, and pull them all together into one plot. Here is the plot summary:

> *A fight between evildoers and heroes. Planet Man is taking Princess Prine to Kondavolin. She's going to bring a top-secret formula for a machine to go back in time to the king there. She is captured by two monsters, the Horlock and the Mudagoo. The secret was handed down from her father before he died. If the evil Dr. Galaxy gets it, he can control the galaxy after he builds the machine. Planet Man is trying to save the Princess but he is vulnerable to Cyplonite. He is stopped by the monsters with Cyplonite.*
>
> *Meanwhile, the monsters take Princess Prine to another planet, Sisen, and Dr. Galaxy and the Horlock and the Mudagoo torture her. Starben, faithful partner of Planet Man, rescues him. They both go to Sisen to rescue Princess Prine. They have a war in space against Dr. Galaxy's forces. Planet Man and Starben and the good guys barely win, by a hair, a hairsbreadth. They land and have a land fight. They rescue the Princess and get the secret, capture the evildoers and live happily ever after (p. 298).*

When the plot was written, the future film was titled *The Adventures of Planet Man.*

c. *Storyboards:* After a plot has been hatched, the next step in filmmaking is the preparation of a storyboard. Storyboard forms are mimeoed papers with three large empty squares in the middle. The filmmaker draws visuals in these squares and writes shooting directions, technical notes, sound effects, description, dialogue, or whatever will be of help in planning on either side. The scenes must be ordered precisely as a guide to shooting them in sequence.

The storyboard script for *The Adventures of Planet Man,* for example, was prepared by three groups, each group turning one third of the plot idea into a story board (see Figure 11–5). The group came together as a whole to edit, make additions and subtractions, iron out transitions, and pull together an ending satisfying to everyone.

d. *Gathering Properties:* Properties, backgrounds, and sets can be kept as a minimum for filmmaking classes. The children can select whatever art materials they need from school supplies (butcher paper, colored paper, paint, glue, scissors). Leftover materials from Halloween or other occasions can yield fine costumes.

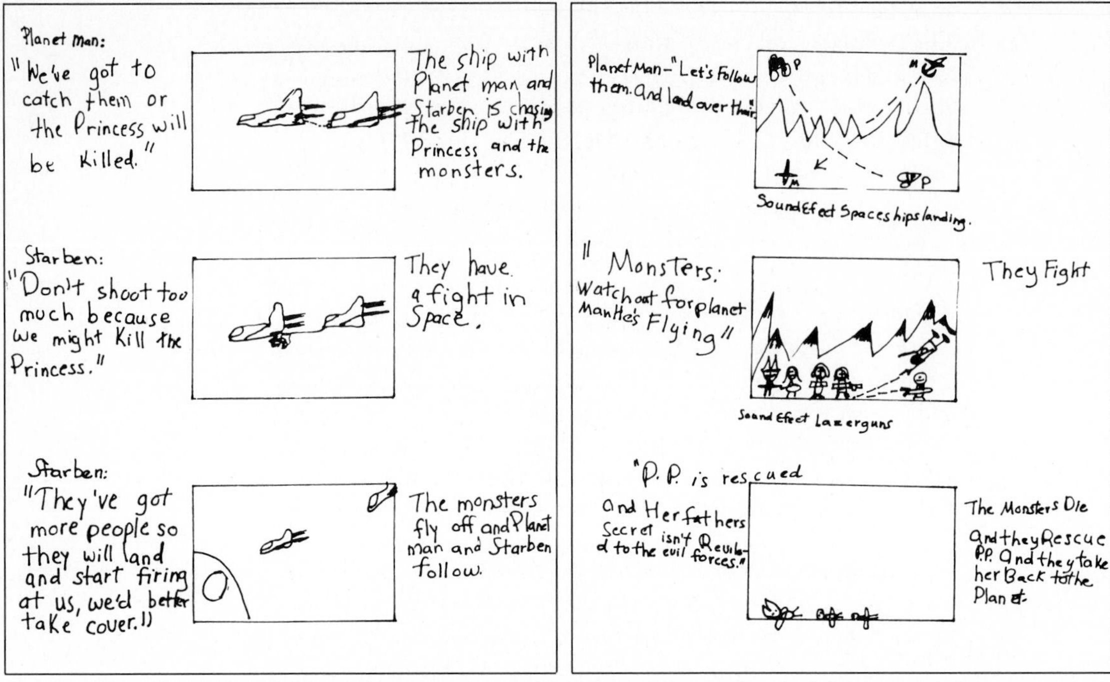

Figure 11–5 *Storyboard Script for "The Adventures of Planet Man"*
From Carole Cox, "Young Filmmakers Speak the Language of Film," *Language Arts* 60 (March 1983): 300.

The pixelation animation technique—filming objects or people one frame at a time and moving them between frames to give the illusion of life to inanimate objects—does not require elaborate sets, background, or costumes. Particularly adaptable to this technique are toys, stuffed animals, and Play-doh. The latter can be metamorphosed into a variety of shapes. The children can bring such items from home, or the teacher can keep a selection on hand for filmmaking.

The only materials required for *Planet Man* are colored 22″ × 28″ poster paper, construction paper, tempera paint, marking pens, and scissors. Credits are formed with cutout letters placed a word at a time on black poster paper. Cutout stars and comets suggest an outer-space setting. When the letters showing the title are removed, a cutout space ship zooms across the scene. The ship's interior consists of light blue poster paper, with a view screen and control panel painted with tempera. The characters are created from construction paper and are in segments so they may be animated: separate heads, torsos, limbs, and features.

e. *Learning to Use the Equipment:* If the children are making their own films, it is necessary for all of them to learn to use the equipment. If a class is making a film as a group, this task could be delegated to a few children for practical purposes, and the others could acquire the skills as the work progressed.

Learning to use a camera is strictly a learning-by-doing affair. It seems that no amount of teacher presentation to the group replaces the chance for the children actually to handle and use the camera. For this reason, I only demonstrate the camera to the group to acquaint them with general features, names, and basic handling and to stress the importance of certain safety features such as keeping the lens cover on when not filming (to prevent scratching the lens) and attaching the camera securely to the tripod (thus preventing the remotest possibility of dropping the camera). After this initial introduction to the camera, the children learn to use it while actually making the film. Because both interest and need are high in this situation, they learn to do it very well.

f. *Filming:* The initial filmmaking periods of forming ideas, writing storyboards, gathering properties, and learning to use the equipment are followed by a period of intense and exciting activity: the filming itself. Filming means lights, camera, action—a lot of action both in front of and behind the camera. The young filmmaker must carefully plan every move made, and must make decisions constantly. It is not possible to erase a filmmaking mistake and not practical to do it over. The children learn quickly that the best policy is careful planning. This begins with the film's inception in the child's mind and continues with the storyboards and the time they spend making properties, but it is most evident during the actual filming. Filming is not hard but it is precise. Children meet this challenge easily, however, since they really want to make films.

Here is a general outline of the steps required to film a shot.

(1) *Set up the backgrounds and properties.* If the children are filming a pixelation sequence, they prepare a background that will fill the camera frame for the objects to be pixelated. They position their objects and make arrangements for them to stand, sit, or whatever position they are to hold while being filmed. Animation layouts can be laid on the floor or a table. Live-action scenes can be set up on location and the children arrange whatever properties—signs, props, actors—they need.

(2) *Secure the camera to the tripod.* If filming is to take place outdoors, it is better to secure the camera to the tripod first and carry the camera outdoors already mounted on the tripod. Mounting is done at the beginning of the period and does not have to be done again.

(3) *Set up the camera.* Setting up the camera is the most exacting procedure. The filmmaker has to adjust the height, angle, and distance of the tripod to frame the shot properly, and then has to choose the proper distance in feet and focus the camera. Any mistakes can result in several types of failures: the edges may show around an animation scene or the camera may move if not properly secured and cause a picture that is wobbly or out of focus. To prevent such failures, which can be very disappointing to young filmmakers, the teacher should check each camera setup before filming. This becomes less urgent as the class progresses and the children become more competent, indeed begin to help each other and check out their own setups.

For *Planet Man,* the poster-paper backdrops were placed on the floor and the camera, attached to a tripod, was angled down. The children who animated the characters sat on the floor and moved the figure parts while others filmed each move with a cable release attachment, which is simply a small cord that will screw into most cameras and, when triggered, shoot one frame at a time. A light was attached to one tripod leg with an adjustable light clamp. I particularly like this method because children are used to working and drawing and painting on poster-paper size; the film's characters are simple to make but very effective on-screen; and working on the floor means nothing can fall off.

g. *Editing:* Editing requires patience, precision, and long fingernails. Children lack only the latter. Despite its demands, this last step is so close to producing a final film that it is usually attacked with relish by young filmmakers.

Especially if made by the whole class or by younger children, films may be edited right in the camera, or shot in sequence so editing is not necessary except to correct mistakes such as a hand filmed by accident during pixelation. If several groups or several individuals are filming on the same roll of film simultaneously, it becomes necessary to splice and edit. When each roll of developed film contains scenes from several films, the children cut out their own scenes. It is better to do this towards the end of the filmmaking period because the film is safer on the roll. Here are the basic steps used during the editing procedure.

(1) *Cutting out the scenes.* Each child views the entire roll of film on an editor or by hand and cuts the desired scenes out of the roll with scissors. It is best if all the children do each roll one at a time since otherwise some scenes could be damaged if not claimed by their owners.

(2) *Using editing bags.* In lieu of an editing bin or similar equipment, each film can be dropped into a large clean paper bag. This keeps the film clean and keeps it from tearing or bending.

(3) *Ordering scenes.* The children place the scenes in the proper sequence by taping each length of film to the inside top of the bag in order with a bit of masking tape, with a number on each piece of tape.

(4) *Splicing.* The Craig Master Splicer, a professional tool that forms a wet splice with cement, is my choice for splicing. Tapes are available and advertised as ideal for the beginner but I find them difficult to use and inferior in quality. It seems worthwhile to teach the professional splicing method because the results are superior.

After the children have demonstrated two good splices on old pieces of film, they can go to work on their film. The following rules were written by children for children:

(a) Keep the emulsion (dull) side up.
(b) The first scene is always on the right.
(c) The top of the picture is always on the right.
(d) Hold the film taut to keep it on the sprockets.
(e) Scrape off all the emulsion.
(f) Use very little glue (wipe the brush).
(g) Replace glue-bottle lid tightly. Spilled glue can ruin a film.
(h) Let the splice dry one minute.

h. *Sound:* Many children's films do not require dialogue. Silent films may have taped music to accompany them. If dialogue and narration are added, the script must be exact, practiced, and then recorded while the film is showing to synchronize sound and visuals.

Making Films without a Camera. The draw-on animation technique, which does not require a camera, is a simple but exciting alternative to filmmaking with a camera. Children simply draw directly on a clear 16-mm film leader with marking pens designed for use on acetate (Cox, 1980).

Buy clear 16-mm film leader where art supplies are sold, or strip the emulsion off an old film in a solution of bleach and water. Wipe dry; store in film can.

For younger children: A whole-class project

1. Brainstorm an idea for a film the whole class can make.
2. Cover a long table with newspaper.
3. Pull a strip of leader the length of the table and secure the reel upright at one end in a blob of clay. Secure the leader in a few places with masking tape.
4. Let three or so children stand on each side of the table and draw on the film in any way they wish.
5. When the film is covered, release the reel and drop the drawn-on film into a large paper bag at the end of the table, pull out a new length of film, resecure the reel, and let a new group of children draw on it.
6. Continue until all the children have had a chance to draw. Repeat if they are still interested.
7. Wind the drawn-on film back around the reel and show as you would any 16-mm film.

A few tips for creating concrete images: 16 frames = 1 second on screen; write words in reverse; move objects slightly to show action.

For older children: Small-group or center filmmaking

See the draw-on films of Norman McLaren, such as *Begone, Dull Care* and *Hen Hop,* available from International Film Bureau, 332 S. Michigan Avenue, Chicago, IL 60604.

35-mm film is the same size as a filmstrip, so you may also begin with a roll of 35-mm exposed film or an unexposed roll of film (this will be harder to clean).

1. Older children may work individually in a center or in small groups.
2. Brainstorm an idea, create a storyboard script, and transfer this to a 16-mm film gauge (see Figure 11–6). In addition to the abstract forms younger children usually make, older students can create concrete representational images of simple shapes and letters, numbers and words. Children love to experiment with this technique and create simple images of flowers growing, eggs hatching, fish swimming, and words dancing across the screen.

Making Filmstrips. An easy introduction or alternative to filmmaking is the making of filmstrips (Cox, 1987). The children create images and write words on blank 35-mm filmstrip the same way they do on clear film leader (see Figure 11–6). Clean off old filmstrips the same way you clean the emulsion off old 16-mm film. Discarded filmstrips can be found in school libraries.

Develop a storyboard and transfer it to a filmstrip gauge. Tape the filmstrip over the gauge and trace the images with pens designed for use on

Figure 11–6 *(1) 16-mm film gauge; (2) 35-mm filmstrip gauge; (3) slide gauge with 35-mm film superimposed to show relative size*

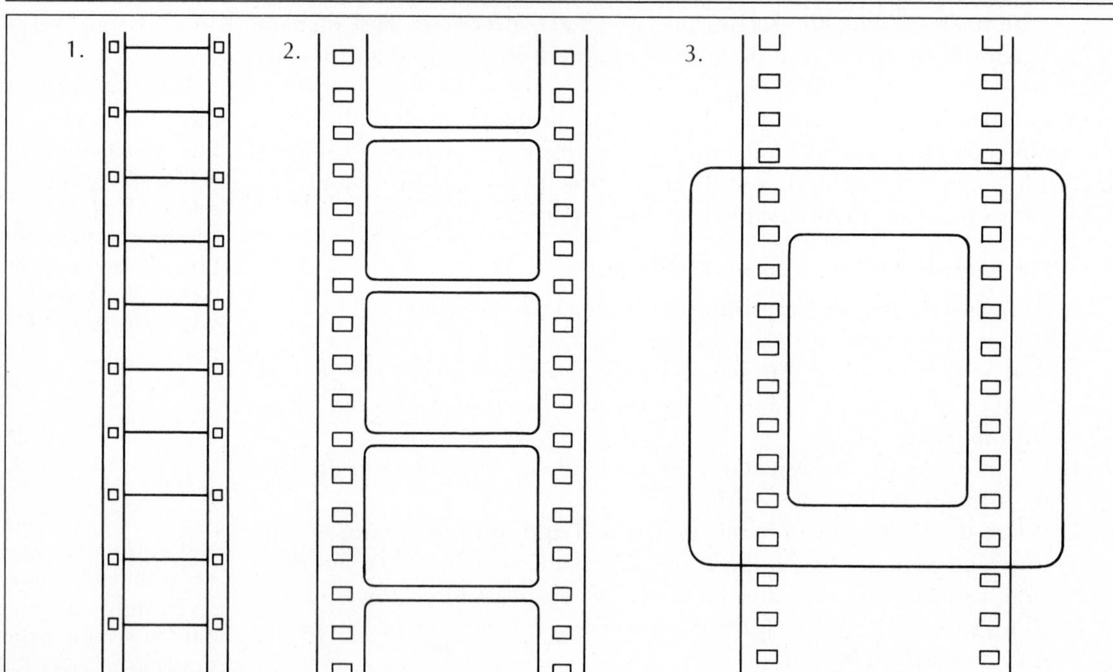

acetate. Add a frame at the beginning for *focus, start tape* (if you use a sound tape to accompany), and a *title.*

Making Slides without a Camera. Use a clean 35-mm gauge blank film (35-mm negative strip or filmstrip) (Figure 11–6) and cut it to fit the size of a paper or plastic slide mount available from discarded slides or at a photographic supply store. The children can brainstorm a sequence of ideas and images, draw directly on the slides, and show the results on a slide projector with the addition of taped sound effects for a slide–tape presentation.

Making Transparencies. Children can also draw on blank transparencies with marking pens designed for use on acetate for a variety of purposes: sharing a favorite book they have read with others, storytelling, or reporting research from the content areas. Since blank transparencies and overhead projectors are available in most schools, this is an extremely easy way for children to make and use the media.

The students may use one transparency at a time or a sequence of several. Or they can attach three transparencies together to form a tryptich with three images that will develop into one when they show the middle one first, fold one side over it to add to the image, and fold the third over the first two to complete the idea or image. The transparencies are joined at the long edge with transparent tape.

Television and Sound and Video Recording

Critical Television Viewing

Critical television skills may be developed in many ways, ways that are ideal to encourage thinking, talking, reading, and writing in the classroom. Here are some strategies that can be done over a short period, or throughout the school year, as children learn to become critical consumers of television.

Keeping a Television Journal. A television journal can be a source of ideas for thinking and talking about television.

- *Record personal television viewing.* The students can note shows they watched, why they chose them, their reactions, and critical comments.
- *React to specific shows.* The children can record their responses to shows the entire class has watched, such as specials, programs related to content area study, and controversial or popular shows. They can also note comparisons of different types of shows.
- *Analyze television treatment of current issues.* Evaluate coverage; compare across networks; compare to the other media (radio, newspapers, news magazines).
- *Collect ideas for videoproduction.* Note possibilities for media production: filmmaking, sound recording, videotaping.

Talking about Television Show Stories. Here are some questions for analyzing literary elements (adapted from Sloan, 1984):

1. *Setting and plot*
   a. Where and when does the show take place? How do you know? If the place and time of the show were different, how would the director and the set designer change it?
   b. With what problem, conflict, or situation does the show start? How did the director get your interest or create suspense?
   c. Tell the main events of the show in order.
   d. Did the show end as you expected? How did you know it would end this way? If you were the director, and changed the ending, how would you change the rest of the show to fit the new ending?
2. *Characters*
   a. Who are the main characters? What kind of persons are they? Describe the actions and dialogue of the actors that let you know this.
   b. Do any characters change in the show? How? Why?
   c. Choose a bit player from the show. Why is this character necessary to the show's story?
3. *Point of view:* Who is telling the show's story? If a character in the story, how is this different from a narrator not in the show?
4. *Mood and theme*
   a. What is the mood of the show? How does the director create it?
   b. Did you have strong feelings as you watched? What did the director or actors do to make you feel this way?
5. *General questions*
   a. Is this show like any other shows you have watched or stories you have read? Does it follow a pattern? What is the pattern?
   b. Are any of the characters similar to those you have seen on other shows?

Talking about Television Show Technical Elements. Here are some questions to ask with regard to the technical elements (adapted from Bilowit, 1981):

1. *Casting:* Did the actors fit their roles? Who else might have played that role? Might the role have been played by someone older, younger, shorter, taller? How would different casting change the nature of the program? Would different casting contribute to or detract from the theme and the overall thrust of the program?
2. *Makeup and costumes:* Were the actors' costumes and makeup appropriate to the actors, the time, the place, and the situation? How might they have been different?
3. *Music and sound effects:* Was the choice of music appropriate for the scene, and did it make the scene better than it would have been with-

out music? Were the sound effects believable? Necessary? Too much? Too little?

4. *Special effects:* Did they look real? How do you think they were done? How else might they have been done? Were they necessary?

Resources for Teaching Critical Television Viewing. Consult the following resources:

American Broadcasting Company
1330 Avenue of the Americas
New York, NY 10019

Columbia Broadcasting System/CBS Reading Program
51 West 52nd Street
New York, NY 10019

National Broadcasting Company
50 Rockefeller Plaza
New York, NY 10021

Prime Time School Television (CBS)
120 S. La Salle, Rm 810
Chicago, Illinois 60603

Critical Television Viewing Skills Curriculum
Southwest Educational Development Laboratory
211 East 7th St.
Austin, Texas 78701

Action for Children's Television
46 Austin St.
Newtonville, MA 02160

The Television Reading Program
Capitol Cities Communications, Inc.
4100 City Lane Ave.
Philadelphia, PA 19131

Teacher's Guides to Television
699 Madison Avenue
New York, NY 10021

Videotaping

Most schools today have a VCR system: a camera in a portapak and other mobile setup, recording deck, and a playback monitor (television). And even very young children are very familiar with television and take readily to this easy-to-use medium. Furthermore, since video is so easy to erase and start over, it lends itself to more spontaneous, improvisational, and on-the-spot experiences, just like its grown-up parent, television. Here is a list of experiences to try as children imagine, think, express themselves, and construct and invent meaning through videotaping.

1. ***Self-reflective modes***
   - *Self-portraits:* The students create self-portraits by collecting images and sounds of places, people, and events that capture their world. Older students can collect art out of school as well. Younger ones can bring objects and people from home.
   - *Role-playing:* The children improvise situations based on an experience they might have: conflict among friends, misunderstanding with a teacher, a meeting with parents and principal. After playback, these can be analyzed and discussed. (This technique can also be applied to historical, social, and cultural situations learned about in the content areas).

See Picture #3 in "Centering Ideas."

2. ***Improvisational/dramatic modes***
   - *Teleplay:* The students act out a situation from life—for example, your best friend tells you she likes someone else better—and develop a storyboard and create a teleplay.
   - *Dramatic reading:* Tapes can be made of reader's theatre, of story dramatizations created to go with wordless picture books, or of students reading their own writing.
   - *Play:* Tapes can be made of creative dramatics or story dramatics.
   - *Television shows and commercials:* Children love to create their own versions of television shows and commercials.

3. ***Documentary/journalistic modes***

   With portable equipment:
   - *Street interviews:* Street interviews can be planned among groups of children with questions related to a specific issue, in or out of the school setting.
   - *Portraits:* Students choose a person that interests them and develop the interview as they go along, creating a portrait of their subject.

   With nonportable equipment:
   - *Newscasting:* Students plan and produce an entire newscast: headlines, sports, weather, on-the-spot reports, commentary, and commercials. The newscast may have a special focus or slant: humorous or fantasy (News from the Moon) or it may be a way of reporting on study in the content areas (News from the Sante Fe Trail, 1890).
   - *In-depth interviews:* Older students may choose a person and develop an in-depth interview on an interesting subject, such as the principal or school discipline. They may also dramatize an interview with a person from the past.

Newspapers

Newspapers can be used in innumerable ways in the classroom. Here is a strategy for introducing the newspaper in middle and upper grades. Many school systems use or have access to a Newspapers in Education program through which sets of newspapers are available for each class in the school throughout the year. If your school system does not have this program, the students may bring newspapers from home to share.

The first thing is to set up a center for the study of newspapers. Gather resources—books and other information on newspapers—and invite the children to do the same. Designate a bulletin board for displaying examples of the parts of a newspaper. Center a discussion around the function of a newspaper and brainstorm a list of student ideas. Chart and save these ideas to refer to later. Each day, give the students time to read whatever they want to in the newspaper and then have an open-ended discussion of what they have read.

Day One. Focus on the general makeup of the newspaper. Together examine the front page, the index, other news pages, the editorial page, and sports stories, feature articles, photographs, charts, maps, puzzles, comics, and advertising. Then have the students find and cut out examples of different news stories: local, county, state, national, and international; features such as editorials, letters to the editor, and editorial cartoons; and display ads and classified ads. In small groups, they can discuss the characteristics and unique features of each.

Day Two. Focus on the organization of a news story. Discuss the stories the children have read that day and what makes them newsworthy. Let them find a story they like and then identify the five *W*s and the *H* of each: What, When, Where, Who, Why, and How.

Day Three. Focus on how news is gathered, on datelines, and on news agencies. Discuss different sources of news. Have them find and cut out examples of news items supplied by the Associated Press and by United Press International; a local story with a byline; syndicated features (by NEA or King Features, for example), and stories datelined in other states and other countries.

Day Four. Focus on the headlines. Discuss some, and have the students rewrite others. You can also have them invent headlines for fanciful news based on a nursery rhyme, a class event, or a story.

Day Five. Focus on sports. Discuss the stories of that day and why sports should (or should not) be in the newspaper. Find articles from different sports classifications: professional, amateur, spectator, seasonal, participation. Have the children write a sports story

Newspapers are an important part of the language arts program

of their own choice about a local college or professional team, a school sports event, or a fictitious sports event.

Subsequent Days. Focus on other parts and functions of the newspaper: comics, entertainment, advertising, business and finance, editorials, advice columns, the weather, horoscopes, and so on. Many of these topics will begin to spill into their discussion and writing and into the content areas. Producing a class newspaper is a logical extension of learning about newspapers.

See Chapter 4, "Writing Class and School Newspapers."

Here are two teacher resources on using and producing newspapers:

American Newspaper Publishers Association (ANPA)
P.O. Box 17407
Dulles International Airport
Washington, DC 20041

Teaching Reading Skills through the Newspaper, 2nd ed.
by Arnold B. Cheyney
International Reading Association, 1984

Magazines

In turn, a logical extension of producing a class newspaper is producing a class magazine or submitting art work or writing to many of the children's magazines that publish children's work. The following magazines accept contributions from children, subject to the limitations described. If your students are interested in sending material to one or more of them, suggest that they first study several representative issues from the library to get a feel for the kind of writing the editors are looking for. Also be sure they look for guidelines that describe the form in which the magazine wants contributions submitted.

Child Life, P.O. Box 567B, Indianapolis, IN 46206. Prints artwork, poetry, stories and letters. (Ages 9–14)

Cricket, Cricket League, Box 100, La Salle, IL 61301. Has monthly contest open to subscribers. Prints story, poetry, and artwork winners. (Ages 5–12)

Ebony, Jr. 820 S. Michigan Avenue, Chicago, IL 60605. Prints letters, riddles, jokes, games, artwork, poetry, short stories. Major works appear as winners of annual writing contest. (Ages 6–12)

The Electric Company Magazine, Editor, Children's Television Workshop, 1 Lincoln Plaza, New York, NY 10023. Runs a monthly joke and cartoon page containing reader submissions. (Ages 7–11)

Highlights for Children, 803 Church St., Honesdale, PA 18431. Prints all forms of original work in "Our Own Page" section. (Ages 5–14)

Jack and Jill, P.O. Box 567B, Indianapolis, IN 46206. Prints articles, letters, artwork, poetry, and stories. (Ages 8–12)

Ranger Rick's Nature Magazine, 1412 14th St., N.W., Washington, DC 20036. Prints poetry, jokes, riddles, games, and letters, and occasionally requests submissions about a specific topic. (Ages 7–12)

Sesame Street Magazine, Art Editor, Children's Television Workshop, 1 Lincoln Plaza, New York, NY 10023. Prints artwork. (Ages 3–6)

Stone Soup, Box 83, Santa Cruz, CA 95063. Entire contents by children: fiction, poetry, artwork, and photography. (Ages up to 13)

The Weewish Tree. American Indian Historical Society, 1451 Masonic Ave., San Francisco, CA 94117. Prints contributions from American Indians. (All ages)

Photojournalism

Many schools and media centers in school systems have cameras for use in the classroom, and I have always found parents willing to loan such equipment, or let students bring their own cameras to use, from 35-mm to Instamatic to Polaroid, the easiest to use. This last is especially effective for use with younger children because the film is processed right in the camera. Even the youngest students can take photos that fall into the following broad areas of composing, expressing, and recording with a camera.

1. *The photo portrait.* Primary students may produce photo essays entitled *All About Me,* using pictures brought from home that document their lives. The pictures they take themselves can form the basis for lan-

guage experience stories and can be bound into books in the classroom. Older students may choose another subject for such a photo essay: a family member or a friend, school personnel, and so on.

2. *The photo illustration.* Photos are one way to illustrate books, newspapers, magazines, and research projects. Younger students can photograph subjects of interest in the content areas, community and school helpers, science projects, pets in the classroom, or field trips. Older ones can use photos in their own newspapers.
3. *The photo essay.* In a photo essay, pictures become the content of the essay rather than merely illustrating the written word. Younger students can take photographs of their family and pets and assemble these and write captions. These photo essays can be displayed on a bulletin board or bound into a book. Older students may create their own fictional or fantasy essay with photographs.
4. *The photo exhibit.* An excellent way for students to share their photographic work is through a class or school photo exhibit of selected works with an audience invited to view and appreciate the children's mediamaking efforts.

Here are examples of some activities, shown roughly in order of ease of use—although all could be used at any level and, once introduced, could become a part of a student's repertoire of media skills.

Order xeroxes of photographs of special events from September 1851 to present from: The New York Times Information Office, 207 West 43rd Street, New York, NY 10036.

- Have students bring in baby pictures and see if the others can guess who they are.
- Examine the works of a variety of well-known photographers, such as Ansel Adams, and compare and contrast their work.
- Make a photo collage of each student by filling in the outlines of their bodies, traced on butcher paper, with photographs of themselves.
- Have students keep a photographic journal, taking pictures at frequent intervals.

Computer Technology

Computers have had a tremendous impact on our culture and on education in recent years and are a familiar part of the landscape of many schools. You may find one in your classroom when you begin teaching, along with a roomful of children who are growing up with computers. The question is no longer whether or not to use computers. The pressing issue in education today is the predominance of computer-assisted instruction, a drill-and-practice approach, in language arts education. Many educators, however, maintain that this offers too narrow a view of the potential of computers in education, and that the teacher's primary role in teaching this new technology and the language arts is to create more situations where children are in control of their own language and learning and are able to explore fully the great range of computer uses (Chandler, 1984; Costanzo, 1985; Newman, 1984, 1985; Papert, 1980; Zaharias, 1983).

Newman (1984) suggests four questions we need to ask about software and computer-based language-learning activities, based on what we know about how children learn to use language, before we proceed to facilitate their learning to use computers.

1. What role does the computer play in language-learning experiences?
2. What is the teacher's role?
3. To what extent does this software let learners take control of their own learning?
4. Does it facilitate a sharing of knowledge?

Keep these questions in mind as we look at the many uses of computers in education, with specific emphasis on language arts education.

Computer Literacy

Four-year-old Gordon comes home from a computer class for preschool children and shows his family a three-piece puzzle he has made of the parts of the computer. As he shows that he knows how to put it together, he starts to talk:

> *Gordon:* Do you know what the parts of the computer are?
> *Parent:* What are they?
> *Gordon:* First you have the CPU. Right here. It goes like this. Then you have the monitor. Here. And then you have a keyboard. You tap, tap, tap, on the keyboard [*simulates with his fingers*]. And then you have a picture on the monitor. It's fun. I like it.

Gordon is taking a first step towards computer literacy. Not so surprising, despite his age, since the culture he lives in surrounds him with the means to become curious and to experiment and even discover for himself what computers are all about. He sees computers on television, at his school, in the dentist's office, and in department stores and watches his high-school-age brother use the computer for schoolwork and to play games with his friends. Gordon often tries to join in these games and play with the computer himself. The computer is as familiar a part of the landscape of his world as his tricycle, his toys, his books, the television, and the illustration from *Goodnight Moon* or the dinosaur posters on his bedroom wall.

What then, is computer literacy? For Gordon, it means recognizing computers and their uses, using them at his own level, and beginning to learn the names that describe them. Computer literacy is what elementary and middle school students need to learn about computers and how to learn with computers. The extent to which this is done, and specific content and skills, will depend on the age and development of the child, what is relevant according to each child's individual interests and needs.

Clements (1985) suggest a scope and sequence of computer literacy for early and primary education based on three assumptions:

1. that teachers should decide how and when to use computers to meet their needs in early childhood education,
2. that computers should be integrated into the curriculum, and
3. that their use should remain consistent with the underlying principles and usual practices of the program (see Table 11–1).

Clement also implies that the development of the whole child is paramount; that computers will not be taught in a unit isolated from language arts, reading, science, social studies; and that different children will learn different things about the computer and how to use it based on their specific needs, interests, and abilities.

What is a Computer? by M. Ball (Houghton, Mifflin, 1972); *Be a Computer Literate,* by M. Ball and S. Charp (Creative Computing Press, 1978); *Computers—A First Look,* by L. O'Brien (Franklin Watts 1978); *COM-LIT: Computer Literacy for Kids,* by C. Horn and C. Collins (Sterling Swift, 1983)

The primary way to help children learn computers, of course, is to provide opportunities to use them. These opportunities should be supported and extended through social interaction: discussions, with another child or small groups of children, about what they are doing; talk with the teacher; or whole-class discussions guided by the teacher. A room environment that includes a computer use center with a bulletin board and related materials such as children's books will also support efforts towards computer literacy (D'Angelo, 1983).

Computer literacy can be integrated into many areas. For example, you might create a bulletin board that shows the basic parts of the computer with labels for computer terminology. These words can be added to children's word lists, used in writing—as in a computer journal—or put on cards and used in spelling and word games. Computer uses can also be learned in the context of social studies learning, as children take note of computers in their environment.

Computer-Assisted Instruction

In computer-assisted instruction, or CAI, the computer serves as a teaching aide, a kind of electronic tutor to teach specific skills, facts, or concepts from the traditional curriculum, such as reading, spelling, grammar, or punctuation. Coburn et al. (1982) have classified these modes as:

1. drill and practice,
2. tutorials,
3. educational games,

Table 11-1 *Teaching Young Children* About *Computers: A Suggested Outline*

	Preschool	Kindergarten	Grades 1	2	3
I. Hardware, Software, Outerwear, and Underwear: What Should Young Children Understand?					
A. What is a computer? How does a computer work?					
1. Models for understanding hardware and software	I	I	I	D	D
2. Computers need instructions	I	I	D	D	D
3. Computers can do many jobs	I	D	D	D	D
4. Computers work with letters, words, numbers, sound, and pictures	I	D	D	D	D
B. What are the parts of a computer? What do they do?					
1. Computer systems and components (parts)		I	D	D	D
2. Models for understanding parts of a computer and what they do		I	D	D	D
C. What different kinds of computers are there?					
1. History					I
2. Types of computers		I	I	D	D
D. Capabilities and limitations					
1. What computers can and cannot do	I	I	D	D	D
2. Artificial intelligence			I	I	D
II. How Are Computers Used in the Neighborhood?					
A. Local applications of computers		I	D	D	D
B. Impact of computers			I	D	D
III. How Can *We* Use Computers?					
A. Getting started: using computers, typing, and problem solving	I	I	D	D	D
B. Computer programming: Now we teach the computer	I	D	D	D	D
C. Using computers as tools: learning what is in the curriculum with computers	I	D	D	D	D

I—Incidental, Informal, Introduction. D—Directed activities, Discussions.

From Douglas H. Clements, *Computers in Early and Primary Education,* © 1985, pp. 54, 101, 92–93. Reprinted by permission of Prentice-Hall, Inc., Englewood Cliffs, New Jersey.

4. simulation, and
5. demonstrations.

The most frequently used of these modes is drill and practice.

Software Cautions. Since CAI represents the most common use of computers in the classroom, language arts teachers should be aware of some of the negative aspects of such commercial software (Nicholl, 1982):

1. The program may be incompatible with the hardware available for use in the school.
2. It may be too costly to merit purchase.
3. It may contain factual errors.
4. It may be pedagogically unsound.
5. It may not quite fit the needs of the class and cannot be modified by the teacher to do so.
6. It may fail to take advantage of the computer's capabilities and, therefore, may be little more than an electronic workbook.
7. Its instructions may be so complicated that students cannot follow them or so verbose that students lose interest before they begin or finish the exercises.
8. Its response times may be too long or too short.
9. Adequate documentation for the program may not be available.

Evaluating Software. Figure 11–7 includes an evaluation checklist that teachers can use to make sure that any program they use is compatible not only with the hardware available in the school but with sound principles of child development and learning language (Clements, 1985).

Information Processing

In addition to CAI, there are many other uses of computers in the classroom that give students more control of their own learning across the curriculum, which fall into the category of information processing: word processors, numerical analysis programs, data processors, instrument monitoring devices, and graphics software (Zaharias, 1983).

Word-processing Programs. Word-processing programs—which allow text editing—and printers—which produce a hard, or paper, copy of the text—allow students to organize, enter, edit, format, and print out anything they write. Writers compose at the computer and can make changes before committing anything to paper. Revision is greatly simplified, without erasing, crossing out, cutting and pasting, and recopying.

I. Establish goals first. Make sure you know exactly what you want the program to do, and insist that it does it.

II. Look into the organizations and journals dedicated to helping teachers locate and evaluate software. If you have any access to a computer, there may be a computerized data base that will allow you to search quickly for the programs you want.

III. When locating software, ensure that service is available (including someone who will answer questions).

IV. Obtain the basic documentation and program.
   A. If you cannot obtain the program for preview, check the following:
      1. Did you attempt to submit a purchase order with "on approval" written on it? Make sure that the company must take back the program if you do not approve the purchase.
      2. Are there demonstration disks or tapes available?
      3. Was field testing done? (Some, e.g., Psychotechnics, do conduct field tests. Write to the sites.)
      4. Are reviews available? (Check who the reviewer was: the closer they are to your situation, the better.)
      5. Is it a reputable company?

      Note: Many organizations, such as the Education Products Information Exchange (EPIE), believe that educators should refuse to buy materials from producers who do not allow preview.
   B. If you can obtain the program:
      1. Go through the program as a successful student would. Test the "intelligence" of the program by making creative or different responses.
      2. Go through the program as a less successful or more "active" student (like "Billy the Bullet") would. Respond incorrectly, not only by making mistakes but also by typing numbers instead of words, hitting the RESET (or RESTORE, BREAK, RUN/STOP, etc.) key, not following directions, and so on. Repeat the same incorrect responses and try different kinds of incorrect responses. What happens? Is the program "bullet-proof"?
      3. If possible, observe several students using the program. Are they interested? Do they understand the program? Do they have any difficulties?
      4. Read the documentation, running through other parts of the program as needed.

V. Complete the evaluation checklist.

Evaluation Checklist

A. Content
   1. Appropriateness of content
      a. Does it match your curriculum? _______
      b. Is it educationally significant? _______
      c. Is it suitable for young children? _______

Figure 11–7 *Steps for Evaluating Software*

From Douglas H. Clements, *Computers in Early and Primary Education,* © 1985, pp. 54, 100, 92–93. Reprinted by permission of Prentice-Hall, Inc., Englewood Cliffs, New Jersey.

2. Is the content accurate? ______

3. Are the values explicitly presented those of your program? ______

B. Instructional considerations

1. Is it consistent with the principles of your educational program? ______

2. Instructional design

a. Are the objectives and purpose well defined? ______

b. Are the prerequisite skills listed? ______

c. Are the learning activities well designed? ______

d. Are the assessments viable? ______

3. Can it be modified for individual students? ______

4. Appropriateness of characteristics

a. Is the teaching strategy appropriate? ______

b. Does it stimulate convergent and/or divergent thinking appropriately? ______

c. Does the child control the rate and sequence appropriately? ______

d. Is the feedback appropriate? ______

e. Does it employ graphics (color and animation) and sound appropriately? ______

f. Is the management appropriate? ______

5. Is field test data available? ______

C. Social/emotional

1. Will the program motivate and sustain interest? ______

2. Will it build self-concept? ______

3. Is there an appropriate balance of cooperation and competition? ______

4. Does it encourage social problem solving? ______

5. Does it encourage sharing? ______

D. Performance/operation

1. Ease of use

a. Can it be used with little effort? ______

b. Are instructions simple? ______

Figure 11–7 *Continued*

c. Is input appropriate? _______

d. Are directions, menus, and on-line help available? _______

e. Is the level of difficulty appropriate? _______

f. Is the presentation clear and consistent? _______

2. Error handling

a. Is the program reliable (free of bugs)? _______

b. Are keys that are not used disabled? _______

c. Can children correct mistakes? _______

d. Does the program limit the number of errors it allows before offering help? _______

e. Can the program handle diverse input? _______

3. Is the operation fast (i.e., loading before and during operation)? _______

E. Is the documentation for teachers and students adequate? _______

1. Are clear directions for loading the program included? _______

2. Is there a full description of the program, including objectives, background, prerequisite skills, etc.? _______

3. Are support materials supplied? _______

F. Global evaluation (1 to 5) _______

G. Comments (strengths, weaknesses, potential):

____

____

____

____

Rating scale: 0–5

0 Characteristic does not exist in program
1 Strongly disagree
2 Disagree
3 No opinion
4 Agree
5 Strongly agree

Figure 11–7 *Continued*

Coburn et al. (1982) report on the use of word processors in schools:

> Schools using word-processing programs have found that even young children will revise their work to correct punctuation, spelling, word selection, sentence structure, and the dozens of errors common to students' writing, such as word and letter juxtaposition. Using word-processing programs encourages students to write who might otherwise avoid writing. All students using such programs tend to write longer, more detailed stories and essays. As a side benefit, learning to use such programs properly often results in the students' overall improvement in following directions (p. 38).

The applications of word-processing programs in elementary classroom are tremendous. In primary grades, teachers can record students' words, ideas, and sentences, and then help them compose language-experience stories, revising and editing as they watch, and discuss the composing process in action (Barber, 1982; Bradley, 1982). Where printing capabilities are available, each child in the class can receive a copy of the story to save for use as a basis for more writing, spelling, or word game experiences. Middle elementary students in small groups may use this same process to record and retrieve research in one of the content areas, as their teacher records for them. Students who know how to use the word processor may also work in small groups, with one student filling the role of the teacher and recording for the others.

Story Maker (Bolt, Beranek and Newman)

Some programs have been created to support children's writing efforts. *Story Maker,* a word processing program developed for use by first-grade children, helps young children to construct stories by offering them choices in the ways a story could be developed. Jo Phenix (Phenix and Hannan, 1984) piloted this program in her own classroom. She describes the effects that using computers for word processing had on her students, including Tim, a reluctant writer who took enthusiastically to the word processor and for the first time did not have to be tricked into writing, wrote increasingly longer, more elaborate pieces, and when he could not get time on the computer, talked the librarian into letting him use her typewriter. Other effects of the computer on children's writing behavior in Jo Phenix's classroom included the following.

- The children wrote and revised more since their writing from the previous day could be loaded on the screen. They then reread what they had written, usually chose to write more on it, and became more critical of their work through conferences and group interaction.
- The children took more risks in writing since it was much easier to insert, delete, rewrite, and erase.
- The children gained confidence in their writing. Since the printout was neat and easy to read, and all writing looked the same, they did not need to worry about letter formation, neatness, and so on.

- Children's transcribing skills improved, for example, spacing between words and standard spelling.

Quill, a word-processing program for older students, was observed in use in a sixth-grade classroom taught by a teacher with a strong media orientation, including computer-assisted writing with particular attention to audience in writing (Bruce et al., 1985). What the observer-researchers noticed most about the use of the word processor in this classroom was the influence not on the technology of writing (speed, printed output, ease of revision), but on the larger classroom writing system. Students interacted with each other more as they milled around the computer waiting for their turn to get on, read each other's writing, and discussed their work together. As a result, these students had a strong sense of purpose for writing and a strong sense of audience. Open-ended programs, like *Quill,* and other word-processing programs, such as *Bank Street Writer, Scriptist,* and *Applewriter,* encourage—in fact, demand—more active involvement and collaboration among students and teachers than do the more commonly used drill-and-practice software used to teach skills in isolation.

Choosing a Word Processor. Here, by way of guidelines for choosing a word processor for children (Piazza & Dawson, 1984), are the attributes to look for in a word processor for children:

1. displays upper- and lower-case letters,
2. automatically moves a whole word to the following line instead of splitting it inappropriately,
3. screen display uses large print with space between lines,
4. words on screen are static rather than scrolled across the page,
5. editing commands are few and easy to remember,
6. editing commands are available on-screen,
7. mnemonic devices are related to some commands,
8. programs can be copied,
9. warning system is available when deleting, and
10. password protect is possible.

Introducing the Word Processing. Here are some suggested steps to follow in introducing the word processor to students (Piazza & Dawson, 1984):

1. The teacher learns the word-processing program.
2. The teacher trains small groups of students to use the word processor.
3. Each student is allowed to explore the word-processing program to see what it can do.
4. The teacher shows the children basic computer commands, such as adding and replacing.
5. Students are allowed to use word processing for short writing periods.

The Uses of a Word Processor. Word processors can be used for a great many purposes through the grades (Newman, 1984):

1. Developing a list of topics. One teacher used an *Applewriter IIe* to prepare a text file called *Topics,* which included headings such as "Things I like to do," "People in my neighborhood," "Things I hate," with spaces for students to list things under each heading.
2. Electronic newspaper. Electronic messages between schools.
3. Written conversations between students or with a teacher.
4. Story dialogue developed from written conversations.
5. Scripts developed from story dialogue.
6. Journal writing.

Computer Graphics

In addition to word processing, children are also learning to produce computer graphics. Genishi, McCollumn, and Stravel (1985) observed kindergarten children using LOGO, a computer language designed as a tool for the discovery of geometric principles (Papert, 1980). Children use a triangle-shaped "turtle" that moves around the screen in response to the child's commands: FD (forward), BK (back), RT (right), and LT (left). The turtle leaves a trail and the child programs the computer to create a shape, picture, or design.

What these researchers noted, above all, was the great amount of social interaction and oral language that occurred among the children and their teacher. In fact, the researchers made two discoveries that somewhat dispel the notion of the computer as either a replacement for the teacher or a dehumanizing, isolating mechanical instrument in the classroom. First, the teacher was at the center of all the activity as the children learned to use the computer; she was in constant demand for help, and transmitted enthusiasm and confidence to the children. Second, these kindergarten children were lively, enthusiastic, and sociable. They were motivated and encouraged to talk and share ideas in a rich set of social interactions as they made discoveries about using computers—precisely the sort of context that encourages all forms of language and learning, whether media-related or not. And this is simply one of many examples that are beginning to show the great potential of computers, and of all the new technologies, in learning and teaching the language arts.

But what exactly happens when one or two or three computers are added to a class of twenty-five students and one teacher? Assuming that teachers really want to take advantage of the potential of computers in the classroom, and also assuming that they may not receive much guidance from a school system itself ambivalent about the use of computers in education, how do you think computers should be used? What is it you are really trying to do when you put children and computers together?

Featured Teacher Joyce Ryder: Using Computers in the Classroom

Joyce Ryder has been using computers in her fourth- and fifth-grade classroom for three years. She shares them with other teachers and has from one to three at a time in her classroom. Here is what she has to say about why and how to use computers.

> What excites me most about using computers in the classroom is the amount of thinking involved. In the past, I often had a hard time doing what I though a good teacher ought to do—help children think, solve problems, and be in control of their own learning. This is hard when you are faced with using one math or spelling text for the whole class. All I taught were facts, and it nagged at me that it was wrong.
>
> With computers, you put children in small groups, let them talk out the problem they are trying to solve, and they immediately begin to handle new information, apply skills, and pay great attention to detail as they work through tasks of many kinds. I'm amazed at the amount of planning, thinking, and the time kids will spend dealing with ideas on their own that has to go on *before* they sit down. I believe it's the motivation of seeing their pictures or words on the screen. The motivational aspects of computers are tremendous.

The following list presents Joyce's approach to using the computers with a limited amount of time and a class of students with very different levels of computer experience.

1. *Computer literacy*

At the beginning of the year, the class becomes acquainted with the computer together; kids who have more experience can help the others. The class discusses what a computer is and how it works and learns new terms and concepts (bits, bytes, information processing, binary, off/on, etc.). Joyce explains things like "When you type the letter A; it goes to the memory box and the computer translates it into an electronic impulse."

Each child buys a disc and initializes it, which means writing a short program. Joyce introduces commands and demonstrates through examples, working at the computer with the students as much as time allows. As Joyce explains, "You can't teach the whole language from A to Z. But they learn about options in creating a program. It doesn't matter what problem you solve. What matters is that when they initialize a disc, they learn by experience to plug it in, turn it on, and communicate with the computer."

2. *Graphics*

The class learns about graphics next because they only require a limited number of commands, the results are immediate, and the students are excited when they see their images on the screen. A number of activities are possible: writing a title, a caption, or a story about a picture; stringing them together to make a story; merging several students' graphics to create a book-length story. Again, Joyce comments:

> We use a graphics worksheet which I introduce in a whole-class lesson with many math concepts: coordinates and points, *x* and *y*. I can go as deep as I want. More with fifth-graders, less with third. I use a large laminated sheet and simple ideas. They work on individual sheets. I like this activity because they have to organize their ideas, order them, plan, and put them on paper, and think about the best way to do it all the time. They learn different ways of ordering information they are dealing with. They can get very elaborate. My students also use *Koala Pad,* a free drawing graphics tablet.

3. *Software*

The class begins to use software available at school or some that Joyce has acquired free through book clubs. Joyce does not use drill-and-practice software; instead, she uses software that increases higher-level thinking, such as simulations. One she likes is Heath Science Software's *Life in the Ocean,* which is used during the unit on oceanography; students read maps, go on underwater missions, keep a ship log, and so on.

Joyce also uses data-base software, which helps students organize information, such as Scholastic's *Secret Filer* and Grolier's *Friendly File.* Another recent discovery she likes is *The Newsroom,* a complete guide to creating a newspaper with all the work areas: banner, photolab, copy desk, layout, wire service, and printing press. It has icons, offers print choices,

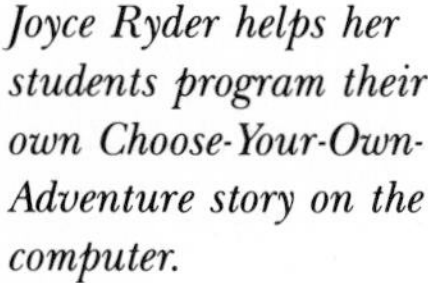

Joyce Ryder helps her students program their own Choose-Your-Own-Adventure story on the computer.

clip art, helps find topics, explains what's in a newspaper, and will print the final product.

4. ***Word processing***

When the class begins word processing, it uses *Bank Street Writer* and starts with simple activities: a letter to parents or a class newsletter. Another project is producing a newspaper with *The Newsroom.*

In the Choose-Your-Own-Adventure activity, students write stories in small groups or as individuals. According to Joyce, "they have to use everything they know for this one," and go through the following steps:

See Chapter 5, "Featured Teacher Phyllis Fuglaar: Writing and Publishing Choose-Your-Own-Adventure Books."

a. Create a flow chart sequence.
b. Add a Roman numeral to every scene.
c. For each Roman numeral, create a scene on one page.
d. Each page has a program line that they have to determine when they create an outline so they don't use someone else's.

Joyce Ryder sums up her approach to using computers in the classroom as follows:

> We do many other activities, and once they have acquired a skill or experience it becomes part of their repertoire and they continue to use it throughout the year, although I'm always introducing new uses. Everything we do is integrated into the rest of the curriculum, and offers great opportunities for each child to do individual projects and solve problems. When there's a bug in their Choose-Your-Own program they have to find it first. They choose to use the computer on their own, and graphics is their favorite. Kids also learn from other kids, and spin off each other's ideas. Computer use just keeps expanding in my room, and mushrooms into wonderful things.
>
> I know teachers feel some barriers to using computers: they feel unprepared; it's time consuming; there are too few computers and sometimes little support from the system; and pressure for a test-teach-text program of instruction. But I had no special courses or instruction. I attended some inservice meetings at my school and then learned along with my students. I do use many guides and idea books—*Basic Apple Basic* is my Bible.
>
> But my students are thinking and programming from the beginning. I don't use a lock-step, literacy-to-software sequence, but rather provide experiences where students are able to learn and practice on their own, and we all learn from each other as we gain control over our own learning.

Summing Up

The photographs at the beginning of this chapter show children using the media arts in the classroom in a variety of ways and for a variety of purposes. No longer technical oddities or for adults only, media such as forms of film, television, and sound and video recording, print- and photojournalism, and computer technology are becoming an integral part of the lives of children both at home and in the classroom.

The National Council of Teachers of English has put forward a rationale for integrating the media into the teaching of English and language arts that is supported by many years of research on the role, effects, and importance of the media in relation to literacy development. The research suggests that students need experiences with these new media that have changed and will continue to change our culture forever.

Many strategies are open to teachers who would help students become literate in nonprint as well as print media: film study, filmmaking with and without a camera, and making filmstrips, slides, and transparencies; critical television viewing and sound and video tape recording; understanding and appreciating the newspaper and creating newspapers and print and photojournalism projects; and learning to understand and use computers.

Teachers who integrate the media arts into their classrooms have found that they offer tremendous opportunities for children to think, solve problems, and create and retrieve meaning as they learn to use language.

Looking Further

1. What kinds of experiences with media have you had? Discuss with others in your class in small groups.

2. Visit your school system's media center and ask to preview several children's films. Start a file of these films, with annotated information shown on the response guide to children's films.

3. Show one of these films to children, direct watch-and-talk groups, and plan activities to extend the film on the response guide to children's films.

4. Ask children to rate several films with the film preference instrument. Rate the films yourself and compare your ratings to theirs.

5. Observe a teacher who makes films with children in the classroom.

6. Make a draw-on film, filmstrip, slides, or transparencies yourself, or with children.

7. Visit the education department of your local newspaper and find out what kind of services and materials they provide for use in the elementary classroom.

8. Observe children using computers in the classroom. Identify which of the aspects of learning about and with computers described in this chapter are evident.

9. Evaluate a piece of computer software for language arts.

10. Start a bibliography of books about computers for children, and resources about computers for teachers.

Chapter Twelve

Research and Study Skills

Objectives

Look for answers to the following questions as you read this chapter.

- How can research and study skills be used in the elementary- or middle-school classroom?
- What are study skills, how should they be taught, and how are they effectively learned?
- How can a teacher teach research and study skills in an already overcrowded curriculum?
- What are some specific strategies for teaching students to find, transcribe, organize, study, and present information?

A Child's View

Here are the comments of four third-grade students interviewed about an independent study project they had done on a topic of interest chosen by themselves.

Mathew on moviemaking: "I liked writing the report and making the movie, even though the rough draft was hard and it took me two whole times of doing the whole thing to get it right. But it took me five times to get the movie right and now I want to start another report and movie—fiction this time. A space monster movie."

Amy on cats: "I've done reports before but this was the only time it was fun. It was a better topic. I got to pick it. I got an idea for my next report after my cat got run over. Bones and fossils and stuff like that."

Thomas on the Chicago Bears: "This was a good thing to do because I wanted to do it because I like the Bears and because I didn't have to have a lot of help. Me and my father got the materials and I found out a lot I didn't know until I read a lot of books about them. It was fun. I want to study a baseball team next."

Robert on killer whales: "I liked the report the best because I liked the writing. And I didn't have any homework. I just worked on the report every night!"

One day towards the end of the school year, Sandi Kim and her mother rode the bus to school dressed in traditional Korean costume. They created a sensation with the bus driver and other bus riders. In Willa Richardson's third-grade classroom they created another when Sandi shared her costume, her mother, and some special Korean food, and reported on an independent project she had done on the topic of Korea.

First, she identified the specific questions she had asked when she began this project.

What are the people in Korea like?
How do they live?
What is their alphabet and language like?

Next, she reported some of the information she had found in answer to these questions:

- People always have to bow because long ago they began to bow to important people like adults and their parents. There is also a special Children's Day in Korea.
- They used to wear very complicated clothes like we're wearing, but now it is more simple, and they wear the same kind as we do. They wear these costumes just on holidays. It's fun to wear the older clothes though. When you raise your arms the shoulder part looks just like a bird's wing.
- The people of Korea aren't very rich because of all the wars they've had. Sometimes they feel like just a little shrimp between the two big whales, China and Japan.
- Girls and ladies like my mother don't have freedom. They can't just walk around anywhere as we can here.
- Seoul is very crowded and most people live in apartments. Children would be lost for sure for sure if they went alone to the markets. There are few cars. Just buses, like in China.
- They used to write Chinese or Japanese but King Sejong didn't like that because it took lots of pages for one sentence so he invented a new alphabet that was simple.
- When a child says "I love my mother" in English, a child would say "I love our mother" in Korean in case they had a brother or sister who would feel sad if they said only "my mother."

Then, she told why she had chosen her topic and where she had found her information.

> My parents are Korean but I was born in Alabama. I wanted to find out more about Korea. We have lots of books at home and I got a lot more from the library. I also read the encyclopedia, magazines, the newspaper, and some pamphlets.
>
> I interviewed my Dad. He was a captain in the Marines and told me all about the war of North and South. He has a little scar on his neck, but his hair hides it.

Finally, she commented on how she felt about doing this research project: "It was fun to do this. I especially like wearing the dress to school. If it had been something the teacher had made me, I wouldn't like it as much. But I liked it a lot so I made it long."

As we saw at the beginning of this chapter, other students in Willa Richardson's class reported on other topics, which cut across the curriculum and were all generated and chosen by the students themselves with the assistance of their teacher and parents. And even though these are all important topics in themselves, what is most important to Mrs. Richardson is that her students practice problem solving and learn critical thinking skills, research skills, and study skills as they question, organize, outline, and gather information from many sources on a topic of interest they chose themselves.

Making Connections

A Reference Point for Research and Study Skills

Devine (1981) describes study skills as

> those competencies associated with acquiring, recording, organizing, synthesizing, remembering, and using information and ideas found in school. Many should be valuable in non-academic settings, but all seem more or less indispensable for school success. All are teachable at all levels to all students (p. 4).

Reading and studying information in the content areas, or researching and writing a report, has less to do with the specific subject or content to be studied or researched, in one sense, than it does with how well a learner is able to identify and solve a problem, and really leads us far beyond the idea of only memorizing information to the idea of processing it and through this to the development of higher mental processes: problem solving, application of principles, analytical skills, and creativity and thinking. In fact, we remember ways to do so long after we have forgotten the specific content learned (Bloom, 1984) since we really do not simply absorb ideas ready made, but construct meaning for ourselves and continue to reconstruct it over time.

Sandi Kim and her mother share traditional Korean dress and food with Sandi's class during Sandi's report on what she learned from her research on Korea.

Students who succeed in school in all subjects and at all levels have learned to do this very well. Whimbey (1984) reports on research (Bereiter & Englemann, 1966; Bloom & Broder, 1950; Frankenstein, 1979; Sadler, 1979; Whimbey & Lochhead, 1983) that has compared students who have succeeded through the school years to those who have not. This research characterizes low- versus high-aptitude students as having contrasting thinking and problem-solving styles.

Low-Aptitude Students: One-Shot Thinking

1. tolerate gaps in knowledge
2. attitude of indifference towards achieving accurate and complete understanding of problems
3. careless and superficial in problem solving
4. spend little time looking for answers to problems
5. choose answers on the basis of only a few clues
6. answers often founded simply on a feeling, impression, or guess

High-Aptitude Students: Precision Thinking

1. actively attack problems
2. use a lengthy sequential analysis to arrive at an answer

3. begin with what they understand of the problem, draw on other information to further clarify, and carefully proceed through a chain of steps that finally arrive at an answer
4. practice an extended, sequential process of constructing understanding and meaning

Research such as this suggests again that what we are really teaching is not content but how to think and solve problems, whatever the content. Students who possess study and research skills are learning to ask and answer their own questions through identification of a problem, are learning where to go to find information, are gaining skill in organizing and finally presenting what they find—a thoroughly understood model of the problem solving process.

The teaching of study skills has become a feature of most basal readers. But Rogers (1984) emphasizes that while study-reading skills are easily adaptable to basal workbooks without relation to a topic the child has chosen or is interested in, they are most meaningfully taught and learned when they enable students to gain information or take action as a result of their ability to use and process reading materials:

Study skills taught in basals: recognizing main idea; noting examples/details; text organization; predicting outcomes; using graphic aids, index, a table of contents.

> Contrived situations such as often occur when students are asked to complete worksheet pages from published materials are not as effective for assessing and teaching study-reading. One of the aims of instruction in study-reading skills is to help young people experience the joy of investigating something of interest to them. This aim cannot be realized by having a student work through a workbook on following directions, summarizing, or previewing (p. 352).

Inquiry across the Curriculum

What is important is that all subjects be taught as methods of inquiry into the nature of the subjects taught, the ways of thinking they represent, as well as for their traditional content. Inquiry learning such as this is characterized by the use of observations, reflections on these observations, direct experience, experiments with real objects and phenomena, and the use of firsthand primary data as well as primary and secondary printed sources.

Ways to do this with children are often surprisingly simple, and appropriate even for very young children. In fact it is often the children themselves—even very young ones—who demonstrate, to parents and teachers, an inquiry approach to learning content and using language. Clem and Feathers (1986) describe a period of "kidwatching" when they both observed five-year-old Joshua at work learning about spiders and learning to use language. One of the authors is his mother; she noted a piece of writing he had done and left lying on the floor. It said: "I LIC SPIDRS CS' SPIDRCR GUD." The authors comment that "Joshua was doing what many middle-school and high-school teachers wish their students would do—he is learning, he is integrating knowledge by forming attitudes toward the subject of study, and he is expressing his learning and his attitudes in writing" (p.143).

To learn more about how Joshua was learning, his observers provided him with many opportunities to investigate subjects of interest to him and to listen, read, talk, and write about them. He observed spiders. He had received the book *Read about Spiders* from a children's book club and reading this book prompted him to draw pictures and ask questions and discuss spiders with his family. He was taken to the library to find more spider books. He was read *Charlotte's Web* as a bedtime story, a few chapters a night. He received a homemade tape recording of *Read about Spiders,* which he often listened to as he read the book. Attempts were made to have him dictate stories about spiders, but the results were stilted. He did initiate some of his own, however, and dictation was given up in favor of the more spontaneous talking, drawing, and writing that Joshua chose.

After a period of watching Joshua learn about spiders and other things of interest to him, the adult observers came to the following insights about how children learn content and use language.

1. Content learning is integrated with other subjects over a period of time; subjects come and go and pique interest in other topics.
2. Content learning is integrated with other aspects of the learner's life and language.
3. Content learning is facilitated when it is learner controlled.
4. Content learning is directly related to the functional use of language.

This study has a number of implications for teaching young children in the classroom:

1. Provide children with more than just story materials or basal reading material, such as nonfiction books, tapes, magazines, newspapers, and encyclopedias.
2. Allow children to investigate more than one topic at a time, and begin inquiry into new subjects as soon as they arise.
3. Provide support for children's self-initiated activities: answer their questions and direct them to where answers might be found.
4. Encourage children to explore their environment and make hypotheses based on their subsequent observations, and then help them to test these hypotheses.
5. Accept and encourage children's self-generated activities and writing.
6. Establish time and space for children to interact in groups and share their ideas, information, and writing with others.
7. Choose a method of evaluation that will not restrict the kind of learning characterized by these suggestions.

Sandi Kim, the third-grader described in "Centering Ideas," did her individual project on Korea in Willa Richardson's class as the culminating activity of a year-long focus on research and study skills that Willa begins on the first day of school. She explains why, in a school day already crowded with basic skills, required subjects, and everything from collecting lunch money to School Adoption Day, she spends more and more time on research and study skills.

Featured Teacher Willa Richardson: Helping Children Solve Problems Themselves

Willa Richardson sums up her own personal philosophy of education as follows:

> We must help children learn how to solve problems themselves. I enjoy it and I think my enthusiasm spills over into the classroom, and whatever we are researching spills over into all other areas of the curriculum. I want to stimulate children to be observant, identify problems, and then know how to gather the data to solve them.

Here's how Willa applies her philosophy, from the first day of school.

Beginning Study Skills: An Environmental Unit

Observing. Willa takes the class outside, to her "outdoor classroom"—a space outside the room where her classes have planted plants and trees and kept animals. Willa asks the students to simply spend some time to use their eyes, and to observe.

Brainstorming. Inside, the class talks about what they saw and learn the scientific method:

1. stating the problem
2. forming the hypothesis
3. observing data
4. interpreting data
5. drawing conclusions

Taking Notes. Willa writes down everything the students noticed that first time to show them how to take notes. "I tell them to be quick, concise, and pick out the main idea." Willa uses the overhead projector and asks questions like, "What did you see?" and "Why do you think it was there?"

Sandi Kim and a friend observe a leaf and take notes in Willa Richardson's "outdoor classroom."

I encourage them to observe everywhere now, correlate their observations with what they already know, and share what they see and read when they come to school. Even though this appears to be science, I try to integrate all this with other subjects: writing, math, reading, social studies, art, music, and learning about the neighborhood. Everything.

Solving a Real Problem: Creating an Aquarium

After a period of observing, brainstorming, and note taking in the outdoor classroom and on other things the students see in the environment, Willa sets up the specific problem of creating an aquarium and asks the class to find out how to create a living environment in it. "This is my way of creating a learning environment where children are in charge of the information they are processing."

Everyone goes to the library and looks for information on tropical fish; the librarian shows filmstrips and films on fish. This then becomes serious research because the students must select (1) the type of water environment they want to create and (2) the type of fish they like and that are compatible. They must then create a real world, choosing from the many types of water worlds of fish.

The students are now solving problems in many areas:

- *Mathematics.* How much do the fish and materials cost? (The class has a limited budget.) Which shop has the best prices and merchandise?
- *Writing.* Willa introduces several poetry forms as the fish are brought into the classroom, especially poetry patterns and haiku.
- *Social studies and science.* Willa skips around in both social studies and science textbooks and uses material related to the aquarium topic—anything on the environment and the ecology of living things.

- *Reading.* Willa's primary goal is to encourage students to look and create questions, "not just ask questions that they think I should tell them the answer to." This carries over into reading, as the students begin to look for the main idea and set up a sequence of steps for problem solving. "I want them to begin to think this way."

Putting It All Together: A Trip to a Wildlife Refuge

In January, this very broad environmental study becomes more focused and culminates with preparation for a trip to a wildlife refuge. The class visits Sabine National Park and Holly Beach and spends the night in the Rockefeller Wildlife Refuge. "Since we live in Louisiana our emphasis all along has been on wetlands. We take microscopes and do observations at the beach and take notes and collect specimens."

This is obviously a big event in the year, one that requires a lot of preparation and parental involvement. This year, twenty children and fifteen parents went along on the trip. They write to government agencies for pamphlets and also become experts in map skills. Willa xeroxed a map of the area and they planned a route, figured mileage, places to stop, and a timed itinerary. They had the most fun planning their menus and what they would take to eat.

> But the best part is all the things that happen after we return, and the children have this great wealth of impressions, ideas, and data to draw on. The writing that follows is wonderful. They are perfectly primed up. Until I began to do this, I didn't know children had such insight. And it all expands and gets bigger. In reading and spelling, they become intensely interested in books on the subject, and correctly spelling words they will use to write thank you letters, and letters of inquiry for more information. There is so much opportunity to learn so many things.

Independent Project:
Children Choose and Research a Topic

This is an opportunity for each child to choose some area that they really want to learn more about and use all of the skills they have learned to work on an independent study project.

Choosing a Topic. After the trip, Willa asks the children to make a list of the things they are interested in. Then, she schedules a private conference with each one to talk about his or her interests and help pinpoint a topic. "It takes a while to focus and they haven't always been asked to do this." With Willa's help, each student narrows it down to three choices and then takes another week to think it over: this time, they each talk it over with their parents to choose one final topic. Willa involves parents because this is a big project and the children often need help getting supplies and going to the library. But the children must choose from three topics they have developed themselves; parents are not supposed to choose for them. But everyone works as a three-way team: child/parent/teacher.

Schedule. Each child works independently on his or her own topic, using the following schedule of dates when everything is due.

Schedule of Important Dates for Independent Project

1. Choose topic	Week 1	_______	
2. Develop questions	Week 2	_______	
3. Find information & take notes	Weeks 3–4	_______	
4. Rough draft	Weeks 5–6	_______	Revising and editing drafts during writing period (Items 4–9)
5. Outline	Week 7	_______	
6. Bibliography	Week 7	_______	
7. Creative product	Week 7	_______	
8. Cover & illustration	Week 8	_______	
9. Complete report	Week 9	_______	

Card Files. Students record each source of information and ideas on 3 × 5 cards. This is one of the ongoing activities that becomes important now.

Developing Questions. After the students have done some reading and developed a card file of references, they need to develop specific questions. The class has already talked about the important where, when, why, how, and who questions and developed ten or twelve questions to talk about. Willa helps the children make the questions broad enough, because if they are too narrow, students will not find enough data. "It is hard at first to get them to think big, to look for underlying ideas. They get picky. When was someone born? When did they die?"

Finding Sources of Information. Willa's class must use five different types of data.

1. *Magazines.* The children learned to use magazines during the nine weeks of library study. Right after the children have chosen their topics and received their packet of materials, Willa schedules an evening for children and parents in the main public library. They talk about where and how to find information and the project schedule. The librarian uses transparencies to show them how to use the *Reader's Guide.* Students are familiar with the card catalogue and have used the *National Geographic* guide already in the classroom. Afterwards, Willa works with parents and children as they begin to look up information and handle the magazines.

Students can collaborate on a research project using the encyclopedia as a source of information.

2. *Encyclopedias.* Students use more than are in class, in the library, and at home.

3. *Books.* This project is an opportunity for students to really put to use what they have learned about the card catalogue and Dewey Decimal System.

4. *Newspapers and pamphlets.* Willa brings a newspaper to class every day and the students all look for related topics of information. During the environmental unit, the class found lots of information related to pollution control and waste dumping in Louisiana.

5. *Interview.* Each student must do one interview, and they really enjoy it. Willa has developed a file of sources each semester. Her students have interviewed the head coaches of Louisiana State University and Southern University, the mayor, the head of the zoo, and the like. They also interview their parents (like Sandi Kim) or other teachers. Students use a question guide, develop specific questions, tape record the interview, and take pictures.

Writing the Report. The class spends a lot of time writing: transcribing notes and ideas; writing summaries; writing paragraphs; organizing; outlining; drafting; conferencing with Willa and other students in peer editing groups. They follow the schedule Willa has set up, and she discusses each student's progress with him or her each week.

The finished report will include:

- Title Page: Tile, Name, Date
- Table of Contents: Each section follows the outline, with page numbers
- Outline
- Introduction: Why they chose the topic and what they did
- Body of the paper
- Bibliography (Willa only requires author and title for third-graders.)

Other creative products; puzzles, poetry, commercials, mobiles, dioramas, maps, comic strips, costumes, experiments.

Creative Products. Students brainstorm ideas, and Willa suggests possible creative products. The parents really become involved here because a third-grader needs help and it often becomes a family project. Students need guidance and background.

Others become involved. One child had the whole School of Veterinary Medicine and the graduate students helping. Here are some possible products—some easy and some more elaborate.

- *Poster.* This is the simplest. It can be photos of the interview, pictures cut out of a newspaper or magazine, or an original design.
- *Game.* Some children enjoy this and adapt their topic to a popular game: Trivial Pursuit, Life, Monopoly.
- *Costumes and food.* Sandi Kim and her mother came to school in traditional Korean dress and prepared Korean food.
- *Build a model.* One boy made a solar energy focusing collector, which used aluminum foil, and cooked a hot dog. It took all day, but it worked, and he was really proud.
- *Mediamaking.* One child made a Super-8 film, another made overhead projector transparencies, and a third did a slide show.
- *Artistic effort.* Melody wrote a song for her project on music and singing. Another student did block prints of scenes from U.S. history.

Sharing. The students all share with the class. Willa encourages them to share their creative product with another class but doesn't require it. All products are displayed in library, and they have an open house when the parents come.

After Willa Richardson helped the children to identify a problem and generate questions and hypotheses aimed at solving it, she set in action a sequence of several steps for problem solving—and thinking, research, and study skills. Grouped here under the broad categories of finding, transcribing, organizing, studying, and presenting information, are these and other strategies you can use to encourage children to observe, question, hypothesize, collect data, experiment, and think as they learn. Many of these strategies cut across all grade levels, from primary to middle school, although many are most appropriate for upper elementary- and middle-school students. For instance, certain reference tools such as the *Reader's Guide to*

Periodical Literature are not usually available until middle school. Consider these ideas as triggers to set off your own thinking, as you encourage children to do the same.

Finding Information

There are many sources of information for elementary and middle school students. See Table 12–1 for a listing.

Table 12–1 *Sources of Information for Elementary- and Middle-School Students*

	Primary Sources				
	Personal Experiences	*Field Trips*	*Guest Speakers*	*Experiments*	
In School	Memory On-going Classroom School	Library Cafeteria Principal's office Maintenance	Teacher Other teacher School personnel	Observations Hypotheses tested (see ESS units)	
Out of School	Trips Extracurricular activities	Business Govt. agencies Parks & zoos Museums Monuments Entertainment events	Professionals Experts in field (develop a resource person file; check Yellow Pages)	Surveys Interviews	
	Secondary Sources				
	Children's Literature	*Periodicals*	*References*	*Vertical File*	*Media*
Library/ Media Center	Fiction Nonfiction Biography Magazines	Journals Newspapers Reports	Dictionary Thesaurus Encyclopedia Atlas	Pictures Pamphlets Clippings Miscellaneous	Study pictures Slides Filmstrips Films Tapes Records Videotapes Games Transparencies Dioramas Models Specimens

Interviews

Interviews are an excellent source of primary information. Willa Richardson required her third-graders to conduct interviews as part of their independent projects. (When I interviewed them about their projects, they all said they enjoyed the interview most.)

Interview Questions. To prepare the children, Willa gave them the following set of sample questions, which they adapted for the person they chose to interview, either on tape or by taking notes.

1. What is your job title?
2. What does your job involve?
3. What special training or experience did you need for your job?
4. How did you find your job?
5. What do you like about your job? Dislike?

Younger children, too, can gather information through interviews by asking questions in a whole-class situation with a guest in the classroom or as part of a trip to another part of the school or community.

In a description of a first-grade classroom where all the children interviewed a police officer (one of a series of community helpers to visit the classroom), Haley-James and Hobson (1980) enumerate the benefits of an interviewing program for these and older students: the students observed are able to assume adult language roles; the drive to communicate is encouraged as they ask questions; they are eager to write and read the results of the interview; they are in control of their own language and learning; any child can succeed; interviewing unifies all the language processes; and children discover language rules and conventions about language based on their own experiences and observations. Observable outcomes in this first-grade class were that the children wrote longer personal and group language-experience stories; they used more sophisticated language; they learned to spell the special vocabularies of the policeman, the artisan, the author, the newspaper editor, the nurse, the pilot, and the state representative; and their communicative drive was reinforced as they shared what they had written with others.

The researchers suggest the following guidelines for teachers who wish to initiate an interviewing program:

1. *Practice interviews.* Simulate a practice interview. The children may interview you about an interest of yours (bring an object to start questions).
   - Give them only the information they ask for. If they ask only yes/no questions, give only yes/no answers. Help them develop broader, higher-level questions.
   - Evaluate the interview. Ask which questions solicited the most information. Develop more practice questions.

- Have the students interview each other in pairs, and evaluate in the same way.

2. *Writing up the interview.* Support children's writing, and help them clarify the meaning through questions during conferencing. Teach needed spelling and conventions in context.

3. *Sharing the interview results.* Encourage the children to read or describe their interviews to others in the class, in school, or at home. Interviews may be shared in many other ways: in a research report, through bookmaking, and through many mediamaking activities—documentary filmmaking, making filmstrips, slides, or transparencies, sound or video tape recording—or through student-produced newspapers or magazines.

Using Books

Tradebooks. Perhaps the richest source of information for students are good children's tradebooks, both fiction and nonfiction. You will, of course, have a classroom library of these. But if you plan to launch students into an area of inquiry, particularly at the beginning of the year—as Willa Richardson did with the problem-solving project of setting up an aquarium—you can develop a specialized temporary collection of books with the children's help. Willa did this when her students learned to use the library by finding books on fish.

A Great Aquarium Book, by Jane Sarnoff (Scribner's, 1977); *Caring For Your Fish,* by Mark McPherson (Troll, 1985); *What Do You Want to Know about Guppies?* by Seymour Simon (Four Winds Press, 1977)

References for teachers that list books by subject, or will guide you to useful books, include:

Subject Guide to Children's Books in Print (Annual) (Bowker)
Children's Catalog (Annual) (H. W. Wilson)
The Elementary School Library Collection (Annual) (Bro-Dart)

Textbooks. Elementary textbooks in the content areas are available in all schools. Students should know how to use the various parts of these, not only when they are used for a unit of study but as another source of information for children on self-chosen topics. For example, Willa Richardson selected all chapters on the environment in the social studies and science texts in her room to integrate with students' observations, aquarium building, and a field trip to a nature refuge. The skills that children learn by using a textbook then become tools they can use with any nonfiction or reference book.

The parts of the textbook that children should know about and be able to use are listed below, with sample questions a teacher could use to guide the whole class through an introduction to the textbook. This is a good way to assess how well children are able to use textbooks. The questions here refer to a fourth-grade social studies text, a page of which is reproduced in Figure 12–1.

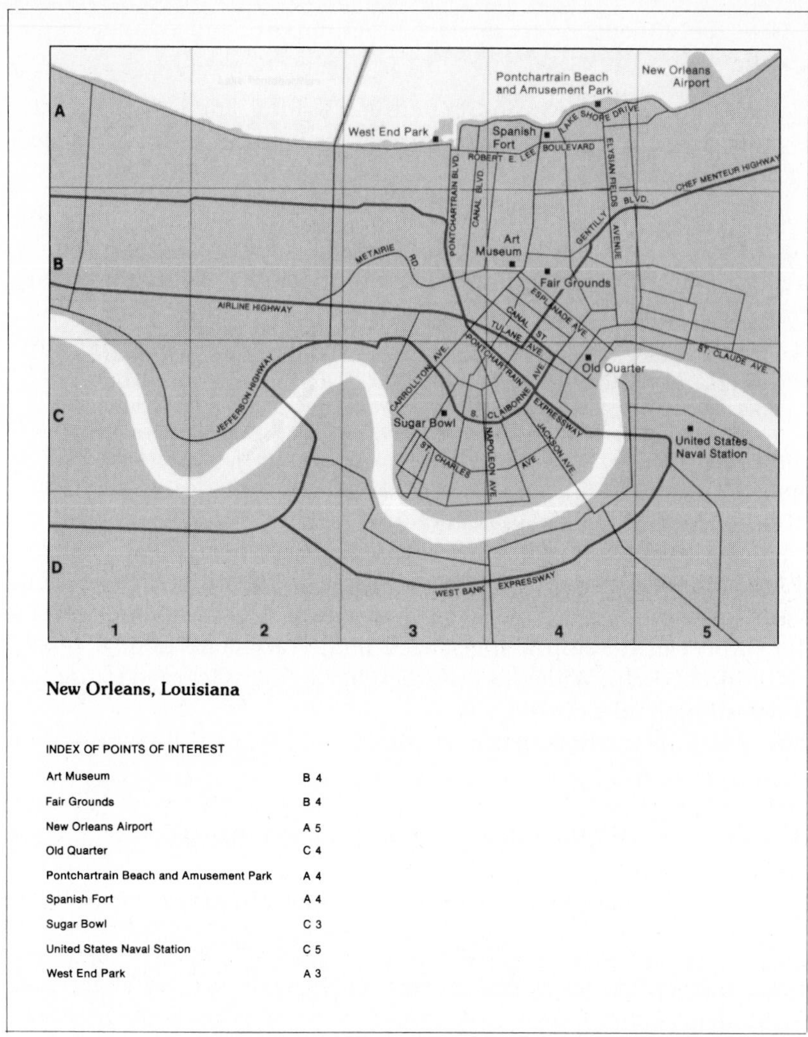

Figure 12–1
Example of a Fourth-grade Social Studies Text

From *Regions Near and Far* (D. C. Heath & Co.: Lexington, MA, 1985), p. 157.

1. Table of Contents
   - "This book tells something about a city in Louisiana. Which city?" (New Orleans)
   - "What page?" (158)
   - "Which chapter?" (9, "Living in the Southeast")
   - "Which unit?" (The Southeast: A Forest Region)

2. Glossary
    - "Turn to p. 158. Skim the section on New Orleans. Look for two words in boldface print (darker than the others). What are they?" (*Dike, process*)
    - "Look these words up in the glossary at the back of the book. What do they mean?"

3. Index
    - "Turn to the index in the back of the book. See whether New Orleans is listed and whether there are any other pages with information about it." (pp. 147, 157, 158–160)
    - "What does *m* mean? Look at the key at the beginning of the index to help you find the answer."

4. Maps
    - "Find the map of New Orleans. Locate the places listed in the legend, or key."

5. Pictures
    - "Find the pictures of the Old Quarter in New Orleans located between pages 158 and 160. Read the caption."
    - "What kind of music do you think this band is playing in the Old Quarter? Why do you think that?"

Continue this type of introductory questioning and informal assessment with other parts of the textbook: diagrams, charts, tables, graphs, study questions, and study aids.

Reference Books. Students learn to use reference books by using them. A good introduction for primary through upper elementary children is to have them create their own reference work, such as a class telephone directory, at the beginning of the year. Individually or in small groups, students can create their own encyclopedias or biographical index on a particular interest or passion, alphabetized according to subject. For example: sports, hobbies, pets, favorite entertainers.

Share and describe the use of reference books appropriate for your students (and do not underestimate the children—it is amazing what they can master when they are interested in finding something out). Explain what kind of information can be found in each type of reference book and how to go about finding it and emphasize the value of reference materials for finding out what one needs to know in order to solve a particular problem. Establish a classroom library of reference materials you inherit from other teachers or collect from parents, or find at garage sales—a terrific source of good books.

Encyclopedias. Most libraries have several encyclopedias. Show them all to your students. Point out that the encyclopedia is a good place to start learning about something because each article introduces the reader to the most important information on a topic, a kind of general overview with a list of related topics at the end. Show the children how to look up an article by first letter of topic, and do this with them. Let them suggest topics of interest. Point out that many are cross-referenced to other articles to help them find out more. Here is a list of encyclopedias commonly found in school and public libraries.

Late Primary

Britannica Junior Encyclopaedia
The New Book of Knowledge

Middle Elementary

The World Book Encyclopedia
Challenger: The Student's Encyclopedia

Upper Elementary and Middle School

Compton's Encyclopedia

Middle and High School

Collier's Encyclopedia
Encyclopedia International

High School, College, and Adult

Encyclopedia Americana
The Encyclopaedia Britannica

Specialized Reference Books. There is a rich variety of specialized reference materials in any school library, among them atlases, almanacs, yearbooks, directories, gazetteers, and biographic dictionaries. Here is a sample of reference works you can expect to find in a school library.

World Atlas
Atlas of American History
World Almanac and Book of Facts
Information Please Almanac
Who's Who in America
Contemporary Authors
Book of Junior Authors
Bartlett's Familiar Quotations

Dictionaries. Show the students some of the many types of dictionaries available, some of which should be a permanent part of the class collection.

The examples listed below range from the simplest to more complex ones and also include specialized dictionaries. Figure 12–2 shows a sample page from an elementary dictionary.

Picture Dictionaries for Primary Grades

The Cat in the Hat Beginner Book Dictionary (Random House)
The Golden Picture Dictionary (Western Publishing Co.)
My First Picture Dictionary, revised edition (Lothrop/Scott, Foresman)
My Pictionary (Lothrop/Scott, Foresman)
My Second Picture Dictionary (Lothrop/Scott, Foresman)
The New Golden Picture Dictionary (Western Publishing Co.)
Storybook Dictionary (Western Publishing Co.)
The Strawberry Picture Dictionary (Larousse)

Elementary School Dictionaries

The Charlie Brown Dictionary (Random House)
Scott, Foresman Beginning Dictionary (Doubleday/Scott, Foresman)
Troll Talking Picture Dictionary (Troll Associates)
Macmillan Dictionary for Children (Macmillan)
Weekly Reader Beginning Dictionary (Grosset & Dunlap) or *The Ginn Beginning Dictionary* (Ginn)
Xerox Intermediate Dictionary (Grosset & Dunlap) or *The Ginn Intermediate Dictionary* (Ginn)

Middle School Dictionaries

The American Heritage School Dictionary (Houghton Mifflin)
Macmillan School Dictionary (Macmillan)
Thorndike-Barnhart Intermediate Dictionary (Doubleday)
The Random House Dictionary (Random House)
Webster's Intermediate Dictionary (Merriam)

High School and Adult Dictionaries

American Heritage Dictionary (Houghton Mifflin)
Webster's New World Dictionary of American Language (World Publishing)
Oxford Dictionary (Oxford University Press)

Students learn to use a dictionary most easily when they actually have a need for it. But there are several skills that do need to be taught directly. (This also helps avoid the syndrome of the teacher telling children to look up a word in the dictionary when they do not know how to spell the word or how to use the word once they do find it.) The best way to use a dictionary is as a source of definitions and word meanings, and as a general

See "Fun in the Word Factory: Exercises with the Dictionary," by Rosemary M. Laughlin, in *Language Arts,* 55 (1978), 319–321.

A a

hat, āge, fär; let, ēqual, tėrm; it, īce;
hot, ōpen, ôrder; oil, out; cup, pu̇t, rüle; ch, child;
ng, long; sh, she; th, thin; ᴛʜ, then; zh, measure;

ə represents *a* in about,
e in taken, *i* in pencil, *o* in lemon, *u* in circus.

A or **a** (ā), the first letter of the alphabet. There are two *a*'s in *afraid. noun, plural* **A's** or **a's.**

a (ə *or* ā), 1 any: *Is there a pencil in the box?* 2 one: *My mother wants a pound of butter.* 3 every: *Thanksgiving comes once a year. adjective* or *indefinite article.*

a back (ə bak′). **taken aback,** suddenly surprised: *He was taken aback by his friend's angry answer. adverb.*

ab a cus (ab′ə kəs), frame with rows of counters or beads that slide back and forth. Abacuses are used in China, Japan, and Korea for counting. *noun, plural* **ab a cus es, ab a ci** (ab′ə sī).

a ban don (ə ban′dən), 1 give up entirely: *She abandoned her hope of being a nurse.* 2 desert, forsake, or leave without intending to return: *A good mother would not abandon her baby. verb.*

a ban doned (ə ban′dənd), deserted: *The boys often play in the abandoned house. adjective.*

a base (ə bās′), bring down; make lower: *A man who betrays his country abases himself. verb,* **a based, a bas ing.**

a bashed (ə basht′), embarrassed and confused: *The shy little girl was abashed when she saw the room filled with strangers. adjective.*

a bate (ə bāt′), 1 make less: *The medicine abated his pain.* 2 become less: *The storm has abated. verb,* **a bat ed, a bat ing.**

ab bess (ab′is), woman who is the head of an abbey of nuns. *noun, plural* **ab bess es.**

ab bey (ab′ē), 1 the building or buildings where monks or nuns live a religious life. 2 the monks or nuns living there. *noun, plural* **ab beys.**

ab bot (ab′ət), man who is the head of an abbey of monks. *noun.*

ab bre vi ate (ə brē′vē āt), make shorter: *We can abbreviate "hour" to "hr." verb,* **ab bre vi at ed, ab bre vi at ing.**

ab bre vi a tion (ə brē′vē ā′shən), a shortened form: *"Dr." is an abbreviation for "Doctor." noun.*

ab di cate (ab′də kāt), give up (office, power, or authority); resign: *When the king abdicated his throne, his brother became king. verb,* **ab di cat ed, ab di cat ing.**

ab di ca tion (ab′də kā′shən), resigning. *noun.*

ab do men (ab′də mən), 1 the part of the body containing the stomach, the intestines, and other important organs; belly. 2 the last of the three parts of the body of an insect. *noun.*

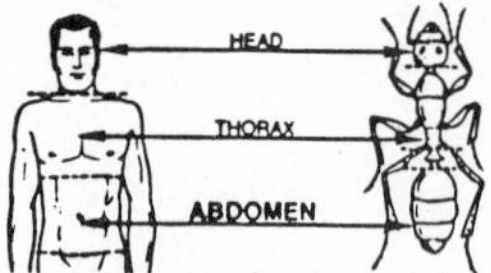

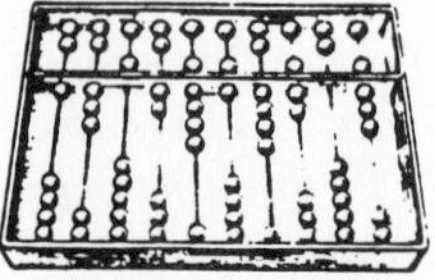

abacus—beads above middle bar, 5 each when lowered toward bar; beads below middle bar, 1 each when raised toward bar. Beads above and below the middle bar are totaled in each row. Numbers are shown below each wire for the setting of 1,352,964,708.

ab dom i nal (ab dom′ə nəl), of the abdomen; in the abdomen; for the abdomen: *Bending the body exercises the abdominal muscles. adjective.*

ab duct (ab dukt′), kidnap. *verb.*

ab duc tion (ab duk′shən), kidnaping. *noun.*

ab hor (ab hôr′), shrink away from with horror; feel disgust for; hate very, very much: *Many people abhor snakes. verb,* **ab horred, ab hor ring.**

a bide (ə bīd′), 1 put up with; endure: *A good housekeeper cannot abide dust.* 2 stay; dwell: *Abide with me for a time. verb,* **a bode** or **a bid ed, a bid ing.**
abide by, 1 accept and follow out: *Both teams will abide by the umpire's decision.* 2 remain faithful to: *Abide by your promise.*

a bid ing (ə bī′ding), permanent; lasting: *The old sailor had an abiding love of the sea. adjective.*

a bil i ty (ə bil′ə tē), 1 power: *A horse has the ability to work.* 2 skill: *Washington had great ability as a general.* 3 power to do some special thing; talent: *Musical ability often shows itself early in life. noun, plural* **a bil i ties.**

ab ject (ab′jekt), 1 wretched; miserable: *Many people still live in abject poverty.* 2 deserving contempt: *Shame on you for your abject fear! adjective.*

a blaze (ə blāz′), on fire; blazing. *adjective.*

a ble (ā′bəl), 1 having enough power or skill: *A cat is able to see in the dark.* 2 having more power or skill than most others have: *She is an able teacher. adjective,* **a bler, a blest.**

-able, suffix meaning "that can be _____ed." Enjoy*able* means *that can be* enjoy*ed.*

a bly (ā′blē), in an able manner; with skill; well. *adverb.*

ab nor mal (ab nôr′məl), not as it should be; very different from the ordinary conditions; unusual: *It is*

Figure 12–2 *Example of a Children's Dictionary*

From *Scott, Foresman Beginning Dictionary* by E. L. Thorndike & Clarence L. Barnhart.

reference tool. Here are some examples of skills to teach to middle- and upper-elementary students; these skills are best taught in the context of content that interests children or that they have a real need to know.

The Scott, Foresman Beginning Dictionary provides an excellent introduction to the dictionary around the theme of zoo animals and ecology.

1. *Alphabetical order.* Make sure that your students know the alphabet. (A simple check is to have them write out the letters in order.)

2. *Guide words.* Knowing how to use guide words can save children the time and frustration of looking through an entire letter. Show them a sample page on the overhead projector, and tell them how to use guide words.

- **a.** Make a list of words that the children suggest and have them find the guide words for the page for each. They could work in groups, each with a different list.
- **b.** Give the children a page number in the dictionary, with its guide words. Next, give them a list of words and have them circle the words that would be on that page, without checking the page. Have them verify by checking in the dictionary.

3. *Parts of a dictionary entry.* Using a word the students need to know as an example, explain the parts of a dictionary entry, and let them answer questions. A good way to do this is with a transparency for overhead projector; check with your library to see if commercial ones are available. If not, you can prepare your own. Students in small groups can also create study sheets for other students, exchange them, and verify each other's answers.

4. *More than one meaning.* Choosing the correct meaning of a word is a critical aspect of dictionary use. Even through middle school, students often think all the dictionary meanings (for a given word) are interchangeable, since they are all in the dictionary. Encouraging students to pinpoint meaning and see that all meanings are not identical is important. This is best done as the need arises.

5. *Reference use of a dictionary.* The dictionary is also a source of information. Teachers can copy a page and create questions for students to answer in an area of interest to practice this skill.

Thesauruses. Another essential reference tool for the classroom is the thesaurus, and students are never too young to begin to use it as they become interested in finding more than one word for a given meaning. Here are three thesauruses, listed in order of complexity, from easiest to most difficult.

In Other Words: A Beginning Thesaurus (Scott, Foresman)
Words to Use: A Junior Thesaurus (Sadlier)
Roget's Thesaurus (Random House)

Phyllis Crawford (1981) describes how her students created their own thesaurus and dictionary after the following "If I Were" pattern writing:

If I Were

If I were a pig, a plump filthy pig,
If I were a pig, this is what I would do.
I would grunt, grunt, grunt, grunt, grunt.
That's what I would do.

As Phyllis explains, "Students find other words for some of the words in their pattern. Example: *dirty, unclean, grimy, grubby,* etc., can be substituted for *filthy* when putting the pattern together. *Fat, stout, corpulent,* can be substituted for *plump.*" This activity can be used with any pattern and the pattern can be used for any subject. Here is an example using the subject *wreaths:*

If I were a wreath, *a* splendid hanging wreath,
If I were a wreath, *this is what I would do.*
I would delight, delight, delight, delight, delight.
That's what I would do.

This time the class took the word *wreath* and decided to make a class dictionary that contained only *wr* words. They considered this an unusual word because the *w* is silent. Each page contained the following:

Wrist—*rist, name word (noun). The part of the arm between the forearm and the hand. "The heavy girl broke her left* wrist."

The pages were put together in alphabetical order. The class also did this activity with *kn* and *gn* words, which were brought up after use by the class or an individual student in writing another creative pattern.

Phyllis Fuglaar asked her students to use a thesaurus to find substitutes for the words in the titles of well-known stories. Then she read the new titles aloud for the whole class to guess what they were. Can you guess?*

1. *Trio of Diminutive Hogs*
2. *The Petite Scarlet Fowl*
3. *Slumbering Symmetry*
4. *The Treasure Effect*
5. *Mouser in Soles*
6. *The Diminutive Vermillon Biddy*
7. *Elderly Belle That Dwelled in a Pump*

**Answers:* 1. The Three Little Pigs. 2 & 6. The Little Red Hen. 3. Sleeping Beauty. 4. The Golden Touch. 5. Puss-in-Boots. 7. The Old Woman Who Lived in a Shoe.

The Library Media Center

Arrangement and Use. Walk the students through the library and identify the location of the following.

- the circulation desk
- the card catalogue
- the vertical file
- shelves for:
    - picture books
    - easy-to-read books
    - oversized books
    - fiction
    - nonfiction
    - biography
    - reference books
    - periodicals
    - audiovisual materials

Describe the types of materials in each category. Have the students make a map of the library, with a key identifying the different parts. In small groups, have the children compare and revise their maps and start a loose-leaf notebook with information on how to use the library.

Card Catalogue. Show the students a book on a subject of interest and then show them an enlarged version of the three types of cards used for such books (see Figure 12–3). You can use poster paper or the overhead projector.

Explain that if you are looking for a book by title, you look under the first letter of the first important word in the title; you will be using the title card. Two other cards for each book include the same information in a different arrangement, except that the subject card also lists the topic of the book; this is one way students can search the card catalogue itself for information. All the cards are arranged in alphabetical order by the first important word in the title, the author's last name, or the first important word of the topic, in the drawers of a cabinet labeled with the letters of the alphabet. Some larger libraries will have a separate cabinet for each type of card. Children may understand these cards better if they make their own for books they have written for their classroom library. They can compile their own card catalogue of student-authored books, and keep it in a 3 × 5 file card box.

The Dewey Decimal System. Once the children have found the card for a book they want, they need to know how to find the book on the shelf. The Dewey Decimal System groups nonfiction books in categories with corresponding numbers; these are known as call numbers (see Figure 12–4). (Another system is the Library of Congress system, but most schools use Dewey Decimal.)

Subject Card

```
     AQUARIUMS

x639.34      Sarnoff, Jane.
           A great aquarium book: the putting-
        it-together guide for beginners/by Jane
        Sarnoff and Reynold Ruffin. - New York:
        Scribner, c1977.
                47p.:col.ill.;26cm.
        SUMMARY:A beginner's guide to creating
        a basic aquarium, with information on
        selecting fish and providing for them
        a comfortable, healthy environment.
```

Title Card

```
     Great aquarium book.

x639.34      Sarnoff, Jane.
           A great aquarium book: the putting-
        it-together guide for beginners/by Jane
        Sarnoff and Reynold Ruffin. - New York:
        Scribner, c1977.
                47p.:col.ill.;26cm.
        SUMMARY:A beginner's guide to creating
        a basic aquarium, with information on
        selecting fish and providing for them
        a comfortable, healthy environment.
```

Author Card

```
x639.34      Sarnoff, Jane.
           A great aquarium book: the putting-
        it-together guide for beginners/by Jane
        Sarnoff and Reynold Ruffin. - New York:
        Scribner, c1977.
                47p.:col.ill.;26cm.
        SUMMARY:A beginner's guide to creating
        a basic aquarium, with information on
        selecting fish and providing for them
        a comfortable, healthy environment.
```

Figure 12-3
Subject, Title, and Author Cards

000–099	Reference books
100–199	Psychology, ethics
200–299	Religion, myths
300–399	Social Sciences: almanacs; political science; community life; banking, trade & money; conservation; commerce; law; United Nations; police; citizenship; armed forces; vocations; transportation, communication; handicrafts; postal service, stamps; railroads, trains; waterways, ships; costumes; families, houses; holidays; etiquette; fairy tales & folklore.
400–499	Language: dictionaries; grammar.
500–599	Science: nature study; mathematics; astronomy; physics, electricity, atomic energy; chemistry; geology, rocks; weather; prehistoric life; anthropology; wildlife; plants, trees; seashore life, shells; insects, worms; birds; animals.
600–699	Useful Arts: industries; inventions; health, fire protection, safety; aviation; radio, television; highways, roads, bridges; cars, trucks, machines; farming, gardening, lumber; domestic animals, food, clothing; printing.
700–799	Fine Arts: drawing; photography; motion pictures; music; games, sports.
800–899	Literature: poetry; plays.
900–999	History & Geography: atlases; regions, continents & countries of the world; biography; world & U.S. history.
E	Easy Book
F	Fiction

Figure 12–4
The Dewey Decimal System for Elementary Schools

Periodicals. Information can also be found in newspapers, magazines, and other periodicals. The *Reader's Guide to Periodical Literature,* indexed and bound in annual volumes, lists articles from such publications by author and subject. (Note that not all elementary school libraries have a *Reader's Guide*; most middle and junior high schools do, however.)

Since her school library did not have a *Reader's Guide,* Willa Richardson scheduled a field trip for parents and students at the public library to show them how to use the *Reader's Guide* and to encourage the children to use the public library as well as the school library.

Each elementary library has its own collection of magazines, such as:

National Geographic World
Creative Computer
Cricket

Ranger Rick
Newsweek
Consumer Reports

Checklist for Library Use. Here is a guide, which can also be used as an informal assessment device, of suggested elementary- and middle-school library experiences. These will vary according to the ability and interests of each student.

Preschool and Kindergarten

1. *Introduce the library:* the librarian and the pleasures of library: books to look at, storytelling, films, filmstrips, records, and special programs such as puppets, guest speakers, book fairs, or displays.
2. *The care of books:* how to hold a book, turn pages, use a bookmark, replace on the shelf, place on the desk, how to care for books taken home.
3. *Locate a picture book or an easy-to-read book:* by the first letter of the author's last name. (Picture books are usually grouped on a shelf according to one letter only.)
4. *Use of media equipment:* record and tape players, filmstrip projectors are all ideal for young children to use themselves and begin to learn mediamaking; tapes and filmstrips.

Primary: 1–2

1. *Locate books:* in fiction section, by author.
2. *Use reference materials:* primary dictionary, picture dictionaries, thesaurus, encyclopedia, atlas.
3. *Basic skills to build study skills:* alphabetizing; using table of contents, index.
4. *Sharing creative work in the library:* art; models; books the children have made; reading to younger children; creative dramatics.

Middle and Upper-Elementary (Middle) School

1. *Learn to use card catalogue* (Dewey Decimal) and *Reader's Guide.*
2. *Learn to use various types of each of the reference materials.*
3. *Prepare displays:* as research conducted in library.
4. *Use library independently:* during class and free time.

A Study Guide for Library Use. Over a period of several weeks or a semester, students could practice using the library to search for information on a topic of interest. For example, the students in Willa Richardson's class could practice in small groups, moving from one library skill to another, gathering information about tropical fish, water environments, and building an aquarium. In these small groups, they could answer specific questions related to the environment of the aquarium they have decided to set up.

What kinds of water environments are there?
Which kind should we create?
What belongs in such an environment?
What kind of water? Plant? Fish?
Where can we find these things?
How do we put them together?
How can we maintain such an environment?
What do we need to know about each of the fish?

A study guide could be developed from this or any other topic of interest to be worked through by having each of several groups use a different area of the library on different days. An example is given below, using the setting up of an aquarium as a problem to solve. The teacher can substitute any other topic by replacing the italicized words, *fish, aquarium,* and *tropical fish* with words relating to your topic of choice.

Group 1: ***The card catalogue and the Dewey Decimal System***
Look under the topics *aquarium, fish, tropical fish*. List some books you would like to use to help you set up the aquarium. Locate three of these books. Who are the authors? List other books on the subject by these authors. Locate these books on the shelf and check out the ones you think would be useful.

Group 2. ***Periodicals***
Check the newspaper for any information on *fish.* Use the index. List two magazines that might have information on *fish.* Look through several issues for information. Take notes.

Group 3. ***Encyclopedias and other reference books***
Make a list of all the encyclopedias found in the library. Note where each is kept on your map of the library. Look up *aquarium, fish,* and *tropical fish* in an encyclopedia. Take notes on any information that will help you with your project. At the end of the article you will find topics of related interest. Look up at least one more article. Repeat with at least one other encyclopedia in the library.

Group 4. ***The vertical file***
Check the vertical file for pamphlets, clippings, and other materials under the headings of *aquarium, fish,* and *tropical fish.* Ask the librarian to suggest other words, titles, or headings. Take out any useful material you find.

Group 5. ***Audiovisual materials***

Make a list of media on the subject of *fish* and ask the librarian to let you view a filmstrip or film or a set of slides or transparencies, or listen to a record. Take notes on any information that will help you with your project.

Group 6. ***Dictionaries and thesauruses***

Make a list of the different dictionaries and thesauruses in the library. Look up *aquarium, fish,* and *tropical fish* in each one. Compare what you find. Take notes on anything you think would help you with your project.

Once a study guide has been designed to fit the topic and needs of the class, the children can work through each of the library resources each time they go to the library. Assign a group for each number and rotate through the groups on each visit. Prepare the children for taking notes and recording the source of the information on card files, on a data chart, or in a loose-leaf folder. As they work, you can circulate from group to group. After each session, allow time for the children to discuss what they have found and how it relates to the problem they are solving.

The kind of preparation described above will lead children to see the library as a storehouse of useful information, as readily accessible to them as to the teacher or librarian. Discuss with your librarian times when the children can come to the library to find answers. Library use improves with practice, and problem solving improves with library use. Students who learn early how to gather and use information gain control over their own learning in a way no amount of textbook reading and exercises can achieve. Knowing where to find information and how to use it to solve a problem is a skill students will use throughout their lives.

Transcribing Information

Once students have found information, they need to record it and make some sense of it. Here are some ways to do this.

Underlining

An obvious way to read and remember important information is underlining, a time-honored practice in college education. In public schools, however, most students are not allowed to write in books. Still, older students can practice and learn underlining skills on consumable print such as newspapers, periodicals not in the permanent library collection, and xeroxed materials. Teachers can demonstrate underlining on the overhead projector, emphasizing the following points:

1. Look for *main ideas.* Look for *keywords* you will want to remember and find again.
2. Find any words you do not know the meaning of. *Underline* them and put a *question mark* in the margin. Look up the meaning.
3. *Note questions or ideas* in the margin.

Media Recording

The electronic media have drastically changed the way we are able to record and process information today. Many of the new technologies available in schools allow children to record information: cassette tape recorders, video tape recorders, data-processing computer programs, photographs, slides, transparencies, and Super-8 films. Students can practice selecting the most important ideas for a project and transcribing these, as Sandi Kim and her classmates did when they recorded the interview for their independent project.

See Chapter 11, "The Media Arts," for ideas on using new technologies for recording and processing information.

Taking Notes

Note-taking can take a variety of forms, from very young children dictating to the teacher in a language experience setting to older students taking their own notes. Notes can be taken on real experiences, from primary sources, and from books and reference materials.

Teacher Takes Dictation. In language experience lessons, the teacher writing down what young children dictate is a model for note-taking, which they can practice by copying the story over themselves for other purposes such as illustrating it and preparing it for display or bookmaking, or making puzzles and games. Older students, too, learn to take notes when the teacher writes their ideas on the board, helps them to phrase research questions, and records these on chart paper for later reference.

Notepaper for Discussions. Middle- and upper-elementary students should have small pieces of notepaper available whenever they read several texts or other resources leading to class discussions. Each child writes down at least one idea to share in the discussion. Later, they can build up to three or more. Keep the pieces of notepaper small: the point is not to copy down everything they read but to note down ideas that seem important to them to bring up for discussion. These notes can be words, phrases, or sketches.

Notes for Writing. When students understand the reason for taking notes and have a purpose of their own to do so, they can use this skill for research, as Willa Richardson's class did in their independent studies.

Here are some ideas to suggest to the children as they take notes.

1. Look for main ideas, ideas that seem important and interesting to you.
2. Put ideas into your own words; avoid simply copying what is already there.
3. Identify important names, dates, and other specifics: size, quantity, technical names.
4. Note ideas of your own as you read: ask questions about what you are reading as they occur to you—these may later form questions you wish to answer as you write your report.

5. Combine and synthesize ideas as you note them; produce some general ideas; use note-taking as a way of clarifying, elaborating, and organizing your thinking.

Summarizing

Simply transcribing what others say or parts of what is read is relatively easy. Summarizing it, synthesizing it into a condensed description, requires more of the learner. But practice in summarizing can be helpful throughout the grades, the school year, and across all subjects and contexts.

Summarizing What Others Say. At the beginning of the year, the teacher can explain simple class procedures, management rules, or rituals—such as collecting money, or household chores—and have the children summarize this information briefly.

Summarizing What You Say for Others. Show-and-tell, current events, and sharing periods all provide opportunities for children to talk at length, and then briefly synthesize what they have said in conclusion.

Summarizing What You or Others Have Written. Students may summarize their own writing before reading it to others, or summarize what they have understood as others read their own writing during peer-editing conferences.

Summarizing What You Have Read. Students may want to write a summary of a book for individualized reading conferences, to recommend it to others during a sharing period prior to library time, or as part of an individualized reading record. Key information can be recorded on a chart for a research project by breaking a central question down into important parts before summarizing. The chart gives the central question, and has columns for noting *what, when, who, why,* and *how.*

Organizing Information

Classifying Data

A system of noting and classifying data is useful for children learning how to organize information. There are several ways to do this.

Card File. Willa Richardson's third-grade students began to organize the data they collected from books and reference sources from the very beginning of their reports. Once they had identified their topic and developed questions, and learned how to use the card catalogue, reference books, and other library resources to find information on their topic and to locate further materials (books, magazines, encyclopedias, pamphlets, newspapers) they used 5 × 7 note cards on which they recorded the important information they wanted to use and remember for their report (see Figure 12–5), and which they organized according to the questions they had asked.

Data Chart. Fourth- and fifth-grade teacher Suzanne Brady (Jacobs, 1984) uses simple data charts to help children break down and organize information. She prefers to see children impose their own order on the information they are gathering in order to retain control over what they are learning. Her students use a large piece of newsprint paper folded several times so that it is sectioned into several boxes. The children write one research question in each box, and then write down relevant information they find to help them answer each question.

Loose-leaf Notebook. Students may also organize information in a loose-leaf notebook in the same way they would use a card file or a data chart. They can write one question on each page and record the information they find under the appropriate headings. (Children love to use the section-divider tabs!)

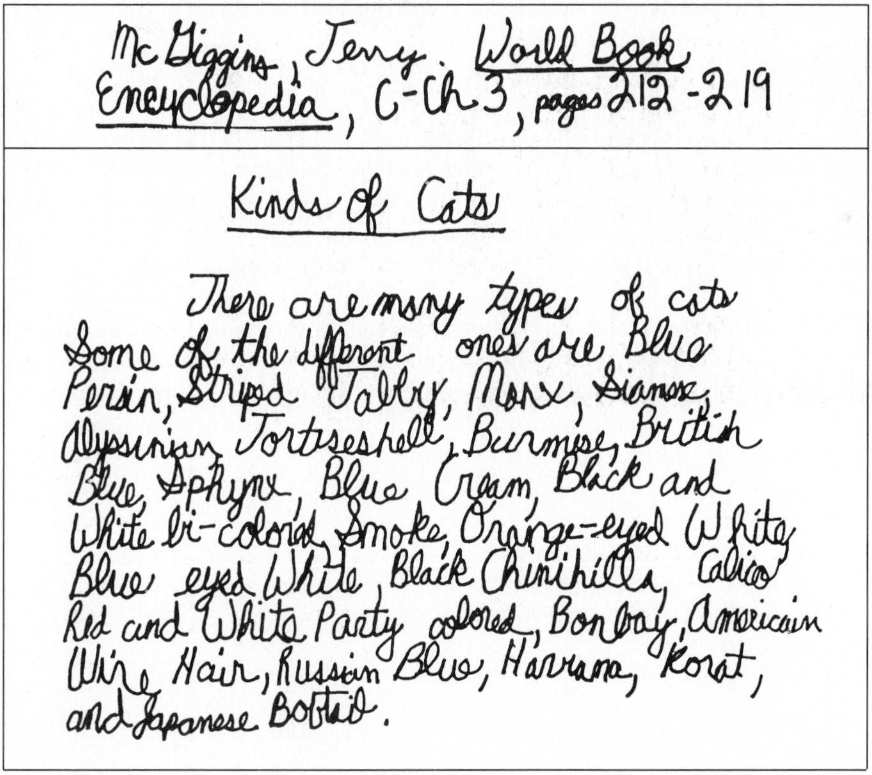

McGiggins, Terry. World Book Encyclopedia, C-Ch 3, pages 212-219

Kinds of Cats

There are many types of cats Some of the different ones are, Blue Persin, Striped Tabby, Manx, Siamese, Abyssinian Tortiseshell, Burmise, British Blue, Sphynx, Blue Cream, Black and White bi-colored, Smoke, Orange-eyed White Blue eyed White, Black Chinihilla, Calico Red and White Party colored, Bombay, Americain Wire Hair, Russin Blue, Havana, Korat, and Japanese Bobtail.

Figure 12–5
Kinds of Cats

Computer File. Students who have access to computers may use a data file to store and retrieve information in preparation for writing and reporting on what they find.

The Student's Own Organizational Scheme. Jacobs (1984) observed Suzanne Brady's approach to investigative writing that focused on the subject of flight. Jacobs identifies two general principles about teaching investigative writing to children ages eight to twelve.

1. Children intuitively develop their own organizational schemes. Bracewell (1980) also found that children do not respond well to explicit instructions on how to organize their writing, even when they are trained to do so.
2. Peer-response groups can help children organize their writing and develop focused questions and can provide feedback on the effect the writing has on the audience.

The broad implications for teaching are that when children choose, research, and write about a topic of interest to them, they should be encouraged to develop their own organization rather than to follow a step-by-step pattern modeled after adult versions of research papers. The more personal their style, the better their writing and the firmer their control over their own ideas and language.

Outlining

Outlining is a way of thinking as much as it is a skill—a way to synthesize, identify main ideas, clarify the relationships among ideas, classify them, and establish a sequence for presenting these ideas and relationships and syntheses. Outlining is often taught in isolation as a simple skill, but it is a process that can and should be used all day long, at every level.

Class Procedures. The teacher can outline class procedures on the board, as the class identifies main activities in general terms and then in more specific categories. Thus a class schedule can be worked out on the board, with the teacher explaining and the children discussing and identifying main headings, subheadings, and sequence.

I. Morning
- **A.** Putting things away
  - **1.** Coats and lunches
  - **2.** Books and homework
- **B.** Business
  - **1.** Notes
  - **2.** Lunch money
  - **3.** Announcements

C. Sharing
  1. Personal
  2. Current events
  3. Planning for the day

II. Afternoon
  A. Reading aloud
    1. Discussion
    (and so on)

Class Experiences. Phyllis Crawford teaches her middle elementary students outlining through cooking experiences. For example, students who are about to work in small groups to make tacos first plan what will happen in each group.

Making Tacos

I. Preparing the ingredients
  A. Lettuce
    1. Wash
    2. Pull off dead leaves
    3. Slice fine
  B. Tomatoes
    1. Wash
    2. Peel
    3. Chop fine
  C. Cheese
    1. Take off wrapper
    2. Cut in small hunks
    3. Grate
  D. Meat
    1. Turn on electric frying pan
    2. Put meat in
    3. Poke meat with wooden spoon until brown, not pink
  E. Onions
    1. Peel
    2. Close your mouth (to keep from crying)
    3. Chop fine

II. Putting the tacos together
  A. Food
    1. Put all of one kind of food on a big plate
    2. Put plates in a line on a long table
    3. Open box of taco shells and put at beginning of table
  B. Making the taco
    1. Get a plate
    2. Get a taco shell

3. Put in the ingredients (you don't have to eat onions or other things you don't like)

C. Eating
   1. Go to your seat
   2. Start to eat
   3. Use a napkin

Blank Outlines. Children can use blank outlines for small-group and individual work after they have had practice in outlining together for many class activities. Blank outlines show the general structure of an outline (including the headings *Main topic, Subtopic, Detail,* and *Subdetail*). When introducing her students to library reference works, Willa Richardson uses the World Book Encyclopedia to show how each article is outlined. Then the students use a blank outline sheet to record the information they have gathered from various sources, after having written several paragraphs on their topic. Figure 12–6 shows an outline written by one of Willa's students, who chose the topic of music for her independent project.

Studying Information

While most elementary students are not expected to study and remember specific material for content testing, upper elementary- and middle-school students are often faced with the shift from a process-oriented, activity-centered learning environment to a lecture-text-test pattern, and many are unprepared for this. To avoid this situation, older students can be introduced to a variety of prereading and studying techniques for learning and remembering material for testing. Many of these techniques also help to improve reading comprehension and information processing in general, although some educators question the validity of these structured methods for interpreting and remembering information (Bloom, 1984; Robinson, 1970; Pearson & Johnson, 1978).

Some of the most commonly used techniques for prestudy for reading and remembering text (Graham & Robinson, 1984) are described below, with references for further reading on each type.

Prereading Strategies

Advance Organizer. The advance organizer is a brief passage that reflects a high level of generality and helps to create interest in the longer passages to be read, allows students to connect their own experiences, and encourages them to predict and set goals for their reading. These organizers can be a paragraph or so in length, and can be written by the teacher or taken from another source (Ausubel, 1963; Karahalios, Tonjes & Towner, 1979).

Questions. There are many ways teachers can help students set goals for reading through questioning before reading. Most textbooks have preread-

I. Introduction
A. Why I chose singing in the back
1. Musical Talent
2. Other music I like
B. Man and sound
1. Early man
2. How sounds are made
II. Types of Music
A. Overview of rock
1. Soft rock
2. Hard rock
B. Overview of Opera
1. Story
2. Training
C. Country and Western
1. Folk
2. Cowboy
D. Folk
1. Story
2. English and Irish songs
III. John Denver
A. Folk singer
1. records
2. concerss
B. Settings
1. Audience
2. Screens

IV. Placido Domingo
A. Opera singer
1. Born in Spain
2. Alway at the theater
B. Operas & Culture
1. Old and New
2. Worked with father
V. William Haley
A. Rock singer
1. Soft rock
2. Music in home
B. Group
1. Comets
2. Famous song
VI. Kenny Rogers
A. Country and Western singer
1. First was a rock singer
2. Cross over music
B. Tells stories
1. Voice
2. Popular

La-La-La-La!

La!

Figure 12–6 *A Third-grader's Outline: Music*

ing questions in the teacher's guide, and review questions in the student's edition to guide reading and reviewing. Teachers may also ask their own questions adapted to the needs of their students.

Semantic Maps. The results of students' brainstorming on a topic can be recorded on a semantic map. Teachers read first to identify the main topic, list key vocabulary, frame directed questions, and list more ideas and vocabulary contributed by students, and then organize the material into a structured overview together with the class for discussion. Directed reading that follows can serve to answer questions raised, verify suggestions, and revise meanings as necessary in a postreading discussion (Pearson & Johnson, 1978).

See Chapter 2, "Semantic Mapping."

Study Strategies

Class Discussions. Postreading discussions with the whole class and in small groups can focus on answers to the prereading questions, responses to advance organizers, and semantic maps. The teacher should encourage active participation and thinking, however, not simply check to see whether the students have actually read or are able to answer prereading questions. Graham and Robinson (1984) suggest the following guidelines for class discussions:

1. Guide the students' discussion—don't lead it yourself.
2. Take care to see that each student gets an opportunity to participate.
3. Allow students time to prepare for discussion of specific topics or certain questions—not broad, general areas of common knowledge.
4. Differentiate assignments—vary the difficulty of the assignment to suit the ability of the individual student.
5. Direct the students back into the text as necessary for reference.
6. Encourage students to use media aids, such as the chalkboard, in their presentations.
7. Establish some form of "discussion etiquette" or parliamentary procedure.
8. Allow time after the discussion for self-evaluation and constructive criticism of peers.
9. Take time to review the important points of the discussion and how they were made.
10. Monitor the ways in which students organize and present information and ideas: Are the purposes clear? Is material presented logically? Are major points highlighted?

Gloss. The gloss technique requires teachers to prepare study guides, with marginal notes on a separate piece of paper, that will direct the students' attention to specific sentences (noted on the guide) in the text, ask questions that the students answer on the guide, and generally help students organize information as they are reading it. Here is an example of gloss notations for a science text (Richgels & Hansen, 1984):

> Fill in the blanks:
>
> 1. The continental shelf is located next to ________. It has a gentle downward slope (12 feet for every mile).
> 2. The abyssal plain is located at the bottom of the continental slope. It can be described as ________.
>
> Now think about your answers and show how sure you are that you are right:
>
> Question 1: sure not sure
> Question 2: sure not sure
>
> Now find the sections of the text by their subheads, "Continental Shelf and Slope" and "Abyssal Plain," in order to check the answers you were not sure of (p. 318).

Review Techniques. Several sequential study strategies have been developed, primarily for the purpose of comprehending and remembering content reading. SQ3R (Robinson, 1970) is one of the most widely described. Here is how it works.

S—Survey: Students skim the whole text before reading, checking the following: title; beginning and conclusion; headings and subheading; charts, pictures, graphs, illustrations, and captions; and notes, advance organizers, or summaries.
Q—Question: On a piece of paper, students note questions they have or turn headings into prereading questions.
R—Read: Students read to answer a question they have posed, note answers and more questions, and focus on the author's main purpose.
R—Review: Students remember what they have read, keeping the questions and main ideas in mind.
R—Recite: Students explain to others what they have found or write a summary for themselves or for others to read.

It is important to note again that study methods are only effective if they engage the learner's focused attention. In a review of research on study skills, Armbruster and Anderson (1981) found that no one technique could be proven superior to another. And in a similar review that focused on SQ3R, Graham (1982) found that it was not superior to other study methods or, perhaps more importantly, to methods of study devised by the learners themselves. Teachers may do well to observe, note, encourage, and support the methods that successful students have developed individually, and help less successful students to develop methods of their own.

Presenting Information

What should students do after they find, transcribe, and organize information? Willa Richardson's students gave both a written and an oral report, and made a creative product as well. In any given classroom, students may do some or all of these and more. Here are some other ways they may present information.

book discussion	construction	fact file
brochure	costume	film strip
bulletin board	data/results	graph
chart	diagrams	journal
chronology	diorama	learning center
collection	editorial	lesson
comic strip	essay	mobile
commercial	experiment	model

museum
newspaper
picture
plan
play
poem
problem
puppet show
puzzle
scrapbook
slide show
song
speech
story
survey
tape
timeline
video tape
vocabulary list

What is most important in the end is that students are thinking and solving problems as they use research and study skills. The ripple effect of energy and ideas that is generated when students are in control of their own language and learning will do more than any amount of carefully prepared teacher's plans, units, or study guides. Or, as Sandi Kim puts it in the beginning of this chapter, "If it had been something the teacher had made me, I wouldn't like it as much. But I liked it a lot so I made it long."

Summing Up

Teachers today do much more than teach a measurable content and the skills that go along with that particular content. They must teach students how to think, to solve problems, and to gain control over their own learning as they learn how to identify their interests, ask questions and hypothesize about them, find and organize information, and share it with others. These thinking, research, and study skills are not bound by content or skills drawn from a scope and sequence form, a text book, or other commercial materials. They require that both teachers and students understand how to solve a problem and learn by actually doing.

Willa Richardson systematically sets out to do this with her third-grade classes, beginning by teaching the children study skills in the context of learning about the environment, helping them solve the problem of creating an aquarium, planning a field trip to a wildlife refuge in Louisiana, and guiding them through an extended independent project as they choose a topic, research it by reading, interviews, and data collection, organize and write it in report form, make a creative product, and share what they have learned with the rest of the class and the school.

There are many ways teachers can teach thinking, research, and study skills in the elementary- and middle-school classroom. An important aspect of these is learning to find information: from interviews and books, and through extended use of the library. Students also need to know how to record and transcribe information, and then organize and process that information into meaningful content to be presented to others. Older students need to learn how to read, remember, and study content material for test-taking.

All of these skills can be learned and used when students choose to pursue topics of interest to them. It is important to remember that, in the end, the best thinking, research, and study strategies may be those that students—encouraged and supported by teachers—will develop for themselves.

Looking Further

1. Develop an interest inventory to help children choose a topic for an independent research project. Try it out with a child. Revise and refine it according to how well it helped identify a topic for that child.

2. With others in your class, brainstorm as many different types of creative products for an independent research project as you can.

3. Choose an area of social studies, mathematics, fine arts, or science and develop a bibliography of related children's books. Choose an area you think you might want to teach, or one that interests you or you know something about.

4. Develop a set of questions to introduce a class to the use of a content area textbook with specific book.

5. Create a lesson for a specific grade level to learn the use of the dictionary or thesaurus. Teach the lesson if possible.

6. Visit a school library media center and develop an introductory study guide for the grade level you are teaching or hope to teach.

7. Ask a group of children to organize data they are working with in any way they like. Compare their systems of organization.

8. Try out one of the study techniques described in this chapter. Comment on its effectiveness and note how you might revise it to meet the needs of that particular group of children.

Chapter Thirteen

Language Arts for Every Child

Objectives

Look for answers to the following questions as you read this chapter.

- How do different teachers organize, individualize, manage, and evaluate the teaching of language arts?
- What factors affect learning in school?
- What are some questions to consider when making decisions about organizing, individualizing, managing, and evaluating instruction?
- What are the main approaches to organizing, individualizing, managing, and evaluating instruction and how can they be implemented in the classroom?

A Teacher's View

Here is how six teacher–artists describe their basic philosophies and approaches to the art of teaching language arts to every child:

Mauretta Hurst (Kindergarten): "I draw on the children's own experiences and then relate language, literature, and lots of drama experiences to them."

Nora Miller (First Grade): "Motivating students to work and learn using their own ideas in small groups is critical."

Glynn Wink (Second Grade): "What's most important is that they are involved. I do centers and individualized reading because it puts children in control."

Willa Richardson (Third Grade): "I want my students to learn how to solve problems and begin to think that way and correlate their learning in all subjects."

Avril Font (Fourth Grade): "Until we teach the process of learning, the only process children will learn is the regurgitation of facts. And children learn in different ways. The trick is to get each child to make their best effort, feel a sense of achievement, and meet their own self-fulfilling prophesy."

Joyce Ryder (Fourth and Fifth Grades): "I've always thought a good teacher should help children solve problems and be in control of their own learning: putting them in groups, letting them talk, and work out problems themselves."

Centering Ideas

Beginning at 9:30 one morning in the same city school district, here is what is happening in the classrooms of several different teachers, some of whom you have met in earlier chapters.

Different Teachers' Styles

Kindergarten: Mauretta Hurst

The Three Billy Goats Gruff by Marcia Brown (Harcourt Brace Jovanovich, 1957)

After sharing their ideas about a class field trip to the zoo, the children draw pictures of the zoo and then dictate a language experience story to Mauretta Hurst. The story is called *The Adventures of a Baby Elephant.* Mauretta then reads *The Three Billy Goats Gruff* aloud, and the children dramatize it after they discuss it.

First Grade: Nora Miller

May I Bring a Friend? by Beatrice Schenk de Regniers, ill. by Beni Montresor (Atheneum, 1965)

Nora Miller reads Beni Montresor's picture book *May I Bring a Friend?* and discusses it with the class to help the children develop skills of sequencing, predicting, and learning the names of the days of the week, before they go to one of five centers designed to reinforce these skills.

Second Grade: Glynn Wink

Her students come one at a time to Glynn Wink for a conference about their personal reading for the week. They then move through listening, reading, and writing centers with activities focused around the theme of dinosaurs.

Third Grade: Willa Richardson

A period of directed reading lessons in basal reader groups is followed by activities in a language arts and spelling text, and a period of creative writing.

Fourth Grade: Avril Font

Avril Font's students share topics of personal interest and plan their activities every day during this time before they do self-directed small-group work.

Fourth and Fifth Grades: Joyce Ryder

Joyce Ryder's students are either in small groups making their own film-strips after brainstorming ideas and writing a script, or programming their own Choose-Your-Own-Adventure story on the computer.

What They Have in Common

There are differences in how each of these teachers teaches language arts, and for different reasons. They teach different grade levels and different types of students, and they have different teaching interests and styles. No matter how much these factors vary, however, every teacher must deal with the following questions when planning how to teach:

- How do I organize for instruction?
- How do I provide for individualized instruction, to meet the needs of every child?
- How do I manage my classroom?
- How do I evaluate children and my own teaching?

Making Connections

How will you answer questions about organizing, individualizing, managing, and evaluating instruction, in terms of your own students, teaching situation, and personal philosophy and teaching style? Deciding how to put together everything you know about the art of teaching language arts is a problem with no single, simple answer, and with sweeping implications. Step back a moment from your concern with minute-to-minute, day-to-day, week-to-week plans for teaching and consider all the elements at work in learning in any subject.

Factors That Affect Learning in School

Walberg (1984) has identified nine factors that require the teacher's attention in order for learning to take place:

Student Aptitude

1. Ability or prior achievement (measured by standardized tests).
2. Development (measured by chronological age or stage of maturity).
3. Motivation and self-concept (as indicated by the student's willingness to persevere on learning tasks).

Instruction

4. Time spent on learning tasks.
5. Quality of instruction (including psychological and instructional aspects).

Environmental Factors

6. The home.
7. The classroom social group.

8. The peer group outside school.
9. Use of leisure time (specifically, television viewing).

Factors That Teachers Can Influence

In a macroanalysis of a synthesis of research related to the factors that teachers can influence, Walberg (1984) identified the following effects:

1. Reinforcement and reward.
2. Instructional cues, engagement, and feedback.
3. Accelerated programs with advanced activities.
4. Reading instruction which emphasizes learner adaptability to reading for a purpose.
5. Cooperative team learning by students in small groups.
6. Personalized and adaptive instruction, tutoring, and individualized diagnosis (as opposed to batch-processing students—thus freeing them from the pervasive seatwork and recitation in groups).
7. Higher-order questioning.
8. Inquiry teaching.
9. Higher teacher expectations.

In terms of environment, the psychological morale or climate of the classroom group was found to have strong effects on instruction. This climate includes cohesiveness, satisfaction, goal direction, and other social-psychological factors as perceived by the students; homework that is graded and commented upon; and school–parent programs to improve academic conditions in the home. All these factors were found to be more important than socioeconomic status or amount of television viewing.

What does such information suggest to the teacher faced with organizing, individualizing, managing, and evaluating the teaching of language arts, and other subjects as well? Walberg (1984) cautions that it would be erroneous to emphasize one or more factors since it is the *interaction* of all these factors that affect learning.

In a review of Walberg's research synthesis, Tyler (1984) cautions that we should not expect research and the resulting theories and models to provide a how-to manual for improving teaching and learning, since research can only evaluate the results of practices that have already been tried out. He advises that teachers become researchers themselves, with their own students and in their own classrooms, using previous research as a guide about the kinds of questions they must ask.

Organizing Instruction

Here are some questions to consider in organizing instruction in the language arts.

The Classroom Environment

- How will you arrange and use furniture and equipment?
- How will you establish a class library or reading center, permanent process centers (listening, writing), and temporary special-interest centers?
- How will you provide for flexible use of permanent displays, for school business, and for small-group activities?
- How will you use bulletin boards for permanent displays, for school business, and for student use?
- How will you arrange supplies (storage, access by the children)?
- How will you provide for access to texts and reference materials?

Scheduling

- As you plan a schedule, and block out time for regular daily activities such as recess, lunch, and special classes, how will you evaluate the remaining blocks of time to determine their use?
- To what extent will you follow state and local requirements for suggested allotments per subject, taking into consideration what this means in an integrated curriculum when you may be doing many subjects at one time?
- How will you resolve time use according to your own approach, your teaching style, and the abilities and needs of your students?

Subject Matter

- How will you determine what to teach?
- To what extent will you use state or local curriculum guides?
- Will you use texts or programmed materials, in combination with other strategies, or not at all?
- What will determine how you make your decisions: state or local guidelines? directives from your principal? models of other teachers around you? student interests? thematic or unit approaches? parental expectations? your own interests? other influences?

The Students

- How will you find out everything you can about your students?
- How will you individualize instruction?
- How will you group students?

Individualizing Instruction

Here are some questions to consider in individualizing instruction in the language arts.

- How will you determine the needs of each student?
- How will you establish methods of diagnosis and record keeping?
- Will you create a pupil profile to plan appropriate experiences?
- How will you group students for instruction?
- How will you plan for special differences and language and cultural differences?
- How will you evaluate students and make appropriate changes?

You often assume that some day, perhaps even on a given day, you will really know how to teach children. What really happens is that you will constantly move through stages of learning how to teach each child. I learned this from Robbie, age 8, when I returned to school after an illness and immediately noticed that the clock face had been broken. I also noticed that lumps of clay had been lobbed at the walls all around the room. The children were glad to see me, as most children are when their regular teacher returns after a stint with substitutes, and a few told me in hushed confidence, "Robbie was bad. He broke the clock." Robbie had black hair and light-brown freckles, and glasses that always seemed to glint mischieviously. He marched up to my desk—he *always* took the offensive—pointed to the broken clock face, and demanded accusingly, "Where *were* you? You *know* I can't sit in my chair all day!"

Robbie was right. He could not, and I knew it. Robbie was extremely active, and when his energy was orchestrated and directed through many changes such as drama and discussions, activities, a fast pace, and a lot of movement, he did fine. Things were not so fine when he was expected to sit in his seat all day. His need to move would frustrate him, and verbal outbursts or attacks on clocks and walls with clay would result.

Robbie is an example of just one of the sets of learning and cognitive styles that each child brings to school, and this factor needs to be considered and respected by the teacher when planning, teaching, and evaluating: individualizing for each child. And while teachers cannot teach twenty-five different children in twenty-five different ways in a day, neither can they teach all the children in one way all year long.

Student Learning Styles

Specific and identifiable learning styles evinced by students have been suggested by Fischer and Fischer (1979).

1. Incremental learner—needs a highly structured approach design to permit the student to reach a generalization.
2. Intuitive learner—unsystematic, sporadic learner who often is unable to explain what has been learned in any organized manner.
3. Sensory specialist—relies upon one sense (e.g., visual or auditory) even though all are sufficiently operating.
4. Sensory generalist—depends upon all senses.
5. Emotionally involved—requires an environment both physically and mentally stimulating to "cause a high emotional charge."

6. Emotionally neutral—requires a "low-key" atmosphere.
7. Explicitly structured—needs clear objectives and organized lesson.
8. Open-ended structure—prefers an open-ended rather than highly structured environment.
9. Damaged learner—a physically normal student with a damaged self-concept and social skills, and who has a negative attitude toward learning.
10. Eclectic learner—can alter learning styles to fit the occasion despite having a preference for one or another (p. 245).

In addition to noting the learning styles of students, you must also take into account other factors such as ability, prior knowledge, and achievement. Other effects on instruction are important when individualizing: the task, teacher–student rapport, the time of the year, class size, the learning context, and the school setting. Furthermore, it appears that students can adapt to many types of high-quality instructional modes even if not their first choice, and in a real classroom setting, a teacher may be better able to manage one main approach that stems from their strengths, but continue to develop a variety of teaching approaches so that children will be provided with a learning environment made up of multiple styles and combinations that will ultimately match their learning styles.

Grouping Students

Grouping students for instruction is a key factor in individualizing instruction.

Ways to Group

- *Whole class/large group.* Certain experiences are best done in a large group: sharing; planning; discussion of issues that concern the whole class (behavior, rules, procedures, projects, themes, or unit questions); skills or content at the beginning of a series of experiences and/or that everyone needs to know (how to write a formal letter, how to use the encyclopedia, casting a play); and guest speakers, storytelling, reading aloud, film and other media-viewing experiences, and any other experiences that are best shared by the whole class.

- *Small group.* Other experiences lend themselves best to small groups: topics of mutual interest for research; planning an activity; peer-editing groups; skill centers; games; writing a newspaper.

- *Partners.* Sometimes a group of two is ideal: researching a subject of mutual interest; building a model; conducting an experiment.

Reasons to Group

- *Achievement.* Achievement is a traditional reason to group children for reading, spelling, and mathematics, when these subjects are taught with a single text; the magic number for these groups is three. Such grouping has not always been a practice in teaching the language arts. Many argue that spelling is best taught not with a text but with an individualized problem-solving approach. In addition, children's achievement in spoken language, listening, writing, and other areas of language arts learning has never been as massively assessed as in reading and spelling, so that each child's achievement is more often evaluated on a personal rather than on a grade-level basis. Besides, there are many other reasons to group children.

- *Ability.* Factors such as intelligence, giftedness, or special talents may be reasons to put children together.

- *Age and maturity.* Older or very mature children may work best in small groups, and may be able to do so without extensive teacher guidance. Younger, less mature children may work best in centers with structured guidance from the teacher or aide.

- *Interest and purpose.* There are strong reasons for bringing children together who have a mutual interest—from sports to spiders—or a similar purpose—they want to make a film or produce a play.

- *Compatibility.* Social interaction is important in forming groups, and children who work well together may do so no matter what their age, ability, achievement, or interest. (And you may not be able to keep best friends like Barbara and Faith—described in Chapter 6—apart, even though they fight.)

- *Serendipity.* Chance happenings will form groups: children may have visited the same state or foreign country and will pool their knowledge to report; some may have the same pets, hobbies, or other experiences, and will get together for those reasons.

Varying Groups. Groups should be flexible and subject to change whenever a better instructional pattern is discovered according to size and reasons to group. What is encouraging about small-group instruction is that the students themselves will often make decisions about group changes and dynamics as they gain increasing control over their own learning.

Public Law 94–142, Education for All Handicapped Children Act of 1975

Pupil Appraisal Handbook, Department of Education, State of Louisiana, 1983

Mainstreaming Students with Special Needs

Federal legislation stipulates that all exceptional children have a right to be educated in "the least restrictive environment." The popular term for accomplishing this is **mainstreaming.**

Here is how this law has been implemented in Louisiana, for example, by defining what is meant by *exceptional* and by identifying specific types of exceptionalities.

What Makes a Child Exceptional? For a child to be considered **exceptional**, the assessment data must indicate that (1) an impairment is present, or a requisite is present, such as exceptionally high abilities, and (2) an assessment of the current and past learning environment and the educational progress of the child demonstrates a need for special educational services.

Only when both of these factors are true is the child considered exceptional. Misclassification can occur in evaluating children when it is assumed that (1) all impaired children need special educational services, or (2) all children with special educational needs are exceptional.

Types of Exceptionalities. The various types of exceptionalities are defined as follows.

- *Autism.* Developmental disabilities including disturbances of developmental rates and sequences, response to sensory stimuli, speech, language-cognitive, and nonverbal communication, or the capacity to relate appropriately to people, events, or objects, are classified as **autism.**

- *Speech impairments or language disorders.* The term **speech impairment** refers to a communication disorder such as stuttering, impaired articulation, or a language or voice impairment. A **language disorder** interferes with the development, formation, and expression of language.

- *Behavior disordered (emotionally disturbed).* A **behavior disordered** or **emotionally disturbed** child shows a pattern of situationally inappropriate personal behavior over an extended period of time, which cannot be explained by intellectual, sensory, neurological, or general health factors. Such manifestations include unhappiness, depression, withdrawal, or development of physical symptoms or fear associated with personal or school problems.

- *Hearing and vision impairment.* Students are considered to have a **hearing** or **vision** impairment if their auditory sensitivity and acuity (hard-of-hearing or deaf) or visual acuity (partially seeing or blind), or both, even with correction, adversely affects their educational performance.

- *Educationally handicapped (slow learner).* An **educationally handicapped** child, often called a **slow learner,** is one whose rate of acquisition and/or degree of retention of information or educational skills is significantly slower than the rate expected for students of the same age.

- *Learning disabled.* A **learning disabled** student is one who has severe and unique learning problems as a result of significant difficulties in the acquisition, organization, or expression of specific academic skills or concepts. This disability is typically manifested in school as significantly poor performance in such areas as reading, writing, spelling, arithmetic reasoning or calculation, oral expression or comprehension, or the acquisition of basic concepts. The learning problems are generally due to factors other than

  lack of educational opportunity,
  emotional stress in the home or school,

difficulty adjusting to school,
curricular change or temporary crisis situations,
other handicapping conditions,
environmental, cultural, or economic disadvantage, and/or
lack of motivation.

• *Mentally retarded.* A **mentally retarded** child exhibits significantly sub-average general intellectual functioning existing concurrently with deficits in adaptive behavior.

• *Orthopedically handicapped.* An **orthopedically handicapped** student has a severe orthopedic impairment that adversely affects educational performance: muscular or neuromuscular handicaps, or skeletal deformities or abnormalities that significantly limit the ability to move about, sit, or manipulate the materials required for learning.

• *Gifted and talented.* Students who possess demonstrated abilities and give evidence of high performance in academic and intellectual aptitude or the visual and/or performing arts are said to be **gifted** or **talented.**

Individual instruction interventions recommended, both during the period of determining whether a given child learns like an exceptional or a nonexceptional student, and during the student's period in the regular classroom, include:

1. restructuring the classroom and the school environment,
2. peer tutoring,
3. classroom-based reinforcement techniques,
4. behavior modification and therapy in the classroom,
5. combined home and school behavior-change programs,
6. individual or group counseling or therapy, and
7. modifications of the curriculum and/or instructional approach.

Meeting the Needs of Exceptional Children. In some instances, regular classroom teachers need special help for special children. One way to meet these needs is with the help of trained support staff such as aides and tutors. A recent report by the National Educational Association (Needham, 1986), however, cites that two thirds of all handicapped students are not in special classes but in regular classes from which they are pulled out for extra instruction. These students include the learning disabled, the physically handicapped with normal intelligence, and the mildly retarded. Evaluation of these programs reveal that the key to success is having enough appropriately trained staff and good administrative arrangements and support.

See *Dealing With Differences,* ed. by G. Stanford, (NCTE, 1980).

According to one of the principals writing this report, one result of Public Law 94–142 is that, since teachers have had to write individualized education plans for exceptional children, these same teachers are diagnosing and meeting the needs of *all* their students more effectively, thus going beyond the demands of this law to what public educational programs should be doing anyway: meeting each child's needs.

Language- and Culturally Different Children

Legislation has also been passed to meet the special needs of language-different and culturally different students. The Bilingual Education Act refers to education in two languages, one of which is English; a Supreme Court decision maintains that a school district with at least ten limited-English speaking children must consider offering a **bilingual program. ESL** (English as a second language) **programs,** which provide special help for such students to understand and speak English, and then to read and write in English, take several different forms in schools today.

Title VII, ESEA—Elementary and Secondary Education Act, 1968; Supreme Court, *Law v. Nichols,* 1974

Bilingual Classrooms. In a regular classroom, Sunny McMullen teaches a first-grade bilingual English/Spanish class in Los Angeles. Along with other southwestern states and New York City, Los Angeles is one of the areas of the country with a large Spanish-speaking population. Some California demographics (Southern California Research Council, 1985) may help explain why such a classroom exists.

See *Mainstreaming the Non-English Speaking Student,* by R. J. Rodrigues and R. H. White (NCTE, 1981).

For kindergarten through twelfth grade in California, minority students constitute 43 percent of total enrollments; by the year 2000, Hispanics will comprise the largest single segment of the school-age population. In Los Angeles County, more than 70 percent of the students in public schools are ethnic minorities; among them, they speak more than eighty languages. And although California is responsible for educating students who speak numerous native languages, Spanish is the language of three fourths of California students whose English is limited. California offers two options for these students:

1. *Bilingual classroom.* A bilingual classroom includes ten or more students who speak the same primary language other than English, and is taught by a bilingual teacher or aide (ideally, both). Parents must give consent for their children to be in such a class.
2. *BILP (Bilingual Individual Learning Plan).* In cases where there are fewer than ten children whose primary language is not English, or when parents do not consent to having their children in a bilingual classroom, there must be bilingual support—from a teacher, an aide, a parent, or a volunteer—and an Individual Learning Plan is written for each child and carried out in the context of the regular classroom.

The basic approach recommended in bilingual or BILP classrooms is:

1. Teach the basic subject matter in the primary language to the greatest extent possible, and at the same time introduce English in informal speaking situations.

2. Gradually add formal English in reading instruction, continuing the dual program, until the child can successfully pass state tests in mathematics, reading, and spelling, scoring at a minimum competency level comparable to that of a native speaker. Ideally this happens at the end of second grade if the child entered the program in the first grade.

Sunny's Approach. Sunny, not a native speaker but of Spanish-speaking heritage, renewed her limited Spanish after she began teaching. To help in her class, Sunny employed my mother, Alice Shirreffs, as a bilingual aide. Alice learned Spanish after she retired from running her own business, because she enjoys traveling to Mexico. Here, Alice describes how Sunny taught the whole class and how she worked as an aide with small groups of children (Shirreffs, 1986).

> Sunny taught the whole class in both Spanish and English. From the first day, when she gave a direction that everyone needed to follow, she did it in both languages. She also taught whole-class and large-group lessons in both. She grouped the students for language arts, reading, mathematics, and spelling at first according to their knowledge of English and, as the non-English speakers became more proficient, rearranged the groups.
>
> I taught small groups of three or four at a time in another section of the classroom. I began solely in Spanish and gradually added English when I thought the children were ready. At first we learned colors, the alphabet, numbers, and other simple concepts and vocabulary. I used many real objects such as fruits and vegetables, and pictures. I also used a lot of games I made. One they enjoyed was building a house with popsicle sticks as they worked with names of the parts of a house.

Sunny and Alice planned a number of basic bilingual activities:

- Everything in the room was labeled in both Spanish and English.
- The walls were covered with pictures of scenes of Mexico with labels in both languages. (All these children had only recently moved to California from Mexico.)
- They read stories in Spanish and English.
- A listening center, with a record player and tape recorder, was used with small groups, playing the same songs and stories in Spanish and English.
- Children wrote their own books with pictures at first and then added words in Spanish and then English.
- Students shared and presented programs in English and Spanish: songs they had learned, their books, and creative dramatics.
- Mexico became the focus in much of what the class studied.

Alice has a number of guidelines for working with language and culturally different children, no matter in what kind of classroom, what subject you are teaching, or in what language.

1. ***Respect the native culture of the children.***

"In addition to posters and pictures of Mexico, we often cooked familiar foods in the classroom. Flan was their favorite. We would pass it around and have a party. We held a big Cinco de Mayo celebration for the whole school. We put up posters, decorations, encouraged the children to wear native costumes if they had them, and had Mexican food, music, dances, and a big parade around the playground."

2. ***Pay attention to each child as an individual and give them responsibilities.***

"In the small groups I encouraged them to tell me about their family, their pets, and their interests. I also let them help me teach: they graded their own papers; recorded their grades (I had to keep daily records of their progress); and put their own stars on their work and themselves, and helped each other."

3. ***Praise and reward them to reinforce interest in school and school learning.***

"Sunny did this extensively. Praise was the way she approached everything and she worked hard to make children feel they were accomplishing something. We used concrete rewards a great deal too: popcorn, little toys, hair ribbons. They would bring us little presents in return."

Alice sums up her experience in Sunny's classroom:

> The most important thing I have learned, however, I learned from the children. I learned that they will use language when they have a real reason to say something, in Spanish or English. Even though I worked very hard to teach colors and numbers the first few weeks, the first thing they learned to say well was "Señora Shirreffs, gimme a kiss!" when I got to school in the morning.
>
> One boy who had not made much progress was absent for two weeks. He had gone to Mexico because his uncle had died. The first thing he said to me when he came back was to ask very innocently and very sadly, in English, "How will he get out of the ground to get to Heaven?"
>
> The best thing for me was to come back after the first year and see how well they spoke English at the beginning of the second grade. It was amazing. They were becoming fluent in both languages.

See "Literacy Instruction for ESL Children" by E. A. Franklin, *Language Arts,* 63 (1986): 51–60; "Developing Contexts to Support Second Language Acquisition," by V. G. Allen, *Language Arts,* 63 (1986): 61–65.

ESL Classrooms. Pat Abbott teaches in a HILT (High Intensive Language Training) classroom in Baton Rouge, Louisiana, a part of the bilingual education program there. In Pat's class, the students speak many different languages, representative of the bilingual population in Baton Rouge schools: 500 students from 60 different language groups—although the two main target languages are Spanish and Vietnamese.

The thrust of these classrooms is to provide special help for children who come from homes where English is not the dominant language. The teachers are all ESL certified and provide an English-speaking model using

ESL teacher Pat Abbott uses computers extensively with her students who are learning English as a second language.

ESL methodology. They are assisted by aides who are native language speakers, primarily Spanish and Vietnamese.

The approach is that of undercutting the content areas for each child in their regular classroom. In the beginning, the HILT teacher develops basic vocabulary and concepts used in the classroom, and some basal ESL texts are also used. The primary emphasis, however, is on respect for the cultural and linguistic heritage of each child, and on making all the children feel good about themselves and their potential to learn in school.

See "Raddara's Beautiful Book," by P. Shea and S. Fitzgerald, *Language Arts,* 58 (1981): 156–161.

Pat Abbott uses a variety of strategies with her students: sharing, storytelling, and the flannel board and language experience techniques. She also works with students from kindergarten through grade five at one time, putting them together in small interest groups. In addition, she has made extensive use of computers lately.

Managing Instruction

Here are some questions to consider in managing instruction in the language arts.

- How will you organize, sequence, motivate, individualize, group, and create active involvement of students with content?
- How will you structure your time, class policies and rules, rewards and punishments, and consequences for behavior?

- How will you create a participatory democracy?
- How will you build a sense of community, communication, and cooperation in your room that will preclude discipline problems?
- How will you plan problem-solving sessions to deal with problems when they arise?
- What kind of language will you use when you discuss problems?
- How will you build your students' self-image and feeling of self-worth?
- What commonsense procedures will you use in managing your day?
- How will you use parents and paraprofessionals in your management plan?

Management can mean many things in education: creating a classroom environment the week before school starts; settling on a schedule during the first week of school; changing groups as the semester wears on; developing a system of work habits, routing routines, learning centers, and traffic patterns; household chores. The really big underlying concept of management is discipline, often cited as the number one problem or issue of concern in public education.

Discipline Development

Stages of Discipline Development. McDaniel (1984) suggests that classroom management and discipline are developmental aspects of a teacher's growing professional competence, and include certain premises, attitudes, skills, and language competencies (see Table 13–1). They do not exist in isolation, but exist together. He suggests that

1. teachers must master the elements of classroom instruction: knowing how to organize, sequence, motivate, individualize, and create active involvement of students with content;
2. teachers must master behavior management: classroom structure, rules, consequences, rewards, which lead to an ordered learning environment; and
3. teachers must master a humanistic stage beyond teaching and control: encouraging self-discipline among students, facilitating participatory democracy, and building community and communication in the classroom based on mutual respect and reasonable expectations.

Problem-Solving Sessions. One way in which teachers can master the humanistic stage is through problem-solving sessions on classroom issues (Gordon, 1974), in which the teacher and the students follow these steps:

1. Define the problem.
2. Generate possible solutions.
3. Evaluate the solutions.
4. Decide which solution is best.
5. Determine how to implement the solution.
6. Assess how well the solution solved the problem (p. 228).

Table 13–1 *Stages of Discipline Development for Professional Teachers*

Level 1. Instructional Stage

Premise:	Effective discipline begins with a teacher's knowledge of subject matter, curriculum, and methods of instruction and evaluation.
Attitudes:	1. Schools exists to promote learning. 2. Teachers are responsible for organizing and facilitating learning. 3. Students can learn and behave in responsible ways.
Skills:	1. Organizing unit and daily plans 2. Motivating students by a variety of techniques 3. Designing a range of learning experiences and teaching methods: learning centers, small- and large-group instruction, audiovisuals, games, and so on 4. Providing evaluation and feedback in ways that provide success and monitor progress
Language Competencies:	1. Clear written and oral expression to ensure clear communication 2. Precise directions 3. Unambiguous evaluation instruments

Level 2. Behavioral Management Stage

Premise:	Effective discipline requires a teacher to provide both control and support of student actions.
Attitudes:	1. Schools have a responsibility to help children learn. 2. Teachers should work with students to develop rules for behavior. 3. Students should be reinforced for appropriate behavior.
Skills:	1. Rule setting and teaching of rules 2. Setting limits in classroom encounters 3. Enforcing rules by action, not anger or threats, and with logical consequences 4. Using praise, rewards, cues, and modeling to reinforce
Language Competencies:	1. Clear, specific, assertive commands ("I need you to . . .") with proper gestures, eye contact, proximity, tone of voice 2. Soft reprimand and "broken record" technique 3. Praising ("I like the way . . ."), cueing, ignoring

Level 3. Humanistic Stage

Premise:	Effective discipline depends ultimately on students developing self-discipline, internal controls for behavior, and mature decision-making processes.
Attitudes:	1. Schools exist to help students grow into responsible, wise adults. 2. Teachers need to respect the worth of students as individuals. 3. Student should have opportunities to assume responsibility.

Skills:	1. Establishing participatory rule-setting and problem-solving sessions 2. Counseling techniques 3. Contract negotiation 4. Making solution-oriented plans with students who break rules
Language Competencies:	1. Stating problems clearly and brainstorming solutions 2. Reflecting feelings, active listening, congruent communication 3. Glasser's response-set to a rule breaker ("What are you doing? Is it helping you? What should you be doing? Can you make a plan?")

From Thomas R. McDaniel, "Developing the Skills of Humanistic Discipline," *Educational Leadership, 41,* 8 (May 1984): 71–74 (p. 72). Reprinted with permission of the Association for Supervision and Curriculum Development.

Language Style of Acceptance. Ginnott (1972) suggests a language style of acceptance that teachers would use in the same way they would talk to visitors in their homes:

1. Addresses situation rather than personalities.
2. Describes rather than evaluates.
3. Uses "I messages" rather than "you messages."
4. Avoids commands while inviting cooperation.
5. Reflects feelings.
6. Does not label (p. 101).

Reality Therapy. Glasser (1977) proposes a reality therapy approach designed to promote students' decision-making abilities.

1. Ask "What are you doing?" in a nonthreatening, nonpunitive way to encourage students to confront the reality of their behavior and encourage them to analyze their decisions.
2. After students have verbalized, ask "Did this help you or others?" to encourage them to evaluate their own behavior.
3. Ask the children to come up with alternative behavior as a solution to the problem, which might become the basis for a plan of action that the teacher might help monitor: "What should you be doing? Can you make a plan?"

All of these approaches reflect a humanistic model of education, one which would replace punishment with solution-oriented practices and would stress personal relationships, democratic classrooms, supportive language, decision-making techniques, and acknowledgment of the worth of each individual.

Example of a Discipline Problem. Here is an example of a discussion between fourth-grade teacher Avril Font and some of her students about a behavior problem. Try to identify which, if any, of these techniques the teacher is using. Are there other techniques of her own at work here? How would you have handled this same situation?

See Chapter 1 for more on Avril Font's classroom.

As the students stream into the classroom after physical education, several of them at once are excitedly telling the teacher about an incident that occurred between Donald and Heather.

Child: Look, Donald did this to her.
Child: They were fistfighting, then Heather slapped him in the face.
Child: Donald kept on messing with Heather.
Child: That boy kept messing with her and Heather slugged him.

Heather is flushed, and hovers over her diary at her desk writing intently. Donald stands as close as he can to the teacher without exactly putting his head on her shoulder. She puts her arm around him and talks quietly to him. Then she addresses both him and Heather:

Avril: How did this all start? Tell me what was happening.
Donald: Well, before PE . . .
Heather [rushing up]: See, when I was down here [points under the table] . . . and I accidentally kicked him.
Donald: Yeah, she accidentally kicked me hard, too.
Avril: Accidentally?
Heather: Well he was bothering me and I was trying to write in my diary and he kept on bothering me and talking to me.
Donald: You was talking to me too.
Avril: Did this help either one of you? Did it help to talk to her when she was writing? Did it help to kick him? [silence]. What should you do next time something like this happens?
Donald: Next time she kicks me I won't hit her and I'll be a big hero.
Heather: Next time you bother me, I'm gonna move to another table.

Home/School Cooperation

The role of the parents and the home environment is often referred to as a factor, both negative and positive, in school achievement. Walberg (1984) and others have found that home/school programs designed to improve academic learning situations in the home have had an outstanding success in increasing students' achievement in school and is more than twice as predictive of this success than socioeconomic status.

What these researchers refer to as "the alterable curriculum" of the home includes such factors as:

1. informal parent–child discussions of school and other events,
2. support and discussion of recreational reading,

3. discussions and joint monitoring of television viewing and peer-group activities,
4. support for long-term achievement goals, and
5. interest in school and personal activities.

Research such as this suggests that schools and teachers should make greater efforts to directly solicit help and support cooperation between themselves and the home and parents.

Another study (Janhom, 1983) suggests how such cooperation might be achieved.

1. Meetings between parents and teachers, ideally two hours twice a month for six months. Formats of these meetings would focus on ways parents could support their child's learning in school. Teachers could present ideas about one of the following factors that influenced this learning, followed by a discussion with the whole group of teachers and parents present for implementing them:
   a. work routines and emphasis on school in the family,
   b. support and direct help with schoolwork at home,
   c. stimulating learning experiences within the family,
   d. encouraging language development and correct and effective use of language, and
   e. interest in and expectations for school achievement;
2. teacher visits to home,
3. newsletters on the above topics and other relevant information sent to the home twice a month for six months.

Evaluating Instruction

Here are some questions to ask about evaluating instruction.

- What are your purposes for instruction?
- What approach to meeting these purposes will you use?
- What do you want your students to learn?
- What will determine what you teach: textbook tests, state or local minimum-competency tests, local curriculum guides, your own ideas about the curriculum, students' needs?
- How will you diagnose students' needs?
- How will you keep records?

In a recent article, Bloom (1984) notes that even after one million copies of *Taxonomy of Educational Objectives—Cognitive Domain* (Bloom et al., 1956) have been sold, the curricula of American education remain largely determined by textbooks, instructional materials, teaching methods, and tests that "rarely rise above the lowest category of the taxonomy: knowledge" (p. 14). Bloom further compares this trend in the United States to other countries where methods of inquiry of each subject are emphasized, and instruction methods and evaluation center on problem solving, application of principles, analytical skills, and creativity.

What does this mean in terms of evaluating the language arts? The current hard push for minimum-competency testing by state and local systems focuses on the three areas of reading, writing, and mathematics. Two of these three are within the domain of language learning. Teachers, then, are faced with the dilemma of finding ways to help students pass these tests, which is often an ultimate requirement for high school graduation regardless of the amount of course work taken, even though what the tests claim to measure often flies in the face of what research, theory, and teachers' knowledge indicate about how children really do become proficient language users.

For example, a reading test may require students to circle a word choice in isolation, making no attempt to have the students read and interpret what they have read. A writing test may consist of simple multiple-choice questions, or ask students to correct punctuation, making no attempt to have the students really *write*—the whole point of teaching writing.

Alternatives to standardized tests are various types of informal assessment of the language arts. Many informal means for diagnosing students' language competency and performance have been described throughout this text, each with the intended purpose of giving teachers a way in which they can learn more about students in order to plan more effectively how to teach them.

1. Finding out about children and their interests
   a. observe children (kidwatching)
   b. writing autobiographies
   c. Most Important Person display
   d. journal writing
   e. parent conferences
   f. sharing
   g. interest inventory
2. Finding out about children's language behavior
   a. gain awareness of how children learn language
   b. keep anecdotal records
   c. use an observation sheet for language use
   d. questions to guide observation
3. Evaluating listening and talking: observation sheet
4. Evaluating writing
   a. writing folders for each child
   b. anecdotal records
   c. holistic evaluation
   d. teacher conference

    e. peer-editing
    f. revision and self-evaluation

5. Evaluating underlying knowledge of grammar: informal evaluation system
6. Evaluating spelling, handwriting, and writing conventions
    a. stages of spelling development
    b. phases in handwriting development
    c. diagnosis and individualized spelling instruction
    d. diagnosis and evaluation of handwriting and record keeping: observation guide and samples
    e. diagnosis of writing conventions: writing samples, individual conferences, record keeping, peer conferences
7. Evaluating growth in literature
    a. question guide to assess children's literature interests
    b. question guide to assess children's understanding of literary elements
    c. question guide to assess story structure
8. Evaluating reading: naturalistic assessment methods
9. Evaluating growth in drama: student's response
10. Evaluating growth in use of media
    a. film preference instrument
    b. response guide to children's films
11. Evaluating growth in study skills: checklist of library use

All of these diagnostic means fall into categories of observing, recording, collecting, and interacting that can be applied to any aspect of the language arts and that all teachers can use at any time. Undoubtedly, the best evaluation devices will be those that you develop yourself and that will yield the information you need in order to plan for teaching time.

Teaching Children

The following examples show how six different teachers—all of whom are considered teacher artists by their school system, principal, peers, parents, and students—go about organizing, individualizing, managing, and evaluating instruction based on their own personal philosophy, teaching style, and chosen approach and techniques. Despite differences in scheduling, types of activities, management systems, and means of evaluating, note that all six teachers place great emphasis on instruction that is individualized, interactive, and integrated across the curriculum through the language arts.

Subject Matter Blocks of Time

Willa Richardson (Third Grade)

See Chapter 12 for more on Willa Richardson's classroom.

Willa Richardson schedules her subjects in blocks of time. She uses basal readers and a spelling text, and groups her third-grade students in four to six groups for each of these subjects. She uses a language arts text for whole-class lessons three times a week, and a creative writing period two times. Here is what her schedule looks like, including her extensive and in-depth approach to teaching thinking, research, and study skills, which she blocks under Science/Social studies.

Time Block	*Subject Areas/Days*
9:00–9:30	Sharing and business (announcements, notes, money collection)
9:30–12:00	Language arts block: Reading basals: 4–6 groups/M–F Spelling text: 4–6 groups/M–F Language arts text: MWF Creative writing: Tu/Th
12:00–12:30	Lunch
12:30–3:00	Math/science/social studies block: Math: Individualized, small-group modules/M–F Science/social studies: Units (selected), texts, teacher units, the scientific method, the environment, independent project

Willa Richardson makes a particular effort to individualize instruction for her highly motivated, high-achieving students. She writes a plan for each one and uses an interest inventory to determine topics for their independent projects. She also has a small chalkboard on an easel with the title "Talk to the Teacher" at the top. Each day, children who wish to talk to her for any reason write their names on this board, and she schedules a private conference for them. Since she has an aide in her room, this is not difficult, and she has a private corner of her room petitioned off with a screen where conferences can go on undisturbed.

Mauretta Hurst (Kindergarten)

Mauretta Hurst, who teaches kindergarten, also uses large subject blocks of time. For younger, and lower-achieving, students her schedule looks slightly different from that of Willa Richardson.

Time Block	*Subject Areas*
9:00–9:30	Roll call
9:30–10:55	Language arts (Thu: Music, 10:05–10:30)
10:55–11:00	Restroom

11:00–11:15	Recess
11:15–11:45	Mathematics
11:45–12:15	Science/social studies
12:15–12:40	Lunch
12:40–12:45	Restroom
12:45–1:00	Recess
1:00–1:45	Storytime/dramatic play/physical education (Mon: Guidance, 1:00–1:30; Tues: Library, 1:05–1:35)
1:45–3:00	Rest/review/prepare for dismissal
3:00–3:15	Dismissal for bus riders
3:15	Dismissal for walkers

Notice that, while Mauretta designates traditional subjects such as language arts, mathematics, and science and social studies, she has an equally large block of time for storytime and dramatic play—important experiences for her five-year-olds. She also believes in integrating the curriculum across these subject matter designations, as we see in this description of the learning experiences of her class during the course of one day—all of

Students revising a story board in preparation for making a filmstrip in Joyce Ryder's class.

which reflect her belief in the importance of using the language arts to integrate the curriculum.

• *Sharing.* Students share on any subject. Then when Mauretta asks them about their trip to the zoo the day before, many of them talk about their impressions of this field trip.

See Chapter 9, "Featured Teacher Gene Hughes: Using the Language Experience Approach with Remedial Readers."

• *The language arts.* The children draw pictures of what they have talked about with regard to the zoo. Then they gather around the teacher, who asks them to tell her their ideas for a language experiences story about their trip to the zoo. She writes their ideas on chart paper, encourages them to share, discusses what they say with others, and talks over word choice, spelling, and punctuation, as they write and read their story, *The Adventures of a Baby Elephant,* together.

• *Storytime/dramatic play.* Mauretta Hurst reads aloud Marcia Brown's picture book *The Three Billy Goats Gruff.* During a second reading she encourages the children to fill in whatever words they know in this repetitive-pattern story. The children begin to imitate her gestures of making a long nose with her hand for the troll and patting the floor to make a sound like "trip-trap," and then first softly and then more loudly begin to anticipate and then chant the words "trip-trap."

See Chapter 10, "Story Dramatization."

After discussing the story and each of the characters, the class does a story dramatization of it. The whole group first acts out the characterization of each of the characters and then chooses one child for each character to play the stories. The rest of the class have rhythm sticks to "trip-trap" like a Greek chorus. The scene is set with green carpet squares for grass and a wooden bridge (often standard play equipment in a kindergarten class). A narrator is chosen to tell the story with help from the teacher. The story is played through several times until every child has had a chance to play in a scene. The period ends with finger plays, such as "Where is Thumbkin?"

• *Rest and review.* After a rest period, the students work in groups through all of the following activities:

1. *Listening center.* Children listen to a tape as they look at a book, *The Story of Little Thumb.*
2. *Reading.* With the teacher, small groups reread their language experience story and read a list of the names of other zoo animals that Mauretta wrote down before they decided to write about elephants.
3. *Drawing and writing.* They continue to draw pictures of the zoo and begin to label them with the names of animals from the list they made earlier during language arts. Some write their names; others write picture titles, captions, and short stories independently or dictate them to the teacher as she circulates among them.

The integrating theme of this day was started by a trip to the zoo, and reinforced by books, pictures, filmstrips, and other materials gathered by

Mauretta Hurst on this theme. The integrating force here comes from the children's ideas and impressions expressed through the language arts as they talk, list new vocabulary words, discuss and dictate, spell words for, and read their own language experience story, listen to and respond to literature through dramatic play and media, and draw and write down their impressions of the zoo.

Team Teaching

An alternative organizational approach to completely self-contained classrooms is a team approach.

Joyce Ryder (Fourth and Fifth Grades)

See Chapter 11, "Featured Teacher Joyce Ryder: Using Computers in the Classroom."

Joyce Ryder enjoys working with children and with computers. She is part of a team at her school that coordinates the teaching of three classes. She works with two other teachers, each teaching subjects they like and which they feel are their strengths.

Their seventy-five fourth- and fifth-grade students are high achieving and highly motivated. (These qualities are not prerequisite for this approach but do contribute to its success.) The students move from room to room with plastic workbaskets containing the items they will need in all classes. The books and materials for the subjects each teacher teaches are kept in the respective classrooms. Here's what a weekly schedule looks like:

Time Block	*Joyce Ryder: Mathematics/science*	*Teacher #2: Reading/spelling*	*Teacher #3 Language/social studies*
9:00–10:05	Fifth	Fourth/fifth	Fourth
10:05–11:30	Fourth	Fifth	Fourth/fifth
11:30–12:45		Recess	
12:45–2:15	Lunch, Physical education, French, Teacher planning time (varies for each teacher)		
2:15–2:45		Wind-up (scheduled weekly)	

The subject blocks designated for each teacher have more to do with the grading system they must use than with anything else. Each of the six subjects is one for which a grade is required on the report card. And this does not imply, however, that the curriculum can be neatly divided into thirds or sixths, or that these six subjects are more important than several others that might have been listed, such as writing, drama, or literature. Here is a case where the evaluation is what has determined at least the name given to the subjects to be taught, rather than a case where evaluation follows what has been taught.

Each of the three teachers cuts across all the subjects in teaching, and the integrating force for all of them is language arts. Thus, for example, during the course of one week, the following learning activities were initiated and integrated in all three classrooms.

Kindergarten students in Mauretta Hurst's class dictate a language experience story about their trip to the zoo.

Mathematics/Science

See Chapter 11, "Making Filmstrips."

1. *Making filmstrips.* The students brainstorm, write a script, and make filmstrips in small groups on any subject they choose. They begin by cleaning off old filmstrips in a solution of bleach and water.
2. *Solutions.* Students observe what happens when they make a solution to clean off old filmstrips, and experiment with other types of solutions and with rates of evaporation in a study of heat and energy in science.

See Chapter 5, "Featured Teacher Phyllis Fuglaar: Writing and Publishing Choose-Your-Own-Adventure Books."

3. *Programming choose-your-own-adventure stories on the computer.* After reading some of these books, and writing their own books in small groups, the students create an outline and a flow chart and program their own story.

Reading/Spelling

1. *Basal readers.* The students continue reading their basals, and begin reading Greek and Roman myths after one such story is introduced in the basal.
2. *Mt. Olympus.* Students construct a model of Mt. Olympus, which they attach to the reading loft in their room. They also make maps of Greece, noting the location of Mt. Olympus and other significant places (Athens, Delphi) in the lives of the ancient Greeks.
3. *Playwriting.* The children begin to draft several short plays based on the Greek myths to dramatize at the end of the semester.

Language/Social Studies

1. *Biographies.* The students have been reading biographies of famous Americans during the period of the Westward Expansion.
2. *Dramatic characterizations.* Grouped together according to the biography they have read, the children characterize and dramatize their subject to share with the rest of the class: Lewis and Clark and Sacajawea, Colonel Travis, Davy Crockett, and General Santa Anna.
3. *Historical diaries.* The students put themselves in the role of a character they have created who moved West, and begin to write a diary of what might have happened to them—as settlers from the East moving West by wagon train; as gold miners in California or silver miners in Colorado; as traders and trappers in Santa Fe.

It should be obvious that, although Joyce Ryder's class is called Mathematics/Science, she is doing many other things, as are the other two teachers, that cut across and tie together all these subjects: working in small groups to discuss, plan, brainstorm, write, and edit; drama; literature; mediamaking; experimenting; and writing. This will be true of any departmentalized situation.

These three teachers note the advantage of teaching in this way, especially with more capable students:

1. The teachers are dealing with subjects they particularly enjoy and feel strong about teaching.
2. The teachers can focus their planning, individualizing, and evaluating efforts.
3. The teachers begin to develop strategies and collect materials in depth in certain subjects.
4. The teachers have increased planning time by blocking special subjects.
5. The students become prepared for departmentalized programming in middle school (grades 6 to 8) or junior high (grades 7 to 9).

There are some disadvantages as well:

1. The teachers have to work with three times as many students.
2. The teachers have increased paperwork in keeping records for the greater number of students.
3. The teachers lose contact with children when they leave the room.
4. The teachers are not able to observe students working in all subjects, where particular strengths and weaknesses may show.
5. The students may not be developmentally ready for a departmental program.

Learning Centers

Principal Phyllis Crawford describes how she used learning centers when she taught kindergarten through second grade.*

> There are five centers going on in my classroom every day. There are centers for: listening; reading; writing; art and math. These centers contain high quality, open ended activities so that children on every level can participate, learn, and progress.
>
> Centers are very important to me as a classroom teacher. There are five to six children in each center and I use this time (1) to teach the skill, lesson or activity to the small group, (2) to diagnose learning differences and learning strengths, (3) to help me plan for individual differences, (4) to help me plan future lessons and (5) to observe the children's performances and interactions with each other.
>
> Each child goes to one center a day and by the end of the week has traveled around the room and has participated in all five centers.
>
> Once every five to six week we have catch-up week and I do not introduce new centers. I help those that have been absent, those that need extra help in a particular subject or area, and those that have tried to expand the center idea beyond the original learning intent.

Phyllis has several suggestions on how to begin using learning centers:

1. Involve the students; let them set up the center, arrange furniture, suggest materials, and decide how many students can use the center at one time. Students will take better care of center materials if they helped set up the center in the first place.
2. Work with students on establishing rules for using the center. Children will be more likely to follow rules that they helped establish.
3. Set up only one or two centers, and use them to replace seatwork for a small group of children. An art center or a listening center can provide successful activities for children, requiring little adult supervision. Writing centers also have a definite appeal for all children.
4. Set up centers and activities at different levels of difficulty. Plan so that each student's experience will be a pleasurable one.
5. Teach the children how to use the centers. Slowly walk through the exact procedures for using a center; be sure students know how to operate and care for equipment.
6. Provide time for the students to use the centers. Plan students' use of centers with them while organizing the day, and be sure students know when they can use the centers.
7. Involve students in continuous planning and evaluation. They should be involved in evaluation of how each center is operating and help decide what centers to add.

*From Phyllis Crawford (n.d.), Individualizing instruction through learning centers, unpublished paper, pp. 1–4.

8. Plan a simple, basic format for all centers.
   a. Use the same basic routing system.
   b. Use the same type of directional card, making directions simple, explicit, and easy to read.
   c. Develop a simple coding system that will enable the children to self-check activities.
9. Encourage sharing, solving, and exchanging ideas with friends. Children learn from each other.
10. Evaluate the children's progress, and initiate a group discussion of the center.
11. Note the positive and negative comments students make, and revise the center accordingly.

Phyllis also recommends that centers have a number of "basic ingredients."

1. Each center should clearly state the purpose of the activity, directions, and evaluation procedure. Immediate feedback is desirable.
2. Use of multimedia materials (such as slides, filmstrips, and records) should be included.
3. Provide manipulative materials for exploration and discovery. Use many different types of formats and materials to make centers interesting and attractive.
4. Gear centers to the abilities, interests, and needs of the students.
5. Activities and materials should range from simple to difficult, from concrete to abstract.
6. Have optional as well as required centers.

What is the teacher's role in a learning center?

1. *Preparation:* to select and set up learning centers or supervise their construction.
2. *Introduction:* to introduce the center to the students so they will know what can be done in the center, how each activity is to be used, and how to evaluate efforts.
3. *Encouragement:* to motivate and encourage students to use centers by making them attractive and appealing and by adding new activities and/or excluding unpopular ones.
4. *Accounting:* to provide a procedure for record keeping and evaluating so that the student will know what he or she has accomplished.
5. *Management:* to be responsible for the so-called "housekeeping" involved in keeping a center organized. Close supervision is needed so that centers do not become cluttered and their purposes become indefinable. (Students should take part in this responsibility.)

Nora Miller (First Grade)

See Chapter 9 for more on Nora Miller's classroom.

Nora Miller is a teacher at the school where Phyllis Crawford is now the principal. Nora teaches a transitional first grade composed of thirteen regular but low-achieving children, three transitional (not ready for first grade), and two repeating. Her daily schedule looks like this.

Time Block	*Subject*
9:00–9:15	Business
9:15–9:30	Sustained silent reading
9:30–10:00	Language experience and literature
10:00–11:00	Centers: mathematics, science, art, writing, reading
11:00–11:15	Sharing of writing and art done during centers
11:15–12:00	Lunch/bathroom/playground
12:00–12:30	Basal reading lessons: Group 1 with teacher
12:30–1:00	Basal reading lessons: Group 2 with teacher
1:00–1:30	Recess
1:30–2:00	Basal reading lessons: Group 3 with teacher
2:00–2:30	Mathematics: Whole group, hands-on

See Chapter 9, "A Language- and Literature-based Reading Lesson."

Let us look at what one of these days looks like. Her language experience literature lesson is centered around Beatrice Schenk de Regniers's book *May I Bring a Friend?* Center activities are related to this lesson and integrated with other experiences in other subjects.

- *Math center.* The children fold a large piece of paper into eighths, write the name of the week in each one, and then trace a different plastic template for a different fraction of a circle in each one showing how much pizza they will eat each day, and write in the name of the fraction (the content they have been working on in math). Fractions and names of the days of the week are posted.

- *Art center.* The children cut out a variety of shapes (circles, triangles, squares, and rectangles—another math content) which have been dittoed onto colored construction paper. They glue these shapes onto another piece of paper to make a shape picture, and write a title, caption, or short story to go with it. They share their pictures after center time.

- *Reading center.* The children color in a picture of a castle dittoed on one side of a piece of paper, following a sequence of directions: (1) color castle, (2) write the names of the days of the week on lines dittoed on the other side, (3) cut the paper along those lines, (4) put the puzzle back together (on a bigger sheet of paper) with the days in the right order, and (5) flip the paper over. If the sequence is correct, so is their castle.

See Chapter 2, "Language Patterns for Writing."

- *Writing center.* The children continue an on going project of writing either an "If I Were" pattern about animals or a story about animals. These stories are shared at the end of the center time, and will eventually be bound into books.

- *Science/social studies center.* The children make edible clay: they read the recipe posted on the wall over the table, measure the ingredients, mix them, and then make shapes or play with the edible dough on waxed paper. Nora Miller spends most of her time in this center, guiding, talking, interacting, and laughing with the children.

Recipe for edible clay: 1/2 c. peanut butter, 1/2 c. dry milk, 1/4 c. honey. Mix and have fun.

Each child goes to one center a day, using the following permanent chart as a routing guide. (Each child is assigned a color, which can be changed as needed.)

	Art	***Writing***	***Reading***	***Math***	***Science/ Social Studies***
Monday	pink	red	yellow	purple	blue
Tuesday	blue	pink	red	yellow	purple
Wednesday	purple	blue	pink	red	yellow
Thursday	yellow	purple	blue	pink	red
Friday	red	yellow	purple	blue	pink

First-grade students use all of the language arts as they make edible clay in this learning center.

Glynn Wink (Second Grade)

See Chapter 9 for more on Glynn Wink's classroom.

Glynn Wink teaches a second grade of low- to average-achieving children, including several remedial students and nonreaders. She also believes in centers, but organizes her week in a different way than does Nora Miller. Monday through Wednesday she does whole-class and small-group lessons, and uses the basal reader with three groups. But on Thursday and Friday her students move through centers, an individualized reading conference, and two labs in other rooms in the school. Her schedule for those two days looks like this.

Time Block	*Thursday/Friday*
9:00–9:15	Business
9:15–10:00	Computer lab
10:00–11:00	Centers and individualized reading
11:00–12:00	Science lab
12:00–12:45	Lunch
12:45–2:30	Centers and individualized reading

Glynn explains her schedule and why she uses centers and individualized reading.

> I wanted to get my students out of the basal and its restrictions on thinking and creativity even though we're supposed to use it in our system. I do centers and individualized reading because it puts children in control. I am not telling them what to do. I put an idea out and they respond. It greatly increases the time we have for writing and integrating all subjects. It's a lot of work, but once you get it going, you love it. And they love it. It certainly beats 26 worksheets to follow every lesson.
>
> The kids call it "playing." It's amazing how quiet they become as they get involved in centers and reading. It eliminates behavior problems, and I've got several in here. Even nonreaders become very involved and I provide many activities to meet their needs. What's important is that they are involved.
>
> Perhaps what's the most important part is the sharing time when they tell what they have done, read what they have written, have something to present. You have to give them opportunities to do that.

In addition to scheduling her many centers differently, Glynn also uses slightly different centers, and a routing system. Each week she assigns each child a number. The children begin in the center that has their number tucked into a pocket with its name on a chart. They then go through the rest of the centers, in the routing order.

Children's Number	*Center Name*	*Routing Order (can be varied)*
4	Writing	1
5	Math	2

1	Listening	3
	Special	4
2	Art	5
3	Reading	6

On Thursday mornings, the children each get a plastic mesh basket with the necessary materials to do center work (paper, pencils, art supplies, books they have been reading) for the next two days. They then come together as a group to plan and review the directions for center work. Glynn integrates her science and social studies teaching throughout the centers, and so does not designate a special one for that purpose. The special center is reserved for special projects, or for planning for a holiday or other event, and the like, and so it is not used on a regular basis.

A Self-Directed Classroom

Avril Font (Fourth Grade)

Avril Font's fourth-grade classroom of low to average students is patterned after the British model of an open classroom, which makes concerns about child development and child language central to a curriculum integrated through the language arts. Teachers who organize their classrooms in this way pay particular attention to designing experiences around the interests and responses of students, and experiences that encourage the growth of language and thinking, such as informal classroom talk, group discussions, personal writing, individualized response to literature, and improvisational drama (Applebee, 1974).

See Chapter 1 for more on Avril Font's classroom.

The features of informal, open, self-directed classrooms—independent learning, cooperation, critical thinking, and positive attitudes—have been cited by many educators and parents as more important results of formal education than are standardized test scores or grades (Raven, 1981) and have also shown a high correlation with the grades of those who have attended college and professional schools as well as with many life-success indicators such as income, happiness, and performance at work (Samson et al., 1984).

In addition, several reviews of research on open education (Giaconia & Hedges, 1982; Hedges, Giaconia & Gage, 1981) show that, on the average, more open classrooms show about the same academic achievement outcome as more traditional classes, but increased outcome on nonachievement goals: attitude, creativity, and self-concept. The characteristics of an open education program are:

1. the central role of the child in learning experiences,
2. individualized, diagnostic evaluation,
3. individualized instruction, and
4. multimedia and manipulative materials and activities.

Avril Font's classroom follows the following schedule.

Time Blocks	*Subject Areas*
9:00–9:15	Business (journal writing, newspaper reading, individual projects)
9:15–9:45	Sharing and planning
9:45–10:15	Group work I
10:15–10:30	Recess
10:30–11:00	Sustained silent reading (library books or basal, which students complete on their own and take magazine tests when ready)
11:00–11:30	Physical education
11:30–12:00	Group work II
12:00–12:30	French
12:30–1:00	Lunch
1:00–1:15	Reading aloud
1:15–1:30	Group work III

Avril uses the following routing system for the children as they self-direct through all subjects during group work.

1. Each child has a card (the kind used in library books to check the date) for each of six subjects, with a color bar at the top, the child's name, and spaces for dates and teacher's initials. The colors correspond to the subjects as follows:

   Orange = Language Arts
   Purple = Reading
   Yellow = Diary
   Blue = Social Studies
   Green = Science
   Red = Math

2. The cards are kept in manila library-book pockets attached to a bulletin board, one pocket for each child.
3. Topics for each subject are discussed and planned in the reading center each morning, and through private conferences with Avril Font throughout the day. Each child makes her own decisions about the order of subjects, in concert with others in her small group or with Avril.
4. Each week, Avril checks the cards and discusses each child's work and use of time.

Over the years, Avril Font had become more and more convinced that children learn best when they are in control of their own learning, and has made decisions about organizing, individualizing, managing, and evaluating learning experiences in her classroom based on that premise. She became increasingly dissatisfied after ten years in a school system that she said monitored her every move to the point where if spelling was to be taught at 1:37 P.M. every day, she had better be teaching spelling at that time precisely, with every child doing the same activity on the same page.

Avril Font's present position is at a school with a principal who believes that teachers teach best with their own methods rather than with an alleged fail-proof/teacher-proof method, text, or commercial program used by all. When Avril first suggested that she try to organize her classroom with a more open atmosphere, with small-group work and an emphasis on individual projects and research, her principal supported her. When she later confessed to feeling guilty because she was moving away from a basal reader, or a single text for language arts, spelling, handwriting, and each of the content areas, her supportive and wise principal, Ann Torregrosa, advised her, "Don't worry, you'll get over it." Avril Font explains what she is doing in her classroom, and as she does, she comments on several important issues of putting it all together in any classroom.

1. ***On organizing for instruction***

> I read aloud to the whole class and we talk about the words as we go along. In the morning we come together as a class to share and plan. And of course they have special subjects as a whole class: library, PE, music, and guidance. But the rest of the day students move through the different subjects individually, and work primarily in small groups. The subjects we designate are reading, language arts, math, social studies, and science—traditional subjects. But we choose topics as a class or individually.

At the beginning of the year, Avril takes the state guides and sees what they suggest. Sometimes topics are planned, such as things related to current affairs or the time of year (i.e., the maypole) and sometimes it's just serendipity—what the children are interested in. "My favorite day or week is 'Do-Nothing,' something I reserve for when we don't have any particular topic. But something usually comes up. We had a great 'Hurricane Day' this year. The haiku they wrote was wonderful as we were wondering if the hurricane would hit there and watched the weather change."

Avril doesn't plan any regular, structured lessons. She uses basals daily at the beginning of the semester, then goes down to three times a week, and then to all students reading independently and conferring with her. "I don't teach structured spelling or use books. They learn to spell as they write, as we talk about words a lot and write them on the board and have them in the room, and through word games. But my kids do beautifully on all the state and standardized tests (even though they were very low last year)."

2. *On individualizing instruction*

> Until we teach the process of learning, the only process children will learn is the regurgitation of facts. We need to think about how children learn. When I have a student teacher, my main direction to them is to put yourselves in the children's position and ask: How do children learn? And how does each child learn best? We need to offer a whole gamut of experiences and opportunities for learning. They all learn differently and yet we put them in straight rows.

Avril uses one student, David, as an example. David is bright but totally unmotivated. Since he is very handy, Avril gives him many opportunities to learn that way, also helping her in the classroom.

> Let them do things they're good at. They will feel good and do better. We expect certain things as learners. We go to inservice and complain because we hate being read to or listening to someone talk all day. And yet we teach the same way and wonder why the children are bored. Children learn in different ways. Not one for all. The trick is to get each child to make their best effort, feel a sense of achievement, and meet their own self-fulfilling prophecy.

Avril has a great range of students in this class, from low-second grade to fifth grade in reading and math. Yet even her low students know how to find information and direct their own projects.

> It's expectancy. I expect them to do it. I tell them not to come and tell me they can't. We have some bushes at the end of our driveway. My husband expects me to hit them when I pull out. I only hit them when he is watching. Yet these children, the lowest-achieving class I've ever had, learned the Maypole dance—not an easy thing to do—faster than any other group I've ever had.

3. *On managing the classroom*

> One reason open classrooms are not more widespread is that people think there is no discipline. It's different when it's done right. Children are more disciplined and organized when they are self-directed. The main strategy for management is to provide time for careful planning with the whole class, so they are involved in making decisions about what they will do. We also work hard at working together and helping each other.

Avril has a system for students to work together in teams to acquire "house points" throughout the day; points are earned for anything at all: finding out what a word means; coming up with a good idea; successfully completing projects; helping each other; helping in the classroom. The next morning, the class adds up the points, and whichever team has the most gets the honor of doing all the household chores for the day: office monitor, lunch money, audiovisual aid, and so on. "It doesn't sound like a reward, but it is to them. It gives them great pride and they learn to work together as a team."

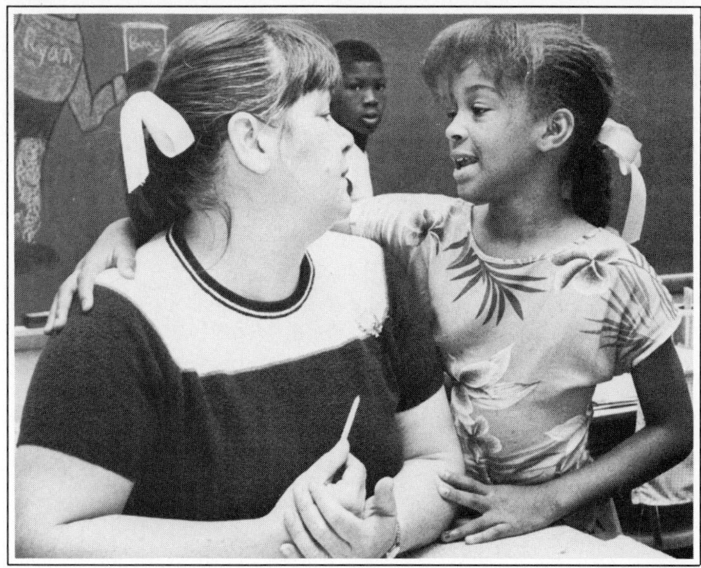

Learning experiences are centered around the individual in Avril Font's self-directed classroom.

Avril acknowledges that she did have behavior problems in her class, which have been resolved. She points to one boy, Michael, who has made the most progress. Michael had spent most of the previous year in a special resource room for low-achieving students. He also had some personal problems; he had been abused by his mother's boyfriend. Michael cried, screamed, misbehaved, and would do no work. Avril comments, "His mother is very protective and very supportive, and Michael has learned to learn. He was classified as a nonreader last year and said he had never read a book. Today he is reading a biography of Abraham Lincoln and will write a report on him."

Another child, Cory, was also a problem. "He is thirteen years old in the fourth grade and has been retained two times, the maximum allowed in this state. He says this is the first year he has liked school and would like to be retained again so he could spend another year in this classroom."

4. *On evaluating children*

Avril explains that hers is not truly an open classroom, especially in terms of evaluation; there are many restrictions on teachers. For instance, in the school's system, teachers have to use the following forms of evaluation:

- *Basal readers:* the basal magazine, test, or the system's criterion-referenced test.
- *Criterion-referenced test:* created by the system; strictly a subskills test.
- *State basic skills test:* not absolutely required but expected.

Even though Avril's class was considered very low in terms of ability, students did fine on all of these tests.

Avril is particularly proud of one other record. "We give an attendance certificate in this system to any child who missed only three days or less of class. All but four of my students will receive this. This is a big change from their record last year. And none of these children will be retained."

Avril sums up, explaining that her own system of evaluation is based on her observations and anecdotal records of what she sees the children doing in class, and how their writing develops.

> Since we spend most of the day in small-group or individual activities, I move from group to group, child to child, and conference and interact with them constantly. My evaluation of them evolves as I spend time with them, noting their progress, identifying areas where they need help, and helping them identify activities to do that will give them more control over their own learning processes.

Summing Up

How will you help children learn and gain control over their own learning processes as you practice the art of teaching language arts? In order to answer that question, you will, of course, develop a personal philosophy and teaching style that may draw from several theories and models as you develop your own unique approach. But no matter how that approach develops and emerges, you will always have to answer these basic questions: How will I organize, individualize, manage, and evaluate instruction in my classroom?

You will need to consider some factors in general, such as those which affect learning in school: student aptitude, instruction, and environmental factors. Specifically, you will have to decide how to organize your room environment, time, subject matter, and—most importantly—your students. You will have to consider how to individualize through instruction, through learning all you can about each child, planning how to teach each child, and how to evaluate each child. Other factors to consider include grouping, mainstreaming special learners, and teaching students who are language- and culturally different. The skill you develop in managing all this will be based on the skill you develop in planning for instruction and guiding students' behavior to the point where they can guide their own as you develop a humanistic atmosphere for dealing with discipline. Finally, the evaluation of children for language arts should be an ongoing process of observing, recording, collecting, and interacting with children, and using this information to plan for instruction as you learn the art of teaching language arts.

Looking Further

1. Interview at least one teacher at each grade level from kindergarten through grade five. Ask them what is their main approach to organizing, individualizing, managing, and evaluating instruction, and why they have chosen that approach.

2. Observe in the classrooms of the teachers you interviewed in Question 1. Note how what they do is a reflection of their philosophy of approaching teaching.

3. Observe in a classroom to identify two children with different learning styles. Describe how they are different, what the teacher does to meet their needs, and what you would do.

4. Observe in a class where special learners are mainstreamed. What does their teacher do to meet their needs?

References

CHAPTER ONE

Ashton-Warner, S. (1963). *Teacher.* New York: Simon and Schuster.

Berman, W. H., & McLaughlin, M. (1978). *Federal programs supporting educational change: Vol. 8. Implementing and sustaining innovations.* Santa Monica, CA: The Rand Corporation.

Brookover, W. B. (1976). *Elementary school climate and school achievement.* East Lansing, MI: Michigan State University, College of Urban Development.

Brophy, J., Downing, D., Evertson, C., & Anderson, L. (1979). Characteristics of effective English teaching in the junior high school. *English in Texas, 10,* 54–56.

Goodman, K. S., & Goodman, Y. M. (1981). *A whole-language comprehension centered view of reading development.* (Occasional paper No. 1.) Tucson, AZ: University of Arizona.

Goodman, Y. M. (1978). Kidwatching: An alternative to testing. *The National Elementary Principal, 57,* 41–45.

Harste, J., Woodward, V., & Burke, C. (1984). *Language stories and literacy lessons.* Portsmouth, NH: Heinemann.

Loban, W. (1976). *Language development: Kindergarten through grade twelve.* Urbana, IL: National Council of Teachers of English.

Loban, W. (1979). Relationships between language and literacy. *Language Arts, 56,* 485–486.

Merek, A., Howard, D., & Goodman, Y. M. (1984). *A kidwatching guide: Evaluation for whole language classrooms* (Occasional paper No. 9). Tucson, AZ: University of Arizona.

Peters, W. H., & Blues, A. G. (1978). Teacher intellectual disposition as it relates to student openness in written response to literature. *Research in the Teaching of English, 12,* 127–136.

Piaget, J. (1952). *The origins of intelligence in children.* New York: International Universities Press.

Piaget, J. (1964). Development and learning. In R. E. Ripple & V. N. Rockcastle (Eds.), *Piaget rediscovered: A report of the conference on cognitive studies and curriculum development.* Ithaca, NY: Cornell University.

Rosenshine, B., & Berliner, D. (1978). Academic engaged time. *British Journal of Teacher Education, 4,* 3–16.

CHAPTER TWO

Baldwin, J. (1981). If black English isn't a language, then tell me what is? In M. Shugrue (Ed.), *The essay.* New York: Macmillan.

Bradley, N. R. (1979). *A two-year investigation of the relation of oral language proficiency and reading achievement of first-grade children with a French linguistic background.* Unpublished doctoral dissertation, University of Texas, Austin.

Chomsky, C. (1969). *The acquisition of syntax in children from 5 to 10.* Cambridge, MA: MIT Press.

Chomsky, N. (1968). *Language and mind.* New York: Harcourt, Brace and World.

Chukovsky, K. (1971). *From two to five.* Berkeley, CA: University of California Press.

Crawford, P. (1981). *Reading.* Unpublished manuscript.

Cunningham, P. M. (1976–1977). Teachers' correction responses to black dialect miscues which are non-meaning changing. *Reading Research Quarterly, 12,* 637–653.

Fechter, E. (1978). *The relation between bidialectal oral language performance and reading achievement of black elementary school children.* Unpublished doctoral dissertation, New York University.

Geller, L. (1981). Riddling: A playful way to explore language. *Language Arts, 58,* 669–674.

Goodman, K. S. (1965). Dialect barriers to reading comprehension. *Elementary English, 42,* 853–860.

Goodman, K. S. (1978). *Reading of American children whose language is a stable rural dialect of English and a language other than English, Final Report.* Washington, DC: U.S. Department of Health, Education, and Welfare, National Institute of Education.

Gunther, V. A. (1979). *A comparison of bilingual oral language skills among limited English-speaking students from Spanish-speaking backgrounds.* Unpublished doctoral dissertation, Northwestern University.

Hall, R. (1984). *Sniglets.* New York: Macmillan.

Halliday, M. A. K. (1973). *Explorations in the functions of language.* New York: Elsevier North-Holland.

Harber, J., & Beatty, J. (1978). *Reading and the black English speaking child.* Newark, DE: International Reading Association.

Johnson, D. (1970). *An investigation of the oral language and oral reading of black first-grade children.* Unpublished doctoral dissertation, Ohio State University.

Johnson, D., & Pearson, P. D. (1984). *Teaching reading vocabulary* (2nd ed). New York: Holt, Rinehart and Winston.

Labov, W. (1972). *Language in the inner city: Studies in the black English vernacular.* Philadelphia: University of Pennsylvania Press.

Labov, W. (1978). *The study of non-standard English.* Urbana, IL: National Council of Teachers of English.

Liu, S. (1973). *An investigation of oral reading miscues made by nonstandard dialect speaking black children.* Unpublished doctoral dissertation, University of California.

Loban, W. (1963). *The language of elementary school children.* Urbana, IL: National Council of Teachers of English.

Lucas, A. (1983). *Language diversity and classroom discourse* (Final Report to NIE). Washington, DC: Center for Applied Linguistics.

Mae, C. (1980). *The dependency relation between oral language and reading in bilingual children.* Unpublished doctoral dissertation, Boston University.

Melmed, P. (1971). *Black English phonology: The question of reading interference.* Berkeley, CA: Language Behavior Research Laboratory, University of California.

Monroe, M., & Rogers, B. (1964). *Foundation for reading: Informal prereading procedures.* Chicago, IL: Scott, Foresman.

Piaget, J. (1962). *Language and thought of the child.* New York: Humanities Press.

Politzer, R., & Hoover, U. (1977). *Teacher and pupil attitudes toward black English speech varieties and black pupil achievement.* Stanford, CA: Center for Education Research.

Rigg, P. (1974). *A psycholinguistic analysis of the oral reading miscues generated by speakers of rural black dialect compared to the miscues of speakers of an urban black dialect.* Unpublished doctoral dissertation, Wayne State University.

Ruddell, R. B. (1965). The effect of oral and written patterns of language structure on reading comprehension. *The Reading Teacher, 18,* 270–275.

Shuy, R. (1969). Some language and cultural differences in a theory of reading. In K. S. Goodman & J. Fleming (Eds.), *Psycholinguistics and the teaching of reading.* Newark, DE: International Reading Association.

Sims, R. (1972). *A psycholinguistic description of miscues generated by selected young readers during the reading of text material in black dialect and standard English.* Unpublished doctoral dissertation, Wayne State University.

Strickland, R. G. (1962). *The language of elementary school children: Its relationship to the language of reading textbooks and the quality of reading of selected children.* Bulletin of the School of Education. Bloomington, IN: Indiana University.

Tizard, B., Carmichael, H., Hughes, M., & Pinkerton, G. (1980). Four-year-olds talking to mothers and teachers. In L. A. Hersov (Ed.), *Language and language disorders in childhood.* Oxford: Pergamon.

Torrey, J. W. (1972). The language of black children in the early grades. *Studies in developing competence in standard English.* Research report, National Institute of Child Health and Human Development.

Vygotsky, L. S. (1962). *Thought and language.* Cambridge, MA: MIT Press.

Vygotsky, L. S. (1978). *Mind in society: The development of higher psychological processes.* Cambridge, MA: Harvard University Press.

Watkins, K. (1981). *History of language / Origin of words unit plan.* Unpublished manuscript.

Wells, G., & Wells, J. (1984). Learning to talk and talking to learn. *Theory into Practice, 23,* 190–197.

CHAPTER THREE

Barnes, D. (1971). *Language, the learner, and the school.* Hammondsworth, Middlesex, England: Penguin.

Barnes, D. (1976). *From communication to curriculum.* Hammondsworth, Middlesex, England: Penguin.

Britton, J. (1970). *Language and learning.* Hammondsworth, Middlesex, England: Penguin.

Brown, K. L. (1967). Speech and listening in language arts textbooks. *Elementary English, 44,* 336–346.

Cazden, C. (1983). Adult assistance to language development: Scaffolds, models, and direct instruction. In R. P. Parker & F. A. Davis (Eds.), *Developing literacy: Young children's use of language.* Newark, DE: International Reading Association.

Cazden, C. (1985). Research currents: What is sharing time for? *Language Arts, 62,* 182–188.

Childers, P. R. (1970). Listening ability as a modifiable skill. *Journal of Experimental Education, 38,* 13.

Chomsky, C. (1972). Stages in language development and reading exposure. *Harvard Educational Review, 42.*

Christenbury, L., & Kelly, P. P. (1983). *Questioning: A path to critical thinking.* Urbana, IL: National Council of Teachers of English.

Clay, M. (1979). *What did I write?* Auckland, New Zealand: Heinemann.

Cox, C. (1984). Oral language development and its relationship to reading. In R. A. Thompson & L. L. Smith (Eds.), *Reading research review.* Minneapolis, MN: Burgess.

Cullinan, B., Jaggar, A., & Strickland, D. (1974). Language expansion for black children in the primary grades: A research report. *Young Children, 29,* 98–112.

Davidson, D. (1968). Trends in curriculum guides. *Elementary English, 45,* 891–897.

Davis, F. A. (1983). Developing literacy: Observation, analysis, and mediation in schools. In R. P. Parker & F. A. Davis (Eds.), *Developing literacy.* Newark, DE: International Reading Association.

Devine, T. G. (1978). Listening: What do we know after fifty years of research and theorizing? *Journal of Reading, 21,* 296–304.

Dyson, A. H., & Genishi, C. (1982). Whatta ya tryin' to write? Writing as an interactive process. *Language Arts, 59,* 126–132.

Flanders, N. (1970). *Analyzing teaching behavior.* Reading, MA: Addison-Wesley.

Flanders, N., King, M. L., & Cazden, C. B. (1974). Functions of language in the classroom, two reviews and a reply. *Research in the Teaching of English, 8,* 46–65.

Fox, S. (1983). Oral language development: Past studies and current directions. *Language Arts, 60,* 234–243.

Goodlad, J. (1984). *A place called school: Prospects for the future.* New York: McGraw-Hill.

Haley-James, S., & Hobson, C. D. (1980). Interviewing: A means of encouraging the drive to communicate. *Language Arts, 57,* 497–502.

Halliday, M. A. K. (1973). *Explorations in the function of language.* New York: Elsevier North-Holland.

Huey, E. B. (1908). *The psychology and pedagogy of reading.* New York: Macmillan.

Hunt, M. A. (1983). *A multimedia approach to children's literature.* American Library Association.

Levy, B. K. (1973). Is the oral language of inner city children adequate for beginning reading instruction? *Research in the Teaching of English, 7,* 51–60.

Manzo, A. (1969). The ReQuest procedure. *Journal of Reading, 13,* 123–126.

Marten, M. (1978). *Classroom relevant research in the language arts.* Washington, D.C.: Association for Supervision and Curriculum Development.

Moffett, J., & Wagner, B. J. (1983). *Student centered language arts and reading, K–13: A handbook for teachers.* Boston: Houghton Mifflin.

Pace, S. F. (1981). Viewpoints: Listening and talking. *Language Arts, 58,* 152–153.

Parnes, S. J., Noller, R. B., & Biondi, A. M. (1977). *Guide to creative action.* New York: Charles Scribner's Sons.

Pearson, P. D., & Fielding, L. (1982). Research update: Listening comprehension. *Language Arts, 59,* 617–629.

Rankin, P. T. (1928). The importance of listening ability. *English Journal, 17,* 623–630.

Redfield, D. L., & Rousseau, E. W. (1981). A meta-analysis of experimental research on teacher questioning behavior. *Review of Educational Research, 51,* 237–245.

Rosen, H. (1982). *Nurture of narrative.* Paper presented at the International Reading Association Annual Convention, Chicago, IL.

Ross, R. R. (1980). *Storyteller* (2nd ed). Columbus, OH: Charles E. Merrill.

Sharpes, D. K. (1982). Improving oral language skills for American Indian speaking students. *Resources in Education, August,* ED 214 191.

Silberman, C. (1970). *Crisis in the classroom: The remaking of American education.* New York: Random House.

Simpson, A. K. (1977). *Are first-grade Indian children ready to read?* Paper presented at the Annual Convention of the International Reading Association, Miami Beach, FL.

Snow, C. E., Dubber, C., & de Blauw, A. (1980). *Routines in mother–child interaction.* Unpublished manuscript.

Staton, J. (1984). Thinking together: Interaction in children's reasoning. In C. J. Thaiss & C. Suhor (Eds.), *Speaking and writing, K–12: Strategies and the new research.* Urbana, IL: National Council of Teachers of English.

Stauffeur, R. G. (1980). *The language-experience approach to the teaching of reading* (2nd ed). New York: Harper & Row.

Teale, W. H. (1981). Parents reading to their children: What we know and what we need to know. *Language Arts, 58,* 902–912.

Tough, J. (1979). *Talk for teaching and learning.* London: Ward Lock.

Trelease, J. (1985). *The read aloud handbook.* New York: Penguin.

Vygotsky, L. (1978). *Mind in society: The development of higher psychological processes.* Cambridge, MA: Harvard University Press.

Wells, G., & Wells, J. (1984). Learning to talk and talking to learn. *Theory Into Practice, 23,* 190–197.

Wilcox, M. (1976). When children discuss: A study of learning in small groups. *Elementary School Journal, 76,* 302–309.

Wilt, M. E. (1950). A study of teacher awareness of listening as a factor in elementary education. *Journal of Educational Research, 43,* 626–636.

Wilt, M. E. (1974). Listening: What's new? In J. de Stefano & S. Fox (Eds.), *Language and the language arts.* Boston: Little, Brown.

Wolfe, D. (1984). Research currents: Learning about language skills from narratives. *Language Arts, 61,* 844–850.

CHAPTER FOUR

Applebee, A. N. (1978). *The child's concept of story.* Chicago: University of Chicago Press.

Applebee, A. N., Langer, J. A., & Mullis, I. V. S. (1986). *The writing report card: Writing achievement in American schools.* Princeton, NJ: National Assessment of Educational Progress.

Bissex, G. (1980). *GNYS AT WRK: A child learns to read and write.* Cambridge, MA: Harvard University Press.

Britton, J. (1970). *Language and learning.* Coral Gables, FL: University of Miami Press.

Britton, J. (1982). Spectator role and the beginnings of writing. In M. Nystrand (Ed.), *What writers know: The language, process, and structure of written discourse.* New York: Academic Press.

Chomsky, C. (1971). Write first, read later. *Childhood Education, 47,* 296–299.

Clark, M. M. (1976). *Young fluent readers.* London: Heinemann.

Clay, M. (1975). *What did I write?* Auckland, New Zealand: Heinemann.

Clay, M. (1979). *Reading: The patterning of complex behavior.* Auckland, New Zealand: Heinemann.

Cook-Gumperz, J., & Gumperz, J. (1981). From oral to written culture: The transition to literacy. In M. F. Whiteman (Ed.), *Variation in writing.* Hillsdale, NJ: Erlbaum.

De Ford, D. E. (1981). Literacy: Reading, writing, and other essentials. *Language Arts, 58,* 652–658.

Donaldson, M. (1978). *Children's minds.* New York: Norton.

Durkin, D. (1966). *Children who read early.* New York: Teachers College Press.

Dyson, A. H. (1982). Reading, writing, and language:

Young children solving the written language puzzle. *Language Arts, 59,* 829–839.

Dyson, A. H. (1983). Research currents: Young children as composers. *Language Arts, 60,* 884–891.

Elbow, P. (1973). *Writing without teachers.* London: Oxford University Press.

Elliott, S., Nowosad, J., & Samuels, P. (1981). Me at school, me at home: Using journals with preschoolers. *Language Arts, 58,* 688–691.

Emig, J. (1978). Hand, eye, brain: Some "basics" in the writing process. In C. R. Cooper & L. Odell (Eds.), *Research on composing.* Urbana, IL: National Council of Teachers of English.

Evans, C. S. (1984). Writing to learn in math. *Language Arts, 61,* 828–835.

Ferreiro, E. (1978). What is written in a written sentence? A developmental answer. *Journal of Education, 160,* 25–39.

Fulwiler, T., & Young, A. (1982). *Language connections: Reading and writing.* Urbana, IL: National Council of Teachers of English.

Goodman, Y. (1980). The roots of literacy. In M. Douglass (Ed.), *Claremont Reading Conference 44th Yearbook.* Claremont, CA: Claremont Graduate School.

Graves, D. (1983). *Writing: Teachers and children at work.* Portsmouth, NH: Heinemann.

Graves, D., & Hansen, J. (1983). The author's chair. *Language Arts, 60,* 176–183.

Hailey, J. (1978). *Teaching writing K–8.* Berkeley, CA: Instructional Laboratory, University of California.

Harste, J., Burke, C., & Woodward, V. (1982). *The young child as writer, reader, and informant.* Final Report, NIE Study. Bloomington, IN: Indiana University.

Hipple, M. L. (1985). Journal writing in kindergarten. *Language Arts, 62,* 255–261.

Holdaway, D. (1978). *The foundations of literacy.* Sydney, Australia: Ashton Scholastic.

Kelly, G. (1963). *A theory of personality.* New York: Norton.

King, M. L., & Rentel, V. (1979). Toward a theory of early writing development. *Research in Teaching English, 13,* 243–253.

Levine, D. S. (1985). The biggest thing I learned but it really doesn't have to do with science . . . *Language Arts, 62,* 43–47.

Mathews, K. (1984). Community journals. *Livewire, 1,* 2–3.

Miller, G. (1977). *Spontaneous apprentices.* New York: Seabury.

Read, C. (1975). *Children's categorization of speech sounds in English.* Urbana, IL: National Council of Teachers of English.

Russell, C. (1983). Putting research into practice: Conferencing with young writers. *Language Arts, 60,* 333–340.

Smith, F. (1981). Myths of writing. *Language Arts, 58,* 792–798.

Taylor, D. (1983). *Family literacy.* Portsmouth, NH: Heinemann.

Vygotsky, L. S. (1978). *Mind in society: The development of higher psychological processes.* Cambridge, MA: Harvard University Press.

Wells, G. (1981). *Learning through interaction: The study of language development.* Cambridge: Cambridge University Press.

CHAPTER FIVE

Bissex, G. (1980). *GNYS AT WRK: A child learns to read and write.* Cambridge, MA: Harvard University Press.

Britton, J. (1970). *Language and learning.* Coral Gables, FL: University of Miami Press.

Britton, J. (1975). *The development of writing abilities, 11–18.* London: Macmillan.

Bruner, J. S. (1975). The ontogenesis of speech acts. *Journal of Child Language, 2,* 1–19.

Calkins, L. M. (1983). *Lessons from a child.* Exeter, NH: Heinemann.

Frye, N. (1964). *The educated imagination.* Bloomington, IN: Indiana University Press.

Giacobbe, M. E. (1982). A writer reads, a reader writes. In S. Newton & N. Atwell (Eds.), *Understanding writing: Ways of observing, learning, and teaching.* Chelmsford, MA: The Northeast Regional Exchange.

Graves, D. (1983). *Writing: Teachers and children at work.* Exeter, NH: Heinemann.

Halliday, M. A. K. (1975). *Learning how to mean: Explorations in the development of language.* London: Edward Arnold.

Jones, F. (1986). Talk worth promoting in the writing classroom. Paper presented at the Annual Convention of the National Council of Teachers of English, San Antonio, TX.

Koch, K. (1970). *Wishes, lies, and dreams.* New York: Random House.

Langer, S. (1967). *Mind: An essay on human feeling.* Baltimore, MD: Johns Hopkins University Press.

Murray, D. (1985). *A writer teaches writing.* Boston, MA: Houghton Mifflin.

Newkirk, T. (1984). Archimedes's dream. *Language Arts, 61,* 341–350.

Smith, F. (1982). *Writing and the writer.* New York: Holt, Rinehart & Winston.

Smith, F. (1983). Reading like a writer. *Language Arts, 60,* 558–567.

Taylor, D. (1983). *Family literacy.* Exeter, NH: Heinemann.

Torrance, E. P. (1962). *Guiding creative talent.* Englewood Cliffs, NJ: Prentice-Hall.

Warrington, J. (1963). *Aristotle's Poetics.* London: J. M. Rent.

Whale, K. B., & Robinson, S. (1978). Modes of students' writing: A descriptive study. *Research in the Teaching of English, 12,* 349–355.

CHAPTER SIX

Braddock, R., Lloyd-Jones, R., & Schoer, L. (1963). *Research in written composition.* Urbana, IL: National Council of Teachers of English.

Chomsky, C. (1972). Stages in language development and reading exposure. *Harvard Educational Review, 42,* 1–33.

Chomsky, C. (1980). Developing facility with language structure. In G. S. Pinnell (Ed.), *Discovering language with children.* Urbana, IL: National Council of Teachers of English.

Chomsky, N. (1957). *Syntactic structures.* The Hague, The Netherlands: Mouton.

Cox, C. (1985). An interview with Crosby Bonsall: A writer for beginning readers. *Children's Literature in Education, 16,* 93–101.

Dudley, J. A. K. (1983). *A meta-analysis of the effects of sentence-combining practice on syntactic maturity, writing quality, and reading comprehension.* Unpublished dissertation proposal, Louisiana State University.

Duffy, G. (1982). Response to Borko, Shavelson, and Stern: There's more to instructional decision-making in reading than the empty classroom. *Reading Research Quarterly, 17,* 295–300.

Ebel, R. L. (1969). *Encyclopedia of educational research.* New York: Macmillan.

Gunderson, D. (1980). Evaluation in language education. In G. S. Pinnell (Ed.), *Discovering language with children.* Urbana, IL: National Council of Teachers of English.

Harris, C. W. (1960). *Encyclopedia of educational research.* New York: Macmillan.

Hunt, K. W. (1965). *Grammatical structures written at three grade levels.* Urbana, IL: National Council of Teachers of English.

Lilja, L. D. (1980). Measuring the effectiveness of language education. In G. S. Pinnell (Ed.), *Discovering language with children.* Urbana, IL: National Council of Teachers of English.

Loban, W. (1976). *Language development: Kindergarten–grade twelve.* Urbana, IL: National Council of Teachers of English.

Malstrom, J. (1968). *Introduction to modern English grammar.* Rochelle Park, NJ: Hayden.

Meckel, H. C. (1963). Research in teaching composition and literature. In N. L. Gage (Ed.), *Handbook of research on teaching.* Chicago, IL: Rand McNally.

Mellon, J. C. (1969). *Transformational sentence-combining.* Urbana, IL: National Council of Teachers of English.

Monroe, W. S. (1950). *Encyclopedia of educational research.* New York: Macmillan.

Petrosky, A. R. (1977). Grammar instruction: What we know. *English Journal, 66,* 86–88.

von Bracht Donsky, B. (1984). Trends in elementary writing instruction, 1900–1959. *Language Arts, 61,* 795–803.

Weaver, C. (1979). *Grammar for teachers: Perspectives and definitions.* Urbana, IL: National Council of Teachers of English.

CHAPTER SEVEN

Ames, W. (1965). A comparison of spelling textbooks. *Elementary English, 42,* 146–150.

Beers, C. S. (1980). The relationship of cognitive development to spelling and reading abilities. In E. Henderson & J. W. Beers (Eds.), *Developmental and cognitive aspects of learning to spell.* Newark, DE: International Reading Association.

Beers, C. S., & Beers, J. W. (1981). Three assumptions about learning to spell. *Language Arts, 58,* 573–580.

Beers, J. W., Beers, C. S., & Grant, K. (1977). The logic behind children's spelling. *Elementary School Journal, 77,* 238–242.

Beers, J. W., & Henderson, E. H. (1977). A study of developing orthographic concepts among first graders. *Research in the Teaching of English, 11,* 133–148.

Chao, Y. (1968). *Language and symbolic systems.* Cambridge, England: Cambridge University Press.

Cordeiro, P., Giacobbe, M. E., & Cazden, C. (1983). Apostrophes, quotation marks, and periods: Learning punctuation in the first grade. *Language Arts, 60,* 323–332.

Cramer, R. L. (1978). *Writing, reading, and language growth: An introduction to language arts.* Columbus, OH: Charles E. Merrill.

DiStefano, P., & Hagerty, P. (1983). An analysis of high frequency words found in commercial spelling series and misspelled in students' writing. *Journal of Educational Research, 76,* 185.

Gentry, J. R. (1981). Learning to spell developmentally. *The Reading Teacher, 34,* 378–381.

Gillet, J. W., & Kita, J. M. (1979). Words, kids, and categories. *The Reading Teacher, 32,* 538–542.

Gillet, J. W., & Kita, J. M. (1980). Words, kids, and categories. In E. H. Henderson & J. W. Beers (Eds.), *Developmental and cognitive aspects of learning to spell.* Newark, DE: International Reading Association.

Graves, D. H. (1977a). Research update: Spelling texts and structural analysis methods. *Language Arts, 54,* 86–90.

Graves, D. H. (1977b). Research update: Language arts textbooks: A writing process evaluation. *Language Arts, 54,* 817–823.

Graves, D. H. (1978). Research update: Handwriting is for writing. *Language Arts, 55,* 393–399.

Graves, D. H. (1980). Research update: When children want to punctuate: Basic skills belong in context—Lucy McCormick Calkins. *Language Arts, 57,* 567–573.

Graves, D. H. (1983). *Writing: Teachers and children at work.* Exeter, NH: Heinemann.

Greene, H. S. (1977). *The new Iowa spelling scale.* Iowa City, IA: University of Iowa.

Hammill, D. D., Larsen, S., & McNutt, G. (1977). The effects of spelling instruction: A preliminary study. *Elementary School Journal, 78,* 67–72.

Hanna, P. R., Hanna, J. S., Hodges, R. E., & Rudorf, E. H. (1966). *Phoneme–grapheme correspondences as cues to spelling improvement.* Washington, DC: Government Printing Office, U. S. O. E.

Henderson, E. H. (1980). Word knowledge and reading disability. In E. H. Henderson & J. W. Beers (Eds.), *Developmental and cognitive aspects of learning to spell.* Newark, DE: International Reading Association.

Henderson, E. H., & Beers, J. W. (1980). *Developmental and cognitive aspects of learning to spell.* Newark, DE: International Reading Association.

Hinrichs, R. (1975). An old but valid procedure. *Elementary English, 52,* 249–252.

Hodges, R. E. (1981). *Learning to spell.* Urbana, IL: National Council of Teachers of English.

Manolakes, G. (1975). The teaching of spelling: A pilot study. *Elementary English, 52,* 246.

Read, C. (1971). Pre-school children's knowledge of English phonology. *Harvard Educational Review, 41,* 1–34.

Read, C. (1975). *Children's categorization of speech sounds in English.* Urbana, IL: National Council of Teachers of English.

Strever, E. F. (1980). Dialect and spelling. In E. H. Henderson & J. W. Beers (Eds.), *Developmental and cognitive aspects of learning to spell.* Newark, DE: International Reading Association.

Sulzby, E. (1980). Word concept development activities. In E. H. Henderson & J. W. Beers (Eds.), *Developmental and cognitive aspects of learning to spell.* Newark, DE: International Reading Association.

Templeton, S. (1979). Spelling first, sound later: The relationship between orthography and higher order phonological knowledge in older students. *Research in the Teaching of English, 13,* 255–264.

Tompkins, G. E. (1980). Let's go on a bear hunt! A

fresh approach to penmanship drill. *Language Arts, 57,* 782–786.

Zutell, J. (1979). Spelling strategies of primary school children and their relationship to the Piagetian concept of decentration. *Research in the Teaching of English, 13,* 69–80.

CHAPTER EIGHT

Abrahamson, R. F. (1980). An analysis of children's favorite picture story books. *The Reading Teacher, 34,* 167–170.

Felsenthal, H. (1978). The tradebook as an instructional tool: Strategies in approaching literature. In J. W. Stewig and S. Sebesta (Eds.), *Using literature in the elementary classroom.* Urbana, IL: National Council of Teachers of English.

Greenlaw, M. J. (1983). Reading interest researched children's choices. In N. Roser & M. Frith (Eds.), *Children's choices: Teaching with books children like.* Newark, DE: International Reading Association.

Hickman, J. (1980). Children's response to literature: What happens in the classroom. *Language Arts, 57,* 524–529.

Hopkins, L. B. (1981). Poetry is many things. *Early Years, November,* 321–324.

Lukens, R. J. (1982). *A critical handbook of children's literature* (2nd ed.). Glenview, IL: Scott, Foresman.

Mandler, J. M., & Johnson, N. S. (1977). Remembrance of things parsed: Story structure and recall. *Cognitive Psychology, 9,* 111–151.

Mattson, M. (1986) *Teaching reading through classics: A model based on* Treasure Island. Unpublished paper.

McGee, L. M., & Tompkins, G. E. (1983). Wordless picture books are for older readers too. *Journal of Reading, 27,* 120–123.

Monson, D., & McClenathan, A. (1979). *Developing active readers: Ideas for parents, teachers, librarians.* Newark, DE: International Reading Association.

Pearson, P. D., & Johnson, D. D. (1978). *Teaching reading comprehension.* New York: Holt, Rinehart & Winston.

Polyani, M. (1958). *Personal knowledge.* London: Routledge & Kegan Paul.

Purves, A., & Beach, R. (1972). *Literature and the reader: Research in response to literature, reading interests and the teaching of literature.* Urbana, IL: National Council of Teachers of English.

Rumelhart, D. (1975). Notes on a schema for stories. In D. G. Bobrow (Ed.), *Representation and understanding: Studies in cognitive science.* New York: Academic.

Sadow, M. W. (1982). The use of story grammar in the design of questions. *The Reading Teacher, 35,* 518–522.

Sebesta, S. (1979). What do young people think about the literature they read? *Reading Newsletter #8.* Boston: Allyn & Bacon.

Sloan, G. D. (1984). *The child as critic* (2nd ed.). New York: Teachers College Press.

Terry, A. (1974). *Children's poetry preferences: A national survey of upper elementary grades.* Urbana, IL: National Council of Teachers of English.

Whaley, J. F. (1981). Story grammar and reading instruction. *The Reading Teacher, 34,* 762–771.

CHAPTER NINE

Anderson, R. C., Hiebert, E., Scott, J., & Wilkinson, I. (1985). *Becoming a nation of readers: The report of the Commission on Reading.* Washington, DC: National Institute of Education, The National Academy of Education.

Applebee, A. N. (1978). *The child's concept of story.* Chicago, IL: University of Chicago Press.

Ashton-Warner, S. (1963). *Teacher.* New York: Simon and Schuster.

Au, K. H. (1979). Using the experience–text–relationship method with minority children. *The Reading Teacher, 32,* 677–679.

Austin, M. C. (1958). Evaluating status and needs in reading. In H. M. Robinson (Ed.), *Evaluation of reading.* Supplementary Educational Monographs, No. 88. Chicago, IL: University of Chicago Press.

Bettelheim, B., & Zelan, K. (1982). *On learning to read:*

The child's fascination with meaning. New York: Random House.

Blair, T. R. (1984). What makes an "effective reading program" effective? In R. A. Thompson & L. L. Smith (Eds.), *Reading research review.* Minneapolis, MN: Burgess.

Bond, G. L., & Dykstra, R. (1967). The cooperative research program in first grade reading instruction. *Reading Research Quarterly, 2,* 1–42.

Chall, J. (1967). *Learning to read: The great debate.* New York: McGraw-Hill.

Chomsky, C. (1972). Stages in language development and reading exposure. *Harvard Educational Review, 42,* 1–33.

Clark, M. (1976). Young fluent readers. London: Heinemann.

Cohen, D. (1968). The effect of literature on vocabulary and reading. *Elementary English, 45,* 209–213, 217.

Cox, C. (1984). Oral language development and its relationship to reading. In R. A. Thompson & L. L. Smith (Eds.), *Reading research review.* Minneapolis, MN: Burgess.

Crawford, P. (1984). *Sustained silent reading.* Unpublished paper.

Cunningham, P. M. (1982). Diagnosis by observation. In J. J. Pikulski & T. Shanahan (Eds.), *Approaches to the Informal Evaluation of Reading,* Newark, DE: International Reading Association.

DeFord, D., & Harste, J. C. (1982). Child language research and curriculum. *Language Arts, 59,* 590–600.

Durkin, D. (1961). Children who read before grade one. *The Reading Teacher, 14,* 163–166.

Durkin, D. (1978–1979). What classroom observations reveal about reading comprehension instruction. *Reading Research Quarterly, 14,* 481–533.

Durkin, D. (1981). Reading comprehension instruction in five basal reader series. *Reading Research Quarterly, 16,* 515–544.

Flood, J. (1977). Parental styles in reading episodes with young children. *The Reading Teacher, 30,* 864–867.

Goodman, K. S. (1970). Behind the eye: What happens in reading. In K. S. Goodman & O. S. Niles (Eds.), *Reading: Process and Program.* Urbana, IL: National Council of Teachers of English.

Goodman, K. S. (1976). Reading: A psycholinguistic guessing game. In H. Singer & R. Ruddell (Eds.), *Theoretical models and processes of reading* (2nd ed.). Newark, DE: International Reading Association.

Goodman, K. S., for the Reading Commission, NCTE. (1986). Basal readers: A call for action. *Language Arts, 63,* 358–368.

Goodman, Y. (1978) Kidwatching: An alternative to testing. *The National Elementary Principal, 57,* 41–45.

Gordon, C., & Pearson, P. D. (1983). *The effects of instruction in metacomprehension and inferencing on children's comprehension abilities* (Technical Report). Urbana, IL: University of Illinois, Center for the Study of Reading.

Gough, P. B. (1976). One second of reading. In H. Singer & R. Ruddell (Eds.), *Theoretical models and processes of reading* (2nd ed.). Newark, DE: International Reading Association.

Hall, M. A. (1981). *Teaching reading as language experience.* Columbus, OH: Charles E. Merrill.

Hansen, J. (1981). The effects of inference training and practice on young children's reading comprehension. *Reading Research Quarterly, 16,* 391–417.

Hansen, J., & Pearson, P. D. (1983). An instructional study: Improving the inferential comprehension of fourth grade good and poor readers. *Journal of Educational Psychology, 75,* 821–829.

Hepler, S. (Ed.). (1982). *The best of the web.* Columbus, OH: Center for Reading, Language Arts, and Children's Literature, Ohio State University.

Holdaway, D. (1979). *The foundations of literacy.* Sydney, Australia: Ashton Scholastic.

Holdaway, D. (1982). Shared book experience: Teaching reading using favorite books. *Theory Into Practice, Autumn,* 293–300.

Johns, J., & Ellis, D. (1976). Reading: Children tell it like it is. *Reading World, 16,* 115–128.

Kinerk, N. S. (1984). Education of effective teachers of reading. In R. A. Thompson & L. L. Smith (Eds.), *Reading research review.* Minneapolis, MN: Burgess.

Koeller, S. (1981). Twenty-five years of advocating children's literature in the reading program. *The Reading Teacher, 34,* 552–556.

LaBerge, D., & Samuels, S. J. (1976). Towards a theory of automatic information processing in reading. In H. Singer and R. B. Ruddell (Eds.), *Theoretical models and processes of reading.* Newark, DE: International Reading Association.

Mason, J. M., & Au, K. H. (1986). *Reading instruction for today.* Glenview, IL: Scott, Foresman.

Mavrogenes, N. A. (1986). What every reading teacher should know about emergent literacy. *The Reading Teacher, 40,* 174–178.

Moore, D. W. (1983). A case for naturalistic assessment of reading comprehension. *Language Arts, 60,* 957–969.

Pearson, P. D., & Johnson, D. D. (1978). *Teaching reading comprehension.* New York: Holt, Rinehart & Winston.

Pearson, P. D., & Raphael, T. E. (1984). Reading comprehension: A selected review. In R. A. Thompson & L. L. Smith (Eds.), *Reading research review.* Minneapolis, MN: Burgess.

Raphael, T. E. (1982). Question-answering strategies for children. *The Reading Teacher, 36,* 186–190.

Rumelhart, D. E. (1977). Toward an interactive model of reading. In S. Dornic (Ed.), *Attention and performance.* Hillsdale, NJ: Erlbaum, 1977.

Rumelhart, D. E. (1981). Schemata: The building blocks of cognition. In J. T. Guthrie (Ed.), *Comprehension and teaching: Research reviews.* Newark, DE: International Reading Association.

Shannon, P. (1982). Some subjective reasons for teachers' reliance on commercial reading materials. *The Reading Teacher, 35,* 884–889.

Shannon, P. (1983). The use of commercial reading materials in American schools. *Reading Research Quarterly, 14,* 481–533.

Singer, H., McNeil, J. D., & Furse, L. L. (1984). Relationship between curriculum scope and reading achievement in elementary schools. *The Reading Teacher, 37,* 608–612.

Spiegel, D. L. (1981). Six alternatives to the Directed Reading Activity. *The Reading Teacher, 34,* 914–920.

Stauffeur, R. G. (1975). *Directing the reading thinking process.* New York: Harper & Row.

Stauffeur, R. G. (1980). *The language experience approach to the teaching of reading.* New York: Harper & Row.

Strang, R. (1964). *Diagnostic teaching of reading.* New York: McGraw-Hill.

Teale, W. (1982). Toward a theory of how children learn to read and write naturally. *Language Arts, 59,* 555–570.

Thorndike, R. (1973). *Reading comprehension in 15 countries: An empirical study.* (Vol. 3, International Studies in Education.) New York: Holsted-Wiley.

Van Allen, R. (1976). *Language experiences in communication.* Boston: Houghton Mifflin.

Veatch, J. (1986). *Reading in the elementary school* (2nd ed.). New York: Richard C. Owen.

Veatch J., Sawicki, F., Elliott, G., Flake, E., & Blakeley, J. (1979). *Key words to reading.* Columbus, OH: Charles E. Merrill.

West, R. (1964). *Individualized reading instruction.* Port Washington, NY: Kennikat Press.

CHAPTER TEN

Blank, W. E. (1953). *The effectiveness of creative dramatics in developing voice, vocabulary, and personality in the primary grades.* Unpublished doctoral dissertation, University of Colorado, Denver.

Carlton, L. (1963). *A report on self-directive dramatization in the regular elementary school classroom and relationships discovered with progress in reading achievement and self-concept changes.* Unpublished doctoral dissertation, University of Houston.

Carlton, L., and Moore, R. H. (1966). The effects of self-directive dramatization on reading achievement and self-concept of culturally disadvantaged children. *The Reading Teacher, 20,* 125–30.

Cox, C. (1980). Shakespeare and company: The best in classroom reading and drama. *The Reading Teacher, 33,* 438–441.

Cox, C. (1985). Stirring up Shakespeare in the elementary school. In C. Carter (Ed.), *Literature—News that stays news.* Urbana, IL: National Council of Teachers of English.

Cox, C. (In press). Scriptwriting in small groups. In Jeff Golub (Ed.), *Student to student: Classroom practices in teaching English, 1988.* Urbana, IL: National Council of Teachers of English.

Davis, J. H., & Behm, T. (1978). Terminology of drama / Theatre with and for children: A redefinition. *Children's Theatre Review, 27,* 10–11.

Duke, C. (1974). *Creative dramatics and English teaching.* Urbana, IL: National Council of Teachers of English.

Heathcote, D. (1981). Drama as education. In N. McCaslin (Ed.), *Children and drama* (2nd ed). New York: Longman.

Kelly, E. F. (1981). Curriculum drama. In N. McCaslin (Ed.), *Children and drama* (2nd ed.). New York: Longman.

Mearns, H. (1958). *Creative power.* New York: Dover.

Pellegrini, A. D., & Galda, L. (1982). The effects of thematic-fantasy play training on the development of children's story comprehension. *American Educational Research Journal, 19,* 443–452.

Piaget, J. (1962). *Play, dreams, and imitation in childhood.* New York: Norton.

Siks, G. B. (1983). *Drama with children.* New York: Harper & Row.

Ward, W. (1957). *Playmaking with children* (2nd ed.). New York: Appleton-Century-Crofts.

Way, B. (1967). *Development through drama.* New York: Humanities.

Yawkey, T. D. (1980). Effects of social relationships curricula and sex differences on reading and imaginativeness in young children. *Alberta Journal of Educational Research, 26,* 159–167.

CHAPTER ELEVEN

Atkinson, R. (1973). Computer assisted instruction in initial reading: Individualized instruction based on optional procedures. *Educational Technology, 1,* 27–37.

Atkinson, R. (1974). Teaching children to read using the computer. *American Psychologist, 29,* 169–178.

Barber, B. (1982). Creating BYTES of language. *Language Arts, 59,* 472–475.

Bennett, D. (1974). The effects of domestic television on the academic performance of the child. *Visual Education, April,* 25–32.

Berryman, C. (1971). The newspaper in the elementary school: A research report to ANPA foundation. Athens, GA: University of Georgia.

Bilowit, D. W. (1981). Critical television viewing: A public station reaches out. In M. Ploghoft & D. Anderson (Eds.), *Education for the television age.* Athens, OH: Ohio University Press.

Board of Education (1970). *Report of the 1968–1969 city-wide testing program.* Chicago, IL: City of Chicago.

Bradley, U. N. (1982). Improving students' writing with microcomputers. *Language Arts, 59,* 732–743.

Bruce, B., Michaels, S., & Watson-Gegeo, K. (1985). How computers can change the writing process. *Language Arts, 62,* 143–149.

Chandler, D. (1984). *Young learners and the microcomputer.* Philadelphia, PA: Open University Press.

Childers, P., & Ross J. (1973). The relationship between television and student achievement. *Journal of Educational Research, 66,* 317–319.

Clements, D. H. (1985). *Computers in early and primary education.* Englewood Cliffs, NJ: Prentice-Hall.

Coburn, P., Kelman, P., Roberts, N., Snyder, T. F., Watt, D. H., & Weiner, C. (1982). *Practical guide to computers in education.* Reading, MA: Addison-Wesley.

Cook, T., & Conner, R. (1976). Sesame Street around the world: The educational impact. *Journal of Communication, 26,* 155–164.

Costanzo, W. (1985). Language, thinking, and the culture of computers. *Language Arts, 62,* 516–523.

Cox, C. (1975a). Film is like your grandma's preserved pears. *Elementary English, 52,* 515–519, 533.

Cox, C. (1975b). The liveliest art and reading. *Elementary English, 52,* 771–775, 807.

Cox, C. (1978). Films children like—and dislike. *Language Arts, 55,* 334–338, 345.

Cox, C. (1980). Making films without a camera. *Language Arts, 57,* 274–279.

Cox, C. (1982). Children's preferences for film form and technique. *Language Arts, 59,* 231–238.

Cox, C. (1983a). Young filmmakers speak the language of film. *Language Arts, 60,* 296–304, 372.

Cox, C. (1983b). Reading and film, the liveliest art.

In J. E. Cowen (Ed.), *Teaching reading through the arts.* Newark, DE: International Reading Association.

Cox, C. (1983c). *The elementary teacher as literature activist: Children rate and react to film.* Paper presented at the National Council of Teachers of English Spring Conference, Seattle, WA.

Cox, C. (1984). *Film and interest: An analysis of elementary school children's preferences for the liveliest art.* Paper presented at the American Educational Research Association, New Orleans, LA.

Cox, C. (1985). Film preference instrument. In W. T. Fagan, J. M. Jensen, & C. R. Cooper (Eds.), *Measures for research and evaluation in the English language arts, Vol. 2.* Urbana, IL: National Council of Teachers of English.

Cox, C. (1987). Making and using Media as a Language Art. In C. R. Personke and D. Johnson (Eds.), *Language arts instruction and the beginning teacher.* Englewood Cliffs, NJ: Prentice-Hall.

Dalzell, B. (1976). Exit Dick & Jane. *American Education, 12,* 9–13.

D'Angelo, K. (1983). Computer books for young students: Diverse and difficult. *Reading Teacher, 36,* 626–633.

Dech, R. (1975). *Story-related films in eighth-grade reading. Resources in Education,* August, ED 096 608.

Diaz-Guerrero, R. (1976). Sesame Street around the world. Plaza Sesouro in Mexico: An evaluation. *Journal of Communication, 26,* 145–154.

Fletcher, J. D., & Atkinson, R. (1972). Evaluation of the Stanford CAI program in initial reading. *Journal of Educational Psychology, 63* (6), 597–602.

Fletcher, J. D. and Suppes, P. (1972). Computer assisted instruction in reading: Grades 4–6. *Educational Technology, 12,* 45–49.

Flood, J. (1976). *Predictors of reading achievement: An investigation of selected antecedents to reading.* Unpublished doctoral dissertation, Stanford University.

Genishi, C., McCollumn, P., & Stravel, E. (1985). Research currents: The interactional richness of children's computer use. *Language Arts, 62,* 526–532.

Goddard, L. (1977). Photography and LEA: Open to suggestion. *Journal of Reading, 21,* 199–200.

Hamilton, H. (1975). *The relationship between televiewing and the reading interests of seventh-grade pupils.* Unpublished doctoral dissertation, Boston University.

Hawkins, J., Sheringold, K., Gerhart, M., & Berger, C. (1982). Microcomputing in schools: Impact on the social life of elementary classrooms. *Journal of Applied Developmental Psychology, 3,* 361–373.

Hunter, B. (1984). *My students use computers.* New York: Restan.

Ienatsch, G. P. (1974). *The effectiveness of teacher interaction on television instruction designed to supplement a reading program for second grades.* Unpublished doctoral dissertation, University of Iowa.

Irwin, J. (1976). Contributions of technology to reading success. In J. E. Merritt (Ed.), *New horizons in reading.* Newark, DE: International Reading Association.

Lamb, P. (1976). Reading and television in the United States. In J. Merritt (Ed.), *New horizons in reading.* Newark, DE: International Reading Association.

National Assessment of Education Progress. (1981). *Reading, thinking, and writing: Results from the 1979–1980 National Assessment of Reading and Literature.* Denver, CO: Education Commission of the States.

National Council of Teachers of English (1984). *A rationale for integrating media into English and the language arts. A report from the Commission on Media.* Urbana, IL: National Council of Teachers of English.

Newman, J. M. (1984). Online: Some Reflections on learning and computers. *Language Arts, 61,* 414–417.

Newman, J. M. (1985). Online: Vision and wisdom. *Language Arts, 62,* 295–300.

Nicholl, J. R. (1982). Computers in English instruction: The dream and the reality. *North Carolina English Teacher, 39,* 1–6.

Papert, S. (1980). *Mindstorms: Children, computers, and powerful ideas.* New York: Basic Books.

Phenix, J., & Hannan, E. (1984). Word processing in the grade one classroom. *Language Arts, 61,* 804–812.

Piazza, C., & Dawson, J. C. (1984). Choosing a word processor for writing instruction. *Computers, Reading and Language Arts, Summer / Fall,* 10–12.

Reid, M. (1972). *Evaluation of "A newspaper in my classroom" project: Second school.* Report made to Vancouver Board of School Trustees, Department of Planning and Evaluation, Vancouver, B.C., Canada.

Saracho, O. N. (1982). The effects of a computer-assisted instructional program on basic skills achievement and attitudes toward instruction of Spanish-speaking migrant children. *American Educational Research Journal, 19,* 201–219.

Schneeberg, H. (1973). The Listen and Read Project: Motivating students through dual modalities. *Elementary English, 50,* 900–904.

Sloan, G. D. (1984). *The child as critic* (2nd ed.). New York: Teachers College Press.

Smith, L., & Morgan, G. (1973). *Cassette tape recording as a primary method in the development of early reading materials. Resources in Education,* October.

Stetson, E. G. (1977). *The effectiveness of newspaper use on reading achievement of special education students. Resources in Education,* April.

West, C. E. (1983). Computers in the 80s. In M. T. Grady & J. D. Gawranski (Eds.), *Computers in curriculum and instruction.* Alexandria, VA: Association for Supervision and Curriculum Development.

Zaharias, J. A. (1983). Microcomputers in the language arts classroom: promises and pitfalls. *Language Arts, 60,* 990–995.

CHAPTER TWELVE

Armbruster, B. B., & Anderson, T. H. (1981). Research synthesis on study skills. *Educational Leadership, 39,* 154–156.

Ausubel, D. P. (1963). Cognitive structure and the facilitation of meaningful verbal learning. *Journal of Teacher Education, 14,* 217–222.

Bereiter, C., & Englemann, S. (1966). *Teaching disadvantaged children in the preschool.* Englewood Cliffs, NJ: Prentice-Hall.

Bloom, B. J., (1984). The search for methods of group instruction as effective as one-to-one tutoring. *Educational Leadership, 11,* 4–17.

Bloom, B. J., & Broder, L. (1950). *Problem-solving processes of college students.* Chicago, IL: University of Chicago Press.

Bracewell, R. (1980). Writing as a cognitive activity. *Visible Language, 14,* 400–422.

Clem, C., & Feathers, K. M. (1986). I LIC SPIDRS: What one child teaches us about content learning. *Language Arts, 63,* 143–147.

Crawford, P. (1981). *Reading.* Unpublished paper.

Devine, T. G. (1981). *Teaching study skills.* Boston: Allyn & Bacon.

Frankenstein, C. (1979). *They think again.* New York: Van Nostrand.

Graham, K. G., & Robinson, H. A. (1984). *Study skills handbook.* Newark, DE: International Reading Association.

Graham, S. (1982). Comparing the SQ3R method with other study techniques for reading improvement. *Reading Improvement, 19,* 44–47.

Haley-James, S. M., & Hobson, C. D. (1980). Interviewing: A means of encouraging the drive to communicate. *Language Arts, 57,* 497–502.

Jacobs, S. E. (1984). Investigative writing: Practice and principles. *Language Arts, 61,* 356–363.

Karahalios, S. M., Tonjes, M. J., & Towner, J. C. (1979). Using advance organizers to improve comprehension of a content text. *Journal of Reading, 22,* 706–708.

Pearson, P. D., & Johnson, D. D. (1978). *Teaching reading comprehension.* New York: Holt, Rinehart & Winston.

Richgels, D. J., & Hansen, R. (1984). Gloss: Helping students apply both skills and strategies in reading context texts. *Journal of Reading, 27,* 312–317.

Robinson, F. P. (1970). *Effective study.* New York: Harper & Row.

Rogers, D. B. (1984). Assessing study skills. *Journal of Reading, 27,* 346–354.

Sadler, W. (1979). Tapping the potentials of interdisciplinary studies in a freshman core program. *Journal of Interdisciplinary Perspectives, Fall,* 12–19.

Whimbey, A. (1984). The key to higher order thinking is precise processing. *Educational Leadership, 42,* 66–70.

Whimbey, A., & Lochhead, J. (1983). *Problem solving and comprehension: A short course in analytical reasoning.* Philadelphia: Franklin Institute Press.

CHAPTER THIRTEEN

Applebee, A. N. (1974). *Tradition and reform in the teaching of English.* Urbana, IL: National Council of Teachers of English.

Bloom, B. S. (1984). The search for methods of group instruction as effective as one-to-one tutoring. *Educational Leadership, 41,* 4–17.

Bloom, B. S., & Krathwohl, D. (1956). *Taxonomy of educational objectives: Handbook I, cognitive domain.* New York: Longman.

Crawford, P. (n.d.). *Individualizing instruction through learning centers.* Unpublished paper.

Fischer, B. B., and Fischer, L. (1979). Styles in teaching and learning. *Educational Leadership, 36,* 245–254.

Giaconia, R. M., & Hedges, L. V. (1982). *Identifying features of open education.* Stanford, CA: Stanford Center for Educational Research.

Ginnott, H. (1972). *Teacher and child.* New York: Macmillan.

Glasser, W. (1977). Ten steps to good discipline. *Today's Education, 66,* 61–63.

Gordon, T. (1974). *Teacher effectiveness training.* New York: Peter H. Wyden.

Hedges, L. V., Giaconia, R. M., & Gage, N. L. (1981). *Meta-analysis of the effects of open and traditional instruction.* Stanford, CA: Stanford University Program on Teaching Effectiveness.

Janhom, S. (1983). *Educating parents to educate their children.* Unpublished doctoral dissertation, University of Chicago.

McDaniel, T. R. (1984). Developing the skills of humanistic discipline. *Educational Leadership, 11,* 71–74.

Needham, N. R. (1986). Nobody ever said they couldn't do it. *NEA Today, April,* 10–11.

Raven, J. (1981). The most important problem in education is to come to terms with values. *Oxford Review of Education, 7,* 253–272.

Samson, G., Grave, M. E., Weinstein, T., & Walberg, H. J. (1984). Academic and occupational performances: A quantitative synthesis. *American Educational Research Journal, 21,* 311–321.

Shirreffs, A. (1986). Personal communication.

Southern California Research Council. (1985). *Financing quality education in Southern California.* (Report No. 28.) Claremont, CA: Pomona College.

Standford, G. (1980). *Dealing with differences.* Urbana, IL: National Council of Teachers of English.

Tyler, R. W. (1984). A guide to educational troubleshooting. *Educational Leadership, 41,* 27–30.

Walberg, H. J. (1984). Improving the productivity of America's schools. *Educational Leadership, 41,* 19–27.

Index

The author (5th from left on bottom row) gathered with a group of the "Featured Teachers" and other teachers whose photographs appear in the text. Bottom row, left to right: Steve Ketcham, Mauretta Hurst, Margaret Mattson, Ann Torregrossa, the author, Phyllis Crawford, Diane Rushing, Willa Richardson, Gene Hughes. Top row, left to right: Diane Roberts, Pat Peabody, Avril Font, Pat Abbott, Nancy Shaver Toms, Joyce Ryder, Jo Anne LaMotte, Nora Miller, Glynn Wink. "Featured Teachers" not pictured are Sarah Sherman-Siegel, who now teaches in New York City, and Marion Harris and Phyllis Fuglaar, both of whom are now teaching in Europe.